Endangered Birds of the World
THE ICBP BIRD RED DATA BOOK

Compiled by Warren B. King
on behalf of the International Council for Bird Preservation
and the Species Survival Commission of the International
Union for Conservation of Nature and Natural Resources

Published by the Smithsonian Institution Press
in cooperation with the International Council for Bird Preservation
Washington, D.C. 1981

Red Data Book, Vol. 2: *Aves,* series published by the International
Union for Conservation of Nature and Natural Resources, 1110 Morges,
Switzerland, with the financial assistance of
World Wildlife Fund (WWF)
United Nations Environment Programme (UNEP)
First edition, 1966; second, revised edition, 1978 and 1979
Reprint in handbook form, 1981

Library of Congress Catalog Card Number 81-607796
ISBN 0-87474-584-5 (cloth)
ISBN 0-87474-583-7 (paper)

Cover: *California Condor*

FOREWORD

The International Council for Bird Preservation (ICBP) is pleased to offer this reprinted text of Volume II, <u>Aves</u>, in the Red Data Book series of the International Union for the Conservation of Nature and Natural Resources (IUCN). This volume was originally published in a loose-leaf format in two parts in 1978 and 1979 by IUCN, Morges, Switzerland, and is made available here for the first time in a convenient, inexpensive paperbound version.

The information presented on these pages will retain value and currency for many years, even though the status of a few of the birds in this volume may change in the intervening years, and new information received by ICBP may alter our perception of the status of others. Updating these sheets in the course of preparing a fully revised edition is an unending process which continues with increasing efficiency at the ICBP Secretariat in Cambridge, England, in facilities shared with the recently established Species Conservation Monitoring Unit of the IUCN Species Survival Commission, the arm of IUCN responsible for preparing the several other volumes in the Red Data Book series. Hence, ICBP perceives the most urgent matter to be the widest possible dissemination of this information with the conviction that only through an understanding of the detail and extent of the problems confronting endangered birds will appropriate conservation action be achieved.

ICBP extends appreciation to its United States National Section for assisting the publication of this reprint financially, and to the Smithsonian Institution Press for undertaking its production and distribution.

Warren B. King
April 1, 1981

PREFACE

The International Council for Bird Preservation (ICBP) is the oldest extant
international conservation organization, dating back to 1922. It has worked
closely with the International Union for Conservation of Nature and Natural
Resources (IUCN) since the latter's foundation in 1948, particularly on preservation of rare and threatened species and the habitats on which they depend.
An agreement of long standing between the two organizations provides that ICBP
should take responsibility for and advise IUCN and its Survival Service Commission on all matters relating to the conservation status and needs of birds.

An example of the close working relationship between ICBP and IUCN is the
preparation by ICBP of Volume Two, Aves, of IUCN's Red Data Book. The first
edition of this volume was compiled by Colonel Jack Vincent in 1966, while serving as ICBP Liaison Officer at IUCN headquarters in Morges, Switzerland; he
continued to be responsible for regular updating of the material until 1972. The
present revision has been in preparation since 1974. It uses a format similar
to that of the other four Volumes of the series and differs only in minor details
of arrangement and scope from the previous edition. Its aim remains that of
providing encapsulated information pertinent to the conservation of threatened
species and subspecies of birds on a worldwide basis. Each Data Sheet, by its
initial wording and coding, indicates the degree of threat to the taxon
concerned and summarizes what is known of its status, distribution, population
size and trend, measures to conserve it (either already taken or proposed for
immediate or eventual consideration), and a selected list of the most important
references.

The value of the Red Data Book to governments, organizations and individuals
concerned with conservation of endangered species is directly related to the
accuracy and timeliness of the information provided. The ICBP is therefore
always very grateful for information that bears on the status of taxa already
included in this volume and also for suggestions as to additional taxa that
merit consideration in the course of future revisions. It should be understood
that the selection of taxa for inclusion is inevitably a somewhat subjective
process, involving as it does the professional judgment of a compiler who is
relying on an enormous number of informants. Misinterpretation and oversight
of information are in such circumstances bound to occur from time to time; but
the lists are flexible and when the status of a particular taxon can be assessed
more precisely on the basis of advice or criticisms received, the necessary
additions, deletions or modifications will be made.

Although concern for and information on threatened species have proliferated
encouragingly since 1966, the task of compiling this volume has been greatly
facilitated by the pioneer work of all those whose efforts led to the publication of the first edition. In addition to Colonel Vincent, those whose
contributions stand out include J.C. Greenway, Jr., S.D. Ripley, Sir Peter
Scott and the late James Fisher. ICBP is moreover indebted to literally
hundreds of contributors of information, including the members of its National

Sections and Working Groups, many governments and many private conservation organizations, without whose excellent cooperation this compilation would not have been possible.   Sir Hugh Elliott, Scientific Editor for IUCN of the Red Data Book series, has also done much in helping to ensure the accuracy of the text, for which the compiler is grateful.   Finally, ICBP acknowledges with thanks the financial support for the preparation of this new edition received from -

American Conservation Association
Anne S. Richardson Fund
Edward John Noble Foundation
Ford Foundation
Marcia Brady Tucker Foundation
Milton S. Erlanger Bequest
Seth Sprague Foundation
Smithsonian Institution
World Wildlife Fund

31 October 1979   Warren B. King
                                International Council for Bird Preservation
                                Smithsonian Institution, Washington, D.C.20560

ARRANGEMENT OF CONTENTS

The sheets are arranged in two main blocks: Preamble and Data Sheets. The Preamble is subdivided into sections as follows:

1. Preface
2. Arrangement of Contents
3. Red Data Book Categories
4. List of Avian Families
5. List of Threatened Avian Taxa in Systematic Order
6. Taxa listed in the First Edition of this Volume, but omitted from this Second Edition except for four 'out-of-danger' taxa
7. Threatened Birds listed in Red Data Book Vol. 2 arranged on a Zoogeographical/Geopolitical basis
8. List of Birds known or thought to have become Extinct since 1600

The Data Sheets are arranged in the numbered systematic order of Families (Preamble 4). At Generic, Specific and Subspecific levels sheets are arranged in strict alphabetical sequence.

Identification of sheets

A line at the bottom of each sheet gives information as follows:

1. Reference to the IUCN Red Data Book Volume 2 (RDB-2).
2. Retention of copyright by ICBP (ICBP © 1979).
3. In parentheses the "issue number" of the sheet, i.e. whether it appears for the first time (1) or is a revision of the sheet published in the previous edition (2).
4. Code numbers (for rapid filing and reference):
   (a) Preamble Sheets are identified by the letter P., followed by the section number (see list above) and the sheet number within the section.
   (b) Data Sheets are identified by the Family number (as listed in P.4), followed by the first five letters of the name of genus, the first three letters of the name of the species, and where applicable the first three letters of the name of the subspecies. Sheets should accordingly be kept in the numerical (Family) order and thereafter in the strict alphabetical order of the two or sometimes three groups of letters.
5. Initial letter of Red Data Book Category (see Preamble 3).

RED   DATA   BOOK   CATEGORIES

The following categories are designated by the Survival Service Commission. The letter in parentheses after the category name is used as a code symbol at the end of the reference line on each data sheet.

1. Endangered (E)

Taxa in danger of extinction and whose survival is unlikely if the causal factors continue operating.

Included are taxa whose numbers have been reduced to a critical level or whose habitat has been so drastically diminished and/or degraded that they are deemed to be in immediate danger of extinction. Also included are a few taxa that may already be extinct.

2. Vulnerable (V)

Taxa believed likely to move into the endangered category in the near future if the causal factors continue operating.

Included are taxa of which most or all the populations are decreasing because of overexploitation, extensive destruction of habitat or other environmental disturbance; taxa with populations that have been seriously depleted and whose ultimate security is not yet assured; and taxa with populations that are still sizeable but are under threat from serious adverse factors throughout their range.

3. Rare (R)

Taxa with small world populations that are not at present endangered or vulnerable, but are at risk.

These taxa are usually localized within restricted geographical areas or habitats or are thinly scattered over a more extensive range.

4. Out of danger (O)

Taxa formerly included in one of the above categories, but which are now considered relatively secure because effective conservation measures have been taken or the previous threat to their survival has been removed.

5. Indeterminate (I)

Taxa that are suspected of belonging to one of the first three categories but for which insufficient information is currently available.

N.B. Categories E and V may include, temporarily, taxa of which the populations are beginning to recover as a result of conservation measures, but not yet to an extent that would justify transfer to another category. A taxon at sub-specific level which might qualify for the V category has not been included if no other subspecies of the species concerned is in a threatened (E, V, R or I) category.

LIST OF AVIAN FAMILIES

The nomenclature and taxonomic sequence follow Peters, J.L. 1931 (Check-List of Birds of the World 15 Vols. - Nos. 8 and 11 in preparation; Cambridge, Harvard Univ. Press) and Morony, J.J., Jr., Bock, W.J. and Farrand, J., Jr. 1975 (Reference List of the Birds of the World; New York, American Museum of Natural History). Included are all Families extant since 1600 A.D.

Differences from the List of Families in the first edition of Vol. 2 of the Red Data Book - AVES, include the addition of seven Families or Subfamilies (viz. Platysteirinae, Rhipidurinae, Aegithalidae, Remizidae, Rhabdornithidae, Climacteridae and Cardinalinae) and the deletion of four Families or Subfamilies (viz. Brachypteraciidae, Prionopidae, Regulinae and Coerebidae). There are also some slight changes in the sequence of Orders and Families. The reference number of each Family or Subfamily is the principal ordinal element in the code for each taxon, as explained in Preamble 2 (Arrangement of Contents) and shown at the foot of each Data Sheet.

Order	No.	Family	
STRUTHIONIFORMES	1	STRUTHIONIDAE	Ostriches
RHEIFORMES	2	RHEIDAE	Rheas
CASUARIIFORMES	3	CASUARIIDAE	Cassowaries
	4	DROMAIIDAE	Emus
AEPYORNITHIFORMES	5	AEPYORNITHIDAE	Elephantbirds
DINORNITHIFORMES	6	ANOMALOPTERYGIDAE	Moas
APTERYGIFORMES	7	APTERYGIDAE	Kiwis
TINAMIFORMES	8	TINAMIDAE	Tinamous
SPHENISCIFORMES	9	SPHENISCIDAE	Penguins
GAVIIFORMES	10	GAVIIDAE	Loons
PODICIPEDIFORMES	11	PODICIPEDIDAE	Grebes
PROCELLARIIFORMES	12	DIOMEDEIDAE	Albatrosses
	13	PROCELLARIIDAE	Petrels, shearwaters
	14	HYDROBATIDAE	Storm petrels
	15	PELECANOIDIDAE	Diving petrels

Order	No.	Family	
PELECANIFORMES	16	PHAETHONTIDAE	Tropicbirds
	17	PELECANIDAE	Pelicans
	18	SULIDAE	Boobies, gannets
	19	PHALACROCORACIDAE	Cormorants
	20	ANHINGIDAE	Darters, anhingas
	21	FREGATIDAE	Frigatebirds
CICONIIFORMES	22	ARDEIDAE	Herons, egrets, bitterns
	23	COCHLEARIIDAE	Boat-billed herons
	24	BALAENICIPITIDAE	Whale-headed storks
	25	SCOPIDAE	Hammerheads
	26	CICONIIDAE	Storks
	27	THRESKIORNITHIDAE	Ibises, spoonbills
	28	PHOENICOPTERIDAE	Flamingos
ANSERIFORMES	29	ANHIMIDAE	Screamers
	30	ANATIDAE	Ducks, geese, swans
FALCONIFORMES	31	CATHARTIDAE	New World vultures
	32	SAGITTARIIDAE	Secretarybirds
	33	ACCIPITRIDAE	Hawks, eagles, harriers, Old World vultures
	34	PANDIONINAE	Ospreys
	35	FALCONIDAE	Falcons, caracaras
GALLIFORMES	36	MEGAPODIIDAE	Megapodes
	37	CRACIDAE	Curassows, guans, chachalacas
	38	TETRAONIDAE	Grouse
	39	PHASIANIDAE	Pheasants, francolins, quails, peafowl
	40	NUMIDIDAE	Guineafowl
	41	MELEAGRIDIDAE	Turkeys
	42	OPISTHOCOMIDAE	Hoatzins

Order	No.	Family	
GRUIFORMES	43	MESOENATIDAE	Roatelos or mesites
	44	TURNICIDAE	Button quails
	45	PEDIONOMIDAE	Collared hemipodes
	46	GRUIDAE	Cranes
	47	ARAMIDAE	Limpkins
	48	PSOPHIIDAE	Trumpeters
	49	RALLIDAE	Rails
	50	HELIORNITHIDAE	Finfoots, sun-grebes
	51	RHYNOCHETIDAE	Kagu
	52	EURYPYGIDAE	Sun-bitterns
	53	CARIAMIDAE	Seriemas
	54	OTIDIDAE	Bustards
CHARADRIIFORMES	55	JACANIDAE	Jacanas
	56	ROSTRATULIDAE	Painted snipe
	57	HAEMATOPODIDAE	Oystercatchers
	58	CHARADRIIDAE	Plovers, surfbirds
	59	SCOLOPACIDAE	Snipes, woodcocks, sandpipers
	60	RECURVIROSTRIDAE	Avocets, stilts
	61	PHALAROPODIDAE	Phalaropes
	62	DROMADIDAE	Crab plovers
	63	BURHINIDAE	Thick-knees
	64	GLAREOLIDAE	Coursers, pratincoles
	65	THINOCORIDAE	Seed snipe
	66	CHIONIDIDAE	Sheathbills
	67	STERCORARIIDAE	Skuas, jaegers
	68	LARIDAE	Gulls, terns
	69	RHYNCHOPIDAE	Skimmers
	70	ALCIDAE	Auks, murres, puffins

Order	No.	Family	
COLUMBIFORMES	71	PTEROCLIDAE	Sandgrouse
	72	RAPHIDAE	Dodos, solitaires
	73	COLUMBIDAE	Pigeons, doves
PSITTACIFORMES	74	PSITTACIDAE	Lories, parrots, macaws
CUCULIFORMES	75	MUSOPHAGIDAE	Turacos
	76	CUCULIDAE	Cuckoos, roadrunners, anis
STRIGIFORMES	77	TYTONIDAE	Barn owls
	78	STRIGIDAE	Owls
CAPRIMULGIFORMES	79	STEATORNITHIDAE	Oilbirds
	80	PODARGIDAE	Frogmouths
	81	NYCTIBIIDAE	Potoos
	82	AEGOTHELIDAE	Owlet frogmouths
	83	CAPRIMULGIDAE	Nightjars
APODIFORMES	84	APODIDAE	Swifts
	85	HEMIPROCNIDAE	Crested swifts
	86	TROCHILIDAE	Hummingbirds
COLIIFORMES	87	COLIIDAE	Mousebirds or colies
TROGONIFORMES	88	TROGONIDAE	Trogons
CORACIIFORMES	89	ALCEDINIDAE	Kingfishers
	90	TODIDAE	Todies
	91	MOMOTIDAE	Motmots
	92	MEROPIDAE	Bee-eaters
	93	LEPTOSOMATIDAE	Cuckoo rollers
	94	CORACIIDAE	Rollers
	95	UPUPIDAE	Hoopoes
	96	PHOENICULIDAE	Wood hoopoes
	97	BUCEROTIDAE	Hornbills

Order	No.	Family	
PICIFORMES	98	GALBULIDAE	Jacamars
	99	BUCCONIDAE	Puffbirds
	100	CAPITONIDAE	Barbets
	101	INDICATORIDAE	Honeyguides
	102	RAMPHASTIDAE	Toucans
	103	PICIDAE	Woodpeckers
PASSERIFORMES	104	EURYLAIMIDAE	Broadbills
	105	DENDROCOLAPTIDAE	Wood-hewers
	106	FURNARIIDAE	Ovenbirds
	107	FORMICARIIDAE	Ant thrushes
	108	CONOPOPHAGIDAE	Ant pipits
	109	RHINOCRYPTIDAE	Tapaculos
	110	COTINGIDAE	Cotingas
	111	PIPRIDAE	Manakins
	112	TYRANNIDAE	Tyrant-flycatchers
	113	OXYRUNCIDAE	Sharp-bills
	114	PHYTOTOMIDAE	Plant-cutters
	115	PITTIDAE	Pittas
	116	ACANTHISITTIDAE	New Zealand wrens
	117	PHILEPITTIDAE	Sunbird-asitys
	118	MENURIDAE	Lyrebirds
	119	ATRICHORNITHIDAE	Scrub-birds
	120	ALAUDIDAE	Larks
	121	HIRUNDINIDAE	Swallows, martins
	122	MOTACILLIDAE	Wagtails, pipits
	123	CAMPEPHAGIDAE	Cuckoo shrikes
	124	PYCNONOTIDAE	Bulbuls

Order	No.	Family	
PASSERIFORMES (cont.)	125	IRENIDAE	Leafbirds
	126	LANIIDAE	Shrikes
	127	VANGIDAE	Vanga shrikes
	128	BOMBYCILLIDAE	Waxwings
	129	DULIDAE	Palm chats
	130	CINCLIDAE	Dippers
	131	TROGLODYTIDAE	Wrens
	132	MIMIDAE	Thrashers, mockingbirds
	133	PRUNELLIDAE	Accentors
		MUSCICAPIDAE	
	134	TURDINAE	Thrushes
	135	ORTHONYCHINAE	Logrunners
	136	TIMALIINAE	Babblers
	137	PANURINAE	Parrotbills
	138	PICATHARTINAE	Picathartes
	139	POLIOPTILINAE	Gnatcatchers
	140	SYLVIINAE	Old World warblers
	141	MALURINAE	Australian warblers
	142	MUSCICAPINAE	Old World flycatchers
	143	PLATYSTEIRINAE	Puffbacked flycatchers, wattle-eyes
	144	MONARCHINAE	Monarchs
	145	RHIPIDURINAE	Fantails
	146	PACHYCEPHALINAE	Whistlers, piopio
	147	AEGITHALIDAE	Long-tailed or bush tits
	148	REMIZIDAE	Penduline tits
	149	PARIDAE	Titmice, chickadees
	150	SITTIDAE	Nuthatches

Order	No.	Family	
PASSERIFORMES (cont.)	151	CERTHIIDAE	Creepers
	152	RHABDORNITHIDAE	Philippine treecreepers
	153	CLIMACTERIDAE	Australian treecreepers
	154	DICAEIDAE	Flowerpeckers
	155	NECTARINIIDAE	Sunbirds
	156	ZOSTEROPIDAE	White-eyes
	157	MELIPHAGIDAE	Honey-eaters
		EMBERIZIDAE	
	158	EMBERIZINAE	Buntings
	159	CATAMBLYRHYNCHINAE	Plush-capped finches
	160	CARDINALINAE	Cardinal-grosbeaks
	161	THRAUPINAE	Tanagers
	162	TERSININAE	Swallow tanagers
	163	PARULIDAE	Wood warblers
	164	DREPANIDIDAE	Hawaiian honeycreepers
	165	VIREONIDAE	Vireos, peppershrikes
	166	ICTERIDAE	Troupials, grackles
	167	FRINGILLIDAE	Grosbeaks, finches
	168	ESTRILDIDAE	Waxbills
		PLOCEIDAE	
	169	VIDUINAE	Widow finches
	170	BUBALORNITHINAE	Buffalo weavers
	171	PASSERINAE	Old World sparrows
	172	PLOCEINAE	Weavers
	173	STURNIDAE	Starlings
	174	ORIOLIDAE	Orioles
	175	DICRURIDAE	Drongos
	176	CALLAEIDAE	New Zealand wattlebirds

Order	No.	Family	
PASSERIFORMES (cont.)	177	GRALLINIDAE	Magpie larks
	178	ARTAMIDAE	Wood swallows
	179	CRACTICIDAE	Bell magpies
	180	PTILONORHYNCHIDAE	Bowerbirds
	181	PARADISAEIDAE	Birds of Paradise
	182	CORVIDAE	Crows

LIST OF THREATENED AVIAN TAXA IN SYSTEMATIC ORDER

This list includes the 437 taxa to which data sheets have been assigned in the two issues making up the Second Edition of the Red Data Book Vol. 2. A replacement sheet for one taxon, Code 11/PODIC/GAL, covered in the first issue has been included in the second issue. The numeral preceding the name of each Family accords with the numbered List of Avian Families (Preamble 4). The letter preceding the name of each taxon refers to its Red Data Book Category (Preamble 3). For a list of taxa included in the First Edition but omitted from this Second Edition (except for four 'out-of-danger' taxa) see Preamble 6.

R H E I F O R M E S

   2. RHEIDAE

      E   Pterocnemia pennata tarapacensis   Puna Rhea

T I N A M I F O R M E S

   8. TINAMIDAE

      I   Crypturellus saltuarius   Magdalena Tinamou
      E   Tinamus solitarius pernambucensis   Pernambuco Solitary Tinamou

S P H E N I S C I F O R M E S

   9. SPHENISCIDAE

      V   Spheniscus demersus   Jackass Penguin

P O D I C I P E D I F O R M E S

   11. PODICIPEDIDAE

      E   Podiceps andinus   Colombian Grebe
      R   Podiceps gallardoi   Hooded Grebe
      R   Podiceps taczanowskii   Junin Grebe
      E   Podilymbus gigas   Atitlan Grebe
      V   Tachybaptus rufolavatus   Madagascar Red-necked Grebe

P R O C E L L A R I I F O R M E S

   12. DIOMEDEIDAE

      E   Diomedea albatrus   Short-tailed Albatross

   13. PROCELLARIIDAE

      E   Procellaria parkinsoni   Black Petrel
      V   Procellaria westlandica   Westland Black Petrel
      E   Pterodroma aterrima   Reunion Petrel
      E   Pterodroma cahow   Cahow
      E   Pterodroma cookii cookii   New Zealand Cook's Petrel
      V   Pterodroma hasitata   Black-capped Petrel
      E   Pterodroma hypoleuca axillaris Chatham Island Petrel
      R   Pterodroma leucoptera leucoptera Gould's Petrel
      I   Pterodroma macgillivrayi   MacGillivray's Petrel
      E   Pterodroma magentae   Chatham Island Taiko

13. PROCELLARIIDAE (continued)

R Pterodroma mollis madeira   Madeiran Soft-plumaged Petrel
E Pterodroma phaeopygia phaeopygia   Galapagos Dark-rumped Petrel
E Pterodroma phaeopygia sandwichensis Hawaiian Dark-rumped Petrel
I Pterodroma rostrata becki   Beck's Petrel
I Puffinus heinrothi   Heinroth's Shearwater
V Puffinus puffinus newelli   Newell's Shearwater

PELECANIFORMES

17. PELECANIDAE

V Pelecanus crispus   Dalmatian Pelican

18. SULIDAE

E Sula abbotti   Abbott's Booby

19. PHALACROCORACIDAE

R Nannopterum harrisi   Galapagos Flightless Cormorant
R Phalacrocorax carunculatus
     carunculatus   King Shag

21. FREGATIDAE

V Fregata andrewsi   Christmas Frigatebird
R Fregata aquila   Ascension Frigatebird

CICONIIFORMES

22. ARDEIDAE

V Egretta eulophotes   Chinese Egret
I Tigrisoma fasciatum fasciatum   Fasciated Tiger-heron

26. CICONIIDAE

E Ciconia ciconia boyciana   Oriental White Stork
I Ciconia episcopus stormi   Storm's Stork
V Mycteria cinerea   Milky Stork

27. THRESKIORNITHIDAE

R Geronticus calvus   Bald Ibis
E Geronticus eremita   Waldrapp
V Lophotibis cristata   Madagascar Crested Ibis
E Nipponia nippon   Japanese Crested Ibis
I Pseudibis davisoni   White-shouldered Ibis
R Thaumatibis gigantea   Giant Ibis
R Threskiornis aethiopica abbotti   Aldabra Sacred Ibis

ANSERIFORMES

30. ANATIDAE

V Anas aucklandica   New Zealand Brown Teal
V Anas bernieri   Madagascar Teal
R Anas laysanensis   Laysan Duck

30. ANATIDAE (continued)

E	Anas "oustaleti"	Marianas Mallard
V	Anas (platyrhynchos) wyvilliana	Koloa
R	Anser albifrons elgasi	Tule White-fronted Goose
V	Aythya innotata	Madagascar Pochard
R	Branta canadensis leucopareia	Aleutian Canada Goose
V	Branta sandvicensis	Nene
V	Cairina scutulata	White-winged Wood Duck
V	Chloephaga rubidiceps	Ruddy-headed Goose
V	Dendrocygna arborea	West Indian Whistling Duck
I	Mergus octosetaceus	Brazilian Merganser
I	Mergus squamatus	Scaly-sided or Chinese Merganser
I	Netta erythrophthalma erythrophthalma	South American Pochard

FALCONIFORMES

31. CATHARTIDAE

E	Gymnogyps californianus	California Condor

33. ACCIPITRIDAE

R	Accipiter fasciatus natalis	Christmas Brown Goshawk
E	Accipiter francesii pusillus	Anjouan Sparrow Hawk
R	Accipiter striatus fringilloides	Cuba Sharp-shinned Hawk
R	Accipiter striatus venator	Puerto Rican Sharp-shinned Hawk
E	Aquila heliaca adalberti	Spanish Imperial Eagle
R	Buteo galapagoensis	Galapagos Hawk
R	Buteo platypterus brunnescens	Puerto Rican Broad-winged Hawk
R	Buteo solitarius	Hawaiian Hawk
E	Chondrohierax uncinatus mirus	Grenada Hook-billed Kite
R	Chondrohierax uncinatus wilsonii	Cuban Hook-billed Kite
E	Eutriorchis astur	Madagascar Serpent Eagle
V	Gyps coprotheres	Cape Vulture
V	Haliaeetus albicilla	White-tailed Eagle
E	Haliaeetus leucocephalus leucocephalus	Southern Bald Eagle
E	Haliaeetus vociferoides	Madagascar Sea Eagle
R	Harpia harpyja	Harpy Eagle
I	Leucopternis occidentalis	Grey-backed Hawk
I	Leucopternis polionota	Mantled Hawk
R	Morphnus guianensis	Crested Eagle
E	Pithecophaga jefferyi	Philippine or Monkey-eating Eagle
R	Rostrhamus sociabilis plumbeus	Florida Everglade Kite

35. FALCONIDAE

R	Falco araea	Seychelles Kestrel
I	Falco kreyenborgi	Kleinschmidt's Falcon
R	Falco newtoni aldabranus	Aldabra Kestrel
V	Falco peregrinus	Peregrine Falcon
E	Falco peregrinus anatum	American Peregrine Falcon
R	Falco peregrinus fruitii	Iwo Peregrine Falcon
R	Falco peregrinus madens	Cape Verde Peregrine Falcon
E	Falco peregrinus tundrius	Tundra Peregrine Falcon
E	Falco punctatus	Mauritius Kestrel

G A L L I F O R M E S

36. MEGAPODIIDAE

V	Macrocephalon maleo	Maleo
R	Megapodius laperouse laperouse	Marianas Megapode
R	Megapodius laperouse senex	Palau Megapode

37. CRACIDAE

E	Aburria jacutinga	Black-fronted Piping Guan
V	Crax alberti	Blue-billed Curassow
E	Crax blumenbachii	Red-billed Curassow
I	Crax fasciolata pinima	Northern Bare-faced Curassow
E	Crax mitu mitu	Eastern Razor-billed Curassow
R	Crax rubra griscomi	Cozumel Curassow
E	Oreophasis derbianus	Horned Guan
E	Ortalis vetula deschauenseei	Utila Chachalaca
E	Penelope albipennis	White-winged Guan
E	Penelope perspicax	Cauca Guan
E	Pipile pipile pipile	Trinidad Piping Guan

38. TETRAONIDAE

| E | Tetrao urogallus cantabricus | Cantabrian Capercaillie |
| R | Tympanuchus cupido attwateri | Attwater's Prairie Chicken |

39. PHASIANIDAE

E	Catreus wallichii	Cheer Pheasant
E	Colinus virginianus ridgwayi	Masked Bobwhite Quail
V	Crossoptilon crossoptilon	White Eared Pheasant
E	Crossoptilon mantchuricum	Brown Eared Pheasant
R	Francolinus ochropectus	Tadjoura Francolin
I	Francolinus swierstrai	Swierstra's Francolin
E	Lophophorus lhuysii	Chinese Monal
R	Lophophorus sclateri	Sclater's Monal
V	Lophura bulweri	Bulwer's Wattled Pheasant
V	Lophura edwardsi	Edwards's Pheasant
V	Lophura imperialis	Imperial Pheasant
V	Lophura swinhoii	Swinhoe's Pheasant
E	Odontophorus strophium	Gorgeted Wood-Quail
V	Pavo muticus	Green Peafowl
E	Perdix perdix italica	Italian Grey Partridge
V	Polyplectron emphanum	Palawan Peacock Pheasant
R	Rheinardia ocellata	Crested Argus Pheasant
E	Syrmaticus ellioti	Elliot's Pheasant
R	Syrmaticus humiae	Hume's Bar-tailed Pheasant
V	Syrmaticus mikado	Mikado Pheasant
R	Tragopan blythii	Blyth's Tragopan
E	Tragopan caboti	Cabot's Tragopan
E	Tragopan melanocephalus	Western Tragopan

G R U I F O R M E S

43. MESOENATIDAE

R	Mesoenas unicolor	Brown Mesite
R	Mesoenas variegata	White-breasted Mesite
R	Monias benschi	Bensch's Monias

46. GRUIDAE

E	Grus americana	Whooping Crane
R	Grus canadensis nesiotes	Cuba Sandhill Crane
E	Grus canadensis pulla	Mississippi Sandhill Crane
V	Grus japonensis	Japanese Crane
E	Grus leucogeranus	Siberian White Crane
V	Grus monacha	Hooded Crane
I	Grus nigricollis	Black-necked Crane
V	Grus vipio	White-naped Crane

49. RALLIDAE

I	Coturnicops novaeboracensis goldmani	Goldman's Yellow Rail
R	Cyanolimnas cerverai	Zapata Rail
R	Dryolimnas cuvieri aldabranus	Aldabra White-throated Rail
R	Fulica americana alai	Hawaiian Coot
R	Fulica cornuta	Horned Coot
R	Gallinula chloropus guami	Marianas Gallinule
E	Gallinula chloropus sandvicensis	Hawaiian Gallinule
E	Notornis mantelli	Takahe
I	Pareudiastes sylvestris	San Cristobal Mountain Rail
E	Rallus longirostris levipes	Light-footed Clapper Rail
V	Rallus longirostris obsoletus	California Clapper Rail
V	Rallus owstoni	Guam Rail
I	Rallus pectoralis muelleri	Auckland Island Rail
E	Rallus poecilopterus	Barred-wing Rail
V	Rallus semiplumbeus	Bogotá Rail
E	Tricholimnas sylvestris	Lord Howe Wood Rail

51. RHYNOCHETIDAE

E	Rhynochetos jubatus	Kagu

54. OTIDIDAE

E	Choriotis nigriceps	Great Indian Bustard

C H A R A D R I I F O R M E S

57. HAEMATOPODIDAE

E	Haematopus chathamensis	Chatham Island Oystercatcher
E	Haematopus moquini meadewaldoi	Canarian Black Oystercatcher

58. CHARADRIIDAE

E	Thinornis novaeseelandiae	New Zealand Shore Plover
I	Vanellus macropterus	Javanese Wattled Lapwing

59. SCOLOPACIDAE

R	Coenocorypha aucklandica	New Zealand Snipe
R	Limnodromus semipalmatus	Asian Dowitcher
E	Numenius borealis	Eskimo Curlew
V	Prosobonia cancellatus	Tuamotu Sandpiper
I	Tringa guttifer	Nordmann's Greenshank

60. RECURVIROSTRIDAE

R Himantopus himantopus knudseni   Hawaiian Stilt
E Himantopus novaezelandiae   Black Stilt

68. LARIDAE

R Larus audouinii   Audouin's Gull
R Larus relictus   Relict Gull
E Sterna albifrons browni   California Least Tern
R Sterna balaenarum   Damara Tern
I Sterna zimmermanni   Chinese Crested Tern

C O L U M B I F O R M E S

73. COLUMBIDAE

E Caloenas nicobarica pelewensis   Palau Nicobar Pigeon
V Claravis godefrida   Purple-winged Ground-Dove
I Columba inornata exigua   Jamaica Plain Pigeon
E Columba inornata wetmorei   Puerto Rican Plain Pigeon
E Columba junoniae   Laurel Pigeon
R Columba palumbus azorica   Azores Wood Pigeon
V Columba trocaz   Long-toed Pigeon
V Didunculus strigirostris   Tooth-billed Pigeon
V Drepanoptila holosericea   Cloven-feathered Dove
V Ducula aurorae   Society Islands Pigeon
E Ducula galeata   Marquesas Pigeon
V Ducula goliath   Giant Imperial Pigeon
I Ducula oceanica ratakensis   Radak Micronesian Pigeon
E Ducula oceanica teraokai   Truk Micronesian Pigeon
V Ducula whartoni   Christmas Imperial Pigeon
I Gallicolumba erythroptera   Society Islands Ground-Dove
I Gallicolumba rubescens   Marquesas Ground-Dove
E Hemiphaga novaeseelandiae
     chathamensis   Chatham Island Pigeon
I Leptotila conoveri   Tolima Dove
I Leptotila wellsi   Grenada Dove
E Nesoenas mayeri   Pink Pigeon
R Ptilinopus huttoni   Rapa Fruit-Dove
V Ptilinopus roseicapillus   Marianas Fruit-Dove
E Streptopelia picturata rostrata   Seychelles Turtle Dove
R Treron australis griveaudi   Moheli Green Pigeon

P S I T T A C I F O R M E S

74. PSITTACIDAE

E Amazona arausiaca   Red-necked Parrot
E Amazona brasiliensis   Red-tailed Parrot
E Amazona guildingii   St. Vincent Parrot
E Amazona imperialis   Imperial Parrot
R Amazona leucocephala bahamensis   Bahamas Parrot
R Amazona leucocephala hesterna   Cayman Brac Parrot
V Amazona pretrei   Red-spectacled Parrot
E Amazona versicolor   St. Lucia Parrot
E Amazona vittata   Puerto Rican Parrot
E Anodorhynchus glaucus   Glaucous Macaw
E Anodorhynchus leari   Lear's Macaw
I Ara ambigua guayaquilensis   Guayaquil Great Green Macaw

74. PSITTACIDAE (continued)

I	Ara caninde	Wagler's Macaw
V	Aratinga guarouba	Golden Parakeet
I	Bolborhynchus ferrugineifrons	Rufous-fronted Parakeet
E	Coracopsis nigra barklyi	Seychelles Lesser Vasa Parrot
V	Cyanopsitta spixii	Spix's Macaw
E	Cyanoramphus auriceps forbesi	Chatham Island Yellow-crowned Parakeet
E	Cyanoramphus malherbi	Orange-fronted Parakeet
E	Cyanoramphus novaezelandiae cookii	Norfolk Island Parakeet
E	Eunymphicus cornutus uvaeensis	Uvea Horned Parakeet
I	Geopsittacus occidentalis	Night Parrot
I	Hapalopsittaca amazonina fuertisi	Indigo-winged Parrot
R	Neophema chrysogaster	Orange-bellied Parakeet
O	Neophema pulchella	Turquoise Parakeet
R	Neophema splendida	Splendid Parakeet
V	Ognorhynchus icterotis	Yellow-eared Conure
E	Pezoporus wallicus flaviventris	Western Ground Parrot
V	Pezoporus wallicus wallicus	Eastern Ground Parrot
R	Psephotus chrysopterygius chrysopterygius	Golden-shouldered Parakeet
R	Psephotus chrysopterygius dissimilis	Hooded Parakeet
E	Psephotus pulcherrimus	Paradise Parakeet
E	Psittacula echo	Mauritius Parakeet
R	Pyrrhura cruentata	Ochre-marked Parakeet
V	Rhynchopsitta pachyrhyncha pachyrhyncha	Thick-billed Parrot
E	Rhynchopsitta pachyrhyncha terrisi	Maroon-fronted Parrot
E	Strigops habroptilus	Kakapo
R	Touit melanonota	Brown-backed Parrotlet
I	Touit surda	Golden-tailed Parrotlet
R	Vini peruviana	Tahiti Lorikeet
R	Vini ultramarina	Ultramarine Lorikeet

CUCULIFORMES

75. MUSOPHAGIDAE

R	Tauraco fischeri zanzibaricus	Zanzibar Red-crested Lourie

76. CUCULIDAE

E	Neomorphus geoffroyi dulcis	South-eastern Rufous-vented Ground-Cuckoo
I	Neomorphus geoffroyi maximiliani	Bahia Rufous-vented Ground-Cuckoo
I	Pachycoccyx audeberti audeberti	Madagascar Thick-billed Cuckoo

STRIGIFORMES

77. TYTONIDAE

E	Tyto soumagnei	Soumagne's Owl

78. STRIGIDAE

R	Asio clamator oberi	Tobago Striped Owl
R	Asio flammeus ponapensis	Ponape Short-eared Owl
I	Athene blewitti	Forest Little Owl
R	Bubo poensis vosseleri	Nduk Eagle Owl
I	Ninox novaeseelandiae undulata	Norfolk Boobook Owl
R	Ninox squamipila natalis	Christmas Island Owl
E	Otus elegans botelensis	Lanyu Scops Owl
R	Otus insularis	Seychelles Owl
R	Otus ireneae	Morden's Scops Owl
I	Otus magicus beccarii	Papuan Scops Owl
R	Otus nudipes newtoni	Virgin Islands Screech Owl
E	Otus rutilus capnodes	Anjouan Scops Owl

C A P R I M U L G I F O R M E S

83. CAPRIMULGIDAE

R	Caprimulgus noctitherus	Puerto Rican Whippoorwill

A P O D I F O R M E S

86. TROCHILIDAE

I	Coeligena prunellei	Black Inca
E	Eulidia yarrellii	Chilean Woodstar
E	Glaucis dohrnii	Hook-billed Hermit
E	Phaethornis margarettae	Klabin Farm Long-tailed Hermit
R	Phaethornis nigrirostris	Black-billed Hermit
E	Threnetes grzimeki	Black Barbthroat

T R O G O N I F O R M E S

88. TROGONIDAE

V	Pharomacrus mocinno	Resplendent Quetzal

C O R A C I I F O R M E S

89. ALCEDINIDAE

E	Halcyon cinnamomina cinnamomina	Guam Micronesian Kingfisher

94. CORACIIDAE

R	Atelornis crossleyi	Crossley's Ground Roller
R	Atelornis pittoides	Pitta-like Ground Roller
R	Brachypteracias leptosomus	Short-legged Ground Roller
R	Brachypteracias squamigera	Scaled Ground Roller
I	Eurystomus orientalis irisi	Ceylon Broad-billed Roller
V	Uratelornis chimaera	Long-tailed Ground Roller

97. BUCEROTIDAE

I	Rhinoplax vigil	Helmeted Hornbill

P I C I F O R M E S

100. CAPITONIDAE

V	Semnornis ramphastinus	Toucan Barbet
R	Stactolaema olivacea woodwardi	Ngoye Green Barbet

103. PICIDAE

E	Campephilus imperialis	Imperial Woodpecker
E	Campephilus principalis bairdii	Cuban Ivory-billed Woodpecker
E	Campephilus principalis principalis	American Ivory-billed Woodpecker
R	Dendrocopos leucotos owstoni	Owston's White-backed Woodpecker
I	Dryocopus galeatus	Helmeted Woodpecker
E	Dryocopus javensis richardsi	Tristram's Woodpecker
I	Melanerpes superciliaris bahamensis	Grand Bahama Red-bellied Woodpecker
R	Melanerpes superciliaris nyeanus	San Salvador Red-bellied Woodpecker
V	Picoides borealis	Red-cockaded Woodpecker
R	Picoides tridactylus inouyei	Inouye's Three-toed Woodpecker
R	Picus awokera takatsukasae	Takatsukasa's Green Woodpecker
E	Sapheopipo noguchii	Okinawa Woodpecker

P A S S E R I F O R M E S

105. DENDROCOLAPTIDAE

R	Xiphorhynchus picus altirostris	Trinidad Straight-billed Wood-creeper

107. FORMICARIIDAE

V	Formicivora iheringi	Narrow-billed Antwren
I	Grallaria alleni	Moustached Antpitta
R	Grallaria guatimalensis aripoensis	Trinidad Scaled Antpitta
I	Grallaria milleri	Brown-banded Antpitta
E	Myrmotherula erythronotos	Black-hooded Antwren
E	Pyriglena atra	Fringe-backed Fire-eye
V	Rhopornis ardesiaca	Slender Antbird

109. RHINOCRYPTIDAE

I	Merulaxis stresemanni	Stresemann's Bristlefront
I	Scytalopus novacapitalis	Brasilia Tapaculo

110. COTINGIDAE

I	Calyptura cristata	Kinglet Calyptura
V	Cephalopterus penduliger	Long-wattled Umbrellabird
V	Cotinga maculata	Banded Cotinga
V	Procnias averano averano	Marcgrave's Bearded Bellbird
V	Xipholena atropurpurea	White-winged Cotinga

112. TYRANNIDAE

I	Polystictus pectoralis bogotensis	Bogotá Bearded Tachuri

115. PITTIDAE

    I   Pitta gurneyi   Gurney's Pitta

116. ACANTHISITTIDAE

    E   Xenicus longipes   New Zealand Bush Wren

117. PHILEPITTIDAE

    I   Neodrepanis hypoxantha   Small-billed Wattled Sunbird

119. ATRICHORNITHIDAE

    E   Atrichornis clamosus   Noisy Scrub-bird
    R   Atrichornis rufescens   Rufous Scrub-bird

120. ALAUDIDAE

    R   Alauda razae   Razo Lark

121. HIRUNDINIDAE

    I   Kalochelidon euchrysea euchrysea   Jamaican Golden Swallow
    I   Pseudochelidon sirintarae   White-eyed River Martin

122. MOTACILLIDAE

    R   Anthus sokokensis   Sokoke Pipit

123. CAMPEPHAGIDAE

    R   Coracina newtoni   Réunion Cuckoo-Shrike
    V   Coracina typica   Mauritius Cuckoo-Shrike

126. LANIIDAE

    E   Lanius ludovicianus mearnsi   San Clemente Loggerhead Shrike
    E   Malaconotus alius   Black-capped Bush Shrike
    R   Malaconotus kupeensis   Kupe Mountain Bush Shrike

127. VANGIDAE

    I   Oriolia bernieri   Bernier's Vanga
    E   Xenopirostris damii   Van Dam's Vanga
    E   Xenopirostris polleni   Pollen's Vanga

130. CINCLIDAE

    I   Cinclus schultzi   Rufous-throated Dipper

131. TROGLODYTIDAE

    V   Cistothorus apolinari   Apolinar's Marsh-Wren
    R   Ferminia cerverai   Zapata Wren
    E   Troglodytes aedon guadeloupensis   Guadeloupe Wren
    E   Troglodytes aedon mesoleucus   St. Lucia Wren
    R   Troglodytes troglodytes
           fridariensis   Fair Isle Wren

132. MIMIDAE

E   Cinclocerthia ruficauda gutturalis Martinique Trembler
R   Nesomimus trifasciatus
     trifasciatus   Charles Mockingbird
E   Ramphocinclus brachyurus
     brachyurus   Martinique White-breasted Thrasher
E   Ramphocinclus brachyurus
     sanctaeluciae   St. Lucia White-breasted Thrasher

134. (MUSCICAPIDAE) TURDINAE

R   Alethe montana   Usambara Robin-Chat
E   Cichlherminia lherminieri
     sanctaeluciae   St. Lucia Forest Thrush
E   Copsychus sechellarum   Seychelles Magpie-Robin
E   Erithacus komadori subrufa   Southern Ryukyu Robin
E   Modulatrix orostruthus   Dappled Mountain-Robin
R   Myadestes genibarbis sibilans   St. Vincent Solitaire
R   Nesocichla eremita eremita   Tristan Starchy
E   Phaeornis obscurus myadestina   Kauai Thrush
E   Phaeornis obscurus rutha   Molokai Thrush
E   Phaeornis palmeri   Puaiohi
E   Turdus poliocephalus poliocephalus Grey-headed Blackbird
I   Zoothera dauma major   Amami Ground Thrush

135. (MUSCICAPIDAE) ORTHONYCHINAE

O   Psophodes nigrogularis   Western Whipbird

137. (MUSCICAPIDAE) PANURINAE

I   Paradoxornis heudei heudei   Lower Yangtze Kiang Crow-Tit

138. (MUSCICAPIDAE) PICATHARTINAE

V   Picathartes gymnocephalus   White-necked Picathartes
V   Picathartes oreas   Grey-necked Picathartes

140. (MUSCICAPIDAE) SYLVIINAE

E   Acrocephalus caffer aquilonis   Eiao Polynesian Warbler
E   Acrocephalus caffer longirostris   Moorea Polynesian Warbler
R   Acrocephalus caffer postremus   Hatutu Polynesian Warbler
R   Acrocephalus familiaris kingi   Nihoa Millerbird
E   Bebrornis rodericana   Rodrigues Brush Warbler
O   Bebrornis sechellensis   Seychelles Brush Warbler
R   Megalurus pryeri pryeri   Japanese Marsh Warbler
R   Nesillas aldabranus   Aldabra Brush Warbler
I   Regulus calendula obscura   Guadalupe Kinglet
E   Trichocichla rufa   Long-legged Warbler

141. (MUSCICAPIDAE) MALURINAE

I   Amytornis goyderi   Eyrean Grass Wren
E   Bowdleria punctata wilsoni   Codfish Island Fernbird
R   Dasyornis brachypterus
     longirostris   Western Bristlebird
E   Dasyornis broadbenti littoralis   Western Rufous Bristlebird

142. (MUSCICAPIDAE) MUSCICAPINAE

I	Newtonia fanovanae	Fanovana Newtonia
E	Petroica traversi	Chatham Island Black Robin

144. (MUSCICAPIDAE) MONARCHINAE

R	Metabolus rugensis	Truk Monarch
V	Pomarea dimidiata	Rarotonga Flycatcher
I	Pomarea iphis fluxa	Eiao Flycatcher
E	Pomarea mendozae mendozae	Hivaoa Flycatcher
R	Pomarea mendozae mira	Uapou Flycatcher
E	Pomarea mendozae nukuhivae	Nukuhiva Flycatcher
E	Pomarea nigra nigra	Tahiti Flycatcher
R	Terpsiphone bourbonnensis desolata	Mauritius Paradise Flycatcher
E	Terpsiphone corvina	Seychelles Black Paradise Flycatcher

150. SITTIDAE

R	Sitta ledanti	Kabylian Nuthatch

155. NECTARINIIDAE

R	Anthreptes pallidigaster	Amani Sunbird

156. ZOSTEROPIDAE

R	Rukia longirostris	Ponape Greater White-eye
E	Rukia ruki	Truk Greater White-eye
E	Zosterops albogularis	White-breasted Silvereye
I	Zosterops conspicillata rotensis	Rota Bridled White-eye
E	Zosterops luteirostris luteirostris	Gizo White-eye
R	Zosterops modesta	Seychelles White-eye
V	Zosterops olivacea chloronothos	Mauritius White-eye

157. MELIPHAGIDAE

E	Apalopteron familiare familiare	Mukojima Bonin Honeyeater
E	Meliphaga melanops cassidix	Helmeted Honeyeater
E	Moho braccatus	Kauai 'O'o
V	Notiomystis cincta	Stitchbird

158. (EMBERIZIDAE) EMBERIZINAE

R	Ammodramus maritimus mirabilis	Cape Sable Seaside Sparrow
E	Ammodramus maritimus nigrescens	Dusky Seaside Sparrow
E	Amphispiza belli clementeae	San Clemente Sage Sparrow
R	Camarhynchus heliobates	Mangrove Finch
I	Geospiza magnirostris magnirostris	Floreana Large Ground Finch
E	Melospiza melodia amaka	Amak Song Sparrow
R	Nesospiza wilkinsi	Grosbeak Bunting
R	Torreornis inexpectata	Zapata Sparrow

161. (EMBERIZIDAE) THRAUPINAE

E	Nemosia rourei	Cherry-throated Tanager
I	Tangara cabanisi	Azure-rumped Tanager
V	Tangara fastuosa	Seven-colored Tanager

163. PARULIDAE

E   Dendroica kirtlandii   Kirtland's Warbler
E   Dendroica petechia petechia   Barbados Yellow Warbler
I   Geothlypis rostrata rostrata   New Providence Bahama Yellow-throat
E   Leucopeza semperi   Semper's Warbler
E   Vermivora bachmanii   Bachman's Warbler

164. DREPANIDIDAE

E   Hemignathus lucidus affinus   Maui Nukupu'u
E   Hemignathus lucidus hanapepe   Kauai Nukupu'u
E   Hemignathus obscurus procerus   Kauai 'Akialoa
E   Hemignathus wilsoni   'Akiapola'au
E   Loxioides bailleui   Palila
V   Loxops coccinea coccinea   Hawaii 'Akepa
E   Loxops coccinea ochracea   Maui 'Akepa
R   Melamprosops phaeosoma   Po'o Uli
V   Palmeria dolei   Crested Honeycreeper
R   Paroreomyza maculata bairdi   Kauai Creeper
E   Paroreomyza maculata flammea   Molokai Creeper
E   Paroreomyza maculata maculata   Oahu Creeper
V   Pseudonestor xanthophrys   Maui Parrotbill
E   Psittirostra psittacea   'O'u

166. ICTERIDAE

V   Agelaius xanthomus monensis   Mona Yellow-shouldered Blackbird
V   Agelaius xanthomus xanthomus   Puerto Rican Yellow-shouldered
                                    Blackbird

167. FRINGILLIDAE

I   Atlapetes flaviceps   Olive-headed Brush-Finch
E   Pyrrhula pyrrhula murina   São Miguel Bullfinch
E   Spinus cucullatus   Red Siskin
I   Sporophila insulata   Tumaco Seedeater

168. ESTRILDIDAE

R   Erythrura kleinschmidti   Pink-billed Parrotfinch
I   Erythrura trichroa pelewensis   Palau Blue-faced Parrotfinch

172. (PLOCEIDAE) PLOCEINAE

E   Foudia flavicans   Rodrigues Fody
E   Foudia rubra   Mauritius Fody
R   Foudia sechellarum   Seychelles Fody
R   Ploceus golandi   Clarke's Weaver
R   Ploceus olivaceiceps nicolli   Usambara Weaver

173. STURNIDAE

V   Aplonis pelzelni   Ponape Mountain Starling
R   Aplonis santovestris   Santo Mountain Starling
E   Leucopsar rothschildi   Rothschild's Starling

176. CALLAEIDAE

E   Callaeas cinerea cinerea   South Island Kokako
V   Callaeas cinerea wilsoni   North Island Kokako
O   Creadion carunculatus   Saddleback

178. ARTAMIDAE

R   Artamus leucorhynchus pelewensis   Palau White-breasted Wood-Swallow

179. CRACTICIDAE

E   Strepera graculina crissalis   Lord Howe Currawong

182. CORVIDAE

E   Corvus kubaryi   Marianas Crow
E   Corvus tropicus   Hawaiian Crow

TAXA LISTED IN THE FIRST EDITION OF RED DATA BOOK VOL. 2

BUT OMITTED FROM THIS SECOND EDITION

except for four 'out-of-danger' taxa

Ninety-five taxa included in the First Edition of this Volume and listed below, have for a variety of reasons been omitted from this Second Edition, except that in four cases enough reliable information is available to justify the issue of 'green' data sheets. This denotes that they are now considered 'out of danger', their status having improved as the direct or indirect result of conservation measures taken. Of the remaining 91, two have been omitted on taxonomic grounds and the rest are now known or thought not to be at risk, in the light of the latest reports on their population trends and the security of their habitats. Some of them, however, have relatively small populations or restricted ranges, others are still poorly known, though there is nothing to suggest that they are at risk: in both cases their status is of conservation concern and needs to be kept under continuing surveillance.

8	TINAMIDAE	
	Crypturellus atrocapillus atrocapillus	Black-headed Tinamou
	Crypturellus casiquiare	Barred Tinamou
9	SPHENISCIDAE	
	Spheniscus mendiculus	Galapagos Penguin
11	PODICIPEDIDAE	
	Rollandia micropterum	Titicaca Grebe
13	PROCELLARIIDAE	
	Pterodroma leucoptera longirostris	Japanese Petrel
30	ANATIDAE	
	Cereopsis novaehollandiae	Cereopsis Goose
	Anas diazi	Mexican Duck
33	ACCIPITRIDAE	
	Gypaetus barbatus meridionalis	African Lammergeyer
	Circus maillardi maillardi	Réunion Harrier
35	FALCONIDAE	
	Falco fasciinucha	Teita Falcon
38	TETRAONIDAE	
	Tympanuchus cupido pinnatus	Greater Prairie Chicken
39	PHASIANIDAE	
	Polyplectron malacense schleiermacheri	Malaysian Peacock Pheasant
46	GRUIDAE	
	Grus canadensis pratensis	Florida Sandhill Crane
49	RALLIDAE	
	Rallus longirostris yumanensis	Yuma Clapper Rail
	Aramidopsis plateni	Platen's Celebes Rail

49 RALLIDAE (continued)
Gallirallus australis hectori   Eastern Weka
Nesophylax ater   Henderson Island Rail
Laterallus jamaicensis jamaicensis   Jamaican Black Rail

70 ALCIDAE
Synthliboramphus wumizusume   Japanese Murrelet

73 COLUMBIDAE
Ducula mindorensis   Mindoro Imperial Pigeon
Streptopelia reichenowi   White-winged Dove
Gallicolumba canifrons   Palau Ground Dove

74 PSITTACIDAE
Prosopeia personata   Masked Parakeet
Neophema pulchella   Turquoise Parakeet
Eunymphicus cornutus cornutus   Horned Parakeet
Cyanoramphus unicolor   Antipodes Island Parakeet
Pezoporus wallicus leachi   Tasmanian Ground Parrot

75 MUSOPHAGIDAE
Tauraco ruspolii   Prince Ruspoli's Turaco

76 CUCULIDAE
Coccyzus minor ferrugineus   Cocos Mangrove Cuckoo
Phaenicophaeus pyrrhocephalus   Red-faced Malkoha

78 STRIGIDAE
Otus gurneyi   Giant Scops Owl
Otus podargina   Palau Owl
Asio flammeus portoricensis   Puerto Rican Short-eared Owl

83 CAPRIMULGIDAE
Siphonorhis americanus brewsteri   Hispaniolan Least Pauraque

84 APODIDAE
Apus myoptilus   Scarce Swift
Apus toulsoni   Luanda Swift
Micropanyptila furcata furcata   Pygmy Swift

86 TROCHILIDAE
Phaethornis porcullae   Porculla Hermit
Goldmania violiceps   Violet-capped Hummingbird
Goethalsia bella   Rufous-cheeked Hummingbird
Amazilia castaneiventris   Chestnut-bellied Hummingbird
Amazilia cyaneotincta   Blue Spotted Hummingbird
Amazilia hollandi   Eastern Venezuela Versicolor Emerald
Amazilia luciae   Honduran Emerald
Phlogophilus harterti   Peruvian Piedtail
Hylonympha macrocerca   Scissor-tailed Hummingbird
Metallura malagae   Reddish Metaltail
Augastes lumachellus   Hooded Visorbearer
Loddigesia mirabilis   Marvelous Spatuletail

97 BUCEROTIDAE
Aceros narcondami   Narcondam Hornbill

103 PICIDAE
Melanerpes superciliaris blakei
                                            Abaco Red-bellied Woodpecker

106 FURNARIIDAE
Aphrastura masafuerae   Masafuera Creeper
Asthenes sclateri   Sclater's Spinetail

112 TYRANNIDAE
Nesotriccus ridgwayi
                                            Cocos Island Flycatcher

115 PITTIDAE
Pitta kochi
                                            Koch's Pitta

123 CAMPEPHAGIDAE
Coracina graueri
                                            Grauer's Cuckoo Shrike

124 PYCNONOTIDAE
Hypsipetes borbonicus olivaceus
                                            Mauritius Olivaceous Bulbul

131 TROGLODYTIDAE
Salpinctes obsoletus guadeloupensis   Guadalupe Rock Wren
Thryomanes sissonii   Socorro Island Wren
Troglodytes aedon musicus   St. Vincent Wren
Troglodytes troglodytes alascensis   Pribilov Wren
Troglodytes troglodytes hirtensis   St. Kilda Wren

132 MIMIDAE
Mimodes graysoni
                                            Socorro Island Thrasher

134 (MUSCICAPIDAE) TURDINAE
Erithacus ruficeps   Rufous-headed Robin
Zoothera cinerea   Ashy Ground Thrush
Nesocichla eremita gordoni   Inaccessible Island Starchy
Nesocichla eremita procax   Nightingale Island Starchy
Turdus helleri   Teita Olive Thrush

135 (MUSCICAPIDAE) ORTHONYCHINAE
Psophodes nigrogularis
                                            Western Whipbird

140 (MUSCICAPIDAE) SYLVIINAE
Acrocephalus luscinia rehsei   Nauru Nightingale Warbler
Sericornis nigroviridis   Watut Leaf Warbler
Bebrornis sechellensis   Seychelles Warbler

142 (MUSCICAPIDAE) MUSCICAPINAE
Muscicapa ruecki   Rueck's Blue Flycatcher
Rhipidura lepida   Palau Fantail
Petroica multicolor multicolor   Scarlet-breasted Robin

144 (MUSCICAPIDAE) MONARCHINAE
Monarcha takatsukasae
                                            Tinian Monarch

156 ZOSTEROPIDAE
Speirops brunnea
                                            Fernando Poo Speirops

157 MELIPHAGIDAE
Prosthemadera novaseelandiae chathamensis   Chatham Island Tui

158 (EMBERIZIDAE) EMBERIZINAE
    Pipilo erythrophthalmus carmani   Rufous-sided Towhee
    Passerculus princeps   Ipswich Sparrow
    Junco insularis   Guadalupe Junco
    Compsospiza baeri   Baer's Mountain Finch
    Compsospiza garleppi   Garlepp's Mountain Finch

163 PARULIDAE
    Dendroica petechia aureola   Cocos Yellow Warbler

164 DREPANIDIDAE
    Loxops maculata newtoni   Maui Creeper

165 VIREONIDAE
    Vireo gracilirostris   Slender-billed Vireo

166 ICTERIDAE
    Tangavius armenti   Colombian Red-eyed Cowbird
    Cassidix nicaraguensis   Nicaragua Grackle

167 FRINGILLIDAE
    Carpodacus amplus   Guadalupe House Finch
    Pinaroloxias inornata   Cocos Island Finch
    Paroaria baeri   Baer's Cardinal
    Warsanglia johannis   Warsangli Bunting
    Nesospiza acunhae acunhae   Tristan Bunting
    Nesospiza acunhae questi   Nightingale Island Bunting

176 CALLAEIDAE
    Creadion carunculatus   Saddleback

THREATENED BIRDS LISTED IN RED DATA BOOK VOL. 2

ARRANGED ON A ZOOGEOGRAPHICAL/GEOPOLITICAL BASIS

June 1979

Zoogeographic Regions

The zoogeographic regions first described by Wallace in 1876 are used as a basis for this index.   However, one has been added to provide for Antarctic fauna, and boundaries have been adjusted in one or two cases in order to avoid subdividing a particular political unit.

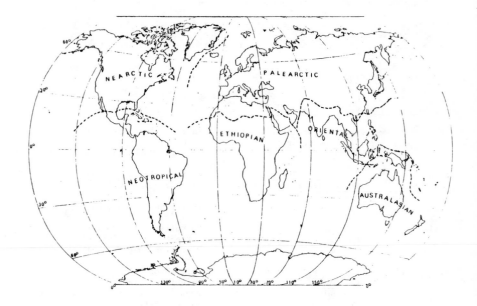

A.   The Palearctic region is the northerly part of the Old World.   It extends over the whole of Europe, USSR and China, including the adjacent offshore islands, and includes the Mediterranean Coast of Africa and northern Arabia.

B.   The Ethiopian region covers southern Arabia, central and southern Africa, and the island of Madagascar with its smaller neighbours.

C.   The Oriental region covers Asia south of China from the western border of Afghanistan and Pakistan east to the Pacific Ocean including the Philippine and the Indonesian Islands.

D.   The Australian region includes the islands of New Guinea, Australia, Tasmania and New Zealand.

E.   The Nearctic region covers all of North America including Greenland, the Aleutian Islands and northern Mexico.

F.   The Neotropical region includes southern Mexico, the Caribbean Islands, Central and South America.

G.   The Antarctic region includes Antarctica and the islands south of the Antarctic Convergence.

H.   Oceans and Oceanic Islands are treated separately.

For the purposes of this listing as well as for clarity and simplicity, it has sometimes been necessary to make arbitrary decisions in placing a species in a particular zoogeographic region.   Where a listed bird is found in more than one political unit, the number of such units in which it regularly occurs is indicated by the figure in brackets following its common name.

This index is confined to threatened birds (i.e. endangered, vulnerable, rare and indeterminate categories) and does not include birds that were formerly threatened but are now considered out of danger (i.e. taxa on green sheets).

A.   PALEARCTIC REGION

Albania	Haliaeetus albicilla	White-tailed Eagle (36)
	Falco peregrinus	Peregrine Falcon (165)
Algeria	Haliaeetus albicilla	White-tailed Eagle (36)
	Falco peregrinus	Peregrine Falcon (165)
	Sitta ledanti	Kabylian Nuthatch
Austria	Haliaeetus albicilla	White-tailed Eagle (36)
	Falco peregrinus	Peregrine Falcon (165)
Bahrain	Falco peregrinus	Peregrine Falcon (165)
Bulgaria	Pelecanus crispus	Dalmatian Pelican (13)
	Haliaeetus albicilla	White-tailed Eagle (36)
	Falco peregrinus	Peregrine Falcon (165)
China	Egretta eulophotes	Chinese Egret (10)
	Ciconia ciconia boyciana	Oriental White Stork (5)
	Nipponia nippon	Japanese Crested Ibis (4)
	Mergus squamatus	Chinese Merganser (4)
	Haliaeetus albicilla	White-tailed Eagle (36)
	Falco peregrinus	Peregrine Falcon (165)
	Tragopan blythii	Blyth's Tragopan (4)
	Tragopan caboti	Cabot's Tragopan
	Lophophorus sclateri	Sclater's Monal (3)
	Lophophorus lhuysii	Chinese Monal
	Crossoptilon mantchuricum	Brown Eared Pheasant
	Crossoptilon crossoptilon	White Eared Pheasant (3)
	Syrmaticus humiae	Hume's Bar-tailed Pheasant (3)
	Syrmaticus ellioti	Elliot's Pheasant
	Pavo muticus	Green Peafowl (9)
	Grus nigricollis	Black-necked Crane (5)
	Grus monacha	Hooded Crane (5)
	Grus japonensis	Japanese Crane (4)
	Grus leucogeranus	Siberian White Crane (5)

	Grus vipio	White-naped Crane (5)
	Tringa guttifer	Nordmann's Greenshank (12)
	Limnodromus semipalmatus	Asian Dowitcher (14)
	Larus relictus	Relict Gull (4)
	Sterna zimmermanni	Chinese Crested Tern (5)
	Paradoxornis heudei heudei	Lower Yangtze Kiang Crow-tit
Cyprus	Falco peregrinus	Peregrine Falcon (165)
	Larus audouinii	Audouin's Gull (9)
Czechoslovakia	Haliaeetus albicilla	White-tailed Eagle (36)
	Falco peregrinus	Peregrine Falcon (165)
Egypt	Pelecanus crispus	Dalmatian Pelican (13)
	Haliaeetus albicilla	White-tailed Eagle (36)
	Falco peregrinus	Peregrine Falcon (165)
Finland	Haliaeetus albicilla	White-tailed Eagle (36)
	Falco peregrinus	Peregrine Falcon (165)
France	Haliaeetus albicilla	White-tailed Eagle (36)
	Falco peregrinus	Peregrine Falcon (165)
	Larus audouinii	Audouin's Gull (9)
German Democratic Republic	Haliaeetus albicilla	White-tailed Eagle (36)
	Falco peregrinus	Peregrine Falcon (165)
Germany, Federal Republic of	Haliaeetus albicilla	White-tailed Eagle (36)
	Falco peregrinus	Peregrine Falcon (165)
Great Britain	Troglodytes troglodytes fridariensis	Fair Isle Wren
	Falco peregrinus	Peregrine Falcon (165)
Greece	Pelecanus crispus	Dalmatian Pelican (13)
	Haliaeetus albicilla	White-tailed Eagle (36)
	Falco peregrinus	Peregrine Falcon (165)
	Larus audouinii	Audouin's Gull (9)
Hong Kong	Egretta eulophotes	Chinese Egret (10)
	Falco peregrinus	Peregrine Falcon (165)
	Tringa guttifer	Nordmann's Greenshank (12)
	Limnodromus semipalmatus	Asian Dowitcher (14)
Hungary	Haliaeetus albicilla	White-tailed Eagle (36)
Iceland	Haliaeetus albicilla	White-tailed Eagle (36)
Iran	Pelecanus crispus	Dalmatian Pelican (13)
	Haliaeetus albicilla	White-tailed Eagle (36)
	Falco peregrinus	Peregrine Falcon (165)
	Grus leucogeranus	Siberian White Crane (5)
Iraq	Pelecanus crispus	Dalmatian Pelican (13)
	Haliaeetus albicilla	White-tailed Eagle (36)
	Falco peregrinus	Peregrine Falcon (165)
Ireland	Falco peregrinus	Peregrine Falcon (165)
Israel	Falco peregrinus	Peregrine Falcon (165)

| Italy | Falco peregrinus | Peregrine Falcon (165) |
| | Perdix perdix italica | Italian Grey Partridge |

Japan	Diomedea albatrus	Short-tailed Albatross
	Egretta eulophotes	Chinese Egret (10)
	Ciconia ciconia boyciana	Oriental White Stork (5)
	Nipponia nippon	Japanese Crested Ibis (4)
	Branta canadensis leucopareia	Aleutian Canada Goose (4)
	Haliaeetus albicilla	White-tailed Eagle (36)
	Falco peregrinus	Peregrine Falcon (165)
	Grus monacha	Hooded Crane (5)
	Grus japonensis	Japanese Crane (4)
	Grus vipio	White-naped Crane (5)
	Tringa guttifer	Nordmann's Greenshank (12)
	Limnodromus semipalmatus	Asian Dowitcher (14)
	Picoides tridactylus inouyei	Inouye's Three-toed Woodpecker
	Megalurus pryeri pryeri	Japanese Marsh Warbler

| Jordan | Falco peregrinus | Peregrine Falcon (165) |

Korea	Egretta eulophotes	Chinese Egret (10)
	Ciconia ciconia boyciana	Oriental White Stork (5)
	Nipponia nippon	Japanese Crested Ibis (4)
	Mergus squamatus	Chinese Merganser (4)
	Haliaeetus albicilla	White-tailed Eagle (36)
	Falco peregrinus	Peregrine Falcon (165)
	Grus monacha	Hooded Crane (5)
	Grus japonensis	Japanese Crane (4)
	Grus vipio	White-naped Crane (5)
	Tringa guttifer	Nordmann's Greenshank (12)
	Dryocopus javensis richardsi	Tristram's Woodpecker

| Kuwait | Pelecanus crispus | Dalmatian Pelican (13) |
| | Falco peregrinus | Peregrine Falcon (165) |

| Lebanon | Falco peregrinus | Peregrine Falcon (165) |
| | Larus audouinii | Audouin's Gull (9) |

| Libya | Falco peregrinus | Peregrine Falcon (165) |

| Malta | Falco peregrinus | Peregrine Falcon (165) |

Mongolia	Pelecanus crispus	Dalmatian Pelican (13)
	Haliaeetus albicilla	White-tailed Eagle (36)
	Falco peregrinus	Peregrine Falcon (165)
	Grus monacha	Hooded Crane (5)
	Grus vipio	White-naped Crane (5)
	Limnodromus semipalmatus	Asian Dowitcher (14)
	Larus relictus	Relict Gull (4)

Morocco	Geronticus eremita	Waldrapp (8)
	Aquila heliaca adalberti	Spanish Imperial Eagle (3)
	Falco peregrinus	Peregrine Falcon (165)
	Larus audouinii	Audouin's Gull (9)

| Norway | Haliaeetus albicilla | White-tailed Eagle (36) |
| | Falco peregrinus | Peregrine Falcon (165) |

| Oman | Falco peregrinus | Peregrine Falcon (165) |

Poland	Haliaeetus albicilla Falco peregrinus	White-tailed Eagle (36) Peregrine Falcon (165)
Portugal	Aquila heliaca adalberti Falco peregrinus	Spanish Imperial Eagle (3) Peregrine Falcon (165)
Qatar	Falco peregrinus	Peregrine Falcon (165)
Rumania	Pelecanus crispus Haliaeetus albicilla Falco peregrinus	Dalmatian Pelican (13) White-tailed Eagle (36) Peregrine Falcon (165)
Saudi Arabia	Geronticus eremita Falco peregrinus Limnodromus semipalmatus	Waldrapp (8) Peregrine Falcon (165) Asian Dowitcher (14)
Spain	Aquila heliaca adalberti Falco peregrinus Tetrao urogallus cantabricus Larus audouinii	Spanish Imperial Eagle (3) Peregrine Falcon (165) Cantabrian Capercaillie Audouin's Gull (9)
Sweden	Haliaeetus albicilla Falco peregrinus	White-tailed Eagle (36) Peregrine Falcon (165)
Switzerland	Falco peregrinus	Peregrine Falcon (165)
Syria	Haliaeetus albicilla Falco peregrinus	White-tailed Eagle (36) Peregrine Falcon (165)
Taiwan	Egretta eulophotes Ciconia ciconia boyciana Haliaeetus albicilla Falco peregrinus Lophura swinhoii Syrmaticus mikado Tringa guttifer Otus elegans botelensis	Chinese Egret (10) Oriental White Stork (5) White-tailed Eagle (36) Peregrine Falcon (165) Swinhoe's Pheasant Mikado Pheasant Nordmann's Greenshank (12) Lanyu Scops Owl
Tunisia	Haliaeetus albicilla Falco peregrinus Larus audouinii	White-tailed Eagle (36) Peregrine Falcon (165) Audouin's Gull (9)
Turkey	Pelecanus crispus Geronticus eremita Haliaeetus albicilla Falco peregrinus Larus audouinii	Dalmatian Pelican (13) Waldrapp (8) White-tailed Eagle (36) Peregrine Falcon (165) Audouin's Gull (9)
USSR	Pelecanus crispus Egretta eulophotes Ciconia ciconia boyciana Nipponia nippon Mergus squamatus Haliaeetus albicilla Falco peregrinus Grus monacha Grus japonensis Grus vipio Grus leucogeranus Larus relictus Tringa guttifer Limnodromus semipalmatus	Dalmatian Pelican (13) Chinese Egret (10) Oriental White Stork (5) Japanese Crested Ibis (4) Chinese Merganser (4) White-tailed Eagle (36) Peregrine Falcon (165) Hooded Crane (5) Japanese Crane (4) White-naped Crane (5) Siberian White Crane (5) Relict Gull (4) Nordmann's Greenshank (12) Asian Dowitcher (14)

United Arab Emirates	Falco peregrinus	Peregrine Falcon (165)
Western Sahara	Falco peregrinus	Peregrine Falcon (165)
Yugoslavia	Pelecanus crispus	Dalmatian Pelican (13)
	Haliaeetus albicilla	White-tailed Eagle (36)
	Falco peregrinus	Peregrine Falcon (165)

B. ETHIOPIAN REGION

Angola	Falco peregrinus	Peregrine Falcon (165)
	Francolinus swierstrai	Swierstra's Francolin
	Sterna balaenarum	Damara Tern (9)
Benin	Falco peregrinus	Peregrine Falcon (165)
Botswana	Gyps coprotheres	Cape Vulture (5)
	Falco peregrinus	Peregrine Falcon (165)
Burundi	Falco peregrinus	Peregrine Falcon (165)
Cameroon	Falco peregrinus	Peregrine Falcon (165)
	Sterna balaenarum	Damara Tern (9)
	Malaconotus kupeensis	Kupe Mountain Bush Shrike
	Picathartes oreas	Grey-necked Picathartes (2)
Central African Empire	Falco peregrinus	Peregrine Falcon (165)
Chad	Falco peregrinus	Peregrine Falcon (165)
Congo	Falco peregrinus	Peregrine Falcon (165)
	Sterna balaenarum	Damara Tern (9)
Djibouti	Falco peregrinus	Peregrine Falcon (165)
	Francolinus ochropectus	Tadjoura Francolin
Equatorial Guinea	Falco peregrinus	Peregrine Falcon (165)
	Sterna balaenarum	Damara Tern (9)
Ethiopia	Geronticus eremita	Waldrapp (8)
	Falco peregrinus	Peregrine Falcon (165)
Gabon	Falco peregrinus	Peregrine Falcon (165)
	Sterna balaenarum	Damara Tern (9)
	Picathartes oreas	Grey-necked Picathartes (2)
Gambia	Falco peregrinus	Peregrine Falcon (165)
Ghana	Falco peregrinus	Peregrine Falcon (165)
	Picathartes gymnocephalus	White-necked Picathartes (5)
Guinea-Bissau	Falco peregrinus	Peregrine Falcon (165)
Ivory Coast	Falco peregrinus	Peregrine Falcon (165)

Kenya	Falco peregrinus	Peregrine Falcon (165)
	Otus ireneae	Morden's Scops Owl
	Anthus sokokensis	Sokoke Pipit (2)
	Anthreptes pallidigaster	Amani Sunbird (2)
	Ploceus golandi	Clarke's Weaver
Lesotho	Geronticus calvus	Bald Ibis (3)
	Gyps coprotheres	Cape Vulture (5)
	Falco peregrinus	Peregrine Falcon (165)
Liberia	Falco peregrinus	Peregrine Falcon (165)
	Picathartes gymnocephalus	White-necked Picathartes (5)
Madagascar	Tachybaptus rufolavatus	Madagascar Red-necked Grebe
	Lophotibis cristata	Madagascar Crested Ibis
	Anas bernieri	Madagascar Teal
	Aythya innotata	Madagascar Pochard
	Eutriorchis astur	Madagascar Serpent Eagle
	Haliaeetus vociferoides	Madagascar Sea Eagle
	Falco peregrinus	Peregrine Falcon (165)
	Mesoenas variegata	White-breasted Mesite
	Mesoenas unicolor	Brown Mesite
	Monias benschi	Bensch's Monias
	Brachypteracias leptosomus	Short-legged Ground Roller
	Brachypteracias squamigera	Scaled Ground Roller
	Atelornis pittoides	Pitta-like Ground Roller
	Atelornis crossleyi	Crossley's Ground Roller
	Uratelornis chimaera	Long-tailed Ground Roller
	Pachycoccyx audeberti audeberti	Madagascar Thick-billed Cuckoo
	Tyto soumagnei	Soumagne's Owl
	Neodrepanis hypoxantha	Small-billed Wattled Sunbird
	Newtonia fanovanae	Fanovana Newtonia
	Oriolia bernieri	Bernier's Vanga
	Xenopirostris polleni	Pollen's Vanga
	Xenopirostris damii	Van Dam's Vanga
Malawi	Falco peregrinus	Peregrine Falcon (165)
Mali	Falco peregrinus	Peregrine Falcon (165)
Mauritania	Geronticus eremita	Waldrapp (8)
	Falco peregrinus	Peregrine Falcon (165)
Mozambique	Falco peregrinus	Peregrine Falcon (165)
	Modulatrix orostruthus	Dappled Mountain-Robin (2)
Niger	Falco peregrinus	Peregrine Falcon (165)
Nigeria	Falco peregrinus	Peregrine Falcon (165)
	Sterna balaenarum	Damara Tern (9)
Rhodesia/Zimbabwe	Gyps coprotheres	Cape Vulture (5)
	Falco peregrinus	Peregrine Falcon (165)
Rwanda	Falco peregrinus	Peregrine Falcon (165)
Senegal	Falco peregrinus	Peregrine Falcon (165)

Sierra Leone	Falco peregrinus	Peregrine Falcon (165)
	Picathartes gymnocephalus	White-necked Picathartes (5)
Somalia	Geronticus eremita	Waldrapp (8)
	Falco peregrinus	Peregrine Falcon (165)
South Africa	Spheniscus demersus	Jackass Penguin
	Geronticus calvus	Bald Ibis (3)
	Gyps coprotheres	Cape Vulture (5)
	Falco peregrinus	Peregrine Falcon (165)
	Sterna balaenarum	Damara Tern (9)
	Stactolaema olivacea woodwardi	Ngoye Green Barbet
South West Africa/ Namibia	Geronticus eremita	Waldrapp (8)
	Gyps coprotheres	Cape Vulture (5)
	Falco peregrinus	Peregrine Falcon (165)
	Sterna balaenarum	Damara Tern (9)
South Yemen	Falco peregrinus	Peregrine Falcon (165)
Sudan	Geronticus eremita	Waldrapp (8)
	Falco peregrinus	Peregrine Falcon (165)
Swaziland	Geronticus calvus	Bald Ibis (3)
	Falco peregrinus	Peregrine Falcon (165)
Tanzania	Falco peregrinus	Peregrine Falcon (165)
	Bubo poensis vosseleri	Nduk Eagle Owl
	Anthus sokokensis	Sokoke Pipit (2)
	Malaconotus alius	Black-capped Bush-Shrike
	Modulatrix orostruthus	Dappled Mountain-Robin (2)
	Alethe montana	Usambara Robin-Chat
	Anthreptes pallidigaster	Amani Sunbird (2)
	Ploceus olivaceiceps nicolli	Usambara Weaver
Togo	Falco peregrinus	Peregrine Falcon (165)
	Picathartes gymnocephalus	White-necked Picathartes (5)
Uganda	Falco peregrinus	Peregrine Falcon (165)
Upper Volta	Falco peregrinus	Peregrine Falcon (165)
Yemen	Falco peregrinus	Peregrine Falcon (165)
Zaire	Falco peregrinus	Peregrine Falcon (165)
	Sterna balaenarum	Damara Tern (9)
Zambia	Falco peregrinus	Peregrine Falcon (165)
Zanzibar	Tauraco fischeri zanzibaricus	Zanzibar Red-crested Lourie

C.   ORIENTAL REGION

Afghanistan	Haliaeetus albicilla	White-tailed Eagle (36)
	Falco peregrinus	Peregrine Falcon (165)
	Grus leucogeranus	Siberian White Crane (5)

Bangladesh	Cairina scutulata	White-winged Wood Duck (6)
	Falco peregrinus	Peregrine Falcon (165)
	Tringa guttifer	Nordmann's Greenshank (12)
Bhutan	Falco peregrinus	Peregrine Falcon (165)
	Tragopan blythii	Blyth's Tragopan (4)
	Grus nigricollis	Black-necked Crane (5)
Burma	Pseudibis davisoni	White-shouldered Ibis (5)
	Cairina scutulata	White-winged Wood Duck (6)
	Mergus squamatus	Chinese Merganser (4)
	Falco peregrinus	Peregrine Falcon (165)
	Tragopan blythii	Blyth's Tragopan (4)
	Lophophorus sclateri	Sclater's Monal (3)
	Crossoptilon crossoptilon	White Eared Pheasant (3)
	Syrmaticus humiae	Hume's Bar-tailed Pheasant (4)
	Pavo muticus	Green Peafowl (9)
	Grus nigricollis	Black-necked Crane (5)
	Limnodromus semipalmatus	Asian Dowitcher (14)
	Tringa guttifer	Nordmann's Greenshank (12)
	Pitta gurneyi	Gurney's Pitta (2)
	Rhinoplax vigil	Helmeted Hornbill (4)
India	Pelecanus crispus	Dalmatian Pelican (13)
	Cairina scutulata	White-winged Wood Duck (6)
	Haliaeetus albicilla	White-tailed Eagle (36)
	Falco peregrinus	Peregrine Falcon (165)
	Tragopan melanocephalus	Western Tragopan (2)
	Tragopan blythii	Blyth's Tragopan (4)
	Lophophorus sclateri	Sclater's Monal (3)
	Crossoptilon crossoptilon	White Eared Pheasant (3)
	Catreus wallichii	Cheer Pheasant (3)
	Syrmaticus humiae	Hume's Bar-tailed Pheasant (4)
	Pavo muticus	Green Peafowl (9)
	Grus nigricollis	Black-necked Crane (5)
	Grus leucogeranus	Siberian White Crane (5)
	Choriotis nigriceps	Great Indian Bustard (2)
	Tringa guttifer	Nordmann's Greenshank (12)
	Limnodromus semipalmatus	Asian Dowitcher (14)
	Athene blewitti	Forest Little Owl
Indonesia	Egretta eulophotes	Chinese Egret (10)
	Mycteria cinerea	Milky Stork (4)
	Ciconia episcopus stormi	Storm's Stork (2)
	Cairina scutulata	White-winged Wood Duck (6)
	Falco peregrinus	Peregrine Falcon (165)
	Macrocephalon maleo	Maleo
	Lophura bulweri	Bulwer's Wattled Pheasant (2)
	Pavo muticus	Green Peafowl (9)
	Vanellus macropterus	Javanese Wattled Lapwing
	Tringa guttifer	Nordmann's Greenshank (12)
	Sterna zimmermanni	Chinese Crested Tern (5)
	Otus magicus beccarii	Papuan Scops Owl
	Rhinoplax vigil	Helmeted Hornbill (4)
	Leucopsar rothschildi	Rothschild's Starling
Kampuchea	Mycteria cinerea	Milky Stork (4)
	Pseudibis davisoni	White-shouldered Ibis (5)
	Thaumatibis gigantea	Giant Ibis (4)

	Falco peregrinus	Peregrine Falcon (165)
	Pavo muticus	Green Peafowl (9)
	Limnodromus semipalmatus	Asian Dowitcher (14)
Laos	Pseudibis davisoni	White-shouldered Ibis (5)
	Thaumatibis gigantea	Giant Ibis (4)
	Falco peregrinus	Peregrine Falcon (165)
	Lophura imperialis	Imperial Pheasant (2)
	Rheinardia ocellata	Crested Argus Pheasant (3)
	Pavo muticus	Green Peafowl (9)
Malaysia	Egretta eulophotes	Chinese Egret (10)
	Mycteria cinerea	Milky Stork (4)
	Ciconia episcopus stormi	Storm's Stork (2)
	Cairina scutulata	White-winged Wood Duck (6)
	Falco peregrinus	Peregrine Falcon (165)
	Lophura bulweri	Bulwer's Wattled Pheasant (2)
	Rheinardia ocellata	Crested Argus Pheasant (3)
	Pavo muticus	Green Peafowl (9)
	Tringa guttifer	Nordmann's Greenshank (12)
	Limnodromus semipalmatus	Asian Dowitcher (14)
	Sterna zimmermanni	Chinese Crested Tern (5)
	Rhinoplax vigil	Helmeted Hornbill (4)
Nepal	Falco peregrinus	Peregrine Falcon (165)
	Catreus wallichii	Cheer Pheasant (3)
Pakistan	Pelecanus crispus	Dalmatian Pelican (13)
	Haliaeetus albicilla	White-tailed Eagle (36)
	Falco peregrinus	Peregrine Falcon (165)
	Tragopan melanocephalus	Western Tragopan (2)
	Catreus wallichii	Cheer Pheasant (3)
	Choriotis nigriceps	Great Indian Bustard (2)
Philippines	Egretta eulophotes	Chinese Egret (10)
	Pithecophaga jefferyi	Philippine Eagle
	Falco peregrinus	Peregrine Falcon (165)
	Polyplectron emphanum	Palawan Peacock Pheasant
	Limnodromus semipalmatus	Asian Dowitcher (14)
	Sterna zimmermanni	Chinese Crested Tern (5)
Singapore	Falco peregrinus	Peregrine Falcon (165)
	Tringa guttifer	Nordmann's Greenshank (12)
	Limnodromus semipalmatus	Asian Dowitcher (14)
Sikkim	Falco peregrinus	Peregrine Falcon (165)
Sri Lanka	Falco peregrinus	Peregrine Falcon (165)
	Eurystomus orientalis irisi	Ceylon Broad-billed Roller
Thailand	Egretta eulophotes	Chinese Egret (10)
	Pseudibis davisoni	White-shouldered Ibis (5)
	Thaumatibis gigantea	Giant Ibis (4)
	Cairina scutulata	White-winged Wood Duck (6)
	Falco peregrinus	Peregrine Falcon (165)
	Syrmaticus humiae	Hume's Bar-tailed Pheasant (4)
	Pavo muticus	Green Peafowl (9)
	Limnodromus semipalmatus	Asian Dowitcher (14)

	Sterna zimmermanni	Chinese Crested Tern (5)
	Rhinoplax vigil	Helmeted Hornbill (4)
	Pitta gurneyi	Gurney's Pitta (2)
	Pseudochelidon sirintarae	White-eyed River Martin
Vietnam	Mycteria cinerea	Milky Stork (4)
	Pseudibis davisoni	White-shouldered Ibis (5)
	Thaumatibis gigantea	Giant Ibis (4)
	Falco peregrinus	Peregrine Falcon (165)
	Lophura imperialis	Imperial Pheasant (2)
	Lophura edwardsi	Edwards's Pheasant
	Rheinardia ocellata	Crested Argus Pheasant (3)
	Pavo muticus	Green Peafowl (9)
	Grus nigricollis	Black-necked Crane (5)
	Limnodromus semipalmatus	Asian Dowitcher (14)
	Larus relictus	Relict Gull (4)

D. AUSTRALIAN REGION

Australia	Pterodroma leucoptera leucoptera	Gould's Petrel
	Falco peregrinus	Peregrine Falcon (165)
	Geopsittacus occidentalis	Night Parrot
	Pezoporus wallicus wallicus	Eastern Ground Parrot
	Pezoporus wallicus flaviventris	Western Ground Parrot
	Neophema chrysogaster	Orange-bellied Parakeet
	Neophema splendida	Splendid Parakeet
	Psephotus chrysopterygius chrysopterygius	Golden-shouldered Parakeet
	Psephotus chrysopterygius dissimilis	Hooded Parakeet
	Psephotus pulcherrimus	Paradise Parakeet
	Atrichornis clamosus	Noisy Scrub-bird
	Atrichornis rufescens	Rufous Scrub-bird
	Amytornis goyderi	Eyrean Grass-wren
	Dasyornis brachypterus longirostris	Western Bristlebird
	Dasyornis broadbenti littoralis	Western Rufous Bristlebird
	Meliphaga melanops cassidix	Helmeted Honeyeater
New Zealand	Pterodroma cookii cookii	New Zealand Cook's Petrel
	Procellaria parkinsoni	Black Petrel
	Procellaria westlandica	Westland Black Petrel
	Phalacrocorax carunculatus carunculatus	King Shag
	Anas aucklandica chlorotis	Brown Teal
	Notornis mantelli	Takahe
	Himantopus novaezeelandiae	Black Stilt
	Strigops habroptilus	Kakapo
	Cyanoramphus malherbi	Orange-fronted Parakeet
	Xenicus longipes	New Zealand Bush Wren
	Bowdleria punctata wilsoni	Codfish Island Fernbird
	Callaeas cinerea cinerea	South Island Kokako
	Callaeas cinerea wilsoni	North Island Kokako
	Notiomystis cincta	Stitchbird

Papua New Guinea   Falco peregrinus   Peregrine Falcon (165)

E.   NEARCTIC REGION

Canada   Branta canadensis leucopareia Aleutian Canada Goose (4)
                Falco peregrinus   Peregrine Falcon (165)
                Falco peregrinus anatum   American Peregrine Falcon (3)
                Falco peregrinus tundrius   Tundra Peregrine Falcon (41)
                Grus americana   Whooping Crane (3)
                Numenius borealis   Eskimo Curlew (9)
                Dendroica kirtlandii   Kirtland's Warbler (3)

Greenland   Haliaeetus albicilla   White-tailed Eagle (36)
                Falco peregrinus tundrius   Tundra Peregrine Falcon (41)

Mexico   Rhynchopsitta pachyrhyncha
                  pachyrhyncha   Thick-billed Parrot
                Rhynchopsitta pachyrhyncha
                  terrisi   Maroon-fronted Parrot
                Branta canadensis leucopareia Aleutian Canada Goose (4)
                Harpia harpyja   Harpy Eagle (18)
                Haliaeetus leucocephalus
                  leucocephalus   Southern Bald Eagle (2)
                Falco peregrinus anatum   Tundra Peregrine Falcon (41)
                Colinus virginianus ridgwayi   Masked Bobwhite Quail (2)
                Grus americana   Whooping Crane (3)
                Coturnicops novaeboracensis
                  goldmani   Goldman's Yellow Rail
                Rallus longirostris levipes   Light-footed Clapper Rail (2)
                Sterna albifrons browni   California Least Tern (2)
                Pharomachrus mocinno   Resplendent Quetzal (7)
                Campephilus imperialis   Imperial Woodpecker
                Tangara cabanisi   Azure-rumped Tanager (2)

USA   Anser albifrons elgasi   Tule White-fronted Goose
                Branta canadensis leucopareia Aleutian Canada Goose (4)
                Gymnogyps californianus   California Condor
                Haliaeetus leucocephalus
                  leucocephalus   Southern Bald Eagle (2)
                Rostrhamus sociabilis
                  plumbeus   Florida Everglade Kite (2)
                Falco peregrinus   Peregrine Falcon (165)
                Falco peregrinus anatum   American Peregrine Falcon (3)
                Falco peregrinus tundrius   Tundra Peregrine Falcon (41)
                Tympanuchus cupido attwateri   Attwater's Prairie Chicken
                Colinus virginianus ridgwayi   Masked Bobwhite Quail (2)
                Grus americana   Whooping Crane (3)
                Grus canadensis pulla   Mississippi Sandhill Crane
                Rallus longirostris levipes   Light-footed Clapper Rail (2)
                Rallus longirostris obsoletus California Clapper Rail
                Numenius borealis   Eskimo Curlew (9)
                Sterna albifrons browni   California Least Tern (2)
                Picoides borealis   Red-cockaded Woodpecker
                Campephilus principalis
                  principalis   American Ivory-billed Woodpecker
                Lanius ludovicianus mearnsi   San Clemente Loggerhead Shrike
                Amphispiza belli clementeae   San Clemente Sage Sparrow

Melospiza melodia amaka	Amak Song Sparrow	
Ammodramus maritimus nigrescens	Dusky Seaside Sparrow	
Ammodramus maritimus mirabilis	Cape Sable Seaside Sparrow	
Vermivora bachmanii	Bachman's Warbler (2)	
Dendroica kirtlandii	Kirtland's Warbler (3)	

F. NEOTROPICAL REGION

Argentina	Pterocnemia pennata tarapacensis	Puna Rhea (4)
	Podiceps gallardoi	Hooded Grebe
	Netta erythrophthalma erythrophthalma	South American Pochard (6)
	Chloephaga rubidiceps	Ruddy-headed Goose (3)
	Mergus octosetaceus	Brazilian Merganser (3)
	Morphnus guianensis	Crested Eagle (15)
	Harpia harpyja	Harpy Eagle (18)
	Leucopternis polionota	Mantled Hawk (3)
	Falco kreyenborgi	Kleinschmidt's Falcon (2)
	Falco peregrinus	Peregrine Falcon (2)
	Falco peregrinus tundrius	Tundra Peregrine Falcon (41)
	Aburria jacutinga	Black-fronted Piping Guan (3)
	Fulica cornuta	Horned Coot (3)
	Numenius borealis	Eskimo Curlew (9)
	Claravis godefrida	Purple-winged Ground-Dove (3)
	Amazona pretrei	Red-spectacled Parrot (3)
	Anodorhynchus glaucus	Glaucous Macaw (3)
	Ara caninde	Wagler's Macaw (3)
	Dryocopus galeatus	Helmeted Woodpecker (3)
	Cinclus schultzi	Rufous-throated Dipper
Bahamas	Dendrocygna arborea	West Indian Whistling Duck (9)
	Falco peregrinus tundrius	Tundra Peregrine Falcon (41)
	Amazona leucocephala bahamensis	Bahamas Parrot
	Melanerpes superciliaris bahamensis	Grand Bahama Red-bellied Woodpecker
	Melanerpes superciliaris nyeanus	San Salvador Red-bellied Woodpecker
	Dendroica kirtlandii	Kirtland's Warbler (3)
	Geothlypis rostrata rostrata	New Providence Bahama Yellow-throat
Barbados	Falco peregrinus tundrius	Tundra Peregrine Falcon (41)
	Numenius borealis	Eskimo Curlew (9)
	Dendroica petechia petechia	Barbados Yellow Warbler
Barbuda	Dendrocygna arborea	West Indian Whistling Duck (9)
	Falco peregrinus tundrius	Tundra Peregrine Falcon (41)
Belize	Harpia harpyja	Harpy Eagle (18)
	Falco peregrinus tundrius	Tundra Peregrine Falcon (41)

Bolivia	Pterocnemia pennata	
	tarapacensis	Puna Rhea (4)
	Morphnus guianensis	Crested Eagle (15)
	Harpia harpyja	Harpy Eagle (18)
	Falco peregrinus tundrius	Tundra Peregrine Falcon (41)
	Fulica cornuta	Horned Coot (3)
	Ara caninde	Wagler's Macaw (3)
Brazil	Tinamus solitarius	
	pernambucensis	Pernambuco Solitary Tinamou
	Tigrisoma fasciatum fasciatum	Fasciated Tiger-Heron
	Netta erythrophthalma	
	erythrophthalma	South American Pochard (6)
	Mergus octosetaceus	Brazilian Merganser (3)
	Morphnus guianensis	Crested Eagle (15)
	Harpia harpyja	Harpy Eagle (18)
	Leucopternis polionota	Mantled Hawk (3)
	Falco peregrinus tundrius	Tundra Peregrine Falcon (41)
	Aburria jacutinga	Black-fronted Piping Guan (3)
	Crax mitu mitu	Eastern Razor-billed Curassow
	Crax blumenbachii	Red-billed Curassow
	Crax fasciolata pinima	Northern Bare-faced Curassow
	Numenius borealis	Eskimo Curlew (9)
	Claravis godefrida	Purple-winged Ground-Dove (3)
	Amazona pretrei	Red-spectacled Parrot
	Amazona brasiliensis	Red-tailed Parrot
	Pyrrhura cruentata	Ochre-marked Parakeet
	Touit surda	Golden-tailed Parrotlet
	Touit melanonota	Brown-backed Parrotlet
	Anodorhynchus leari	Lear's Macaw
	Cyanopsitta spixii	Spix's Macaw
	Aratinga guarouba	Golden Parakeet
	Neomorphus geoffroyi dulcis	South-eastern Rufous-vented
		Ground-Cuckoo
	Neomorphus geoffroyi	
	maximiliani	Bahia Rufous-vented Ground-
		Cuckoo
	Threnetes grzimeki	Black Barbthroat
	Glaucis dohrnii	Hook-billed Hermit
	Phaethornis margarettae	Klabin Farm Long-tailed Hermit
	Phaethornis nigrirostris	Black-billed Hermit
	Dryocopus galeatus	Helmeted Woodpecker (3)
	Formicivora iheringi	Narrow-billed Antwren
	Rhopornis ardesiaca	Slender Antbird
	Pyriglena atra	Fringe-backed Fire-eye
	Myrmotherula erythronotos	Black-hooded Antwren
	Merulaxis stresemanni	Stresemann's Bristlefront
	Scytalopus novacapitalis	Brasilia Tapaculo
	Procnias averano averano	Marcgrave's Bearded Bellbird
	Xipholena atropurpurea	White-winged Cotinga
	Calyptura cristata	Kinglet Calyptura
	Cotinga maculata	Banded Cotinga
	Tangara fastuosa	Seven-colored Tanager
	Nemosia rourei	Cherry-throated Tanager
Caymans	Dendrocygna arborea	West Indian Whistling Duck (9)
	Falco peregrinus tundrius	Tundra Peregrine Falcon (41)
	Amazona leucocephala hesterna	Cayman Brac Parrot

Chile	Pterocnemia pennata tarapacensis	Puna Rhea (4)
	Chloephaga rubidiceps	Ruddy-headed Goose (3)
	Falco kreyenborgi	Kleinschmidt's Falcon (2)
	Falco peregrinus	Peregrine Falcon (165)
	Falco peregrinus tundrius	Tundra Peregrine Falcon (41)
	Fulica cornuta	Horned Coot (3)
	Numenius borealis	Eskimo Curlew (9)
	Eulidia yarrellii	Chilean Woodstar
Colombia	Crypturellus saltuarius	Magdalena Tinamou
	Podiceps andinus	Colombian Grebe
	Netta erythrophthalma erythrophthalma	South American Pochard (6)
	Morphnus guianensis	Crested Eagle (15)
	Harpia harpyja	Harpy Eagle (18)
	Falco peregrinus tundrius	Tundra Peregrine Falcon (41)
	Crax alberti	Blue-billed Curassow
	Penelope perspicax	Cauca Guan
	Odontophorus strophium	Gorgeted Wood-Quail
	Rallus semiplumbeus	Bogotá Rail
	Leptotila conoveri	Tolima Dove
	Ognorhynchus icterotis	Yellow-eared Conure (2)
	Hapalopsittaca amazonina fuertisi	Indigo-winged Parrot
	Bolborhynchus ferrugineifrons	Rufous-fronted Parakeet
	Coeligena prunellei	Black Inca
	Semnornis ramphastinus	Toucan Barbet (2)
	Grallaria milleri	Brown-banded Antpitta
	Grallaria alleni	Moustached Antpitta
	Cephalopterus penduliger	Long-wattled Umbrellabird (2)
	Polystictus pectoralis bogotensis	Bogotá Bearded Tachuri
	Cistothorus apolinari	Apolinar's Marsh Wren
	Sporophila insulata	Tumaco Seedeater
	Atlapetes flaviceps	Olive-headed Brush-Finch
	Spinus cucullatus	Red Siskin (2)
Costa Rica	Morphnus guianensis	Crested Eagle (15)
	Harpia harpyja	Harpy Eagle (18)
	Falco peregrinus tundrius	Tundra Peregrine Falcon (41)
	Pharomachrus mocinno	Resplendent Quetzal (7)
Cuba	Dendrocygna arborea	West Indian Whistling Duck (9)
	Accipiter striatus fringilloides	Cuba Sharp-shinned Hawk
	Chondrohierax uncinatus wilsoni	Cuba Hook-billed Kite
	Rostrhamus sociabilis plumbeus	Florida Everglade Kite (2)
	Falco peregrinus tundrius	Tundra Peregrine Falcon (41)
	Grus canadensis nesiotes	Cuba Sandhill Crane
	Cyanolimnas cerverai	Zapata Rail
	Campephilus principalis bairdii	Cuba Ivory-billed Woodpecker
	Ferminia cerverai	Zapata Wren
	Vermivora bachmanii	Bachman's Warbler (2)
	Torreornis inexpectata	Zapata Sparrow

Dominica	Falco peregrinus tundrius	Tundra Peregrine Falcon (41)
	Amazona imperialis	Imperial Parrot
	Amazona arausiaca	Red-necked Parrot
Dominican Republic	Dendrocygna arborea	West Indian Whistling Duck (9)
	Falco peregrinus tundrius	Tundra Peregrine Falcon (41)
Ecuador	Netta erythrophthalma erythrophthalma	South American Pochard (6)
	Leucopternis occidentalis	Grey-backed Hawk (2)
	Morphnus guianensis	Crested Eagle (15)
	Harpia harpyja	Harpy Eagle (18)
	Falco peregrinus tundrius	Tundra Peregrine Falcon (41)
	Ara ambigua guayaquilensis	Guayaquil Great Green Macaw
	Ognorhynchus icterotis	Yellow-eared Conure (2)
	Semnornis ramphastinus	Toucan Barbet (2)
	Cephalopterus penduliger	Long-wattled Umbrellabird (2)
El Salvador	Falco peregrinus tundrius	Tundra Peregrine Falcon (41)
	Pharomachrus mocinno	Resplendent Quetzal (7)
French Guiana	Morphnus guianensis	Crested Eagle (15)
	Harpia harpyja	Harpy Eagle (18)
	Falco peregrinus tundrius	Tundra Peregrine Falcon (41)
Grenada	Chondrohierax uncinatus mirus	Grenada Hook-billed Kite
	Falco peregrinus tundrius	Tundra Peregrine Falcon (41)
	Leptotila wellsi	Grenada Dove
Guadeloupe	Falco peregrinus tundrius	Tundra Peregrine Falcon (41)
	Troglodytes aedon guadeloupensis	Guadeloupe Wren
Guatemala	Podilymbus gigas	Atitlán Grebe
	Harpia harpyja	Harpy Eagle (18)
	Falco peregrinus tundrius	Tundra Peregrine Falcon (41)
	Pharomachrus mocinno	Resplendent Quetzal (7)
	Tangara cabanisi	Azure-rumped Tanager (2)
Guyana	Morphnus guianensis	Crested Eagle (15)
	Harpia harpyja	Harpy Eagle (18)
	Falco peregrinus tundrius	Tundra Peregrine Falcon (41)
Haiti	Pterodroma hasitata	Black-capped Petrel
	Dendrocygna arborea	West Indian Whistling Duck (9)
	Falco peregrinus tundrius	Tundra Peregrine Falcon (41)
Honduras	Morphnus guianensis	Crested Eagle (15)
	Harpia harpyja	Harpy Eagle (18)
	Falco peregrinus tundrius	Tundra Peregrine Falcon (41)
	Ortalis vetula deschauenseei	Utila Chachalaca
	Pharomachrus mocinno	Resplendent Quetzal (7)
Jamaica	Dendrocygna arborea	West Indian Whistling Duck (9)
	Falco peregrinus tundrius	Tundra Peregrine Falcon (41)
	Columba inornata exigua	Jamaica Plain Pigeon
	Kalochelidon euchrysea euchrysea	Jamaican Golden Swallow

Martinique	Falco peregrinus tundrius	Tundra Peregrine Falcon (41)
	Cinclocerthia ruficauda gutturalis	Martinique Trembler
	Ramphocinclus brachyurus brachyurus	Martinique White-breasted Thrasher
Nicaragua	Morphnus guianensis	Crested Eagle (15)
	Harpia harpyja	Harpy Eagle (18)
	Falco peregrinus tundrius	Tundra Peregrine Falcon (41)
	Pharomachrus mocinno	Resplendent Quetzal (7)
Panama	Morphnus guianensis	Crested Eagle (15)
	Harpia harpyja	Harpy Eagle (18)
	Falco peregrinus tundrius	Tundra Peregrine Falcon (41)
	Pharomachrus mocinno	Resplendent Quetzal (7)
Paraguay	Mergus octosetaceus	Brazilian Merganser (3)
	Morphnus guianensis	Crested Eagle (15)
	Harpia harpyja	Harpy Eagle (18)
	Leucopternis polionota	Mantled Hawk (3)
	Falco peregrinus tundrius	Tundra Peregrine Falcon (41)
	Aburria jacutinga	Black-fronted Piping Guan (3)
	Numenius borealis	Eskimo Curlew (9)
	Claravis godefrida	Purple-winged Ground-Dove (3)
	Anodorhynchus glaucus	Glaucous Macaw (3)
	Ara caninde	Wagler's Macaw (3)
	Dryocopus galeatus	Helmeted Woodpecker (3)
Peru	Pterocnemia pennata tarapacensis	Puna Rhea (4)
	Podiceps taczanowskii	Junin Grebe
	Netta erythrophthalma erythrophthalma	South American Pochard (6)
	Leucopternis occidentalis	Grey-backed Hawk (2)
	Morphnus guianensis	Crested Eagle (15)
	Harpia harpyja	Harpy Eagle (18)
	Falco peregrinus tundrius	Tundra Peregrine Falcon (41)
	Penelope albipennis	White-winged Guan
Puerto Rico	Dendrocygna arborea	West Indian Whistling Duck (9)
	Accipiter striatus venator	Puerto Rico Sharp-shinned Hawk
	Buteo platypterus brunnescens	Puerto Rico Broad-winged Hawk
	Falco peregrinus tundrius	Tundra Peregrine Falcon (41)
	Columba inornata wetmorei	Puerto Rico Plain Pigeon
	Amazona vittata	Puerto Rico Parrot
	Caprimulgus noctitherus	Puerto Rico Whippoorwill
	Agelaius xanthomus xanthomus	Puerto Rico Yellow-shouldered Blackbird
	Agelaius xanthomus monensis	Mona Yellow-shouldered Blackbird
St. Lucia	Falco peregrinus tundrius	Tundra Peregrine Falcon (41)
	Amazona versicolor	St. Lucia Parrot
	Troglodytes aedon mesoleucus	St. Lucia Wren
	Ramphocinclus brachyurus sanctaeluciae	St. Lucia White-breasted Thrasher
	Cichlherminia lherminieri sanctaeluciae	St. Lucia Forest Thrush
	Leucopeza semperi	Semper's Warbler

St. Vincent	Falco peregrinus tundrius	Tundra Peregrine Falcon (41)
	Amazona guildingii	St. Vincent Parrot
	Myadestes genibarbis sibilans	St. Vincent Solitaire
Suriname	Morphnus guianensis	Crested Eagle (15)
	Harpia harpyja	Harpy Eagle (18)
	Falco peregrinus tundrius	Tundra Peregrine Falcon (41)
Trinidad and Tobago	Falco peregrinus tundrius	Tundra Peregrine Falcon (41)
	Pipile pipile pipile	Trinidad Piping Guan
	Asio clamator oberi	Trinidad Striped Owl
	Xiphorhynchus picus altirostris	Trinidad Straight-billed Woodcreeper
	Grallaria guatimalensis aripoensis	Trinidad Scaled Antpitta
Uruguay	Falco peregrinus tundrius	Tundra Peregrine Falcon (41)
	Numenius borealis	Eskimo Curlew (9)
	Amazona pretrei	Red-spectacled Amazon (3)
	Anodorhynchus glaucus	Glaucous Macaw (3)
Venezuela	Netta erythrophthalma erythrophthalma	South American Pochard (6)
	Morphnus guianensis	Crested Eagle (15)
	Harpia harpyja	Harpy Eagle (18)
	Falco peregrinus tundrius	Tundra Peregrine Falcon (41)
	Spinus cucullatus	Red Siskin (2)
Virgins	Dendrocygna arborea	West Indian Whistling Duck (9)
	Falco peregrinus tundrius	Tundra Peregrine Falcon (41)
	Otus nudipes newtoni	Virgin Islands Screech Owl

H. OCEANS AND OCEANIC ISLANDS

Atlantic

Ascension	Fregata aquila	Ascension Frigatebird
Azores	Columba palumbus azorica	Azores Wood Pigeon
	Pyrrhula pyrrhula murina	São Miguel Bullfinch
Bermuda	Pterodroma cahow	Cahow
	Numenius borealis	Eskimo Curlew (9)
Canaries	Haliaeetus albicilla	White-tailed Eagle (36)
	Falco peregrinus	Peregrine Falcon (165)
	Haematopus moquini meadewaldoi	Canarian Black Oystercatcher
	Columba trocaz	Long-toed Pigeon (2)
	Columba junoniae	Laurel Pigeon
Cape Verdes	Falco peregrinus madens	Cape Verde Peregrine
	Alauda razae	Razo Lark
Falklands	Chloephaga rubidiceps	Ruddy-headed Goose (3)
	Falco peregrinus	Peregrine Falcon (165)

Madeira	Pterodroma mollis madeira	Madeiran Soft-plumaged Petrel
	Columba trocaz	Long-toed Pigeon (2)
Tristan da Cunha	Nesocichla eremita eremita	Tristan Starchy
	Nesospiza wilkinsi	Grosbeak Bunting

Central Pacific

Hawaii	Pterodroma phaeopygia sandwichensis	Hawaiian Dark-rumped Petrel
	Puffinus puffinus newelli	Newell's Shearwater
	Anas laysanensis	Laysan Duck
	Anas (platyrhynchos) wyvilliana	Koloa
	Branta sandvicensis	Nene
	Buteo solitarius	Hawaiian Hawk
	Gallinula chloropus sandvicensis	Hawaiian Gallinule
	Fulica americana alai	Hawaiian Coot
	Himantopus himantopus knudseni	Hawaiian Stilt
	Phaeornis obscurus myadestina	Kauai Thrush
	Phaeornis obscurus rutha	Molokai Thrush
	Phaeornis palmeri	Puaiohi
	Acrocephalus familiaris kingi	Nihoa Millerbird
	Moho braccatus	Kauai 'O'o
	Hemignathus lucidus affinis	Maui Nukupu'u
	Hemignathus lucidus hanapepe	Kauai Nukupu'u
	Hemignathus obscurus procerus	Kauai 'Akialoa
	Hemignathus wilsoni	'Akiapola'au
	Loxioides bailleui	Palila
	Loxops coccinea coccinea	Hawaii 'Akepa
	Loxops coccinea ochracea	Maui 'Akepa
	Melamprosops phaeosoma	Po'o Uli
	Palmeria dolei	Crested Honeycreeper
	Paroreomyza maculata maculata	Oahu Creeper
	Paroreomyza maculata bairdii	Kauai Creeper
	Paroreomyza maculata flammea	Molokai Creeper
	Pseudonestor xanthophrys	Maui Parrotbill
	Psittirostra psittacea	'O'u
	Corvus tropicus	Hawaiian Crow

East Pacific

Galapagos	Pterodroma phaeopygia phaeopygia	Galapagos Dark-rumped Petrel
	Nannopterum harrisi	Galapagos Flightless Cormorant
	Buteo galapagoensis	Galapagos Hawk
	Nesomimus trifasciatus trifasciatus	Charles Mockingbird
	Geospiza magnirostris magnirostris	Floreana Large Ground Finch
	Camarhynchus heliobates	Mangrove Finch
Guadalupe	Regulus calendula obscura	Guadalupe Kinglet

South Pacific

Antipodes	Coenocorypha aucklandica meinertzhagenae	Antipodes Island Snipe
Auckland	Anas aucklandica aucklandica	Auckland Island Teal
	Rallus pectoralis muelleri	Auckland Island Rail
	Coenocorypha aucklandica aucklandica	Auckland Island Snipe
Australs	Ptilinopus huttoni	Rapa Fruit-Dove
Bismarcks	Puffinus heinrothi	Heinroth's Shearwater
	Falco peregrinus	Peregrine Falcon (165)
Campbell	Anas aucklandica nesiotis	Campbell Island Teal
Carolines	Ducula oceanica teraokai	Truk Micronesian Pigeon
	Asio flammeus ponapensis	Ponape Short-eared Owl
	Metabolus rugensis	Truk Monarch
	Aplonis pelzelni	Ponape Mountain Starling
	Rukia ruki	Truk Greater White-eye
	Rukia longirostra	Ponape Greater White-eye
Chathams	Pterodroma hypoleuca axillaris	Chatham Island Petrel
	Pterodroma magentae	Chatham Island Taiko
	Haematopus chathamensis	Chatham Island Oystercatcher
	Thinornis novaeseelandiae	New Zealand Shore Plover
	Coenocorypha aucklandica pusilla	Chatham Island Snipe
	Hemiphaga novaeseelandiae chathamensis	Chatham Island Pigeon
	Cyanoramphus auriceps forbesi	Chatham Island Yellow-crowned Parakeet
	Petroica traversi	Black Robin
Cooks	Vini peruviana	Tahiti Lorikeet (3)
	Pomarea dimidiata	Rarotonga Flycatcher
Fiji	Pterodroma macgillivrayi	MacGillivray's Petrel
	Falco peregrinus	Peregrine Falcon (165)
	Rallus poecilopterus	Barred-wing Rail
	Trichocichla rufa	Long-legged Warbler
	Erythrura kleinschmidti	Pink-billed Parrotfinch
Lord Howe	Tricholimnas sylvestris	Lord Howe Wood Rail
	Strepera graculina crissalis	Lord Howe Currawong
Loyalties	Falco peregrinus	Peregrine Falcon (165)
	Eunymphicus cornutus uvaeensis	Uvea Horned Parakeet
Marianas	Anas "oustaleti"	Marianas Mallard
	Megapodius laperouse laperouse	Marianas Megapode
	Rallus owstoni	Guam Rail

	Gallinula chloropus guami	Marianas Gallinule
	Ptilinopus roseicapillus	Marianas Fruit-Dove
	Halcyon cinnamomina cinnamomina	Guam Micronesian Kingfisher
	Zosterops conspicillata rotensis	Rota Bridled White-eye
	Corvus kubaryi	Marianas Crow
Marquesas	Ducula galeata	Marquesas Pigeon
	Gallicolumba rubescens	Marquesas Ground Dove
	Vini ultramarina	Ultramarine Lorikeet
	Pomarea iphis fluxa	Eiao Flycatcher
	Pomarea mendozae mendozae	Hivaoa Flycatcher
	Pomarea mendozae nukuhivae	Nukuhiva Flycatcher
	Pomarea mendozae mira	Uapou Flycatcher
	Acrocephalus caffer aquilonis	Eiao Polynesian Warbler
	Acrocephalus caffer postremus	Hatutu Polynesian Warbler
Marshalls	Ducula oceanica ratakensis	Radak Micronesian Pigeon
New Caledonia	Falco peregrinus	Peregrine Falcon (165)
	Rhynochetos jubatus	Kagu
	Drepanoptila holosericea	Cloven-feathered Dove
	Ducula goliath	Giant Imperial Pigeon
New Hebrides	Falco peregrinus	Peregrine Falcon (165)
	Aplonis santovestris	Santo Mountain Starling
Norfolk	Cyanoramphus novaezelandiae cookii	Norfolk Island Parakeet
	Ninox novaeseelandiae undulata	Norfolk Boobook Owl
	Turdus poliocephalus poliocephalus	Grey-headed Blackbird
	Zosterops albogularis	White-breasted Silvereye
Palau	Megapodius laperouse senex	Palau Megapode
	Caloenas nicobarica pelewensis	Palau Nicobar Pigeon
	Artamus leucorhynchus pelewensis	Palau White-breasted Woodswallow
	Erythrura trichroa pelewensis	Palau Blue-faced Parrotfinch
Snares	Coenocorypha aucklandica huegeli	Snares Island Snipe
Societies	Ducula aurorae	Society Islands Pigeon (2)
	Vini peruviana	Tahiti Lorikeet (3)
	Pomarea nigra nigra	Tahiti Flycatcher
	Acrocephalus caffer longirostris	Moorea Polynesian Warbler
Solomons	Pterodroma rostrata becki	Beck's Petrel
	Pareudiastes sylvestris	San Cristobal Mountain Rail
	Zosterops luteirostris luteirostris	Gizo White-eye

Tuamotus	Prosobonia cancellatus	Tuamotu Sandpiper
	Ducula aurorae	Society Islands Pigeon (2)
	Gallicolumba erythroptera	Society Islands Ground Dove
	Vini peruviana	Tahiti Lorikeet (3)
Western Samoa	Falco peregrinus	Peregrine Falcon (165)
	Didunculus strigirostris	Tooth-billed Pigeon

West Pacific

Bonins	Haliaeetus albicilla	White-tailed Eagle (36)
	Apalopteron familiare	
	familiare	Mukojima Bonin Honeyeater
Iwos	Falco peregrinus fruitii	Iwo Peregrine Falcon
Ryukyus	Haliaeetus albicilla	White-tailed Eagle (36)
	Falco peregrinus	Peregrine Falcon (165)
	Picus awokera takatsukasae	Takatsukasa's Green Woodpecker
	Sapheopipo noguchii	Okinawa Woodpecker
	Dendrocopos leucotos owstoni	Owston's White-backed Woodpecker
	Erithacus komadori subrufa	Southern Ryukyu Robin
	Zoothera dauma major	Amami Ground Thrush

Indian Ocean

Christmas	Sula abbotti	Abbott's Booby
	Fregata andrewsi	Christmas Frigatebird
	Accipiter fasciatus natalis	Christmas Brown Goshawk
	Ducula whartoni	Christmas Imperial Pigeon
	Ninox squamipila natalis	Christmas Island Owl
Comoros	Accipiter francesii pusillus	Anjouan Sparrow Hawk
	Falco peregrinus	Peregrine Falcon (165)
	Treron australis griveaudi	Moheli Green Pigeon
	Otus rutilus capnodes	Anjouan Scops Owl
Mauritius	Falco punctatus	Mauritius Kestrel
	Nesoenas mayeri	Pink Pigeon
	Psittacula echo	Mauritius Parakeet
	Coracina typica	Mauritius Cuckoo-Shrike
	Terpsiphone bourbonnensis	
	desolata	Mauritius Paradise Flycatcher
	Zosterops olivacea	
	chloronothos	Mauritius White-eye
	Foudia rubra	Mauritius Fody
Réunion	Pterodroma aterrima	Réunion Petrel
	Coracina newtoni	Réunion Cuckoo-Shrike
Rodrigues	Bebrornis rodericana	Rodrigues Brush Warbler
	Foudia flavicans	Rodrigues Fody
Seychelles	Threskiornis aethiopica	
	abbotti	Aldabra Sacred Ibis
	Falco araea	Seychelles Kestrel
	Falco newtoni aldabranus	Aldabra Kestrel
	Dryolimnas cuvieri	
	sandvicensis	Aldabra White-throated Rail
	Streptopelia picturata	
	rostrata	Seychelles Turtle Dove

Coracopsis nigra barklyi	Seychelles Lesser Vasa Parrot
Otus insularis	Seychelles Owl
Copsychus sechellarum	Seychelles Magpie-Robin
Bebrornis sechellensis	Seychelles Brush Warbler
Nesillas aldabranus	Aldabra Brush Warbler
Terpsiphone corvina	Seychelles Black Paradise Flycatcher
Zosterops modesta	Seychelles White-eye
Foudia sechellarum	Seychelles Fody

LIST OF BIRDS KNOWN OR THOUGHT TO HAVE BECOME

EXTINCT SINCE 1600

Only taxa represented by skins or osseous remains are included.   Greenway (1958, Extinct and Vanishing Birds of the World, p. 9 et seq.) lists hypothetical species, known from verbal descriptions or drawings but not specimen material, and assays the evidence of their existence.

STRUTHIONIFORMES

  1 Struthionidae
     Struthio camelus syriacus   Arabian Ostrich   1966

CASUARIIFORMES

  4 Dromiceiidae
     Dromaius novaehollandiae diemenensis   Tasmanian Emu   1838
     Dromaius novaehollandiae diemenianus   Kangaroo Island Black Emu 1803

AEPIORNITHIFORMES

  5 Aepiornithidae
     Aepyornis maximus   Great Elephantbird   ca 1649

DINORNITHIFORMES

  6 Anomalopterygidae
     Dinornis torosus   Brawny Great Moa   1670
     Eurapteryx gravis   Burly Lesser Moa   ca 1640
     Megalapteryx didinus   South Island Tokoweka 1785

PROCELLARIIFORMES

 13 Procellariidae
     Pterodroma hasitata caribbea   Diablotin   1880

 14 Hydrobatidae
     Oceanodroma macrodactyla   Guadalupe Storm Petrel 1912

PELECANIFORMES

 19 Phalacrocorax perspicillatus   Spectacled Cormorant   1852

CICONIIFORMES

 22 Ardeidae
     Nycticorax caledonicus crassirostris   Bonin Nankeen Night Heron 1889
     Nycticorax megacephalus   Flightless Night Heron 1730

 27 Threskiornithidae
     Lampribis olivacea rothschildi   Principe Olive Ibis   1901

ANSERIFORMES

30 Anatidae
Anas georgica niceforoi .... Niceforo's Pintail 1952
Anas gibberifrons remissa .... Rennel Island Grey Teal 1959
Anas strepera couesi .... Washington Island Gadwall 1874
Camptorhynchus labradorium .... Labrador Duck 1875
Cygnus sumnerensis .... Chatham Island Swan 1590-1690
Mergus australis .... Auckland Island Merganser 1905
Rhodonessa caryophyllacea .... Pink-headed Duck 1944
Tadorna cristata .... Crested Shelduck 1943

FALCONIFORMES

35 Falconidae
Polyborus lutosus .... Guadalupe Caracara 1900

GALLIFORMES

38 Tetraonidae
Tympanuchus cupido cupido .... Heath Hen 1932

39 Phasianidae
Coturnix novaezelandiae .... New Zealand Quail 1875
Ophrysia superciliosa .... Himalayan Mountain Quail 1868

GRUIFORMES

49 Rallidae
Amaurolimnas concolor concolor .... Jamaican Wood Rail 1890
Aphanapteryx bonasia .... Van den Broecke's Red Rail ... 1675
Aphanapteryx leguati .... Rodrigues Blue Rail 1730
Aphanolimnas monasa .... Kusaie Crake 1828
Atlantisia elpenor .... Ascension Flightless Crake ... 1656
Pareudiastes pacificus .... Samoan Wood Rail 1873
Pennula millsi .... Hawaiian Brown Rail 1864
Pennula sandwichensis .... Hawaiian Spotted Rail 1893
Poliolimnas cinereus brevipes ..... Iwo Jima White-browed Rail ... 1925
Porphyrio porphyrio alba .... Lord Howe Purple Gallinule ... 1834
Porphyriornis nesiotes nesiotes ... Tristan Island Hen 1872
Porzanula palmeri .... Laysan Rail 1944
Rallus dieffenbachii .... Chatham Island Banded Rail ... 1840
Rallus modestus .... Chatham Island Rail 1900
Rallus pacificus ecaudata .... Tahiti Red-billed Rail 1925
Rallus philippensis macquariensis . Macquarie Island Banded Rail . 1880
Rallus wakensis .... Wake Island Rail 1945
Tricholimnas lafresnayanus .... New Caledonia Wood Rail 1904

CHARADRIIFORMES

59 Scolopacidae
Coenocorypha aucklandica barrierensis . Little Barrier New Zealand
                                          Snipe 1870
Pisobia cooperi .... Cooper's Sandpiper 1833
Prosobonia leucoptera .... Tahiti Sandpiper 1777

64 Glareolidae
Cursorius bitorquatus .... Jerdon's Courser 1900

CHARADRIIFORMES (continued)

70 Alcidae
    Alca impennis   Great Auk   1844

COLUMBIFORMES

72 Raphidae
    Pezophaps solitaria   Rodrigues Solitaire   1791
    Raphus cucullatus   Dodo   1681

73 Columbidae
    Alectroenas nitidissima   Mauritius Blue Pigeon   1830
    Alectroenas rodericana   Rodrigues Pigeon   1693
    Columba jouyi   Ryukyu Wood Pigeon   1936
    Columba palumbus maderensis   Madeiran Wood Pigeon   1904
    Columba versicolor   Bonin Wood Pigeon   1889
    Hemiphaga novaeseelandiae spadicea   Norfolk Island Kereru   1801
    Microgoura meeki   Choiseul Crested Pigeon   1904
    Phapitreron amethystina frontalis   Cebu Amethyst Brown Fruit
                                                        Dove   1892
    Ptilinopus mercierii mercierii   Nukuhiva Red-moustached
                                                        Fruit Dove   1849
    Ptilinopus mercierii tristrami   Hivaoa Red-moustached Fruit
                                                        Dove   1922

PSITTACIFORMES

74 Psittacidae
    Amazona vittata gracilipes   Culebra Puerto Rican Parrot   1899
    Ara tricolor   Cuban Red Macaw   1885
    Aratinga chloroptera maugei   Puerto Rico Hispaniolan
                                                        Conure   1892
    Conuropsis carolinensis carolinensis   Carolina Parakeet   1914
    Conuropsis carolinensis ludovicianus   Louisiana Carolina Parakeet   1912
    Charmosyna diadema   New Caledonia Lorikeet   1860
    Cyanoramphus novaezelandiae erythrotis   Macquarie Kakariki   1913
    Cyanoramphus novaezelandiae
        subflavescens   Lord Howe Kakariki   1869
    Cyanoramphus ulietensis   Raiatea Parakeet   1774
    Cyanoramphus zealandicus   Tahiti Parakeet   1844
    Lophopsittacus mauritianus   Mauritius Broad-billed Parrot 1638
    Loriculus philippensis chrysonotus   Cebu Hanging Parakeet   1906
    Loriculus philippensis siquijorensis   Siquijor Hanging Parakeet   1908
    Mascarinus mascarinus   Mascarene Parrot   1834
    Necropsittacus rodericanus   Rodrigues Parrot   1730
    Nestor meridionalis productus   Norfolk Island Kaka   1851
    Psittacula eupatria wardi   Seychelles Alexandrine Parrot 1870
    Psittacula exsul   Rodrigues Ring-necked
                                                        Parakeet   1875

CUCULIFORMES

76 Cuculidae
    Coua delalandei   Madagascar Coucal   1930

STRIGIFORMES

78 Strigidae
    Athene murivora   Rodrigues Little Owl   1730
    Ninox novaeseelandiae albaria   Lord Howe Boobook Owl   1940

STRIGIFORMES (continued)

Sceloglaux albifacies albifacies	South Island Laughing Owl	1950
Sceloglaux albifacies rufifacies	North Island Laughing Owl	1889
Speotyto cunicularia amaura	Antigua Burrowing Owl	1890
Speotyto cunicularia guadeloupensis	Guadeloupe Burrowing Owl	1890

CAPRIMULGIFORMES

82　Aegothelidae
　　Aegotheles savesi　　　　　　　　　New Caledonia Owlet Frogmouth 1880

83　Caprimulgidae
　　Siphonorhis americanus americanus　Jamaica Least Pauraque　　　　1859

CORACIIFORMES

89　Alcedinidae
　　Halcyon gambieri　　　　　　　　　Mangareva Kingfisher　　　　1841
　　Halcyon miyakoensis　　　　　　　Ryukyu Kingfisher　　　　　1841

PICIFORMES

103　Picidae
　　Colaptes cafer rufipileus　　　　Guadalupe Flicker　　　　　1906

PASSERIFORMES

112　Tyrannidae
　　Empidonax euleri johnstonei　　　Grenada Euler's Flycatcher　1910

116　Acanthisittidae
　　Xenicus longipes stokesi　　　　North Island Bush Wren　　1955
　　Xenicus longipes variabilis　　Stead's Bush Wren　　　　1972
　　Xenicus lyalli　　　　　　　　Stephen Island Wren　　　1874

123　Campephagidae
　　Coracina coerulescens altera　　Cebu Black Greybird　　　1906
　　Coracina striata cebuensis　　Cebu Barred Greybird　　1906
　　Lalage leucopyga leucopyga　　Norfolk Island Triller　1962

124　Pycnonotidae
　　Hypsipetes siquijorensis monticola　Cebu Slaty-crowned Bulbul　1906

130　Cinclidae
　　Cinclus cinclus olympicus　　　Cyprus Dipper　　　　　1939

131　Troglodytidae
　　Salpinctes obsoletus exsul　　San Benedicto Rock Wren　1952
　　Thryomanes bewickii brevicauda　Guadalupe Bewick's Wren　1897
　　Thryomanes bewickii leucophrys　San Clemente Bewick's Wren　1927
　　Troglodytes aedon martinicensis　Martinique House Wren　1886
　　Troglodytes troglodytes orii　Daito Wren　　　　　　1938

134　(Muscicapidae) Turdinae
　　Copsychus niger cebuensis　　Cebu Black Shama　　　1956
　　Myadestes elisabeth retrusus　Isle of Pines Solitaire　1934
　　Phaeornis obscurus lanaiensis　Lanai Thrush　　　　1931
　　Phaeornis obscurus oahensis　Oahu Thrush　　　　　1825

134 Turdinae (continued)

Saxicola dacotiae murielae	Muriel's Chat	1913
Turdus poliocephalus mareensis	Mare Grey-headed Blackbird	1939
Turdus poliocephalus vinitinctus	Lord Howe Grey-headed Blackbird	1918
Turdus ravidus	Grand Cayman Thrush	1938
Zoothera terrestris	Kittlitz's Thrush	1828

136 Timaliinae

Moupinia altirostris altirostris	Burma Jerdon's Babbler	1941

140 Sylviinae

Acrocephalus familiaris familiaris	Laysan Millerbird	1923
Bowdleria punctata rufescens	Chatham Island Fernbird	1900
Cettia diphone restrictus	Daito Bush Warbler	1922
Gerygone igata insularis	Lord Howe Grey Warbler	1919

142 Muscicapinae

Rhipidura fuliginosa cervina	Lord Howe Grey Fantail	1928

144 Monarchinae

Pomarea nigra pomarea	Maupiti Flycatcher	1823

146 Pachycephalinae

Turnagra capensis capensis	South Island Piopio	1963
Turnagra capensis tanagra	North Island Piopio	1955

149 Paridae

Parus varius orii	Daito Varied Tit	1938

154 Dicaeidae

Dicaeum quadricolor	Four-colored Flowerpecker	1906
Dicaeum trigonostigma pallidus	Cebu Orange-breasted Flowerpecker	1906

156 Zosteropidae

Zosterops everetti everetti	Cebu Everett's White-eye	1906
Zosterops mayottensis semiflava	Seychelles Chestnut-flanked White-eye	1888
Zosterops strenua	Lord Howe White-eye	1928

157 Meliphagidae

Anthornis melanura melanocephala	Chatham Island Bellbird	1906
Chaetoptila angustipluma	Kioea	1859
Moho apicalis	Oahu 'O'o	1837
Moho bishopi	Molokai 'O'o	1915
Moho nobilis	Hawaii 'O'o	1934

158 (Emberizidae) Emberizinae

Melospiza melodia graminea	Santa Barbara Song Sparrow	1967
Pipilo erythrophthalmus consobrinus	Guadalupe Rufous-sided Towhee	1897

164 Drepanididae

Ciridops anna	Ula-ai-Hawane	1892
Drepanis funerea	Black Mamo	1907
Drepanis pacifica	Mamo	1898
Hemignathus lucidus lucidus	Oahu Nukupu'u	1860
Hemignathus obscurus ellisianus	Oahu 'Akialoa	1837
Hemignathus obscurus lanaiensis	Lanai 'Akialoa	1894

164 Drepanididae (continued)

Hemignathus obscurus obscurus	Hawaïi 'Akialoa	1895
Himatione sanguinea freethi	Laysan Honeycreeper	1923
Loxops coccinea rufa	Oahu 'Akepa	1893
Paroreomyza maculata montana	Lanai Creeper	1937
Psittirostra flaviceps	Lesser Kona Finch	1891
Psittirostra kona	Kona Finch	1894
Psittirostra palmeri	Hopue	1896
Viridonia sagittirostris	Greater 'Amakihi	1900

166 Icteridae

Cassidix palustris	Slender-billed Grackle	1910
Icterus leucopteryx bairdi	Grand Cayman Jamaican Oriole	1938

167 Fringillidae

Carpodacus mexicanus mcgregori	McGregor's House Finch	1938
Chaunoproctus ferreorostris	Bonin Grosbeak	1890
Loxigilla portoricensis grandis	St. Kitts Puerto Rican Bullfinch	1880
Spiza townsendi	Townsend's Finch	1833

172 (Ploceidae) Ploceinae

Neospiza concolor	São Tomé Grosbeak Weaver	1888

173 Sturnidae

Aplonis corvina	Kusaie Starling	1828
Aplonis fuscus fuscus	Norfolk Island Starling	1925
Aplonis fuscus hullianus	Lord Howe Starling	1918
Aplonis mavornata	Mysterious Starling	1774
Fregilupus rodericanus	Leguat's Starling	1832
Fregilupus varius	Bourbon Crested Starling	1862

174 Oriolidae

Oriolus xanthonotus assimilis	Cebu Dark-throated Oriole	1906

176 Callaeidae

Heteralocha acutirostris	Huia	1907

PUNA RHEA

Pterocnemia pennata tarapacensis Chubb, 1913

Order RHEIFORMES   Family RHEIDAE

STATUS   Endangered. This rhea is now rare over much of its range, throughout
which it is avidly hunted and chased.

DISTRIBUTION   The Puna zone of the eastern Andes in Puno, Tacna and Moquegua
departments, Peru; Potosí and Oruro departments, Bolivia; Jujuy, Salta and
Catamarca provinces, Argentina; and Tarapacá, Antofagasta and Atacama provinces,
Chile (1-3). It is probable that in a large part of this range the rhea no
longer occurs, although precise details are lacking.

POPULATION   No estimate is available for the population as a whole, although
there is no doubt it is seriously declining because of human persecution. In the
department of Arica, Tarapacá province, in Chile, there are less than 100 rheas (4)
and a further estimated 200-400 survive in the Lauca National Park, where egg
poaching by the indigenous Aymara Indians continues unabated (J. Rottmann 1977,
pers. comm.). However, rheas are considered to be still common in certain places
on the Peruvian side of the border (M. Plenge 1977, pers. comm.).

HABITAT   Puna zone, above 4000 m elevation.

CONSERVATION MEASURES TAKEN   This rhea has been given year-round legal protection
in Chile and, as noted above, it occurs in Lauca National Park, in the extreme
north-east of the country. Protected by law in Peru, although with little effect,
for it is still hunted - with particular avidity near mining centers by people in
dune buggies (M. Plenge 1977, pers. comm. to R. Innes). It is also protected by
Bolivian law; none the less feather-dusters made from its feathers are still
widely sold in the country. Its skin finds a ready market because, when burned,
its smoke has a supposedly beneficial effect on coca plantations (C. Cordier, 1974,
pers. comm.). The species as a whole is listed in Appendix 1 of the 1973
Convention on International Trade in Endangered Species of Wild Fauna and Flora.

CONSERVATION MEASURES PROPOSED   None known.

REMARKS   The nominate subspecies, Pterocnemia pennata pennata, known as Darwin's
Rhea, found in southern Chile and Argentina, still exists in adequate numbers (4).
A third subspecies named P. p. garleppi is here considered identical with
tarapacensis.

REFERENCES   1.   de Schauensee, R.M. 1966. The Species of Birds of South
                    America and their Distribution. Narberth, Pa.: Livingston
                    Publishing Co.
              2.   Olrog, C.C. 1959. Las Aves Argentinas. Univ. Nac. Tucumán.
              3.   Johnson, A.W. 1965. The Birds of Chile and Adjacent Regions
                    of Argentina, Bolivia and Peru. Buenos Aires: Platt
                    Establecimientos Gráficos S.A.
              4.   McFarlane, R.W. 1975. The status of certain birds in northern
                    Chile. Bull. ICBP 12: 300-309.

MAGDALENA TINAMOU

Crypturellus saltuarius Wetmore, 1950

Order TINAMIFORMES   Family TINAMIDAE

STATUS   Indeterminate. This tinamou, known only from the unique type specimen collected in Colombia, is probably extinct as the result of forest destruction.

DISTRIBUTION   The type specimen was taken in 1943, at Ayacucho, 25 km east of La Gloria, in the north-western foothills of the Sierra de Ocaña, just inside Magdalena division, Colombia.

POPULATION   Unknown: there have been no further reports of the species since 1943.

HABITAT   Presumably forested lowlands. The single specimen was taken at an altitude of 150 m. The forests in this area have largely disappeared.

CONSERVATION MEASURES TAKEN   None known.

CONSERVATION MEASURES PROPOSED   None known.

REFERENCES   1.   Wetmore, A. 1950.   Additional forms of birds from the republics of Panama and Colombia. Proc. Biol. Soc. Washington 63: 171-174.

Tinamus solitarius pernambucensis Berla, 1946

Order TINAMIFORMES   Family TINAMIDAE

STATUS   Endangered. Confined to one state in Brazil and very much reduced in population as the result of destruction of the primary forests to which it is restricted, as well as of continual hunting.

DISTRIBUTION   Recorded in the north-eastern Brazilian states of Pernambuco and Alagoas, south to the São Francisco River. Now only known from a few coastal forest patches in Alagoas near São Miguel dos Campos (1; 2).

POPULATION   All estimates are recent, but there can be no doubt that this sub-species was far more abundant when the primary forests of north-eastern Brazil were intact. Only three specimens have been recorded, the latest taken in 1952, although in 1971 one that had been recently killed was seen in São Miguel dos Campos. No more than 100 birds were believed to remain in 1971.

HABITAT   This subspecies probably has habitat requirements similar to those of the nominate subspecies farther south in Brazil, where each bird is said to require about 30 ha of primary forest (2). What is left of the coastal forest providing the requisite conditions in north-eastern Brazil, is now confined to a few areas in Alagoas state, none of those known to be inhabited by this subspecies being in any way reserved or protected.

CONSERVATION MEASURES TAKEN   The species is listed on Appendix 1 of the 1973 Convention on International Trade in Endangered Species of Wild Fauna and Flora.

CONSERVATION MEASURES PROPOSED   Hunting of this subspecies, which goes on continually, should be stopped (2). A reserve which would protect portions of the habitat it shares with the highly endangered Crax mitu mitu (see 37/CRAX/MIT/MIT) has been proposed (H. Sick 1976, pers. comm.).

REMARKS   The nominate subspecies occurs in southern Brazil and Paraguay. It is now much reduced in distribution but occurs in several parks or reserves and is not presently considered at risk (3). It has also been bred in captivity, whereas pernambucensis is not even known to be represented in captive collections (2).

REFERENCES   1.   Amadon, D. 1959.   The subspecies of Tinamus tao and Tinamus solitarius (Aves).   Amer. Mus. Novit. No. 1955.
             2.   Coimbra-Filho, A.F. 1971.   Tres formas da avifauna do nordeste do Brasil ameaçadas de extinçao: Tinamus solitarius pernambucensis Berla, 1946, Mitu m. mitu (Linnaeus, 1766) e Procnias a. averano (Hermann, 1783) (Aves-Tinamidae, Cracidae, Cotingidae).   Rev. Brasil. Biol. 31: 239-247.
             3.   Sick, H. 1972.   A ameaça da avifauna brasileira.   In Espécies da Fauna Brasileira Ameaçadas de Extinção.   Rio de Janiero: Academia Brasileira de Ciências.

JACKASS PENGUIN

Spheniscus demersus (Linnaeus, 1758)

Order SPHENISCIFORMES   Family SPHENISCIDAE

STATUS   Vulnerable.   Although still plentiful this penguin has suffered
substantial population declines in the past from egg harvesting, and is now
subject to further declines from competition for food by a pelagic fishing
industry, from harbour developments near breeding islands and from oil pollution
(1; 2).

DISTRIBUTION   Breeds on 18 islands and their outliers along the coast of south-
western Africa from Hollamsbird Island in South West Africa/Namibia to Bird Island
in the South African republic.   It has been recorded from coastal waters on the
west as far north as Lobito, Angola (12°S), and on the east to Maputo, Mozambique
(26°S) (1).   No changes in distribution have been recorded except for the fact
that Robben Island near Cape Town has not been used by the penguins for nesting
since before 1800 (3).

POPULATION   An initial decline is believed to have taken place between 1844 and
1861, during the period of destructive, uncontrolled guano mining.   Between 1890
and 1930, over 400,000 eggs of this species were collected annually from Dassen
Island (220 ha) and also smaller numbers from other islands.   Dassen is the
largest of the islands on which the species breeds and still supports the highest
population, having been occupied by up to 1.5 million penguins during this period.
After 1930, the annual harvest of eggs (which can be used as a relative indicator
of total population) dwindled to 236,000 by 1940, to 161,000 by 1950, to 129,000
by 1960 and to 35,300 by 1969, when egg collecting was discontinued.   In 1956 and
1972, the Dassen population was 145,000 and 70,000 birds respectively, while the
estimated totals for all islands was 295,400 and 171,710.   The decline from the
first decade of the century is of the order of 90 percent and believed to be
continuing even though the former causes of decline have been eliminated (1).

HABITAT   Breeds on coastal islands and ranges in coastal waters primarily within
the highly productive Benguela current.   This area is traversed by numbers of oil
tankers.   There were 8 significant incidents of oil pollution of waters frequented
by the species between 1969 and 1978.   However, less than 1 percent of the penguin
population is believed to have been affected annually, so that oiling may not yet
be a significant mortality factor.   On the other hand, a major pelagic fishery
off South Africa has seriously depleted local stocks of pilchard Sardinops and
maasbanker Trachurus, and is also heavily exploiting anchovy Engraulis, all species
on which the penguin feeds.   Off South West Africa the commercial catch of
pilchard continues to increase but the anchovy catch is already declining.   This
exploitation may be the most significant cause of the penguins' decline at present,
although industrial projects involving the construction of several new harbours,
if implemented, may ultimately affect about 40,000 or about 25 percent of the
population.

CONSERVATION MEASURES TAKEN   Protection under the South African Sea Birds and
Seals Protection Act of 1973.   Egg collecting was ended in 1969, as the result
of a resolution of the Third Pan-African Ornithological Congress submitted to the
South African government (4), although some still occurs illegally.   The South
African National Foundation for the Conservation of Coastal Birds has developed
an extensive program of oiled bird rehabilitation, but involves some risk of
diverting interest and funds from more pressing conservation needs (1).   A
research project on the penguins' status has been undertaken (5).

CONSERVATION MEASURES PROPOSED   A complete census, further studies of the
penguins' population dynamics, of the effects of the commercial fishery, of the
effects of oil pollution and of the best means of minimizing the latter, and an
evaluation of rehabilitation attempts, in that order of priority, have been
recommended to the South African government (1).

REFERENCES   1.   Frost, P.G.H., Siegfried, W.R. & Cooper, J. 1976.
                    Conservation of the Jackass Penguin (Spheniscus demersus (L.)).
                    Biol. Cons.9: 79-99.
              2.   Rand, R.W. 1971.   Some hazards to seabirds.   Ostrich
                    Suppl. 8: 515-520.
              3.   Westphal, A. & Rowan, M.K. 1971.   Some observations on the
                    effects of oil pollution on the Jackass Penguin.   Ostrich
                    Suppl. 8: 521-526.
              4.   Anon. 1971.   Conservation of Jackass Penguin.   Ostrich
                    Suppl. 8: 527.
              5.   Verwey, J.E.M. 1971.   Conservation programmes for coastal
                    birds in South Africa.   Biol. Cons. 3: 311-312.

COLOMBIAN GREBE

Podiceps andinus (de Schauensee, 1959)

Order PODICIPEDIFORMES   Family PODICIPEDIDAE

STATUS   Endangered.   This grebe still exists in one highland lake in Colombia,
but its population is very low.   Its decline may have to do with the introduction
of trout to this and other lakes within its former range.

DISTRIBUTION   The species was described only fairly recently (as a subspecies of
P. caspicus=nigricollis) from Lake Tota (3015 m elevation), Boyaca, Colombia (1).
It was also known from several other temperate zone lakes north of Bogotá in
Cundinamarca and Boyaca, but since the 1950s it has been reported only on Lake
Tota (J. Hernandez 1974, pers. comm. to M. Rylander; R. Ridgely 1978, pers. comm.).

POPULATION   In the 1940s abundant on Lake Tota (1), where 1968 about 300 were
observed.   In 1972 a visit to the lake revealed only one bird (J. Hernandez 1974,
pers. comm.).   In 1977, one and possibly two more, were seen along the south-west
and north-east shores of the lake, and although the entire lake was not surveyed,
it was evident that very few of the grebes remained (R. Ridgely 1977, pers. comm.).

HABITAT   Temperate zone lakes in northern Colombia.   Presumably this species,
like others of its genus, requires reed beds for nesting.   The reed beds appeared
to be relatively intact on Lake Tota in February 1977 (R. Ridgely, pers. comm.).
Reed harvesting at other times, particularly during the breeding season, could have
a devastating effect on nesting success.   Pesticide contamination of the Tota
basin does not seem to be a problem, although it may have been elsewhere in the
species' range.   Trout were introduced to Lake Tota in 1944.   Competition for
food from trout is the most likely cause of the species' drastic decline
(J. Hernandez 1974, R. Ridgely 1977, pers. comms.).

CONSERVATION MEASURES TAKEN   None known.

CONSERVATION MEASURES PROPOSED   A complete survey of Lake Tota is urgently needed
(R. Ridgely 1977, pers. comm.).

REMARKS   Hunting is not likely to have been a major cause of decline, for
waterbirds more desirable to a hunter than this small grebe are still abundant
on Lake Tota.

REFERENCES   1.   de Schauensee, R.M. 1959.   Additions to the "Birds of the
                    Republic of Colombia".   Proc. Acad. Nat. Sci. Phila. 111:
                    53-75.

HOODED GREBE

Podiceps gallardoi Rumboll, 1974

Order PODICIPEDIFORMES   Family PODICIPEDIDAE

STATUS   Rare.   Restricted during the breeding season to one lake in Argentina,
where its population is quite small.

DISTRIBUTION   Known only from Laguna Las Escarchadas (1 by 3 km, 743 m
elevation), Santa Cruz province, Argentina.   There are numerous other lakes in
the general area, but in none of the others, searched for this species, has it yet
been detected.   It is absent from the lake in winter, when the surface freezes,
and may well repair to the coasts of Argentina or Chile, from which the lake is
about equidistant (1; R. Storer 1976, pers. comm.).

POPULATION   In December 1975, a maximum of 126 was counted.   Reproduction in
1975-1976 and again in 1978-1979 appeared to be negligible, due possibly to
predation by Kelp Gulls Larus dominicanus (R. Storer 1976, F. Erize 1979, pers.
comms).   Whether the population is stable is unknown.

HABITAT   Freshwater lakes, in which the water level depends on snow melt from
nearby mountains and which support mats of the waterweed Myriophyllum.   A
national highway passes along one shore of the only lake from which the species
has been recorded.   The lake is situated on a privately owned sheep station and
there is no human habitation in its vicinity.

CONSERVATION MEASURES TAKEN   A special permit from the Argentine government,
issued at present to one individual, is required to collect this species.

CONSERVATION MEASURES PROPOSED   It appears unlikely that the species is actually
limited to a single lake.   If its presence on other suitable nearby lakes could
be successfully demonstrated, the existing apparent risk of its extinction would
be diminished.

REMARKS   Although a hybrid between this species and the widespread Crested or
Silvery Grebe P. occipitalis has been collected, there is no doubt it is a
distinct and valid species (R. Storer 1976, pers. comm.).

REFERENCES   1.   Rumboll, M.A.E. 1974.   Una nueva especie de macá
                    (Podicipitidae).   Comun. Mus. Argentino Cienc. Nat.
                    Bernardino Rivadavia 4: 33-35.

JUNIN GREBE

Podiceps taczanowskii Berlepsch and Stoltzmann, 1894

Order PODICIPEDIFORMES

Family PODICIPEDIDAE

STATUS   Rare.   Confined to one lake in Peru, where pollution from mine washings may pose a serious threat to the species.   The lake may soon be used as a reservoir for Lima.

DISTRIBUTION   Known only from Lake Junin (4,000 m elevation, 33 by 40 km), Peru. This grebe is flightless, hence now confined to this lake except through human intervention.

POPULATION   In 1938 this species was extremely abundant (1).   In 1961 it remained common (2).   A serious decline was presumed in 1969, as the result of gradual poisoning of the lake from washings from the Cerro de Pasco copper mine, which was said to affect not only this species but all flora and fauna in parts of the lake.   By the end of that year a third of the life in the lake was said to be dead (3).   In 1978, the grebe population was estimated at 300, including about 100 breeding pairs (J. Fjeldso 1978, pers. comm.).

HABITAT   Lake Junin is a large, high altitude, shallow lake bordered by extensive reed beds, in the puna zone of Peru.   This species frequents open water, in contrast to other grebe species on the lake which keep more to the reed beds (2). The vegetation of the lake was said in 1969 to be tinged yellow by decomposition products of sulphur acids and toxic fumes from the copper mine.   Lake levels are controlled by a hydroelectric plant at the outlet.   Trout were introduced by the 1930s and may have replaced native species of fish (3).   Use of the lake as a reservoir for Lima, currently in the planning stage, would cause periodic fluctuations in water level of up to 7 m.   Although the mines near Huallay had efficient purifying plants by 1978, such was not yet the case with the mines toward Cerro de Pasco (J. Fjeldso 1978, pers. comm.).

CONSERVATION MEASURES TAKEN   Lake Junin has been declared a National Reserve. The Peruvian government nationalized Cerro de Pasco mine and is attempting to get the lake free from mine washings (M. Plenge 1977, pers. comm. to R. Innes).

CONSERVATION MEASURES PROPOSED   The possibility of introduction of this grebe to one or more nearby lakes, for example at Carhuacayan or Laguna Punrun, should be investigated (J. Fjeldso 1978, pers. comm.).

REFERENCES   1.   Morrison, A. 1939.   Notes on the birds of Lake Junin,
                     central Peru.   Ibis 1939: 643-654.
              2.   Storer, R.W. 1967.   Observations on Rolland's Grebe.
                     El Hornero 10: 339-350.
              3.   Sherrit, R. 1969.   Junin lagoon marine pollution.
                     Smithsonian Inst. Center for Short-lived Phenomena, 562.

ATITLAN or GIANT PIED-BILLED GREBE

Podilymbus gigas (Griscom, 1929)

Order PODICIPEDIFORMES   Family PODICIPEDIDAE

STATUS   Endangered.   Known from one lake in Guatemala.   Although the small
population of this species has withstood food competition and predation from an
introduced fish, it remains at great risk because of continuing diminution of its
nesting habitat and the threat of a hydroelectric project which would drastically
alter the lake's ecology.

DISTRIBUTION   Lake Atitlán, Guatemala (130 sq. km), where it is mainly restricted
to the sheltered and vegetated southern shore (1).

POPULATION   There were likely never to have been more than about 400 birds (1).
In 1929, the estimate was 100 pairs (2).   This figure was repeated in surveys in
1936 (3) and in 1960 (4).   Following the introduction of bass Micropterus
salmoides and M. dolomieui in 1958 and 1960, the population declined to a low of
80 birds in 1964, thereafter gradually increasing until 1973, when the estimated
total had recovered to about 210.   The lake can presently hold about 280 birds (1).

HABITAT   Inshore waters and dense emergent vegetation, primarily rush or reed
(Scirpus) and cat-tail (Typha).   Only a quarter of the 105 km lake shoreline is
vegetated.   Rushes and cat-tails provide cover and nest sites, but are harvested
by Indians for a local weaving industry.   Introduced bass compete for food,
especially crabs, for the capture of which this grebe is believed to have evolved
its powerful bill and massive head, neck and jaw musculature (5).   In addition
bass are believed to prey on grebe chicks.   Real estate development (113 vacation
homes built between 1960 and 1973) has caused considerable clearing along the shore
line.   Since 1967, the Guatemala National Institute of Electrification has
favoured a proposal for a hydroelectric project, which would divert the flow of
four rivers into the lake.   The resulting substantial drawdown, increased turbidity
and pollution might all be expected to have deleterious effects on the grebe's
habitat (1).   The project has been postponed or revised several times, and a
recent view was that it was not likely to be implemented (J. Ibarra 1977, pers.
comm.).

CONSERVATION MEASURES TAKEN   Listed in Appendix 1 of the 1973 Convention on
International Trade in Endangered Species of Wild Fauna and Flora.   In 1959, the
species was protected by Guatemalan Presidential decree, under which hunting of this
and all waterbirds on Lake Atitlán was prohibited, although a lenient attitude has
been shown to subsistence hunting of coots and gallinules.   A warden with a patrol
boat is on duty at the lake throughout the year and between 1960 and 1968, visits
were made to officials and villagers around the lake to explain the intention of
the 1959 decree and outline the plans for protecting the grebe.   Its adoption as
a local symbol for the purpose of tourism has been promoted and postage stamps
depicting it were issued by Guatemala in 1970.   Regulations decreed in 1968
prohibit reed-cutting from 1 May to 15 August, and specify that only half of each
reed plot be harvested each year.   A special two-hectare refuge for the grebe was
inaugurated in 1968 and two pairs were placed in it, but the gate of the enclosure
was several times torn open by bad weather, allowing the birds to escape, so that
the refuge is now only used as a visitors' center (1).

CONSERVATION MEASURES PROPOSED   None additional known.

REMARKS   The presence of a separate breeding population of the closely related P. podiceps on Lake Atitlán confirms the specific distinctness of the Atitlán Grebe.   The species are segregated by a two-month difference in breeding seasons and by morphological, behavioral and ecological differences (1).   The bulk of the highly commendable conservation and research efforts on behalf of the Atitlán Grebe were carried out by Dr. Anne La Bastille.

REFERENCES   1.   La Bastille, A. 1974.   Ecology and management of the Atitlan Grebe, Lake Atitlán, Guatemala.   Wildl. Monog. 37.
           2.   Griscom, L. 1932.   The distribution of bird life in Guatemala.   Bull. Amer. Mus. Nat. Hist. 64: 1-439.
           3.   Wetmore, A. 1941.   Notes on birds of the Guatemalan highlands.   Proc. U.S. Nat. Mus. 89(3105): 523-581.
           4.   Bowes, A.L. & Bowes, C.V., Jr. 1962.   Recent census and observations of the Giant Pied-billed Grebe.   Auk 79: 707-709.
           5.   Zusi, R.L. & Storer, R.W. 1969.   Osteology and myology of the head and neck of the pied-billed grebes (Podilymbus). Misc. Publ. Mus. Zool. Univ. Mich. 139.

MADAGASCAR RED-NECKED GREBE

Tachybaptus rufolavatus Delacour, 1932

Order PODICIPEDIFORMES   Family PODICIPEDIDAE

STATUS   Vulnerable. Restricted to a few localities in Madagascar where it is
not numerous and where it is threatened by hybridization with a closely related
species.

DISTRIBUTION   Known primarily from Lake Alaotra (35 km by 5 km), north-eastern
Madagascar (1). Specimens have been obtained at Ankazobé, on the Massif de
l'Isalo and near Majunga, and the species was fairly recently observed between
Antsalova and the Antsingy or Bemarah Massif (4).

POPULATION   In 1929, when the species was first collected, it was reasonably
common on Lake Alaotra. Fifteen specimens were collected in 1929 (2). In 1960
an additional 13 were collected out of an estimated 50 birds seen. Although this
species was considered in 1960 to be five times as abundant as T. pelzelnii, more
widespread but rare in Madagascar, it has been shown to hybridize with a third
species of grebe T. ruficollis. Five such hybrids were collected, and in fact the
type specimen of rufolavatus is thought to be a hybrid as well. T. ruficollis
was first recorded on Madagascar in 1945, and is now widespread and common.
Continued hybridization, which seems likely, will result in a population
morphologically intermediate between the two parent types (3).

HABITAT   Reed beds and open shallow water of Lake Alaotra, and presumably similar
habitats elsewhere. Lake Alaotra has suffered introductions of Tilapia and bass
(Micropterus), which have disturbed the lake's ecosystem. The bass prey on chicks
of ducks and grebes.

CONSERVATION MEASURES TAKEN   None known.

CONSERVATION MEASURES PROPOSED   Legal protection of this and other endemic bird
species of Madagascar has been urged.

REFERENCES   1. Milon, P., Petter, J.-J. & Randrianasolo, G. 1973. Faune de
                  Madagascar, 35: Oiseaux. Tananarive and Paris: ORSTOM and
                  CNRS.
              2. Rand, A.L. 1936. The distribution and habits of Madagascar
                  birds. Bull. Amer. Mus. Nat. Hist. 72: 143-499.
              3. Voous, K.H. & Payne, H.A.W. 1965. The grebes of Madagascar.
                  Ardea, 53: 9-31.
              4. Salvan, J. 1971. Observations nouvelles à Madagascar.
                  Alauda, 39: 37-42.

SHORT-TAILED ALBATROSS

Diomedea albatrus Pallas, 1769

Order PROCELLARIIFORMES   Family DIOMEDEIDAE

STATUS   Endangered, because of its low numbers, low reproductive potential, and
very restricted breeding range on islands south of Japan.   There is now some
ground for optimism for the future of this species in view of a slow but
persistently upward trend in the population since the Second World War.

DISTRIBUTION   Known to have bred on Torishima, Izu Islands, on Kita-no-shima and
Nishi-no-shima and possibly Mukoshima and Yomeshima, all of the Bonin Islands
(Ogasawara Gunto), and on Kobisho, Senkaku group, southern Ryukyu Islands.
Probably also bred on Kita-daitojima of the Daito group.   May have bred as well on
the Pescadores between Taiwan and mainland China, Agincourt north of Taiwan, and on
Iwo Jima, the westernmost of the Volcano Islands (Kazan-Retto) south of the Bonins,
although confirmation is lacking (1; 2).   The species presently breeds only on
Tsubakuro Point in the south-east of the 5 sq. km island of Torishima (Y. Yamashina
1974, pers. comm.), although there are unconfirmed reports of its occurrence on
Minami-kojima of the Senkaku group and on Nakodo-shima, Kitano-shima and the
Mukoshima group in the Bonin Islands (3; 5).   The marine range formerly included
most of the North Pacific southward to about latitude 10°N. (4).

POPULATION   This albatross was once abundant, especially on Torishima, where
between 1887 and 1903 thousands were taken by feather hunters.   Large numbers of
bones identified as of this species have also been found in American Indian kitchen
middens along the northern North American coast (4).   By 1929 only 1,400
albatrosses were seen on Torishima, and a decade later there were a mere 30-50
birds.   During the Second World War the species was virtually eliminated from
Torishima, for the sighting of a single bird aroused attention in 1945.
Prematurely considered extinct in 1949, the species was reported nesting again on
Torishima the following year.   In 1954 the estimate was 25 birds, with 6 pairs
breeding, increasing to 12 pairs in 1956 and to 26 pairs by 1964 (2; 3; 5).   A
survey in 1973 revealed 24 fledglings, which suggests a breeding population of about
57 pairs.   In 1974, however, only 11 chicks were counted (Y. Yamashina, 1974, pers.
comm.).   On the basis of the 1973 survey, the total population, including non-
breeders, is less than 200 birds (3).

HABITAT   The species nests on volcanic ash slopes on Torishima, especially where
the grass Miscanthus sinensis is established.   The island is an active volcano,
and fresh lava or volcanic ash covers much of it, including areas previously used
for nesting.   Major eruptions took place in 1902 and 1939.   About 300 people
lived on the island at the turn of the century and again during the Second World
War, and in 1947 a meteorological station was established but was evacuated in 1965
due to threat of an eruption.   Cats and Norwegian rats Rattus norvegicus have
established themselves on the island (2; 3).

CONSERVATION MEASURES TAKEN   The feather-gathering which was primarily responsible
for the near-extinction of this species was banned by government edict in 1906, but
the practice continued until the mid 1930s, by which time the albatross population
was reduced below economic significance (3; 5).   A proposal in 1957 to mine sulphur
on Torishima was turned down because of the precarious status of this species (6)
and in the same year the albatross was designated a Special Natural Monument, the
flora and fauna of Torishima as a whole being similarly designated in 1965.   In
1972, the albatross was designated a Special Bird for Protection (Y. Yamashina 1974,
pers. comm.).

CONSERVATION MEASURES PROPOSED   Management proposals for Torishima Island have included elimination of feral cats and transplanting of turf to unvegetated ash slopes.   The latter has been attempted without notable success, possibly from lack of nutrients in the ash.   Investigation of rumored breeding sites in other island groups has been suggested (3).

REFERENCES   1.   Greenway, J.C. Jr. 1958.   Extinct and vanishing birds of the world.   Amer. Comm. Int. Wildl. Prot. Spec. Pub. No. 13
2.   Fisher, J., Simon, N. and Vincent, J. 1969.   The Red Book: Wildlife in Danger.   New York:Viking Press;   London:Collins.
3.   Tickell, W.L.N. 1975.   Observations on the status of Steller's Albatross (Diomedea albatrus) 1973.   Bull. ICBP 12: 125-131.
4.   Sanger, G.A. 1972.   The recent pelagic status of the Short-tailed Albatross (Diomedea albatrus).   Bio. Cons. 4: 189-193.
5.   Yamashina, Y. 1967.   The status of endangered species in Japan.   Bull. ICBP 10: 100-109.
6.   Yamashina, Y. 1958.   Report on successful preservation of Japanese Crane and Steller's Albatross in Japan.   Bull. ICBP 7: 135-139.

BLACK PETREL

Procellaria parkinsoni Gray, 1862

Order PROCELLARIIFORMES   Family PROCELLARIIDAE

STATUS   Endangered. Breeds on two islands offshore of the north-east coast of
North Island, New Zealand, and possibly on North Island as well. Populations are
small in number and are decreasing rapidly because of predation by cats and
possibly other introduced predators (1).

DISTRIBUTION   Known to breed on Little Barrier Island, Great Barrier Island and
perhaps still on a few mountain ranges of North Island, New Zealand, although no
colonies known to have been active on North Island are presently occupied.
Migrates to the coast of South America. Specimens have been collected near the
Galapagos Islands (1).

POPULATION   On Little Barrier Island there were (1975) 200 to 300 breeding pairs.
Smaller numbers breed on Great Barrier. Taking immature birds into account and
assuming a small population still occurs on mainland North Island, it is estimated
that the total population cannot exceed 2,000 birds. Cats killed 65 and 90
percent of fledglings on Little Barrier Island in 1972 and 1973, respectively, and
100 percent in 1974 and 1975, as well as breeding adults. Between 1971 and 1975
there was a 42 percent decline in breeding birds in a study area on Little Barrier
Island. At the present rate of predation this breeding colony will no longer
exist by 1980 (2). Formerly the species was considerably more widespread and
abundant, although precise figures are lacking. Before the arrival of European
settlers in New Zealand, Maoris took young of this species in numbers for food (1).

HABITAT   Nests in burrows among tree roots on ridges and mountain tops between
300m and 1,000m elevation (1).

CONSERVATION MEASURES TAKEN   The species is fully protected legally. Little
Barrier Island was made a sanctuary in 1890. The Little Barrier population has
been the subject of research by biologists of the New Zealand Wildlife Service.
A campaign to control the cats which are the main predators of the petrel, by
infecting them with feline enteritis virus between 1967 and 1970 killed 80 percent
of the cats but the number has since returned to its former level (1; 2; 3).

CONSERVATION MEASURES PROPOSED   The New Zealand Wildlife Service proposes to make
a further effort to eliminate cats from Little Barrier Island commencing in 1977.

REMARKS   Polynesian rats Rattus exulans are present on Little Barrier Island but
apparently have little impact on the petrel (3).

REFERENCES   1. Imber, M.J. 1973. The petrels of Little Barrier. Wildlife -
                  A review, 4: 5-9.
              2. Imber, M.J. 1975. The Black Petrel. Wildlife - A review, 6:
                  37-39.
              3. Imber, M.J. 1975. Petrels and predators. ICBP Bull. 12:
                  260-263.

WESTLAND BLACK PETREL

Procellaria westlandica Falla, 1946

Order PROCELLARIIFORMES   Family PROCELLARIIDAE

STATUS   Vulnerable. Very restricted in distribution, breeding only in one small
mountain range on South Island, New Zealand, where it is subject to predation by
introduced mammals.   Clearing of indigenous beech forests is proceeding in the
vicinity but beyond the known limits of the colony and will not be permitted within
the area occupied by it (1; 2; 3; 4).

DISTRIBUTION   This recently discovered petrel breeds in a four sq. km area in the
coastal mountain ranges of the west coast of South Island between Barrytown and
Punaikaiki (4).   At sea it is known from Cook Strait and the east coast of South
Island south to the Banks Peninsula, north along the west coast of North Island,
and west to the coast of New South Wales, Australia (2).

POPULATION   In 1956 the population was believed to approach 3,000 pairs (3), but
in 1974 no more than 900 occupied burrows existed (4).   The population is suspected
to have been decreasing slowly throughout the present century, in view of numerous
unoccupied burrows to be found within breeding area.   Introduced cats, stoats and
rats are known to abound in the vicinity.   Goats are also numerous (3; 4).

HABITAT   Nests in burrows near the tops of limestone bluffs, which are mostly
covered with Nothofagus beech forest.   Abandoned burrows have been found in
cleared areas near the present colonies, but it is not certain that clearing and its
associated disturbances caused the desertion of these burrows (3; 4).

CONSERVATION MEASURES TAKEN   Fully protected by law.   A major portion of the
breeding grounds has been reserved.

CONSERVATION MEASURES PROPOSED   Research to determine the effects of predation
and forest clearing on the population of this species.   Extension of the boundaries
of the existing reserve to protect the species' entire breeding area from further
disturbance (4).

REMARKS   In view of the serious decline of several other shearwaters and petrels
on the main islands of New Zealand, it is remarkable that a colony of westlandica
of the present size still manages to exist.

REFERENCES   1.   Falla, R.A., Sibson, R.B. & Turbott, E.G. 1967.   A Field Guide
                   to the Birds of New Zealand and Outlying Islands.   Boston:
                   Houghton Mifflin Co.; London:Collins.
              2.   Ornithological Society of New Zealand, 1970.   Annotated Check-
                   list of the Birds of New Zealand Including the Birds of the
                   Ross Dependency.   Wellington:A.H. & A.W. Reed.
              3.   Jackson, R. 1958.   The Westland Petrel.   Notornis 7: 230-233.
              4.   Best, H.A. & Owen, K.L.   Unpublished report dated August 1974.
                   Distribution of breeding sites of the Westland Black Petrel
                   (Procellaria westlandica).   New Zealand Wildlife Service
                   Fauna Survey Unit Report Series, 3.

REUNION PETREL

Pterodroma aterrima (Bonaparte, 1857)

Order PROCELLARIIFORMES   Family PROCELLARIIDAE

STATUS   Endangered.   This mysterious species was thought to have been extinct
since the last century, but two specimens collected in the 1970s on Réunion,
Indian Ocean, increase the likelihood the species still survives.

DISTRIBUTION   Known only from specimens from Réunion, except for subfossil
skeletal remains from Rodrigues that are attributed to this species (1; 2).   Some
Réunion folk apparently still know of the bird which they say occurs in the ravines
above Entre-Deux.   The two recent specimens were taken at Entre-Deux,and at Bois
Rouge on the north-east coast of Réunion (1; A.S. Cheke 1974, pers. comm.).

POPULATION   Until 1970, four specimens collected last century were the sole
evidence of the occurrence of this species on Réunion (1).   However, examination
of fresh-killed specimens in 1970 and 1974 confirmed its continued existence,
although there is no doubt the population is very small and liable to further
reduction (A.S. Cheke 1974, pers. comm.).

HABITAT   The breeding place of the petrel is unknown, although it is thought to
be in burrows or crevices on the walls of deep ravines inland on Réunion.
Terrestrial predators such as cats, dogs and rats are common in the island and may
well prey on nesting petrels or their chicks.   The birds undoubtedly forage for
food well out at sea, but it is possible this species may be absorbing pesticide
residues harmful to its reproduction, since Pterodroma arminjoniana of Mauritius
probably has a very similar diet and is laying thin-shelled eggs as a result of
organochlorines accumulated in its tissues through its food supply (3).   People may
also take the birds for food, capture of shearwaters (mostly Puffinus lherminieri)
for that purpose threatening accessible petrel nests equally (A.S. Cheke 1977, pers.
comm.).

CONSERVATION MEASURES TAKEN   Legal protection but enforcement ineffective.

CONSERVATION MEASURES PROPOSED   None known.

REFERENCES   1.   Jouanin, C. 1970.   Le Pétrel noir de Bourbon Pterodroma
                   aterrima Bonaparte.   L'Oiseau et R.F.O. 40:   48-68.
              2.   Bourne, W.R.P. 1967.   Birds of Rodriguez.   Ibis 110:   338-344.
              3.   Temple, S.A. 1976.   Observations of seabirds and shorebirds
                   on Mauritius.   Ostrich 47(2 & 3):   123-124.

Pterodroma cahow (Nichols and Mowbray, 1916)

Order PROCELLARIIFORMES   Family PROCELLARIIDAE

STATUS   Endangered.   Confined to islets off Bermuda.   Population and
reproductive potential of the species are very low.   Pesticide contamination
posed a serious threat in the early 1970s but no longer does.   The species has
recovered slightly from its all-time low, but remains a subject of grave concern.

DISTRIBUTION   Formerly nested throughout Bermuda, Atlantic Ocean, but now
confined to five small islets in Castle Harbour on the east coast.   Disperses
widely at sea to feed and when not breeding (1-8).

POPULATION   Colonists in Bermuda at the beginning of the 17th century still
relied heavily on Cahows for food.   The birds were at that time numbered in the
thousands, but as early as 1616 they had mostly disappeared as the result of
persistent overharvesting.   In 1951 the species was rediscovered at its present
breeding grounds after 290 years of presumed extinction (5).   Eighteen pairs
were believed to survive in 1951 and a like number in 1961.   By 1966, the number
of pairs had climbed to 20, but only 6 young were fledged that year, the poor
productivity being attributed to DDT contamination (8).   Since 1966, the number
of pairs has been as high as 26 and the number of chicks fledged once reached 17
(in 1972), although annual production has since averaged 12 (D.B. Wingate, 1974,
1977, pers. comm.).

HABITAT   Formerly the hillsides of Bermuda, but since its rediscovery the Cahow
has been restricted to rocky islets almost devoid of soil.   It was once preyed
upon by semiferal pigs and humans, and is still subject to predation by rats,
although its offshore breeding islets are periodically cleared of that pest.
It also has to compete with the more aggressive tropicbird Phaethon lepturus
for nest sites (6).   At sea its food has been contaminated by pesticides, and
tarring of its plumage by oil slicks is an additional threat which is growing as
that from pesticides declines (9; 10).   Bright lights of nearby U.S. military
installations were believed to be causing the abandonment of 3 islets by this
nocturnally active species (D.B. Wingate 1977, pers. comm.).

CONSERVATION MEASURES TAKEN   The Cahow has full legal protection in Bermuda.
This was first proclaimed in 1616, and a law protecting the species on its nesting
ground was enacted in 1621-1622.   Three of its 5 nesting islets are wildlife
sanctuaries, on which landing is illegal.   Classified as endangered by the United
States government, it is also given protection by the U.S. Endangered Species Act
of 1973.   A rat poisoning campaign is periodically carried out on the nesting
islets.   Artificial nesting burrows, to which the Cahows are now accustomed, have
been constructed and wooden baffles, fitted to the mouths of occupied burrows, permit
access by Cahows but not by the slightly larger tropicbirds, thus eliminating
nestsite competition (1).   A monitoring program has been underway since 1960.
The floodlighting of U.S. military bases situated near the nesting islets, which was
inhibiting establishment of new pairs, has now been modified or reduced to a level
apparently compatible with their breeding requirements.

CONSERVATION MEASURES PROPOSED   It is hoped that Cahows will recolonize Nonsuch
Island (5.8 ha), in the vicinity of the islets to which nesting is at present
confined, where soil conditions would permit thousands of Cahow burrows, free from
competition and predation (D.B. Wingate 1977, pers. comm.).

REMARKS   The measure of improvement in the status of this species as well as all we know of its biology can be attributed to the unceasing efforts and dedication of Mr. David Wingate.

REFERENCES
1. Zimmerman, D.R. 1975.   To Save a Bird in Peril.   New York: Coward, McCann and Geoghegan.
2. Greenway, J.C. Jr. 1958.   Extinct and Vanishing Birds of the World.   Amer. Comm. Internat. Wildl. Prot. Spec. Pub. 13.
3. Palmer, R.S. (ed.) 1962.   Handbook of North American Birds.   Vol. 1.   New Haven and London: Yale University Press.
4. Rogin, G. 1968.   There are problems when man plays god. Sports Illustrated 29(19):   78-90.
5. Murphy, R.C. & Mowbray, L.S. 1951.   New light on the Cahow, Pterodroma cahow.   Auk 68:   266-280.
6. Wingate, D.B. 1960.   Cahow, living legend of Bermuda. Canadian Audubon 22:   145-149.
7. Beebe, W. 1935.   Rediscovery of the Bermuda Cahow.   Bull. New York Zool. Soc. 38:   187-190.
8. Milne, L. & Milne, M. 1968.   The Cahow-10 years to doom? Audubon 70(6):   46-50.
9. Wurster, C.F. Jr. & Wingate, D.B. 1968.   DDT residues and declining reproduction in the Bermuda Petrel.   Science 159: 979-981.
10. Anon. 1971.   Week's Watch.   Time, June 14, 1971:   46.
11. Wingate, D.B. 1977.   In S.A. Temple (ed.) Endangered Birds: Management Techniques for Preserving Threatened Species. Madison: Univ. of Wisconsin Press.

NEW ZEALAND COOK's PETREL

Pterodroma cookii cookii (Gray, 1843)

Order PROCELLARIIFORMES   Family PROCELLARIIDAE

STATUS   Endangered.   Known to breed on two islands off New Zealand and possibly
a third and to migrate great distances to the north and east Pacific.   Introduced
predators occur on all three islands.   The populations on two of the islands have
been reduced to virtual extinction by predators; that on the third is larger and
suffering a lesser and more gradual decline (1; 2; 3; 4).

DISTRIBUTION   Breeds in New Zealand waters on Little Barrier and possibly on
Great Barrier islands off north-east North Island and on Codfish Island off
Stewart Island.   It migrates across the Pacific to the coasts of North and South
America (3).   On the basis of subfossil evidence the species once bred in both
North and South Islands of New Zealand (G. Williams 1976, pers. comm.).

POPULATION   Although Cook's Petrel is suspected of still nesting on Great Barrier
Island, severe predation pressure makes sure that it does so unsuccessfully (4).
Little Barrier Island (3,000 ha) is now the main breeding-place of the subspecies.
Its burrows are still found on high ridges near the summit of the island.   The
population was estimated at perhaps 2,000 individuals in 1973 (1; 4).   However,
Polynesian rats Rattus exulans take up to 30 percent of eggs or chicks annually,
and an unknown but sizeable portion of adults, non-breeders in search of burrows,
and fledglings, are killed by cats (4).   On Codfish Island an estimated 20,000
burrows were believed to be occupied in 1935.   Following the introduction of the
Weka Gallirallus australis scotti, however, the population has declined drastically
to a point where it can only be considered as a remnant.   Polynesian rats are also
present on Codfish Island (2).

HABITAT   Burrows are dug on densely forested ridge tops and slopes of offshore
islands (1).   Feeding takes place far at sea in temperate waters.

CONSERVATION MEASURES TAKEN   The subspecies is fully protected legally.   Little
Barrier Island was made a sanctuary in 1890.   Codfish Island is also a reserve.
Research conducted by the New Zealand Wildlife Service has shed light on the extent
of predation by rats and cats on this and other sea birds.   An attempt to eliminate
cats from Little Barrier Island between 1967 and 1970 using cage traps and feline
enteritis virus failed.   Although 80 percent of the cats were killed recovery of
the cat population was rapid and predation on sea birds has continued (1).

CONSERVATION MEASURES PROPOSED   An ambitious program of total extermination of cats
on Little Barrier Island has been proposed and is now being planned by the New
Zealand Wildlife Service.   Wekas will also be controlled on Codfish Island by the
Wildlife Service.

REMARKS   This subspecies is harassed by massive predation throughout its breeding
range.   Should the cat extermination program on Little Barrier Island succeed the

bird's future would be reasonably secure, for it apparently can tolerate predation by Polynesian rats, but not the additional mortality imposed by a second predator.

REFERENCES   1.   Imber, M.J. 1975.   Petrels and predators.   ICBP Bull. 12: 260-263.
2.   Ellis, B.A. 1975.   Rare and endangered New Zealand birds: the role of the Royal Forest and Bird Protection Society of New Zealand, Inc.   ICBP Bull. 12: 173-186.
3.   Ornithological Society of New Zealand, 1970.   Annotated Checklist of the Birds of New Zealand Including the Birds of the Ross Dependency.   Wellington: A.H. and A.W. Reed.
4.   Imber, M.J. 1973.   The petrels of Little Barrier.   Wildlife - A review 4: 5-9.

BLACK-CAPPED PETREL or DIABLOTIN

Pterodroma hasitata (Kuhl, 1820)

Order PROCELLARIIFORMES   Family PROCELLARIIDAE

STATUS   Vulnerable.   Greatly reduced in breeding range and abundance and now
restricted to certain cliffs of the Massif de la Selle, Haiti, where its numbers
are thought to be stable at present but there is little hope for improvement.

DISTRIBUTION   Once occurred on Guadeloupe, Martinique, Jamaica, Dominica and
Hispaniola, but it disappeared from all but the last by 1870.   In 1963 eleven
separate colonies were found along several cliffs on the Massif de la Selle in
southern Haiti (1).   In recent years individual birds have been observed at sea
in the Caribbean and the western North Atlantic.

POPULATION   Formerly abundant on all its nesting islands, but the populations on
all but Hispaniola declined disastrously in the 1850s.   In 1963 the breeding
population in Haiti was estimated to be at least 4,000 birds, and probably much
higher (1).

HABITAT   The species breeds in burrows in vegetated cliffs in mountains, often
well inland.   It disperses widely to feed at sea in the Caribbean and the North
Atlantic.   Whether it migrates, or once did, is not known.   Its decline has been
attributed to the introduction of the Mongoose Herpestes auropunctatus to its
nesting islands, but this took place in the 1870s, by which time Black-capped
Petrel populations had already seriously decreased.   Although the mongoose may
have completed its extirpation on most islands, capture by man for food and
predation by rats probably were responsible for the bulk of the decline (2).   On
Haiti birds are still taken for the pot when they can be caught.

CONSERVATION MEASURES TAKEN   None known.

CONSERVATION MEASURES PROPOSED   None known, although it would seem that legal
protection of the birds and their breeding grounds might be a useful first step.

REMARKS   The Jamaican race of this species P. h. caribbaea, known locally as the
Blue Mountain Duck, was wholly dark, whereas the populations now or formerly
inhabiting the other islands are white-breasted.

REFERENCES   1.   Wingate, D.B. 1964.   Discovery of breeding Black-capped Petrels
                   on Hispaniola.   Auk 81: 147-159.
              2.   Greenway, J.C. Jr. 1958.   Extinct and Vanishing Birds of the
                   World.   Amer. Comm. Internat. Wildl. Prot. Spec. Pub. No. 113.

CHATHAM ISLAND PETREL

Pterodroma hypoleuca axillaris (Salvin, 1893)

Order PROCELLARIIFORMES   Family PROCELLARIIDAE

STATUS   Endangered.   Known from one island in the Chatham Islands, 800 km east
of New Zealand.   Its population is very small and its future is in question in
view of the apparent recent colonization of the same island by another subspecies
of the same species.   The island is, however, free from introduced predators (1).

DISTRIBUTION   Confined to South-East Island (220 ha), Chatham Islands, and nearby
seas.   The subspecies is not known to migrate (2).

POPULATION   Recent estimates put the population at between 100 and 200 individuals.
The subspecies has always been considered rare (1), and its abundance appears not to
have changed since its discovery in 1892 (G. Williams 1976, pers. comm.).

HABITAT   Known only from lowland flats, where it burrows amongst the roots of the
forest floor and on low coastal slopes (3), while the apparently conspecific Black-
winged Petrel Pt. h. nigripennis was recently discovered to be inhabiting the high,
steep summit area of the island.

CONSERVATION MEASURES TAKEN   In 1954 South-East Island was purchased in the name
of the New Zealand government and was declared a Reserve for the Preservation of
Flora and Fauna.   Since late last century the island has been grazed by up to
1,200 sheep and a few head of cattle, most of which were removed when the island
was acquired for reservation.   The remaining stock was removed by the New Zealand
Wildlife Service in 1961.   No introduced mammals now remain on the island and its
vegetation is recovering dramatically (1).

CONSERVATION MEASURES PROPOSED   A study of the relationship of the Black-winged
Petrel with the Chatham Island Petrel and the reasons for failure of the latter to
increase would be most useful.

REMARKS   Remains of Chatham Island Petrels were found in the middens of skuas
Catharacta skua lonnbergi on South-East Island in 1937 (3), but not recently.
Presumably skuas are natural predators on these petrels, and are not the cause of
the subspecies' very small and restricted population.   However, a substantial
reduction of scrub and forest cover due to livestock grazing may well have made
the petrels much more vulnerable.   The recovery of the vegetation now taking place
may therefore benefit the subspecies (G. Williams 1976, pers. comm.).

REFERENCES   1.   Merton, D.V. & Bell, B.D.   Undated manuscript.   Endemic
                    birds of the Chatham Islands.   New Zealand Wildlife Service.
              2.   Ornithological Society of New Zealand, 1970.   Annotated
                    Checklist of the Birds of New Zealand Including the Birds of the
                    Ross Dependency.   Wellington:A.H. and A.W. Reed.
              3.   Fleming, C.A. 1939.   Birds of the Chatham Islands, Part 1.
                    Emu 38: 380-413.

GOULD'S PETREL

Pterodroma leucoptera leucoptera (Gould, 1844)

Order PROCELLARIIFORMES   Family PROCELLARIIDAE

STATUS   Rare.   Restricted to one small island off the New South Wales coast of
Australia and decidedly low in numbers.   Mammalian predators if introduced to the
island might quickly eliminate this subspecies.

DISTRIBUTION   Known to breed only on Cabbage Tree Island (26 ha) off Port
Stephens, New South Wales, where it occupies portions of the coastal slope,
primarily a single large gully (1).   No change has been recorded.   At sea the
subspecies is relatively sedentary (2), although there are a handful of records
from New Zealand waters.   These may, however, have come from a yet undiscovered
breeding colony (3; 4).

POPULATION   The total population is presently static at about 400 birds (2).
Between 1910 and 1930, there was a decline from a slightly higher number due
primarily to taking of the birds or their eggs for scientific collections (1).   No
further decline has been noted, although the petrels are sometimes found dead as the
result of having become covered by the viscid fruits of Pisonia brunoniana (1; 5)
and avian predators have also been thought to be a source of mortality (6).

HABITAT   Rock-strewn gullies with dense ground cover of vines and dead cabbage
palm (Livistona) fronds on Cabbage Tree Island (maximum elevation 120 m) (1).
The island apparently remains free of potential mammalian predators although it has
been suggested but not proved that rats occur (7).   Peregrines Falco peregrinus,
Ravens Corvus coronoides and Grey Goshawks Accipiter novaehollandiae are considered
to be serious predators (6).   The petrels disperse locally in the subtropical
waters off coastal New South Wales (2).

CONSERVATION MEASURES TAKEN   Fully protected by state law.   Cabbage Tree Island
is a faunal reserve.   In 1943, the island was used for a short time for gunnery
practice but this was quickly suspended following intercession by the Royal
Australian Ornithologists' Union (8).

CONSERVATION MEASURES PROPOSED   The subspecies has been proposed by the
Australian government for Appendix 1 of the 1973 Convention on International Trade
in Endangered Species of Wild Fauna and Flora.

REMARKS   Another subspecies P. l. brevipes is still abundant, breeding in New
Caledonia, New Hebrides and Fiji, and possibly elsewhere in yet undiscovered
colonies.   Stejneger's Petrel Pterodroma longirostris has also been considered a
subspecies of P. leucoptera (P. leucoptera longirostris of the 1966 edition of the
Red Data Book), but it is now widely accepted among marine ornithologists that the
small series of birds taken off Japan, from which the type was described, is
referable to the abundant P. longirostris population based on Masafuera Island,
Juan Fernandez group, off the Chilean coast (3).

REFERENCES   1.   Hindwood, K. & Serventy, D.L. 1941.   The Gould Petrel of
                    Cabbage Tree Island.   Emu 41: 1-20.
               2.   Serventy, D.L., Serventy, V. & Warham, J. 1971.   The Handbook of
                    Australian Sea-birds.   Sydney, Melbourne, Wellington, Auckland:
                    A.H. and A.W. Reed.

3. Falla, R.A. 1942.   Review of the smaller Pacific forms of Pterodroma and Cookilaria.   Emu 42: 111-118.
4. Bull, P.C. 1943.   The occurrence of Pterodroma leucoptera in New Zealand.   Emu 42: 145-152.
5. Hindwood, K.A. & Serventy, D.L. 1943.   Further notes on Pterodroma leucoptera.   Emu 42: 153-155.
6. D'Ombrain, A.F. 1970.   Notes on the Gould Petrel.   Australian Bird Bander 8: 82-84.
7. D'Ombrain, A.F. 1943.   The Cabbage Tree Island colony in the 1941-42 season.   Emu 42: 156-159.
8. Hindwood, K.A. 1944.   Cabbage Tree Island as an artillery target.   Emu 43: 220.

MACGILLIVRAY'S PETREL

Pterodroma macgillivrayi (Gray, 1859)

Order PROCELLARIIFORMES   Family PROCELLARIIDAE

STATUS   Indeterminate.   Only one specimen, a fledgling, of this distinctive
species is known.   It was collected on Ngau Island, Fiji, in October 1855.   It
has not been found subsequently, but it has been looked for on only two occasions,
once by R.H. Beck of the Whitney South Sea Expedition in February 1925 and again
by J.B. Smart in October 1971.   The natives of Ngau do not know of the bird,
although environmental conditions appear to be relatively unchanged from the time
of its discovery (1).

DISTRIBUTION   Ngau Island, Fiji.   Exact location on the island is not known,
but it is felt that the rocky summit of the island is the most likely place to find
the species (1).

POPULATION   It is not known if this species is still extant.

HABITAT   The breeding grounds are unknown.

CONSERVATION MEASURES TAKEN   None known.

CONSERVATION MEASURES PROPOSED   A survey of Ngau Island to determine if the
species still exists.

REFERENCES   1.   Smart, J.B. undated manuscript.   Quest for MacGillivray's
                    Petrel.

CHATHAM ISLAND TAIKO or MAGENTA PETREL

Pterodroma magentae (Giglioli and Salvadori, 1868)

Order PROCELLARIIFORMES   Family PROCELLARIIDAE

STATUS   Endangered.   This gadfly petrel was dramatically rediscovered in 1978,
111 years after the unique type specimen was collected.   It is apparently
restricted to one island near New Zealand where it is clearly threatened by
introduced predators and where the forest, on the floor of which it must nest, is
rapidly deteriorating from the combined impact of several introduced herbivores.

DISTRIBUTION   That the Magenta Petrel, taken at sea in 1867 in the South Pacific
south of Pitcairn Island is identical to the Taiko of Chatham Island has now been
confirmed by photographs and measurements of two birds captured and subsequently
released on Chatham Island in 1978.   Until that year the Chatham Island Taiko had
been known to science only by recent skeletal remains.   The nest sites on Chatham
have not yet been discovered or described, though the Maori inhabitants formerly
collected the breeding birds annually for food.   The traditional collecting place
and locality of the two birds caught in 1978, was inland on ridges along the Tuku
River toward the southern end of the island (1; 2; D.E. Crockett 1978, pers. comm.)
The type specimen was taken at sea in the zone of the Westerlies, at 39o38'S,
125o58'W or about 4500 km ENE of Chatham, three more birds believed to be of the
same species having been later seen further to the north-east towards the Peru
Current.   These observations, if accurate, suggest migration to the south-east
Pacific.

POPULATION   The Taiko was evidently once abundant enough to be considered by
man as a worthwhile food resource.   Its decline took place last century and the
islanders generally considered it to have disappeared from Chatham Island by about
1914, although reports of sightings persisted into the 1930s (2).   Renewed search
of the ridges above the Tuku River in recent years produced sightings in 1973,
1975 and in 1978, the last-mentioned of three birds two of which were captured and
released.   The population is likely to be very small, judging from an almost
complete lack of reports of Taiko in the previous several decades (D.E. Crockett
1978, pers. comm.).

HABITAT   The birds captured in 1978 were flying along a ridge of dense bush
forest, one of the last large stands of native bush in the Chathams.   No nest
burrows have been found in the area.   The bush forest is deteriorating through
the combined effects of wind and introduced herbivores, including Australian
brush-tailed opossums, feral cattle, sheep and pigs.   Predators, including cats,
rats and Wekas Gallirallus australis, are common in this area (D.E. Crockett 1978,
pers. comm.).

CONSERVATION MEASURES TAKEN   The bird itself is protected under New Zealand law,
but the forested area in which it was rediscovered is still unprotected.

CONSERVATION MEASURES PROPOSED   Location of nest burrows followed by conservation
of their immediate and general surroundings (D.E. Crockett 1978, pers. comm.).

REMARKS   The rediscovery of this lost petrel can be attributed to the vision of
Dr. W.R.P. Bourne, who correctly concluded in 1964 that the Magenta Petrel of
Giglioli and Salvadori was the Taiko of the Chatham Islands, and to the
perseverence of David E. Crockett who proved the point after several years of
effort by capturing the first birds seen by ornithologists in more than a century.

REFERENCES   1.   Bourne, W.R.P. 1964.   The relationship between the
                  Magenta Petrel and the Chatham Island Taiko.   *Notornis* 11:
                  139-144.
             2.   Fleming, C.A. 1939.   Birds of the Chatham Islands.
                  Part 1.   *Emu* 38:   380-413.

MADEIRAN SOFT-PLUMAGED PETREL

Pterodroma mollis madeira Mathews, 1934

Order PROCELLARIIFORMES   Family PROCELLARIIDAE

STATUS   Rare. This subspecies, known only from Madeira, is severely restricted
in distribution and also quite rare.   The cause of its decline, if one has taken
place, is not known.

DISTRIBUTION   Madeira (728 sq. km) in the eastern Atlantic, where this petrel
has been found near Curral das Freiras in the mountains behind Funchal, Santo
Antão, and the Ribeira de Santa Luzia, and may occur in other high, inaccessible
mountain areas (1).   The details of its oceanic distribution and feeding grounds
remain unknown.

POPULATION   On the evidence of a few birds heard calling at night in at least
one mountain locality a small population must still exist.   Between 1909, six
years after the first specimen was taken, and 1940 when a live fledgling was picked
up in the city of Funchal the subspecies was considered to be possibly extinct (1)
and it was not until as recently as 1969 that a small breeding population was
rediscovered (A. Zino 1976, pers. comm.).   The reproductive potential of this
and other petrels is low: one egg is laid annually, there is never any re-laying,
and several years are taken to reach breeding maturity.

HABITAT   Mountain slopes above 1600 m are used by this petrel to dig its nest
burrows (1).   Such slopes are inaccessible to all but the most determined
intruders, which should help to deter inroads on what at best must be a rather
small population.

CONSERVATION MEASURES TAKEN   None known.

CONSERVATION MEASURES PROPOSED   None known.

REMARKS   P. m. "deserta" from Bugio, Desertas group, south-east of Madeira, now
considered identical with P. m. feae from the Cape Verde Islands, is another
population which rates as quite rare (only 45-50 nest burrows have been found and
the total number of breeding pairs is unlikely to be much greater).   It is also
rather vulnerable to capture, so altogether must be considered at some risk (2).
However, neither P. m. feae of the Cape Verdes nor nominate P. m. mollis of
subantarctic islands in the Atlantic and Indian Oceans is believed at risk.

REFERENCES   1.   Bannerman, D.A. & W.M. 1965.   Birds of the Atlantic
                    Islands, Vol. 2.   Edinburgh and London: Oliver and
                    Boyd.
              2.   Jouanin, C., Roux, F. & Zino, A. 1969.   Visites aux
                    lieux de nidification de Pterodroma mollis "deserta".
                    l'Oiseau et R.F.O. 39: 161-175.

GALAPAGOS DARK-RUMPED PETREL

Pterodroma phaeopygia phaeopygia (Salvin, 1876)

Order PROCELLARIIFORMES   Family PROCELLARIIDAE

STATUS   Endangered. Declining at a disastrous rate in the Galapagos Islands,
Ecuador, as the result of predation by introduced mammals and destruction of its
habitat for agriculture.

DISTRIBUTION   The breeding distribution of the species on the Galapagos remains
to be fully worked out. It is known to breed above 180 m elevation on Santa
Cruz, San Cristobal, James and Isabela, very likely breeds on Floreana, and may
breed on Fernandina and Pinta (1). The species occurs at sea off the Galapagos
throughout the year, but has also been observed as far east as the South and
Middle American coasts (2).

POPULATION   Population estimates have been made only on Santa Cruz, where in
1971 it was estimated that there were about 10,000 burrows in the "Pampas" or
fern-sedge highlands but only about 4,000 occupied and about 1,600 containing eggs.
A mere 160 birds were later estimated to have fledged (3). Roughly similar
results were obtained in 1966, with four young fledged from 62 occupied burrows,
and in 1967, when no young at all fledged from 26 burrows that had contained eggs
(1), suggesting a bleak future for this particular colony. It is likely that the
same high reproductive failure applies to all populations of this species in the
Galapagos and that they will continue their precipitous decline.

HABITAT   Humid, thickly vegetated uplands. On Santa Cruz the species occurs
in the fern-sedge zone, the Miconia zone and formerly also in the Scalesia zone,
but the two latter have been extensively cleared for agriculture, thus removing
substantial areas of habitat. Introduced predators include dogs, pigs and black
rats Rattus rattus. Short-eared Owls Asio flammeus also prey on this petrel as
at one time did Galapagos Hawks Buteo galapagoensis. Black rats and pigs became
common on Santa Cruz in the 1930s. Pigs are now rare there, but are abundant on
James and also occur on Isabela and Floreana, which are the only two islands where
feral dogs are common. Although intensive predation on the petrel by pigs has
been noted, rats are thought to be the most significant long-term threat. Cattle
also do damage by causing the collapse of nest burrows by their trampling (1; 3).

CONSERVATION MEASURES TAKEN   The areas on James and Santa Cruz where this
species now breeds lie within the Galapagos National Park and some control of
their pig population has been undertaken.

CONSERVATION MEASURES PROPOSED   Poisoning of rats in the vicinity of breeding
areas and exclusion of cattle, pigs and other introduced mammals have been
suggested as the measures most likely to improve the breeding success of the
petrels (3).

REMARKS   The Hawaiian Islands subspecies P. p. sandwichensis is also seriously
threatened.

REFERENCES   1. Harris, M.P. 1970. The biology of an endangered species,
                  the dark-rumped Petrel (Pterodroma phaeopygia), in the
                  Galapagos Islands. Condor 72: 76-84.

2. Murphy, R.C. 1936. <u>Oceanic Birds of South America</u>.
Vol. II. New York: American Museum of Natural History.
3. Jacobs, R.B. Unpub. report dated 1972. A progress
report on the survey and study of the Dark-rumped
Petrel in the Galapagos Islands.

HAWAIIAN DARK-RUMPED PETREL or 'UA'U

Pterodroma phaeopygia sandwichensis (Ridgway, 1884)

Order   PROCELLARIIFORMES   Family   PROCELLARIIDAE

STATUS   Endangered.   Still occurs in relict populations on at least two of the
Hawaiian Islands, where introduced terrestrial predators especially the black rat
Rattus rattus, feral domestic cats, and mongooses (Herpestes auropunctatus)
continue to make inroads, but probably at a slower rate than in the past.   While
mongooses probably caused the bulk of the population decline, the surviving
petrels breed above the normal range of this predator.   Nestlings and eggs are
taken by rats (1; 2; 3).

DISTRIBUTION   Formerly occurred on Hawaii, Maui, Lanai, Molokai and Kauai.
Presently known only from the walls and rim of Haleakala Crater, Maui, and upper
slopes of Mauna Kea, Mauna Loa, and Kilauea on Hawaii (2).

POPULATION   Formerly abundant.   The population is now mainly concentrated on
Haleakala, Maui, where 1,800 birds were estimated in 1971.   On Hawaii three small
scattered colonies are known, the largest of which contains about a hundred birds
(1).

HABITAT   Formerly most numerous in the tree fern belt of moist forest above
600 m elevation on most of the Hawaiian Islands.   Present populations are
confined to very sparsely vegetated weathered lava slopes and cliffs above 2,300 m
elevation on Maui and mainly above 1,700 m on Hawaii (1; 3).

CONSERVATION MEASURES TAKEN   The species is protected by federal and state laws.
The Maui population lies within the boundaries of Haleakala National Park.
Predator control programs have been conducted on the Maui breeding grounds.

CONSERVATION MEASURES PROPOSED   Continuation of predator population monitoring
and, when necessary, control on Maui.   Continuation of population surveys and
studies (2).

REMARKS   The nominate subspecies from the Galapagos Islands is also endangered.

REFERENCES   1.   Banko, W.   Ms.   Status and distribution of two endangered
                     seabirds (Procellariidae) in the Hawaiian Islands.
                     U.S. Fish. Wildl. Ser.
              2.   U.S. Dept. of Interior Bureau of Sport Fisheries and Wildlife,
                     1973.   Threatened Wildlife of the United States.   U.S. Bur.
                     Sport Fish. Wildl. Res. Pub. 114.
              3.   Berger, A.J. 1972.   Hawaiian Birdlife.   Honolulu: University
                     Press of Hawaii.

BECK'S PETREL

Pterodroma rostrata becki Murphy, 1928

Order PROCELLARIIFORMES   Family PROCELLARIIDAE

STATUS   Indeterminate.   The nesting place of this petrel has not been
discovered.   It is known only from two specimens taken at sea in 1928.

DISTRIBUTION   Collected in the south-west Pacific at two localities, the first
east of New Ireland, Bismarck Archipelago, and north of Buka, Solomon Islands,
the second north-east of Rendova Island, Solomon Islands.   It is hypothesized
that this petrel breeds in the Solomons (1; 2).

POPULATION   Unknown.   Only two specimens exist and there have been no records
whatever for half a century.   But the bird occurs in an area in which there has
been relatively little ornithological activity, so that the population could well
be undiminished.

HABITAT   Feeds at sea in tropical waters.   Assuming its habits resemble those
of the nominate race, as is highly likely, it must nest in burrows on mountain
slopes and there are no particular reasons for expecting that such a breeding
habitat is threatened.

CONSERVATION MEASURES TAKEN   None known.

CONSERVATION MEASURES PROPOSED   A survey to determine if and where a population
of this subspecies persists (3).

REMARKS   This petrel was originally described as a full species, but later
considered sufficiently similar to P. rostrata of the south-central Pacific, from
which it apparently differs only in being about three-quarters as large, to be
treated as a subspecies (1; 2).

REFERENCES   1.   Murphy, R.C. 1928.   Birds collected during the Whitney
                   South Sea Expedition, IV.   Amer. Mus. Novit. 322.
              2.   Murphy, R.C. & Pennoyer, J.M. 1952.   Larger petrels
                   of the genus Pterodroma.   Amer. Mus. Novit. 1580.
              3.   Bourne, W.R.P. 1971.   General threats to seabirds.
                   Bull. ICBP 11: 200-218.

HEINROTH'S SHEARWATER

Puffinus heinrothi Reichenow, 1919

Order PROCELLARIIFORMES   Family PROCELLARIIDAE

STATUS   Indeterminate. Known only from a handful of specimens from the northern coast of New Britain and not reported since 1934.

DISTRIBUTION   The breeding site of this shearwater has not been found. It has been observed and collected in Blanche Bay, Talili Bay and the seas around Watom Island, at the north-eastern end of the Gazelle Peninsula, New Britain (1).

POPULATION   Not known. In 1934 the species was described as being not uncommon at sea around Watom Island. Small groups of up to six birds were observed (1). There is no subsequent record.

HABITAT   At sea this species has been observed in offshore tropical waters off north-eastern New Britain. The area is relatively rich in fish resources as the presence of sea bird flocks and Japanese tuna fishing vessels attest (W.B. King, unpublished notes). Its breeding habitat is unknown.

CONSERVATION MEASURES TAKEN   None known.

CONSERVATION MEASURES PROPOSED   None known.

REMARKS   There have been few observations recently in the area where this species has occurred, which may well account for the lack of records for nearly a half century.

REFERENCES   1.   Meyer, O. 1934.   Seltene Vogel auf Neubritannien.   Journ. f. Ornith. 82: 568-578.

NEWELL'S SHEARWATER

Puffinus puffinus newelli Henshaw, 1900

Order PROCELLARIIFORMES   Family PROCELLARIIDAE

STATUS   Vulnerable. Although this seabird has been found to be much less scarce than was initially feared, subsequent reports indicate a continuing decline on its Hawaiian breeding grounds.

DISTRIBUTION   Formerly bred on Kauai, Maui and Molokai, and possibly throughout the high islands of the Hawaiian chain.   There are recent nesting records from Hawaii (W. Banko 1975, pers. comm.), and birds have been found on Oahu from time to time although there is as yet no evidence of breeding.   Kauai is at present the center of breeding distribution.   The shearwater disperses widely in the central Pacific.   It is frequently encountered near Kauai and Niihau between March and November but during the non-breeding season from December to February it is virtually absent from the vicinity of the Hawaiian Islands in the central Pacific and where it goes is still unknown (1).

POPULATION   There are no early estimates of abundance of Newell's Shearwater, although there can be no doubt that it was more abundant by far a century ago when it bred on several islands.   It was believed extinct in this century until the 1940s when reports began to come in of its presumed continued existence.   In 1967 it was estimated to occur at least in the low thousands on the basis of extensive sightings at sea (1).   Nevertheless the population is believed still to be declining.   In particular the largest known breeding colony on Anahola Mountain on Kauai, containing 500 or more birds when it was discovered in 1967, is significantly smaller (2).   A small colony was recently discovered on Hawaii, but it was presumed destroyed by volcanic eruptions (W. Banko 1975, pers. comm.).

HABITAT   Breeds along mountain ridges below 1200 m elevation.   Feeds at sea well away from its breeding islands.   On its breeding grounds the bird is subject to predation from dogs, cats and pigs (2).   The mongoose Herpestes auropunctatus has recently become established on Kauai, giving rise to serious concern for this shearwater's future, since predation by mongoose was the likely cause of its extirpation elsewhere in the Hawaiian islands (1).

CONSERVATION MEASURES TAKEN   Fully protected by U.S. and Hawaii State Law. Classified as vulnerable in the U.S. Secretary of Interior's list of endangered species, and thus protected by the U.S. Endangered Species Act of 1973.

CONSERVATION MEASURES PROPOSED   The control of predators where needed has been proposed (3).   This now appears essential and urgent having regard to the recent establishment of the mongoose on Kauai.

REMARKS   Of the seven other subspecies of Puffinus puffinus only P. p. huttoni of New Zealand is believed to be at risk.   The attraction of this subspecies to bright lights results in a substantial mortality of birds annually and there is no solid evidence that birds thus attracted are in any way sick or infirm.   Like other shearwaters once grounded they are unable to take off from a flat surface or without a headwind (1; 2).

REFERENCES   1.   King, W.B. & Gould, P.J. 1967.   The status of Newell's race of the Manx Shearwater.   The Living Bird 6: 163-186.
              2.   Sincock, J.L. & Swedberg, G.E. 1969.   Rediscovery of the nesting grounds of Newell's Manx Shearwater (Puffinus puffinus newelli) with initial observations.   Condor 71: 69-71.

3. U.S. Dept. of Interior Bureau of Sport Fisheries and Wildlife,
    1973.   Threatened wildlife of the United States.   U.S. Bur.
    Sport Fish. Wildl. Res. Pub. 114.

DALMATIAN PELICAN

Pelecanus crispus Bruch, 1832

Order PELECANIFORMES   Family PELECANIDAE

STATUS   Vulnerable. Declining or already eliminated from most breeding sites
in south-eastern Europe and many in the USSR as well, as a result of wetland
draining and desiccation and also of direct persecution by fishermen, who view
this pelican as a competitor.

DISTRIBUTION   The former breeding range included rivers, deltas, estuaries and
lakes of Europe and central Asia.   Its European distribution has been centered for
some time in the Balkan Peninsula, but historically the species nested as far north
and west as the Scheldt, Rhine and Elbe estuaries and, until 1868, in Hungary.
In Rumania, where its colonies were widespread in the 19th century, particularly
up the Danube as far as Calafat, it has been restricted to the Danube delta since
1963 when the Lake Călăraşi site was drained.   In Bulgaria it still nests at Lake
Srebarna but the 3 colonies known in Albania disappeared by 1940 and in Yugoslavia
of 7 known colonies only the Lake Skadar one remains, while Greece has lost 7,
possibly 8, out of its 9, breeding persisting only at Lake Mikra Prespa and perhaps
in the Arta Gulf.   Elsewhere, known nesting-places in Iran in the 1970s are Lake
Perishan, Dasht-i-Arjan and Bandar-e-Shāhpūr gulf, in Turkey three of the seven
historically known colonies remain occupied - Kizil Irmak delta, the Konya-Ereğli-
Hotamis area, and Lake Manyas -, and in the USSR an undetermined number of colonies
have been lost this century but nesting persists in the vicinity of the Volga
delta, Lake Chernoye, the Kizlyarskiy and Agrakhan Bays of the north-west Caspian,
the Aral Sea, and Zaysan and Manyeh-Gudilo lakes.   Breeding occurred formerly in
Mongolia at Lake Orok Nuur and may yet do so at Lake Buncagan, 120 km to the
north-west.
    The species is partially migratory, European birds moving to Greece, the east
Mediterranean, Black Sea coasts of Turkey and the Gulf of Suez; others winter in
the south Caspian coastlands of Iran and the Azerbaydzhan SSR, the Tigris-Euphrates
marshes of Iraq, on the coast of Kuwait, and not uncommonly from Baluchistan,
Pakistan, to Bengal, India. (1-6).

POPULATION   A serious decline has taken place since the last century when
'millions' were reported in Rumania alone (7).   The world population was estimated
at 665-1000 pairs in 1979, about half of them breeding in the USSR.   In the Danube
delta only about 100 pairs bred in 1975 as against 1300 in 1939.   In Bulgaria
30-90 pairs have bred regularly on Srebarna Lake and in Greece 80-100 pairs on
Lake Mikra Prespa.   The Lake Skadar colony in Yugoslavia contained 55 nests in
1978.   Between 90 and 200 pairs breed in Turkey.   The colonies in Bulgaria, Yugoslavia, Greece and Turkey have remained roughly stable or have increased slightly
since 1970.   Only 5-10 pairs now breed in Iran.   In the USSR the Volga delta
colony declined from 300 pairs in 1949 to 160 pairs in 1974, while several other
colonies reported on in the last few years have contained 50 pairs or fewer. (1-5).

HABITAT   Islands or flooded reedbeds in estuaries, lagoons, rivers, deltas and
lakes, free from human disturbance or terrestrial predators.   In winter ice-free
lakes and coastal waters with a predator-free island for roosting.   Drainage of
wetlands has caused the loss of numerous colonies and the trend is likely to
continue although several key wetlands used by this species now have legal protection.   Sudden rises in water level have also resulted in loss of eggs or young
in certain colonies. (1-3).

CONSERVATION MEASURES TAKEN   The species has legal protection in Rumania,
Bulgaria, Yugoslavia, Greece, Turkey and USSR.   Reserves or national parks give
protection to several breeding colonies including those on Sfîntu Gheorghe island,
Rumania, Lake Srebarna (600 ha), Bulgaria, Lake Skadar, Yugoslavia, Lake Mikra
Prespa (19,380 ha), Greece, and Lake Manyas, Turkey.   Platforms in trees and
floating or fixed rafts have been provided and used by the pelicans for nesting
at Lake Manyas and in the Volga delta (3).

CONSERVATION MEASURES PROPOSED   Protection for all surviving colonies and, where
necessary, of feeding areas.   Construction of flood-proof nesting platforms.
Annual censuses of all colonies.   Investigation of possible effects of pesticides
on reproductive success (3).

REMARKS   The Dalmatian Pelican occasionally nests in mixed colonies with the
White Pelican P. onocrotalus, which has declined seriously over much of its range
for much the same reasons and is now only slightly more secure.   Some authors
consider Pelecanus philippensis, which is still widely distributed in eastern and
south-eastern Asia as far as the Philippines, to be a subspecies of P. crispus (6).
Much of the information on which this sheet is based was generously provided by
Mr. A. Crivelli, Station Biologique de la Tour du Valat, coordinator of the IWRB
Pelican Research Group.

REFERENCES   1. Cramp, S. 1977.   Handbook of the Birds of Europe, the
                   Middle East and North Africa: the Birds of the Western
                   Palearctic, Vol. 1.   Oxford, London and New York:
                   Oxford University Press.
              2. Bauer, K.M. & Glutz von Blotzheim, U. 1966.   Handbuch
                   der Vögel Mitteleuropas, Vol. 1.   Frankfurt am Main:
                   Akademische Verlagsgesellschaft.
              3. Crivelli, A. 1978.   Pelicans in Europe.   Report to IWRB
                   Symposium on Conservation of Colonially Nesting Waterbirds,
                   Carthage, Tunisia.
              4. Flint, V.E. (ed.) 1978.   Part II, Birds.   In Borodin, A.M.,
                   Bannikov, A.G., Syroyetchkovski, E.E. et al. (Editorial
                   Board) The USSR Red Data Book: The Book of Rare and Endangered
                   Species of Animals and Plants.   Moscow: Lesnaya Promyshlennost.
              5. Dementiev, G.P., Gladkov, N.A., Ptushenko, E.S.,
                   Spangenberg, E.P. & Sudilovskaya, A.M. 1951.   Handbook of
                   the Birds of the Soviet Union, Vol. 1.   Moscow.
                   Trans. from Russian by Israel Program for Scientific
                   Translations, Jerusalem, 1966.
              6. Ali, S. & Ripley, S.D. 1968.   Handbook of the Birds of
                   India and Pakistan, Vol. 1.   Bombay, London and New York:
                   Oxford University Press.
              7. Hodek, E. 1873.   Über Verbreitung und Verhalten der
                   Gattung Pelecanus im europäischen Osten.   Verh. zool.
                   bot. Ges. Wien 1873: 1-22.

ABBOTT'S BOOBY

Sula abbotti Ridgway, 1893

Order PELECANIFORMES   Family SULIDAE

STATUS   Endangered.   This booby occurs on one island in the Indian Ocean.   Its
population is small and its reproductive potential is very low.   The areas of
rainforest it selects for nesting coincide with rich phosphate deposits which are
being mined.   The species' future depends on the preservation of sufficient
nesting areas to ensure a viable population.

DISTRIBUTION   There is a subfossil record of this species from Mauritius, and
eighteenth century descriptions and a subfossil bone suggest it occurred on
Rodrigues (1).   Also formerly known from Christmas Island and Assumption Island,
but it has not bred on Assumption since 1930, and it was last seen there in 1936
(2).   The suggestion that this species formerly bred on Glorioso (3; 4) probably
refers to the Red-footed Booby Sula sula (5).   On Christmas Island (142 sq. km) it
is largely restricted to the western part of the inland plateau above 150 m
elevation.   Within this area the species is locally clumped rather than evenly
dispersed (6).   At sea the species apparently forages up to 350 km north-west of
Christmas Island at an upwelling off Java Head (7; 8).

POPULATION   A population estimate in 1939-1940 of 500-750 pairs (9) was probably
low, for in 1967 and again in 1974 careful censuses were carried out of birds
returning to the island from the ocean.   These censuses revealed that 5,000-5,500
birds comprised the total population, including less than 2,000 breeding pairs
(6; 7).   Destruction of breeding habitat between 1967 and 1974 resulted in the
loss of a minimum of 120 pairs (7).   The species lays one egg every two years and
does not breed until 5 or 6 years of age (6).   Observations since 1974 further
refine population figures to at least 8,000 including perhaps 1,300 breeding pairs.
Weather during the monsoon is the most important factor controlling chick survival
and hence recruitment rate (11).

HABITAT   High rainforest above 150 m on Christmas Island.   The areas of
concentration of this species coincide substantially with the areas of richest
phosphate deposit (6).   The British Phosphate Commissioners have conducted large
scale phosphate extraction since 1965.   When it is completed by 1994 at least
30 percent of the island will have been mined (9).   The effect of mining is to
replace a forested area with one described as a moonscape, on which revegetation is
at best slow and sparse (6; 7).   Abbott's Booby is conservative in its nest sites.
It apparently does not move to new areas when previously occupied sites are
destroyed, but settles on the fringe of the destroyed site.   Islands of vegetation
left standing will continue to be used by this species, but may succumb to
dessication if not sufficiently large or protected peripherally by secondary
growth (7).   A relay station requiring about 400 ha of Abbott's Booby habitat,
not otherwise at risk because it is not rich in phosphate,has been proposed by
Radio Australia (10).

CONSERVATION MEASURES TAKEN   Legally protected from killing or capture.   The
species is listed in Appendix 1 of the 1973 Convention on International Trade in
Endangered Species of Wild Fauna and Flora.   Recommendations based on surveys in
1967 and 1974 have been made to the Government of Australia for the preservation of
this species (7; 10).   One of these recommendations, the appointment of a Resident
Conservation Officer, was implemented in 1975.

CONSERVATION MEASURES PROPOSED   Areas of forest in which dense population nuclei
occur are recommended for preservation, particularly if they occur on less than

highest grade phosphate deposits. The extent of areas cleared for support activities should be minimized. Clearing of forest should take place at times of day or during seasons when the species is largely absent from the island. Areas with lower grade deposits should not be cleared until it is certain they will be needed. Mined areas should be reclaimed (7; 10).

REMARKS   This is a classic case of confrontation between the requirements for the preservation of a species and economic exploitation of a natural resource. The species' future may be secured only at the cost of foregoing the extraction of a certain amount of valuable phosphate. Its extirpation from Assumption was caused by disturbance associated with guano mining on that island.

REFERENCES   1. Bourne, W.R.P. 1976. On subfossil bones of Abbott's Booby *Sula abbotti* from the Mascarene Islands, with a note on the proportions and distribution of the Sulidae. *Ibis* 118: 119-123.
2. Betts, F.N. 1940. The birds of the Seychelles, 2. *Ibis* (14)4: 489-504.
3. Nelson, J.B. 1974. The distribution of Abbott's Booby *Sula abbotti*. *Ibis* 116: 368-369.
4. Gibson-Hill, C.A. 1950. Notes on Abbott's Booby. *Bull. Raffles Mus.* 23: 65-76.
5. Benson, C.W., Beamish, H.H., Jouanin, C., Salvan, J. & Watson, G.E. 1975. The birds of the Iles Glorieuses. *Atoll Res. Bull.* 176: 1-34.
6. Nelson, J.B. 1971. The biology of Abbott's Booby *Sula abbotti*. *Ibis* 113: 429-467.
7. Nelson, J.B. 1976. Report on the status and prospects of Abbott's Booby (*Sula abbotti*) in relation to phosphate mining on the Australian Territory of Christmas Island, August 1974. *Bull. ICBP* 12: 131-140.
8. Becking, J.H. 1976. Feeding range of Abbott's Booby *Sula abbotti* at the coast of Java. *Ibis* 118: 589-590.
9. Gibson-Hill, C.A. 1947. Notes on the birds of Christmas Island. *Bull. Raffles Mus.* 18: 87-165.
10. Australia House of Representatives Standing Committee on Environment and Conservation, 1974. Conservation of endangered species on Christmas Island. Canberra:Australian Government Publishing Service.
11. Nelson, J.B. 1977 (unpublished). Abbott's Booby and mining: report and recommendations on the status and prospects of Abbott's Booby, in relation to the British Phosphate Commissioner's mining and conservation policy.

GALAPAGOS FLIGHTLESS CORMORANT

Nannopterum harrisi (Rothschild, 1898)

Order PELECANIFORMES   Family PHALACROCORACIDAE

STATUS   Rare.   Restricted to portions of the coastline of Fernandina and
Isabela islands, Galapagos Islands.   Extremely sedentary, flightless, with a very
small total population, and liable to rapid extermination if net-fishing for
lobsters is permitted in the Galapagos.

DISTRIBUTION   The coastline of Fernandina and western Isabela (363 km), Galapagos
Islands.   This species does not disperse after breeding.

POPULATION   In 1970-1971 there were between 700 and 800 pairs, confined to many
small colonies in not easily accessible terrain.   The species is probably at least
as numerous now as at any time since its discovery.

HABITAT   Breeds along rocky shorelines.   Restricted to within 100 m of coastline
while swimming.   Its range coincides with the coldest, richest waters in the
Galapagos.

CONSERVATION MEASURES TAKEN   Fully protected by law.   A thorough census of
population has been completed.

CONSERVATION MEASURES PROPOSED   Continued prohibition of net-fishing for lobsters
in the Galapagos.

REFERENCES   1.   Harris, M.P. 1974.   A complete census of the Flightless
                   Cormorant (Nannopterum harrisi).   Biol. Cons. 6(3):   188-191.

KING SHAG

Phalacrocorax carunculatus carunculatus (Gmelin, 1789)

Order PELECANIFORMES   Family PHALACROCORACIDAE

STATUS   Rare.   The small population of this subspecies barely replaces itself
annually in its restricted (less than 100 km in diameter) breeding range in New
Zealand.   Formerly collected in excessive numbers for the feather trade and for
museum specimens, but now protected and relatively secure.

DISTRIBUTION   At one time thought to be confined to the White Rocks islets of
Marlborough Sounds, South Island, flanking Cook Strait due west of Wellington.
But between 1933 and 1960, several additional colonies were found and, although
there may be some tendency in the long term for old ones to disappear and new
ones to be established, all of them - Sentinel Rock, Duffer's Reef, North Trio
Island and Te Kuru Kuru Island (also known as 'Bushy' or 'Stewart' Island and not
to be confused with the well-known Stewart Island south of Foveaux Strait) are
still extant (1).

POPULATION   Only about 300 birds, a figure that is not believed to be substantially lower than at the time of the first report of this population in 1773
(1).   A decline may have taken place at the turn of this century as the result
of increased human persecution but there has probably been a subsequent slight
recovery; whether the population is now stable is uncertain (1).

HABITAT   This shag nests on rocky islets on the edge of the subtropical
convergence, dispersing to feed in nearby waters and roosting on headlands near
its breeding sites (1; 2).

CONSERVATION MEASURES TAKEN   Fully protected by law since 1924, although still
occasionally shot by fishermen who accuse it of depleting fish stocks.   Notices
have been erected at breeding sites indicating the birds have full legal
protection and all permanent breeding colonies have been gazetted as wildlife
sanctuaries with access by permit only (1).

CONSERVATION MEASURES PROPOSED   Continued surveillance of this small vulnerable
population is advocated (1).

REMARKS   King or Blue-eyed Shags found on islands south and east of South Island
(one of them, the Stewart Island Shag, also nesting along the south-east coast of
South Island itself, as far north as Dunedin) have been treated by some authors as
subspecies of carunculatus, by others as full species (2) or, in the case of those
in Bounty and Auckland islands, as subspecies of the smaller Campbell Island Shag
P. campbelli.   It is generally agreed, however, that the most nearly related to
the nominate carunculatus of Marlborough Sounds are the Stewart Island Shag,
chalconotus, and the Chatham Island Shag P. (carunculatus) onslowi.   Neither of
them is presently considered at risk, although the total population of chalconotus
may be in the low thousands.

REFERENCES   1.   Nelson, A. 1971.   King Shags in the Marlborough Sounds.
                    Notornis 18:   30-37.
              2.   Falla, R.A., Sibson, R.B. & Turbott, E.G. 1970.   A field
                    guide to the birds of New Zealand (revised ed.).   London:
                    Collins.

CHRISTMAS FRIGATEBIRD

Fregata andrewsi Mathews, 1914

Order PELECANIFORMES   Family FREGATIDAE

STATUS   Vulnerable.   Restricted to one island in the Indian Ocean which is being
intensively mined for phosphate. Disturbance and habitat destruction associated
with mining and illegal capture of the species for food by island residents are
serious threats to its survival.

DISTRIBUTION   Known to breed only on Christmas Island, Indian Ocean, but also
recorded from the Anambas Islands, between the Malay peninsula and Sarawak, and it
may prove to breed there.   Strays have been reported from the Cocos Keeling
Islands, Sri Lanka, India and Sarawak (1).   On Christmas Island the species nests
behind the golf course and on a 3.2 km strip of shore terrace along the north
coastline near the north-east point (2).

POPULATION   The earliest estimate of numbers, for the period 1938-1940, was of
1,000 to 1,500 pairs (1).   In 1967 rather less than 2,000 pairs were estimated to
occur on Christmas Island (2), while one further estimate based on visits to
Christmas Island in 1965, 1972 and 1974 was of less than 1,000 pairs (3).   There
is no firm evidence of a decline, although substantial numbers have been taken by
resident Malays, who have been living on the island for a half-century.   In 1967
the remains of 40 birds were found in one area (2).   This species raises one
young every two years, and doubtless shares the characteristically delayed maturity
of other species in the Frigatebird Family.   Hence, its potential for recouping
population losses is very poor.

HABITAT   Nesting takes place on tall trees along the shore terrace.   The species
disperses widely at sea to feed.   On Christmas Island nests are relatively near
human habitation.   The future security of the species' habitat depends on the
extent of mining of the island's surface for lesser grade phosphate (2).   By 1994,
30 percent of the island's surface will have been mined (4), but fortunately this
species nests in areas of low grade phosphate which may be left untouched.   Some
damage to the species' habitat may, however, be expected from clearing for
activities ancillary to the main mining effort.

CONSERVATION MEASURES TAKEN   Legally protected from killing or capture but birds
are frequently taken illegally, apparently without fear that the law will be
enforced and adequate penalties exacted.   The species is listed on Appendix 1 of
the 1973 Convention on International Trade in Endangered Species of Wild Fauna
and Flora.   A Conservation Officer was appointed on Christmas Island in 1975.

CONSERVATION MEASURES PROPOSED   The long-term resident human population of
Christmas Island will be relocated following completion of mining operations in
about 1994 (4).   Revegetation of mined areas has been proposed but is unlikely on
a large scale.   More effective enforcement of the existing legal protection of
this species has been advocated (2; 4) and is clearly desirable.

REFERENCES   1.   Gibson-Hill, C.A. 1947.   Notes on the birds of Christmas
                    Island.   Bull. Raffles Mus. 18: 87-165.
              2.   Nelson, J.B. 1972.   The biology of the seabirds of the Indian
                    Ocean Christmas Island.   Journ. Mar. Biol. Ass. India 14:
                    643-662.

3. Van Tets, G.F. 1976. A report on the conservation of resident birds on Christmas Island. *Bull. ICBP* 12: 238-242.
4. Australian House of Representatives Standing Committee on Environment and Conservation, 1974. Conservation of endangered species on Christmas Island. Canberra:Australian Government Publishing Service.

ASCENSION FRIGATEBIRD

Fregata aquila (Linnaeus, 1758)

Order PELECANIFORMES   Family FREGATIDAE

STATUS   Rare.   The entire breeding population of this species is confined to
one tiny island in the Atlantic Ocean.

DISTRIBUTION   Formerly occurred on Ascension Island, but extirpated as a
breeding species over a century ago and now only roosting. Presently restricted for
breeding purposes to Boatswainbird Island (5.5 ha), which is separated from eastern
Ascension Island by a turbulent 230 m wide channel (1; 2).

POPULATION   The species was once abundant on Ascension, but rapidly eliminated
following the introduction of cats (1).   On Boatswainbird Island between 8,000
and 10,000 breeding adults were estimated to be present in 1957-1959 (3).

HABITAT   For breeding, lower ash, cinder and lava slopes of the main tropical
mid-ocean island of Ascension were once used.   Now nests are confined to the
summit plateau, ledges and remains of paths cut on the steep flanks of a 100 m high
trachytic but basalt-capped rocky stack.   Feeding grounds not known to extend more
than 150 km from Ascension Island.   Like all members of its family, this species
is vulnerable to predation by introduced predators, in this case having been
extirpated from the main island by cats.

CONSERVATION MEASURES TAKEN   A cat control program has reduced but not eliminated
cats on Ascension.

CONSERVATION MEASURES PROPOSED   None known, although it is obvious that care must
be taken to restrict visits to Boatswainbird Island to prevent the introduction of
predators or disturbance of breeding seabirds.

REFERENCES   1.   Stonehouse, B. 1962.   Ascension Island and the British
                   Ornithologists' Union Centenary Expedition 1957-1959.
                   Ibis 103b: 107-123.
              2.   Olson, S.L. 1977.   Additional notes on subfossil bird
                   remains from Ascension Island.   Ibis 119: 37-43.
              3.   Stonehouse, B. and Stonehouse, S. 1963.   The Frigate
                   Bird Fregata aquila of Ascension Island.   Ibis 103b:
                   409-422.

CHINESE EGRET

Egretta eulophotes (Swinhoe, 1860)

Order CICONIIFORMES   Family ARDEIDAE

STATUS   Vulnerable.   This egret was formerly widely distributed, breeding in
eastern China and wintering in South East Asia.   Recent records suggest it may
have recovered slightly from a serious decline caused by hunting of egrets for
plumes and other direct or indirect human persecution.   Competition from other
egrets may prevent a complete recovery.

DISTRIBUTION   Formerly bred in the maritime provinces of Fukien and Kwangtung,
China (1), North Korea, and possibly Cheju Do (Quelpart I.) in the Yellow Sea (2).
It was found breeding in Hong Kong in 1959 (3).   Its present breeding distribution
is not known precisely but there are recent specimens in Peking from Kwantung,
including Hainan Island, Chekiang, Fukien, Taiwan, Kiangsu and Shantung (Tso-Hsin
Cheng in litt. to J. Vincent, 1964).   It is not known if the species still breeds
in North Korea.   The species disperses widely after breeding.   There are now
regular spring records from Amur-Ussuriland, U.S.S.R. (4), summer and winter
records from Taiwan (S. Severinghaus, 1976, pers. comm.) and formerly at least
winter records from the Philippines, Sulawesi, Peninsular Thailand, Malaysia,
Sarawak, Honshu, Japan, and Natuna Island (3).   More recently there have been
records from coastal South Korea (5), the Ryukyu Islands (6), Sabah (7), Malaya (8)
and the Aleutians.

POPULATION   Not known with any certainty, although believed to be sparse.   The
species declined disastrously at the end of last century with the advent of the
plumage trade in China, and was excessively rare for several decades into this
century.   It apparently never recovered its former numbers, in contrast to the
Little Egret Egretta garzetta which may now have replaced it over much of its
range (3).   A recent report suggests the Chinese Egret may in fact be locally
common once more in China (J. Gerson in litt. to S.D. Ripley, 1975).   Up to 10
pairs bred in Hong Kong until 1962 but by 1969 only 3 pairs remained (3).

HABITAT   Tidal flats, also river banks and paddy fields in parts of its range (3).

CONSERVATION MEASURES TAKEN   Fully protected by law in Hong Kong.   The heronries
of Hong Kong were protected in 1971 and are patrolled by game wardens (3).

CONSERVATION MEASURES PROPOSED   None known.

REMARKS   The decline of this species was documented poorly and only some years
after its occurrence, partly because the species was considered identical with
and even made a synonym of E. sacra for many years (4).

REFERENCES   1.   La Touche, J.D.D. 1931-1934.   A Handbook of the Birds of
                    Eastern China, Vol. 2.   London:Taylor and Francis.
              2.   Austin, O.L., Jr. 1948.   The birds of Korea.   Harvard Mus.
                    Comp. Zool. Bull. 101: 1-301.

REFERENCES (cont.)

3. Murton, R.K. 1972.   The ecology and status of Swinhoe's
    Egret, with notes on other herons of south-eastern China.
    Biol. Cons. 4:   89-96.
4. Fisher, J., Simon, N. & Vincent, J. 1969.   Wildlife in Danger.
    New York:Viking Press; London:Collins.
5. Fennell, C.M. & King, B.F. 1964.   New occurrences and recent
    distributional records of Korean birds.   Condor 66:   239-246.
6. Bruce, M.D. 1975.   Okinawa bird notes.   Bull. Brit. Orn. Cl.
    95:   154-157.
7. Thompson, M.C. 1966.   Birds from North Borneo.   U. Kansas
    Pubs. 17(8):   377-433.
8. Medway, G. & Wells, D.R. 1976.   The Birds of the Malay
    Peninsula, Vol. 5.   London & Malaysia:Witherby & Penerbit
    University.

FASCIATED TIGER-HERON

Tigrisoma fasciatum fasciatum (Such, 1825)

Order CICONIIFORMES   Family ARDEIDAE

STATUS   Indeterminate.   There have been no records of this rare heron of south-eastern Brazil for many years.

DISTRIBUTION   Known from a few specimens from south-eastern Brazil from Rio de Janeiro south to Rio Grande do Sul, also a specimen from Mato Grosso, and two from Bonpland, Misiones, Argentina, taken in 1912 (1).   In what parts of the extensive range indicated by these occurrences this subspecies may still be found is unknown.

POPULATION   Undetermined but never thought to have been large.   The dearth of specimens and absence of recent records, in spite of several attempts to locate this subspecies in the wild, suggest it may now be at serious risk (H. Sick 1977, pers. comm.).

HABITAT   Forested hill country along rocky rapidly-flowing rivers and streams. The forests of south-eastern Brazil have been seriously depleted (2; R. Ridgely 1978, pers. comm.).

CONSERVATION MEASURES TAKEN   Brazilian law protects this species as a whole, but not its habitat.

CONSERVATION MEASURES PROPOSED   None known.

REMARKS   The species is local and uncommon throughout its range.   Another subspecies, Tigrisoma fasciatum pallescens, found in Salta and Tucumán provinces of Argentina, is known only from four specimens and may also be at risk.   The most widespread of the subspecies, T. f. salmoni, ranging from northern Bolivia, Peru, Ecuador, Colombia and Venezuela to Panama and Costa Rica, is, however, unlikely to be at risk.

REFERENCES   1.   Eisenmann, E. 1965.   The Tiger-Herons (Tigrisoma) of Argentina.   Hornero 10: 225-234.
              2.   Sick, H. 1972.   A ameaça da avifauna brasileira.   Pp. 99-153 in Espécies da Fauna Brasileira Ameaçadas de Extinção. Rio de Janeiro: Academia Brasileira de Ciências.

ORIENTAL WHITE STORK

Ciconia ciconia boyciana Swinhoe, 1873

Order CICONIIFORMES   Family CICONIIDAE

STATUS   Endangered. This well-marked race of the White Stork, possibly
deserving recognition as a full species, has ceased to nest in two countries on
the periphery of its range. Recent information on its status in south-eastern
Siberia, where it is thought to be most numerous, indicates that the surviving
population is small.

DISTRIBUTION   The breeding range in Siberia at one time extended from the river
systems of the Lake Khanka basin northwards along the Ussuri and Amur rivers, the
Samarga and Botchi rivers on the east slopes of the Sikhote Alin range, and the
Krasnoi River in Amurland. The stork has also bred in adjacent eastern Manchuria
(1).   Nested in Korea and Japan and a pair has been recorded in Tibet in summer
(3).   In winter, migrants have been recorded with certainty south to Fukien
in eastern China, Taiwan and the southern Ryukyu archipelago, in addition to the
more southerly parts of the former breeding range (3).   The stork no longer breeds
in Japan and South Korea, but is still found over much of the basin of the Amur
River, although thinly distributed (S. Winter 1976, pers. comm.).

POPULATION   The history of the decline of this stork in Korea and Japan is known
in some detail.   The major decline in the once abundant Japanese population took
place from 1868 to 1895, before it was protected.   By the turn of the century it
was only nesting on one hill, called Tsuruyama, in west-central Honshu.   A slight
increase in population resulted from protection of this site and by 1944 the
Japanese population was 50 birds.   However, the illegal shooting of storks
continued and from 1957 increasing use of chemicals, especially mercury, in the
fields near its breeding places caused reproductive failure, and the population
slowly dwindled away.   The last successful breeding took place in 1959, when 3
young were fledged.   Three individuals from the continental population visited
Japan in the winter of 1972-73 (4; 5; 6; Y. Yamashina 1974, pers. comm.).   In
South Korea the stork was a locally common breeder, but by the Second World War
it had ceased to do so, except for one pair, which continued nesting at Umsung
until one of the pair was shot in 1971 (7; 8); in 1977 the lone female laid
infertile eggs (G. Archibald, 1978, pers. comm.).   At least two birds were seen
in South Korea in winter 1973-74 (9).   The status of the population in North Korea
is unknown but the stork was said to be still reasonably common in Manchuria in
1976 (J.A.W. Paludan in litt.to S.D. Ripley, February).   It was never known to be
numerous and may now be declining, although a few were seen recently near
Tsitsihar, Heilungkiang Province (J.H. Gerson in litt.to S.D. Ripley, April 1976).
Lastly, the censuses carried out in the entire Soviet Amur basin in 1974 and 1975
yielded a count of 137 breeding pairs and an estimate of 550 birds, including young
of the year, a conservative figure for certainly not all nests of the region were
found (10; 13).

HABITAT   Marshes with scattered clumps of trees.   In Japan and Korea, cultivated
fields especially rice fields with nearby wooded hillsides, where the nests used to
be sited (1; 5).   In these areas loaches were a favoured food and tended to absorb
the mercury which was frequently used as an agricultural pesticide.   The resulting
concentration of the poison by the storks was often enough to cause mortality or
reproductive failure (11).   The wetlands at the Bureya-Amur confluence in south-
eastern Siberia, another important habitat, are threatened by drainage and
agricultural development (G. Archibald 1976, pers. comm.).

CONSERVATION MEASURES TAKEN   Totally protected by law in USSR, Japan and South
Korea.   Designated a Special Natural Monument in Japan in 1956 (Y. Yamashina
1974, pers. comm.) and in South Korea as Natural Monument No. 199 in 1968 (9).
In 1904, Tsuruyama hill and 15 sq. km around it (Hyogo Prefecture) were made a
reserve and, in 1935, a Natural Monument; in Fukui Prefecture, where the birds
nested in 1957, the area concerned was similarly made a Natural Monument (2; 4).
Captive breeding has been attempted for a number of years in Japan, as yet
unsuccessfully (6; 11).   The stork is listed in Appendix 1 of the 1973 Convention
on International Trade in Endangered Species of Wild Fauna and Flora.

CONSERVATION MEASURES PROPOSED   None additional known.

REMARKS   The breeding ranges of the two other subspecies are, respectively,
Central Asia (C. c. asiatica) and western Asia, Europe and Africa (the nominate
race).   The latter has seriously declined in western Europe.   The oriental
boyciana, dealt with in this data sheet, is widely regarded as sufficiently
distinct to be treated as a species (13; V. Flint 1978, pers. comm.).   There were
17 boyciana in captivity in 1975 in China, Japan and Indonesia, and 2 in Moscow
in 1978 (12; H.F.I. Elliott 1979, pers. comm.).

REFERENCES   1.   Dementiev , G.P., Meklenburtsev, R.N., Sudilovskaya, A.M. &
                   Spangenberg, E.P. 1951.   Birds of the Soviet Union, Vol. 2.
                   Trans. from Russian by Israel Program for Scientific
                   Translations, Jerusalem, 1968.
              2.   Fisher, J., Simon, N. & Vincent, J. 1969.   Wildlife in Danger.
                   New York: Viking Press.
              3.   Vaurie, C. 1972.   Tibet and its Birds.   London:
                   H.F. and G. Witherby.
              4.   Austin, O.L., Jr. & Kuroda, N. 1953.   The birds of Japan:
                   their status and distribution.   Harvard Bull. Mus. Comp. Zool.
                   109(4): 279-637.
              5.   Ornithological Society of Japan, 1974.   Check-list of
                   Japanese Birds, 5th revised ed. Tokyo: Gakken Co.
              6.   Yoshii, M. 1971.   The present status of the Japanese
                   Crested Ibis and the Japanese White Stork.   Bull. ICBP 11:
                   168-169.
              7.   Won, P.-O. 1971.   The status of bird conservation in Korea,
                   1966-1970.   Bull. ICBP 11: 242-247.
              8.   Gore, M.E.J. & Won, P.-O, 1971.   The Birds of Korea.
                   Rutland, Vt. and Tokyo: Charles E. Tuttle Co.
              9.   Won, P.-O. 1974.   Bird Treasures (Natural Monuments)
                   in Korea.   In Korean, English summary.
             10.   Lebedeva, M.I. undated.   Distribution and population of the
                   Far Eastern Stork in the U.S.S.R.   Ms (in Russian).
             11.   Yamashina, Y. 1967.   The status of endangered species
                   in Japan.   Bull. ICBP 10: 100-109.
             12.   Olney, P.J.S. (ed.) 1976.   Census of rare animals in
                   captivity, 1975.   International Zoo Yearbook 16: 411-446.
             13.   Vaurie, C. 1965.   The Birds of the Palearctic Fauna.
                   London: H.F. & G. Witherby.
             14.   Shibaev, I.V., Semenchenko, N.N. & Limin, V.A. 1976.
                   Nesting area of the White Stork on the right bank of the
                   Ussuri River.   In Nature Conservation in the Soviet
                   Far East.   In Russian.

STORM'S STORK

Ciconia episcopus stormi (Blasius, 1896)

Order CICONIIFORMES   Family CICONIIDAE

STATUS   Indeterminate. This stork, which is known from Borneo, peninsular
Malaysia and Sumatra, is believed to be declining as the result of forest
destruction in Borneo. Its status in Sumatra is unknown and in Malaya there are
few recent records.

DISTRIBUTION   This stork has been recorded rather locally in Borneo, in eastern
Sumatra, off the south-west coast of Sumatra on North Pagai, Mentawai Islands, and
in Selangor, Pahang and possibly Taman Negara, peninsular Malaysia. Its present
distribution is not known to be different.

POPULATION   Unknown, but there has clearly been a decline. This subspecies has
never been reported as abundant and it is now considered to be rare everywhere
(D. Wells in litt. to K. Scriven, 1974). In peninsular Malaysia there are
records of four and possibly five birds since 1963 (5).

HABITAT   Fresh water swamps (1). Roosts and nests in trees. The extensive
destruction of forests in Borneo is believed a major factor in the decline of
this subspecies (D. Wells in litt. to K. Scriven, 1974).

CONSERVATION MEASURES TAKEN   Legally protected in Sarawak by the Wild Life
Protection Ordinance of 1957. Also legally protected in Indonesia.

CONSERVATION MEASURES PROPOSED   None known.

REMARKS   The nominate subspecies and two others, from Africa, India and South-
East Asia, respectively, are not known to be at risk. C. e. stormi is sufficiently distinct from the others to have been considered a separate species by several
authors.

REFERENCES   1. Smythies, B.E. 1960. The Birds of Borneo. Edinburgh
                  and London: Oliver and Boyd.
              2. Delacour, J. 1947. Birds of Malaysia. New York:
                  MacMillan Co.
              3. Chasen, F.N. 1939. The Birds of the Malay Peninsula.
                  Vol. 4. London: H.F. and G. Witherby.
              4. White, C.M.N. 1974. Three water birds of Wallacea.
                  Bull. Brit. Ornith. Club 94: 9-11.
              5. Medway & Wells, D.R. 1976. The Birds of the Malay
                  Peninsula. Vol. 5. London: H.F. and G. Witherby.

MILKY STORK

Mycteria cinerea (Raffles, 1822)

Order CICONIIFORMES   Family CICONIIDAE

STATUS   Vulnerable.   Although widely distributed in South East Asia this
striking species has declined and is now threatened throughout most of its range.
It has suffered from military activities in many parts of South East Asia, and from
habitat destruction in Malaya and Java; its status on Sumatra is not known.

DISTRIBUTION   Recorded from the southern half of the Malay Peninsula in western
Malaysia, south of Kedah and Penang, southern Cambodia, southernmost Vietnam,
Sumatra and Java (1).   Its present distribution is not known to differ.

POPULATION   No estimate has been made.   It was considered not uncommon locally
half a century ago (1).   It is now all but extinct in Malaysia, where it is
presently known from one locality in Perak State (D. Wells 1976, pers. comm.).
It is threatened on Pulau Dua, off the coast of north-west Java, where a large
nesting colony is known, and military activities in former Cambodia and South
Vietnam have doubtless also caused a decline, although confirmation is lacking
(D. Wells in litt. to K. Scriven, 1974).   There are no recent reports of the
status of the species in Sumatra, although at least in the south it is still to be
found (D. Wells 1976, pers. comm.).

HABITAT   Lakes, marshes, coastal mudflats and mangroves (2).   Its large colonial
nesting sites are especially vulnerable to disturbance.

CONSERVATION MEASURES TAKEN   Legally protected in Java and Sumatra.   Pulau Dua,
off western Java, is a nature reserve.   In Malaysia it is protected and may not be
killed or taken for food, except by aborigines.

CONSERVATION MEASURES PROPOSED   None known.

REFERENCES   1.   Robinson, H.C. & Chasen, F.N. 1936.   The Birds of the Malay
                    Peninsula.   Vol. 3.   London:H.F. and G. Witherby.
              2.   King, B.F. & Dickinson, E.C. 1975.   A Field Guide to the
                    Birds of South-East Asia.   Boston:Houghton Mifflin Co.;
                    London:Collins.

BALD IBIS

Geronticus calvus (Boddaert, 1783)

Order CICONIIFORMES   Family THRESKIORNITHIDAE

STATUS   Rare. Locally distributed and scarce in south-eastern Africa, this
ibis has declined historically through disturbance and through replacement of
grasslands by karoo vegetation.

DISTRIBUTION   Restricted to South Africa, where it occurs in southern Transvaal,
eastern Orange Free State, north-eastern Cape Province, western Natal and Zululand,
and to Lesotho and, as a non-breeder, to western Swaziland. It was once widespread in the Cape Province but is now limited to one small colony at the
north-eastern corner (1).

POPULATION   About 70 colonies are known. Only 10 pairs continue to breed in
Cape Province, where the greatest population decline has taken place. The
breeding population of Transvaal is about 450. About 1000 breed in Orange Free
State and a further 300 in Natal and Zululand. The total population, including
a substantial non-breeding portion, is 2,000 birds (1). No estimates of the
population were made in the past but, in 1948, this ibis was considered very local
but still reasonably common, although no longer present in parts of its former
range (2).

HABITAT   The species nests on rock cliffs and feeds on relatively level grassveld
It does not wander widely from its nesting-places. In Cape Province large areas
of grassveld have been replaced with karoo vegetation (1).

CONSERVATION MEASURES TAKEN   Protected by law in South Africa, although in
remote areas where enforcement is not possible some still continue to be killed by
the local people.

CONSERVATION MEASURES PROPOSED   It has been recommended that the government
should set aside as special nature reserves one or two selected breeding and
feeding sites of the ibis. Research on which to base management decisions is
also needed (1).

REMARKS   The closely related Waldrapp Geronticus eremita is now restricted to
Turkey and Morocco and is in danger of extinction.

REFERENCES   1. Siegfried, W.R. 1971. The status of the Bald Ibis of
                   southern Africa. Biol. Cons. 3: 88-91.
               2. Vincent, J. & Symons, G. 1948. Some notes on the Bald
                   Ibis. Ostrich 19: 58-62.

WALDRAPP or HERMIT IBIS

Geronticus eremita (Linnaeus, 1758)

Order CICONIIFORMES   Family THRESKIORNITHIDAE

STATUS   Endangered.   This ibis is one of the few bird species to have become
extinct in Europe in historical times.   It is now known to have only one small
breeding colony in Turkey and 15 more scattered over Morocco.   Its population has
declined rapidly in both areas, although intensive management has brought about
a slight amelioration in the Turkish colony.   Without direct aid it could become
extinct within two decades as a result of hunting, disturbance at nest sites,
taking of live birds and eggs for zoos and for food, and possibly reproductive
failure from pesticide residues.

DISTRIBUTION   The species bred in Europe on the upper Rhone and Danube, in the
Italian Alps and in the Swiss Juras until the 17th century, and in Syria until
sometime after 1929 (or according to other authorities only until 1910-1916).
Breeding may have occurred but was never proved in Iraq and the countries bordering
the Red Sea, and was recorded in Algeria until 1930, but not since.   The only
colonies now known are one in Turkey, at Birecik on the upper Euphrates, and at
15 sites in Morocco, 2 in the east (out of the 7 historically occupied), 5 in the
middle and high Atlas (out of 9), 7 in the coastal plains or along the coast (out
of 13) and 1 south of the Atlas (out of the 4 of which there are historical
records).   The Turkish birds migrate during the dry autumn and winter months to
Eritrea and northern Ethiopia, and in smaller numbers to the Sudan, southern
Arabia and Somaliland.   The North African population is also at least partially
migratory but to unknown winter quarters, possibly in the Niger Inundation Zone
of Mali.   There are records from former Spanish Sahara and from Mauritania of
birds presumed to be on passage. (1-4; 11; 13; 14; 16).

POPULATION   Although the population was once substantially above its present
level, there is no evidence the species was ever abundant.   The Birecik colony
was established between 1840 and 1870 and in 1890 numbered some 3000 pairs.   It
had declined to 530 pairs in 1953, 130 pairs in 1962, to 70-75 pairs in 1965, to
45 pairs in 1967 and to 25 pairs in 1972 (3; 5; 6; 14).   Thereafter a slight
increase was indicated by the production of 21 young in 1973 and 64 in 1974, but
further declines followed: 25 pairs produced 36 young in 1975 and 13 pairs
produced 17 young in 1976 (3; 7; 11).   In Morocco the population declined from
1000 pairs to less than 250 pairs between 1930 and 1975.   In eastern Morocco
numbers dropped from 200 to 30 pairs, in the middle and high Atlas from 100 to 50
pairs, in the coastlands from 220 to 100 pairs, and south of the Atlas range from
30 to 10 pairs.   The total Moroccan population, including non-breeders, was
estimated at 600-650 birds in 1975.(3; 11; 14; 17).

HABITAT   Nests gregariously on cliff ledges at traditional sites.   Feeds on
open ground, including cultivated fields.   Reduced reproduction and direct
mortality associated with increased use of persistent pesticides such as DDT and
dieldrin,on croplands where the birds feed and for malaria control, were partly
responsible for the decline between 1956 and 1959, when more than 600 dead birds
were found around Birecik (6; 8; 11), although a chick and an egg sampled in 1972
contained pesticide residues well below those associated with reproductive failure
(9; 11).   Human disturbance of nest sites and climatic changes have been
suggested as causes of the extinction of the species in Europe (3; 4; 16).

CONSERVATION MEASURES TAKEN   Protected by law from hunting or capture in Turkey
and Morocco, but the law is often virtually unenforceable, particularly in Morocco

where nesting and feeding sites are far from human settlements. At Birecik in Turkey, under a World Wildlife Fund-Turkish National Parks conservation project, the ledges used for nesting on a cliff that bisects the town, were enlarged to reduce egg and chick loss, and artificial wooden platforms built, on which 85% of the population nested in 1976. Walls above the cliff were made higher, to discourage throwing of stones and refuse on nest sites, and a festival to celebrate the annual return of the species was revived. In Morocco a privately sponsored conservation education campaign has resulted in effective protection of one important colony in the Atlas Mountains, while provision of funds by a dedicated conservationist has enabled another Moroccan colony to be protected (3; 8; 11).

CONSERVATION MEASURES PROPOSED   The World Wildlife Fund and Turkish National Parks have suggested a project for a park at the foot of the nesting cliff in Birecik. Houses adjacent to the cliff would be demolished and alternative accommodation constructed for their occupants, while the use of pesticides in fields near Birecik favoured by the ibis for feeding would be eliminated. In Morocco, programs for increased surveillance of nesting colonies by game wardens, additional wardens being if necessary recruited for the purpose, and for conservation education campaigns, as in Turkey, which would include showing films of the species, have been advocated by World Wildlife Fund (3; 8). The Swiss Appeal of the Fund has considered reestablishing a wild population through release of captive-bred individuals, but such a release is not yet feasible (10). More recently a project has been launched to relocate the Birecik colony on a nearby but less disturbed cliff site, using captive birds to attract those still occupying the Birecik cliff (15).

REMARKS   The Waldrapp has bred well in captivity for at least 15 years. In 1975, 29 collections housed 215, about threequarters of them captive bred (11). The closely related species G. calvus of southern Africa has been reduced to about 2000 individuals (12) and is now sufficiently at risk to be included in this volume.

REFERENCES   1. Smith, K.D. 1970. The Waldrapp Geronticus eremita (L.).
                   Bull. Brit. Ornith. Club 90: 18-24.
              2. Siegfried, W.R. 1972. Discrete breeding and wintering areas
                   of the Waldrapp Geronticus eremita (L.). Bull. Brit. Ornith.
                   Club 92: 102-103.
              3. Hirsch, U. 1975. L'Ibis Chauve Geronticus eremita au
                   Maroc. Unpub. WWF Report.
              4. Geroudet, P. 1965. Du "Waldrapp" de Gessner aux Ibis
                   Chauves du Maroc. Nos Oiseaux 28: 129-143.
              5. Kumerloeve, H. 1962. Zur Geschichte der Waldrapp-Kolonie in
                   Birecik am oberen Euphrat. Journ. f. Ornith., 103: 389-398.
              6. Kumerloeve, H. 1967. Nouvelles données sur la situation
                   de la colonie d'Ibis chevelus Geronticus eremita (L.) 1758, à
                   Birecik sur l'Euphrate (Turquie). Alauda 35: 194-202.
              7. Mallet, M. 1975. The Waldrapp Ibis (Geronticus eremita)
                   Jersey Wildl. Preserv. Trust Ann. Report 12: 26-31.
              8. Hirsch, U. 1973. Bald Ibis, Turkey. Unpub. WWF interim
                   report, Project 945.
              9. Parslow, J.L.F. 1973. Organochlorine insecticide residues and
                   food remains in a Bald Ibis Geronticus eremita chick from
                   Birecik, Turkey. Bull. Brit. Ornith. Club 93: 163-166.
             10. Grundbecher, B., Lups, P. & Salzmann, H. 1975. Zwischen-
                   bericht "Waldrapp" zuhanden der WWF-Sektion Bern. Unpub.
                   WWF Report.
             11. Hirsch, U. & Schenker, A. 1977. Der Waldrapp (Geronticus
                   eremita): Freilandbeobachtungen und Hinweise für eine artge-
                   mässe Haltung. Zeitschrift des Kölner Zoo 20(1): 3-11.

12. Siegfried, W.R. 1971. The status of the Bald Ibis of southern Africa. Biel. Cons. 3: 88-91.

13. Aharoni, J. 1929. Zur Brutbiologie von Comatibis comata Bp. (Geronticus eremita L.). Beitr. Fortpfl. Vogel 5: 17-19.

14. Hamel, H.D. 1975. Ein Beitrag zur Populationsdynamik des Waldrapps Geronticus eremita (L., 1758). Die Vogelwelt 96: 213-221.

15. World Wildlife Fund. Press release 17 February 1978. Last minute preparations to save rare ibis.

16. Schenker, A. 1977. Das ehemalige Verbreitungsgebiet des Waldrapps Geronticus eremita in Europa. Ornith. Beob. 74: 13-30.

17. Hirsch, U. 1976. Beobachtungen am Waldrapp Geronticus eremita in Marokko und Versuch zur Bestimmung der Alterzusammensetzung von Brutkolonien. Ornith. Beob. 73: 225-235.

MADAGASCAR CRESTED IBIS

Lophotibis cristata cristata (Boddaert, 1783)

Lophotibis cristata urschi Lavauden, 1929

Order CICONIIFORMES   Family THRESKIORNITHIDAE

STATUS   Vulnerable.   Although still widespread in Madagascar, the species has
suffered an obvious decline in distribution and abundance.   It is hunted
excessively and its forest habitat continues to be destroyed.

DISTRIBUTION   L. c. cristata occurs throughout the humid forests of eastern
Madagascar, and into the dry forests of the northern savannah.   L. c. urschi
occurs less widely in the dry forests of western Madagascar south to Tulear.   No
change in the overall distribution of the species has taken place, although within
its range there are now areas where the species is very thinly distributed or
lacking altogether (1).

POPULATION   No estimate has been made, although in 1930 the eastern subspecies
was considered common, the western form rather less so, but still common locally (2).
Since that time there has been a noticeable decline and both subspecies have become
increasingly rare (1; 3).

HABITAT   Humid and dry savannah forest.   The forests of Madagascar are being
destroyed at an accelerating rate by timber harvesting, clearing for agriculture,
and damage from repeated burning of adjacent grasslands.   About 90 percent of
Madagascar's forests have already been destroyed (4), although reserves or parks
total 7,000 sq. km (3).

CONSERVATION MEASURES TAKEN   This is the only endemic bird species of Madagascar
to have been afforded legal protection, although even so it may be shot or captured
upon payment of a small fee.   In practice the species is still hunted avidly and
extensively (1).

CONSERVATION MEASURES PROPOSED   The African Convention on the Conservation of
Nature and Natural Resources of 1968, which the Malagasy government has ratified,
calls for protection of this species, but no additional implementing legislation
has been passed.

REFERENCES   1.   Milon, P., Petter, J.-J., & Randrianasolo, G. 1973.   Faune de
                   Madagascar, 35: Oiseaux.   Tananarive and Paris: ORSTOM
                   and CNRS.
              2.   Rand, A.L. 1936.   The distribution and habits of Madagascar
                   birds.   Bull. Amer. Mus. Nat. Hist. 72: 143-499.
              3.   Keith, G.S., Forbes-Watson, A.D. & Turner, D.A. 1974.   The
                   Madagascar Crested Ibis, a threatened species in an endemic
                   and endangered avifauna.   Wilson Bull. 86: 197-199.
              4.   Curry-Lindahl, K. 1975.   Man in Madagascar.   Defenders of
                   Wildlife 50(2): 164-169.

JAPANESE CRESTED IBIS

Nipponia nippon (Temminck, 1835)

Order CICONIIFORMES   Family THRESKIORNITHIDAE

STATUS   Endangered.   This species is now among the rarest in the world.   It
breeds on one small island in Japan and probably in eastern Manchuria or Siberia,
although precise locations are unknown.   Human persecution, especially by hunting
and deforestation of woodlands, has caused its decline.

DISTRIBUTION   Formerly this species bred in Ussuriland, south-eastern Siberia,
along several rivers of the Lake Khanka basin and the Ussuri River, also in
adjacent eastern Manchuria in China, south to Chekiang and Shensi provinces,
possibly west to Tibet, and in Japan.   The continental population migrated south
as far as Hainan, Taiwan, Korea and the Ryukyu Islands, although lately only an
occasional bird has been reported in Korea in winter, particularly near Panmunjom
in the Demilitarized Zone.   The Japanese population was known to breed on southern
Hokkaido, Honshu and Kyushu, but since 1932 it has been restricted to Sado Island
and the Noto Peninsula of Ishikawa Prefecture, Honshu, and since 1969 to Sado
alone (1; 2; 3; 4; 5; 6).

POPULATION   The Crested Ibis was common on mainland Asia and Japan until a
century ago.   The last breeding record in the U.S.S.R. dates from 1917, except for
a possible one in 1927, although individual birds were observed in 1956 and 1962
near Lake Khanka; the last known colony in China was destroyed by wood cutting in
1958 (2).   In Korea only scattered sightings have been recorded since 1930; 10 were
seen in flight in North Korea in 1965, 3 near Panmunjom in the Demilitarized Zone in
1966 (2), and most recently 4 were seen in winter 1973-74 in the same area
(G. Archibald 1974, pers. comm.).   In Japan few remained after 1875.   By 1925 only
20 birds were found, but these increased slightly to between 25 and 40 by 1930,
divided between Honshu's Noto Peninsula, and Sado Island.   Thereafter the
population dwindled, so that by 1961 only 10 birds remained.   By 1963, only one
remained on the Noto Peninsula.   This was captured and placed in a captive-breeding
facility on Sado Island in 1969 (7; 8).   The population on Sado remained between
9 and 12 until 1973, when it increased to 14 (Y. Yamashina 1974, pers. comm.).
By 1976 it had declined to 8 birds and no young were raised (M. Yoshii 1977, pers.
comm.).

HABITAT   Pine woodlands, where the species nests, and agricultural lands,
especially rice paddies, also marshlands, where it feeds (4; 5).   The present
feeding areas on Sado Island are relatively unpolluted by chemicals, which is not
the case over much of Japan today (7).

CONSERVATION MEASURES TAKEN   Protected by the Japanese as a Natural Monument in
1934, as a Special Natural Monument in 1952, and as a Special Bird for Protection in
1972 (Y. Yamashina 1974, pers. comm.).   The breeding forests on Sado Island were
purchased by the Japanese government in 1962 (7).   A captive breeding facility was
established on Sado Island, with financing supplied in part by World Wildlife Fund.
Two young birds were captured for the project in 1965, but one died in 1966, and an
additional bird captured in 1969 died in 1971.   Only one remains in captivity in
Japan (8; Y. Yamashina 1974, pers. comm.).   The species is also fully protected by
law in the U.S.S.R. (2).   In South Korea the species was designated National
Treasure No. 198 in 1968 (9).

CONSERVATION MEASURES PROPOSED   No additional measures known.

REMARKS   In addition to the bird held in captivity on Sado Island, one is reported from Tientsin Zoo in China (Tso-Hsin Cheng 1975, pers. comm. to S.D. Ripley).

REFERENCES   1. Dementiev, G.P., Meklenburtsev, R.N., Sudilovskaya, A.M. & Spangenberg, E.P. 1951. Birds of the Soviet Union, Vol. 2. Trans. from Russian by Israel Program for Scientific Translations, Jerusalem, 1968.

2. Fisher, J., Simon, N. & Vincent, J. 1969. Wildlife in Danger. New York:Viking Press; London:Collins.

3. Gore, M.E.J. & Won, P.-O. 1971. The Birds of Korea. Rutland, Vt. and Tokyo:Charles E. Tuttle Co.

4. Austin, O.L., Jr. & Kuroda, N. 1953. The birds of Japan: their status and distribution. Harvard Bull. Mus. Comp. Zool. 109(4): 279-637.

5. Ornithological Society of Japan, 1974. Check-list of Japanese birds. Fifth and revised ed. Tokyo:Gakken Co.

6. Vaurie, C. 1972. Tibet and its Birds. London:H.F. and G. Witherby Ltd.

7. Yamashina, Y. 1967. The status of endangered species in Japan. Bull. ICBP 10: 100-109.

8. Yoshii, M. 1971. The present status of the Japanese Crested Ibis and the Japanese White Stork. Bull. ICBP 11:168-169.

9. Won, P.-O. 1971. The status of bird conservation in Korea, 1966-1970. Bull. ICBP 11: 242-247.

WHITE-SHOULDERED IBIS

Pseudibis davisoni (Hume, 1875)

Order CICONIIFORMES   Family THRESKIORNITHIDAE

STATUS   Indeterminate.   Formerly widespread across central South East Asia but
now seriously reduced, although precise data are lacking.

DISTRIBUTION   Formerly resident throughout Burma, Thailand, Cambodia, southern
Vietnam and Laos south to the northern border of Malaysia (1; 2).   Its present
distribution is poorly known for there are no recent records from much of its
former range.   There is an unconfirmed recent report of this species nesting near
Thale Noi Swamp in peninsular Thailand (D. Wells 1976, pers. comm.).

POPULATION   In the 1920s this species was locally common in southernmost Vietnam
and north-eastern Cambodia (3; 4).   There is no population estimate, although it
was considered to be more abundant than the Giant Ibis Thaumatibis gigantea where
the two occurred together (5).   There is but one recent record, and its abundance
elsewhere in South East Asia has surely declined in view of recent hostilities
throughout much of the area, and the consequent dependence of large segments of the
human population on whatever can be caught when a season's harvest has been
disrupted (J. McNeely and D. Wells 1976, pers. comm.).

HABITAT   Marshes, paddyfields and margins of lakes or rivers (2).   Natural
wetlands have been drained for agriculture over much of the species' range.

CONSERVATION MEASURES TAKEN   Protected legally from hunting and capture in
Thailand.

CONSERVATION MEASURES PROPOSED   None known.

REMARKS   The fact that this species is always exceedingly wild and wary (6) may
stand it in good stead as subsistence hunting pressure on all animals large and
small increases in South East Asia.

REFERENCES   1.   Delacour, J. and Jabouille, P. 1931.   Les Oiseaux de l'Indochine
                   Française, Tome 1.   Paris:Exposition Coloniale Internationale.
              2.   King, B. & Dickinson, E.C. 1975.   The Birds of South-east Asia.
                   Boston:Houghton Mifflin Co.;   London:Collins.
              3.   Delacour, J. 1928.   On the birds collected during the Third
                   Expedition to French Indo-China.   Ibis (12)4: 23-51.
              4.   Delacour, J. 1929.   On the birds collected during the Fourth
                   Expedition to French Indo-China.   Ibis (12)5: 193-220.
              5.   Riley, J.H. 1938.   Birds from Siam and the Malay Peninsula in
                   the United States National Museum collected by Drs. Hugh M. Smith
                   and William L. Abbott.   U.S. Nat. Mus. Bull. 172.
              6.   Deignan, H.G. 1945.   The birds of northern Thailand.
                   U.S. Nat. Mus. Bull. 186.

GIANT IBIS

Thaumatibis gigantea (Oustalet, 1877)

Order CICONIIFORMES

Family THRESKIORNITHIDAE

STATUS   Rare.   Occurs in the Mekong River basin in South East Asia.   This shy ibis has always been scarce; agricultural development and recent hostilities in much of its range have doubtless made it more so, although recent reports are lacking.

DISTRIBUTION   Recorded from central and northern Cambodia, southern Laos, south-eastern Thailand and South Vietnam (1).   It has been recorded twice from peninsular Thailand (2).   In 1925 it probably bred near Phu-Rieng, north of Saigon, South Vietnam, near the delta of the Mekong River (3), but it probably no longer occurs in the region.   In Cambodia it is still believed to occur from Tongle Sap northward (4); in 1927 it was frequently observed between Kompong-Thom and Sambor, north-east of Tongle Sap (5).   In Laos it was found in Saravane district in 1925 (3).   In 1964 it was observed along the border between Cambodia and Laos (4).

POPULATION   This species has always been considered uncommon and local.   This is due in part to its retiring nature.   None have been seen in Thailand for well over 10 years (J. McNeely 1976, pers. comm.).   The center of its abundance is probably in Cambodia north of Tongle Sap where it was considered numerous in 1927 (5).   The outbreak of war over much of South East Asia probably resulted in a rapid decline and it has been suggested that its world population may now be only a few hundred birds (4).

HABITAT   Wetlands, wooded plains and humid forest clearings (1).   Wetlands have been drained for agriculture over much of the ibis's range.

CONSERVATION MEASURES TAKEN   Protected legally from hunting or capture in Thailand. It was also fully protected in Cambodia, but with the recent change in government, it is not known if any effective protection still exists.

CONSERVATION MEASURES PROPOSED   None known, but investigation of the present status of the species would be an obvious first step.

REFERENCES   1.   Delacour, J. & Jabouille, P. 1931.   Les Oiseaux de l'Indochine Française, Tome 1.   Paris:Exposition Coloniale Internationale.
             2.   Chasen, F.N. 1939.   The Birds of the Malay Peninsula, Vol. 4. London:H.F. and G. Witherby.
             3.   Delacour, J. 1928.   On the birds collected during the Third Expedition to French Indo-China.   Ibis (12)4: 23-51.
             4.   Fisher, J., Simon, N. & Vincent, J. 1969.   Wildlife in Danger. New York:Viking Press; London:Collins.
             5.   Delacour, J. 1929.   On the birds collected during the Fourth Expedition to French Indo-China.   Ibis (12)5: 193-220.

ALDABRA SACRED IBIS

Threskiornis aethiopica abbotti (Ridgway, 1893)

Order CICONIIFORMES   Family THRESKIORNITHIDAE

STATUS   Rare. Restricted to Aldabra Atoll, western Indian Ocean, where its
numbers are very low and it is very subject to disturbance while nesting.
Formerly this tame ibis was hunted by temporary workers on Aldabra, which doubtless
caused its decline, but it is now protected.

DISTRIBUTION   Restricted to Aldabra, where it once occurred throughout the atoll,
but now virtually absent from West, Polymnie and Middle Islands, although it was
always very rare on the latter two. It seems to be now largely confined to the
south-eastern end of South Island (1).

POPULATION   Formerly believed to have been somewhat more abundant, although
precise data are not available. An estimate in 1964 of about 1,000 birds (2) may
have been optimistic for, in 1967 and 1968, there were believed to be no more than
200 and possibly as few as 150. Considerable egg loss occurs at breeding colonies
from desertion or trampling of eggs by birds returning to their nests (1).
Desertion is probably more related to frequency and quantity of wet season rains
than to human disturbance (R. Prys-Jones 1977, pers. comm.).

HABITAT   Feeds around pools on flat coralline limestone pavement, also along the
shores of the lagoon. Nests and roosts colonially in low bushes over or near
water. Feral cats are present on South Island, as are black rats Rattus rattus.
Predation on this subspecies has not however been noted. Disturbance by dogs may
have been a disrupting factor in nesting attempts, but two dogs formerly present
at the south-east end of South Island (see 4) are now dead (R. Prys-Jones, loc.
cit.).

CONSERVATION MEASURES TAKEN   Aldabra was spared from massive development as a
military air base when Diego Garcia was selected as the site of the base (3; 4).
A research station of the British Royal Society was established in 1970. Aldabra
was made into a nature reserve and this subspecies is now legally protected and can
no longer be hunted.

CONSERVATION MEASURES PROPOSED   Too close an approach to a nesting colony of this
ibis has been shown to entail a serious risk of nest abandonment. Visitors to
Aldabra should therefore take extreme care not to disturb it when it is nesting
and any question of placing a research station at the south-eastern end of Aldabra
should take full account of this disturbance factor (1).

REMARKS   Neither of the two other subspecies, found respectively in Madagascar and
in Africa south of the Sahara, southern Arabia and formerly Egypt (5), is known to
be at risk.

REFERENCES   1.   Benson, C.W. & Penny, M.J. 1971. The land birds of Aldabra.
                    Phil. Trans. Roy. Soc. London B260: 417-527.
              2.   Gaymer, R. 1966. Aldabra - The case for conserving this
                    coral atoll. Oryx 8: 348-352.
              3.   Stoddart, D.R. 1968. The Aldabra affair. Bio. Cons. 1:
                    63-69.
              4.   Stoddard, D.R. 1971. Settlement, development and conservation
                    of Aldabra. Phil. Trans. Roy. Soc. London B260: 611-628.
              5.   Peters, J.L. 1931. Check-list of Birds of the World, Vol. 1.
                    Cambridge:Harvard University Press.

NEW ZEALAND BROWN TEAL

Anas aucklandica (Gray, 1844)

Order ANSERIFORMES   Family ANATIDAE

STATUS   Vulnerable.   Three subspecies, two of which are flightless.
A. a. aucklandica (Gray, 1844) is common on several of the Auckland Islands (1).
A. a. chlorotis Gray, 1845 is distributed widely on New Zealand but only in small
relict populations.   Severely depleted or absent from most of its former range,
it is now primarily restricted to areas remote from human population centers.
The Brown Teal's decline has been caused by drainage of swamps, which the species
frequents, by the introduction of predators and by excessive shooting; it has been
suggested that a poultry disease may have been a major contributing factor as well
(2).   A. a. nesiotis (Fleming, 1935) from Campbell Island is now very rare and
confined to one islet offshore of that island.

DISTRIBUTION   The Auckland Island Flightless Teal occurs on all larger islands of
the Auckland Islands not inhabited by cats or rats.   It no longer is found on
Auckland Island itself (1; 3; 4).   In the 19th Century chlorotis, the Brown Teal,
occurred throughout the lowlands of New Zealand and on the Chatham Islands.   It is
now only found on Great and Little Barrier Islands, in parts of Northland, Southern
Fiordland and on Stewart Island (1; 2).   The Campbell Island Teal, nesiotis,
was believed extinct until rediscovered in 1975 on Dent Island, a small islet about
1 km off-shore at the extreme south end of the entrance to Northwest Bay of
Campbell Island (G. Williams 1976, pers. comm.).

POPULATION   The Auckland Island Teal is now extirpated from Auckland Island
proper which is infested by cats, but still found on six of the small islets in
numbers estimated at 1,200-1,500 (M.W. Weller 1974, pers. comm.).   The Brown Teal
was formerly considered to be abundant throughout New Zealand.   A major decline
occurred in the second decade of this century, and a second decline, even affecting
some of the more remote populations, took place starting around 1930.   Populations
in the remote corners of New Zealand are very small but apparently stable and the
total is put at 1,000 birds, the majority being on Great Barrier Island (D.V. Merton
1974, pers. comm.).   In December 1975, four Campbell Island Teal were seen on Dent
Island.   Prior to this observation only about a dozen had ever been seen, most
recently in 1958, when four birds, presumably of this subspecies, were seen on
Campbell Island (5).   Expeditions to Campbell Island in 1970 and 1971 did not
encounter it (G. Williams 1976, pers. comm.).

HABITAT   The Auckland Island Teal lives on rocky shorelines and along fresh water
courses but, as previously mentioned, not on main Auckland Island, where introduced
cats, rats and pigs are present (4).   The Brown Teal is found along estuarine
reaches at slack water and in tidal streams, in ponds, lagoons and head of fiords,
and in swamps with open water, feeding in nearby grasslands at night as well as on
aquatic vegetation.   The clearing of the lowlands by European settlers probably
added to the feeding grounds of the species and may have caused an increase in its
population last century, but draining of swamplands and other factors have more
than cancelled this out (1; 2).

CONSERVATION MEASURES TAKEN   The species is fully protected by law.   The Brown
Teal is still shot occasionally, especially in areas where its occurrence is not
expected.   It has been raised in captivity, notably by the New Zealand Wildlife
Service at Mt. Bruce Native Bird Reserve and by the Wildfowl Trust in England.
Birds reared at the Mt. Bruce Reserve have been liberated with some success on
Kapiti Island and in several other locations (6).

CONSERVATION MEASURES PROPOSED   It has been suggested that the establishment of numerous private sanctuaries where groups of landowners prohibit hunting over substantial areas of likely range is the only hope of permitting the Brown Teal to return to anything like its former abundance (2).

REMARKS   The Campbell Island Teal is only marginally distinct from the subspecies of the Auckland Islands.   It has been suggested that the teal found on Campbell have been merely stragglers from the Aucklands, less than 250 km distant (4).

REFERENCES   1. Fisher, J., Simon, N. & Vincent, J. 1969.   Wildlife in Danger. New York:Viking Press; London:Collins.
2. McKenzie, H.R. 1971.   The Brown Teal in the Auckland Province. Notornis 18: 280-286.
3. Scott, D. 1971.   The Auckland Island Flightless Teal. Wildlfowl 22: ˙44-45.
4. Weller, M.W. 1975.   Ecological studies of the Auckland Island Flightless Teal.   Auk 92: 280-297.
5. Bailey, A.M. & Sorensen, J.H. 1962.   Subantarctic Campbell Island.   Denver Mus. Nat. Hist. Proc. 10.
6. Reid, B. & Roderick, C. 1973.   New Zealand Scaup Aythya novaeseelandiae and Brown Teal Anas aucklandica chlorotis in captivity.   Internat. Zoo Yearbook 13: 12-15.

MADAGASCAR TEAL

Anas bernieri (Hartlaub, 1860)

Order ANSERIFORMES   Family ANATIDAE

STATUS   Vulnerable.   This little known species has been collected only in a few localities in Madagascar.   It is rare and is pursued mercilessly along with other waterfowl of the Grande Ile by "sportsmen" and commercial hunters.

DISTRIBUTION   Restricted to swamps and lakes of the western coast of Madagascar near Morombe, the small Bemamba and Masama lakes between Antsalova and Maintirano, and near Ambilobe (1; 2).

POPULATION   Always considered to be rare, although there has been no estimate of total population.   An expedition in 1929 and 1930 produced a single specimen (3). One was collected at Ambilobe in 1969, 13 were collected at Lake Masama in 1970 by "sportsmen" soon after 60 had been reported as seen there (4), in 1971 another two were seen (5), and in 1973 120 were estimated to be present on Lake Bemamba (6), the largest concentration recorded recently.   The species may be somewhat more common than these figures indicate, for areas in which it may be found are seldom visited by ornithologists.

HABITAT   Marshes, lakes and mangroves, also brushy savannahs and dense deciduous forest (2).   Neither the species nor its habitat are presently protected.   An airstrip recently opened at Ambereny has provided easy access for hunters to the area in which it appears to be most abundant (7).

CONSERVATION MEASURES TAKEN   None known.

CONSERVATION MEASURES PROPOSED   The creation of one or more reserves on the lakes or other wetlands between Antsalova and Maintirano, to provide a refuge for this species, has been strongly advocated (2; 7).

REMARKS   The Madagascar Teal is one of the few ducks in the world not represented in collections of captive wildfowl.

REFERENCES   1. Milon, P., Petter, J.-J. & Randrianasolo, G. 1973.   Faune de Madagascar, 35: Oiseaux.   Tananarive and Paris: ORSTOM and CNRS.
              2. Salvan, J. 1970.   Remarques sur l'évolution de l'avifaune malgache depuis 1945.   Alauda 38: 191-203.
              3. Rand, A.L. 1936.   The distribution and habits of Madagascar birds.   Bull. Amer. Mus. Nat. Hist. 72: 143-499.
              4. Curry-Lindahl, K. 1972.   Let Them Live.   New York: William Morrow & Co.
              5. Forbes-Watson, A.D. & Turner, D. 1973.   Bird preservation in Madagascar.   Part 3, Appendix I.   Unpublished report presented to ICBP.
              6. Scott, D. & Lubbock, J. 1975.   Preliminary observations on waterfowl of western Madagascar.   Wildfowl 25: 117-120.
              7. Salvan, J. 1972.   Remarques sur l'avifaune malagasy et la protection d'espèces aviennes mal connues ou menacées.   Comptes rendus de la Conference internationale sur la Conservation de la Nature et de ses Ressources à Madagascar.   IUCN Document Supplémentaire No. 36, communication 26.

LAYSAN DUCK

Anas laysanensis Rothschild, 1892

Order ANSERIFORMES   Family ANATIDAE

STATUS   Rare.   It was thought that this species had recovered fully from
near-extinction brought about by denudation of the vegetation of Laysan Island,
north-western Hawaiian Islands, by European rabbits (Oryctolagus cuniculus).
The last rabbits were eliminated in 1923.   Subsequent surveys have shown the
population to fluctuate considerably.   By 1957 it appeared to be near saturation
point for the restricted habitat, but since 1969 it has declined from unknown
causes to the point where it is once more vulnerable to extinction (1; 2; 3; 4; 5;
E. Kridler 1974, pers. comm.).

DISTRIBUTION   Laysan Island (4 sq. km), north-western Hawaiian Islands.   A
report of this species from neighboring Lisianski Island in 1828, is thought to be
erroneous (2; 3).

POPULATION   Never very common, the population declined to its lowest level
between 1920 and 1930.   A thorough census in 1930 revealed only a single female
(2).   By 1957, however, numbers had increased again to about 600 and fluctuated
between 200 and 600 until 1969.   In 1970 only 75 birds could be found (1; 2; 3).
In 1972 the estimate rose again to 175, but a census in the late summer of 1973
yielded a figure of less than 40 birds (E. Kridler 1974, pers. comm.).

HABITAT   All plant associations on Laysan Island, but this duck tends to be
concentrated in the low sedges and vines around the central lagoon (2; 4; E. Kridler
1974, pers. comm.).

CONSERVATION MEASURES TAKEN   Laysan Island is included in the Hawaiian Islands
National Wildlife Refuge.   Landings on islands in the Refuge are allowed on permit
only.   The species is protected by federal and state law.   Censuses of its
population are conducted periodically by the U.S. Fish and Wildlife Service.   An
attempt to introduce twelve of these ducks to Pearl and Hermes Reef in 1968 failed
(1; 2; E. Kridler 1974, pers. comm.).   The species is listed in Appendix 1 of the
1973 Convention on International Trade in Endangered Species of Wild Fauna and
Flora.

CONSERVATION MEASURES PROPOSED   Increased patrolling of Laysan Island to prevent
unauthorized landings and prevent introduction of additional pest plants, insects
and predators such as dogs, cats and rats.   A study of the ecology of this duck on
Laysan has been proposed.   Introduction of captive bred birds to another Pacific
island with suitable habitat (1).

REMARKS   This species now has a larger population in captivity than in the wild.
Over 150 are in zoos and private collections.   It breeds readily in captivity (5).

REFERENCES   1.   U.S. Department of Interior Bureau of Sport Fisheries and
                    Wildlife, 1973.   Threatened Wildlife of the United States.
                    U.S. Bureau Sport Fish. Wildl. Res. Publ. 114.
              2.   Ely, C.A. & Clapp, R.B. 1973.   The natural history of Laysan
                    Island, Northwestern Hawaiian Islands.   Atoll Research Bull.
                    No. 171.

REFERENCES (cont.)

3. Berger, A.J. 1972. Hawaiian Birdlife. Honolulu: University Press of Hawaii.
4. Warner, R.E. 1963. Recent history and ecology of the Laysan Duck. Condor 65: 2-23.
5. Ripley, S.D. 1960. Laysan Teal in captivity. Wilson Bull. 72: 244-247.

MARIANAS MALLARD

Anas "oustaleti" Salvadori, 1894

Order ANSERIFORMES   Family ANATIDAE

STATUS   Endangered.   Known from the southern Mariana Islands, Western Pacific,
where now very rare and decreasing because of the drainage of wetlands.   Hunting
of ducks, including this species, continues in the Marianas.

DISTRIBUTION   Recorded from Guam (541 sq. km), Tinian (101.2 sq. km), Saipan
(121.7 sq. km) and possibly Rota (85.5 sq. km), southern Marianas.   It was never
widespread on Guam, and is now extinct there (N. Drahos 1976, pers. comm.).   Its
presence on Rota has never been confirmed.   It is presumed to occur still in the
reeds of Lake Hagoi on Tinian and possibly on Lake Susupe on Saipan, and it may do
so elsewhere in suitable habitat on these two islands (R. Owen 1975, pers. comm.).
The possibility of movement between islands has also been suggested (2).

POPULATION   Although there are no precise records, the Marianas mallard was
clearly more abundant even in the 1940s than it is presently.   Between 1931 and
1940, 38 specimens were collected on Saipan and Tinian and two flocks of 50 to 60
birds each were seen on Tinian in 1940 (1).   In 1945, 12 was the maximum seen at
one time on either one of these islands (2).   During more recent brief surveys
none was seen on Saipan, while a number of ducks were heard in the reed beds but
not specifically identified on Tinian.   However, two, believed to be of this
species, were seen on Saipan in 1976 (R. Owen 1975, pers. comm.).   It no longer
occurs on Guam (N. Drahos 1976, pers. comm.), where the most recent published
record is of three seen between December 1945 and July 1946 (5).   The effects of
troops being stationed in the Marianas during World War II were doubtless strongly
detrimental to populations of this duck (3).

HABITAT   Wetlands, particularly freshwater lakes with reedbeds, but also lagoons,
stream beds and flooded fields (1).   Wetland areas have been drained extensively
in the Marianas and there are now only two major areas of prime habitat remaining.
The essential habitat of this species at Lake Hagoi, Tinian, is not protected.

CONSERVATION MEASURES TAKEN   The species is on Appendix 1 of the 1973 Convention
on International Trade in Endangered Fauna and Flora.

CONSERVATION MEASURES PROPOSED   It has been suggested that the prohibition of
hunting of all ducks on Fena Valley Reservoir, Guam, by the U.S. Navy, which has
jurisdiction of the area, would be greatly beneficial to the species.   It is
included in the proposed list of endangered species of the U.S. Trust Territories
(R. Owen 1975, pers. comm.).

REMARKS   There are two morphs of oustaleti, one rather similar to the Mallard
Anas platyrhynchos and the other similar to the Australian Grey Duck Anas
superciliosa.   This situation is responsible in part for the widely accepted view
that the form is of hybrid origin (4).   It is significant, however, that no
individual of either presumed parental species has been recorded in the Marianas (6),
so that the population has maintained itself in geographic isolation at least for
the duration of the ornithological history of the Marianas, starting from the first
half of the nineteenth century.   It is a matter of considerable scientific interest
and importance that this experiment in the evolution of a species through
hybridization should continue uninterruptedly and that protection of the population,
regardless of its taxonomic status, should be assured.

REFERENCES   1.   Baker, R.H. 1951.   The avifauna of Micronesia, its origin,
                  evolution, and distribution.   Univ. Kansas Pubs. Mus. Nat.
                  Hist. 3(1): 1-359.
             2.   Marshall, J.T., Jr. 1949.   The endemic avifauna of Saipan,
                  Tinian, Guam and Palau.   Condor 51: 200-221.
             3.   Baker, R.H. 1948.   Report on collections of birds made by
                  United States Naval Medical Research Unit No. 2 in the Pacific
                  War Area.   Smithsonian Misc. Coll. 107(15): 1-74.
             4.   Yamashima, Y. 1948.   Notes on the Marianas Mallard.   Pac. Sci.
                  2: 121-124.
             5.   Kibler, L.F. 1950.   Notes on the birds of Guam.   Auk 67:
                  400-403.
             6.   Owen, R.P. (in prep.).   Checklist of the birds of
                  Micronesia.

KOLOA or HAWAIIAN DUCK

Anas (platyrhynchos) _wyvilliana_ Sclater, 1878

Order   ANSERIFORMES   Family   ANATIDAE

STATUS   Vulnerable.   Restricted to Kauai, Hawaiian Islands, where its population
is not large.   Continual reduction in acreage of taro and rice fields, in which
this bird often feeds, and drainage of other wetland areas prevent the full
recovery of this species.   The recent establishment of mongoose _Herpestes auro-_
punctatus on Kauai increases the threat to this ground-nesting duck from predation.
Introduced rats, cats and especially dogs are already serious predators (1; 2; 3).

DISTRIBUTION   Formerly occurred on Hawaii, Maui, Molokai, Oahu, Kauai and Niihau,
Hawaiian Islands.   Presently restricted to Kauai.   Extirpated from Oahu as
recently as 1964.   Captive-bred birds were released in 1968 on Oahu and in 1959
on Hawaii, and there is some evidence that they may have bred at least on Hawaii
(2; 4).

POPULATION   About 3,000 in the wild on Kauai in 1967.   Formerly much more
abundant and widespread (1; 3)

HABITAT   Lowland marshes, reservoirs, taro patches, pastures, drainage ditches,
agricultural lands in the lowlands.   Also wooded stream valleys at higher
elevations.   This species is adaptable to a wide variety of habitats and climatic
conditions (2; 3).

CONSERVATION MEASURES TAKEN   Protected by federal and state law.   Hunting of
this duck has been prohibited since 1930.   Important habitat in Hanalei Valley,
Kauai, acquired by federal government as National Wildlife Refuge.   Restoration
project on Kauai conducted by Hawaii Division of Fish and Game with funds
provided by World Wildlife Fund.   Captive-bred birds have been introduced to
former range on Oahu and Hawaii, but apparently unsuccessfully except perhaps on
Hawaii (1; 4).

CONSERVATION MEASURES PROPOSED   Acquisition of wetland areas as refuges.
Continued program of reintroduction to former range.   Continued survey of life
history and ecology of species (1).

REMARKS   At least 181 in captivity in many collections around the world.
Breeds readily in captivity (5).   Average clutch size 8.3 eggs (2).

REFERENCES   1.   U.S. Department of Interior Bureau of Sport Fisheries and
                     Wildlife, 1973.   Threatened Wildlife of the United States.
                     U.S. Bur. Sport Fish. Wildl. Res. Pub. 114
              2.   Berger, A.J. 1972.   _Hawaiian Birdlife._   Honolulu: University
                     Press of Hawaii.
              3.   Swedberg, G.E. 1967.   _The Koloa._   Honolulu: Hawaii Dept.
                     of Land and Nat. Res.
              4.   Swedberg, G.E. 1969.   Sighting of wild Koloa on the island of
                     Hawaii and history of a past release.   _Elepaio_ 29: 87-88.
              5.   Duplaix-Hall, N. (ed.) 1974.   Census of rare animals in
                     captivity, 1973.   _International Zoo Yearbook_ 14: 396-429.

TULE WHITE-FRONTED GOOSE

Anser albifrons elgasi Delacour and Ripley, 1975

Order ANSERIFORMES   Family ANATIDAE

STATUS   Rare.   A race of the White-fronted Goose recently described from a
small population wintering in California and breeding in an as yet undiscovered
area presumably of Alaska.   Hunted heavily on its wintering grounds.

DISTRIBUTION   It has been suggested that the breeding area of this goose may be
the Alaskan taiga west of the main Alaskan mountain ranges.   It has been
collected on migration in coastal Alaska and southern Oregon and is known to
winter on several wildlife refuges in the Sacramento river valley, California,
particularly the Sacramento Refuge near Willows, the Delavan Refuge and the Butte
Sink area, the Colusa Refuge, and the Napra and Suisun marshes and vicinity of
Merced (1; B. Elgas 1974, pers. comm.).

POPULATION   It is not known if a decline has taken place.   Estimated numbers
in 1973-1974 were 1200-1500 birds, 400 of them in the Sacramento Refuge.   Hunting
on the Sacramento Refuge accounts for about a quarter of the latter annually
(B. Elgas 1974, pers. comm.).

HABITAT   For breeding presumably taiga.   In winter small ponds, with a heavy
growth of reeds, cattails and millet and often adjacent to clumps of willow,
are favoured and the Tule Goose seldom visits ricefields in the manner of the far
more numerous race Anser albifrons frontalis, which in general tends to prefer
more open situations.   The total area of winter habitat in the Tule Goose's
range is less than 4050 ha (1).

CONSERVATION MEASURES TAKEN   The Tule Goose in winter occurs mostly in U.S.
National Wildlife Refuges; but hunting is permitted in such refuges and that of
this goose is subject to the California state hunting regulations.   It appears to
suffer a heavier annual mortality from hunting than A. a. frontalis with which it
shares a number of refuges.   Several unsuccessful searches for its breeding
grounds have been made.

CONSERVATION MEASURES PROPOSED   Further efforts to discover where the Tule Goose
nests in order to ensure that any such locality is safeguarded from disturbance.
Careful assessment of the impact of hunting on mortality of the small population
(1; B. Elgas 1977, pers. comm.).

REMARKS   Before it was distinguished under the new subspecific name of elgasi,
the Tule Goose was always ascribed to, and in the previous edition of Vol. 2 of
the Red Data Book listed as, the subspecies Anser a. gambelli, which however
breeds in the taiga east of the main mountain ranges of North America and winters
along Gulf of Mexico coasts in Louisiana, Texas and northern Mexico.   Apart from
A. a. elgasi, the race gambelli is the only one, out of five recognized subspecies
of White-fronted Goose ranging throughout the northern Holarctic, which may be at
risk and as such have to be included again in the Red Data Book, although for the
time being it has only been replaced.

REFERENCES   1.   Delacour, J. & Ripley, S.D. 1975.   Description of a
                    new subspecies of the White-fronted Goose Anser albifrons.
                    Amer. Mus. Novit. 2565.

MADAGASCAR POCHARD

Aythya innotata (Salvadori, 1894)

Order ANSERIFORMES   Family ANATIDAE

STATUS   Vulnerable.   Of restricted distribution in Madagascar and believed to be
decreasing as the result of excessive overhunting.

DISTRIBUTION   Found primarily on Lake Alaotra and other wetlands of the high
central plateaux (1).   In 1930 it was seen at a pond near Antsirabe (2) and in
1970 observed at Lake Ambohibao.

POPULATION   This species was considered common in 1930, when 27 were collected on
Lake Alaotra (2).   The paucity of subsequent reports suggests that a serious
decline has taken place.   None have been seen on Lake Alaotra by recent visitors
(4).

HABITAT   Wetlands, including open fresh water lakes, where it feeds, and marshes,
where it breeds.   Introduced bass Micropterus in Lake Alaotra may prey on chicks
of this as of other species.   But it is likely that the continued excessive
hunting of all waterfowl by "sportsmen" and commercial hunters has contributed
most significantly to its decline (4).

CONSERVATION MEASURES TAKEN   None known.   The pochard, like most endemic birds
on Madagascar, being classified as 'game', may be hunted by any person who has
taken out a permit.

CONSERVATION MEASURES PROPOSED   This and many other endemic species in Madagascar
have been strongly recommended for complete legal protection (K. Curry-Lindahl in
litt. to G. Ramanantsoavina, Director, Service des Eaux et Forêts, Chasse et
Pêche, Jan. 1973).

REMARKS   The species was frequently bred in captivity prior to World War II, but
it is not presently represented in captive collections (5).

REFERENCES   1.   Milon, P., Petter, J.-J. & Randrianasolo, G. 1973.   Faune de
                    Madagascar, 35: Oiseaux.   Tananarive and Paris: ORSTOM
                    and CNRS.
              2.   Rand, A.L., 1936.   The distribution and habits of Madagascar
                    birds.   Bull. Amer. Mus. Nat. Hist. 72: 143-499.
              3.   Salvan, J. 1970.   Remarques sur l'évolution de l'avifaune
                    malgache depuis 1945..   Alauda 38: 191-203.
              4.   Forbes-Watson, A.D. & Turner, D.A. 1973.   Bird preservation
                    in Madagascar.   Unpublished report presented to ICBP.
              5.   Delacour, J. 1959.   The Waterfowl of the World, Vol. 3.
                    London:Country Life Ltd.

ALEUTIAN CANADA GOOSE

Branta canadensis leucopareia Brandt, 1836

Order ANSERIFORMES   Family ANATIDAE

STATUS   Rare. An integrated rehabilitation program for this goose, involving
release to the wild of captive-bred birds, predator removal from selected islands
and closing of hunting on its wintering grounds, shows every likelihood of success;
but until breeding populations become self-sustaining on more than one island some
risk remains.

DISTRIBUTION   Formerly bred in the western Aleutian Islands from Attu to Atka,
the Komandorski and northern Kuril islands of the U.S.S.R., and possibly the
Pribilofs, and migrated in winter to Japan and to western North America from
British Columbia south mainly to inland valleys of California and, recently,
occasionally to Arizona and Sonora, Mexico. It was extirpated from the Kurils
and Komandorskis by 1914 and from all islands in the Aleutians except Buldir by
1961, and no longer winters in Japan or north of California.(1-5; J. Aldrich
1977, pers. comm.).

POPULATION   Formerly numbered in thousands in the Aleutians, but declined
drastically in the 1920s and the mid-1930s following introduction of the blue fox
Alopex lagopus to almost all of the Aleutians. The decline in the Kurils was
from the same cause but earlier; foxes were apparently indigenous on the Koman--
dorskis and geese were never abundant there. Only about 200 breeding pairs
persisted on fox-free Buldir Island in the Aleutians. Counts of what is believed
to be virtually the entire population at a staging area near Crescent City,
California, showed 790 in the spring of 1975, 900 in spring 1976, 1150 in spring
1977, and 1600 in fall 1977. This increase is believed to be real and the result
of hunting being prohibited on wintering grounds.(4; 5; 6; 7; P. Springer 1977,
pers. comm.).

HABITAT   The nesting habitat includes stream banks, marshes, lagoons and sea
cliffs cut by watercourses. Birds move inland to small ponds for moulting (2; 4).
In winter the geese utilize agricultural croplands and pastures. At the Crescent
City staging ground, used on passage in California, one 5.2 ha offshore island,
Castle Rock, provides a roost for virtually the entire population (6). Predation
by Arctic foxes introduced for fur-farming on almost every island in the goose's
breeding range has been the most serious cause of decline (5; 7). Predation by
Bald Eagles Haliaeetus leucocephalus has contributed to failure of releases of
captive bred birds on Amchitka island in the Aleutians (8).

CONSERVATION MEASURES TAKEN   The goose is protected by U.S., Canadian and
Japanese laws and listed in Appendix 1 of the 1973 Convention on International
Trade in Endangered Species of Wild Fauna and Flora. A recovery team, appointed
by the U.S. Fish and Wildlife Service, has drafted and is implementing a plan for
rehabilitating the subspecies. The surviving wild population of geese on Buldir
Island has been under study since 1974 and, elsewhere in the Aleutians, foxes had
been eliminated from Amchitka, Nizki and Alaid and nearly from Agattu by 1977.
Captive breeding at Patuxent Wildlife Research Center, Laurel, Maryland, began in
1963, and over 380 goslings were produced between 1966 and 1977. Additional
captive breeding began in 1975, at Northern Prairies Wildlife Research Center,
Jamestown, North Dakota. In 1977, 100 captive-bred birds were sent to Amchitka
to establish a third unit. Releases of captive-bred birds on Amchitka in 1971
and 1976 were unsuccessful, but on Agattu, following a release in 1974, young were
reared locally. Buldir birds were brought to Agattu to act as guides on migration

and Agattu-released birds were subsequently observed in northern California; but
none of them were detected on Agattu or Buldir in 1975. Areas frequented in
winter by the subspecies, in northern California, the Sacramento valley and the
San Joaquin valley, have been closed to hunting since 1976. (5; 6; 8; 9;
R. Erickson, P. Springer 1977, pers. comms).

CONSERVATION MEASURES PROPOSED   Foxes are to be removed from Agattu and Kanaga
islands. The aim of the Aleutian Canada Goose Recovery Plan is to establish 3
additional island populations each of at least 50 breeding pairs (5; 8).

REMARKS   The subspecies B. c. asiatica, described from the Kuril and Komandorski
islands and previously listed as extinct in Red Data Book, Vol. 2, is now
considered identical with B. c. leucopareia (J. Aldrich 1977, pers. comm.).
Recognized subspecies, varying in number from 7 to 10 depending on the author
consulted, span the northern North American continent and extend to Greenland and,
as introductions, to the British Isles, Norway, Sweden and New Zealand (2; 3).
None is believed to be seriously at risk, although B. c. maxima was once thought
to be extinct (it is now relatively common) and it has recently been suggested
that B. c. occidentalis is threatened by reason of its circumscribed distribution
in the Copper River Valley and near Valdez, Alaska. This is an area affected by
major recent developments, where many geese are killed by hunters and where, due to
flooding, nesting success has latterly been poor (10).

REFERENCES   1. Delacour, J. 1954. The Waterfowl of the World Vol. 1.
                  London: Country Life Ltd.
              2. Palmer, R.S. (ed.) 1976. Handbook of North American Birds.
                  Vol. 2. New Haven: Yale University Press.
              3. Delacour, J. 1951. Preliminary note on the taxonomy of
                  Canada Geese, Branta canadensis. Amer. Mus. Novit. 1537.
              4. Murie, O.J. 1959. Fauna of the Aleutian Islands and
                  Alaska Peninsula. U.S. Fish and Wildlife Service
                  North Amer. Fauna 61.
              5. Byrd, G.V. & Springer, P.F. 1976. Recovery program for the
                  endangered Aleutian Canada Goose. Cal.-Neva. Wildl. Trans.
                  1976: 65-73.
              6. Woolington, D.W. & Springer, P.F. 1977. Population,
                  distribution and ecology of Aleutian Canada Geese on
                  their migration and wintering areas. U.S. Fish and
                  Wildlife Service Research Field Station, Humboldt State
                  University, Arcata, Calif. Unpub. report: 15 pp.
              7. Jones, R.D., Jr. 1963. Buldir Island, site of a remnant
                  breeding population of Aleutian Canada Geese. Wildfowl
                  14: 80-84.
              8. American Ornithologists' Union, 1977. Report of the
                  Committee on Conservation: The recovery team-recovery plan
                  approach to conservation of endangered species: a status
                  summary and appraisal. Auk 94 (4, Suppl.): 1DD-19DD.
              9. American Ornithologists' Union, 1976. Report of the Committee
                  on Conservation. Auk 93 (4, Suppl.): 1DD-19DD.
             10. Resolution passed by International Wild Waterfowl Association
                  at its annual meeting, Denver, Colorado, 20 October 1977.

NENE or HAWAIIAN GOOSE

<u>Branta</u> <u>sandvicensis</u> (Vigors, 1883)

Order ANSERIFORMES   Family ANATIDAE

<u>STATUS</u>   Vulnerable. Occurs on the flanks of Mauna Loa, Hualalai and Mauna Kea
mountains, Hawaii.   Also introduced to Haleakala Crater, Maui, between 1962 and
1970.   It is not known if the populations can remain stable or increase in the
wild without additional introductions.   The introduced population on Maui is
clearly not maintaining itself.   The future of the species in the wild is still in
jeopardy until it can be shown that reproduction is sufficient to offset losses
from all sources.   Formerly hunting was a major factor in population decline.
Presently it is believed that introduced rats, cats, dogs and mongooses preying
heavily on eggs and flightless goslings, are preventing the population from
expanding (1; 2; 3; 4).

<u>DISTRIBUTION</u>   Breeds in the winter between 1,525 and 2,440 m on the lava slopes
of Mauna Loa and Hualalai, Hawaii, in the summer also on the flanks of Mauna Kea,
Hawaii.   Somewhat more widespread before the population declined, occupying an
estimated 6,475 sq. km as compared to 3,100 sq. km today.   Its former breeding
on Maui rests only on hearsay evidence.   It is now found on Maui primarily at the
eastern end of Haleakala Crater, where it has been introduced repeatedly (1; 2;
3; 4).

<u>POPULATION</u>   About 25,000 at the end of the eighteenth century.   By the early
1940s about 50 remained, decreasing to perhaps 30 by 1952 (2; 4).   Captive
breeding began in 1949, and first releases back to the wild were in 1960, between
which time and 1975, 1061 birds have been released on Hawaii and 391 on Maui (5).
By 1972 fewer than 1000 birds were estimated to occur in the wild (1), but in 1971
seven broods of goslings were known to have been raised in the wild on Hawaii by
released pairs of captive-bred geese, and 19 additional broods had one captive-bred
parent.   On Maui at least three goslings have fledged from nests in the wild (3),
while nine have been raised by a captive pair held near Haleakala National Park
headquarters before release (A.F. Hewitt, Jr., 1974, pers. comm.).

<u>HABITAT</u>   Sparsely vegetated old lava flows between 1,525 and 2,440 m elevation.

<u>CONSERVATION MEASURES TAKEN</u>   Totally protected by federal and state law.   Hunting
is prohibited.   The Hawaii Division of Fish and Game has conducted a captive-
breeding program, funded by the U.S. Fish and Wildlife Service.   Over 1400 birds
from several sources have been released to the wild.   Four temporary refuges
totalling over 20,250 hectares have been established.   Portions of the range of the
Nene lie within Hawaii Volcanoes National Park and Haleakala National Park.
Listed in Appendix 1 of the 1973 Convention on International Trade in Endangered
Species of Wild Fauna and Flora.

<u>CONSERVATION MEASURES PROPOSED</u>   Field studies to determine fate of released
captive-bred birds.   Control of predators and grazing animals in breeding areas.
Establishment of permanent refuges (1).   Continuation of captive breeding program
if field studies show these are warranted.   Comparison of "gentle release", "Nene
park" and other techniques for returning the birds to the wild.

<u>REMARKS</u>   The perpetuation of the species, at least in captivity, seems assured.
Several Nene populations in zoos and private collections around the world are now
self-sustaining.

REFERENCES   1.   U.S. Dept. of Interior Bureau of Sport Fisheries and
                  Wildlife, 1973.   Threatened Wildlife of the United States.
                  U.S. Bur. Sport Fish. Wildl. Res. Pub. 114.
             2.   Berger, A.J. 1972.   Hawaiian Birdlife.   Honolulu: University
                  Press of Hawaii.
             3.   State of Hawaii Division of Fish and Game, 1972.   A report
                  of the Nene Restoration Program.
             4.   Ripley, S.D. 1965.   Saving the Nene, world's rarest goose.
                  Nat. Geogr., November 1965:   745-754.
             5.   State of Hawaii Department of Land and Natural Resources, 1976.
                  Nene restoration project: 1 July 1972 to 30 January 1975.
                  Elepaio 36:   104-108.

WHITE-WINGED WOOD DUCK

Cairina scutulata (S. Müller, 1842)

Order ANSERIFORMES   Family ANATIDAE

STATUS   Vulnerable. This species has declined seriously throughout its extensive
range in South East Asia due to massive decreases in the total area of suitable
habitat, isolation of local populations, increased disturbance, increased hunting of
adults and collection of young, and increased pollution of available waters.

DISTRIBUTION   Formerly occurred in northern and eastern Assam, India, Bangladesh
and south through Burma, western Thailand and western or Peninsular Malaysia to
Sumatra and Java (1; 2).   Presently known as still occurring in several Reserve
Forests in Lumding, Doom Dooma and Digboi districts, north-eastern Assam; in the
Pablakhi Sanctuary and the Ranga Mutti forest tract,near Chittagong, in Bangladesh;
and in Burma where it was reported in Kyatthin Sanctuary in 1955, Pidaring Sanctuary,
Myitkyina district, in 1959, and in the Mansi Tract, Bhamo district of Kadim State.
There have been no observations of the species in Thailand or Peninsular Malaysia
since before 1960.   Recently there have been reports of its occurrence near the
Batang Hari River, Jambi, Sumatra, on the neighbouring island of Siberut, and in
the Udjung Kulon Reserve of north-western Java (3).

POPULATION   Once considered by no means uncommon although nowhere numerous (1).
In north-eastern Assam the total known population is 15 pairs in six Reserve
Forests, a reduction since 1969-1970 of some 18 pairs, but it is believed to occur
in small numbers in several additional areas.   Two small groups were recorded in
Bangladesh in 1971.   Its population is not known in Burma, although a number of
suitable areas remain.   It has probably been extirpated in Thailand and Peninsular
Malaysia.   Only in Sumatra, and possibly elsewhere in Indonesia are there likely
to be substantial populations (4).   Outside of Indonesia small population groups
are usually isolated in individual forest areas.'   One pair per 100 ha of ideal
habitat is considered maximal in north-eastern Assam (3).

HABITAT   Dense primary evergreen rainforest interspersed with slow streams and
sheltered pools, and in the dry season also open swamp (1; 2; 3).   Reported from
sea level to 1,500 m elevation (5), although most upland forests have unsuitably
fast-flowing rivers.   The clearing of the primary forests of South East Asia
began to intensify after 1945, and in the 1960s and 1970s has increased drastically,
when clear-felling and replanting with selected fast-growing tree species replaced
selective logging in many areas.   The decrease in total area of suitable habitat
is considered the most important factor in the species' decline although various
disturbances, including hunting made possible by increased access to forests, have
also contributed to it (3).

CONSERVATION MEASURES TAKEN   Listed in Appendix 1 of the 1973 Convention on
International Trade in Endangered Species of Wild Fauna and Flora, and thus
subject to strict regulation in trade by ratifying nations.   Legally protected in
Indonesia.   In Assam 2.59 sq. km blocks within each Reserve Forest are now
reserved as sanctuaries.   With careful selection these sanctuaries could provide
essential habitat protection for this species (3).

CONSERVATION MEASURES PROPOSED   Selection of sanctuaries based on ecological
surveys is held to be essential.   Effective protection of these sanctuaries,
prohibiting logging, cane cutting, fishing, shooting and grazing within sanctuaries,

and restricting activities to daytime use in a surrounding buffer zone, is considered an essential corollary. Captive breeding followed by reintroduction of captive stock to suitably protected areas of presently unoccupied habitat has also been advocated (3).

REMARKS   This species was first held in captivity in Europe in 1851, but did not breed in captivity until 1936 (1). Captive breeding was established on a regular basis at the Wildfowl Trust, Slimbridge, England, in 1971. By 1976, about 70 birds were held in captive wildfowl collections in Europe, North America and Asia. All birds outside Asia are related to the Wildfowl Trust stock (3).

REFERENCES   1.   Delacour, J. 1959.   The Waterfowl of the World.   Vol. 3.
                     London:Country Life Ltd.
              2.   Ali, S. & Ripley, S.D. 1968.   Handbook of the Birds of India
                     and Pakistan.   Vol. 1.   Bombay, London, New York:Oxford
                     University Press.
              3.   Mackenzie, M.J.S. & Kear, J. 1976.   Unpublished report.
                     The White-winged Wood Duck.   Slimbridge, England:Wildfowl Trust.
              4.   Hoogerwerf, A. 1950.   De Witvleugeleend, Cairina scutulata, van
                     de Grote Soenda eilanden.   Ardea 38: 64-69.
              5.   Deignan, H.G. 1945.   The birds of northern Thailand.   U.S.
                     Nat. Mus. Bull., 186: 1-616.

WHITE-WINGED WOOD DUCK

Cairina scutulata (S. Müller, 1842)

Order ANSERIFORMES   Family ANATIDAE

STATUS   Vulnerable.   This species has declined seriously throughout its extensive
range in South East Asia due to massive decreases in the total area of suitable
habitat, isolation of local populations, increased disturbance, increased hunting of
adults and collection of young, and increased pollution of available waters.

DISTRIBUTION   Formerly occurred in northern and eastern Assam, India, Bangladesh
and south through Burma, western Thailand and western or Peninsular Malaysia to
Sumatra and Java (1; 2).   Presently known as still occurring in several Reserve
Forests in Lumding, Doom Dooma and Digboi districts, north-eastern Assam; in the
Pablakhi Sanctuary and the Ranga Mutti forest tract, near Chittagong, in Bangladesh;
and in Burma where it was reported in Kyatthin Sanctuary in 1955, Pidaring Sanctuary,
Myitkyina district, in 1959, and in the Mansi Tract, Bhamo district of Kadim State.
There have been no observations of the species in Thailand or Peninsular Malaysia
since before 1960.   Recently there have been reports of its occurrence near the
Batang Hari River, Jambi, Sumatra, on the neighbouring island of Siberut, and in
the Udjung Kulon Reserve of north-western Java (3).

POPULATION   Once considered by no means uncommon although nowhere numerous (1).
In north-eastern Assam the total known population is 15 pairs in six Reserve
Forests, a reduction since 1969-1970 of some 18 pairs, but it is believed to occur
in small numbers in several additional areas.   Two small groups were recorded in
Bangladesh in 1971.   Its population is not known in Burma, although a number of
suitable areas remain.   It has probably been extirpated in Thailand and Peninsular
Malaysia.   Only in Sumatra, and possibly elsewhere in Indonesia are there likely
to be substantial populations (4).   Outside of Indonesia small population groups
are usually isolated in individual forest areas.   One pair per 100 ha of ideal
habitat is considered maximal in north-eastern Assam (3).

HABITAT   Dense primary evergreen rainforest interspersed with slow streams and
sheltered pools, and in the dry season also open swamp (1; 2; 3).   Reported from
sea level to 1,500 m elevation (5), although most upland forests have unsuitably
fast-flowing rivers.   The clearing of the primary forests of South East Asia
began to intensify after 1945, and in the 1960s and 1970s has increased drastically,
when clear-felling and replanting with selected fast-growing tree species replaced
selective logging in many areas.   The decrease in total area of suitable habitat
is considered the most important factor in the species' decline although various
disturbances, including hunting made possible by increased access to forests, have
also contributed to it (3).

CONSERVATION MEASURES TAKEN   Listed in Appendix 1 of the 1973 Convention on
International Trade in Endangered Species of Wild Fauna and Flora, and thus
subject to strict regulation in trade by ratifying nations.   Legally protected in
Indonesia.   In Assam 2.59 sq. km blocks within each Reserve Forest are now
reserved as sanctuaries.   With careful selection these sanctuaries could provide
essential habitat protection for this species (3).

CONSERVATION MEASURES PROPOSED   Selection of sanctuaries based on ecological
surveys is held to be essential.   Effective protection of these sanctuaries,
prohibiting logging, cane cutting, fishing, shooting and grazing within sanctuaries,

and restricting activities to daytime use in a surrounding buffer zone, is
considered an essential corollary.   Captive breeding followed by reintroduction of
captive stock to suitably protected areas of presently unoccupied habitat has also
been advocated (3).

REMARKS   This species was first held in captivity in Europe in 1851, but did not
breed in captivity until 1936 (1).   Captive breeding was established on a regular
basis at the Wildfowl Trust, Slimbridge, England, in 1971.   By 1976, about 70
birds were held in captive wildfowl collections in Europe, North America and Asia.
All birds outside Asia are related to the Wildfowl Trust stock (3).

REFERENCES   1.   Delacour, J. 1959.   The Waterfowl·of the World.   Vol. 3.
                    London:Country Life Ltd.
               2.   Ali, S. & Ripley, S.D. 1968.   Handbook of the Birds of India
                    and Pakistan.   Vol. 1.   Bombay, London, New York:Oxford
                    University Press.
               3.   Mackenzie, M.J.S. & Kear, J. 1976.   Unpublished report.
                    The White-winged Wood Duck.   Slimbridge, England:Wildfowl Trust.
               4.   Hoogerwerf, A. 1950.   De Witvleugeleend, Cairina scutulata, van
                    de Grote Soenda eilanden.   Ardea 38: 64-69.
               5.   Deignan, H.G. 1945.   The birds of northern Thailand.   U.S.
                    Nat. Mus. Bull., 186: 1-616.

RUDDY-HEADED GOOSE

Chloephaga rubidiceps Sclater, 1860

Order ANSERIFORMES   Family ANATIDAE

STATUS   Vulnerable.   The southern South American population of this sheldgoose
has shown a disastrous decline and is now endangered, probably mainly as a result
of the introduction of foxes to Tierra del Fuego, where it breeds.   The Falkland
Islands population, although still sizable, is unprotected and subject to control
measures.

DISTRIBUTION   Breeds in the grasslands of northern Tierra del Fuego, Chile and
Argentina, and migrates in winter to the grasslands of southern Argentina north
to Buenos Aires province (1; 2).   In the Falklands the species is sedentary and
generally distributed on East and West Falkland and outlying islands (3).

POPULATION   In Tierra del Fuego the species seems to have substantially
increased in abundance at the turn of the century as brushwood gave way to grasslands under grazing pressure from sheep (4).   By the 1950s it was one of the
commonest sheldgeese in northern Tierra del Fuego, constituting more than half of
the countless thousands of sheldgeese in certain areas (5; 6).   In 1961, however,
a report indicated that it had declined in that area and now accounted for no more
than 10 percent of the sheldgeese present (7), the proportion dropping by 1973 to
a mere 0.1 percent (six out of a total of 6,000 counted).   This decline is
paralleled on its wintering grounds, recent censuses in southern Buenos Aires
Province showing this species to comprise between 0.45 and 0.7 percent of the
sheldgeese observed.   A 1976 estimate quoted the total population at less than
1000 individuals (8; 9).   On the Falklands the species remains relatively
abundant, although the least so of the three common sheldgeese of the islands,
reaching its maximum abundance in drier coastal grasslands of West Falkland (10).
No decline has in fact been documented and the total population is estimated at
between 38,000-141,000, even though up to 100,000 were killed during the period
1905-1912, and an undetermined number are still killed annually (J. Harradine 1977,
pers. comm.).

HABITAT   Grasslands.   The goose is said to compete with sheep for grassland
resources, although no serious scientific study has yet been made to prove the
point.   Nevertheless, a bounty for destroying eggs of this and other sheldgeese
has been in effect since about 1970 on Tierra del Fuego breeding grounds, while
the Argentine government's Sanidad Vegetal has eradication of sheldgeese on their
wintering grounds under consideration.   Bounties are also paid in the Falkland
Islands.   But of greater significance than bounties for the future of sheldgeese
was the introduction in the late 1940s of the Patagonian Grey Fox Dusicyon griseus
to Tierra del Fuego to control introduced rabbits.   The fox like the Ruddy-headed
Goose is restricted to grasslands (other species of sheldgeese nesting in wooded
or ecotonal areas), so decline of the goose has coincided with the fox's increase
(8; 11; M. Rumboll 1975, pers. comm.).

CONSERVATION MEASURES TAKEN   A study of the goose's feeding habits has been
undertaken in the Falklands, where the species has no legal protection.   It is
still on the Argentine government's "plague" list.   The foxes now preying on
sheldgeese in Tierra del Fuego are protected in the Chilean sector but are
poisoned and trapped on the Argentine side of the island (8).

CONSERVATION MEASURES PROPOSED   Removal of the species from the Argentine
"plague" list and according it legal protection have been recommended (M. Rumboll
1975, pers. comm.).

REMARKS The Ruddy-headed Goose breeds regularly in captivity. None of the other four Chloephaga species is presently at risk.

REFERENCES
1. Delacour, J. 1954. The Waterfowl of the World. Vol. 1. London: Country Life Ltd.
2. Humphrey, P.S. , Bridge, D., Reynolds, P.W. & Peterson, R.T. 1970. Birds of Isla Grande (Tierra del Fuego). Washington, D.C.: Smithsonian Institution.
3. Woods, R.W. 1975. The Birds of the Falkland Islands. Oswestry, Shropshire: Anthony Nelson.
4. Crawshay, R. 1907. The Birds of Tierra del Fuego. London: Bernard Quaritch.
5. Scott, P. 1954. South America-1953. Wildfowl Trust Annual Rept. 6: 55-69.
6. Ripley, S.D. 1950. A small collection of birds from Argentine Tierra del Fuego. Postilla 3: 1-11.
7. Plotnik, R. 1961. La Avutarda de Pecho Rayado. Instituto de Patalogia Vegetal IDIA No. 157: 9-22 (Not seen).
8. Rumboll, M.A.E. Undated ms. The status of the Ruddy-headed Goose (Chloephaga rubidiceps) of Tierra del Fuego.
9. Rumboll, M.A.E. 1975. El Cauguen de Cabeza Colorada (Chloephaga rubidiceps): Una nota de alarma. El Hornero 11: 315-316.
10. Weller, M.W. 1972. Ecological studies of Falkland Islands' waterfowl. Wildfowl 23: 25-44.
11. Weller, M.W. 1975. Habitat selection by waterfowl of Argentine Isla Grande. Wilson Bull. 87: 83-90.

WEST INDIAN WHISTLING DUCK

Dendrocygna arborea (Linnaeus, 1758)

Order ANSERIFORMES   Family ANATIDAE

STATUS   Vulnerable. This species is now scarce and believed still to be
declining throughout most of its range in the West Indies as the result of excessive
hunting.

DISTRIBUTION   Recorded in the Bahamas from Andros, San Salvador, Long, Crooked,
Inagua, New Providence and probably Abaco islands (1; 2; 3; J. Patterson 1973,
pers. comm.) and on Cuba, Isle of Pines, Hispaniola, Ile à Vache, Jamaica, Cayman
Islands, Puerto Rico, Mona, Vieques, Virgin Islands, Barbuda and possibly Antigua
(1; C. Kepler, B. Sorrie 1973, pers. comm.). Its present distribution is
virtually unchanged, except that it no longer appears to be present in Jamaica.

POPULATION   In the Bahamas there is a small but apparently secure population on
Inagua and possibly Andros (A. Sprunt 1973, pers. comm.), but the species is rare
elsewhere. On Cuba there has been some decline, although it is still reasonably
common (O. Garrido 1974, pers. comm.). It was rare in Lanier Swamp on Isle of
Pines in 1955 (4). There has probably been some decline on Hispaniola (5). The
species has not been seen on Jamaica since before 1960 (A. Downer 1973, pers. comm.).
It is still resident and reasonably common on Grand Cayman and Little Cayman, and
less so on Cayman Brac (D. Johnston 1973, pers. comm.). It is now very rare on
Puerto Rico although about 80 were reported recently from two swamps in the north-
eastern part of the island (H. Raffaele 1973, pers. comm.). It was only recently
reported from Mona and Vieques (C. Kepler, B. Sorrie 1973, pers. comm.) and was
also seen recently on Barbuda (A. Diamond 1974, pers. comm.). However, Cuba and
Hispaniola undoubtedly now support the bulk of the surviving populations.

HABITAT   Freshwater and brackish swamps (1). On the Greater Antilles swamps
have been extensively drained, thus removing much of the suitable habitat.

CONSERVATION MEASURES TAKEN   Listed in Appendix 2 of the 1973 Convention on
International Trade in Endangered Species of Wild Fauna and Flora. Hunting of the
species is prohibited in the Bahamas, Cuba, Puerto Rico, the Virgin Islands and
Jamaica, although enforcement is generally non-existent. The species is not
protected in Hispaniola and is frequently shot in Cuba where a related species, the
Fulvous Whistling Duck, Dendrocygna bicolor, occurs, which may be legally hunted,
and in the company of which arborea is quite often to be found (O. Garrido, 1974,
pers. comm.).

CONSERVATION MEASURES PROPOSED   A close season during the breeding season of the
West Indian Whistling Duck has been proposed in the Dominican Republic (5).

REMARKS   This species is widely represented in waterfowl collections around the
world. At least 131 were in captivity in 1974, of which three-quarters were
captive-bred (6).

REFERENCES   1. Bond, J. 1956. Check-list of Birds of the West Indies.
                  Philadelphia Acad. Nat. Sci.
              2. Bond, J. 1971. Sixteenth supplement to the Check-list of
                  Birds of the West Indies (1956). Philadelphia Acad. Nat. Sci.
              3. Bahamas National Trust, undated. Endangered and threatened
                  species and subspecies in the Bahama Islands. Mimeo., 3 pages.

4. Ripley, S.D. & Watson, G.E., 3rd, 1956.   Cuban bird notes.
   Yale Peabody Museum <u>Postilla</u> 26: 1-6.
5. Ottenwalder, S.A. 1973.   Algunas sugerencias para la conserva-
   ción de nuestra fauna.   Dominican Republic Dept. de Caza y
   Pesc. 36 pages.
6. Duplaix-Hall, N.   Census of rare animals in captivity, 1974.
   <u>Internat. Zoo Yearbook</u> 15: 397-429.

BRAZILIAN MERGANSER

Mergus octosetaceus Vieillot, 1817

Order ANSERIFORMES   Family ANATIDAE

STATUS   Indeterminate.   Sparsely distributed in Brazil, Paraguay and Argentina,
this shy little-known merganser is nowhere common.   Human disturbance may have
caused its disappearance from portions of its range.

DISTRIBUTION   Occurs along small tributaries in the Parana and Tocantins river
drainages in the Brazilian states of Minas Gerais, São Paulo, Paraná, Santa
Catarina and Goias, in the Argentine province of Misiones, and in eastern
Paraguay (1; 2; 3).   Its range is not known to have declined over all.

POPULATION   Unknown.   In the past three decades scattered reports indicate a
sparsely distributed, small population in suitable areas throughout the range.
The species is sedentary, although widely dispersed, and only rarely is more than
one pair to be seen in an area (1; 2; 3).

HABITAT   Small streams and water courses towards the headwaters of the Paraná
and Tocantins drainage systems, surrounded by tropical forest.   Larger rivers are
shunned.   The upper Tocantins river basin is increasingly subject to human
disturbance from nearby Brasilia.   On the Paraná river and its tributaries
several dams under construction or being planned will almost certainly affect this
merganser adversely (R. Ridgely 1978, pers. comm.).

CONSERVATION MEASURES TAKEN   The species is legally protected in Brazil.

CONSERVATION MEASURES PROPOSED   None known.

REMARKS   This species has only been kept in captivity in South America itself,
and none of the specimens held captive have survived long enough to breed.

REFERENCES   1.   Delacour, J. 1959.   The Waterfowl of the World. Vol. 3.
                     London: Country Life Ltd.
              2.   Sick, H. 1972.   A ameaça da avifauna brasileira.
                     Pp. 99-153 in Espécies da Fauna Brasileira Ameaçadas de
                     Extinção.   Rio de Janeiro: Academia Brasileira de
                     Ciências.
              3.   Partridge, W.H. 1956.   Notes on the Brazilian Merganser
                     in Argentina.   Auk 73: 473-488.

CHINESE MERGANSER

Mergus squamatus Gould, 1864

Order ANSERIFORMES   Family ANATIDAE

STATUS   Indeterminate.   Believed to be locally distributed in small numbers in
south-eastern Siberia.

DISTRIBUTION   This little-known species breeds in the mountains of south-eastern
Siberia and north-eastern Manchuria.   There are winter records from Korea,
Szechwan, south-west Yunnan, Tibet and Burma, but it appears that the bulk of
the population remains further north within the breeding range, keeping to areas
of open water of rivers that flow east from the eastern slope of the Sikhote Alin
range (1; 2; 3).

POPULATION   The species has been called common in parts of its restricted
breeding range (1), although recent information is lacking.   In the vast
Khabarovsk territory isolated pairs are still to be found and it has been
suggested that several hundred pairs of this species may still exist (Y. Yamashina
1973, pers. comm. to S.D. Ripley).

HABITAT   Rivers and lakes.   Nests have been found in tree cavities on forested
river banks and on rocky islands in lakes (1).

CONSERVATION MEASURES TAKEN   The Sikhote Alin Reserve and the Sudzukhe Sanctuary
include parts of the range of this merganser and therefore give it limited
protection.

CONSERVATION MEASURES PROPOSED   None known.

REFERENCES   1. Dementiev, G.P. & Gladkov, N.A. (eds) 1953. Birds of the
                  Soviet Union. Vol. 4.   Trans. from Russian by Israel
                  Program for Scientific Translation, Jerusalem, 1967.
              2. Delacour, J. 1959.   The Waterfowl of the World. Vol. 3.
                  London: Country Life Ltd.
              3. Vaurie, C. 1972.   Tibet and its Birds.   London:
                  H.F. and G. Witherby Ltd.

SOUTH AMERICAN POCHARD

Netta erythrophthalma erythrophthalma (Wied, 1832)

Order ANSERIFORMES   Family ANATIDAE

STATUS   Indeterminate. This subspecies, despite its wide distribution across
the northern half of South America, has recently all but disappeared throughout
much of its range.   The causes of this dramatic but little noted decline are
unknown.

DISTRIBUTION   Has been recorded locally in Zulia and Aragua departments,
Venezuela; the Caribbean coast, temperate parts of the eastern Andes, the Cauca
Valley and the south-east of Colombia; San Pablo and near Quito, Ecuador; west
of the Andes from Lambayeque to Arequipa, Peru; Arica department, Chile (one
record in 1883); Ceará, Pernambuco, Alagoas, Bahia and Rio de Janeiro in eastern
Brazil; and Jujuy, Argentina (1; R. McFarlane 1977, pers. comm.).   There is a
specimen taken in Trinidad a century ago (2).   Present distribution is poorly
known, though it is reliably reported as still to be found in Venezuela, Colombia
and Peru (R. Ridgely, M. Plenge 1977, pers. comm.).   It may in fact no longer
occur in the remainder of its range.

POPULATION   Unknown. This subspecies has always been sparsely distributed
but it is apparent that a serious decline has taken place.   Recent records from
Venezuela suggest that this does not apply to parts of that country (P. Schwartz
1978, pers. comm.), some still inaccessible marshes, for example at the southern
end of Lago de Maracaibo, probably supporting a population.   There is only one
recent sighting in Colombia, one likely sighting of several pochards in the early
1970s near Guayaquil, Ecuador, and one sighting of a pair in 1962 in a coastal
marsh south of Mollendo, Peru (M. Plenge 1977, R. Ridgely 1978, pers. comms.).
In Brazil it was not considered rare and was breeding at Lagoa Feia near Rio de
Janeiro in 1966, an area largely drained and planted up with sugarcane a decade
later, while reports of the subspecies in other Brazilian states date back to
1958 (H. Sick 1977, pers. comm.).

HABITAT   Open and shallow ponds, marshes and large rivers. The South American
subspecies is apparently not migratory (3).

CONSERVATION MEASURES TAKEN   None known.

CONSERVATION MEASURES PROPOSED   None reported.

REMARKS   N. c. brunnea, a weakly differentiated subspecies, is widespread in
southern and eastern Africa, where it is not at risk.   The nominate South
American subspecies was represented in The Wildfowl Trust at Slimbridge, England,
until the late 1960s (M. Lubbock 1977, pers. comm.).   It is quite possible that
some are still held by South American zoos, but there is no information on the
point.

REFERENCES   1.   de Schauensee, R.M. 1966.   The Species of Birds of South
                    America and their Distribution.   Narberth, Pa.: Livingston
                    Publishing Co.
              2.   ffrench, R. 1973.   A Guide to the Birds of Trinidad and
                    Tobago.   Wynnewood, Pa.: Livingston Publishing Company.
              3.   Delacour, J. 1959.   The Waterfowl of the World. Vol. 3.
                    London: Country Life Ltd.

CALIFORNIA CONDOR

Gymnogyps californianus (Shaw, 1797)

Order FALCONIFORMES   Family CATHARTIDAE

STATUS   Endangered.   Gradually dwindling in California despite extreme
measures.   Reproduction appears inadequate to compensate for small annual losses
in this long-lived bird.   Extinction is inevitable under existing circumstances.

DISTRIBUTION   Once distributed along the Pacific coast of North America from
British Columbia, Canada, south through Washington, Oregon and California, U.S.A.,
to northern Baja California, Mexico and, prehistorically, eastwards across the
southern United States to Florida (1; 2; 3).   There is no proof of breeding north
of San Francisco or in Baja California and by 1850 condors were all but absent
north of California.   Rumours that a small isolated population might survive in
the Sierra San Pedro de Martir of Baja California have not been confirmed and by
1932 the species had virtually disappeared from that area.   Condors now occur
only in a U-shaped area of up to 45,000 sq. km, from Santa Barbara along the Coast
Range to San Jose and along the western foothills of the Sierra Nevadas to
southern Madera County, north-east of Fresno.   The populations in the two ranges
concerned are no longer believed to mix.   Three nesting areas are known, Hi
Mountain-Beartrap region east of San Luis Obispo, Sisquoc area north of Santa
Barbara, and the Sespe-Piru area in Ventura and Los Angeles counties, of which the
last has been the most important (1; 3; 5; 6; 7; 12).

POPULATION   The California Condor probably reached a peak in numbers during the
Pleistocene.   It was widespread and often seen, although not abundant, in the
19th and early 20th centuries.   In the 1940s the first surveys produced an
estimate of 60 birds (1), a figure now thought to have been about 40 too low (4).
Counts in the early 1960s suggested a population decline of about 30 percent,
with only 60-70 birds (4) or only 40 according to a review of the counts in 1965
(5), remaining.   Between 1966 and 1971 the population was 50 to 60 (6), between
1972 and 1975 no more than 50 (7) and by 1977 perhaps as few as 40 (8; 12).   For
a decade the Coast Range population has numbered only about 10 birds, all the
others ranging from the Sespe area north along the Sierra Nevada foothills.
Although adult survival may be as high as 95 percent a year (exact figures are not
known), only about 2 birds on average have fledged annually in the decade 1967-
1977, the number of birds in subadult plumage has declined about 60 percent and
very few pairs are even attempting to breed (3; 4).

    The population decline in the 19th and 20th centuries is attributed to
shooting, trapping, poisoning and egg-collecting.   About half of the 288 condor
specimens and 71 eggs known to have been collected were taken between 1881 and
1910.   Disturbance by human activity near nest sites can impair breeding success
and condors in any case have a low reproductive potential.   They lay a single egg,
only nest alternate years except possibly under optimal conditions, and do not
reach maturity until the age of 6 or even later.   On the other hand, a condor may
live for half a century or more (1; 3; 5; 12).

HABITAT   For nesting, cavities on cliffs in mountainous terrain free from human
disturbance and with nearby exposed roost sites.   Food is sought in open grasslands, generally within 40-50 km of the nest, a dependable supply of carrion being
essential, which in this century usually means dead cattle (1; 3; 5).   Food
shortage within range of nest sites has been suggested as a likely cause of recent
poor breeding success (3; 10; 12).   Eagles may compete with condors for food and

nest sites. Development of grasslands, for oil production and urbanization, and more efficient removal of livestock carcasses have reduced feeding habitat and the amount of food available (3). Pesticide contamination may be a significant cause of reproductive failure; recent samples show seriously high DDE concentrations in body tissues and eggshells, the latter 23-57 percent thinner than pre-DDT samples (12).

CONSERVATION MEASURES TAKEN   The condor is fully protected under the U.S. Endangered Species Act and by California law, and is listed in Appendix 1 of the 1973 Convention on International Trade in Endangered Species of Wild Fauna and Flora.   The U.S. Fish and Wildlife Service appointed a recovery team for the Condor and the Recovery Plan was ready by 1974, but the indications are that it may not suffice to arrest the condor's decline.   A contingency plan for captive breeding has been drafted and is under consideration.   Portions of the bird's range are on U.S. National Forests, National Parks and State managed lands that afford good protection of the species and its habitat.   The Sespe Condor Sanctuary and Sisquoc-San Rafael, Hi Mountain-Beartrap, Mt. Pinos and Matilija Condor areas are all on Los Padres National Forest land.   Management has concentrated on securing nesting habitat and minimizing human disturbance.   A supplemental feeding program was begun in 1971.   Conservation education has also been stressed and has been fruitful (3; 8; 9).

CONSERVATION MEASURES PROPOSED   Captive breeding has been proposed by the Recovery Team as the last hope for saving the condor from extinction, and has received tentative approval of the U.S. Fish and Wildlife Service (3), but the details still have to be worked out.   Investigation of sources and levels of pesticides and other toxic substances found in condors, their competitors and their food has been advocated and other recommendations are: artificial nest sites in southern Kern County, where part of the Sespe-Piru Condor population now winters; acquisition of additional habitat, especially for feeding; study of changes in vegetation structure and their possible effect on condor; and, finally, much more extensive studies of the life history, biology, ecology and behaviour, based on identifiable individuals, which are so badly needed for effective management (3; 4; 8; 12; C. Koford 1977, pers. comm.).

REMARKS   The related Andean Condor Vultur gryphus, which ranges the length of the Andes from Venezuela to Tierra del Fuego, has also declined seriously in the northern part of its range (11), but elsewhere survives in fair numbers.   It is a borderline case for inclusion in the Red Data Book in the vulnerable category, and certainly calls for a close watch on any further deterioration of its status. There is a single California Condor in captivity in Los Angeles.

REFERENCES   1.   Koford, C.B. 1953.   The California Condor.   Nat. Audubon Soc. Res. Rept. 4.
            2.   Wilbur, S.R. 1973.   The California Condor in the Pacific Northwest.   Auk 90: 196-198.
            3.   Wilbur, S.R., Carrier, W.D., Muldowney, B.K., Mallette, R.D., Borneman, J.C. & Radtkey, W.H. 1974.   California Condor recovery plan.   U.S. Fish and Wildlife Service.
            4.   Verner, J. Undated report.   An appraisal of the continued involvement of Forest Service research in the California Condor Recovery Program.   U.S. Forest Service Pacific Southwest Forest and Range Experiment Station.
            5.   Miller, A.H., McMillan, I.I. & McMillan, E. 1965.   The current status and welfare of the California Condor. Nat. Audubon Soc. Res. Rept. 6.
            6.   Wilbur, S.R., Carrier, W.D., Borneman, J.C. and Mallette, R.W. 1972.   Distribution and numbers of the California Condor, 1966-1971.   Amer. Birds 26: 819-823.

7. Wilbur, S.R. 1976.   Status of the California Condor, 1972-1975.   Amer. Birds 30: 789-790.
8. American Ornithologists' Union. 1977.   Report of the Committee on Conservation.   Auk 94(4, Suppl.): 1DD-19DD.
9. Wilbur, S.R., Carrier, W.D. & Borneman, J.C. 1974. Supplemental feeding program for California Condors. Journ. Wildl. Mgmt. 38: 343-346.
10. Wilbur, S.R. 1972.   Food resources of the California Condor.   Admin. Rept., Patuxent Wildlife Research Center, U.S. Dept. of Interior.
11. McGahan, J. 1971.   The status of the Andean Condor in Peru. Bull. ICBP 11: 127-132.
12. Wilbur, S.R. 1978.   The California Condor, 1966-76: a look at its past and future.   U.S. Dept. of Interior North American Fauna 72.

CHRISTMAS BROWN GOSHAWK

Accipiter fasciatus natalis (Lister, 1889)

Order FALCONIFORMES   Family ACCIPITRIDAE

STATUS   Rare.   Restricted to one island in the Indian Ocean, where it is scarce.
It is shot as a predator of poultry, and its forest habitat has been dissected and
extensively destroyed by mining for phosphate.

DISTRIBUTION   Known only from Christmas Island, Indian Ocean, where it occurs
over the entire island (142 sq. km) except in areas of human habitation (1) and
mined areas devoid of vegetation.

POPULATION   In 1938-1940, this subspecies was considered fairly common (1).   By
1963-1964, only 12 birds were seen in a two-year period, and a decline was implied
(A.J. Pearson in litt. to J. Vincent, 1965).   An estimate of less than 100 birds
was made on the basis of visits in 1965, 1972, and 1974 (2), but by 1977, it was
noted as being once more on the increase (J.B. Nelson, unpublished report).

HABITAT   Forest, especially of the inland plateau but also along the shore terrace
(1).   By 1994, when phosphate mining operations are scheduled to end, at least
30 per cent of Christmas Island's surface will have been denuded (3).   There will
nevertheless probably remain sufficient forest to support a population of this
subspecies, unless it is decided to exploit lower grade phosphate deposits as well
as the higher grade deposits presently being mined.   The Australian Kestrel Falco
cenchroides has been introduced into the island and is now common, but it is not
known whether there is any competition between it and the Brown Goshawk.

CONSERVATION MEASURES TAKEN   Protected by law from killing or capture, but birds
are still shot as predators on poultry.   A Conservation Officer for Christmas
Island was appointed in 1975.

CONSERVATION MEASURES PROPOSED   Preservation of islands of vegetation to safeguard breeding sites of Abbott's Booby Sula abbotti will also benefit the goshawk.
Re-afforestation of mined areas has been recommended.   Most of the 3,000 people
now living on Christmas Island will be evacuated following completion of mining
activities in 1994 (3).

REMARKS   Ten other subspecies of the goshawk are recognized, ranging over much of
Australasia, none of them known to be at risk.

REFERENCES   1.   Gibson-Hill, C.A. 1947.   Notes on the birds of Christmas Island.
                    Bull. Raffles Mus. 18: 87-165.
              2.   Van Tets, G.F. 1976.   A report on the conservation of resident
                    birds on Christmas Island.   Bull. ICBP 12: 238-242.
              3.   Australian House of Representatives Standing Committee on
                    Environment and Conservation, 1974.   Conservation of endangered
                    species on Christmas Island.   Canberra:Australian Government
                    Publishing Service.

ANJOUAN SPARROWHAWK

Accipiter *francesii pusillus* (Gurney, 1875)

Order FALCONIFORMES   Family ACCIPITRIDAE

STATUS   Endangered.   Known only from Anjouan Island, Comoro group, western
Indian Ocean and now exceedingly rare.   Anjouan is heavily populated by man, and
what little remains of the indigenous evergreen forests has been seriously
degraded by human activity as well as by periodic cyclones.

DISTRIBUTION   On Anjouan this subspecies was formerly widespread but it is now
restricted to the scant 9,000 ha of forest along the mountainous backbone of the
island (1).

POPULATION   Although no early estimates are available, the fact that 30 specimens
were taken in the 19th century and a further 14 in 1906 and 1907, while only one
was seen during a whole month of extensive surveys in 1958 (1) and none at all in
3 days in 1965 (2), is indicative of the decline that must have taken place.   The
subspecies is now believed to be near extinction.

HABITAT   Evergreen forest and forest edges.   Two small areas of evergreen forest
remained on Anjouan in 1958, 7,000 ha and 2,000 ha respectively, and both were
seriously degraded by banana plantations and the destructive effects of cyclones;
soil erosion is severe in places.   The human population density in the 378 sq. km
of Anjouan in 1958 was 164 per sq. km (1).

CONSERVATION MEASURES TAKEN   None known.

CONSERVATION MEASURES PROPOSED   None known.

REMARKS   Three other subspecies of this sparrowhawk inhabiting Madagascar,
Mayotte and Grand Comoro are not known to be at risk, although A. f. griveaudi
from Grand Comoro was noted as being not at all common in 1958 (1).

REFERENCES   1.   Benson, C.W. 1960.   The birds of the Comoro Islands: Results
                    of the British Ornithologists' Union Centenary Expedition 1958.
                    Ibis 103b: 5-106.
              2.   Forbes-Watson, A.D. 1969.   Notes on birds observed in the
                    Comoros on behalf of the Smithsonian Institution.   Atoll
                    Research Bull. 128: 1-23.

CUBAN SHARP-SHINNED HAWK

Accipiter striatus fringilloides Vigors, 1827

Order FALCONIFORMES   Family ACCIPITRIDAE

STATUS   Very rare and decreasing.   Only found very locally in certain forested
mountains of Cuba.   The species is shot by hunters and farmers, and the forests
where it normally occurs continue to decrease in area as they are felled or cleared.

DISTRIBUTION   Formerly more widely distributed in Cuban montane forests, but now
known only from the Cordillera de los Organes at the western end of the island,
except for one shot recently in the central Sierra de Trinidad (O.H. Garrido 1974,
pers. comm.).

POPULATION   No estimates have been made, but the population has clearly declined.
The species is now considered Cuba's rarest bird of prey (O.H. Garrido 1974, pers.
comm.).

HABITAT   Montane forests, occasionally intermontane valleys and, formerly at
least, in the lowlands (1).

CONSERVATION MEASURES TAKEN   Protected by law, but all birds of prey are still
shot as a matter of course by local hunters and farmers (O.H. Garrido 1974, pers.
comm.).

CONSERVATION MEASURES PROPOSED   None known.

REMARKS   Another subspecies, A. s. venator, is very rare on Puerto Rico, but
eight others ranging from the tree line in northern North America south to
northern Argentina and Paraguay, and including the West Indian island of
Hispaniola (2), are not known to be at risk.

REFERENCES   1.   Bond, J. 1961.   Birds of the West Indies.   Boston:Houghton
                    Mifflin Co.; London:Collins.
              2.   Brown, L. & Amadon, D. 1968.   Eagles, Hawks and Falcons of the
                    World.   Feltham, Middlesex:Hamlyn Publishing Group.

PUERTO RICAN SHARP-SHINNED HAWK

Accipiter striatus venator Wetmore, 1914

Order FALCONIFORMES   Family ACCIPITRIDAE

STATUS   Rare.   Although the range of this subspecies extends to several different areas of Puerto Rico, its total population is quite low.

DISTRIBUTION   Known to be as widespread now as at any time since its discovery, this hawk occurs in Maricao, Toro Negro, Luquillo Forest, possibly along much of the Cordillera Central in suitable forest, and also in the Carite-Guavate Commonwealth Forest (N. Snyder, 1975, pers. comm.).

POPULATION   A total of 100-200 birds has been estimated as the entire population. Possibly 40 occur at Toro Negro, up to 24 at Maricao, no more than 20 in Luquillo Forest, and the rest probably scattered along the Cordillera Central (N. Snyder 1975, pers. comm.).

HABITAT   Montane forest.   In Luquillo Forest, and possibly elsewhere in its range, nestlings are frequently infested by bot fly warbles, which can be fatal if the warbles are sufficiently numerous.   The range of the bot fly is not known, but it is apparently uncommon in lowland areas (N. Snyder, 1975, pers. comm.).

CONSERVATION MEASURES TAKEN   Fully protected by Puerto Rico Commonwealth law and by U.S. Federal law, although in practice enforcement is often impossible. Portions of the hawk's habitat are protected in Commonwealth Forests or U.S. National Forests.   A biologist of the U.S. Fish and Wildlife Service has made preliminary studies of the subspecies.

CONSERVATION MEASURES PROPOSED   Thorough study of the hawk's distribution and abundance, and of the factors affecting its survival (1).

REMARKS   Of the ten subspecies distributed throughout the Americas and in the Caribbean islands, only this subspecies and the one from Cuba (A. s. fringilloides) are rare.

REFERENCES   1.   U.S. Fish and Wildlife Service, 1973.   Threatened Wildlife of the United States.   U.S. Bur. Sport Fish. Wildl. Res. Pubs. 114.

SPANISH IMPERIAL EAGLE

Aquila heliaca adalberti Brehm, 1860

Order FALCONIFORMES   Family ACCIPITRIDAE

STATUS   Endangered.   Now restricted to southern Spain and Portugal, where it is
subject to poisoning, shooting, habitat destruction, pesticides and the danger of
striking overhead powerlines.

DISTRIBUTION   Formerly throughout the drier parts of the Iberian Peninsula as
far as the Pyrenees, northern Morocco and north-eastern Algeria south to the
Atlas Mountains.   There is no record of breeding in Morocco or Algeria for many
years, but a pair was seen in the Atlas of Morocco in spring 1977, and young birds
have been seen in autumn flying over Gibraltar to Africa.   It presently occurs
in central, western and southern Spain (where its stronghold is in the Coto de
Doñana)and Portugal (1; 2; 3; 4; J. Garzon 1978, pers. comm.).

POPULATION   There are no estimates of past populations although the eagle was
doubtless once far more plentiful than it is today.   Over the past 10 years the
population has been stable: about 45-50 pairs are known in Spain, mainly in the
west-centre, primarily in Caceres Province and in the Coto de Doñana National Park,
Andalucia (13 pairs). (1; 4; 5; 6; 7; J. Garzon 1978, pers. comm.).   Because many
pairs breed on private land, access to which is restricted, a thorough census has
yet to be made, but 60-80 breeding pairs are thought to remain in Spain, while
seven more known pairs in Portugal indicate a real total of 15-20 pairs in that
country   (J. Garzon 1978, pers. comm.).

HABITAT   For nesting,low trees on dry brushy hills are favoured.   Forests
throughout much of the Spanish range and in northern Africa have been cleared
indiscriminately and overgrazing by livestock causes serious erosion.   In Spain,
also, the use of poisoned baits to control mammalian predators on game species
has resulted in serious population declines of several birds of prey (4; 5).

CONSERVATION MEASURES TAKEN   This eagle has been accorded full legal protection
in Spain, but in practice still suffers from the Spanish farmers' traditional
abuse of birds of prey.   Listed in Appendix 1 of the 1973 Convention on International Trade in Endangered Species of Wild Fauna and Flora, although none of
this subspecies is known to be in captivity at the present time (1978).   The
effective wildlife and habitat conservation within the Doñana National Park affords
protection for at least a portion of the remaining population of this eagle.

CONSERVATION MEASURES PROPOSED   In 1972, an imaginative management technique was
applied to this subspecies.   The third and fourth nestlings, which are smaller
than their siblings and never survive, were taken from nine nests and placed in
nests containing no or one young.   The fledging success was thereby increased by
43 percent (8).   The technique holds great promise for augmentation of this
beleaguered population.   The creation of a reserve in Caceres Province has been
proposed by ADENA, the Spanish appeal of World Wildlife Fund.

REMARKS   The nominate subspecies occurs in eastern and south-eastern Europe,
Turkey and eastwards across southern Russia to Transbaikalia, northern India and
China, eastern populations migrating for the winter to south and south-east Asia,
western populations to north-eastern and north central Africa.   It has declined
seriously on the western periphery of its range (9), but cannot yet be considered
at risk in view of the substantial numbers remaining in the U.S.S.R. and Iran.
A recent taxonomic study of the Spanish form has concluded that it is specifically
distinct (10).

REFERENCES   1.   Bijleveld, M. 1974.   Birds of Prey in Europe.   London:
                  Macmillan.
             2.   Meyburg, B.-U. 1975.   On the biology of the Spanish Imperial
                  Eagle (Aquila heliaca adalberti).   Ardeola 21:   245-283.
             3.   Etchécopar, R.D. & Hüe, F. 1967.   The Birds of North
                  Africa.   Edinburgh and London: Oliver and Boyd.
             4.   Mills, S.P. Unpub. report dated 1976.   Spanish Imperial
                  Eagle-Morocco.   WWF report, project 1264.
             5.   Garzon Heydt, J. 1972.   Especies en peligro: El Aguila
                  Imperial.   ADENA 4:   8-11.   (Not seen).
             6.   Valverde, J.A. 1960.   La population d'Aigles impériaux
                  des marismas du Guadalquivir; son évolution depuis un siècle.
                  Alauda 28:   20-26.
             7.   Meyburg, B.-U. 1973.   Observations sur l'abondance relative
                  des rapaces (Falconiformes) dans le nord et l'ouest de
                  l'Espagne.   Ardeola 19:   129-150.
             8.   Meyburg, B.-U. & Garzon Heydt, J. 1973.   Sobre la protecion
                  del Aguila Imperial (Aquila heliaca adalberti) aminorando
                  artificialmente la mortandad juvenil.   Ardeola 19:   107-128.
             9.   Glutz von Blotzheim, U.N., Bauer, K.M. & Bezzel, E. 1971.
                  Handbuch der Vögel Mitteleuropas.   Band 4.   Falconiformes.
                  Frankfurt am Main: Akademische Verlagsgesellschaft.
            10.   Hiraldo, F., Delibes, M. & Calderon, J. 1976.   Sobre el
                  status taxonomico del Aguila Imperial Iberica.   Doñana
                  Acta Vertebrata 3:   171-180.

GALAPAGOS HAWK

Buteo galapagoensis (Gould, 1837)

Order FALCONIFORMES   Family ACCIPITRIDAE

STATUS   Rare. This remarkably confiding hawk has declined both in abundance
and in its range in the Galapagos Islands, Ecuador, because of human disturbance.

DISTRIBUTION   Once found on almost all of the main Galapagos Islands, but now
absent from San Cristobal, Floreana, Daphne, Seymour and Baltra.   Still survives
on Barrington, Duncan, James, Isabela, Fernandina, Pinta, Marchena, Santa Cruz
and Hood, although it is very much reduced on Santa Cruz (1; 2; 3).

POPULATION   As recently as 1930 this species was so common on some islands
that chickens could not be kept (3), yet by 1974 only 130-150 pairs remained, the
majority on James and Barrington islands (1; 2).

HABITAT   Most of the Galapagos island habitats, covering a total area of about
7,000 sq. km, are visited by this bird but its nesting is confined to a much
smaller area of about 1,000 sq. km.   It is believed to be subject to a good deal
of predation by feral cats and is now absent from most areas of easy access to
humans.

CONSERVATION MEASURES TAKEN   Killing of this species is expressly forbidden by
law.   Much of its range lies within the Galapagos National Park.

CONSERVATION MEASURES PROPOSED   None additional known.

REFERENCES   1. DeVries, Tj. 1973.   The Galapagos Hawk. Amsterdam: Free
                  University Press.   (Not seen).
              2. Harris, M.P. 1974.   A Field Guide to the Birds of
                  Galapagos.   New York: Taplinger Publishing Co.
              3. Brosset, A. 1963.   Le comportement de la Buse des
                  Galapagos Buteo galapagoensis.   Alauda 31: 5-21.

PUERTO RICAN BROAD-WINGED HAWK

Buteo *platypterus* *brunnescens* Danforth and Smyth, 1935

Order FALCONIFORMES   Family ACCIPITRIDAE

STATUS   Rare.   Restricted to two forested areas of Puerto Rico, West Indies.
The total population is quite small.   The reasons for the hawk's rarity are not
known.

DISTRIBUTION   Considered to be widespread in inland forests of Puerto Rico last
century, but by 1927 was thought to be extinct or excessively rare (1).   Recent
observations indicate that the subspecies is restricted to the upper Mamayes River
drainage, in the north-east part of Luquillo Experimental Forest at the eastern end
of Puerto Rico, and near Utuado in the Toro Negro region in the center of the
island (N. Snyder 1974, pers. comm.).

POPULATION   Last century the subspecies was common, but by 1900 it had become
very rare (1).   There are now at the most 30-40 birds in the Luquillo Forest, and
probably fewer in the Toro Negro area.   A maximum of 75 birds has been estimated
for the entire poopulation (N. Snyder, 1974 pers. comm.).

HABITAT   Tropical montane rainforest, formerly also in lowland forest (1).   The
subspecies presently occupies only a small portion of what appears to be suitable
habitat.

CONSERVATION MEASURES TAKEN   Fully protected by Puerto Rican and U.S. Federal law.
The bulk of the population occurs within the boundaries of a national forest.   A
biologist of the U.S. Fish and Wildlife Service has made preliminary surveys of
the population recently.

CONSERVATION MEASURES PROPOSED   Further surveys to determine the distribution and
abundance of this subspecies and to identify the factors limiting its present
numbers (N. Snyder 1974, pers. comm.).

REMARKS   Four other subspecies occur in the Caribbean and are non-migratory.
A fifth breeds in North America and winters south to Central and South America.
Only the Puerto Rico subspecies is presently at risk.

REFERENCES   1.   Wetmore, A. 1927.   Scientific survey of Porto Rico and the
                     Virgin Islands.   New York Acad. Sci. 9(3):   322-323.

HAWAIIAN HAWK or 'IO

Buteo solitarius   Peale, 1848

Order   FALCONIFORMES   Family   ACCIPITRIDAE

STATUS   Rare.   Restricted to the island of Hawaii, where it is widespread but
not common.   Occasionally killed illegally and subject to habitat alteration from
infiltration of the forests by grazing animals and clearing of substantial tracts
of forest (1; 2).

DISTRIBUTION   Kohala Mountains and the slopes of Mauna Kea, Hualalai, and Mauna
Loa, Hawaii.   Not known to have changed much from former times (1; 2; W. Banko
1974, pers. comm.).

POPULATION   Estimated to be in the low hundreds.   Thought to have increased
slightly in Hawaii Volcanoes National Park in the past 30 years (1; 3; 4).

HABITAT   Woody vegetation of any type below 2,600 m elevation (3).

CONSERVATION MEASURES TAKEN   Protected by federal and state law from killing,
capture or harassment.   A portion of the species' range lies within a National
Park.

CONSERVATION MEASURES PROPOSED   Research on population, life history and
ecological requirements of the species.   Surveillance for chemical contamination
and other environmental pollution (1).

REMARKS   Three birds in captivity at the Honolulu Zoo in 1975 (5).

REFERENCES   1.   U.S. Department of Interior Bureau of Sport Fisheries and
                   Wildlife, 1973.   Threatened Wildlife of the United States.
                   U.S. Bur. Sport Fish. Wildl. Res. Pub. 114.
              2.   Berger, A.J. 1972.   Hawaiian Birdlife.   Honolulu: University
                   Press of Hawaii.
              3.   Morrison, G.T. 1969.   Hawaiian Hawk.   Elepaio 29: 75-78.
              4.   Baldwin, P.H. 1969.   The Hawaiian Hawk from 1938 to 1949.
                   Elepaio 29: 95-98.
              5.   Duplaix-Hall, N. 1975.   Census of rare animals in captivity,
                   1974.   International Zoo Yearbook 15: 397-429.

GRENADA HOOK-BILLED KITE

Chondrohierax uncinatus mirus Friedmann, 1934

Order FALCONIFORMES   Family ACCIPITRIDAE

STATUS   Endangered.   Known from Grenada, Lesser Antilles, West Indies, where it
is thought to be on the verge of extinction, if in fact it still exists.   At least
three factors may have contributed to its decline: hunters, a decrease in
abundance of snails on which this species feeds, and destructive hurricanes, the
one in 1955 being especially severe (1).

DISTRIBUTION   Presumably ranging widely in Grenada, but it is by no means certain
that it still survives.   It would be most likely to occur in the mountain forests.

POPULATION   Never known to have been common at any time since its discovery,
although presumed to have been more so before much of Grenada's forested land was
cleared.   One was seen in 1929, two collected in 1935, and a pair shot by a
hunter in 1968 (1; 2).   Two visits to the island in 1971 failed to yield further
information (3), although one was seen in 1972 in open secondary forest at 600 m
elevation on Morne Fedon (O.M. Buchanan 1976, pers. comm. to S. Temple).

HABITAT   Mountain forest, also occasionally in the lowlands.   A decrease in the
abundance of giant land snails Strophoceilus has undoubtedly had a marked effect on
the kite population, these snails being its chief food (1).

CONSERVATION MEASURES TAKEN   None known.   According to the Grenada Wildlife
Ordinance of 1956, birds of prey may be legally shot between September and February.

CONSERVATION MEASURES PROPOSED   None known.

REMARKS   Another subspecies C. u. wilsonii of Cuba has become rare and is now
endangered.   Two other subspecies are widespread in Central and South America.

REFERENCES   1.   Bond, J. 1961.   Extinct and near extinct birds of the West
                    Indies.   Pan-American Section, ICBP, Res. Rep. No. 4.
              2.   Bond, J. 1968.   Thirteenth supplement to the Check-list of
                    Birds of the West Indies.   Phila. Acad. Nat. Sci.
              3.   Lack, D. and Lack, A. 1973.   Birds on Grenada.   Ibis 115:
                    53-59.

CUBAN HOOK-BILLED KITE

Chondrohierax uncinatus wilsonii (Cassin, 1847)

Order FALCONIFORMES   Family ACCIPITRIDAE

STATUS   Rare.   This species is very rare and local in eastern Cuba, where now
confined.   Its dependence for food on snails of the genus Polymita, the beautiful
shells of which are collected by Cubans in large numbers, makes it exceptionally
vulnerable (O.H. Garrido 1974, pers. comm.).

DISTRIBUTION   Formerly more widespread in the east and south of Cuba, as far west
as Cochinos Bay, near Zapata Peninsula, but presently restricted to a small area at
the eastern end of the island between Moa and Baracoa, Oriente Province (1;
O.H. Garrido 1974, pers comm.).

POPULATION   Once considerably more common, although no precise population figures
are available.   An observation of this species in 1974, is the first by an
ornithologist in many years, although farmers in the Baracoa area know the species
and say it is not uncommon (O.H. Garrido 1974, pers. comm.).

HABITAT   Along rivers and streams in wooded areas where the tree snail Polymita
is plentiful.   The snail is the kite's chief food (2).

CONSERVATION MEASURES TAKEN   Protected by law.

CONSERVATION MEASURES PROPOSED   It has been suggested that the Cuban government
should prohibit collection of the shells of the tree snail on which this species
is dependant for food (O.H. Garrido 1974, pers. comm.).

REMARKS   Another subspecies C. u. mirus of Grenada is critically endangered; two
more inhabiting continental tropical America are widespread and not threatened.
C. u. wilsonii has sometimes been regarded as a full species, C. wilsonii, as in
the previous edition of the Red Data Book, Vol. 2.

REFERENCES   1.   Bond, J. 1956.   Check-list of the Birds of the West Indies.
                    Philadelphia Acad. Natural Sci.
              2.   Bond, J. 1961.   Birds of the West Indies.   Boston:Houghton
                    Mifflin Co.;   London:Collins.

MADAGASCAR SERPENT EAGLE

Eutriorchis astur Sharpe, 1875

Order FALCONIFORMES   Family ACCIPITRIDAE

STATUS   Endangered, if in fact it still exists.   Known only from a few specimens and nothing has been heard or seen of this species since 1930.   Its forest habitat has been extensively cleared.

DISTRIBUTION   Restricted to the forests of eastern Madagascar between Maroantsetra and Farafangana and last found, in the vicinity of Maroantsetra, in 1930.

POPULATION   No estimate was ever made but it was already considered rare in 1930, when two were seen and collected, and is doubtless far more so today, if in fact it still exists (1; 2).

HABITAT   Dense humid forest from sea level to at least 600 m elevation (2). The forests of Madagascar have been severely depleted, and there is presently little indication that this trend will be checked.

CONSERVATION MEASURES TAKEN   This serpent-eagle and all other birds of prey on Madagascar were scheduled for total protection by the 1968 African Convention on the Conservation of Nature and Natural Resources, which the Malagasy Government signed and ratified.   However, the species has not yet been given specific legal protection.

CONSERVATION MEASURES PROPOSED   It has been recommended to the Malagasy Government that this and most other endemic birds of Madagascar should be legally protected (K. Curry-Lindahl in litt. to G. Ramanantsoavina, Director, Service des Eaux et Forêts, Chasse et Pêche, Jan. 1973).

REFERENCES   1.   Rand, A.L. 1936.   The distribution and habits of Madagascar birds.   Bull. Amer. Mus. Nat. Hist. 72(5):   143-499.
             2.   Milon, P., Petter, J.-J. & Randrianasolo, G. 1973.   Faune de Madagascar, 35: Oiseaux.   Tananarive and Paris: ORSTOM and CNRS.

CAPE VULTURE

Gyps coprotheres (J.R. Forster, 1798)

Order FALCONIFORMES   Family ACCIPITRIDAE

STATUS   Vulnerable.   Of increasingly restricted distribution in southern Africa.
Its decline in population is due to insufficient rate or success of reproduction,
which in turn has been brought about by the killing of the bird itself, disturbance at nest sites and calcium deficiency in parts of its range.

DISTRIBUTION   Southern Africa south of the Zambesi and Cunene Rivers.   Breeds
from near Shangani, Rhodesia, and Waterberg, South West Africa, to the southern
Cape Province but excluding a substantial area of the central plateau.   No change
has been recorded in the over all range, although the species has ceased to breed
in many areas, notably parts of the southern Cape Province.   Within its extensive
range individuals travel widely, although breeding adults normally remain close by
their breeding cliffs throughout the year (1; 2).

POPULATION   Now highest in the Transvaal.   The vulture was formerly abundant in
Cape Province and it is there that the most serious declines have occurred.
Altogether the sites of 60 colonies are known, some of them now abandoned, and a
colony may contain up to 250 pairs.   The total population in 1977 was of the
order of 10,000 birds, assuming that those nesting comprised half the total
number.   Certain areas such as Lesotho and the Transkei, have not yet been
adequately searched, but it is unlikely the population estimate will be increased
materially by discovery of new colonies.   Although some colonies, particularly in
the Transvaal, appear stable or even increasing, the population as a whole has
been declining and at an increasing rate for more than a century.   This has
recently been confirmed by analysis of recoveries of banded (ringed) birds.
Adults must breed for a minimum of 8 years to replace themselves but adult life
expectancy is only about 6 years (1; 2; P. Mundy 1977, pers. comm.).

HABITAT   Cliff ledges provide the breeding habitat, while open mountainous
country, plains and agricultural lands are all frequented for scavenging (1; 4).
Where populations of large carnivores and hyaenas are absent the vultures are
unable to provide their chicks with sufficient bone fragments, resulting in
mortality because the growing chick is weakened by calcium deficiency (1; 5).
In areas where livestock, particularly sheep, are grazed vultures are poisoned and
shot as potential predators (1; 2).   Immatures are often electrocuted on pylons
carrying power lines or their wings are broken by flying into the wires: in one
area of the Transvaal mortality from this cause was noted in 148 cases in a single
year (6).   Disturbance of birds at nest sites by humans and fire also have caused
losses (7; 8; 9).

CONSERVATION MEASURES TAKEN   The Cape Vulture is protected by provincial laws
in South Africa, except when causing damage to property.   One small colony is
within a protected area, the Umtamvuna (gorge) Nature Reserve in southern Natal.
A large colony in the Transvaal is protected by the private owner of the farm on
which the nesting cliff is located.   Nesting cliffs at Mannyelanong, Botswana,
are protected by a concerned, vigilant game scout of the Department of Wildlife
and National Parks.   A 5-year research project mainly on the population dynamics
of the species began in 1973 and has been assisted by the fact that a certain
number of Cape Vultures have been banded since 1948 (1; 7; P. Mundy 1977, pers.
comm.).

CONSERVATION MEASURES PROPOSED   Protection of certain additional nesting sites
(3).   Continuation of population studies, including analysis of pesticide
residues, management and feeding ecology (P. Mundy 1977, pers. comm.).

REMARKS   Four specimens in the National Zoological Gardens at Pretoria; they
have not yet bred (3).

REFERENCES   1.   Mundy, P.J. 1976.   The Cape Vulture.   In Proceedings of a
                   Symposium on Endangered Wildlife in Southern Africa held
                   in Pretoria, 22-23 July 1976.   Pp. 116-118.
              2.   Jarvis, M.F.J., Siegfried, W.R. & Currie, M.H. 1974.
                   Conservation of the Cape Vulture in the Cape Province.
                   Journ. S. Afr. Wildl. Mgmt. 4: 29-34.
              3.   Siegfried, W.R., Frost, P.G.H., Cooper, J. & Kemp, A.C. 1976.
                   South African Red Data Book-Aves.   S. Afr. Nat. Sci. Prog.
                   Rept. 7.
              4.   Brown, L. & Amadon, D. 1968.   Eagles, Hawks and Falcons of the
                   World.   London & New York: Country Life; McGraw-Hill.
              5.   Mundy, P.J. & Ledger, J.A. 1976.   Griffon Vultures,
                   carnivores and bones.   S. Afr. Journ. Sci. 72: 106-110.
              6.   Markus, M.B. 1972.   Mortality of vultures caused by
                   electrocution.   Nature 283: 228.
              7.   Ledger, J. & Mundy, P. 1975.   Research on the Cape Vulture:
                   1974 progress report.   Bokmakierie 27(2): 2-7.
              8.   Ledger, J. & Mundy, P. 1976.   Cape Vulture research in 1975.
                   Bokmakierie 28(1): 4-8.
              9.   Mundy, P.J.& Ledger, J.A. 1975.   The effects of fire on a
                   Cape Vulture colony.   S. Afr. Journ. Sci. 71: 217.

WHITE-TAILED EAGLE

Haliaeetus albicilla (Linnaeus, 1758)

Order FALCONIFORMES   Family ACCIPITRIDAE

STATUS   Vulnerable. Widely but locally distributed in the northern Palearctic
and Greenland, but declining in most of the European part of its range from human
persecution, habitat destruction and pollution. Its status in Asia may be stable,
but information on populations is lacking.

DISTRIBUTION   Breeds in western Greenland, Iceland, Scandinavia and along the
northern coast of U.S.S.R. to Kamchatka, the Kurils and Japan. It ranges north
to about 70°N in the west and to 75°N in the east, and south to the Baltic Sea
coast in western Europe, farther south in central and south-eastern Europe,
sparsely through the Balkan peninsula to Greece and thence through Turkey, Iraq,
Transcaucasia, northern Iran, the Caspian region and Turkestan to Zaisan Nor,
Mongolia, Transbaikalia, Amurland, northern Manchuria, Sakhalin and Ussuriland.
Immatures, only, are migratory-to southern Europe, the Mediterranean, north Africa,
Iraq, Iran, Afghanistan, Pakistan, occasionally north-western India, central and
southern China, Korea, Japan and off-shore islands of South East Asia.   Formerly
bred in the Faroes, Ireland, Scotland, Denmark, Austria, Corsica, Sardinia, Egypt
and Israel (1; 2; 5; 8).

POPULATION   The West Greenland population was about 200 adults with an unknown
but smaller number of juveniles in 1974, having declined from an uncertain but
larger figure (3).   In the same year the European population was estimated at
500-750 breeding pairs (4).   The Norwegian population (300-350 pairs, currently
stable) (6) is the most important in Europe, but Sweden (80 pairs, declining) (7),
the German Democratic Republic (50-100 pairs, declining) and Poland (45-50 pairs,
of which 30 or less breed successfully) also have significant populations.
Iceland, Finland, Rumania, Federal Republic of Germany, Czechoslovakia, Hungary,
Greece, Albania, Yugoslavia, Turkey and possibly Bulgaria have smaller populations,
most of which have declined and show poor reproduction (1; 4; 9).   The populations
in various parts of U.S.S.R. are uncertain, but again some decreases have been
noted, e.g. in the Ukraine, along the Volga River, and in Kamchatka and Amurland,
although the species is apparently still abundant on the Caspian Sea (1; 10).
Rates as a rare breeding bird in Japan in the north-east of Hokkaido and Hondo (11).
In China no longer breeds along the lower Yangtze Valley (5).

HABITAT   Rocky coasts, inland lakes and large river valleys.   Areas where there
is repeated human disturbance are usually abandoned.   Shooting and poisoning,
particularly in eastern Europe where poisoned baits are still occasionally set out
to kill wolves, has had a serious impact on this eagle and wetlands on which it
was formerly dependant have been extensively drained throughout Europe.   Contamination by pesticides such as DDT and by heavy metals such as mercury has
caused deaths and has contributed to seriously reduced breeding success,
particularly along the Baltic coast (4; 9).

CONSERVATION MEASURES TAKEN   This eagle or its nest is legally protected in
almost all countries in which it breeds (4; 12).   It is listed in Appendix 1 of
the 1973 Convention on International Trade in Endangered Species of Wild Fauna and
Flora.   In Sweden protective measures include guarding of selected nest sites from
human disturbance during the breeding season (7) and winter feeding with pesticide-
free meat is practised in Finland (13).

CONSERVATION MEASURES PROPOSED   Since lawfully protected birds are still occasionally shot or their nest contents robbed in Europe, more effective protection is important, including the safeguarding of more breeding sites by creation of nature reserves.   Continual monitoring of toxic chemicals in the eagle's environment, control, where necessary, of the use of such chemicals and supplemental feeding with uncontaminated food, are among the other measures which have been recommended (4).

REMARKS   The Greenland population is recognized by some authors as a subspecies H. a. groenlandicus, separable by its larger size from continental populations (14).   However, it is also treated as being the end point of a cline of increasing size which can be traced through Europe from south-east to north-west (1).

REFERENCES   1.   Glutz von Blotzheim, U.N., Bauer, K.M. & Bezzel, E. 1971. Handbuch der Vögel Mitteleuropas.   Band 4.   Falconiformes. Frankfurt am Main: Akademische Verlagsgesellschaft.
2.   Dementiev, G.P. & Gladkov, N.A. (eds) 1951.   Birds of the Soviet Union.   Vol. 1.   Translated from Russian 1966. Jerusalem: Israel Program for Scientific Translations.
3.   Hanson, K. 1977.   The Greenland White-tailed Eagle. In Report of Proceedings World Conference on Birds of Prey (R.D. Chancellor ed.).   London: ICBP.   Pp. 73-74.
4.   Parslow, J.L.F. 1974.   Study of birds in need of special protection in Europe.   Council of Europe.
5.   Vaurie, C. 1965.   The Birds of the Palearctic Fauna. Non-Passeriformes.   London: H.F. and G. Witherby Ltd.
6.   Willgohs, J.F. 1977.   Birds of prey in Norway.   In Report of Proceedings World Conference on Birds of Prey (R.D. Chancellor ed.).   London: ICBP.   Pp. 143-148.
7.   Segnestam, M. & Helander, B. 1977.   Birds of prey in Sweden. In Report of Proceedings World Conference on Birds of Prey (R.D. Chancellor ed.).   London: ICBP.   Pp. 170-178.
8.   Paz, U. Undated.   The rehabilitation of the Huleh Reserve. Government of Israel Nature Reserves Authority.
9.   Bijleveld, M. 1974.   Birds of Prey in Europe.   London: Macmillan.
10.   Galushin, V.M. 1977.   Recent changes in the actual and legislative status of birds of prey in the USSR. In Report of Proceedings World Conference on Birds of Prey (R.D. Chancellor ed.).   London: ICBP.   Pp. 152-159.
11.   Yamashina Inst. for Ornithology, no date.   Save these Birds. Tokyo: The Kasumikaikan.   In Japanese.
12.   Conder, P. 1977.   Legal status of birds of prey and owls in Europe.   In Report of Proceedings World Conference on Birds of Prey (R.D. Chancellor ed.).   London: ICBP. Pp. 189-193.
13.   Bergman, G. (compiler) 1977.   Birds of prey: the situation in Finland.   In Report of Proceedings World Conference on Birds of Prey (R.D. Chancellor ed.).   London: ICBP.   Pp. 96-102.
14.   Brown, L. & Amadon, D. 1968.   Eagles, Hawks and Falcons of the World.   London & New York: Country Life Books; McGraw-Hill Book Co.

SOUTHERN BALD EAGLE

Haliaeetus leucocephalus leucocephalus (Linnaeus, 1766)

Order FALCONIFORMES   Family ACCIPITRIDAE

STATUS   Endangered.   All populations of this widely distributed eagle have
declined, some seriously, due to pesticide contamination, habitat loss and
disturbance.   Strict protection, especially on wintering grounds and of nesting
habitat, and the banning of most organochlorine pesticides have led to stabilization of status in some areas.

DISTRIBUTION   The United States, south of 40°N latitude, and northern Mexico.
Breeds mostly on seacoasts but also inland in some states, along major waterways
and lakes, in northern California, Baja California (Mexico), Arizona, New Mexico,
Utah, Colorado, Texas, Louisiana, Mississippi, Tennessee (doubtful), Florida,
the Carolinas, Virginia, Maryland, Delaware and New Jersey.   Formerly bred in
California along most of the coast south to the Channel Islands and in some
interior valleys, western Nevada, along the Mississippi River, below its junction
with the Ohio River, and coastal Georgia (1-6).   The dividing line between the
nominate subspecies and H. l. alascanus of Canada and the northern third of the
United States including Alaska, is arbitrarily set at 40°N: in fact populations
are more or less continuous, increasing in size clinally from south-east to north-
west.   During the non-breeding season many northern birds move south into the
range of the southern subspecies and some southern birds move north (7; 16).

POPULATION   A strong downward trend has been apparent since 1950, although
population estimates based on counts of nests have been available only comparatively recently for most parts of the breeding range.   Fewer than 500 breeding
pairs exist, two-thirds of which are in Florida.   In northern California there
were about 20 breeding pairs in 1976-1977, only one of which was south of the 40°N
parallel.   Only 2 breeding pairs are known in Baja California.   In 1976-77
Arizona had about 7 pairs and Texas and Louisiana about 8 pairs each, although it
used to nest more frequently and more extensively in both these states.   Also in
1976-77, Mississippi, New Jersey and possibly Tennessee were each credited with
single breeding pairs.   In Florida the population has declined by at least 50
percent in the last 30 years; it is estimated that 300-325 pairs are left but they
are still slowly decreasing.   In South Carolina 16 pairs bred in 1976-77.   In
the Chesapeake Bay region of Virginia and Maryland, 72 pairs attempted to breed in
1975-76, but only 28 were successful, fledging 39 young.   However, in 1977, 63
fledged from 78 active nests in what was the most successful season for at least
30 years.   Four nests were active in Delaware in 1976-77.   (1; 3; 4; 5; 8; 12;
17; S. Sprunt, W. Clark 1978, pers. comms.).

HABITAT   For breeding, usually the vicinity of water - viz. the rivers, estuaries
lakes or marshes, from which this eagle obtains most of its food.   Nests are
generally high up in tall trees or on cliffs.   Contamination of habitat and prey
by toxic chemicals, such as DDT, dieldrin, heavy metals and PCB's, has had a
markedly adverse effect on breeding success and has sometimes been directly
responsible for mortality (9; 10).   Disturbance at nests and deterioration or
destruction of feeding habitats are other significant factors in the eagle's
decline (11).

CONSERVATION MEASURES TAKEN   Protected in the U.S.A. by the 1973 Endangered
Species Act and the Bald Eagle Act, by numerous state laws and by the U.S.-Mexico
and U.S.-Canada Migratory Bird Treaties, the species is also listed in Appendix 1
of the Convention on International Trade in Endangered Species of Wild Fauna and

Flora. The U.S. Fish and Wildlife Service has appointed several recovery teams.
Management plans for Wildlife Refuges and National Forest Lands restrict access to
nests or protect timber within 0.8 km of nests. An undetermined but substantial
number of active nests are sited on public lands subject to some degree of control
over disturbance or habitat destruction. In Florida, restrictions on land use
have been secured by the Florida Audubon Society on 9308 sq. km of nesting habitat.
Extensive research and conservation programs involving banding, productivity
studies, pesticide contamination, surveillance of individual nests, public
education, law enforcement and purchase of breeding sites and winter roosts are
being undertaken by U.S. federal and state agencies, national, state and conservation organizations, universities and private individuals. Since 1963, the
National Audubon Society has coordinated research and more recently the National
Wildlife Federation has begun a program of land acquisition, communication, and
information exchange and storage. (1-5; 11; W. Clark 1978, pers. comm.).

CONSERVATION MEASURES PROPOSED   Continuation of most existing programs.   These
include protection of the birds and of their nesting, feeding and roosting
habitat, by identifying their presence on public lands, law enforcement, land
acquisition or special arrangements with landowners; further research on population
dynamics and environmental pollution; banning of hunting from aircraft; modification of traps set for predators; and the reintroduction of eagles into suitable
areas. (1-5; 11; W. Clark 1978, pers. comm.).

REMARKS   The northern subspecies has seriously declined over much of its range,
e.g. Maine, eastern Canada, the Great Lakes and the U.S. Pacific North-west, but
it is still widespread and common in Alaska and adjacent western Canada, so is not
yet rated as gravely threatened (2; 3).   Bald Eagles have rarely been reared in
captivity and only two of the 111 (subspecies not determined) present in 61
zoological collections in 1976, were captive-bred (13; 14).

REFERENCES   1. Jordan, J. & Brandt, F. 1977.   Southern Bald Eagle
                   (Haliaeetus leucocephalus leucocephalus Linnaeus).
                   U.S. Fish and Wildlife Service; ms.
              2. Snow, C. 1973.   Habitat management series for endangered
                   species, report No. 5: Southern Bald Eagle Haliaeetus
                   leucocephalus leucocephalus and Northern Bald Eagle
                   Haliaeetus leucocephalus alascanus.   U.S. Bur. Land Mgmt.
                   Technical Note.
              3. Marshall, D.B. & Nickerson, P.R. 1976.   The Bald Eagle:
                   1776-1976. Natl. Parks and Conserv. Mag. July: 14-19.
              4. Peterson, D.W. & Robertson, W.B., Jr. 1976.   The Southern
                   Bald Eagle.   In J.N. Layne (ed.) Inventory of Rare and
                   Endangered Biota of Florida, pp. 735-745.   Florida Audubon
                   Soc. and Florida Defenders of Environment.
              5. Stumpf, W.A. & Creighton, D.E., Jr. 1977.   The Bald Eagle
                   of the Southwest.   U.S. Bureau of Reclamation; ms.
              6. Small, A. 1975.   The Birds of California.   New York:
                   Winchester Press.
              7. American Ornithologists' Union, 1957.   Check-list of North
                   American Birds.   5th ed. Amer. Ornith. Union.
              8. Sprunt, A., IV. 1969.   Population trends of the Bald Eagle
                   in North America.   In J.J. Hickey (ed.) Peregrine Falcon
                   Populations, pp. 347-351.   Madison, Milwaukee, and London:
                   Univ. of Wisconsin Press.
              9. Wiemeyer, S.N., Mulhern, B.M., Ligas, F.H., Hensel, R.J.,
                   Mathisen, J.E., Robards, F.C. & Postupalsky, S. 1972.
                   Residues of organochlorine pesticides, polychlorinated
                   biphenyls, and mercury in Bald Eagle eggs and changes in
                   shell thickness - 1969 and 1970.   Pesticides Monit. Journ.
                   6: 50-55.

10. Belisle, A.A., Reichel, W.L., et al. 1972.   Residues of organochlorine pesticides, polychlorinated biphenyls, and mercury and autopsy data for Bald Eagles, 1969 and 1970. Pestic. Monit. Journ. 6: 133-138.

11. Hamerstrom, F., Ray, T., White, C.M. & Braun, C.E. 1975. Conservation Committee report on status of eagles. Wilson Bull. 87: 140-143.

12. Sprunt, A. IV, Robertson, W.B., Jr., Postupalsky, S., Hensel, R.J., Knoder, C.E. & Ligas, F.J. 1973. Comparative productivity of six Bald Eagle populations. Trans. N. Amer. Wildl. Nat. Resour. Conf. 38: 96-106.

13. Maestrelli, J.R. & Wiemeyer, S.N. 1975.   Breeding Bald Eagles in captivity.   Wilson Bull. 87: 45-53.

14. Olney, P.J.S. (ed.) 1977.   Census of rare animals in captivity, 1976.   Internat. Zoo Yearbook 17: 337-371.

15. American Ornithologists' Union 1975.   Report of the Committee on Conservation, 1974-75. Auk 92(4, Suppl): 1B-16B.

16. Spencer, D.A. 1976.   Wintering of the Migrant Bald Eagle in the lower 48 States.   Washington, D.C.: National Agricultural Chemicals Assoc.

17. Henny, C.J., Anderson, D.W. & Knoder, C.E. 1978. Bald Eagles nesting in Baja California.   Auk 95: 424.

MADAGASCAR SEA EAGLE

Haliaeetus vociferoides Des Murs, 1845

Order FALCONIFORMES   Family ACCIPITRIDAE

STATUS   Endangered.   Although there is little up to date information, it is
clear that this eagle has undergone a widespread and massive decline as a result
of constant persecution, so much so that only a few pairs are now believed to
survive.

DISTRIBUTION   Towards the end of the 19th century this species was to be found in
all coastal regions of Madagascar and presumably also in the vicinity of some of
the larger inland lakes and rivers (6).   It disappeared from the east coast many
years ago but as recently as 1930 was still common along the north-west coast (2).
It is now believed to be largely restricted to a small area in the centre of the
western coastal belt from Antsalova south to Bekopaka and the Manambolo River and
thence westwards to the sea.   Within this area the eagle population is probably
at its largest around Lakes Masama and Bemamba (3; B.-U. Meyburg 1977, pers. comm.).

POPULATION   The species was reported as generally common in the 19th century, but
no more precise estimate is available.   That it occurred widely and in considerable concentrations, until at least fairly recently, is suggested by the collection
in 1930 of eight specimens within a 1 km radius in a bay on the north-west coast
opposite the island of Nosy Bé.   In July 1970, eight of the birds were seen in
the Antsalova, Bekopaka, Manambolo River, sea coast area, but by 1978 no more than
10 pairs were believed to exist and the breeding place of only one pair was known
(1-3; A. Peyrieras, G. Randrianasolo 1978 pers. comm. to B.-U. Meyburg).

HABITAT   Coasts, lakes and rivers.   Persecution by humans, rather than habitat
destruction, has been largely responsible for the decline of the species.

CONSERVATION MEASURES TAKEN   Although all birds of prey were scheduled for total
protection by the 1968 African Convention on the Conservation of Nature and
Natural Resources, which the Malagasy Government signed and ratified, there is as
yet no specific legal protection for this eagle.

CONSERVATION MEASURES PROPOSED   Full legal protection of the eagle and inclusion
within a nature reserve of mangroves, lakes and swamps in the area where it is
presumed to exist in greatest numbers (4).   Effective protection of such a
reserve, including strict prohibition of hunting, would also benefit the vulnerable
Madagascar Teal Anas bernieri.   Aerial surveys of likely breeding sites, followed
by a two year study of the breeding biology, ethology and ecology of the eagle,
have also been recommended (B.-U. Meyburg proposal to IUCN/WWF/ICBP dated 16 March
1979).

REMARKS   One specimen is known to be in captivity, in the Zoological Garden in
Tananarive.   The possibility of obtaining eggs or young from the wild to build up
a captive population, using the methods developed by Meyburg (5), should be
investigated.

REFERENCES   1.   Milon, P., Petter, J.-J. & Randrianasolo, G. 1973.
                    Faune de Madagascar, 35: Oiseaux.   Tananarive and Paris:
                    ORSTOM and CNRS.
              2.   Rand, A.L. 1936.   The distribution and habits of
                    Madagascar birds.   Bull. Amer. Mus. Nat. Hist. 72(5):
                    143-149.

3. Albignac, R. 1970. Rapport ORSTOM sur la mission conjointe Armée Française-ORSTOM dans la région de Bekopaka Antsalova. Tananarive.

4. UICN, 1972. Comptes rendus de la Conférence internationale sur la Conservation de la Nature et de ses Ressources à Madagascar. Tananarive 7-11 Octobre 1970. Morges: IUCN new series Suppl. Papers No. 36.

5. Meyburg, B.-U. 1978. Productivity manipulation in wild eagles. In T.A. Geer (ed.) Bird of Prey Management Techniques, pp. 81-93. Oxford: British Falconers' Club.

6. Milne-Edwards, A & Grandidier A. 1879-1886. Histoire Physique, Naturelle et Politique de Madagascar, Vol. XII, Histoire Naturelle des Oiseaux. Paris.

HARPY EAGLE

Harpia harpyja (Linnaeus, 1758)

Order FALCONIFORMES   Family ACCIPITRIDAE

STATUS   Rare.   Ranges widely in Central and South America but scarce throughout
and relentlessly shot by hunters wherever it occurs.   Forest destruction has
doubtless also caused significant diminution in its range.   A prime indicator
species of largely undisturbed tropical lowland forest.

DISTRIBUTION   South-eastern Mexico through Middle and South America to Paraguay
and northern Argentina.   West of the Andes extends south only to the Chocó
division of Colombia.   Unrecorded in El Salvador.   (1; 2).

POPULATION   Nowhere numerous and particularly sparse in Mexico and Middle
America, where eastern Dari{é}n, Panama, is one of the very few places which may
still have a viable population.   A century ago it was still considered fairly
common in Panama.(3; 4; 11).   Now said to be encountered with greater regularity
than elsewhere in the Guyanan region where most of what is known of its biology
has been recorded (5; 6; 7; 8; 9).   It probably also occurs in relatively stable
numbers in remote parts of eastern Peru, Bolivia and the upper Amazon basin of
Brazil (10; J. O'Neill 1977, pers. comm.).   Its numbers can be assumed to have
decreased wherever regular human access to lowland forest is possible.   Hunters
not only shoot the eagle but also reduce the abundance of its prey species.

HABITAT   Lowland tropical and to a lesser extent subtropical forest, usually
undisturbed but also occasionally after modification (8).   The nest tends to be
built in a tall tree, often a silk cotton, Ceiba pentandra, emerging from the
forest canopy.   Each pair of eagles is said to require a vast but as yet not
precisely determined area of forest.   Except in Amazonia few areas of lowland
forest of sufficient size to sustain viable populations have been set aside or
are planned as national parks or reserves.   This is particularly true of south-
eastern Mexico and Middle America.

CONSERVATION MEASURES TAKEN   Nominally given legal protection in several
countries including Brazil, Surinam and Panama, the eagle is unlikely in practice
to be effectively protected, since locations in which it is apt to be found are
too remote and inaccessible.

CONSERVATION MEASURES PROPOSED   None known.

REMARKS   The Crested Eagle Morphnus guianensis (q.v.) has a similar but rather
more restricted distribution and is even rarer than the Harpy Eagle.   Problems
of human persecution and habitat destruction apply equally to both.   There are
several pairs of Harpy Eagles in captivity (6) but no success has yet been
achieved in breeding them.

REFERENCES   1.   de Schauensee, R.M. 1966.   The Species of Birds of South
                   America and their Distribution.   Narberth, Pa.: Livingston
                   Publishing Co.
              2.   Blake, E.R. 1977.   Manual of Neotropical Birds.   Vol. 1.
                   Chicago and London: University of Chicago Press.
              3.   Ridgely, R. 1976.   Birds of Panama.   Princeton:
                   Princeton University Press.

4. Wetmore, A. 1965.   The birds of the Republic of Panama.
   Part 1.   Tinamidae (Tinamous) to Rhynchopidae (Skimmers).
   Smithsonian Misc. Coll. 150.
5. Fowler, J.M. & Cope, J.B. 1964.   Notes on the Harpy Eagle in
   British Guiana.   Auk 81: 257-273.
6. Gochfeld, M., Kleinbaum, M. & Tudor, G. 1978.   Observations
   on behavior and vocalizations of a pair of wild Harpy Eagles.
   Auk 95: 192-194.
7. Rettig, N. 1977.   In quest of the snatcher.   Audubon 79(6):
   26-49.
8. Haverschmidt, F. 1968.   Birds of Surinam.   Edinburgh and
   London: Oliver and Boyd.
9. Snyder, D.E. 1966.   The Birds of Guyana.   Salem: Peabody
   Museum.
10. Sick, H. 1972.   A ameaça da avifauna brasileira.   In
    Espécies da Fauna Brasileira Ameaçadas de Extinção, pp. 99-153.
    Rio de Janeiro: Academia Brasileira de Ciências.
11. Ridgely, R. undated.   Preliminary list of endangered bird species
    in the Republic of Panama.   Report to ICBP.   Mimeo, 8 pages.

GREY-BACKED HAWK

Leucopternis occidentalis Salvin, 1876

Order FALCONIFORMES   Family ACCIPITRIDAE

STATUS   Indeterminate.   Believed to have declined seriously in Ecuador as the
result of forest destruction.

DISTRIBUTION   Endemic to western Ecuador from Pichincha province south to Rio
Tumbes on the Peruvian border (1).   Agricultural development in this zone has
been rapid and widespread during the last two decades.   The hawk is now most
often seen in the southern part of its range, for instance in the forested hills
inland from Naranjal, south-east of Guayaquil and west of Cuenca.

POPULATION   Unknown, although it is certain that a great decline has taken place.
One was seen recently in a small reserve of about 200 ha near Rio Palenque
(R. Ridgely 1977, pers. comm.).   Some 8 or 9 were observed over a period of four
days in the Parque Nacional Puerto Lopez y Machalilla in Manabi Province, on the
coast south-west of Quito, in 1978 (R. Ridgely 1978, pers. comm.).

HABITAT   Tropical and subtropical forest, the extent of which within the range
of this species has been seriously reduced in recent years.

CONSERVATION MEASURES TAKEN   As noted above the hawk occurs in a 200 ha reserve
at Rio Palenque and also in the Puerto Lopez y Machalilla National Park (35,000 ha,
only a small portion of which is, however, suitable habitat).

CONSERVATION MEASURES PROPOSED   None known.

REMARKS   The closely related Leucopternis polionota from south-eastern Brazil,
northern Argentina and eastern Paraguay is also reduced in abundance and believed
to be at risk (see relevant data sheet).   These two species, together with
L. albicollis, a more widespread species of Middle and northern South America, are
considered to comprise a superspecies (1).

REFERENCES   1.   de Schauensee, R.M. 1966.   The Species of Birds of South
                     America and their Distribution.   Narberth, Pa.: Livingston
                     Publishing Co.

MANTLED HAWK

Leucopternis polionota (Kaup, 1847)

Order FALCONIFORMES   Family ACCIPITRIDAE

STATUS   Indeterminate.   The status of this hawk of the high forest of south-
eastern South America has deteriorated as the result of widespread deforestation.

DISTRIBUTION   Eastern Brazil from Alagoas and Bahia south to Santa Catarina,
eastern Paraguay, and Misiones, Argentina (1; 2).   There is no up to date
information on the distribution of this species, but it was seen in 1951 and 1953
in the forested mountains near Rio de Janeiro (3) and again recorded in 1964,
1967, and 1971 near Teresopolis, 60 km north of Rio de Janeiro (H. Sick 1977,
pers. comm.).   Immense areas within the range of this species have been
deforested and are no longer occupied by it (4).

POPULATION   Unknown, but a decline is certain, especially in Brazil.   Although
this hawk soars freely and is conspicuous, it could not be found during recent
searches in eastern Paraguay (R. Ridgely 1978, pers. comm.).

HABITAT   Primary forest.   The coastal forests of eastern Brazil have suffered
serious destruction as to a similar extent have the Araucaria-dominated forests
of southern Brazil and adjacent parts of Argentina (4).

CONSERVATION MEASURES TAKEN   This hawk is seen regularly in two protected areas:
Itatiaia National Park, Rio de Janeiro state (150 km NW of the city) and Iguazu
National Park, Misiones, Argentina (R. Ridgely 1978, pers. comm.).   Legally
protected in Brazil.

CONSERVATION MEASURES PROPOSED   None known.

REMARKS   This species is closely related to L. occidentalis of western Ecuador,
whose status is also in question (see relevant data sheet).   The two species,
together with L. albicollis, a more widespread species of Middle and northern
South America, are considered to form a superspecies (1; 2).   Three mantled
hawks are in captivity in São Paulo and Santa Catarina, Brazil (H. Sick 1977,
pers. comm.).

REFERENCES   1.   de Schauensee, R.M. 1966.   The Species of Birds of South
                  America and their Distribution.   Narberth, Pa.: Livingston
                  Publishing Co.
             2.   Brown, L. & Amadon, D. 1968.   Eagles, Hawks and Falcons of the
                  World.   London & New York: Country Life; McGraw-Hill.
             3.   Mitchell, M.H. 1957.   Observations on Birds of South-
                  eastern Brazil.   Toronto: University of Toronto Press.
             4.   Sick, H. 1972.   A ameaça da avifauna brasileira.
                  In Espécies da Fauna Brasileira Ameaçada de Extinção,
                  pp. 99-153.   Rio de Janeiro: Academia Brasileira de
                  Ciências.

CRESTED EAGLE

Morphnus guianensis (Daudin, 1800)

Order FALCONIFORMES   Family ACCIPITRIDAE

STATUS   Rare.   Widely distributed in lowland Central America and South America,
but everywhere scarce.   Liable like other large eagles to be shot whenever it
occurs in areas accessible to hunters.   Forest destruction has reduced its
habitat in parts of its range.   The species is an excellent indicator of the
presence of still largely undisturbed lowland tropical forest.

DISTRIBUTION   Recorded from Honduras south through Central America and South
America to northern Paraguay and Misiones, Argentina (1).   Not known to have
been extirpated in any significant portion of its extensive range, but observed
so rarely that its total disappearance might easily go unnoticed for decades.

POPULATION   Certainly not large in spite of the immense area from which the
species has been reported.   There are only two records from Honduras, most
recently in 1902 (2).   It is extremely rare in Nicaragua, and there is but one
record, in 1904, from Costa Rica (3).   It is rare in Panama, but there are a
number of records from the Caribbean and Pacific slopes (4; 5) and also quite a
number of records from all but the south-western part of Colombia (6).   It may
be more common in Panama and north-western South America than elsewhere in its
range (R. Ridgely 1978, pers. comm.).   In Venezuela there have been only two
records (7), it is rare in Guyana (8) and occasional in Surinam.   Rated as
endangered in Brazil, it has been recorded only in the states of Amazonas, Bahia
and São Paulo (10; 11).   There are no clues as to its population size elsewhere
in South America.

HABITAT   Dense lowland jungle in humid tropical areas, particularly in riverine
situations.   It frequently perches or nests in tall trees protruding from the
forest canopy (12).   Forest destruction in many parts of this eagle's range has
been extensive, but how far this has affected its distribution has not been
precisely determined, although in some areas, such as Darién, the Guianas and the
upper Amazon basin, the amount of lowland forest still seems ample for its
requirements.

CONSERVATION MEASURES TAKEN   Legal protection is of little avail in the forests
where this eagle is likely to be found, since it appears to be a prize which few
hunters can be persuaded to ignore.

CONSERVATION MEASURES PROPOSED   None known.

REMARKS   The distribution and conservation problems of the Crested Eagle are
nearly identical to those of the Harpy Eagle Harpia harpyja (q.v.).

REFERENCES   1.   de Schauensee, R.M. 1966.   The Species of Birds of South
                    America and their Distribution.   Narberth, Pa.: Livingston
                    Publishing Co.
               2.   Monroe, B.L., Jr. 1968.   A distributional survey of the
                    birds of Honduras.   Amer. Ornith. Union Ornith. Monog. 7.
               3.   Slud, P. 1964.   The birds of Costa Rica.   Bull. Amer.
                    Mus. Nat. Hist. 128.
               4.   Ridgely, R. 1976.   A Guide to the Birds of Panama.
                    Princeton, N.J.: Princeton University Press.

5. Wetmore, A. 1965. The Birds of the Republic of Panama.
   Part 1. Tinamidae (Tinamous) to Rhynchopidae (Skimmers).
   Smithsonian Misc. Coll. 150.
6. de Schauensee, R.M. 1949. The birds of the Republic of
   Colombia. Part II. Caldasia 5: 381-644.
7. Phelps, W.H. & Phelps, W.H., Jr. 1958. Lista de aves
   de Venezuela con su distribución. Tome II. Bol. Soc.
   Venez. Cienc. Nat. 19(90).
8. Snyder, D.E. 1966. The Birds of Guyana. Salem: Peabody
   Museum.
9. Haverschmidt, F. 1968. Birds of Surinam. Edinburgh
   and London: Oliver and Boyd.
10. Sick, H. 1972. A ameaça da avifauna brasileira. In
   Espécies da Fauna Brasileira Ameaçadas de Extinção, pp. 99-153.
   Rio de Janeiro: Academia Brasileira de Ciências.
11. Pinto, O.M. de O. 1938. Catalogo das Aves do Brasil.
   1 Parte. Revista Mus. Paulista 22.
12. Brown, L. & Amadon, D. 1968. Eagles, Hawks and Falcons
   of the World. London & New York: Country Life; McGraw-Hill.

MONKEY-EATING EAGLE

Pithecophaga jefferyi Ogilvie-Grant, 1897

Order FALCONIFORMES   Family ACCIPITRIDAE

STATUS   Endangered.   Restricted in distribution to primary forest on three
islands in the Philippines, where its population is low and widely dispersed.   It
is frequently shot or captured alive and its range decreases annually because of
the clearing of forests.

DISTRIBUTION   Formerly known from Samar, Luzon, Leyte, Mindanao, a small island
in the Surigao Straits north of Mindanao, and possibly from Negros (1; 2; 3; 4).
It has not been seen on Samar since 1934 and is believed to be extinct there (5).
On Luzon it occurred in the Sierra Madre Range in Cagayan, Isabella, Nueva Vizcaya
and Quezon provinces in 1960, and was most recently seen in 1963 (6).   On Leyte it
was recently rediscovered in Southern Leyte province.   On Mindanao it is still
widespread, having been reported in 15 of the 17 provinces in the last decade,
although now absent from much of the lowlands formerly covered by dipterocarp
forest (4).

POPULATION   Continues on a gradual decline.   An estimate of 1,200 birds was made
for Mindanao in 1910, on the basis of the extent of forest habitat existing at that
time (65 per cent of the island) and assuming a home range of 100 sq. km per pair
(2).   Also on Mindanao, where the bulk of the population still occurs, estimates
made between 1968 and 1970 varied from 36 to 60 only (1; 2; 3).   A careful
reappraisal of all data available up to 1973, yielded an estimate of 309 to 580
birds, based on three different types of calculations; the lower figure is believed
more accurate.   The home range was shown to be as small as 12 to 25 sq. km in some
cases.   Shooting and trapping are responsible for the removal of 5 to 10 per cent
of the population annually, but this mortality is of much less significance than is
habitat destruction.   Eight to ten were believed to survive on Leyte in 1970.   The
population on Luzon is not known but believed quite small.

HABITAT   Primary evergreen forest between sea level and 2,000m elevation, also
some secondary forest.   In 1910, 65 per cent of Mindanao was forested; in 1973
only 30 per cent (29,000 sq. km) remained suitable forest habitat (4).   About
650 sq. km of forest are cleared annually in the island (7).

CONSERVATION MEASURES TAKEN   The species is fully protected; to hunt, kill or
possess it is illegal and capture for zoos is strictly controlled.   In spite of
this, shooting of the eagles for stuffing as private trophies is a serious source
of mortality.   Numbers are also captured, often illegally, for zoos and private
collections (1; 2; 3).

CONSERVATION MEASURES PROPOSED   Selective logging and reforestation, utilizing
native tree species, have been recommended as a measure to prevent total destruction
of the eagle's habitat.   Preserves of at least 200 sq. km in extent should be
established in mountain ranges where logging and agriculture are not feasible.
Logging in National Parks should be prohibited.   Laws regulating capture and
possession of this species should be enforced.   The eagle has been proposed as the
national bird of the Philippines.   It has been suggested that conservation
education is one of the most important long-term measures necessary for its
conservation (1; 2; 4).

<u>REMARKS</u>   There were 6 captive monkey-eating eagles in 4 collections outside the
Philippines in 1976.   Exchanges to promote captive breeding were made between the
New York, Philadelphia and Los Angeles Zoos in 1973 and 1975, without success
(W.G. Conway 1976, pers. comm.).   There are at least another 18 in captivity in
the Philippines, including 8 held by the Philippine Parks and Wildlife Office for
release back to the wild (8).   Although this species has so far never bred in
captivity, recently developed housing methods and techniques, including artificial
insemination, could be applied to the birds presently held and might produce
satisfactory results.   Under present arrangements there is little likelihood that
the captive birds in the Philippines will breed (R. Fyfe 1975, pers. comm.).
Captive birds have laid a total of 6 eggs (9).

<u>REFERENCES</u>   1.   Rabor, D.S. 1968.   The present status of the Monkey-eating
                            Eagle, <u>Pithecophaga</u> <u>jefferyi</u> Ogilvie-Grant, of the Philippines.
                            In <u>Conservation in Tropical South East Asia</u>, pp. 312-314.
                            Morges:IUCN Publ. N.S. 10.
                     2.   Gonzales, R.B. 1971.   Report on the 1969 status of the Monkey-
                            eating Eagle on Mindanao Island, Philippines.   <u>Bull. ICBP</u> 11:
                            154-168.
                     3.   Alvarez, J.B., Jr. 1970.   A report on the 1969 status of the
                            Monkey-eating Eagle of the Philippines.   In <u>Problems of</u>
                            <u>Threatened Species: Proceedings of 11th Technical Meeting of</u>
                            <u>IUCN, New Delhi</u>, Vol. 2, pp. 68-73.   Morges:IUCN Publ. N.S. 18.
                     4.   Kennedy, R.S. undated.   Notes on the biology and population
                            status of the Monkey-eating Eagle in the Philippines.   Unpub-
                            lished ms.
                     5.   Rabor, D.S. 1971   The present status of conservation of the
                            Monkey-eating Eagle of the Philippines.   <u>Philippine Geogr.</u>
                            <u>Journal</u> 15: 90-103.
                     6.   Gonzales, R.B. 1968.   A study of the breeding biology and
                            ecology of the Monkey-eating Eagle.   <u>Silliman Univ. Journal</u>
                            15: 461-491.
                     7.   Basan, A.C. 1975.   Winged lightning.   <u>Internat. Wildl</u>. 6(1):
                            19.
                     8.   Kennedy, R.S. in prep.   Measurements of Monkey-eating Eagles
                            with notes on individuals in captivity.
                     9.   Wylie, S.R. 1974.   Notes on egg-laying in the Monkey-eating
                            Eagle.   <u>Auk</u> 91: 191.

FLORIDA EVERGLADE KITE

Rostrhamus sociabilis plumbeus Ridgeway, 1874

Order FALCONIFORMES   Family ACCIPITRIDAE

STATUS   Rare.   The population of this kite in the Florida peninsula is very
seriously reduced by habitat alteration but has now been stable since 1973.   It
is no longer considered subspecifically distinct from the population in Cuba and
the Isle of Pines, the status of which is not adequately known.

DISTRIBUTION   Formerly extended throughout the widespread freshwater marshes of
the Florida peninsula, United States, but by 1937 had been substantially reduced
(1).   In recent times this kite has been found mainly in the headwaters of the
St. John's River (the St. John's River marshes were a former stronghold), the
south-western side of Lake Okeechobee, parts of Everglades National Park and
Loxahatchee National Wildlife Refuge, and in Broward, Dade and Palm Beach
counties; in the past few years most of the successful nests have been near Lake
Okeechobee (2; 3).   Occurs on Cuba and the Isle of Pines wherever suitable
marshlands are found (10).

POPULATION   Common in Florida at least until 1909, this kite had decreased
alarmingly by 1937 (1).   In 1950 it was estimated that there were no more than
100 and probably fewer than 60 (4) and in 1956 a partial survey suggested that
20 or less remained (5).   However, at least 20 were known to be still surviving
in 1966 (2) and by 1973 the population was back to about 100 and remained
constant at that level to 1976 (3).   In 1956 it was considered locally common
in western Cuba though rather rare and local on the Isle of Pines (10).   In 1975
it was still common in certain marshes such as Laguna del Tesoro and the Zapata
Swamp (11).

HABITAT   Freshwater marshes with shallow open water vegetated by saw grass
sedge Cladium jamaicensis and spike-rush Eleocharis sp., often interspersed with
tree or shrub islands.   Drying of marshes, which has happened occasionally,
is especially detrimental to populations of the apple snail Pomacea paludosa,
on which the kite almost entirely subsists (2; 3; 6).   Nest contents are
commonly predated by mammals, snakes and some birds.   Modification of the
habitat for agricultural purposes (e.g. citrus orchards and pasture), for flood
control or in the urbanization process, is largely responsible for the kite's
decline.   For example, by 1967 a 56 percent decrease in the extent of the
Everglades to less than 4000 sq. km, had been noted.   Invasion of open water
by water hyacinth Eichhornia crassipes and other aggressive plants has also
reduced the feeding grounds available to the kite (2).

CONSERVATION MEASURES TAKEN   The kite is protected from killing, capture or
harassment by the U.S. Endangered Species Act of 1973.   The U.S. Fish and
Wildlife Service has appointed a recovery team for the Florida population.
Portions of its range lie within Everglades National Park, Loxahatchee National
Wildlife Refuge and a private sanctuary of the National Audubon Society on the
margin of Lake Okeechobee.   Kites have accepted artificial nesting platforms
which reduce the chance of loss of nests from storms and some predators (7).
Habitat management for the kite has been undertaken at Loxahatchee Refuge (8).

CONSERVATION MEASURES PROPOSED   Additional habitat acquisition, protection from
hunters in the hunting season, including the establishment of 330m-radius no
entry zones around nests, and maintenance of adequate surface water levels (3).
An intensive study of the kite's life history and ecology was due to begin in
1978.

<u>REMARKS</u>   In 1975 Amadon showed that the subspecies described from Cuba and the
Isle of Pines, <u>R</u>. <u>s</u>. <u>levis</u>, was inseparable taxonomically from <u>R</u>. <u>s</u>. <u>plumbeus</u>
(9).   There are two other subspecies in Mexico and in Central and South America
respectively: they are not at risk, although there is recent evidence of heavy
mortality of these kites in Surinam following pesticide treatment of rice fields
(12).

<u>REFERENCES</u>   1.   Bent, A.C. 1937.   Life histories of North American birds
of prey.   Part 1.   <u>U.S. Nat. Mus. Bull.</u> 167.
2.   Stieglitz, W.O. & Thompson, R.L. 1967.   Status and life
history of the Everglade Kite in the United States.
U.S. Fish and Wildlife Service <u>Spec. Sci. Rept. Wildl.</u> 109.
3.   Sykes, P.W., Jr. 1976.   The Everglade Kite.   In
J.N. Layne (ed.) <u>Inventory of Rare and Endangered Biota</u>
<u>of Florida</u>, pp. 675-676.   Florida Audubon Society and
Florida Defenders of Environment.
4.   Sprunt, A., Jr. 1950.   Vanishing wings over the Everglades.
<u>Audubon Mag.</u> 52(6):   380-386.
5.   Wachenfeld, A. 1956.   <u>Linnaean Newsletter</u> 10(3).
6.   Snyder, N.F.R. & Snyder, H.R. 1969.   A comparative
study of mollusk predation by Limpkins, Everglade Kites,
and Boat-tailed Grackles.   <u>Living Bird</u> 8:   177-223.
7.   Sykes, P.W., Jr. & Chandler, R. 1974.   Use of artificial
nest structures by Everglade Kites.   <u>Wilson Bull.</u> 86:
282-284.
8.   Martin, T.W. & Doebel, J.H. 1973.   Management techniques
for the Everglade Kite, preliminary report.   <u>Proc.</u>
<u>Southeast Assoc. Game Fish Comm. Ann. Conf.</u> 27:   225-236.
9.   Amadon, D. 1975.   Variation in the Everglade Kite.
<u>Auk</u> 92:   380-382.
10.   Bond, J. 1956.   <u>Check-list of Birds of the West Indies</u>.
Philadelphia: Academy of Natural Sciences.
11.   Garrido, O.H. & Garcia, F.M. 1975.   <u>Catalogo de las</u>
<u>Aves de Cuba</u>.   Havana: Academia de Ciencias de Cuba.
12.   Vermeer, K., Risebrough, R.W., Spaans, A.L. & Reynolds, L.M.
1974.   Pesticide effects on fishes and birds in rice fields
of Surinam, South America.   <u>Environ. Pollut.</u> 7:   217-236.

SEYCHELLES KESTREL

Falco araea (Oberholser, 1917)

Order FALCONIFORMES   Family FALCONIDAE

STATUS   Rare.   This species has declined in the past, but now appears to have a
small but stable population in the Seychelles.

DISTRIBUTION   Occurred on most of the islands of the Seychelles as recently as
1939 (1), yet by 1965 was believed to be restricted to Mahé (2).   Subsequently,
it has been shown as still occurring on Mahé, Silhouette and Praslin.   On Mahé
(137 sq. km), the largest of the Seychelles, it is found throughout the island.
It is equally widely distributed on the small 21 sq. km Silhouette (A.W. Diamond,
1975, pers. comm.) but is very restricted on Praslin (67 sq. km) (3).

POPULATION   The kestrel population on Mahé was given as possibly less than 30
birds in 1965 (2), but a subsequent study in 1972 and 1973 revealed a minimum of
49 pairs and a likely total population of upwards of 100 pairs in the light of the
wide distribution of the species and its small home range (82.8 ha per pair).   At
least 10 pairs occupied Silhouette, but only one or two birds were found on Praslin
between 1970 and 1973 (3).

HABITAT   The species occurs both in open country and in dense forest, the former
being probably a secondary adaptation, having regard to the fact that the extent of
forest in the Seychelles was much greater before the islands were settled by man in
the eighteenth century.   Competition for nest sites with introduced Barn Owls
Tyto alba may have contributed to the decline of the kestrel on some islands, while
human disturbance has doubtless also had an adverse effect on this confiding species
(3; 4).

CONSERVATION MEASURES TAKEN   Legally protected from capture or shooting.   This
species and all other falcons are listed in Appendix 2 of the 1973 Convention on
International Trade in Endangered Species of Wild Fauna and Flora.   A program of
conservation education in the Seychelles has brought about a welcome decrease of
shooting and disturbance of the kestrel (S.A. Temple 1974, pers. comm.).

CONSERVATION MEASURES PROPOSED   Control of Barn Owls should, if vigorously pursued,
promote the welfare of this and several other native bird species (4; 5).

REFERENCES   1.   Vesey-Fitzgerald, D. 1940.   The birds of the Seychelles, 1.
                   Ibis (14)4:   480-489.
              2.   Gaymer, R., Blackman, R.A.A., Dawson, P.G., Penny, M. & Penny,
                   C.M. 1969.   The endemic birds of Seychelles.   Ibis 111:
                   157-176.
              3.   Feare, C.J., Temple, S.A. & Procter, J. 1974.   The status,
                   distribution and diet of the Seychelles Kestrel Falco araea.
                   Ibis 116:   548-551.
              4.   Penny, M. 1968.   Endemic birds of the Seychelles.   Oryx 9:
                   267-275.
              5.   Procter, J. 1970.   Conservation in the Seychelles: Report of
                   the Conservation Advisor, 1970.   Seychelles Government Printer.

KLEINSCHMIDT'S FALCON

Falco kreyenborgi Kleinschmidt, 1929

Order FALCONIFORMES   Family FALCONIDAE

STATUS   Indeterminate. Almost nothing is known about this very rare falcon
of southernmost South America.

DISTRIBUTION   Recorded only from a rocky islet off the southern, Chilean, coast
of Tierra del Fuego, from the vicinity of Viamonte on the east coast of Tierra
del Fuego and from the Cerro Piltriquitron in the extreme south-west corner of
Rio Negro province, Argentina. The bird collected at this last locality, over
1200 km to the north of the others, could have been a winter migrant from the
south (1; 2).

POPULATION   Unknown. A total of five specimens is known, the most recent
taken in 1961 (1). There are no other records.

HABITAT   Presumably windswept rocky subantarctic coastlines. The winter
specimen, an immature male collected in August, came from the eastern foothills
of the southern Andes.

CONSERVATION MEASURES TAKEN   Listed in Appendix 2 of the Convention on
International Trade in Endangered Species of Wild Fauna and Flora.

CONSERVATION MEASURES PROPOSED   None known.

REMARKS   Some doubt exists as to the taxonomic status of this little known
bird. It is generally agreed, in the absence of adequate material on which a
more comprehensive review could be based, that it is a valid species, most
closely related to the Peregrine Falco peregrinus (1).

REFERENCES   1. Stresemann, E. & Amadon, D. 1963. What is Falco
                  kreyenborgi Kleinschmidt? Ibis 105: 400-402.
              2. Brown, L. & Amadon, D. 1968. Eagles, Hawks and Falcons
                  of the World,Vol. 2. London & New York: Country Life Books;
                  McGraw Hill Book Co.

ALDABRA KESTREL

Falco newtoni aldabranus Grote, 1928

Order FALCONIFORMES   Family FALCONIDAE

STATUS   Rare.   This kestrel occurs only on the atoll of Aldabra, western Indian
Ocean.   Its population is very low, although there is no indication of a decline.
In view of the decision to construct a military air base on Diego Garcia rather
than Aldabra, there is presently no threat to this species other than those inherent
in small populations.

DISTRIBUTION   Known only from Aldabra, where it has been encountered most
frequently on South and West islands, and considerably less so on Polymnie and
Middle islands (1).

POPULATION   Not very common in 1892 (2), by 1964 less than 100 were estimated to
occur throughout the atoll (3) and it has since been suggested there may in fact be
considerably fewer (1).   However, in 1977 the population remained at about 100,
which may be as many as the habitat can support (R. Prys-Jones 1977, pers. comm.).

HABITAT   Open vegetation and areas of human habitation.   Benson and Penny
suggest this species is a recent colonizer of Aldabra, having arrived only after
man and being dependent for nest sites on buildings, introduced palms or old nests
of Pied Crows Corvus albus, which themselves probably did not arrive until man's
activities became apparent on the atoll (1).

CONSERVATION MEASURES TAKEN   Legally protected from killing or capture.   The
Royal Society maintains a research station on Aldabra.   This species and all other
falcons are listed in Appendix 2 of the 1973 Convention on International Trade in
Endangered Species of Wild Fauna and Flora.   Aldabra is a nature reserve.

CONSERVATION MEASURES PROPOSED   The provision of nest-boxes might augment the
population, particularly where a lack of natural nest sites may be a limiting
factor (Prys-Jones, pers. comm.).

REMARKS   Benson and Penny demonstrate considerable overlap in wing measurements
between aldabranus and nominate F. n. newtoni of Madagascar, and for that reason
suggest that aldabranus should no longer receive formal taxonomic recognition (1).
However, specimens from Aldabra have measurements consistently on the lower side of
the average for Madagascar specimens, so there is at least an indication of
incipient differentiation.   This, coupled with the population's obviously
precarious position in view of its rarity, seems to justify the retention of the
form in the Red Data Book.

REFERENCES   1.   Benson, C.W. & Penny, M.J. 1971.   The land birds of Aldabra.
                      Phil. Trans. Roy. Soc. London B260:   417-527.
               2.   Ridgway, R. 1895.   On birds collected by Doctor W.L. Abbott
                      on the Seychelles, Amirantes, Gloriosa, Assumption, Aldabra and
                      adjacent islands, with notes on habits, etc., by the collector.
                      Proc. U.S. Nat. Mus. 18:   509-546.
               3.   Gaymer, R. 1967.   Observations on the birds of Aldabra in 1964
                      and 1965.   Atoll Research Bull. 118:   113-125.

PEREGRINE FALCON

Falco peregrinus Tunstall, 1771

Order FALCONIFORMES   Family FALCONIDAE

STATUS   Vulnerable. Declining or already rare over large portions of its North
American and European range; extirpated from eastern U.S.A. and Canada south of the
boreal forests. Continuing to decline in North American arctic. There is a
slight recovery in the British Isles. Holding up well in Aleutian Islands and
perhaps Greenland, although egg shell thinning has been detected in these populations, as it has from NW Europe and Siberia to Africa and south-eastern Australia,
indeed almost everywhere except for isolated populations in central and west
Australia and in Indonesia. Moderate levels of chlorinated hydrocarbons have been
found in Chilean populations. The status of Peregrines in Africa and in South
East Asia and Indonesia is poorly known. Everywhere the major threat appears to
be contamination from chlorinated hydrocarbons; killing and capture have played a
contributory role in some areas, particularly when populations were already small.
Habitat loss has also been significant.(1-9).

DISTRIBUTION   Nearly cosmopolitan except for New Zealand, Antarctica, most of
Micronesia and Polynesia, northern South America and Central America. Breeds as
far north as 76°N and as far south as 55°S. Some northern hemisphere populations
migrate to temperate equatorial or southern hemisphere regions, most other
populations are resident (10).

POPULATION   There are no reliable estimates for numbers on a worldwide basis,
although populations of certain regions are well known, e.g. Aleutian Islands
c. 400 pairs (stable), boreal Canada and U.S. c. 50 pairs (formerly 900 pairs,
still declining), Alaskan and Canadian tundra c. 250 pairs (formerly c. 2200),
Great Britain 420 pairs (up from c. 300 pairs in 1963 but still well below the
pre-1950s), Europe excluding Iberia and Russia c. 1000 pairs (declining), Spain
c. 2000 pairs (stable). Extirpated from Belgium, Denmark, Hungary and eastern U.S.
In parts of Europe the decline has been up to 95 percent of the population level of
the 1940s, due in most cases to pesticides, sometimes exacerbated by human
predation. One of two populations studied on Siberian breeding grounds declined
seriously in the last decade, the other remained stable (V. Flint 1978, pers.comm.).
Essentially nothing is known of the populations of South America, Africa,
Madagascar, Indonesia, Malaysia and New Guinea or of Australia, excluding Victoria
and parts of South Australia, New South Wales and Tasmania. (1-5; 8).

HABITAT   Breeds in nearly all habitats from tundra to tropical rainforest where
suitable ledges for nests are available or, in a few areas and very rarely
elsewhere, suitable trees. As a vagrant has even occurred in Hawaii. Some
populations (e.g. the Spanish) are well adjusted to the presence of man or habitat
modification by him. Disturbance or destruction of nest sites has elsewhere been
a serious problem, but not as significant as contamination of food by chlorinated
hydrocarbons and other pollutants. Persistent chlorinated hydrocarbons such as
DDT are now banned or stringently controlled in some areas (U.S., Canada, several
European countries) but not in others (Central and South America, Africa, Australia).

CONSERVATION MEASURES TAKEN   Legally protected in most countries of the northern
hemisphere and many southern hemisphere ones, the peregrine is also listed in
Appendix 1 of the 1973 Convention on International Trade in Endangered Species of
Wild Fauna and Flora. In the U.S. and Canada captive breeding and reintroduction
to its former range are now underway. Protection of individual eyries, while
expensive, has been given in areas where eyasses are often taken for falconry.

CONSERVATION MEASURES PROPOSED   Full legal protection in all countries.
Effective reduction and strict control of organochlorine pesticides throughout
the Peregrine's range.   Protection of nesting and feeding habitats.   Surveys
to determine the status of this falcon in parts of its range where it is as yet
undetermined. (1-4).

REMARKS   The Peregrine has proved to be resistant to persecution and tolerant
of changes in its habitat, and may survive in acceptable numbers if organochlorines and other such environmental poisons can be controlled on an
international basis.   About 18 subspecies are currently recognized, of which
F. p. anatum and F. p. tundrius of North America are endangered, F. p. fruitii
of the Volcano Islands and F. p. madens of the Cape Verde Islands are rare,
several populations, notably F. p. peregrinus in Europe, are vulnerable, while
the status of several such as F. p. babylonius and F. p. pelegrinoides of the
Middle East and Central Asia, which are in particular demand for falconry, is
unknown.   Dr. C.M. White kindly contributed to the preparation of this sheet.

REFERENCES   1.   Fyfe, R.W., Temple, S.A. & Cade, T.J. 1976.   The 1975
                    North American Peregrine Falcon survey.   Canad. Field-Nat.
                    90: 228-273.
              2.   Several papers in Chancellor, R.D. (ed.) 1977.   World
                    Conference on Birds of Prey, Vienna, 1975, Report of
                    Proceedings.   London: ICBP.
              3.   Parslow, J.L.F. 1974.   Threatened birds.   Strasbourg;
                    Council of Europe.
              4.   Bijleveld, M. 1974.   Birds of Prey in Europe.   London
                    and Basingstoke: Macmillan Press.
              5.   White, C.M. & Jones, S.G. 1976.   Peregrine Falcon study
                    in Victoria.   Victoria, Australia, Fisheries and Wildlife
                    Division, unpubl. report.
              6.   Walker, W., II, Risebrough, R.W., Mendola, J.T. & Bowes, G.W.
                    1973.   South American studies of the Peregrine: an
                    indicator species for persistent pollutants.   Antarctic
                    Journ. U.S. 8: 29-31.
              7.   Walker, W., II, Mattox, W.G. & Risebrough, R.W. 1973.
                    Pollutant and shell thickness determinations of Peregrine
                    eggs from West Greenland.   Arctic 26: 256-258.
              8.   Hickey, J.J. 1969.   Peregrine Falcon Populations: their
                    Biology and Decline.   Madison, Milwaukee, and London:
                    University of Wisconsin Press.
              9.   Peakall, D.B. & Kiff, L.F. 1979.   Eggshell thinning and
                    DDE residue levels among Peregrine Falcons Falco peregrinus:
                    a global perspective.   Ibis 121(2): 200-204.
             10.   Brown, L. & Amadon, D. 1968.   Eagles, Hawks and Falcons
                    of the World.   London & New York: Country Life Books;
                    McGraw Hill Book Co.

AMERICAN PEREGRINE FALCON

Falco peregrinus anatum Bonaparte, 1838

Order FALCONIFORMES   Family FALCONIDAE

STATUS   Endangered.   Status well known for U.S., boreal Canada and boreal
Alaska, but not for Mexico.   Extinct in eastern U.S. and eastern boreal Canada.
About 50 pairs remain in western U.S. and western boreal Canada.   Perhaps 100-
150 pairs in boreal Alaska.   No estimates for Mexico.   Contamination of birds
and eggs by persistent pesticides and killing and capture, whether on breeding
or wintering grounds or on passage, have been the main causes of decline.

DISTRIBUTION   Boreal forest, extending from south of the tree line to about
20°N, in Alaska, Canada, the entire U.S. and Mexico, except for the outermost
Pacific coastlands of British Columbia and Alaska, which are occupied by F. p.
pealei.

POPULATION   Within boreal Alaska less than 100 pairs remain of an estimated
200-250 that may have bred prior to 1950.   About 400-500 pairs bred in eastern
U.S. and boreal Canada in the 1940s.   Today there are none in the eastern U.S.
(excepting the captive-bred birds now being released).   In western boreal Canada
and U.S. about 50 pairs remain of the 400 estimated to have bred formerly.   The
population of west Texas and central Mexico may still exceed 100 pairs, while in
the Gulf of California the estimate is about 35-50.   The west coast of Baja
California population, once perhaps 25 pairs, is now believed to be extinct.
In the western U.S. states, Washington, Oregon, Montana and Idaho, there may be
up to 13 occupied nest sites compared with the former 150.   In the Rocky
Mountains 6 of the 27 former sites were occupied in 1975, and in Utah and
eastern Nevada only 1 out of 42.   Fifteen pairs remain in New Mexico, where the
decline is perhaps less serious.   In Arizona, 35 historical sites are known but
only six of the 20 visited in 1975 were occupied.   Only 8-9 pairs remain of a
pre-1940s population of about 100 pairs in California (1; 8; 10; W.G. Hunt 1977,
pers. comm.).

HABITAT   In Alaska, river valleys of the boreal forest region, up to altitudes
of about 800 m.   In western Canada, varying between boreal forest, open
deciduous forest and arid open country.   In the U.S., distinctly different -
closed to semi-closed deciduous forest in the east and arid to semi-alpine in the
west, though usually overlooking a water source.   However, many eyries are in
extremely arid desert.   Lastly, in Mexico, this Peregrine seems to keep largely
to the main cordilleras.

CONSERVATION MEASURES TAKEN   Full protection has been given under the Mexican-
U.S. and Canadian-U.S. migratory bird treaties, the U.S. Endangered Species Act
of 1973, and by laws in several states.   The species is also listed in Appendix
1 of the 1973 Convention on International Trade in Endangered Species of Wild
Fauna and Flora.   The U.S. Fish and Wildlife Service has constituted regional
recovery teams for the Peregrine, to prepare and implement plans for its
rehabilitation (2).   Captive-bred individuals are being released in three regions
(6; 7).   Persistent chlorinated hydrocarbons are tightly controlled or banned in
the U.S. and Canada, but not in Mexico.   Studies of the Peregrine's life history
are underway in the western U.S. and Mexico to determine causes of continuing
decline.

CONSERVATION MEASURES PROPOSED   Increased legal protection; preservation of
natural habitat (especially nest sites); evaluation of pesticide contamination;

management of wild populations; captive propagation for augmenting dwindling populations and restocking vacated range; education and dissemination of information; and national and international cooperation and coordination (3; 4; 5).

REMARKS   Although the causes of decline apply equally to most of North America, the problems of maintaining or reintroducing populations differ from east to west.   In the east it is mainly a matter of reintroducing young birds, bred and reared in captivity, into areas where the species no longer exists.   In the west efforts have to be divided between safeguarding the remaining Peregrines and augmenting numbers by placing in the nests of wild pairs eggs or young which have been laid or hatched in captivity.   If reintroduction is successful in the east it will involve a genetically mixed stock bred from several subspecies, for no pure F. p. anatum stock is any longer available (3).   Of the other subspecies, F. p. tundrius of northern North America is also rated as endangered, F. p. fruitii and F. p. madens rare, while the Peregrine Falcon species as a whole is placed in the vulnerable category.

Dr. C.M. White's contribution to the preparation of this data sheet is gratefully acknowledged.

REFERENCES   1.   Fyfe, R.W., Temple, S.A. & Cade, T.J. 1976.   The 1975 North American Peregrine Falcon survey.   Canadian Field-Nat. 90: 228-273.
2.   Porter, R.D. & Marshall, D.B. 1977.   The recovery team approach to restoration of endangered species.   ICBP World Conference on Birds of Prey Proc.:   314-319.
3.   Clement, R.C. (ed.) 1974.   Proceedings of a conference on Peregrine Falcon recovery.   Audubon Conservation Reports 4.
4.   Rocky Mountain/Southwest Peregrine Recovery Team, 1977. Rocky Mountain/Southwest Peregrine Recovery Plan (draft). U.S. Fish and Wildlife Service.
5.   American Ornithologists' Union, 1977.   Report of the Committee on Conservation 1976-77. Auk 94 (Suppl.):   1DD-19DD.
6.   Fyfe, R. 1976.   Rationale and success of the Canadian Wildlife Service Peregrine Breeding Project.   Canad. Field-Nat. 90:   308-319.
7.   Cade, T.J. & Dague, P.R. (eds) 1976.   The Peregrine Fund Newsletter No. 4.   Cornell Univ. Lab. of Ornith.
8.   Hickey, J.J. (ed.) 1969.   Peregrine Falcon Populations: Their Biology and Decline.   Madison, Milwaukee, London: Univ. of Wisconsin Press.
9.   Cade, T.J. (ed.) 1974.   The Peregrine Fund Newsletter No. 2.   Cornell Univ. Lab. of Ornith.
10.   Hunt, W.G. undated.   The Peregrine Falcon population in the Chihuahuan Desert and surrounding mountain ranges: an evaluation through 1976.   Alpine, Texas: Chihuahuan Desert Research Institute.

IWO PEREGRINE FALCON

Falco peregrinus fruitii Momiyama, 1927

Order FALCONIFORMES   Family FALCONIDAE

STATUS   Rare.   This subspecies of the Peregrine breeds on one island in the
Kazan-retto or Volcano Islands south of Japan.

DISTRIBUTION   Known to breed only on Kita-iwo-jima (6.36 sq. km) in the Volcano
Islands (1).   It is thought to be extinct on Naka-iwo-jima and its status on
Minami-iwo-jima is unknown (2).   An individual of this race has been recorded on
Torishima at the extreme southern end of the Izu Islands, half way between Iwo Jima
and Japan (1).

POPULATION   Not known, but unquestionably small, in view of the very restricted
size of the island in which the subspecies breeds.   Islands of comparable size in
the Aleutians would support about 4 pairs of Peregrines (C.M.N. White 1975, pers.
comm.).   The series of specimens from which the type was taken and described,
numbered 10 birds (4).

HABITAT   Not described, but presumed to be sea cliffs.   Prior to World War II,
Kita-iwo-jima had a human population of about 100 (3).

CONSERVATION MEASURES TAKEN   Hunting of this subspecies would be illegal in Japan.
The legal basis of its protection is the U.S.-Japan Migratory Bird Treaty of 1973.

CONSERVATION MEASURES PROPOSED   None known.

REMARKS   Several of the 18 or so named subspecies of the Peregrine, a species of
worldwide distribution, are either endangered (F. p. anatum, F. p. tundrius),
vulnerable (F. p. peregrinus), or rare (F. p. madens); in fact the entire species
is at some risk because of its tendency to concentrate pesticide residues in its
tissues, resulting in reproductive debilitation, and also because of being in great
demand for falconry.

REFERENCES   1.   Ornithological Society of Japan, 1974.   Check-list of Japanese
                    Birds.   Tokyo:Gakken Co.
              2.   Hasuo, K. 1970.   Fauna of the Bonin Islands.   In Survey Report
                    on Nature Conservation of Bonin Islands, Vol. 2, pp. 193-224.
                    Tokyo:Metropolitan Government. (In Japanese)
              3.   Douglas, G. 1969.   Draft Check List of Pacific Ocean islands.
                    Micronesica 4: 327-463.
              4.   Momiyama, T.T. 1927.   Descriptions of twenty-five new birds
                    and three additions from Japanese territories.   Annot. Ornith.
                    Orient. 1: 81-102.

CAPE VFRDE PEREGRINE FALCON

Falco peregrinus madens Ripley and Watson, 1963

Order FALCONIFORMES   Family FALCONIDAE

STATUS   Rare. This subspecies survives in apparently undiminished but very low numbers in the Cape Verde Islands.

DISTRIBUTION   Described from the Cape Verde Islands, where it has been recorded from Brava, Cima (Rombos group), São Tiago, almost certainly São Vincente, and according to a reliable second-hand report also Santo Antão (1; 2; 3; 4).

POPULATION   A pair nests on Cima, a pair on Brava, and probably no more than a pair or two on the other islands from which it has been reported, making the total population no more than about 6 pairs. No decline is believed to have occurred (3; 4).

HABITAT   This Peregrine nests on cliffs, particularly near seabird colonies or overlooking other areas where the birds on which it preys are plentiful.

CONSERVATION MEASURES TAKEN   The species is listed in Appendix 1 of the 1973 Convention on International Trade in Endangered Species of Wild Fauna and Flora.

CONSERVATION MEASURES PROPOSED   Protected status in the Cape Verdes for this as yet unprotected subspecies has been recommended to the Portuguese authorities (5).

REMARKS   The Peregrine is now considered to be vulnerable throughout its nearly worldwide range. F. p. anatum and tundrius of North America are in the endangered category, and F. p. fruitii of the Volcano Islands south of Japan, like the Cape Verde subspecies, rates as rare.

REFERENCES   1. Ripley, S.D. & Watson, G.E. 1963.   A new Peregrine Falcon from the Cape Verde Islands, Eastern Atlantic Ocean. Postilla 77.
2. Bannerman, D.A. & Bannerman, W.M. 1968.   History of the Birds of the Cape Verde Islands. Edinburgh: Oliver and Boyd.
3. de Naurois, R. 1969.   La population de Faucons Pèlerins (Falco peregrinus madens Ripley et Watson) de l'archipel du Cap-Vert. Effectif, écologie et signification zoogéographique.   Alauda 37: 301-314.
4. de Naurois, R. 1969.   Notes brèves sur l'avifaune de l'archipel du Cap-Vert.   Faunistique, endémisme, écologie. Bull. Inst. Fond. Afr. Noire 31(ser. A): 143-218.
5. de Naurois, R. 1964.   Les oiseaux des îles du Cap-Vert. Garcia de Orta (Lisboa) 12: 609-620.

TUNDRA PEREGRINE FALCON

Falco peregrinus tundrius White, 1968

Order FALCONIFORMES   Family FALCONIDAE

STATUS   Endangered.   Status incompletely known, in absence of data from most of
Greenland.   The subspecies ranges widely north of the treeline from mainland
western coastal Alaska through Canada to Greenland.   Status well known for
Alaska (serious and widespread diminution and low productivity) (1-3), for most of
Canada (declines in some regions) (1; 4) and in a few places in western Greenland
(production possibly holding its own but eggshells showing considerable thinning)
(1; 5).   The factors responsible for the decline are apparently nothing to do with
the breeding grounds but derive from accumulation of chlorinated hydrocarbons in
the wintering grounds used by the subspecies in Latin America.

DISTRIBUTION   Tundra regions north of the treeline across North America including
western Greenland (6).   Intergradation occurs where tundrius meets the boreal
forest form F. p. anatum, especially in Canada at localities such as the Upper
Mackenzie River, Anderson River and Koksoak River in Ungava.   Greenland
individuals are the least distinctive and the limits of their distribution are
poorly known, but tundrius is not known to have been extirpated anywhere in its
range.   In the winter it migrates south through eastern and central North America
to the U.S. Gulf Coast, Middle America and South America as far as Argentina and
Chile.

POPULATION   On the Alaska tundra believed at one time to have numbered about
150-200 pairs but now no more than 50-75 pairs (1; 2; 3).   Canadian populations
are less well known, possibly because of the much greater area they occupy.
There may well have been more than 2,000 pairs in the Canadian tundra, reduced
today to perhaps 200 pairs (4).   Alaskan and Canadian populations are still
declining.   The Greenland population is practically unknown but could well be
significant.   Thus in western Greenland, in the region of Søndre Strømfjord,
the density of active sites is one pair/200 sq. km (5).   If the exact geographic
limits were known an estimate of population size could be made.

HABITAT   Tundra ecosystem.   In Alaska primarily along rivers and seacoasts.
In Canada along rivers, coasts and lakeshores, also occasionally away from water.
In Greenland no particular habitat type seems to be preferred.

CONSERVATION MEASURES TAKEN   The U.S. Fish and Wildlife Service has set up a
recovery team to establish criteria for bringing the subspecies back to its
1960 population level (7).   Pairs are being reared in captivity both in the U.S.
and Canada, with the eventual hope of releasing them into the wild.   The subspecies is fully protected in the U.S., Canada and Greenland.   It also receives
protection by convention in some countries of Latin America.   The species as a
whole is listed in Appendix 1 of the 1973 Convention on International Trade in
Endangered Species of Wild Fauna and Flora.

CONSERVATION MEASURES PROPOSED   Discourage use of persistent chlorinated hydrocarbons in Latin America; determine precise Latin American wintering range by
satellite telemetry; monitor toxic chemical residue levels in the Peregrine's prey
species in Latin America; and give further protection on breeding grounds by such
means as nest site stabilization.

REMARKS   This subspecies is the North American counterpart of the Siberian
Peregrine F. p. calidus.   The general level of threat to the peregrine on a

worldwide basis is now great enough for it to be regarded as vulnerable. F. p. anatum of North America like F. p. tundrius is rated as endangered, while F. p. fruitii of the Volcano Islands and F. p. madens of the Cape Verde Islands, which have very small populations, fall into the 'rare' category.

Dr. C.M. White very kindly supplied the information for this sheet.

REFERENCES

1. Fyfe, R.W., Temple, S.A. & Cade, T.J. 1976. The 1975 North American Peregrine Falcon survey. Canad. Field-Nat. 90: 228-273.

2. White, C.M. & Cade, T.J. 1977. Long term trends of Peregrine populations in Alaska. ICBP World Conf. Birds of Prey Proc.: 63-71.

3. White, C.M. & Cade, T.J. 1971. Cliff-nesting raptors and ravens along the Colville River in Arctic Alaska. Living Bird 10: 107-150.

4. Fyfe, R.W. 1977. Status of Canadian raptor populations. ICBP World Conf. Birds of Prey Proc.: 34-39.

5. Burnham, W.A. et al. 1974. Falcon research in Greenland, 1973. Arctic 27(1): 71-74.

6. White, C.M. 1968. Diagnosis and relationships of the North American tundra-inhabiting Peregrine Falcons. Auk 85: 179-191.

7. Porter, R.D. & Marshall, D.B. 1977. The recovery team approach to restoration of endangered species. ICBP World Conf. Birds of Prey Proc.: 314-319.

MAURITIUS KESTREL

Falco punctatus Temminck, 1823

Order FALCONIFORMES   Family FALCONIDAE

STATUS   Critically endangered.   Very rare, restricted in range, declining in
numbers and close to extinction.   The main threats to its existence are habitat
destruction and nest predation by introduced mammals.   It has until recently been
shot by hunters (local name is Mangeur de Poules).

DISTRIBUTION   Found only on the island of Mauritius in the Indian Ocean and never
identified elsewhere; restricted to the very limited areas of native forest in the
Black River Gorges in the south-west of the island (1).   Formerly occurred throughout the greater part of the island from sea level to the mountains (2; 3).   Its
decline has paralleled the decrease in the extent of forest on the island.

POPULATION   Once common (2; 3), the species dwindled gradually until in 1974 the
total population numbered only six individuals (1; 4); but had increased to twelve or
perhaps thirteen by 1977, inclusive of two captive birds (S. Temple; D. McKelvey
1977, pers. comm.).

HABITAT   Limited exclusively to indigenous evergreen forests, where it can hunt
small birds, lizards and insects and find nest cavities in hollow trees or cliffs
(1).   Forest covered most of Mauritius at one time, but now what is left of the
indigenous forest accounts for less than one per cent of the land surface (4; 5).
Moreover, introduced macaque monkeys Macaca irus are abundant in this remnant and
are serious nest predators (1).

CONSERVATION MEASURES TAKEN   Fully protected by laws forbidding the killing or
capture of native birds.   A small portion of the kestrel's range is in officially
declared reserves.   During 1972-1976 ecological studies were carried out to
determine the status and requirements of the species and in 1974 a pair having been
taken into captivity bred that year and again in 1975; so far, no young have been
reared successfully (6).   This species and all other falcons are listed in Appendix
2 of the 1973 Convention on International Trade in Endangered Species of Wild Fauna
and Flora.

CONSERVATION MEASURES PROPOSED   Continued protection and management of the remnant
native forests is essential to the bird's survival.   A management plan for a
system of nature reserves and national parks has been submitted to the Mauritius
Government.   Protection of nest sites and control of macaque monkeys is a
prerequisite of breeding success.   Eventual release of captive-produced kestrels
into suitable habitat on Mauritius and possibly also the neighbouring island of
Réunion is anticipated (1; 7; 8).

REMARKS   Like most kestrels, F. punctatus appears to nest quite readily in
captivity.

REFERENCES   1.   Temple, S.A., Staub, J.J.F. & Antoine, R. Unpublished report
                     dated 1974.   Some background information and recommendations
                     on the preservation of the native flora and fauna of Mauritius.
                     Report submitted to the Mauritius Government.
              2.   Newton, E. 1861.   Ornithological notes from Mauritius.
                     II.   Ibis (1)3: 270-277
              3.   Meinertzhagen, R. 1912.   On the birds of Mauritius.   Ibis
                     (9)6: 82-108.

4.   Temple, S.A. 1974.   Wildlife in Mauritius today.   _Oryx_ 12:
     584-590.
5.   Vaughan, R.E. & Wiehe, P.O. 1937.   Studies on the vegetation
     of Mauritius, I.   A preliminary survey of the plant communities.
     J. Ecol. 25:   289-343.
6.   Temple, S.A. 1975.   World Wildlife Yearbook, 1974-75, pp. 210-
     212.   Morges:World Wildlife Fund.
7.   Scott, P.   Unpublished IUCN report dated 1973.   Conservation
     in Mauritius.   Report to the Prime Minister of Mauritius.
8.   Procter, J. & Salm, R.   Unpublished IUCN report dated 1974.
     Conservation in Mauritius, 1974.   Report to the Mauritius
     Government.

MALEO

Macrocephalon maleo S. Muller, 1846

Order GALLIFORMES   Family MEGAPODIIDAE

STATUS   Vulnerable.   Restricted to parts of Sulawesi, Indonesia, where it is
rare, locally distributed and heavily exploited.

DISTRIBUTION   Occurs in the northern and south-eastern peninsulas as well as in
central Sulawesi, and said to have been introduced to the Kepulauan-Sangihe island
chain, between Sulawesi and the Philippines, last century (1-4).   Its overall
distribution is unchanged although it has been exterminated in several localities
(5).

POPULATION   In northern Sulawesi the numbers of Maleo in the 13 known colonies
vary from 30 to 1250 adult birds.   Assuming each female lays 30 eggs annually,
an estimated population of about 3000 adult birds may be made for north Sulawesi;
a rougher estimate of 5,000-10,000 has been made for the whole of Sulawesi.
Several colonies, e.g. those at Panua, Imandix and Honayono, have been drastically
reduced, and a colony at Batu-putih vanished 6 years after a nearby human settlement was established in 1913 (5).

HABITAT   Feeding habitat is primary lowland rainforest.   Nesting occurs
communally, often at some distance from primary forest, in areas of loose sandy
soil heated either by subterranean hot springs or by the sun, for example certain
seaside beaches and forest clearings.   Eggs are buried up to 1 m deep in this
loose substrate but this does not prevent them from being dug up by humans, pigs,
monitor lizards and, at least formerly, by crocodiles.(1; 2; 3; 5).

CONSERVATION MEASURES TAKEN   Full protection under Indonesian law since 1970;
adults and young birds were in fact protected since the 1930s but nesting beaches
were leased by the government to local villagers for egg collecting.   Although
now illegal, such collecting is not effectively controlled.   Maleo populations
are, however, or will be protected within existing or planned reserves from Pulau
Garat (at the northern tip of the Kepulauan chain) to Tangkoko-Batuangus, Panua,
Manembo Nembo, Bone, Dumoga and Lore Kalamanta.   The species is listed in
Appendix 1 of the 1973 Convention on International Trade in Endangered Species of
Wild Fauna and Flora.

CONSERVATION MEASURES PROPOSED   An additional reserve is being sought for an area
where the Maleo occurs in south-eastern Sulawesi.   A three-year conservation-
oriented ecological study was started in northern Sulawesi in 1977.   The
possibility of reestablishing former maleo colonies, by removing and reburying eggs
at the old sites, should be investigated.   Careful wardening to prevent overexploitation is essential (5).

REMARKS   In 1978 there were 3 pairs of Maleos in Surabaja Zoo, a single specimen
in Jakarta Zoo, and a pair each at San Diego and Bronx Zoos.   Breeding in
captivity has not yet been successful.

The contribution of Mr. C. Savage to this data sheet is gratefully acknowledged.

REFERENCES   1.   Stresemann, E. 1941.   Die Vögel von Celebes.   Teil 3.
                   Systematik und Biologie.   Journ. f. Ornith. 89: 1-102.

2. Meyer, A.B. & Wiglesworth, L.N. 1898. The Birds of
    Celebes and the Neighboring Islands. Vol. 2. Berlin:
    R. Friedlander und Sohn.
3. Lint, K.C. 1967. The Maleo - a mound builder from the
    Celebes. Zoonooz, October: 4-8.
4. Coomans de Ruiter, L. 1930. De Maleo (Megacephalon maleo
    (Hartl.)). Ardea 19: 16-19.
5. MacKinnon, J. 1978. Sulawesi megapodes. World Pheasant
    Assoc. Journ. 3: 96-103.

MARIANAS MEGAPODE

Megapodius laperouse laperouse Gaimard, 1823

Order GALLIFORMES   Family MEGAPODIIDAE

STATUS   Rare.   Restricted to several of the Mariana Islands, Western Pacific
Ocean, where its total population is probably not large.

DISTRIBUTION   Once almost certainly inhabited all the Mariana Islands.   Farallon
de Medinilla (0.9 sq. km) is now the only island in the group for which evidence of
present or prior occurrence is lacking.   Recent information suggests the continuing
presence of the megapode on Asuncion, (7.3 sq. km), Agrihan (47.4 sq. km), Pagan
(48.4 sq. km), Alamagan (11.1 sq. km) and Tinian (101.2 sq. km).   The species was
thought to have been extirpated from Tinian by 1945, but natives of that island
report that a bird fitting the description of the megapode is still to be found.
In addition there is now evidence that it occurs on Uracas (2.1 sq. km), Maug
(2.1 sq. km), Guguan (4.2 sq. km), Sarigan (4.9 sq. km) and Anatahan (32.4 sq. km)
(1).   It is surely gone from Saipan (121.7 sq. km), Rota (85.5 sq. km) and Guam
(541 sq. km) (2; 3).   On Agiguan (7.3 sq. km) it was last reported in 1955 (1).

POPULATION   Formerly abundant, at least on the larger of the Marianas; doubtless
far less so on the smaller islands (2).   No estimates of existing populations
are available.   The species is still present on islands with and without human
populations.

HABITAT   Thickets of brush fringing some of the beaches; also in the hills of the
higher islands (4).   Some of the northern Marianas, such as Uracas, have very
little vegetation (1).   All islands of less than 10 sq. km are at present
uninhabited, Agiguan is overrun by goats and Saipan has feral pigs and monitor
lizards, which pose a direct threat to the megapode (1).

CONSERVATION MEASURES TAKEN   Fully protected by law under the U.S. Endangered
Species Act of 1973, and by the Trust Territory Endangered Species Act of 1975.
The latter permits taking of this species or its eggs for subsistence by indigenous
people.

CONSERVATION MEASURES PROPOSED   Several of the uninhabited islands of the
Marianas were proposed as 'islands for science' (reserved for scientific studies)
by the C.T. (conservation of terrestrial communities) section of the International
Biological Program in view of their relatively or completely undisturbed state (5).
One of these, Farallon de Medinilla, has recently begun to be used as a bombing
range by U.S. defense forces (1).

REMARKS   The inhabitants of the Marianas prefer to use the megapode eggs rather
than the adult birds for food (2).   Another subspecies, M. l. senex of the Palau
group, is also still relatively widespread but likewise under pressure because of
the collection of its eggs by the local human inhabitants.

REFERENCES   1.   Falanruw, M.V.C. 1975.   Notes on the distribution of the
                      Micronesian Megapode Megapodius laperouse in the northern
                      Mariana Islands.   Micronesica 11: 149-150.
              2.   Baker, R.H. 1951.   The avifauna of Micronesia, its origin,
                      evolution, and distribution.   Univ. Kansas Pubs. Mus. Nat.
                      Hist. 3(1): 1-359.
              3.   Marshall, J.T. Jr. 1949.   The endemic avifauna of Saipan,
                      Tinian, Guam and Palau.   Condor 51: 200-221.

4.   Greenway, J.C. Jr. 1958.   Extinct and Vanishing Birds of the
     World.   Amer. Comm. Internat. Wild Life Prot. Spec. Publ. No. 13.
5.   Douglas, G. 1969.   Draft check list of Pacific Ocean islands.
     Micronesica 5(2):   327-463.

PALAU MEGAPODE

Megapodius laperouse senex Hartlaub, 1867

Order GALLIFORMES   Family MEGAPODIIDAE

STATUS   Rare.   Small populations still occur on several of the Palau Islands in
the south-west Pacific.   The eggs are highly sought after by their human inhabitants
and this probably prevents the megapode's numbers increasing.   Aids to mobility,
such as the use of speed boats, facilitate frequent trips to raid islands formerly
seldom visited (R. Owen 1975, pers. comm.).

DISTRIBUTION   Once occurred on almost all islands of the Palau group (1).   It is
still present on most, including Peleliu, Ngesebus, Urukthapel, Auluptagel, Koror,
Babelthuap and Kayangel, as well as many of the smaller uninhabited islands; but is
now gone from Malakal, Arekabesan and Angaur, and its existence is precarious on
Babelthuap (R. Owen 1975, pers. comm.).

POPULATION   Probably rather larger in the more distant past.   Estimates in 1945
of the total numbers on Peleliu, Garakayo, Ngabad and Angaur came to only 45 to 70
birds (1).   There are no more recent estimates although the fact that the megapode
is still widely distributed suggests a reasonably secure basic population.

HABITAT   Forest on deep soil in the interior of large islands, on rocky knife-
edged ridges with little soil, also on small raised limestone islands.   The
megapode forages in soil and leaf litter under the forest canopy (2).   Burgeoning
human populations have caused habitat disturbance on some islands: Angaur is
overrun by the crab-eating macaque Macaca irus and Babelthuap has numerous wild pigs
Sus scrofa.   However, there is still much undisturbed forest remaining (R. Owen
1975, pers. comm.).

CONSERVATION MEASURES TAKEN   The species is protected by U.S. Federal law and U.S.
Trust Territories law.   Nevertheless, illegal taking of its eggs is widespread.

CONSERVATION MEASURES PROPOSED   The Ngerukewid Islands, a group of 70 small
islands, on some of which this subspecies occurs, have been a wildlife sanctuary
since 1958, but have been recommended for inclusion in a larger National Park (3).

REMARKS   The nominate subspecies from the Mariana Islands still occurs in small
numbers on several islands of that group but is also classified as rare.

REFERENCES   1.   Baker, R.H. 1951.   The avifauna of Micronesia, its origin,
                    evolution, and distribution.   Univ. Kansas Pubs. Mus. Nat. Hist.
                    3(1): 1-359.
              2.   Marshall, J.T., Jr. 1949.   The endemic avifauna of Saipan,
                    Tinian, Guam and Palau.   Condor 51: 200-221.
              3.   Douglas, G. 1969.   Draft check list of the Pacific Ocean
                    islands.   Micronesica 5(2): 327-463.

BLACK-FRONTED PIPING GUAN

Aburria jacutinga (Spix, 1825)

Order GALLIFORMES   Family CRACIDAE

STATUS   Endangered.   Now much reduced in distribution, absent from large
portions of its former range and believed to be less numerous elsewhere.
Although it is still avidly hunted, its most serious losses are attributable to
forest destruction.

DISTRIBUTION   This guan once ranged through south-eastern Brazil, from south-east
Bahia to Rio Grande do Sul, and thence to south-eastern Paraguay and the Misiones
and Corrientes provinces of Argentina (1).   It still occurs in the north-east of
the state of Rio de Janeiro and in the Serra do Mar of coastal Espirito Santo and
Paraná, although it has apparently disappeared from inland forests in these states.
It has again been quite recently reported in the states of Santa Catarina and Rio
Grande do Sul and in Corrientes and Misiones (1; 2).   In the 19th century, before
it became scarce, seasonal movements of this species were noted during the
southern winter (3).

POPULATION   Unknown, but certainly far lower today than formerly.   In the 1950s
hunters were still killing large numbers of this species and it could be purchased
in the Porto Alegre markets (2).   Now it is uncommon even in parks and it is
uncertain whether any of the areas where it is presently known supports a viable
population (R. Ridgely 1978, pers. comm.).

HABITAT   Tropical forest, the destruction of which over much of its former range
is seen as the most important cause of this guan's present precarious status.
It still occurs, together with the endangered Red-billed Curassow Crax blumenbachii, in Monte Pascoal National Park, south-eastern Bahia, in the Sooretama
Reserve (24,000 ha) and on Klabin Farm (4,000 ha), where however the future is in
doubt, for felling is reported to have commenced in 1977 and is scheduled to clear
about one-quarter of the forest (R. Ridgely 1978, pers. comm.).   Sooretama and
Klabin Farm contain the only remaining tracts of Amazonian primary forest in
Espírito Santo.

CONSERVATION MEASURES TAKEN   Hunting of this species has been prohibited since
1951 but this is not enforced.   It is listed in Appendix 1 of the 1973 Convention
on International Trade in Endangered Species of Wild Fauna and Flora and occurs
in at least three national parks or reserves, Sooretama and Monte Pascoal,
mentioned above, and Iguazu National Park, Misiones, Argentina.

CONSERVATION MEASURES PROPOSED   None additional known.

REMARKS   This piping guan has often been kept in captivity and has bred
successfully in Italy as well as Brazil (4; H. Sick 1977, pers. comm.).

REFERENCES   1.   Delacour, J. & Amadon, D. 1973.   Curassows and Related
                    Birds.   New York: Amer. Mus. Nat. Hist.
              2.   Sick, H. 1972.   A ameaçada da avifauna brasileira.   In
                    Espécies da Fauna Brasileira Ameaçadas de Extinção, pp. 99-153.
                    Rio de Janeiro: Academia Brasileira de Ciências.
              3.   Sick, H. 1968.   Vogelwanderungen im kontinentalen Sudamerika.
                    Vogelwarte 24: 217-243.
              4.   Taibel, A.M. 1968.   Osservazioni sulla riproduzione e
                    allevamento di Pipile jacutinga (Spix) (Cracidae-Galliformes)
                    realizzata per la prima volta con esemplari in cattivitá.
                    Ann. Civ. Mus. Stor. Nat. Genova, 77: 33-52.

BLUE-BILLED CURASSOW

Crax alberti Fraser, 1850

Order GALLIFORMES   Family CRACIDAE

STATUS   Vulnerable.   Still fairly widespread in lowland tropical forest in
northern Colombia but steadily declining as the combined result of rapid forest
destruction and ceaseless hunting pressure.

DISTRIBUTION   Northern Colombia from the north and west slopes of the Santa
Marta massif south along the Magdalena River valley to Hondo and the lower Cauca
River valley (1; 2; 3).   Not known to have changed, although extensive areas
within this range now support neither forest nor this curassow.

POPULATION   No figures available, but this curassow is uncommon throughout its
range (2) and now declining alarmingly in all areas accessible to hunters.

HABITAT   Lowland forest up to 600 m, occasionally up to 1200 m (1; 2; 3).
Destruction of this type of forest in northern Colombia is taking place at a rate
which must give rise to serious concern, especially as no significant sample
receives protection.

CONSERVATION MEASURES TAKEN   None known.

CONSERVATION MEASURES PROPOSED   None known.

REMARKS   Crax annulata Todd, 1915, has been shown to be a color phase of the
female C. alberti (4).   A Crax, probably this species but possibly the Yellow-
knobbed Curassow C. daubentoni, occurs in Tayrona National Park, north of
Santa Marta (R. Ridgely 1977, pers. comm.).   The Blue-billed Curassow has
frequently been kept in captivity and in 1977 there were 12 in collections (4).
It has bred only rarely, though hybridization with no less than four other species
of Crax has been recorded (2).

REFERENCES   1. de Schauensee, R.M. 1949.   The birds of the Republic of
                   Colombia.   Part 2.   Caldasia 5: 381-644.
               2. Delacour, J. & Amadon, D. 1973.   Curassows and Related
                   Birds.   New York: American Museum of Natural History.
               3. Todd, W.E.C. & Carriker, M.A., Jr. 1922.   The birds of
                   the Santa Marta region of Colombia: a study in altitudinal
                   distribution.   Ann. Carnegie Mus. 14.
               4. Brown, P. 1977.   WPA census of cracids and megapodes 1977.
                   World Pheasant Assoc. Journal 2: 76-79.
               5. Vaurie, C. 1968.   Taxonomy of the Cracidae (Aves).
                   Bull. Amer. Mus. Nat. Hist. 138(4): 131-260.

RED-BILLED CURASSOW

Crax blumenbachii Spix, 1825

Order GALLIFORMES   Family CRACIDAE

STATUS   Endangered.   Formerly rather widespread in south-eastern Brazil but now restricted to three tracts of protected forest.   Hunting and forest destruction have brought it to the edge of extinction.

DISTRIBUTION   To judge from the occurrence of the native name of this curassow in place names, it once was distributed from southern Bahia to eastern Minas Gerais, Espírito Santo and north-eastern Rio de Janeiro (1; 2).   It is presently restricted to the forests of Sooretama Reserve (24,000 ha) and Klabin Farm (4,000 ha), both in Espírito Santo (A. Ruschi 1977, pers. comm.), and of Monte Pascoal National Park, south-eastern Bahia (R. Ridgely 1978, pers. comm.).   As recently as 1963, it still survived in a forest near São Fidelis, 225 km north-east of the city of Rio de Janeiro, but the forest has now been felled (2).

POPULATION   This species has been considered rare for many years, probably as the result of heavy hunting pressure in accessible forest, although it was said to be still locally common in northern Espírito Santo up to 1939 (2; 3).   Forest destruction has accelerated since the 1940s and with it the decline of this curassow, until it is now among South America's and the world's rarest species. Currently perhaps 60 or more survive in the Sooretama Reserve and possibly as few as 10 on Klabin Farm (A. Ruschi 1977, pers. comm.).   In Sooretama some were to be seen daily in 1973, in a forest camp yard, where grain was scattered for domestic fowls (5).   Numbers in the Monte Pascoal Park are believed to be much less than at Sooretama (R. Ridgely 1978, pers. comm.).

HABITAT   Amazonian primary rainforest.   The extent of this habitat along the coastal states of south-eastern Brazil has been very seriously reduced and only relict patches remain.   The most substantial of these, to which the curassow is now restricted, are the two in Espírito Santo and one in Bahia referred to in the two previous and the next sections.

CONSERVATION MEASURES TAKEN   The species has been given legal protection in Brazil and is also listed in Appendix 1 of the 1973 Convention on International Trade in Endangered Species of Wild Fauna and Flora.   Of the three localities where it survives, Sooretama is a well protected nature reserve, Monte Pascoal a National Park and Klabin Farm is in private ownership.   Forest clearance is reported to have started on Klabin Farm in 1977 and is expected to continue until about a quarter of the forest has been felled (R. Ridgely 1978, pers. comm.).

CONSERVATION MEASURES PROPOSED   None known.

REMARKS   In 1976, twelve Red-billed Curassows were known to be held in six zoos (4).   Young have been successfully reared in captivity in Brazil (H. Sick 1977, pers. comm.).

REFERENCES   1.   Delacour, J. & Amadon, D. 1973.   Curassows and Related
                      Birds.   New York: American Mus. Nat. Hist.
              2.   Sick, H. 1972.   A ameaça da avifauna brasileira.
                      In Espécies da Fauna Brasileira Ameaçadas de Extinção, pp. 99-
                      153.   Rio de Janeiro: Academia Brasileira de Ciências.

3. Sick, H. 1970.   Notes on Brazilian Cracidae.
    Condor 72: 106-108.
4. Olney, P.J.S. (ed.) 1977.   Census of rare animals in
    captivity, 1976.   _Internat. Zoo. Yearbook_ 17: 333-371.
5. Gochfeld, M. & Keith, S. 1977.   The Red-billed Curassow.
    Oryx 14(1): 22-23.

NORTHERN BARE-FACED CURASSOW

Crax fasciolata pinima Pelzeln, 1869

Order GALLIFORMES   Family CRACIDAE

STATUS   Indeterminate.   Likely to be close to extinction, although virtually
nothing is known about its present distribution or abundance.

DISTRIBUTION   North-east Brazil, in the lowlands of Pará and Maranhão states
east of the lower Tocantins River, inland only to about latitude $2^{\circ}30'S$ (1; 2).

POPULATION   Unknown.   Eight specimens have been collected, the most recent
from Moiraba, Rio Tocantins, Pará, in 1955 (2).   This subspecies was considered
extinct in 1968 by Vaurie (3), who was at that time unaware of the 1955 record.
It has been suggested that there may still be a few of these curassows left in the
state of Maranhão.

HABITAT   Tropical forest.   Birds of this subspecies, and all other members of
the genus Crax, are constantly hunted and among the first birds to disappear from
any newly accessible forest, but the reasons for the extreme rarity of this
particular bird are not clear.   There is still a considerable amount of forest
within its range, in north-western Maranhão and north-eastern Para, although none
of it is protected and much is being destroyed in large settlement schemes along
the new roads penetrating into the interior (R. Ridgely 1978, pers. comm.).

CONSERVATION MEASURES TAKEN   Brazilian law at least nominally protects this
curassow and part of its habitat falls within the newly established 10,000 sq. km
Amazonia National Park, which extends into Pará from Amazonas.

CONSERVATION MEASURES PROPOSED   None known.

REMARKS   The species as a whole has often been kept in captivity and successfully
bred in Antwerp Zoo and at Clères in France.   In 1977, this subspecies was
certainly represented in Brazilian collections (H. Sick 1977, pers. comm.)   The
two other subspecies range throughout central Brazil and as far south as Bolivia,
eastern Paraguay and northern Argentina; neither of them is known to be at risk.

REFERENCES   1.   Delacour, J. & Amadon, D. 1973.   Curassows and Related
                   Birds.   New York: American Mus. Nat. Hist.
              2.   Sick, H. 1969.   Aves brasileiras ameaçadas de extinção e
                   noções gerais de conservação de aves no Brasil.   An. Acad.
                   Brasil. Ciênc. 41(Supl.): 205-229.
              3.   Vaurie, C. 1968.   Taxonomy of the Cracidae.   Bull. Amer.
                   Mus. Nat. Hist. 138(4).

EASTERN RAZOR-BILLED CURASSOW

Crax mitu mitu Linnaeus, 1766

Order GALLIFORMES   Family CRACIDAE

STATUS   Critically endangered.   Restricted to pockets of primary forest in the
coastal area of north-eastern Brazil and now possibly extinct as the result of
continual hunting and forest destruction.

DISTRIBUTION   Formerly recorded in the Pernambuco and Alagoas states of Brazil
as far as their southern borders on the Rio São Francisco.   This, the nominate
race of Razor-billed Curassow, was believed to be extinct for a century, until
rediscovered in 1951 near São Miguel dos Campos, about two thirds of the way down
the coast of Alagoas (1).   It was still known to survive there in 1970 (2; 3).

POPULATION   Before the primary forests in the coastlands of north-eastern Brazil
were felled, this subspecies may well have been quite common, though it was
regarded as virtually extinct for over 100 years.   In 1970 it was estimated that
only about 20 birds remained in the 8,500 ha forest near São Miguel dos Campos
(2; 3).

HABITAT   Primary coastal rainforest, a habitat seriously reduced in extent along
the whole north-eastern coast of Brazil.   It was calculated in 1970 that only
about 2000 sq. km of such forest were left in the entire state of Alagoas (3).

CONSERVATION MEASURES TAKEN   The subspecies is listed in Appendix 1 of the
Convention on International Trade in Endangered Species of Wild Fauna and Flora.

CONSERVATION MEASURES PROPOSED   A reserve in Alagoas, to protect at least part
of the habitat of the subspecies has been recommended (H. Sick 1976, pers. comm.).
Up till now none of this habitat has received any kind of legal protection.

REMARKS   The other subspecies, C. m. tuberosa, which is widespread in the
southern Amazon basin despite being ceaselessly harried by hunters, is not
believed to be at risk.   It has often bred in captivity (4), whereas the nominate
race is represented in captive collections only in Brazil (H. Sick 1977, pers.
comm.).

REFERENCES   1.   Pinto, O.M. de O. 1952.   Redescobrimento de Mitu mitu (Linne)
                   no nordeste do Brasil (est de Alagoas).   São Paulo Depto.
                   Zool. Papeis Avulsos 10: 325-334.
              2.   Coimbra-Filho, A.F. 1971.   Tres formas da avifauna do
                   nordeste do Brasil ameaçadas de extinção: Tinamus solitarius
                   pernambucensis Berla, 1946, Mitu m. mitu (Linnaeus, 1766) e
                   Procnias a. averano (Hermann, 1783) (Aves-Tinamidae, Cracidae,
                   Cotingidae).   Rev. Brasil. Biol. 31: 239-247.
              3.   Coimbra-Filho, A.F. 1970.   Sobre Mitu mitu (Linnaeus, 1766) e
                   a validez des suas duas raças geograficas.   Rev. Brasil.
                   Biol. 30: 101-109.
              4.   Delacour, J. and Amadon, D. 1973.   Curassows and Related
                   Birds.   New York: American Museum of Natural History.

COZUMEL CURASSOW

Crax rubra griscomi Nelson, 1926

Order GALLIFORMES   Family CRACIDAE

STATUS   Rare.   Restricted to one island off the N.E. Mexican coast.   Avidly
hunted and now a new road network threatens to make all parts of the island
accessible to hunters.

DISTRIBUTION   Known only from Cozumel Island off the north-east coast of the
Yucatán Peninsula, Mexico, and becoming increasingly restricted to the most
remote parts of the island (1; K. Parkes 1973, pers. comm.).

POPULATION   Unknown.   There was a decline in numbers as the result of heavy
hunting by the inhabitants of the only town in the interior of the island, but the
town was virtually abandoned in 1939, following a hurricane.   Nevertheless, by
the 1960s the curassow had become too scarce to be worth hunting, although any
found during the course of a pig or other game hunt would invariably be taken.
A party of ornithologists saw one in 1968, which is the last known sighting
(K. Parkes 1973, pers. comm.).

HABITAT   Rainforest, which is said to cover two thirds of Cozumel.   A road
built in 1971 bisects the island and another, under construction in 1971,
encircles it.   Human settlements are being established along these roads
(K. Parkes 1973, pers. comm.) and none of the curassow's forest habitat has yet
been accorded any kind of protection.

CONSERVATION MEASURES TAKEN   The subspecies has been given legal protection, but
the law is unenforceable and widely disregarded.

CONSERVATION MEASURES PROPOSED   None known.

REMARKS   The nominate subspecies of what is sometimes known as the Great
Curassow has a wide range in Latin America from Tamaulipas, Mexico, south to
Colombia and Ecuador.   It is constantly pursued by hunters throughout its range
and its forest habitat has seriously decreased in extent in several countries.
However, it is not yet considered to be at sufficient risk to warrant inclusion
in this volume.   The species has been kept and often bred successfully in
captivity, but it is almost certain that all such records refer to birds belonging
to the nominate mainland race and none to the insular form (1).

REFERENCES   1.   Delacour, J. & Amadon, D. 1973.   Curassows and Related
                    Birds.   New York: American Museum of Natural History.

Oreophasis derbianus G.R. Gray, 1844

Order GALLIFORMES   Family CRACIDAE

STATUS   Endangered.   Sparsely distributed in cloud forest in south-eastern Mexico and western Guatemala.   Habitat destruction and continual hunting pressure have contributed to the deterioration of its status.

DISTRIBUTION   Restricted to the Sierra Madre in the state of Chiapas, Mexico, and western Guatemala.   Its former range probably extended along the higher ridges west to Oaxaca and included the upper forested slopes of the volcanos of Fuego, Tolimán, Atitlán, San Pedro, Santa Maria, Tajamulco, Tacaná, the Zunil and Tecpán ridges, and the Sierra de los Cuchumatanes, possibly east along the Alta Vera Paz in Guatemala, as well as several localities along the Sierra Madre in Chiapas including Volcan Tacaná on the border.   The total area is estimated at 18,000 sq. km (1; 2).   In 1965, extensive searches were made for the Horned Guan but it was only found at El Triunfo, Chiapas and Tajamulco, Guatemala (1). However, more recently it has been rediscovered in south-eastern Oaxaca (J. Estudillo 1978, pers. comm.), at Tres Picos on Volcan Tacaná (L. Binford 1973, pers. comm.), again at El Triunfo, Chiapas, and along the Zunil and Tecpán ridges and near Tajamulco, Santiago, Cuchumatanes and Atitlán, Guatemala (3; 9; 10; R. Andrle, T. Parker, M. Alvarez del Toro 1973, J. Estudillo 1978, pers. comms). In short, there are still remote, inaccessible areas where this species will probably survive at least for the immediate future.

POPULATION   No early population estimates are available, but the species was usually considered common in suitable areas.   It tends to be the first bird eliminated by hunters in any newly opened-up area.   Wherever it is known to occur it appears to be very sparsely distributed; Andrle (1973, pers. comm.) suggested that there were less than 1000 left.   During extensive searches in 1965 and 1967 only two were seen and one heard (1; 2; 4).   A few others have been seen in the 1970s, but always in the same few localities.

HABITAT   Dense broadleaf cloud forest between 1500 m and 2500 m elevation. In many places this forest has been cleared for agriculture, including coffee production (5).   It has also been degraded by the browsing of cattle, goats and swine.   These factors are perhaps less important to the welfare of this guan than the intensive subsistence hunting to which it is subjected (9; R. Andrle, M. Alvarez del Toro 1973, pers. comms).

CONSERVATION MEASURES TAKEN   This guan is legally protected from hunting or capture in Mexico and Guatemala, but the laws are unenforced.   It is listed in Appendix 1 of the 1973 Convention on International Trade in Endangered Species of Wild Fauna and Flora.   National Parks or reserves protect parts of its habitat, notably the 10,000 ha reserve maintained on federal land at El Triunfo by the Institute of Natural History of Chiapas.   A private reserve protects some of the cloud forest on Volcan Atitlán (6).

CONSERVATION MEASURES PROPOSED   None additional known.

REMARKS   A few birds derived from eggs or chicks taken in the wild have been kept in captivity in Mexico, but there is no record of captive breeding (3; 7; 8).

REFERENCES   1.   Andrle, R.F. 1967.   The Horned Guan in Mexico and Guatemala. Condor 69: 93-109.

2. Delacour, J. and Amadon, D. 1973. Curassows and Related Birds. New York: American Museum of Natural History.
3. Parker, T.A. III , Hilty, S. & Robbins, M. 1976. Birds of El Triunfo Cloud Forest, Mexico, with notes on the Horned Guan and other species. Amer. Birds 30: 779-782.
4. Andrle, R.F. 1968. Biology and conservation of the Horned Guan. Amer. Philosoph. Soc. Year Book for 1968: 276-277.
5. Veblen, T.T. 1976. The urgent need for forest conservation in highland Guatemala. Biol. Cons. 9: 141-154.
6. La Bastille, A. 1973. Establishment of a Quetzal cloud forest reserve in Guatemala. Biol. Cons. 5: 60-62.
7. Haynes, M.H. 1975. News and views. Avicult. Mag.81: 231-233.
8. Delacour, J. 1977. Two collections of birds in Mexico. Avicult. Mag. 83: 50-53.
9. Alvarez del Toro, M. 1976. Datos biologicos del Pavón. Rev. Univ. Auton. Chiapas 1: 43-54.
10. Cantwell, R. 1978. Bird thou never wert. Sports Illustrated 13 Feb.: 56-66.

UTILA CHACHALACA

Ortalis vetula deschauenseei Bond, 1936

Order GALLIFORMES   Family CRACIDAE

STATUS   Endangered.   Restricted to a single island off the Caribbean coast of
Honduras, where it has been excessively persecuted.

DISTRIBUTION   Known only from Utila Island (11 by 5 km) situated 40 km off
the port of La Ceiba on the north coast of Honduras (1; 2).

POPULATION   Total numbers always considered to have been small given the small
area of the island on which this chachalaca occurs, but there has clearly been a
recent decline following excessive harassment by hunters (B. Monroe 1973, pers.
comm.).   In 1936, it was rated as not uncommon but local, being most abundant
in mangroves of the north of the island (1).   By 1962, it was estimated that 50
to 75 individuals comprised the entire population (3) and by now it may be
extinct (B. Monroe 1977, pers. comm.).

HABITAT   Mangrove swamps; formerly also thick scrub forest.   Mangroves cover
three quarters of Utila Island (1).

CONSERVATION MEASURES TAKEN   None known.

CONSERVATION MEASURES PROPOSED   None known.

REMARKS   The three other subspecies of the Plain Chachalaca range from southern
Texas to western Nicaragua and north-western Costa Rica.   The species as a whole
is subject to widespread hunting but although it is the most important game
species in parts of its range, it is not yet considered to be at risk.   It has
been kept and bred regularly in zoos and private collections, particularly in
warmer climates (2).

REFERENCES   1.   Bond, J. 1936.   Resident birds of the Bay Islands of
                    Spanish Honduras.   Proc. Acad. Nat. Sci. Philadelphia 88:
                    353-364.
              2.   Delacour, J. and Amadon, D. 1973.   Curassows and Related
                    Birds.   New York: Amer. Mus. Nat. Hist.
              3.   Monroe, B.L., Jr. 1970.   Effects of habitat changes on
                    population levels of the avifauna in Honduras.
                    In H.K. Buechner and J.H. Buechner (eds) The Avifauna of
                    Northern Latin America: A Symposium held at the
                    Smithsonian Institution 13-15 April 1966, pp. 38-41.
                    Smithsonian Contrib. Zool. 26.

WHITE-WINGED GUAN

Penelope albipennis Taczanowski, 1877

Order GALLIFORMES   Family CRACIDAE

STATUS   Endangered.   Endemic to Peru and with a restricted range; threatened by
hunting for food and by destruction of a habitat which seems to sustain only a
sparse population.   Legal protection, combined with urgent establishment of
sanctuaries, is essential.

DISTRIBUTION   The species was first described by Taczanowski on the basis of two
skins collected by Stolzmann and by Jelski, respectively, at Santa Lucia,
Department of Tumbes,(the type) and at Hacienda Pabur, Department of Piura, both
in the extreme north-west of Peru (skins at Warsaw and Lima Museums) (1).   There
were no further records until 100 years later Gustavo del Solar and John O'Neill
found a group of four White-winged Guans on 13 September 1977, when they were
exploring an area on the boundary between the Departments of Piura and Lambayeque,
at about 79°50'W and 5°32'S and an altitude of 650 m.

POPULATION   Now said to number several hundred birds, scattered and apparently
diminishing as a result of habitat destruction and some hunting pressure.   This
guan was said to be locally common in the late 1840s but by 1877, the year it was
scientifically described, it was already very rare (1).   Within a fortnight of
its rediscovery in 1977, groups of 8 and 6 were observed in the same locality; two
additional localities are now known, occupied by 6 and 4 birds, respectively, and
in yet another there are said to be 20 birds (J. O'Neill 1977, pers. comm.).

HABITAT   Dry forest and formerly mangroves on the Pacific coast of extreme
north-western Peru, so the species shows some plasticity in its choice of habitat.
Dry forest is extensive in north-western Peru and the species could therefore
range widely in the deep forested valleys of the northern half of Peru, along the
western slopes of the Andes.   During the dry season the guans concentrate around
springs in evergreen groves along the ravines.   Unfortunately the habitat is
rapidly being altered by the practice of charcoal burning.

CONSERVATION MEASURES TAKEN   The new hunting law in Peru does not yet include
this species in the list of endangered species since it was thought to be extinct.
As yet it receives no protection.   In any case enforcement of the new hunting
regulations is difficult in remote and isolated areas.   However, the guan is
believed to occur in one protected area, the Cerros de Amotape Reserve in northern
Piura.   A research project on the species is being undertaken by Mr. E. Ortiz with
the support of the National Parks Department of Peru.

CONSERVATION MEASURES PROPOSED   Legal protection of the species and inclusion in
Peru's endangered species list.   It is the larger of the two species of Penelope
found on the west slopes of the western cordillera of the Andes.   Surveys need to
be carried out along the valleys of north-western Peru to determine its range and
discover the best places for sanctuaries.   The Museo de Historia Natural Javier
Prado of San Marcos University in Lima has recommended to the Dirección General
Forestal y de Fauna of the Ministerio de Agricultura that a sanctuary be established in the very area where the guan was rediscovered.

REMARKS   The information for this data sheet was supplied, in September 1977,
by Dr. Hernando de Macedo-Ruiz, Jefe Titular, Section of Ornithology and Mammalogy,
Museo de Historia Natural Javier Prado, Avenida Arenales 1256, Apartado 1109, Lima,
Peru; and by Mr. Gustavo del Solar, Avenida Santa Victoria 640, Chiclayo, Peru.

REFERENCES   1.   Delacour, J. & Amadon, D. 1973.   Curassows and Related
              Birds.   New York: American Museum of Natural History.

CAUCA GUAN

Penelope perspicax Bangs, 1911

Order GALLIFORMES   Family CRACIDAE

___

STATUS   Endangered.   The large river valley in Colombia to which this guan is
restricted, has been almost entirely deforested.

DISTRIBUTION   This guan was at one time found throughout the middle section of
the Cauca River valley, including both slopes of the western Andes and the western
slope of the central Andes in Valle and Cauca Departments (1).   It has now
disappeared from almost all of its historical range, although it is believed to be
still present in Bosque de Yotoco, on the western Andes slope above Buga, and
possibly elsewhere (R. Ridgely 1977, pers. comm.).

POPULATION   Unknown.   There has undoubtedly been a major decline in numbers,
because practically no suitable habitat remains (2).

HABITAT   Subtropical forest of the middle Cauca.   Only one forest tract in
this area, the Bosque de Yotoco, receives even token protection, while virtually
all the rest of the valley has been cleared.   In 1977, squatters were moving into
the Bosque de Yotoco also (R. Ridgely 1977, pers. comm.).

CONSERVATION MEASURES TAKEN   The administration of the one remaining forest
within the range of the species is being undertaken by a local college.

CONSERVATION MEASURES PROPOSED   None known.

REMARKS   The species has been kept in captivity in Colombia (2), but by 1977 only
one captive specimen was known to survive in South America (3), although at least
one other was in a Mexican collection (4).   Some authorities treat perspicax
as a subspecies of Penelope jacquacu or of P. purpurascens (1; 2).

REFERENCES   1.   de Schauensee, R.M. 1949.   The birds of the Republic of
                    Colombia.   Segunda entrega: Accipitridae-Picidae.
                    Caldasia 5: 381-644.
              2.   Delacour, J. & Amadon, D. 1973.   Curassows and Related
                    Birds.   New York: American Mus. Nat. Hist.
              3.   Brown, P. 1977.   WPA census of cracids and megapodes 1977.
                    World Pheasant Assoc. Journal 2: 76-79.
              4.   Delacour, J. 1977.   Two collections of birds in Mexico.
                    Avicult. Mag. 83: 50-53.

Pipile pipile pipile (Jacquin, 1784)

Order GALLIFORMES   Family CRACIDAE

STATUS   Endangered.   Confined to Trinidad, where it may survive in the eastern
parts of the northern range.   Sighted in the forest-covered mountains at the
southern end of the island in 1969, but not subsequently (1; 2; 3).

DISTRIBUTION   Formerly known from the dense forests of Trinidad's Northern Range
and from the forested mountains in the south.   Not reported recently in the north
and, as indicated above, last report in the south, in the Trinity Hills, was in
1969 (3; R. ffrench 1974, pers. comm.).

POPULATION   Unknown and because these birds seldom leave dense cover not
susceptible to precise assessment.   Under constant pressure from hunters whenever
found.   Recent visits to the Trinity Hills, where two were seen in 1969, have
produced no further sightings.   Vague reports by hunters of the guan's continued
existence in north-east Trinidad continue, however, to be made (R. ffrench 1974,
pers. comm.).

HABITAT   Montane forests.   Forests of the Northern Range continue to be cleared
at a rapid rate, and trails and roads cross most parts of the bird's habitat,
making it accessible to hunters.   Nevertheless, suitable rainforest habitat for
this species still covers over 250 sq. km of Trinidad (R. ffrench 1974; A.M.
Greenhall 1973, pers. comm.).

CONSERVATION MEASURES TAKEN   Protected by law on Trinidad, but the law is
practically unenforceable in remote areas where this bird is likely to be found.
Recent authors have wisely refused to divulge precise locations of sightings
(1; R. ffrench 1974, pers. comm.).

CONSERVATION MEASURES PROPOSED   Formerly when more abundant these guans were kept
in a captive or domesticated state.   Being easily tamed they were often treated as
poultry and one hundred years ago were described as roosting on the roofs of houses
if suitable tree perches were unobtainable (3).   Captive breeding is therefore a
potentially promising measure for increasing the guan's population.   Parts of its
range are within the boundaries of national parks or wildlife sanctuaries and if
hunting regulations in such reservations could be strictly enforced, they could
provide valuable and effective protection for the species (R. ffrench 1974, pers.
comm.).

REMARKS   Generally now considered conspecific with the Red-throated piping guan
of the South American tropics, P. p. cumanensis, which is not known to be at risk.

REFERENCES   1.   Herklots, G.A.C. 1965.   Birds of Trinidad and Tobago.   London:
                   Collins.
              2.   ffrench, R. 1973.   A Guide to the Birds of Trinidad and Tobago.
                   Wynnewood, Pa.:Livingston Publishing Co.
              3.   Delacour, J. & Amadon, D. 1973.   Curassows and Related Birds.
                   New York:American Museum of Natural History.

CANTABRIAN CAPERCAILLIE

Tetrao urogallus cantabricus Castroviejo, 1967

Order GALLIFORMES   Family TETRAONIDAE

STATUS   Endangered.   This recently described form of the capercaillie, found
only in one small area in Spain, where it is subject to hunting and habitat
destruction, is seriously reduced in numbers.

DISTRIBUTION   Recorded in the past along the whole of the Cantabrian range from
northern Portugal through Galicia, Asturias and Leon to Santander in northern
Spain.   Now restricted to isolated pockets in a narrow strip of the range in
Spain. (1).

POPULATION   Formerly more abundant, although precise figures are lacking.   In
the spring of 1972 it was estimated that there were 300-400 males on display
grounds.   The subspecies has become segregated by habitat destruction into
isolated subpopulations and according to a recent estimate the maximum density is
one bird per two to three sq. km. (1).

HABITAT   Relatively undisturbed deciduous forests of oak Quercus, beech Fagus
and birch Betula in the breeding season, but in the winter holly Ilex between 1200
and 1600 m elevation is favoured (1, 2).   In 1972, there were still 12,000 sq. km
of suitable habitat, but in recent years deciduous forests in Spain have been
seriously depleted, the effects on the capercaillie's habitat having been most
severe at the extreme ends of its range.   In Asturias, for example, between 1946
and 1974, the lumber industry felled 700 sq. km of forest, including 37 percent of
the oak and 45 percent of the beech of the entire area.   Non-indigenous conifers
and eucalypts have been largely used for reafforestation. (1).

CONSERVATION MEASURES TAKEN   Hunting of this subspecies is allowed, on licence
only, both on natural reserves and private hunting grounds.   The shooting season
opens before the capercaillie begin to breed and an excessive number have tended
to be taken annually.   In 1975-1976, the quota was reduced and in one area, the
Sierra de los Ancares, hunting was prohibited entirely (J. Castroviejo 1976, pers.
comm.).

CONSERVATION MEASURES PROPOSED   It has been recommended that no more hunting of
this subspecies should be permitted or that, at the very least, the hunting season
should be delayed until after the birds' mating season; also that further alteration of its habitat should be prevented (1; 3).

REMARKS   Capercaillie occur in suitable habitat throughout northern Europe and
north central Asia and no less than ten other subspecies have sometimes been
recognized; but except for cantabricus none are believed at risk even though the
species has disappeared from several parts of its former range in western Europe.

REFERENCES   1.   Castroviejo, J., Delibes, M., Garcia-D., M., Garzon, J.,
                   & Junco, E. 1974.   Census of the Cantabrian Capercaillie
                   (Tetrao urogallus cantabricus).   Proc. Internat. Cong.
                   Game Biol. 11: 203-223.
              2.   Castroviejo, J. 1970.   Premières données sur l'écologie
                   hivernale des vertébrés de la Cordillière Cantabrique.
                   Alauda 38: 126-149.
              3.   Barclay-Smith, P. (ed.) 1971.   Hunting of the subspecies of the
                   Capercaillie.   In Report on XV World Conference of the Inter-
                   national Council for Bird Preservation.   ICBP Bull. 11: 47-53.

ATTWATER'S PRAIRIE CHICKEN

Tympanuchus cupido attwateri Bendire, 1893

Order GALLIFORMES   Family TETRAONIDAE

STATUS   Rare.   The range of this prairie chicken decreased enormously as the
coastal tall-grass prairies were converted to rice cultivation or were overgrazed
and invaded by brush.   Since about 1971 its decline has stopped, the population
having become stabilized at a much reduced level.

DISTRIBUTION   In the 19th century this subspecies was found in the southern
United States, in Cameron and Calcasieu parishes of south-western Louisiana, and
in 21 counties along the Texas coast from its south-east extremity as far west and
south as Aransas County - a total area of about 24,300 sq. km.   It was last
reported in Louisiana in 1919.   By 1937 only 1851 sq. km of the prairie or
agricultural land remained occupied by this prairie chicken (1-3) and by 1967 only
948 sq. km, a historical decline of about 96 percent (4; 5).   Fourteen counties
in Texas still support populations, but the main concentrations are in Austin,
Fort Bend, Colorado and Galveston counties and, 150 km further south and west in
Goliad, Refugio and Victoria counties (6; 8; R. Brownlee 1977, pers. comm.).

POPULATION   Numbers of Attwater's Prairie Chicken have always fluctuated in
response to climatic factors but, at its peak, the 19th century population
probably totalled about a million, with a maximum density of 1/0.4 ha in well-
drained prairie.   By 1937, the population had dwindled to about 8700 and by 1967
to 1070 (1; 3-5).   Between 1971 and 1977 the population varied between 1500 and
2500 (8), being 2335-2350 in 1977, about evenly split between the area around
Colorado County and the area farther south (R. Brownlee 1977, pers. comm.).

HABITAT   Coastal tall-grass prairie, cord-grass (Spartina spartinae) prairie
and, this century, also fallow ricefields and other combinations of pasture and
croplands (5).   A mosaic of well-drained prairie and fallow ricefields (prairie
chickens frequently make use of the third-year fallows, of the 4-year rice-growing
rotation, for nesting) can apparently support more birds than uniform prairie.
On the other hand, overgrazed pastures and agricultural crops of other kinds are
incompatible with prairie chicken needs, particularly as prairie once it has come
under the plough is often invaded by woody brush of such species as mesquite, live
oak and wax myrtle.   Rice cultivation has not increased significantly in the last
decade within the bird's remaining range; moreover, in the northern half of that
range, the soybean/rice rotation now under trial poses a threat (R. Brownlee 1977,
pers. comm.).   Other problems which have been noted include major urbanization or
other industrial development, for example around Houston, in what was once prime
prairie habitat; significant losses through skunk and possibly coyote predation
(this in northern not southern habitats, though parts of the latter probably had
more skunks, raccoons, opossums, cats, dogs and feral pigs, all likely predators,
than prairie chickens); occasional flooding on poorly drained land (this in the
southern sector); and intensive spraying of rice fields with persistent pesticides
and herbicides, though the adverse effects of this have not been proved (3; 5; 9;
10; R. Brownlee 1977, pers. comm.).

CONSERVATION MEASURES TAKEN   The subspecies now has full protection under the
U.S. Endangered Species Act and Texas state law (it was first legally protected in
1937) and is listed in Appendix 1 of the 1973 Convention on International Trade in
Endangered Species of Wild Fauna and Flora.   A recovery team appointed by the

state of Texas was reconstituted in 1977, and research into the ecology and biology of the subspecies, and on burning as a technique for managing its prairie habitat, is being undertaken. Some of the habitat is protected by the 4050 ha Attwater Prairie Chicken National Wildlife Refuge (up to 100 birds have been counted there but usually only about 10) and by the Aransas National Wildlife Refuge (the Tatton Unit of which contains 2000 ha and about 50 birds).

CONSERVATION MEASURES PROPOSED   Better habitat management and predator control have been urged for the northern sector of the range; creation of more 'edge effect', by promoting small areas of cultivation in large expanses of uniform prairie, has been suggested as a means of increasing the southern population (3; 5; R. Brownlee 1977, pers. comm.).

REMARKS   The nominate race Tympanuchus cupido cupido, the Heath Hen of coastal east central United States, became extinct in 1932. T. c. pinnatus, the Greater Prairie Chicken of the central plains of the U.S. and southern Canada, was classified as rare and decreasing in the previous edition of the Red Data Book. But although both its range and abundance are known to have been reduced, it is no longer considered as falling within any Red Data Book category, the facts being that even today it numbers upwards of a million birds in 8 states; in some states can sustain an annual hunting season; and has populations protected in several refuges (7).

REFERENCES   1.   Lehmann, V.W. 1941.   Attwater's Prairie Chicken: its life history and management.   North American Fauna 57.
2.   Oberholser, H.C. 1974.   The Bird Life of Texas, Vol. 1. Austin and London: University of Texas Press.
3.   Lehmann, V.W. & Mauermann, R.G. 1963.   Status of Attwater's Prairie Chicken.   Journ. Wildl. Mgmt. 27: 713-725.
4.   Lehmann, V.W. 1971.   Attwater's Prairie Chicken. Natl. Parks Cons. Mag. 49(9): 25-28.
5.   Lehmann, V.W. 1968.   The Attwater's Prairie Chicken: current status and restoration opportunities.   Trans. North Am. Wildl. Nat. Res. Conf. 33: 398-407.
6.   American Ornithologists' Union, 1975.   Report of the Committee on Conservation.   Auk 92(4, Suppl.): 1B-16B.
7.   U.S. Department of Interior Bureau of Sport Fisheries and Wildlife, 1973.   Threatened wildlife of the United States.   U.S. Bur. Sport Fish. Wildl. Res. Pub. 114.
8.   Brownlee, W.C. 1977.   Attwater's Prairie Chicken population census.   Texas Dept. of Parks and Wildlife Fed. Aid Proj. W-100-R-8, job no. 3.
9.   Brownlee, W.C. 1977.   Attwater's Prairie Chicken production. Texas Dept. of Parks and Wildlife Fed. Aid Proj. W-100-R-8, job no. 4.
10.   Brownlee, W.C. 1977.   Requirements of Attwater's Prairie Chicken.   Texas Dept. of Parks and Wildlife Fed. Aid Proj. W-100-R-8, job no. 9.

CHEER PHEASANT

Catreus wallichii (Hardwicke, 1827)

Order GALLIFORMES   Family PHASIANIDAE

STATUS   Endangered in most parts of its range, and possibly extinct in Pakistan.
Becoming increasingly rare and local in the western Himalayan foothills, where
habitat destruction and hunting have caused a serious deterioration in its status.

DISTRIBUTION   Hazara district, Pakistan, and Kashmir, India, south-east through
Himachal Pradesh and northern Uttar Pradesh along the Himalayan foothills to
Pokhara, central Nepal (1).   The present distribution of the species in India is
similar to its historical distribution, except that it is now absent from many
areas formerly occupied (K.L. Mehta in litt. to P. Wayre, 1968.).   It was believed,
in 1976, that it might still occur in Azad Kashmir (C. Savage 1977, pers. comm.).
In Nepal, however, the species appears to be holding its own and a small extension
of range has been noted (C. Fleming in litt. to C. Savage, 1975).

POPULATION   No estimates have been made.   The species was once considered far
from rare (2), but the populations in Kashmir, Punjab, Himachal Pradesh and
northern Uttar Pradesh have all decreased seriously (K.L. Mehta in litt. to P. Wayre
1968), while subject to the report previously mentioned it was thought as long ago
as 1970 to be nearing extinction in Azad Kashmir (3).   Its population in Nepal,
however, has not significantly deteriorated (J. Roberts 1976, pers. comm. to
P. Wayre).   Hunters have persecuted this species relentlessly and family groups
remain sedentary for several months at a time, even when under constant fire, which
makes them especially vulnerable (2).

HABITAT   Precipitous moist or dry temperate oak forest, scrub and open meadow
between 1,220m and 3,355m, and at somewhat lower elevations in winter (1).

CONSERVATION MEASURES TAKEN   The species is now totally protected in Pakistan,
although it may no longer be present.   In some reserved forests within its range
in India there is a close season during spring and summer, although poaching
continues to be a problem.   In 1971, 12 pairs, bred at the Pheasant Trust, Norwich,
England, were presented to the State Government of Himachal Pradesh for release in
a reserved forest near Simla.   In 1973 a further 12 pairs were released in the
same area (P. Wayre 1975, pers. comm.).   The species is listed in Appendix 2 of the
Convention on International Trade in Endangered Species of Wild Fauna and Flora of
1973, so that exploitation is subject to regulation by parties to the Convention.

CONSERVATION MEASURES PROPOSED   Additional reintroductions of captive-bred birds
into suitably protected areas of natural habitat have been proposed, for example in
Pakistan (4).   Captive bred birds have now been provided to India and Pakistan to
supply the needs of aviculture and for reintroduction trials in suitable areas.

REMARKS   The Cheer Pheasant first bred in captivity in Europe in 1858, was common
in avicultural collections until the First World War, when captive stocks dwindled
away.   In 1933, they reappeared in collections (5) and numbers in captivity have
gradually mounted to more than 800 birds by 1976 (C. Savage, pers. comm.).   Most
of these were bred in captivity.

REFERENCES   1.   Ali, S. & Ripley, S.D. 1969.   Handbook of the Birds of India and Pakistan.   Vol. 2.   Bombay, London, New York:Oxford University Press.

2.   Beebe, W. 1922.   A Monograph of the Pheasants, Vol. 3. London:H.F. and G. Witherby

3.   Roberts, T.J. 1970.   A note on the pheasants of West Pakistan. Pakistan Journal of Forestry 20:   319-326.

4.   Wayre, P. Undated.   Pheasant conservation in Pakistan with special reference to the Tragopan.   Lahore:Pakistan Wildlife Appeal;   Great Witchingham, Norwich:The Pheasant Trust.

5.   Delacour, J. 1951.   The Pheasants of the World.   London: Country Life, Ltd.;   New York:Charles Scribner's Sons.

MASKED BOBWHITE QUAIL

Colinus virginianus ridgwayi Brewster, 1885

Order GALLIFORMES   Family PHASIANIDAE

STATUS   Endangered.   Nearing extinction throughout its range, due to overgrazing of its grassland habitat by cattle, exacerbated by periodic drought.
Establishment of a population from captive stock in an area from which it has been
absent for 75 years is the best remaining hope for the survival of this distinctive
bobwhite subspecies.

DISTRIBUTION   Occurred in the United States in southern Arizona between the
Altar and Santa Cruz river valleys, and over a substantially larger area of
northern and central Sonora, Mexico.   It was effectively lost to Arizona by the
end of the 19th century, although sightings persisted until the 1930s.   In Sonora,
dates of its last recorded presence in areas formerly frequented were: Sásabe-
Molinos, on the northern border, 1884; Tecoripa-Rancho 1a Cuesta 1931; La
Misa-San Marcial 1942; Rancho Agua Fria-Valle de Agua Caliente 1950; and Mazatán-
Cobachi 1968.   But it has survived in the Benjamin Hill-Carbo area, north of
Hermosillo, up to the present. (1-4).

POPULATION   Once numerous within its limited range, the subspecies suffered
major declines during 1892 and 1893 in Arizona and between 1940 and 1950 in Sonora.
By 1972, it was estimated that at least 1000 were still present near Benjamin Hill,
but all other populations had been reduced to a small size and were not expected to
persist (2).   Subsequent habitat deterioration in the Benjamin Hill area was
reflected in a steady decline, with extinction in Sonora predicted for 1979,
although a few isolated birds or coveys might of course survive for several years.
Captive stocks are sizeable (6853 eggs were produced by the U.S. Fish and Wildlife
Service in 1976), but although release experiments have been attempted in Arizona
with increasing sophistication since 1937, a wild population has not yet become
established, due largely to unavailability of suitably protected habitat (4).

HABITAT   Desert grasslands between 300 and 1200 m elevation.   This habitat has
been extensively and significantly degraded by overgrazing of cattle and when this
is aggravated by persistent drought the soil is laid bare and the grasses do not
recover or are replaced by woody species (2; 3).   Despite pleas by conservationists, deterioration of the last two ranches in Sonora known to have populations of
Masked Bobwhites has been allowed to continue throughout the 1970s and they are no
longer capable of supporting the birds (4).

CONSERVATION MEASURES TAKEN   The subspecies is protected by law in the U.S. and
Mexico and listed in Appendix 1 of the 1973 Convention on International Trade in
Endangered Species of Wild Fauna and Flora.   A Recovery Team for the Masked
Bobwhite has been appointed by the U.S. Fish and Wildlife Service.   Private
conservation bodies and the Fish and Wildlife Service have been working since 1937
and 1965, respectively, on captive breeding of Masked Bobwhites for release to the
wild.   Breeding and release techniques have now reached the operational stage,
with over 650 releases in 1975 and over 800 in 1976.   In one area where some of
the released birds had established territories in 1976, incursions by cattle
prevented successful breeding (4).

CONSERVATION MEASURES PROPOSED   Purchase by the U.S. government of suitable land
for management as refuges for the subspecies.   Parallel negotiations with private
cattle ranches to ensure the long term preservation of suitable grassland habitat.
Mexico's Departamento de Fauna Silvestre is cooperating with the U.S. Fish and
Wildlife Service in a proposal to acquire a sanctuary in Sonora (4).

REMARKS   Four other subspecies of the Bobwhite, none of which are at risk, occur naturally in many of the contiguous areas of the United States and as far as southern Ontario in Canada.   They have also been introduced to several north-western U.S. states, British Columbia, Hawaii, Cuba, Jamaica, Haiti, St. Croix and New Zealand.

REFERENCES   1.   Ligon, J.S. 1952.   The vanishing Masked Bobwhite. Condor 54: 48-50.
              2.   Tomlinson, R.E. 1972.   Current status of the endangered Masked Bobwhite Quail.   Trans. N. Am. Wildl. Nat. Res. Conf. 37: 294-310.
              3.   Tomlinson, R.E. 1972.   Review of literature on the endangered Masked Bobwhite.   U.S. Fish Wildl. Svc. Res. Pubs. 108.
              4.   Ellis, D.H. & Serafin, J.A. 1977.   A research program for the endangered Masked Bobwhite.   World Pheasant Assoc. Journ. 2: 16-31.

WHITE EARED PHEASANT

Crossoptilon crossoptilon (Hodgson, 1838)

Order GALLIFORMES   Family PHASIANIDAE

STATUS   Vulnerable.   Distributed through the mountains of Assam, Burma and
western China including Tibet, and formerly relatively abundant in parts of its
range, although now believed to be threatened by forest destruction and by excessive
hunting.

DISTRIBUTION   Recorded from eastern Tibet north to southern Tsinghai, east to
eastern Sikang and south to northern Assam, northern Burma and north-western Yunnan
(1).   The present distribution is not known to differ materially from the
historical range but is presumed to be less widespread (P. Wayre 1975, pers. comm.).

POPULATION   The White Eared Pheasant was formerly described as locally abundant
in parts of its range (2; 3; 4) and was protected on religious grounds in Tibet,
where it became quite confiding.   There is no information from Tibet since the
Chinese occupation, but the paucity of birds offered to western collectors may be
an indication that the species is now scarce (P. Wayre 1975, pers. comm.).

HABITAT   High elevation forests, grasslands and alpine scrub between 3,000m and
the snowline (1; 2).   Some destruction of the forests is believed to have taken
place.

CONSERVATION MEASURES TAKEN   The species is listed in Appendix 1 of the 1973
Convention on International Trade in Endangered Species of Wild Fauna and Flora, and
is subject to strict regulation in international trade by contracting nations.

CONSERVATION MEASURES PROPOSED   A proposed Himalayan reserve in the Mishmi Hills
of northern Assam will increase protection of this species in India (C. Savage 1976,
pers. comm.).   In China some work may have been done on its domestication in
certain communes in Szechwan (5).   Attempts are being made to breed it in captivity
with a view to subsequent release of stocks in suitably protected natural habitat
(P. Wayre 1975, pers. comm.).

REMARKS   Five subspecies have been described, although one has recently been
considered so distinct from the others (C. c. harmoni) as to be a borderline case in
speciation (6).   White Eared Pheasants were first shown in western collections in
1891, but not bred until 1938.   A small number were imported to Europe and the
United States between the wars (2).   More recently one was imported in 1960 to the
Pheasant Trust, 6 pairs were sent to several European zoos in 1965, 2 pairs in 1966
to the Jersey Wildlife Preservation Trust, and in 1974 the Pheasant Trust received
2 pairs of the nominate race from the Peking Zoo.   One of these two pairs raised
20 young in 1976 (P. Wayre 1977, pers. comm.), but the majority of the 200 or more
now in captivity in Britain, Europe, and North America are descended from the
Jersey pairs (C. Savage 1976, pers. comm.).

REFERENCES   1.   Vaurie, C. 1965.   The Birds of the Palearctic Fauna.
                    Non-Passeriformes.   London:H.F. and G. Witherby.
               2.   Delacour, J. 1951.   The Pheasants of the World.   London:
                    Country Life Ltd.; New York:Charles Scribner's Sons.
               3.   Ludlow, F. 1944.   The birds of south-eastern Tibet.   Ibis
                    86: 43-86, 176-208, 348-389.
               4.   Beebe, W. 1918.   A Monograph of the Pheasants.   Vol. 1.
                    London:Witherby.

5. Cheng, Tso-Hsin, 1963. <u>China's Economic Fauna: Birds</u>. Peiping:Science Publishing Society. In Chinese, translated by U.S. Dept. Commerce Office of Tech. Services, 1964.

6. Vaurie, C. 1972. <u>Tibet and its Birds</u>. London:H.F. and G. Witherby.

BROWN EARED PHEASANT

Crossoptilon mantchuricum Swinhoe, 1862

Order GALLIFORMES   Family PHASIANIDAE

STATUS   Endangered.   This pheasant occurs in the mountains of northern China.
It is believed to be quite scarce due to human persecution and forest destruction,
although no new information on its status in the wild has been received since 1949.

DISTRIBUTION   The mountains of southern Chahar, Inner Mongolia, north-western
Hopei province and north and central Shansi province (1).   Believed to have been
extirpated in Hopei by 1931, but one bird from that province was bought in Peking in
1933 (2).   Its present distribution elsewhere is not known.

POPULATION   Not known, but believed to be quite small.   In 1862, the species was
already rare in parts of its range, although as recently as a few years before 1951,
it was still numerous in the mountains of Shansi (2).   The Peking Museum has
received no specimens or records of its occurrence since the inauguration of the
People's Republic in 1949 (Tso-Hsin Cheng in litt. to J. Vincent, 1964), although
the Peking Zoo has recently received several wild-caught birds (C. Savage 1976,
pers. comm.).

HABITAT   Stunted montane forest, shrub and grasslands (1).   Some destruction of
the forests has taken place (2; 3).

CONSERVATION MEASURES TAKEN   Listed in Appendix 1 of the 1973 Convention on
International Trade in Endangered Species of Wild Fauna and Flora, and subject to
strict regulation in international trade by contracting nations.

CONSERVATION MEASURES PROPOSED   Captive breeding with a view to release in
suitably protected natural habitat has been advocated (P. Wayre 1975, pers. comm.).

REMARKS   The Brown Eared Pheasant was first imported to Europe in 1864, when a
male and two females were sent to Paris, and successfully bred in 1866, in which
year two males were sent to London Zoo.   All 849 in captivity outside China in
1976 are descended from the 3 original importations (2; C. Savage 1976, pers.
comm.).   There were also 7 individuals at the Peking Zoo in 1975 (K.C. Searle 1977,
pers. comm.).   Despite the present abundance of the species in captivity,
inbreeding poses a problem to its future existence unless the gene-pool can be
enlarged by wild-caught birds.   However, two pairs were shipped to the Pheasant
Trust in England from China in 1976, of which three still survive.   All are
unrelated to those previously in captivity (P. Wayre 1977, pers. comm.).

REFERENCES   1.   Vaurie, C. 1965.   The Birds of the Palearctic Fauna.
                    Non-Passeriformes.   London:H.F. and G. Witherby.
              2.   Delacour, J. 1951.   The Pheasants of the World.   London:
                    Country Life, Ltd.;   New York:Charles Scribner's Sons.
              3.   Beebe, W. 1918.   A Monograph of the Pheasants.   Vol. 1.
                    London:Witherby.

TADJOURA FRANCOLIN

Francolinus ochropectus Dorst and Jouanin, 1952

Order GALLIFORMES   Family PHASIANIDAE

STATUS   Rare. This is a species of very restricted distribution; it is only
known from a small area of juniper forest in north-eastern Africa, which may well
have been considerably reduced in extent.

DISTRIBUTION   Occurs with certainty only in about 20 sq. km of juniper forest on
the Plateau du Day, Goda Massif, Cercle de Tadjoura, Djibouti (1; 2).

POPULATION   Unknown, but likely to be small in view of its extremely limited
distribution.   In 1954 total numbers were thought to be no more than a few
hundred (2).

HABITAT   The dominant species in the relict forest of the Plateau du Day,
inhabited by this francolin, are Juniperus procera and Buxus hildebrantii, but
Ficus spp., along the valleys that dissect the plateau, also provide an important
food source.   The altitude range within which the species occurs is 1100 to
1700 m.   Its principal predator is said to be one of the genets (2), but
destruction of its forest habitat undoubtedly poses a more serious threat to its
future.   No information about the precise state of the forest is presently
available; its character is such that livestock are unlikely to be tempted to
invade it, but on the other hand it may well be suffering from gradual deterioration as a result of continual lopping for fuel or building materials.

CONSERVATION MEASURES TAKEN   The Plateau du Day forest has been given protection,
as the Parc National du Daï, by the Djibouti government.   The Tadjoura Francolin
is listed in Appendix 2 of the 1973 Convention on International Trade in
Endangered Species of Wild Fauna and Flora, of which however Djibouti is not yet
a signatory.

CONSERVATION MEASURES PROPOSED   None known.

REMARKS   F. ochropectus is considered to be intermediate between F. erckelii,
which frequents the open grasslands of the high plateaux of northern Ethiopia,
and F. castaneicollis of montane evergreen forests in southern Ethiopia and
neighbouring Somalia, but sufficiently distinct from both to be treated as a valid
but weakly marked species, being isolated from its close relatives by some 240 km
(2-5).   It is not known to have been kept in captivity.

REFERENCES   1.   Dorst, J. & Jouanin, C. 1952.   Description d'une espèce
                    nouvelle de francolin d'Afrique orientale.   l'Oiseau et
                    R.F.O. 22: 71-74.
              2.   Dorst, J. & Jouanin, C. 1954.   Précisions sur la position
                    systématique et l'habitat de Francolinus ochropectus.
                    l'Oiseau et R.F.O. 24: 161-170.
              3.   Hall, B.P. & Moreau, R.E. 1962.   A study of the rare birds
                    of Africa.   Bull. Brit. Mus. (Nat. Hist.) Zool. 8(7): 313-378.
              4.   Hall, B.P. 1963.   The francolins, a study in speciation.
                    Bull. Brit. Mus. (Nat. Hist.) Zool. 10(2): 105-204.
              5.   Snow, D.W. (ed.) 1978.   An Atlas of Speciation in African
                    Non-passerine Birds.   London: Trustees of the British
                    Museum (Natural History).

SWIERSTRA's FRANCOLIN

Francolinus _swierstrai_ (Roberts, 1929)

Order GALLIFORMES   Family PHASIANIDAE

STATUS   Indeterminate.   This francolin is locally distributed in south-western
Angola.   Forest destruction is likely to have reduced its numbers.

DISTRIBUTION   Known from the Bailundu highlands, the Mombolo plateau and the
Chela escarpment, Angola, this species must have been more widespread, before so
much of the montane forest of that country was destroyed (1; 2).

POPULATION   Not known but likely to be small.   A decline has undoubtedly taken
place.

HABITAT   Montane evergreen forest and forest edges.   This francolin's habitat
has been fragmented by forest destruction, leaving only a few relict patches of a
few square kilometers each, for example on Moco and Soque mountains, and some
smaller patches along the Chela escarpment, 320 km to the south (1).

CONSERVATION MEASURES TAKEN   Listed in Appendix 2 of the 1973 Convention on
International Trade in Endangered Species of Wild Fauna and Flora, of which
Angola became a signatory in 1977.

CONSERVATION MEASURES PROPOSED   None known.

REMARKS   This francolin is not known to be represented in captive collections.

REFERENCES   1.   Hall, B.P. & Moreau, R.E. 1962.   A study of the rare
                    birds of Africa.   Bull. Brit. Mus. (Nat. Hist. Zool.
                    8(7): 313-378.
              2.   Snow, D.W. (ed.) 1978.   An Atlas of Speciation in
                    African Non-passerine Birds.   London: Trustees of the
                    British Museum (Natural History).

CHINESE MONAL

Lophophorus lhuysii Geoffroy Saint Hilaire, 1866

Order GALLIFORMES   Family PHASIANIDAE

STATUS   Endangered.   Rare throughout its restricted range in western China and
under heavy pressure from hunters who seek this bird avidly.

DISTRIBUTION   In north-eastern Sikang, western and north-western Szechwan, south-
eastern Tsinghai, and possibly southern Kansu, western China (1).   Not known to
have altered.

POPULATION   No estimates have been made.   In 1877 it was already considered rare
throughout its range and likely to disappear before long (2).   In 1910 and 1951 the
same assessment was made (3; 4).   There is no recent information.

HABITAT   High montane coniferous forests with an undergrowth of rhododendron up
into alpine meadows and tundra at 3050m to 4880m altitude but in winter down to
2745m (1).   No part of the habitat of this pheasant is known to be protected;
however, hunting rather than habitat destruction is responsible for its precarious
state (2; 3; 4).

CONSERVATION MEASURES TAKEN   Listed in Appendix 1 of the 1973 Convention on
International Trade in Endangered Species of Wild Fauna and Flora, traffic in it
therefore being subject to strict control by ratifying nations.

CONSERVATION MEASURES PROPOSED   None known.

REMARKS   Held in captivity only very rarely and has never bred in the western
world (5).   The only captive birds recently reported were in Peking Zoo, where
there were five in 1974 (6); but by 1975 only one male was seen there (S.D. Ripley
pers. comm.) and none in 1976 (C. Savage pers. comm.).

REFERENCES   1.   Vaurie, C. 1965.   The Birds of the Palearctic Fauna.
                     Non-Passeriformes.   London:H.F. and G. Witherby.
              2.   David, A. & Oustalet, M.E. 1877.   Les Oiseaux de la Chine.
                     Paris:G. Masson.
              3.   Beebe, W. 1918.   A Monograph of the Pheasants.   Vol. 1.
                     London:Witherby.
              4.   Delacour, J. 1951.   The Pheasants of the World.   London:
                     Country Life Ltd.;   New York:Charles Scribner's Sons.
              5.   Wayre, P. 1969.   A Guide to the Pheasants of the World.
                     London, New York, Sydney, Toronto:Country Life.
              6.   Duplaix-Hall, N. 1975.   Census of rare animals in captivity,
                     1974.   Internat. Zoo Yearbook 15: 397-405.

SCLATER'S MONAL

Lophophorus sclateri   Jerdon, 1870

Order GALLIFORMES   Family PHASIANIDAE

STATUS   Rare over much of its range in southern Asia, but tolerably abundant in at
least part of it in Burma.   Human persecution is believed to be the major threat
to this species.

DISTRIBUTION   South-eastern Tibet, Assam from the Abor and Mishmi Hills east to
the mountains of northern Burma and western Yunnan, China, and south to the Shweli-
Salween divide where it crosses the Burma-Yunnan border (1; 2; 3).   Not known to
have changed, although there have been few reports since the 1930s.

POPULATION   No estimates have been made.   It was already considered rare in 1910
(4), and is doubtless still more so today in most parts of its range.   Naga
trappers in Assam have long been unable to find this species (P. Wayre 1975, pers.
comm.).   However, a report in 1968 indicated that the species was still quite
common in parts of Burma, particularly at elevations between 2,440m and 2,745m
(U Tun Yin in litt. to J. Vincent).

HABITAT   Montane forest with dense rhododendron understory (1).   None of this
monal's habitat is known to be protected.

CONSERVATION MEASURES TAKEN   Listed in Appendix 1 of the 1973 Convention on
International Trade in Endangered Species of Wild Fauna and Flora, and traffic in it
therefore subject to some degree of restriction.   The educational efforts on the
bird's behalf, among people living in the vicinity of its range, by U Zanhta Sin,
Chairman of the Rawang Cultural Committee, who was also at that time compiling a
book on the birds of the Kachin State, were exemplary (U Tun Yin in litt. to
J. Vincent, 1968).

CONSERVATION MEASURES PROPOSED   The proposed Himalayan Reserve in the Mishmi
Hills may protect a part of this monal's range (Ranjitsinh 1976, pers. comm. to
C. Savage).

REMARKS   The species is almost unknown in captivity, except for the type
specimen which was sent alive to London Zoo in 1870 and lived there for 20 months
(4).   None are known to be held in collections at the present time (P. Wayre 1975,
pers. comm.).   Recently birds from the eastern end of the range of the species,
from north-east Burma and north-west Yunnan south along the Shweli (Lung-chuan
Chiang)-Salween (Nu Chian) watershed, have been separated as a subspecies L. s.
orientalis from typical L. s. sclateri occupying the rest of the range (5).

REFERENCES   1.   Ali, S. & Ripley, S.D. 1969.   Handbook of the Birds of India
                     and Pakistan.   Vol. 2.   Bombay, London, New York:Oxford
                     University Press.
              2.   Delacour, J. 1951.   The Pheasants of the World.   London:
                     Country Life Ltd.;   New York:Charles Scribner's Sons.
              3.   Rothschild, 1926.   On the avifauna of Yunnan, with critical
                     notes.   Nov. Zool. 33: 189-343.
              4.   Beebe, W. 1918.   A Monograph of the Pheasants.   Vol. 1.
                     London:Witherby and Co.
              5.   Davison, G.W.H. 1974.   Geographical variation in Lophophorus
                     sclateri.   Bull. Brit. Ornith. Club 94: 163-164.

BULWER'S WATTLED PHEASANT

Lophura _bulweri_ (Sharpe, 1874)

Order GALLIFORMES   Family PHASIANIDAE

STATUS   Vulnerable.   Restricted to the island of Borneo, where it is widespread
but locally distributed.   The opening up of the forests for logging poses a
potential threat to its survival.

DISTRIBUTION   This pheasant is widespread in submontane primary forests of Sabah,
Sarawak, and Kalimantan but decidedly local (1).   Its range is not known to
have altered significantly up to 1974 (T. Harrisson _in_ _litt._ to P. Wayre).

POPULATION   No estimates have been made.   In 1910, Bulwer's Wattled Pheasant was
locally not uncommon, although there were extensive unoccupied areas between the
localities where it was found (1).

HABITAT   Primary forest between 300m and 750m in altitude (1; T. Harrisson _in_
litt. to P. Wayre, 1974).   Although extensive suitable forests remain, much of the
primary forest is scheduled for cutting and much has already been cut.   Virtually
all primary forests of Borneo have been contracted out to lumber companies,
including forest reserves and at least some national parks.   Exceptions, where some
primary forest will probably be protected, include Mt. Kinabalu National Park
(712 sq. km) and Pulau Gaya National Park (1276 ha), Sabah, and there are possibly
a small number of other areas.   One-third of Kutai National Park (3,060 sq. km),
Kalimantan, has already been cleared of forest; oil exploitation is also in progress
within its boundaries.   If existing logging schedules are adhered to, all primary
forest, excluding the few areas mentioned above, will be converted to agricultural
lands or second growth, by 1980 in Sabah and by 1995 in Kalimantan (W. Meijer 1976,
pers. comm.).

CONSERVATION MEASURES TAKEN   None beyond the creation of the parks and reserves
mentioned above.   The species is not protected by law, although further collection
of specimens for export has been stopped.

CONSERVATION MEASURES PROPOSED   A highland forest reserve is under consideration
in central Kalimantan.   The area, called Bakit Raya, would include the mountain
Gunung Bondang, on which the pheasant is known to occur (D. Soerodjo 1976, pers.
comm. to C. Savage).

REMARKS   This species is only one of many on Borneo that depend on primary forest.
All will be eliminated when existing forestry plans have been carried out by the
turn of the century.   Bulwer's Wattled Pheasant first appeared in western
collections in 1876, and has been kept sporadically up to the present day (2),
although breeding did not take place until 1974, in a private collection in Mexico.
By 1975, there were at least 34 birds in collections in the United States, Europe
and Mexico (3).

REFERENCES   1.   Beebe, W. 1921.   A Monograph of the Pheasants.   Vol. 2.
                    London:H.F. and G. Witherby.
              2.   Delacour, J. 1951.   The Pheasants of the World.   London:
                    Country Life Ltd.;   New York:Charles Scribner's Sons.
              3.   Sivelle, C. 1975.   Bulwer's Wattled Pheasants.   Amer.
                    Pheasant and Waterfowl Soc. Mag. 75(2):   11-15.

EDWARDS'S PHEASANT

Lophura edwardsi (Oustalet, 1896)

Order GALLIFORMES   Family PHASIANIDAE

STATUS   Vulnerable.   Rare and localized in Vietnam.   Its habitat has recently
been subjected to the ravages of war, although to unknown effect.

DISTRIBUTION   Apparently confined to a restricted area in Quangtri, Hue and
Faifo provinces, just south of the former demarcation line between north and
south Vietnam (1).   No evidence of any recent alteration in its range.

POPULATION   No estimates have been made; this little-known species has always
been considered difficult to observe, rare and localized (1; 2).   A report from
Vietnam in 1975 stated that Edwards's Pheasants were thriving in secondary growth
following defoliation and were more numerous than ever known before.   They were
often sighted and also killed for food by U.S. military personnel (C. Savage 1978,
pers. comm.).

HABITAT   Rugged limestone hills covered by damp forest with thick underbrush (2).
The habitat was sprayed extensively with herbicides by U.S. forces during the
Vietnam war, which may have caused mortality of forest animals, at least locally
(3), and probably had both direct and indirect effects on pheasant populations,
through poisoning and habitat destruction, although the extent of these effects
has not been documented.

CONSERVATION MEASURES TAKEN   The species is listed in Appendix 1 of the 1973
Convention on International Trade in Endangered Species of Wild Fauna and Flora,
and traffic in it is subject to strict regulation by contracting nations.   A
studbook to record all captive specimens is maintained by the World Pheasant
Association.

CONSERVATION MEASURES PROPOSED   The World Pheasant Association has recommended
to the Vietnam government protection of the species as a national monument
(C. Savage 1978, pers. comm.).   Planned exchanges of captive birds have been made
recently with beneficial results.   Reintroduction of captive stocks to the wild
at some later date, should it prove to be advisable, has also been suggested
(P. Wayre 1975, C. Savage 1978, pers. comms).

REMARKS   Edwards's Pheasant first entered western collections in 1924, breeding
successfully the following year.   Additional wild-caught birds have contributed
from time to time to the gene pool (2) and by 1976 there were 635 captive specimens
in Europe and North America.   Signs of degeneration due to inbreeding can be
reversed by management of the captive stock based on the studbook (C. Savage 1978,
pers. comm.).

REFERENCES   1.   Delacour, J. & Jabouille, P. 1925.   On the birds of Quangtri,
                   central Annam; with notes on others from other parts of
                   French Indo-China.   Ibis (12th series)1: 209-260.
              2.   Delacour, J. 1977.   The Pheasants of the World. 2nd Ed.
                   London: Spur Publications and the World Pheasant Association.
              3.   Hickey, G.C. 1974.   Perceived effects of herbicides used in
                   the highlands of South Vietnam.   In The Effects of Herbicides
                   in South Vietnam.   Washington, D.C.: Academy of Sciences
                   - National Research Council.

IMPERIAL PHEASANT

Lophura imperialis (Delacour and Jabouille, 1924)

Order GALLIFORMES   Family PHASIANIDAE

STATUS   Vulnerable. Known only from the vicinity of the former demarcation line between north and south Vietnam and from adjacent Laos where it is scarce.

DISTRIBUTION   Recorded from the Vietnamese provinces of Dong Hoi (formerly in North) and Quangtri (formerly in the South) and neighbouring parts of Laos (1). Not known to have altered but access to this area has been severely restricted for many years by the political situation and also by the natural obstacles of dense vegetation and rugged terrain.

POPULATION   Not known, although believed to be small (2); whether there has been a recent decline is also quite unknown.

HABITAT   Dense forest and brush of chaotically rough limestone mountains (1). Part of the habitat was sprayed by defoliants by U.S. military forces during the Vietnam war. Some forest animals are believed to have been poisoned by ingestion of large amounts of the herbicides (3). The effects on the Imperial Pheasant are not documented, but are likely to have been both direct, through poisoning, and indirect, through habitat destruction. The actual border area or so-called Demilitarized Zone received heavy defoliant application (4).

CONSERVATION MEASURES TAKEN   Listed in Appendix 1 of the 1973 Convention on International Trade in Endangered Species of Wild Fauna and Flora, and traffic in it subject to strict regulation in international trade by contracting nations.

CONSERVATION MEASURES PROPOSED   Captive breeding to perpetuate the species for eventual reintroduction was planned at the Pheasant Trust, Norwich, England, although a shortage of suitable breeding stock has hampered success (P. Wayre 1975, pers. comm.).

REMARKS   The Imperial Pheasant is closely related to the equally vulnerable Edwards's Pheasant Lophura edwardsi replacing it geographically, immediately to the north (2). The pair of Imperial Pheasants on which the original description of the species was based was imported alive to Clères, France, in 1924 and bred the following year (1). The 27 birds in captivity in 1976 were all descended from them. There are also 17 birds of hybrid origin in collections (C. Savage 1976, pers. comm.) but without an infusion of fresh blood existing captive stocks are likely to die out.

REFERENCES   1. Delacour, J. 1951. The Pheasants of the World. London: Country Life Ltd.; New York:Charles Scribner's Sons.
              2. Delacour, J. & Jabouille, P. 1925. On the birds of Quangtri, central Annam; with notes on others from other parts of French Indo-China. Ibis (12th series) 1: 209-260.
              3. Hickey, G.C. 1974. Perceived effects of herbicides used in the highlands of South Vietnam. In The Effects of Herbicides in South Vietnam. Washington, D.C.:National Academy of Sciences - National Research Council.
              4. Carrier, J.M. 1974. Estimating the Highlander population affected by herbicides. In The Effects of Herbicides in South Vietnam. Washington, D.C.:National Academy of Sciences - National Research Council.

SWINHOE's PHEASANT

Lophura swinhoii (Gould, 1862)

Order GALLIFORMES   Family PHASIANIDAE

STATUS   Vulnerable.   Unique to Taiwan, where the preferred habitat of the
species is under mounting pressure from many competing land use practices.   It is
still live-trapped for commercial trade, although less so now than previously.

DISTRIBUTION   Found widely in the mountains of Taiwan, including the central
mountains, the East Coast Range and the northern hills near Taipei, from close to
sea level in some places to 2000m elevation, occasionally higher (S. Severinghaus
1975, pers. comm.).

POPULATION   More common in the past, but still probably fairly numerous,
totalling perhaps a few thousand individuals today.   The population is likely to
be declining as preferred habitat decreases, although this may be offset to some
extent by adaptation to man-altered environments (S. Severinghaus 1975, pers. comm.).

HABITAT   Primary hardwood forests on mountainsides with a slope of less than 40°,
but also mature secondary hardwood forests and to some extent other second growth.
Hardwood forests below 2000m are steadily being cleared for agriculture, forestry,
mining, hydro-electric power, tourism, transportation and developments associated
with these activities.   General harassment of the species is increasing with
easier access to and increased development of the mountainous areas (S. Severinghaus
1977, pers. comm.).

CONSERVATION MEASURES TAKEN   Protected by the Japanese as a natural monument from
1919 to the end of World War II.   The Taiwan Government declared the species to be
fully protected in 1967 and in 1974 passed a law prohibiting the export of wildlife,
including pheasants (D. Poltock in litt. to P. Wayre).   Further protection is
afforded by a three-year ban on hunting of wildlife, instituted in 1972 and renewed
in 1975 for three more years.   Also in 1974 the Taiwan Government created a 3680-
hectare high-altitude reserve, principally for the protection of Swinhoe's Pheasant
and the likewise vulnerable Mikado Pheasant Syrmaticus mikado (S. Severinghaus 1975,
pers. comm.).   In 1967, six males and five females bred at the Pheasant Trust near
Norwich, England, were released in the Che Chi experimental forest belonging to
National Taiwan University, near Hsitou in the central mountains (1).   A further
six pairs were released in the same area in 1968 and the pheasant has subsequently
been seen several times in the release area (2).   The species is listed in
Appendix 1 of the 1973 Convention on International Trade in Endangered Species of
Wild Fauna and Flora, so that traffic in it should now be strictly controlled by
ratifying nations.

CONSERVATION MEASURES PROPOSED   Additional portions of the range of Swinhoe's
Pheasant have been proposed as national parks or nature reserves (3), including five
areas specifically recommended to the Taiwan Forestry Bureau and National Science
Council, all of which are known to hold Swinhoe's Pheasant or are potentially
suitable.   The species has also been suggested as an appropriate "Provincial Bird"
for Taiwan, symbolizing the uniqueness and value of the island's avifauna.   Thirdly,
to ensure its survival, it has been recommended that main efforts should be
concentrated on saving tracts of primary hardwood forests (S. Severinghaus 1977,
pers. comm.).

REMARKS   There were at least 1693 Swinhoe's Pheasants in captivity in 1976
(C. Savage, pers. comm.).

REFERENCES   1.   Wayre, P. 1967.   Swinhoe's Pheasants for Taiwan.   Ornamental
                     Pheasant Trust Annual Report 1967: 11-18.
              2.   Wayre, P. 1972.   Breeding endangered species of pheasants in
                     captivity as a means of ensuring their survival.   Pheasant
                     Trust Annual Report 1972.
              3.   Wayre, P. 1967.   Advisory report on the wildlife of Taiwan with
                     proposals for its conservation.   Published by the author.

GORGETED WOOD-QUAIL

Odontophorus strophium (Gould, 1844)

Order GALLIFORMES   Family PHASIANIDAE

STATUS   Endangered. This secretive wood-quail has not been found at its type
locality in Colombia for 60 years, but it may still survive in some of the forest
patches elsewhere in the country.

DISTRIBUTION   Known from two old "Bogotá" skins and from two additional
specimens taken at Subia near Bogotá, Colombia, in about 1915 (1).   A specimen,
which is likely to prove to belong to this species, was taken about 1972 on the
east slope of the Eastern Andes near Betulia, in the Santander division.   There
are still scattered patches of forest in this area where this wood-quail may yet
be found (J. Hernandez 1977, pers. comm. to R. Ridgely).

POPULATION   Unknown. The survival of this species is still in doubt.

HABITAT   Temperate zone forest. Small patches of forest remain in the area
where specimens were collected over 60 years ago, but are probably too small and
disturbed to harbour this species. The recent specimen, awaiting final confirmation, was taken in oak (Quercus) forest, of which some suitable areas are still to
be found in Santander, although none are protected (J. Hernandez 1977, pers. comm.
to R. Ridgely).

CONSERVATION MEASURES TAKEN   None known.

CONSERVATION MEASURES PROPOSED   None known.

REMARKS   It has been suggested that Odontophorus strophium may be conspecific
with O. dialeucus of Darién, Panama (2; 3). The recent Santander specimen is
reported to be on display at a college in Tunja, Boyaca division.

REFERENCES   1. de Schauensee, R.M. 1966. The Species of Birds of South
                  America and Their Distribution.   Narberth, Pa.: Livingston
                  Publishing Co.
              2. Wetmore, A. 1963.   The Birds of the Republic of Panama.
                  Part 1.   Tinamidae (Tinamous) to Rynchopidae (Skimmers).
                  Smithsonian Misc. Coll., 150.
              3. Kuroda, N. 1970.   Odontophorinae and Perdicinae of the
                  World.   Ornithological Society of Japan.

GREEN PEAFOWL

Pavo muticus Linnaeus, 1766

Order GALLIFORMES   Family PHASIANIDAE

STATUS   Vulnerable.   The species used to be widespread in South East Asia, but
has recently suffered a serious decline and is now absent from large parts of its
former range.   The principal causes of its disappearance have been human pot-
hunting and large-scale modification of its habitat for the purposes of
agriculture.

DISTRIBUTION   There are three subspecies: 1. Nominate P. m. muticus is recorded
from Java and the Malay Peninsula north to the Isthmus of Kra (1); it is now
severely restricted, occurring only in the Udjong Kulon and Baluran Reserves in
west and east Java, respectively (J. Blower & S. Somadikarta 1976, pers. comm. to
C. Savage).   There is no longer any positive news of its presence in peninsular
Malaysia (2; D. Wells 1978, pers. comm. to C. Savage) and a recent report from
Terutao Island off the west coast of Thailand just north of the Malaysian border
requires confirmation (J. McNeely 1976, pers. comm.).   2. P. m. imperator
formerly ranged widely through Indo-China, southern Yunnan (China), Thailand south
to the Isthmus of Kra, and eastern Burma (1).   It was not found in intensive
searches of south Thailand between the Malaysian border and Trang province from
1972 to 1974 (D. Wells pers. comms, to P. Wayre 1975 and to C. Savage 1978).   It
certainly still occurs in north-east Thailand in the Petchabun Range and in north-
west Thailand along the Burmese border (J. McNeely 1976, pers. comm.).   Its
distribution in Indo-China may be similarly reduced and there is no up to date
information from Yunnan or Burma.   3. P. m. spicifer has been recorded from the
Chittagong and Lushai hills of south-east Assam, where it had disappeared by 1975
(M.J.S. Mackenzie 1975, pers. comm. to C. Savage), Manipur, North Cachar and mid
Assam, where it had disappeared by 1951 (1)   Its distribution in western Burma
is not known to have changed, although it is certainly persecuted in the more
accessible areas (3).

POPULATION   The species was considered locally common as recently as 1951 (1),
since when there have been serious but undocumented declines.   As already
mentioned, the Javan population is restricted to Udjong Kulon and estimated at
less than 50 in 1965, and to Baluran, where there were about 200 in that year
(J. Blower & S. Somadikarta 1976, pers. comm. to C. Savage).   Small populations
have also been recorded on the islands of Pucang off Udjong Kulon, on Panaitan in
the Sunda Strait (R. Schenkel 1978, pers. comm. to C. Savage) and, reputedly, on
Terutao Island, Thailand.   It would appear to be extinct or nearly so in
peninsular Malaysia and Assam.   Fair numbers of P. m. imperator are reported only
in north-east and north-west Thailand, where they may well be adversely affected
by the disturbed political situation, and this subspecies was already becoming
scarce in western Burma by 1942 (3; 4).

HABITAT   River banks, clearings and park-like country, with long grass and
patches of jungle, from near sea level to 1220 m elevation (1).   In Java vast
stretches of countryside which were Green Peafowl haunts are now completely
devoted to agriculture and devoid of suitable cover (D. Wells 1975, pers. comm.).

CONSERVATION MEASURES TAKEN   Protected by law in Indonesia since 1973, totally
protected by the 1973 Wildlife Act in Malaysia, and also protected in Thailand.
Two protected areas in Indonesia, Udjong Kulon and Baluran, are known to support
stable populations.   What is said to be a well-protected national park of
149,000 ha has been established on Terutao Island.

<u>CONSERVATION MEASURES PROPOSED</u>   None additional known.

<u>REMARKS</u>   This peafowl is widely represented in collections.   There were about 500 in captivity in 1976 (C. Savage 1976, pers. comm.), but it is doubtful if they include any pure <u>P</u>. <u>m</u>. <u>muticus</u> (D. Wells 1978, pers. comm. to C. Savage).

<u>REFERENCES</u>   1.   Delacour, J. 1977.   <u>The Pheasants of the World</u>, 2nd Ed. London: Spur Publications and the World Pheasant Association.
2.   Lord Medway & Wells, D.R. 1976.   <u>The Birds of the Malay Peninsula</u>.   Vol. 5.   London: H.F. and G. Witherby.
3.   Smythies, B. 1953.   <u>The Birds of Burma</u>.   Edinburgh and London: Oliver and Boyd.
4.   Smith, H.C. 1942.   <u>Notes on Birds of Burma</u>.   Simla: H.C. Smith.

ITALIAN GREY PARTRIDGE

Perdix perdix italica Hartert, 1917

Order GALLIFORMES   Family PHASIANIDAE

STATUS   Endangered. This subspecies of the Grey Partridge has been severely
reduced in distribution and abundance by hunting, changes in agricultural
practice, competition from introduced game birds, and genetic swamping from
introduced Grey Partridges of other subspecies.   Few pure populations continue
to exist.

DISTRIBUTION   Formerly extended over the greater part of the Italian peninsula,
but a gradual, continuous decline has occurred, beginning about the turn of the
century.   The subspecies was first eliminated on the periphery of its range,
surviving only in a few hill areas in central Italy (1).   The localities where
pure populations of this subspecies are now known to occur are confined to two
private shooting reserves near Radda and Castellina in Chianti, north of Siena in
Tuscany (2).

POPULATION   The serious decline of this subspecies set in around 1900.   Grey
Partridges from northern and eastern Europe, and captive-bred birds of mixed but
partially italica stock, were repeatedly released, the former up to 1960, the
latter from 1960 to the present day.   Resulting populations, while temporarily
high, have never attained their original abundance (3).   Although no proper
estimates are available, it is feared that the remaining population of unmixed
birds is restricted to a few small coveys (2).

HABITAT   Open areas on hills and lower mountains.   The advent of monoculture
in agriculture, in conjunction with use of herbicides and pesticides, has had a
serious impact on partridge populations.   Competition for food from introduced
pheasants Phasianus colchicus may also have been important in certain areas (3).

CONSERVATION MEASURES TAKEN   The shooting season for this species in Italy has
been limited to the period between the last Sunday in August and 1 January, but
it is estimated that there is one hunter for every 10 ha of land in which shooting
takes place (3).

CONSERVATION MEASURES PROPOSED   It is hoped that newly enacted regional hunting
regulations in Italy will help protect the small remaining population of P. p.
italica (2; 4).

REMARKS   None of the nine other subspecies of Grey Partridge is known to be at
risk.   This subspecies like the others could doubtless be bred readily in game
farms, but it would probably suffer from the same disabilities - loss of
adaptiveness and vitality - when released into the wild.

REFERENCES   1.   Ghigi, A. 1968.   Fagiani, Pernici e Altri Galliformi da
                      Caccia e da Voliera.   Bologna: Edizioni Agricole.
                2.   Lovari, S. Undated report.   The Italian Grey Partridge
                      (Perdix perdix italica Hartert): a subspecies in danger of
                      extinction.
                3.   Renzoni, A. 1974.   The decline of the Grey Partridge in
                      Italy.   Biol. Cons. 6: 213-215.
                4.   Renzoni, A. 1975.   Hunting regulations in Italy: a move
                      in the right direction.   Biol. Cons. 8: 185-188.

PALAWAN PEACOCK PHEASANT

Polyplectron emphanum Temminck, 1831

Order GALLIFORMES   Family PHASIANIDAE

STATUS   Vulnerable.   Restricted to Palawan, Philippines, where it is still
reasonably common but under constant pressure from habitat destruction, due to
logging, and from trapping.

DISTRIBUTION   Widespread in the lowlands and in some places, at least, in the
hills of the 480 km by 24 km island, the southwesternmost of the large islands of
the Philippines, but locally it has been extirpated, although still found near some
settlements.   In 1974 and 1975, it was confirmed as present throughout the south-
eastern two-thirds of the island (1).

POPULATION   Considered less common than formerly but recently referred to as not
yet a particularly rare bird, although undoubtedly decreasing as suitable habitat
decreases (1).

HABITAT   Primary forests of the coastal plain and, at least in parts of its range,
the more arid woodland and scrub of the foothills.   It is possible, though not yet
demonstrated, that the species may now be adapting to rough cut-over forest growth.
The entire exploitable forest area of Palawan, which unlike many islands in the
Philippines is restricted to the coastal plain, is under lease, but by 1975 only a
portion of the forests on the east coast had been felled (1).   There are no
protected natural areas on the island.

CONSERVATION MEASURES TAKEN   Totally protected by law but in practice trapped
widely and openly for food and for export to aviculturists (1).   These exports of
live birds were at one time estimated to be in the region of 70 to 100 per year
(I. Grimwood in litt. to P. Wayre 1974), but only a fifth of those captured survive
to the export stage, because of the unsuitable conditions under which they are kept
(H. Bregulla 1974, pers. comm.).

CONSERVATION MEASURES PROPOSED   The key to the future of this pheasant is its
ability to adapt to scrub and cut-over forest, for the primary forests of Palawan
are doomed.   If the species proves to be not wholly dependent on a climax forest
habitat, its future should be relatively secure (1), but otherwise the only way to
ensure its survival would be to preserve tracts of primary forest.

REMARKS   The congeneric Bornean Peacock Pheasant Polyplectron malacense
schleiermacheri was included in the previous edition of the Red Data Book, but is no
longer considered as particularly rare nor threatened.   The number of Palawan
Peacock Pheasants in captivity is now 364 (C. Savage 1976, pers. comm.).   Over
100 have been bred by Dr. K.C. Searle, Botanic Gardens, Hong Kong, in the past ten
years and the species appears to be well established in captivity.   It is to be
found in collections in three continents and at least 60 are being bred in captivity
annually (C. Savage 1976, pers. comm.).

REFERENCES   1.   Grimwood, I. 1974.   Report to P. Wayre, Hon. Director,
                   Pheasant Trust.   In Pheasant Trust Annual Report: 9-10.

CRESTED ARGUS PHEASANT

Rheinardia ocellata ocellata (Elliot, 1871)

Rheinardia ocellata nigrescens (Rothschild, 1902)

Order GALLIFORMES   Family PHASIANIDAE

STATUS   Rare. Known from rather limited areas in Vietnam, Laos and the Malay
peninsula respectively. The Malayan subspecies has always been considered quite
rare and its status is unlikely to have changed recently.

DISTRIBUTION   The nominate race is found in central Vietnam and Laos and has
been recorded from Qui Nhon, Vietnam, at $14^{o}N$, to Vinh and Tranninh, between
Vientiane and Luang Prabang in Laos, at $19^{o}N$ (1-3); but it has not been seen in the
field by any ornithologist for over 50 years. R. o. nigrescens has been recorded
in three localities of north Pahang and south Kelantan, Malaysia (1; D. Wells in
litt. to P. Wayre, Feb. 1975).

POPULATION   No estimate has been made for the nominate race, although it was
considered common within parts of its restricted range in 1924 (4).   Half a
century ago R. o. nigrescens was described as by no means uncommon though
excessively wary (1), and there is no evidence that it has declined.   On Gunong
Rabong in Taman Negara National Park, south Kelantan, Davison estimated 15 males
with dancing grounds and a total population of probably less than 50.   On Gunong
Benom in Pahang he found that it was very local and that there were large sections
of the mountain where it was apparently absent; conversely he considered that it
almost certainly occurred on another as yet uninvestigated Malayan mountain and
probably on a few more (5; G. Davison 1978, pers. comm. to C. Savage).

HABITAT   Dense undergrowth in forests between sea level and 915 m altitude,
occasionally up to 1,525 m (1; 2).   The altitudinal range in Malaysia is only
800 m to 1050 m (G. Davison 1978 in litt. to C. Savage).   The range of both
subspecies has been affected by forest destruction and may have been aggravated in
the case of the nominate race by military activities, including repeated defoliation by herbicides (7); however the precise effects of this on the pheasant remain
unknown.

CONSERVATION MEASURES TAKEN   A portion of the range of R. o. nigrescens lies
within Taman Negara National Park, as already noted.   In Malaysia this pheasant
is totally protected, but some of the population is bound to be displaced by
future logging (G. Davison 1978, pers. comm. to C. Savage).

CONSERVATION MEASURES PROPOSED   None known.

REMARKS   The nominate subspecies was first brought to Europe in captivity in 1924
and was bred regularly thereafter until the Second World War, by the end of which
no captive specimens survived in the West (2).   R. o. nigrescens is not known
to be in captivity (2; 3).

REFERENCES   1.   Beebe, W. 1918-22.   A Monograph of the Pheasants, Vol. 4.
                    London: H.F. and G. Witherby.
               2.   Delacour, J. 1977.   The Pheasants of the World. 2nd Ed.
                    London: Spur Publications and the World Pheasant Association.
               3.   Wayre, P. 1969.   A Guide to the Pheasants of the World.
                    London, New York, Toronto: Country Life.

4. Delacour, J. & Jabouille, P. 1925. On the birds of Quangtri, central Annam; with notes on others from other parts of French Indo-China. Ibis (12th series)1: 209-260.

5. Davison, G.W.H. 1977. Studies of the Crested Argus. 1. History and problems associated with the species in Malaysia. World Pheasant Assoc. Journ. 2: 50-56.

6. Davison, G.W.H. 1978. Studies of the Crested Argus. 2. Gunong Rabong. World Pheasant Assoc. Journ. 3: 46-53.

7. Carrier, J.M. 1974. Estimating the Highlander population affected by herbicides. In The Effects of Herbicides in South Vietnam. Washington, D.C.: National Academy of Sciences - National Research Council.

ELLIOT'S PHEASANT

Syrmaticus ellioti (Swinhoe, 1872)

Order GALLIFORMES   Family PHASIANIDAE

STATUS   Endangered.   Occurs in the mountains of eastern China, where its forest
habitat has been largely destroyed and where it is subject to uncontrolled hunting.

DISTRIBUTION   Recorded from Kiangsi, southern Anhwei, Chekiang, Fukien and
northern Kwangtung provinces, eastern China (1).   It is less widespread than
formerly.

POPULATION   No estimates have been made.   Already by 1910, it was described as
not common and extremely local (2) and, in 1951, it was considered widespread but
nowhere abundant, with habitat destruction contributing to its scarcity (3).   It
is presumed to have become increasingly rare since that time.

HABITAT   Thick montane jungle, broken by steep ravines, at moderate elevations (2).
The forests of eastern China have suffered extensive destruction and what remains is
increasingly accessible to hunters and trappers, who doubtless have also had a
negative influence on the population of this species (3).   As far as is known no
part of the habitat of this pheasant is included in any form of reserve.

CONSERVATION MEASURES TAKEN   Elliot's Pheasant is listed in Appendix 1 of the 1973
Convention on International Trade in Endangered Species of Wild Fauna and Flora, and
traffic in it is therefore subject to strict regulation by ratifying nations.   It
has legal protection in China, but how effective it may be is uncertain.

CONSERVATION MEASURES PROPOSED   It has been suggested that a program of reintroducing captive-reared birds into suitably protected natural habitats should be
put into effect whenever such habitats become available (P. Wayre 1975, pers. comm.).

REMARKS   This species first bred in captivity in Europe in 1880 (3) and stocks
now number more than 1,500 birds (C. Savage 1976, pers. comm.).   The only additions
of wild-trapped birds to captive stocks since 1960 have been two males sent to the
Pheasant Trust, Norwich, England in 1974 (P. Wayre 1975, pers. comm.), and a male
in Hong Kong in 1975 (C. Savage 1976, pers. comm.).   Zoo collections accounted for
121 birds in 1975 (5).

REFERENCES   1.   Cheng, Tso-Hsin 1955.   Record of the Distribution of Chinese
                   Birds.   Vol. 1.   Peiping.
              2.   Beebe, W. 1922.   A Monograph of the Pheasants.   Vol. 3.
                   London:H.F. and G. Witherby.
              3.   Delacour, J. 1951.   The Pheasants of the World.   London:
                   Country Life Ltd.;   New York:Charles Scribner's Sons.
              4.   Wayre, P. 1969.   A Guide to the Pheasants of the World.
                   London, New York, Sydney, Toronto:Country Life.
              5.   Olney, P.J.S. (ed.) 1976.   Census of rare animals in captivity,
                   1975.   Internat. Zoo Yearbook 16:   411-446.

HUME'S BAR-TAILED PHEASANT

Syrmaticus humiae humiae (Hume, 1881)

Syrmaticus humiae burmanicus (Oates, 1898)

Order GALLIFORMES   Family PHASIANIDAE

_____

STATUS   Rare.   The species is found in northern Burma and adjacent hill country
in China, including Tibet, and in Assam, where it is sufficiently numerous not to
be immediately threatened, although its populations merit careful watching.

DISTRIBUTION   The nominate race S. h. humiae occurs from the hills of northern
Burma west of the Irrawaddy River to Manipur, Naga, Patkai and the Lushai Hills of
Assam, India, south through Burma's Chin Hills to Mt. Victoria, and north to the
mountains of the border between Burma, and India and China (1; U Tun Yin in litt.
to J. Vincent, 1968).   S. h. burmanicus occurs east of the Irrawaddy River in
Burma, in the Shan highlands and into south-western Yunnan across the Salween River,
south to north-western Thailand (1).   The distribution of both subspecies is not
known to differ now from what it was in the past.

POPULATION   No estimates have been made.   Recent inquiries in northern Burma
have shown the species to be more abundant than hitherto believed, the typical
race inhabiting practically all the mountains along the Burmese borders with China
and India.   It has been found in considerable numbers in at least three localities
in Kachin State between 1,800m and 2,100m elevation.   S. h. burmanicus was
described as very common north-east of Kawnghong Hpu on the border between Burma and
southern Yunnan, at altitudes of 900m to 1,200m, some being recorded up to as high
as 3,355m elevation.   Neither subspecies is known to have declined seriously in
abundance.   Human trapping and persecution may have had deleterious effects in some
areas, but in northern Burma few birds are killed and the populations of this
species give no cause for concern at present (U Tun Yin in litt. to J. Vincent,
1968).

HABITAT   Mixed open forests interspersed with grass and bracken patches on steep
hillsides (2).

CONSERVATION MEASURES TAKEN   The species is listed in Appendix 1 of the 1973
Convention on International Trade in Endangered Species of Wild Fauna and Flora,
and traffic in it is therefore subject to strict regulation by contracting states.

CONSERVATION MEASURES PROPOSED   Captive propagation with a view to re-introduction
of captive bred stocks in suitably protected areas of natural habitat.   In 1971,
the Pheasant Trust, Norwich, England, presented 5 pairs of young birds bred at the
Trust to the Burmese Government.   They were sent to Rangoon Zoo for the purpose of
launching a captive breeding project (P. Wayre 1975, pers. comm.).   But no reserve
suitable for the reintroduction of the species exists in Burma at present (Col.
Sithu Hla Aung in litt. to P. Wayre, 1970) and the establishment of such a reserve
is obviously necessary.

REMARKS   The nominate subspecies reached western collections as late as 1962,
when 4 pairs were sent to Stagsden, England, where they were bred successfully by
F.E.B. Johnston.   Later, several additional birds were sent to Germany from India
(3).   The captive population now numbers 559 birds in Europe, Japan and North
America (C. Savage 1976, pers. comm.).   One male of the eastern race was held by
the Peking Zoo in 1975 (S.D. Ripley 1977, pers. comm.).

REFERENCES   1.   Delacour, J. 1951.   The Pheasants of the World.   London: Country Life, Ltd.;   New York:Charles Scribner's Sons.

2.   Ali, S. & Ripley, S.D.1969.   Handbook of the Birds of India and Pakistan.   Vol. 2.   Bombay, London, New York:Oxford University Press.

3.   Wayre, P. 1969.   A Guide to the Pheasants of the World. London, New York, Sydney, Toronto:Country Life.

MIKADO PHEASANT

Syrmaticus mikado (Ogilvie-Grant, 1906)

Order GALLIFORMES   Family PHASIANIDAE

STATUS   Vulnerable.   Although unique to and still fairly widespread in Taiwan,
the most significant factor now limiting populations is live-trapping for commercial
trade.   This continues, but has been decreasing substantially in recent years.

DISTRIBUTION   Found widely in the central mountains of Taiwan, usually between
2000 and 3000m elevation, but occasionally as low as 1600m or as high as 3300m
(S. Severinghaus 1975, pers. comm.).

POPULATION   This pheasant is probably fairly common, numbering a few thousand
individuals and possibly maintaining a fairly stable population (S. Severinghaus
1975, pers. comm.).

HABITAT   Steep slopes, usually greater than 40°, covered by coniferous or
coniferous-hardwood primary forest, often with a dense undergrowth of bamboo.   Also
inhabits monoculture conifer plantations, secondary hardwood forests, and dense
second growth of brush and grass on open slopes.   In short, the species is notably
adaptable to man-altered habitats (S. Severinghaus 1975, pers. comm.).

CONSERVATION MEASURES TAKEN   Protected by the Japanese as a national monument from
1919 until the end of the Second World War.   There has again been legal protection
of the species since at least 1966 and its export and that of other wildlife was
formally prohibited in 1974 (D. Poltock in litt. to P. Wayre, 1974).   It is,
moreover, covered by a three-year ban on hunting of wildlife instituted in 1972 and
renewed in 1975 for 3 more years.   In 1974, the Taiwan Government designated a
3680-hectare high-altitude reserve principally to protect this species and the
vulnerable Swinhoe's Pheasant (Lophura swinhoii).   The pheasant is listed in
Appendix 1 of the 1973 Convention on International Trade in Endangered Species of
Wild Fauna and Flora, and trafficking in it is thus subject to strict control by
contracting nations.

CONSERVATION MEASURES PROPOSED   Additional portions of this species' habitat
have been proposed as national parks or nature reserves (1).   Of five specific
areas recommended to the Taiwan Forestry Bureau and National Science Council as
reserves or parks, three contain Mikado Pheasants and their habitat (S. Severinghaus
1977, pers. comm.).

REMARKS   There were 836 Mikado Pheasants in captivity in 1976 (C. Savage 1976,
pers. comm.) and the species now seems able to maintain itself in captivity.   In
1969, no less than 140 young were bred at the Pheasant Trust, Norwich, England
(P. Wayre 1975, pers. comm.).   Swinhoe's Pheasant Lophura swinhoii, also unique to
Taiwan, is now considered at greater risk than this species (S. Severinghaus 1977,
pers. comm.).

REFERENCES   1.   Wayre, P. 1967.   Advisory report on the Wildlife of Taiwan
                   with proposals for its conservation.   Published by author.

BLYTH'S TRAGOPAN

Tragopan blythii blythii (Jerdon, 1870)

Tragopan blythii molesworthi Stuart Baker, 1914

Order GALLIFORMES   Family PHASIANIDAE

STATUS   Rare.   The nominate subspecies is rare in Assam, where it is hunted
excessively, but locally common in Burma.   T. b. molesworthi is known from very few
specimens from south-east Tibet, Bhutan and Assam to the north of the range of the
nominate subspecies.   Its status is poorly known, although the human inhabitants
who share its range are predominantly Buddhist and do not persecute it.

DISTRIBUTION   T. b. blythii formerly occurred south of the Brahmaputra River from
Paona Peak in the Barail Range west to the ranges south-east of Sadiya, Assam, and
the Patkai Range, Burma, and south through the Naga Hills and Manipur to the Lushai
Hills of Assam and the Chin Hills of north-western Burma (1).   Now believed to be
restricted to the Naga Hills in Assam, the Chin Hills and several locations in the
extreme north of Burma (U Tun Yin in litt. to J. Vincent, 1970).   T. b. molesworthi
is known from south-east Tibet and eastern Bhutan eastwards across the bend of the
Brahmaputra River to the Mishmi Hills of Assam (1), although in recent years
reported only from eastern Bhutan and the Dafla Hills of Assam.   For most of its
range the information is, however, insufficient to determine whether a decline of
this subspecies has taken place.

POPULATION   No estimates have been made, but it is clear there has been a serious
decline in the abundance of the nominate subspecies in Assam, where it is now very
rare.   Naga trappers secured only two males in several months of trapping in the
Naga Hills in 1962 (P. Wayre 1966, pers. comm. to J. Vincent).   However, in
northern Burma it was common in the five localities where it was found in 1970
(U Tun Yin in litt. to J. Vincent, 1970).   The difference is to be explained as
the result of human predation and trapping in Assam, whereas in Burma the species
is killed only infrequently, hence its greater abundance.   No one has any idea of
the numbers of T. b. molesworthi, of which only three specimens have ever been
collected (1).

HABITAT   Thick, damp forests between 1,800m and 3,300m in altitude, but in winter
down to 1,525m (1).   None of the habitat of the species is known to be protected.

CONSERVATION MEASURES TAKEN   Blyth's Tragopan is listed in Appendix 1 of the 1973
Convention on International Trade in Endangered Species of Wild Fauna and Flora,
and trafficking in it is thus subject to strict control by contracting parties to
the Convention.

CONSERVATION MEASURES PROPOSED   The proposed Himalayan Reserve in the Mishmi
Hills, Arunuchal Pradesh, may protect part of the range of this species (Ranjitsinh
1976, pers. comm. to C. Savage).   In 1973, the Nagaland government initiated a
captive breeding project with a stock of 2 males and 4 females (R. Banagee in litt.
to P. Wayre, 1973).   By 1976 the captive stock numbered 15 birds (3; C. Savage
1976, pers. comm.).

REMARKS   Blyth's Tragopans first appeared in European avicultural collections in
1870, were first bred in captivity in 1884, and with some regularity thereafter
until after the Second World War when numbers in captivity gradually dwindled for
lack of fresh genetic material from wild-caught birds (2).   Only one is believed to
be in captivity outside of Asia at present (C. Savage 1976, pers. comm.).

REFERENCES

1. Ali, S. & Ripley, S.D. 1969. Handbook of the Birds of India and Pakistan. Vol. 2. Bombay, London, New York: Oxford University Press.

2. Delacour, J. 1951. The Pheasants of the World. London:Country Life Ltd.; New York:Charles Scribner's Sons.

3. Zeliang, D.G. 1975. The tragopan breeds in captivity. The Warrior (Kohima, Nagaland, India), June: 12-14.

CABOT'S TRAGOPAN

Tragopan caboti (Gould, 1857)

Order GALLIFORMES   Family PHASIANIDAE

STATUS   Endangered.   Confined to parts of four provinces in south-eastern China
and now quite rare.   Habitat destruction for agriculture is thought to be the
major factor contributing to the decline of this species.

DISTRIBUTION   There are records from Fukien, Kiangsi, Kwangtung and Hunan
provinces, south-eastern China (1; Tso-Hsin Cheng in litt. to J. Vincent, 1964)
and the species is still thought to occur in these four provinces, although less
widespread (P. Wayre 1975, pers. comm.).

POPULATION   No estimates have been made.   In 1877, the species was very common
in the mountain range separating Fukien from Kiangsi (2), but is believed to have
declined considerably in abundance and to be now very rare (Tso-Hsin Cheng 1975,
pers. comm. to K. Searle.).

HABITAT   Mountain forests between 700m and 1,525m in elevation; also open areas
above treeline (3).   Extensive destruction of the forests combined with increasing
human persecution of the species have contributed to its present precarious status.

CONSERVATION MEASURES TAKEN   Traffic in this species is subject to strict
regulation by the contracting parties to the 1973 Convention on International Trade
in Endangered Species of Wild Fauna and Flora, in Appendix 1 of which Tragopan
caboti is listed.   It has legal protection in China.

CONSERVATION MEASURES PROPOSED   Propagation in captivity is proposed by the
Pheasant Trust, Norwich, England, as a potential means of augmenting wild
populations through eventual release of captive bred stock when suitably safeguarded
natural habitat is available (P. Wayre 1975, pers. comm.).

REMARKS   This species was first held in captivity in Europe in 1882 and bred
successfully in 1884.   It was common in captivity until the First World War, after
which captive stocks dwindled (4).   In 1961, 5 males and 2 females, all wild-
trapped, were sent to the Pheasant Trust through Hong Kong, and by 1974 an
additional male and 2 females had reached the Pheasant Trust (P. Wayre 1977, pers.
comm.).   The total known to be in captivity in 1976 was 19 (C. Savage, pers. comm.).
In the past 15 years 30-40 birds have reached Hong Kong from China, the maximum in
any one year being ten.   Most were in poor health and died quickly (K.C. Searle
1977, pers. comm.).

REFERENCES   1.   Cheng, Tso-Hsin, 1955.   Record of the Distribution of Chinese
                    Birds. Vol. 1.   Peiping.
              2.   Beebe, W. 1918.   A Monograph of the Pheasants. Vol. 1.
                    London:Witherby and Co.
              3.   Caldwell, H.R. & Caldwell, J.C. 1931.   South China Birds.
                    Shanghai:Hester May Vanderburgh.
              4.   Delacour, J. 1951.   The Pheasants of the World.   London:
                    Country Life Ltd.;   New York:Charles Scribner's Sons.

WESTERN TRAGOPAN

Tragopan melanocephalus (J.E. Gray, 1829)

Order GALLIFORMES   Family PHASIANIDAE

STATUS   Endangered.   Seriously reduced in distribution and abundance in north-
western India and Pakistan by excessive hunting and trapping, forest destruction
and general disturbance by man and goats.   Now restricted to a few isolated
localities.

DISTRIBUTION   Historically, the species ranged along the north-western Himalayas
from Swat (Duber valley) to the Bagirathi River, Tehri-Garhwal (1-3).   It was
found in 1953 in the upper Beas River valley in Himachal Pradesh (I. Grimwood in
litt. to J. Vincent, 1969), has recently been recorded in the Neelum and Jhelum
valleys in Azad Kashmir (4), and is present in some adjacent areas of northern
Kashmir (Rashid Wani 1977, pers. comm. to K. Howman), in the Kunhar valley in
Hazara, Indus Kohistan (5) and in the Hunza state of Gilgit (6).   It also survived
in Himachal Pradesh at least until 1969 (I. Grimwood in litt. to J. Vincent).

POPULATION   In 1977 the first population estimates were made in Pakistan and
Azad Kashmir (7), and more comprehensive surveys were planned for 1978.   The
tragopan had become very rare in most parts of Kashmir by 1918 (1), but in 1953
and 1968, respectively, was common enough in two of the localities mentioned in
the previous section, namely the upper Beas River valley in Himachal Pradesh and
the Jhelum valley of Azad Kashmir.   Its stronghold may now be the Neelum valley,
also in Azad Kashmir.   In 1977, in Salkhala reserve, 12 males were heard and 6
birds were flushed in a 31 sq. km area; 9 were recorded in Kuttan reserve in an
area of 26 sq. km, and its presence was also confirmed in 8 sq. km of Machyara
National Park, all in Neelum valley (7).   The population in Gilgit is thought to
be small (T.J. Roberts in litt. to J. Vincent, 1969).   Sightings of 22 birds,
including six pairs, were made during ten months in Himachal Pradesh in 1969
(I. Grimwood in litt. to J. Vincent, 1969).   Small populations are believed to
survive in Hazara Kohistan and the Duber valley, Swat (G. Schaller, A. Khan 1975,
pers. comms.).

HABITAT   Rhododendron, bamboo and other dense undergrowth in conifer or oak
forest between 2,400 m and 3,600 m elevation but as low as 1,350 m in winter (3; 7).
Destruction and fragmentation of forests and increased disturbance by man and goats
within what is left of the forests, have been a major cause of decline, although
another important threat is direct human predation (6; P. Wayre 1975, pers. comm.).

CONSERVATION MEASURES TAKEN   The Western Tragopan is protected by law in Pakistan
and India, and under the 1973 Convention on International Trade in Endangered
Species of Wild Fauna and Flora, where it is listed in Appendix 1.   Exports from
Pakistan of any wildlife may not be undertaken without a permit of the Provincial
Forest Department, while species on the protected list cannot be exported save for
scientific research or for captive breeding (P. Wayre 1974, pers. comm.).
Machyara National Park and reserve forests throughout the Neelum valley in Azad
Kashmir protect portions of the tragopan's habitat.   A three-year ban on hunting
in Azad Kashmir was imposed in 1976 (C. Savage 1977, pers. comm.).

CONSERVATION MEASURES PROPOSED   The Pakistan National Wildlife Council determined
in 1977 that no further birds of this species should be taken from the wild for
captive breeding under any circumstances and that any captive stocks should be
built up gradually from birds hatched from eggs collected from the wild.   Suitable
facilities for hatching and rearing have been set up with trained staff in six

localities in Pakistan; meanwhile a two-year programme of field studies has started which will both survey the current position and provide the information required for development of management plans. A similar 18-months programme in Himachal Pradesh was to have been launched in autumn 1978 (C. Savage 1978, pers. comm.).

REMARKS   One female has been kept at the Pheasant Trust since 1971 and in 1975 was the only Western Tragopan in captivity (P. Wayre, pers. comm.).   The species was frequently kept in European collections in the late nineteenth century and bred a few times, but all captive stock had disappeared by 1900 (2).

REFERENCES   1.   Beebe, W. 1918.   A Monograph of the Pheasants, Vol. 1. London: H.F. and G. Witherby.
2.   Delacour, J. 1977.   The Pheasants of the World, 2nd Ed. London: Spur Publications and the World Pheasant Association.
3.   Ali, S. & Ripley, S.D. 1969.   Handbook of the Birds of India and Pakistan, Vol. 2.   Bombay, London, New York: Oxford University Press.
4.   Mirza, Z.B. 1971.   Notes on the distribution and status of Western Horned Tragopan in Azad Kashmir.   Pheasant Trust Annual Report 1971: 22-23.
5.   Wayre, P. undated.   Pheasant Conservation in Pakistan with special reference to the Tragopan.   Lahore: Pakistan Wildlife Appeal; Great Witchingham, Norwich: The Pheasant Trust.
6.   Roberts, T.J. 1970.   A note on the pheasants of West Pakistan. Pakistan Journal of Forestry 20: 319-326.
7.   Mirza, Z.B. 1976.   Pheasant restoration in Pakistan. Pheasant Trust and Norfolk Wildlife Park Ann. Rept. 1976: 20-24.

BROWN MESITE

Mesoenas unicolor (Desmurs, 1845)

Order GRUIFORMES   Family MESOENATIDAE

_____

STATUS   Rare and very locally distributed in eastern Madagascar.

DISTRIBUTION   Restricted to the forests of eastern Madagascar, where it has been
found in the central region in Sianaka Forest (1) and near Tamatave (2), further
north near Maroantsetra and on the Masoala peninsula (3), and in the south about
70 km north of Fort Dauphin (4).

POPULATION   No estimate has been made but the species has always been considered
rare.   An expedition in 1929 and 1930 failed to find it, although they were able to
purchase six specimens from a local collector (1).   In 1948 two nests were found
(4).   There is no evidence of a decline in population, but the continuing
destruction of forests may be surmised to be having an adverse effect.

HABITAT   Primary moist evergreen forest (5).   Only 10 per cent of Madagascar
remains forested and clearing of indigenous forestland for subsistence agriculture
and for reafforestation with exotic pines and eucalypts continues; an undetermined
amount is also destroyed annually as the result of burning of adjacent grasslands
(6).   Introduced rats infest much of Madagascar and could pose a threat in certain
areas to this and other species (7).

CONSERVATION MEASURES TAKEN   None known.

CONSERVATION MEASURES PROPOSED   Legal protection of this and most other endemic
birds of Madagascar has been recommended to the Malagasy government (K. Curry-
Lindahl in litt. to G. Ramanantsoavina, Director, Service des Eaux et Forêts,
Chasse et Pêche, Jan. 1973.).

REMARKS   This species used to be protected by strong taboos in east central
Madagascar (2), but the Malagasy people no longer respect these taboos as strictly
as formerly (7).

REFERENCES   1.   Rand, A.L. 1936.   The distribution and habits of Madagascar
                    birds.   Bull. Amer. Mus. Nat. Hist. 72: 143-499.
              2.   Lavauden, L. 1931.   Note préliminaire sur les oiseaux
                    appartenant aux Genres Mesoenas et Monias.   Alauda 3: 395-400
              3.   Lavauden, L. 1937.   Supplément to Vol. 12, Oiseaux, in A. and G.
                    Grandidier, Histoire Physique, Naturelle et Politique de
                    Madagascar.   Paris: Société d'Editions Géographiques, Maritimes
                    et Coloniales.
              4.   Rand, A.L. 1951.   The nests and eggs of Mesoenas unicolor of
                    Madagascar.   Auk 68: 23-26.
              5.   Milon, P., Petter, J.-J. & Randrianasolo, G. 1973.   Faune de
                    Madagascar, 35: Oiseaux.   Tananarive and Paris: ORSTOM and
                    CNRS.
              6.   Curry-Lindahl, K. 1975.   Man in Madagascar.   Defenders of
                    Wildlife 50(2): 164-169.
              7.   Forbes-Watson, A.D. & Turner, D.A. 1973.   Report on bird
                    preservation in Madagascar.   Report to ICBP.

WHITE-BREASTED MESITE

Mesoenas variegata (Geoffroy Saint-Hilaire, 1838)

Order GRUIFORMES   Family MESOENATIDAE

STATUS   Rare and extremely localized in western Madagascar.

DISTRIBUTION   Known from western Madagascar, where it was recorded at the
Falaise d'Anakarana near Tsarakibany in 1930 (1), and at Ankarafantsika near
Majunga in 1929 (2) and 1971 (3).   It is not known with certainty whether the
distribution of this species has decreased in extent.

POPULATION   No estimate has been made, although the species has always been
considered rare.   A few were seen in 1971, the only recent sighting (3).

HABITAT   Dry forests, relatively clear of underbrush (1).   The extent of all
forests in Madagascar has declined seriously this century and now accounts for only
10 per cent of the surface area of the island.   The forest destruction, which
continues unabated, arises mainly from clearing for subsistence agriculture and for
forestry projects involving replacement of native species with exotic pines and
eucalypts, and from damage caused by repeated burning of adjacent grasslands (4).

CONSERVATION MEASURES TAKEN   Although this species is not legally protected, it
is known to occur in one protected area: Ankarafantsika Forest Reserve (3).

CONSERVATION MEASURES PROPOSED   The legal protection of this and many other
endemic bird species of Madagascar has been recommended to the Malagasy government
(K. Curry-Lindahl in litt. to G. Ramanantsoavina, Director, Service des Eaux et
Forêts, Chasse et Pêche, Jan. 1973).

REFERENCES   1.   Rand, A.L. 1936.   The distribution and habits of Madagascar
                    birds.   Bull. Amer. Mus. Nat. Hist. 72: 143-499.
              2.   Lavauden, L. 1931.   Note préliminaire sur les oiseaux
                    appartenant aux Genres Mesoenas et Monias.   Alauda 3: 395-400.
              3.   Forbes-Watson, A.D. & Turner, D.A, 1973.   Report on bird
                    preservation in Madagascar.   Report to ICBP.
              4.   Curry-Lindahl, K. 1975.   Man in Madagascar.   Defenders of
                    Wildlife 50(2): 164-169.

BENSCH'S MONIAS

Monias benschi Oustalet and G. Grandidier, 1903.

Order GRUIFORMES   Family MESOENATIDAE

STATUS   Rare.   Distributed locally in a small portion of south-western
Madagascar, where it is presumed to be decreasing as the result of forest
degradation.

DISTRIBUTION   Recorded between the Fiherenana and the Mangoky Rivers, south-west
Madagascar, in a coastal belt with a maximum width of about 70 km, from sea level
to the first line of foothills at an altitude of 130 m (1; 2).   This rather
restricted range is not known to have altered in any way.

POPULATION   Because it has been met with in groups of up to 20 individuals, it
has been described as locally common, although inhabited localities are often
widely separated (1).   It was considered to be fairly numerous near Lake Ihotry in
1930, when 48 specimens were collected in a 10-day period (2).   It is probable,
however, that it has declined in abundance throughout most of its range due to the
degradation of much of its preferred habitat.

HABITAT   Undisturbed primary dry forest with sandy substrate covered thickly with
leaf litter.   Bushes and trees of this forest stand leafless half of each year (1)
and in general this type of forest is only too easy to clear and burn, so that
little of the original forest cover remains today (3).   There are no protected
areas within the range of the species.

CONSERVATION MEASURES TAKEN   None known.

CONSERVATION MEASURES PROPOSED   The legal protection of this and most other
endemic birds of Madagascar has been recommended to the Malagasy government
(K. Curry-Lindahl in litt. to G. Ramanantsoavina, Director, Service des Eaux et
Forêts, Chasse et Pêche, Jan. 1973).

REMARKS   The Monias shares an almost identical range with the Long-tailed Ground
Roller Uratelornis chimaera, a species which falls within the 'vulnerable' category.
Both were at one time protected by 'fady' or taboos, but these are no longer
strictly observed even by the Malagasy countryfolk (4).

REFERENCES   1.   Appert, O. 1968.   Beobachtungen an Monias benschi in Sudwest-
                   Madagascar.   Journ. f. Ornith. 109: 402-417.
              2.   Rand, A.L. 1936.   The distribution and habits of Madagascar
                   birds.   Bull. Amer. Mus. Nat. Hist. 72: 143-499.
              3.   Curry-Lindahl, K. 1975.   Man in Madagascar.   Defenders of
                   Wildlife 50(2): 164-169.
              4.   Forbes-Watson, A.D. & Turner, D.A. 1973.   Report on bird
                   preservation in Madagascar.   Report presented to ICBP.

WHOOPING CRANE

Grus americana (Linnaeus, 1758)

Order GRUIFORMES   Family GRUIDAE

STATUS   Endangered, but gradually recovering as the result of protection of
birds and habitat stemming from an enormous cooperative education effort.   An
experimental program now seeks to establish a separate independent population.

DISTRIBUTION   Known from fossil remains from Idaho, California and Florida.   In
the recent past bred in Louisiana (a non-migratory population extirpated by 1950)
and from Iowa and northern Illinois north across southern Manitoba, Saskatchewan
and Alberta to southern Mackenzie.   On migration occurred from New Jersey west to
Great Salt Lake, Utah, wintering along the Gulf coast in southern Louisiana and
Texas, and as far south as central Mexico.   Since 1922, breeding of the migratory
population has been confined to Wood Buffalo National Park, northern Alberta and
southern Mackenzie, and wintering to Aransas National Wildlife Refuge, Texas, and
adjacent coastlands (1; 2; 11).   A second population, created in 1975 by placing
eggs under Sandhill Crane Grus canadensis foster parents at Grey's Lake National
Wildlife Refuge, Idaho, now winters with its foster parents at Bosque del Apache
National Wildlife Refuge, New Mexico (3; 4).

POPULATION   The maximum size of the original population prior to 1860 was thought
to be about 1300 birds.   Its decline was greatest in the 1890s.   By winter 1912,
56 remained in Texas, 32 in Louisiana.   By 1918 the Louisiana population was gone.
The Texas wintering population reached a low of 15 in 1941, but climbed gradually
to 59 by 1971 and, following a slight decline to 49 in 1974, increased further to
70 in 1977.   In that year 8 wintered with foster parents in New Mexico and an
additional 27 were in captivity. (1; 2; 4-7; 9; 10).   The causes of mortality in
young pre-breeding birds, which in recent years has been high, are not understood
(3; 8).

HABITAT   Wetlands in prairie, aspen parkland, taiga, and transitional areas; in
winter, coastal lagoons, fresh and brackish marshes, and interior prairies.
Extensive disturbance or destruction of wetlands has contributed to this crane's
decline and has slowed its recovery (1).   While its breeding habitat is protected
and to a large extent also its wintering grounds, the risk of pollution of flats
and coastal marshes along the Gulf coast has not been removed: the U.S. Intracoastal Waterway runs through the heart of the crane's winter habitat, bringing
threats from dredging, from erosion by motorboat wakes and from transport of
hazardous substances (12; D. Blankinship 1978, pers. comm.).

CONSERVATION MEASURES TAKEN   Fully protected by the U.S. Endangered Species Act
and by Migratory Bird Treaties between Mexico and the U.S. and Canada and the U.S.
Listed in Appendix 1 of the 1973 Convention on International Trade in Endangered
Species of Wild Fauna and Flora.   The U.S. Fish and Wildlife Service has appointed
a recovery team for this crane.   The breeding area lies wholly within Wood Buffalo
National Park and wintering grounds mostly within Aransas National Wildlife Refuge,
the establishment of which in 1937 has probably been the single most important
conservation measure.   Jurisdiction over important winter habitat on Matagorda
Island, north of Aransas, has been surrendered by the U.S. Air Force but was being
disputed in 1978 by the U.S. Fish and Wildlife Service and the Texas Dept. of Parks
and Wildlife.   Massive education campaigns aimed primarily at reducing hunting
mortality have been undertaken by the U.S. and Canadian governments, National
Audubon Society and several other organizations and individuals.

The ecology of this species has been studied on its wintering grounds but only rather superficially in the area where it nests. The normal clutch is two but almost always only one young from a nest survives, hence "surplus" eggs are available. A population is being established experimentally using a related species as foster parents, "surplus" eggs from Wood Buffalo and captive-laid eggs from Patuxent Wildlife Research Center (4; 13). The Idaho sandhill cranes chosen for this project nest and winter in U.S. National Wildlife Refuges. Migrating cranes do in fact visit a number of such refuges, though in some of them, like Bosque del Apache Refuge, hunting of waterfowl is permitted.

CONSERVATION MEASURES PROPOSED   The Whooping Crane Recovery Team has recommended that marshes in the interior of Matagorda Island be protected as a sanctuary and also that the intracoastal waterway be relocated outside the island, so as to ensure that essential habitat can be properly safeguarded. The team's next priority is documenting and protecting areas used by cranes on migration. The Canadian Wildlife Service proposes to establish a third population, using the foster-parent technique: its nesting area would be in the interlakes region of Manitoba and it would migrate to Florida. The launching of this project will depend on the success of the Grey's Lake, Idaho, experiment (D. Blankinship 1978, pers. comm.).

REFERENCES   1.   Allen, R.P. 1952.   The Whooping Crane.   Nat. Audubon
                    Soc. Res. Rept. 3.
              2.   McNulty, F. 1966.   The Whooping Crane.   New York: E.P. Dutton
                    and Co.
              3.   Zimmerman, D.R. 1975.   To Save a Bird in Peril.   New York:
                    Coward, McCann and Geoghegan.
              4.   Drewein, R. & Bizeau, E.G. 1978.   Cross-fostering Whooping
                    Cranes to Sandhill Crane foster parents.   In S. Temple (ed.)
                    Endangered Birds: Management Techniques for Preserving
                    Threatened Species, pp. 201-221.   Madison: Univ. of
                    Wisconsin Press.
              5.   Kepler, C.B. 1978.   Captive propagation of Whooping Cranes:
                    a behavioral approach.   In S. Temple (ed.) Endangered Birds:
                    Management Techniques for Preserving Threatened Species,
                    pp. 231-242.   Madison: Univ. of Wisconsin Press.
              6.   Novakowski, N.S. 1966.   Whooping Crane population dynamics
                    on the nesting grounds, Wood Buffalo National Park, Northwest
                    Territories, Canada.   Canad. Wildl. Soc. Rept. Series 1.
              7.   Miller, R.S., Botkin, D.B. & Mendelssohn, R. 1974.   The
                    Whooping Crane (Grus americana) population of North America.
                    Biol. Cons. 6: 106-111.
              8.   Erickson, R.C. 1975.   Report on Whooping Crane research and
                    management - 1974.   Bull. ICBP 12: 122-125.
              9.   Pratt, J.J. 1977.   Whooping Crane management: the last ten
                    years.   Whooping Crane Conservation Assoc.
             10.   Anon. 1978.   Whooper population increased in 1977.
                    Grus americana 17(1): 1.
             11.   Walkinshaw, L. 1973.   Cranes of the World.   New York:
                    Winchester Press.
             12.   Blankinship, D.R. 1976.   Studies of Whooping Cranes on the
                    wintering grounds.   Proc. Int. Crane Workshop: 197-206.
             13.   Erickson, R.C. 1976.   Whooping Crane studies at the Patuxent
                    Wildlife Research Center.   Proc. Int. Crane Workshop: 166-176.

CUBAN SANDHILL CRANE

Grus canadensis nesiotes Bangs and Zappey, 1905

Order GRUIFORMES   Family GRUIDAE

STATUS   Rare and local.   This subspecies of the Sandhill Crane is restricted as
far as is known to only four localities in Cuba and the Isle of Pines, and its
total population is quite low.   Nevertheless, it is not in immediate danger of
extinction (O.H. Garrido 1974, pers. comm.).

DISTRIBUTION   Formerly more widespread in Cuba, where it was recorded from all
Provinces but Oriente, the easternmost (1).   Now only known to survive in the
Isle of Pines, the Pinar del Rio swamps and probably one or
more parts of Camaguey Province (O.H. Garrido loc. cit.).

POPULATION   No precise figures are available, but there is no doubt the subspecies
has declined.   In 1951, the population on the Isle of Pines, where the largest
concentrations of the cranes have traditionally occurred, was about 100 birds (1),
while today it is thought to be near 30.   The Zapata swamp population in Cuba
itself also now numbers about 30.   The Pinar del Rio colonies are smaller still and
the numbers remaining in Camaguey are unknown.   The total population is probably
between 100-150 birds (O.H. Garrido loc. cit.).

HABITAT   Park-like dry savannah, sparsely wooded with shrubs and especially pines,
but very seldom marshy (1), although it may border marshland as at Zapata.

CONSERVATION MEASURES TAKEN   None known.

CONSERVATION MEASURES PROPOSED   None known.

REMARKS   Five other subspecies of Sandhill Cranes have been recognized, all in
North America except for one in the extreme north-east of Siberia.   Of these,
G. c. pulla, a recently described population from Mississippi, is in the endangered
category.   But none of the others is now thought to be at risk, including
C. s. pratensis of south-eastern U.S.A., which was rated as 'rare' in the previous
edition.

REFERENCES   1.   Walkinshaw, L. 1973.   Cranes of the World.   New York:
Winchester Press.

MISSISSIPPI SANDHILL CRANE

Grus canadensis pulla Aldrich, 1972

Order GRUIFORMES   Family GRUIDAE

STATUS   Endangered.   Fewer than 50 survive in a small area near the U.S. Gulf
Coast.   Habitat destruction is primarily responsible although illegal hunting is
a continuing concern.   It has been suggested that this small population has
suffered a genetic deterioration which may limit its reproductive potential.

DISTRIBUTION   This subspecies, or undescribed but closely related forms, may
once have been distributed discontinuously, in pockets of suitable habitat, across
the Gulf Coast plains of Louisiana, Mississippi and Alabama.   Although these
cranes have been recorded in summer in Alabama as recently as 1960, their breeding
range is presently restricted to Jackson County, Mississippi, from the Pascagoula
River west to the Jackson-Harrison County line, north to about 6 km north of
Vancleave township and south nearly to the Gulf of Mexico.   Within this general
range there are seven more or less discrete breeding areas, totalling 25 sq. km
and centered near Ocean Springs and Fountainbleau, but about 100 sq. km of
habitat are required for all purposes at various seasons.   The historical range
of the population in Mississippi was only slightly larger than it is today.   In
fall and winter (August to March) the cranes roost in the nearby Pascagoula Marsh
(c. 18 sq. km).   Individuals of other, migratory, Sandhill Crane subspecies may
winter in the Mississippi Crane's range (1-7; 11).

POPULATION   Resident cranes in Mississippi were first reported in 1928, when
there were believed to be at least 50 and possibly 100 (1).   In 1940 the estimate
was 'over 25 pairs' (7), in 1947, '30 birds' and in 1961 'less than 50' (8; 9).
The 1968 estimate of 50-60 birds, including 16 breeding pairs, had declined to 38
to 40 in 1970 (6; 10) and more recently, in 1975, the population was put at 30 to
50 birds, including 10 to 15 breeding pairs (2), figures which still pertained in
1978 (J. Valentine 1978, pers. comm.).   Considerable loss of habitat has taken
place since the 1950s.   As a precaution a captive flock has been established at
Patuxent Wildlife Research Center and now numbers 14, having been gradually built
up by taking the second egg from up to five nests in the wild each year since 1965
(the second egg being considered "surplus" in the sense that crane pairs almost
always rear only a single chick).   The intention is to return birds or eggs to
the wild, but so far only two have been reared in captivity.   The breeding of this
subspecies in captivity appears far more problematical than that of other subspecies of Sandhill Cranes at Patuxent, giving rise to the suggestion that the
stock may have deteriorated genetically, although there is as yet no evidence of
this in the wild (2; R. Erickson 1978, pers. comm.).

HABITAT   Savanna, swampy clearings and open forest; also cornfields and pastures
when feeding, and slightly brackish marshes for winter roosting (1-7).   Since the
mid-1950s timber companies have drained thousands of hectares of savanna for slash
pine Pinus elliottii culture.   Open range cattle grazing ceased at about the same
time as did control of wildfires, resulting in denser cover unsuitable for cranes.
Access roads and fire lanes accompanying the pine planting have permitted increased
human disturbance throughout the crane's range.   Commercial and residential
building along roads and on the outskirts of growing towns have also been a
disturbing factor and eaten into crane habitat.   A major interstate highway was
recently constructed straight through this habitat, destroying over 200 ha of it in
the process, but a highway interchange initially planned for the same area is to be
relocated to minimize such effects (1; 2; 6; 11; J. Aldrich 1978, pers. comm.).

CONSERVATION MEASURES TAKEN   This crane is fully protected by U.S. law, under the Endangered Species Act of 1973, and by Mississippi state law.   It is listed in Appendix 1 of the Convention on International Trade in Endangered Species of Wild Fauna and Flora.   A Mississippi Sandhill Crane National Wildlife Refuge was established in 1975 and will contain over 6000 ha when land acquisitions are completed in 1979.   The U.S. Fish and Wildlife Service has undertaken field studies and has appointed a recovery team, which has prepared a recovery plan. An area of 200 ha was burned in 1977 in an attempt to restore suitable habitat (J. Valentine 1978, pers. comm.).   Private conservation organizations brought a successful suit in 1976, against the U.S. and Mississippi Highway Administrations, to prevent location of a highway interchange in the cranes' breeding habitat.

CONSERVATION MEASURES PROPOSED   Further acquisition of nesting habitat for inclusion in a wildlife refuge.   Appropriate savanna management, including burning, thinning of vegetation and raising the water table by retarding drainage. Establishing plots of selected plants as winter feeding areas and building up breeding populations on properly protected land by releasing captive-bred or wild stock (2).

REMARKS   Of the 5 other subspecies, ranging over much of the central and western U.S. and Canada, Cuba and easternmost Siberia, G. c. nesiotes of Cuba (q.v.) is rare and at some risk but G. c. pratensis of Florida and southern Georgia, also rated rare in the previous edition, although of somewhat limited population and range, is not at present at risk and is no longer included.

REFERENCES   1.   Valentine, J.M., Jr. 1974.   The Mississippi Sandhill Crane (Grus canadensis pulla).   Report to the Crane Working Group, ICBP.
2.   Mississippi Sandhill Crane Recovery Team, 1976.   Mississippi Sandhill Crane Recovery Plan.   U.S. Fish and Wildlife Service.
3.   Walkinshaw, L. 1973.   Cranes of the World.   New York: Winchester Press.
4.   Imhoff, T.A. 1962.   Alabama Birds.   University, Alabama: Univ. of Alabama Press.
5.   Aldrich, J. 1972.   A new subspecies of Sandhill Crane from Mississippi.   Proc. Biol. Soc. Wash. 85: 63-70.
6.   Valentine, J.M., Jr. & Noble, R.E. 1970.   A colony of Sandhill Cranes in Mississippi.   Journ. Wildl. Mgmt. 34: 761-768.
7.   Walkinshaw, L.H. 1949.   The Sandhill Cranes.   Cranbrook Inst. Sci. Bull. 20.
8.   Turcotte, W.H. 1947.   The Sandhill Crane in Mississippi. Miss. Game and Fish June: 8-9.
9.   Turcotte, W.H. 1961.   Sandhill Crane in Jackson County may be threatened by superhighway routing.   Miss. Ornith. Soc. Newsletter 6(5):   1-2.
10.   Strong, L. 1969.   An investigation of the status of the Sandhill Crane in Mississippi.   Miss. Game Fish. Comm. P.-R. Proj. Rep. 10 W-48-R.   Mimeo, 11 pp.
11.   Valentine, J.M., Jr., & Noble, R.E. 1976.   The Mississippi Sandhill Crane - endangered or doomed?   Proc. Internat. Crane Workshop pp. 343-346.

JAPANESE CRANE

Grus japonensis (P.L.S. Müller, 1776)

Order GRUIFORMES   Family GRUIDAE

STATUS   Vulnerable. The species occurs in two disjunct populations, both quite
small. The mainland Asia population breeds in south-eastern Siberia and
Manchuria, whence it migrates to Korea. The Japanese population is sedentary
and severely threatened by alienation of marshland habitat, despite a promising
rise in numbers since the mid-1920s.

DISTRIBUTION   Breeds in eastern Asia in the Lake Khanka basin of Ussuriland,
U.S.S.R., and along tributaries of the Ussuri and Amur river systems; also in
northern and central Manchuria, China. Seen in spring in the southern Kurils,
but not proved to breed (9). These continental populations formerly migrated to
central China (possibly the Yangtze valley marshlands), to northern South Korea,
to southern Kyushu, Japan, and to Taiwan, but only a few remnant individuals have
appeared in Korea in the last two decades. In Japan the species probably once
bred on the four main islands, but since the 1890s has been confined as a breeding
bird to eastern Hokkaido near Otsu, Kushiro, Nemuro and Abashiri. A few
individuals appear sporadically in southern Kyushu in winter. (1-4).

POPULATION   There are no early estimates of mainland populations. In 1964, 30
to 35 pairs were reported on the south-eastern shores of Lake Khanka, Siberia, and
the entire U.S.S.R. population was estimated at 200-300 (2). In Hopei Province,
north China, numerous small flocks of up to 50 birds were observed on spring and
fall migration between 1942 and 1945 (5). In South Korea there were no reports
whatever between 1953 and 1962,but since then a few each year (3; 4). For
example, 41 were seen on the Han River estuary in winter 1974-75 (6) and 50 were
counted near Panmunjom, 20 at Inchon and 100 at Chorwon in winter 1977-78 (10;
G. Archibald 1978, pers. comm.), all tending to confirm the reports of numerous
cranes (species undetermined) wintering in North Korea following the Korean War
(3).   A small colony now breeds and overwinters near Pyongyang Zoo, North Korea
(J.A.W. Paludan in litt. to S.D. Ripley, Feb. 1976).   In Japan the species was
not uncommon until about 1870; it had ceased to inhabit several important breeding
areas, including the Ishikari Plain, western Hokkaido, by 1895.   In 1924, the
population inhabiting the Kushiro Marshes in eastern Hokkaido was discovered.   At
that time it was estimated at only 20 birds, but as a result of protection and
artificial feeding numbers increased rapidly to 175, by 1960, and thereafter much
more gradually.   Fifty-two pairs bred in the marshes in 1973 and the December
count was 233 (3), rising in 1974 to 253, plus 3 that wintered that year on Honshu
for the first time in decades (6).   In 1976-77, 220, including 40 juveniles,
wintered in Hokkaido (Y. Yamashina in litt. to G. Archibald, 1977).

HABITAT   In Siberia the species nests in large clearings, sometimes marshy,
overgrown with bunches of reed grass Calamagrostis (1). In Japan it utilizes a
combination of open water, marshlands of Phragmites reeds and low open alder-sedge
woodland, visiting cultivated country in winter. Here two major and several minor
feeding stations have been set up on farmland, where the birds are fed corn, and
this is mainly responsible for the increase in their numbers in recent decades
(3).   Each pair requires 2 to 7 sq. km of marshland for breeding.   Only 5 percent
of the Hokkaido crane population breeds on protected marshland, the remaining 95
percent nesting in areas currently being developed or scheduled for development
in the near future for dairy farming, forestry, heavy industry and new highways.
The wetland of the Bureya-Amur confluence in south-eastern Siberia, an important
habitat, is also threatened by agricultural development (G. Archibald 1976, pers.
comm.).

CONSERVATION MEASURES TAKEN   In 1892 the Japanese Crane was given protection throughout Japan, in 1935 designated a Natural Monument and in 1952 a Special Natural Monument.   It is also protected by the Japan/U.S.A. and Japan/U.S.S.R. Conventions on migratory birds.   A Japanese Crane Protected Area of 5011 ha has been established in the middle of Kushiro Marsh, but unfortunately only 3 pairs breed within its boundary.   A Society for the Preservation of the Tancho (Japanese Crane) was established in 1935, and has continued to play an active role; artificial feeding of the cranes in winter by farmers and school children is supported by private contributions and a prefectural government subsidy; and a Kushiro Natural Crane Park, established in 1958, now contains about 20 birds (3).   In North Korea the species is legally protected and crane wintering areas in South Hwanghai Province are designated as natural monuments.   In South Korea it was designated Natural Monument No. 202 in 1968.   The Han River Estuary in northern South Korea was declared a provisional Natural Monument in 1974 (5). The crane is protected from hunting in the U.S.S.R. and is listed in Appendix 1 of the 1973 Convention on International Trade in Endangered Species of Wild Fauna and Flora.

CONSERVATION MEASURES PROPOSED   In Japan a major cause of mortality, up to 12% annually, is collision of this crane with electric power lines.   It has been proposed that wires near crane feeding stations, particularly the one at Shimosettsuri, be buried underground or the station moved.   An additional station at Lake Furen has, in any case, also been suggested.   A proposal to expand the Tancho Protected Area to take in two large and several smaller areas, which would protect 52 nesting pairs instead of only 3, has been made to the Japanese government.   Development projects in its marshland habitat are the single most serious threat to this species in Japan; the future conservation of the crane is entirely dependent on strict protection of marshlands (4).

REMARKS   In 1975, 53 Japanese Cranes in 18 zoos, 19 of them bred in captivity, were officially listed (7).   There were thought to be an additional 50 in Korea, 20 in Japan and 24 in China.

REFERENCES   1.   Walkinshaw, L. 1973.   Cranes of the World.   New York: Winchester Press.
2.   Fisher, J., Simon, N. & Vincent, J. 1969.   Wildlife in Danger. New York: Viking Press.
3.   Masatomi, H. 1974.   The Japanese Crane Grus japonensis. Report to ICBP Working Group on Cranes.
4.   Kim, H.K. & Oesting, M. 1974.   Cranes in Korea.   Report to ICBP Working Group on Cranes.
5.   Hemmingsen, A.M. & Guildal, J.A. 1968.   Observations on birds in north eastern China.   Spolia Zool. Mus. Haun. (Copenhagen) 28(2): 1-326.
6.   Anon. 1975.   Winter count of rare cranes completed. The Brolga Bugle 1(2): 1.
7.   Olney, P. (ed.) 1976.   Census of rare animals in captivity 1975.   International Zoo Yearbook, 16: 411-446.
8.   Archibald, G. 1972.   Tancho Conservation Report. Unpub. Report to Japanese Government.
9.   Ostapenko, V.A. undated.   The Manchurian Crane in Kunashir. In Russian.   Unpublished ms.
10.   Won, P.-O. 1977.   Present status of cranes wintering in Korea 1976-1977.   Seoul: Kyung Hee Univ. Inst. of Ornith.

SIBERIAN WHITE CRANE

Grus leucogeranus Pallas, 1773

Order GRUIFORMES   Family GRUIDAE

STATUS   Endangered. Population slowly dwindling. Each pair requires an
enormous area for its territory. The species is easily disturbed and its
reproductive potential quite low, as is true of most cranes. It is sometimes
shot by hunters on its breeding grounds and nests are often destroyed or the
birds disturbed by herds of domesticated reindeer (1).

DISTRIBUTION   Breeds in northern Siberia in two discrete populations, one in
north-eastern Yakutia between the Yana and Kolyma rivers, including the upper
Indigirka basin, and the second on the lower reaches of the Ob River. Its
former breeding distribution may have been continuous between and beyond these
two relict populations, and could also have extended considerably farther south.
The Ob River population migrates to the Keoladeo Ghana Sanctuary in Bharatpur,
Rajasthan, India (1; 2) and at least occasionally drops in at Lake Ab-i-Istada in
Afghanistan (3). It is possible that in some years part of the Yakutia population joins the wintering flocks in India and Afghanistan, but where the remainder
winter is unknown, reports of the species occurring in the lower Yangtze valley
in China being unconfirmed (1). A remnant wintering group was discovered in
1978 at Feredoonkenar in the south Caspian coastlands of Iran (G. Archibald 1978,
pers. comm.).

POPULATION   Presumed to have been much greater than now, although precise
figures are lacking. According to the most recent (1974) estimate, the Yakutia
population numbers only 300 birds (1), which is a considerably more pessimistic
figure than, for example, the one of 700 pairs quoted in 1961 (4). The great
disparity is probably a reflection of differing estimation techniques rather than
of a very sharp decline. White Cranes have seldom been observed during their
migrations. The Ob River birds have been seen in Kazakhstan (about 70 birds
near Aktumsyk north-west of the Aral Sea in 1974) and at a reserve in Astrakhan
(8-14 birds annually) (1; 5); large numbers reported between 1942 and 1945 from
the shore of the Liaotun Gulf of the Yellow Sea, including two flocks (or possibly
just one) of 200-300 birds (6), were almost surely from the Yakutia population,
but their destination is uncertain. Usually between 70 and 80 birds, virtually
the entire Ob River population, winter annually at the Ghana Sanctuary, Bharatpur,
a site used regularly until 1880 and re-occupied since 1960 (2). Occasional
fluctuations, both at Bharatpur and in Afghanistan, when numbers reach as high as
200, suggest that in such years some Yakutia birds join the Ob birds (1). The
Ghana Sanctuary count in winter 1974-75 was 63 (7) and was 57 in 1977, in which
year 56 were later observed at Ab-i-Istada (R.G. Petocz 1977, pers. comm.). Nine
were discovered at Feredoonkenar, Iran, in 1978 (G. Archibald 1978, pers. comm.).

HABITAT   For breeding, bogs in typical tundra, lightly wooded tundra and possibly
also northern edges of the taiga (1); for wintering, wetlands and shallow ponds,
often covered with rush or sedge (2).

CONSERVATION MEASURES TAKEN   This crane has legal protection over much of its
range, its wintering area in India having been declared a bird sanctuary by the
Rajasthan government in 1956, putting to an end the excessive game bird hunting
in what had long been a private shooting preserve (8). It is listed in Appendix
1 of the 1973 Convention on International Trade in Endangered Species of Wild
Fauna and Flora. Ab-i-Istada was gazetted a flamingo and waterfowl sanctuary in

1977 by the Afghanistan government. In 1976 a project was launched to establish a new White Crane population, using Common Cranes Grus grus nesting south of the Urals and wintering at Lake Perishan, Iran, as foster parents (G. Archibald 1977, pers. comm.).

CONSERVATION MEASURES PROPOSED   A reserve to protect the breeding area of this crane in Yakutia from disturbance has been recommended (1).   Better protection of cranes from hunting in Afghanistan and also, especially, at Feredoonkenar, Iran, is also needed (G. Archibald 1978, pers. comm.).

REMARKS   In 1975, 9 White Cranes were in captivity in 7 zoos (9).

REFERENCES   1.   Flint, V.E. & Kistchinski, A.A. 1975.   Distribution, population density, and biology of the Siberian White Crane in Yakutia. Zool. Zh. 54: 1197-1212.   In Russian
2.   Walkinshaw, L. 1973.   Cranes of the World.   New York: Winchester Press.
3.   Koning, F.J. 1972.   Siberische witte kraanvogels in Afghanistan. Vogeljaar 1: 4-8.
4.   Uspenski, S.M. 1961.   Zur Verbreitung und biologie des Nonnenkranichs in Nordost-Siberien. Der Falke 8: 334-337.
5.   Vinogradov, V.V. undated.   Siberian White Cranes in the Caspian Region.   Unpublished ms.   In Russian.
6.   Hemmingsen, A.M. & Guildal, J.A. 1968.   Observations on birds in north eastern China. Spolia Zool. Mus. Haun. (Copenhagen) 28: 1-326.
7.   Anon. 1975.   Winter count of rare cranes completed. The Brolga Bugle 1(2): 1.
8.   LaBastille, A. 1974.   Taj Mahal to Nature. Audubon 76(3): 20-33.
9.   Olney, P.J.S. (ed.) 1976.   Census of rare animals in captivity 1975. International Zoo Yearbook 16: 411-446.

HOODED CRANE

Grus monacha Temminck, 1835

Order GRUIFORMES   Family GRUIDAE

STATUS   Vulnerable.   This species migrates from central Siberia, where it breeds,
to Japan and Korea.   Its population on its main wintering grounds in Japan is
relatively large, but concentrated in two small areas, where it receives supplemental feeding and where, recently, a number are reported to have succumbed to
pesticide poisoning.   Human persecution and habitat destruction are thought to
have been the main causes of the Hooded Crane's decline.

DISTRIBUTION   The presumed breeding range is in central Siberia between Tomsk and
Lake Baikal (1; 2).   The first nest was in fact discovered as recently as 1974,
near Tomsk (I. Neyfeldt 1975, pers. comm. to G. Archibald).   The cranes migrate to
Japan, Korea and, formerly at least, the lower Yangtze Valley in China (1; 2).   In
Korea its winter distribution is poorly understood; individuals or small groups have
been found irregularly in several provinces, in both the North and South; formerly
it was quite widespread (3).   In Japan a century ago it occurred in many localities,
but at present it is restricted to Arasaki on the Izumi Plain, Kagoshima Prefecture,
southern Kyushu and Kumage-machi, Yamaguchi Prefecture, Honshu (4; Y. Yamashina
1974, pers. comm.).

POPULATION   Formerly more numerous on its wintering grounds, the considerable
decline in its abundance in Korea, where only a few birds are now reported annually,
dates from about 1952; at about that time there was some recovery of the numbers
visiting Japan, coinciding with a program of supplemental feeding (3):   in 1939,
3,435 had been recorded but after the end of World War II only about 250 could be
found; thereafter numbers increased annually until 1974, when just over 3,000 were
recorded.   A year earlier, in 1973, 2,793 were at Arasaki and 137 were at Kumage-
machi (Y. Yamashina, pers. comm.; G. Archibald, pers. comm.).   There is no recent
information about numbers in China, although flocks of up to 50 to 100 birds were
observed on spring and fall migration in Hopei Province, north-eastern China,
between 1942 and 1945 (5).

HABITAT   In summer, marshlands on wooded steppes (2); in winter, wetlands and
agricultural lands, especially rice fields (1).   The agricultural areas where this
species winters in Japan are sprayed heavily with pesticides; in 1972, 20 birds were
found dead on the Izumi Plain, presumably as a result of pesticide poisoning.   The
species is said to do considerable damage to wheat and rice fields.

CONSERVATION MEASURES TAKEN   The wintering areas in Japan have been Special
Natural Monuments since 1955.   Supplemental feeding is subsidized by the Japanese
government (Y. Yamashina 1974, pers. comm.).   In South Korea the species was
designated Natural Monument No. 228 in 1970 (6).   It is listed in Appendix 1 of the
1973 Convention on International Trade in Endangered Species of Wild Fauna and Flora.

CONSERVATION MEASURES PROPOSED   No additional measures are known to have been
suggested.

REMARKS   Eighty captive birds were known to be held by 27 zoos in 1973 (7) and
75 by 24 zoos in 1975 (8).   The species has bred only twice in captivity; in
Woburn, England, in 1908, and at the International Crane Foundation, Baraboo,
Wisconsin, U.S.A., in 1976.

REFERENCES   1.   Walkinshaw, L. 1973.   _Cranes of the World_.   New York:
                    Winchester Press.
               2.   Dementiev, G.P., Meklenburtsev, R.N., Sudilovskaya, A.M. &
                    Spangenberg, E.P. 1951.   _Birds of the Soviet Union_ Vol. 2.
                    Trans. from Russian by Israel Program for Scientific
                    Translations, Jerusalem, 1968.
               3.   Kim, H.K. & Oesting, M. 1974.   Cranes in Korea.   Report to
                    ICBP Working Group on Cranes.
               4.   Austin, O.L., Jr. & Kuroda, N. 1953.   The birds of Japan:
                    their status and distribution.   _Bull. Mus. Comp. Zool_.
                    (Harvard) 109(4): 279-637.
               5.   Hemmingsen, A.M. & Guildal, J.A. 1968.   Observations on birds
                    in north-eastern China.   _Spolia Zool. Mus. Haun_. (Copenhagen)
                    28(2): 1-326.
               6.   Won, P.-O. 1974.   _Bird Treasures (Natural Monuments) in Korea_.
                    In Korean with English summary.
               7.   Duplaix-Hall, N. 1974.   Census of rare animals in captivity
                    1973.   _International Zoo Yearbook_ 14: 396-429.
               8.   Olney, P.J.S. 1976.   Census of rare animals in captivity 1975.
                    International Zoo Yearbook 16: 340-375.

BLACK-NECKED CRANE

Grus nigricollis Przevalski, 1876

Order GRUIFORMES   Family GRUIDAE

STATUS   Indeterminate.   Almost no information is available on this least-known species of crane which breeds on the inhospitable Tibetan plateau and winters in western China.

DISTRIBUTION   Believed or known to have bred in the Indus River basin in Ladakh and neighboring Tibet, the upper Brahmaputra River basin in Tibet, and in China near Lake Koko Nor, Tsinghai Province, and the Jalung and Dsachu steppes in western Szechwan.   Recorded as a migrant or in winter along the Brahmaputra River, Tibet, in Bhutan, in the Apa Tani Valley of Assam, India, northern Burma, Szechwan and Yunnan provinces, China, and northern Vietnam.   Its present distribution is unknown but is thought not to have altered significantly (1; 2).

POPULATION   No population estimates have been made, although "thousands" were reported earlier this century on the wintering grounds in China (1; 2).   There is no strong evidence for a decline, but there may well have been one.   About 15 were seen in Bhutan in winter 1974 (3) and 5 adults and a chick were found during an expedition to Ladakh in 1976, in search of this species (4).

HABITAT   Marshes, lake margins and lakes dotted with small islands, at elevations of 3,800 to 4,500m.   In winter lower elevations are resorted to, especially along river valleys with agricultural fields (1).

CONSERVATION MEASURES TAKEN   None known.

CONSERVATION MEASURES PROPOSED   A high-altitude National Park in the Changthang area of Ladakh has been proposed to the Indian government following a recent survey of the area (4).

REMARKS   When information from the seldom visited region inhabited by this species becomes available, it may show it to be relatively abundant and thus inappropriate for Red Data Book listing.   Until that time it seems advisable to draw attention to present ignorance of its status by including it.   Two birds are held in the Peking Zoo and three are in the Shanghai Zoo.   It is not known ever to have bred in captivity.

REFERENCES   1.   Walkinshaw, L. 1973.   Cranes of the World.   New York: Winchester Press.
2.   Oesting, M. & Archibald, G. 1974.   The Black-necked Crane (Grus nigricollis).   Report to ICBP Working Group on Cranes.
3.   Anon. 1975.   News of the world's least known crane.   The Brolga Bugle 1(2): 1.
4.   Ali, S. 1976.   Status and conservation of the Black-necked Crane (Grus nigricollis) and other rare wildlife in Ladakh.   Unpub. report, WWF Project.

WHITE-NAPED CRANE

Grus vipio Pallas, 1811

Order GRUIFORMES   Family GRUIDAE

STATUS   Vulnerable.   The breeding grounds of this species are virtually unknown.
It is found in winter very locally in Japan and Korea, where numbers have declined
and are now low.   The reasons for decline are probably human persecution and
habitat destruction, but this is unproven.

DISTRIBUTION   The summer distribution is centered in northern Mongolia, adjacent
south-eastern Siberia and northern Manchuria (1; 2).   The crane breeds at Lake
Khanka and along the Amur and Bureya rivers, U.S.S.R., and the Halhin, Uldza and
Onon rivers, Mongolia (7).   In winter it occurs in Japan at Arasaki, in Kagoshima
Prefecture, southern Kyushu, and formerly throughout Japan (1; 3).   It also
winters in Korea, once throughout the whole country, but now mainly in North and
South Chungchong Provinces, the Han River Estuary in the Demilitarized Zone being
at present an important staging area (1; 4).   It used also to be found in winter
in the lower Yangtze Valley in China, but there are no recent reports from this
area (1).

POPULATION   Formerly far more abundant.   In Japan 469 of these cranes were
counted in 1939, but by 1955 numbers had declined to 25.   However, it then
increased steadily to 449 in 1973, declining again to about 300 in 1974 (Y. Yamashina 1974, G. Archibald 1975, pers. comms).   It is in Korea that its highest
winter abundance has been recorded, making it at one time quite a common species,
though there has been some decline recently.   In November 1961 a flock of no less
than 2300 was observed at the confluence of the Han and Imjin Rivers (1) and
1500 were seen in the same area in the winter of 1974 and about 2000 in 1977, of
which about half continued their migration to Japan (8), 732 being counted at
Arasaki during that winter (Y. Yamashina in litt. to G. Archibald, 1977).   In
the U.S.S.R. only about 20 pairs are thought to be still nesting, the remainder
presumably in Mongolia and Manchuria.

HABITAT   In summer, along river valleys.   In winter, wetlands and cultivation,
especially rice paddies (1; 2).

CONSERVATION MEASURES TAKEN   This species was designated a Special Natural
Monument in Japan in 1952, and its wintering area at Arasaki ranks as a Special
Bird Protection Area, where feeding of the cranes is subsidized by the Japanese
government (Y. Yamashina 1974, pers. comm.).   In South Korea it was designated
Natural Monument No. 203 in 1968 and the Han River staging area has been made
a provisional Natural Monument (5).   A reed island on the Han has been made a
sanctuary and supplemental feeding has begun (G. Archibald 1977, pers. comm.).
The establishment of the 39 km-wide Demilitarized Zone between North and South
Korea has provided an excellent if unintended additional sanctuary (4).   The
species is listed in Appendix 1 of the 1973 Convention on International Trade in
Endangered Species of Wild Fauna and Flora.

CONSERVATION MEASURES PROPOSED   Recommendations include financial support by the
South Korean government for research and for conservation of the cranes by
expansion of supplemental feeding programs, provision of wardens to protect the
wintering population and public education emphasizing the importance of such
conservation (8).

REMARKS   There were 62 White-naped Cranes in 14 zoos in 1975, 24 of them bred in captivity (6).

REFERENCES

1. Walkinshaw, L. 1973.   The Cranes of the World.   New York: Winchester Press.
2. Dementiev, G.P., Meklenburtsev, R.N., Sudilovskaya, A.M. & Spangenberg, E.P. 1951.   Birds of the Soviet Union, Vol. 2. Trans. from Russian by Israel Program for Scientific Translations, Jerusalem, 1968.
3. Austin, O.L., Jr. & Kuroda, N. 1953.   The birds of Japan: their status and distribution.   Harvard Bull. Mus. Comp. Zool.   109(4): 279–637.
4. Kim, H.K. & Oesting, M. 1974.   Cranes in Korea.   Report to ICBP Working Group on Cranes.
5. Won, P.-O. 1974.   Bird Treasures (Natural Monuments) in Korea.   In Korean, English summary.
6. Olney, P.J.S. (ed.) 1976.   Census of rare animals in captivity 1975.   International Zoo Yearbook 16: 411–446.
7. Kucheruk, V.V. undated.   New data on the distribution of the White-naped Crane.   Unpublished ms.   In Russian.
8. Won, P.-O. 1977.   Present status of cranes wintering in Korea, 1976–1977.   Seoul: Kyung Hee University Inst. of Ornith.   In Korean, English summary.

GOLDMAN'S YELLOW RAIL

Coturnicops noveboracensis goldmani (Nelson, 1904)

Order GRUIFORMES   Family RALLIDAE

STATUS   Indeterminate.   Restricted to one marsh in Mexico which has been
significantly reduced in size and is under continuing pressure of development for
agriculture and for the water supply of Mexico City.

DISTRIBUTION   Known only from the headwater marshes of the Rio Lerma near San
Pedro Techuchulco, Mexico State (1).   The undisturbed portions of the Lerma
marshes now cover about 24 sq. km, one-tenth of their size in 1904, when the
subspecies was discovered (2).

POPULATION   Unknown.   The decline in the extent of marshland has doubtless
caused a similar decline in the population of this subspecies.   Only eight
specimens are known, the most recent one a partial skeleton, the remains of a
predator's meal, found in 1964 (1).

HABITAT   Wet meadows dominated by Typha sp. (cat-tail or bulrush) bordering the
Lerma marsh.   Water is pumped to Mexico City from the springs that form the
source of this marsh.   Ditching and draining for the purpose of agricultural
development have made substantial inroads into the wetlands during the present
century (2; R. Dickerman 1974, pers. comm.).

CONSERVATION MEASURES TAKEN   None known.

CONSERVATION MEASURES PROPOSED   None known.

REMARKS   The nominate race is widely but locally distributed in North America,
wintering in the southern United States.   It is highly secretive and may be more
common than is often believed.   Until 1910, the Lerma marshes supported the
population of the now extinct Slender-billed Grackle Cassidix palustris.

REFERENCES   1.   Dickerman, R.W. 1971.   Notes on various rails in
                   Mexico.   Wilson Bull. 83: 49-56.
              2.   Hardy, J.W. & Dickerman, R.W. 1965.   Relationships between
                   two forms of the Red-winged Blackbird in Mexico.   Living
                   Bird 4: 107-129.

ZAPATA RAIL

Cyanolimnas cerverai Barbour and Peters, 1927

Order GRUIFORMES   Family RALLIDAE

STATUS   Rare and local.   Known from the Zapata Swamp, Cuba, which has thus far
largely escaped from drainage attempts.   Its future is only as secure as the future
of the swamp (1).

DISTRIBUTION   Restricted to a portion of the Zapata Swamp, Las Villas Province,
Cuba, lying north of Santo Tomas woodland, and "apparently confined to within one
mile of the high ground" (2).   Former distribution is not known to have differed
substantially (1; 3; 4), but fossil bones from cave deposits in Pinar del Rio and
on the Isle of Pines have recently been attributed to this species (5).

POPULATION   Not precisely known.   The species was collected most recently in
1931, when two were taken and more were heard (3).   Attempts to locate it in 1935
(6) and 1955 (G.E. Watson 1973, pers. comm.) failed, but there are still no solid
grounds for suggesting a decline in its population.

HABITAT   Dense Myrica brushland with scrub, low trees and stretches of saw grass.
Some areas of the Zapata Swamp have been drained, but these are not extensive and
should cause no harm to the rail's habitat (1).

CONSERVATION MEASURES TAKEN   None known.

CONSERVATION MEASURES PROPOSED   None known.

REMARKS   This unique genus of rail shares its circumscribed habitat with two other
endemic birds, the Zapata Wren Ferminia cerverai and the Zapata Sparrow Torreornis
i. inexpectata.

REFERENCES   1.   Fisher, J., Simon, N. & Vincent, J. 1969.   Wildlife in
                   Danger.   New York:Viking Press; London:Collins.
              2.   Bond, J. 1956.   Check-list of the Birds of the West Indies.
                   Philadelphia Acad. Nat. Sci.
              3.   Bond, J. 1971.   Sixteenth supplement to the Check-list of the
                   Birds of the West Indies (1956).   Philadelphia Acad. Nat. Sci.
              4.   Ripley, S.D. 1977.   Rails of the World.   Boston:Godine.
              5.   Olson, S.L. 1974.   A new species of Nesotrochis from Hispaniola,
                   with notes on other fossil rails from the West Indies (Aves:
                   Rallidae).   Proc. Biol. Soc. Wash. 87(38): 439-450.
              6.   Bond, J. 1973.   Eighteenth supplement to the Check-list of the
                   Birds of the West Indies (1956).   Philadelphia Acad. Nat. Sci.

ALDABRA WHITE-THROATED RAIL

Dryolimnas cuvieri aldabranus (Gunther, 1879)

Order GALLIFORMES   Family RALLIDAE

STATUS   Rare.   Occurs on Aldabra, Indian Ocean, where it is restricted to the
islands of the atoll on which feral cats are not established.   It can apparently
tolerate large populations of rats.   The threat of road construction linking
islands presently with and without cats appears to have been removed by the
decision to construct airbase facilities on Diego Garcia rather than Aldabra.

DISTRIBUTION   Formerly this subspecies almost certainly occurred throughout
Aldabra, but was extirpated from South and West islands shortly after the
intentional introduction of cats in about 1890.   It still occurs on Polymnie,
Middle and some of the neighboring lagoon islets such as Michel and Ile aux Cèdres
(1).   Unfortunately, there has been a recent report that a cat was observed on
Middle Island (3).

POPULATION   No early estimates are on record, although South Island, the largest
of the atoll, may be assumed to have once supported the bulk of the population. In
1967 and 1968, the Middle Island rail population was put at 1000, although the
figures for some habitats such as mangrove were little more than guesses.   The
total population for all islands has been stated to be unlikely to exceed the
probable margin of error in the Middle Island estimate (1).   It will probably
remain stable, barring disasters.

HABITAT   Brush and mangrove, both of the more open and dense varieties.   As
previously stated feral cats have excluded the rails from some of the islands;
rats Rattus rattus are present in abundance throughout the atoll and may well take
eggs or young chicks, as does the land crab Cardisoma carnifex.   Predation may
account for the typical survival of only one young in spite of a normal clutch size
of three or four (1).

CONSERVATION MEASURES TAKEN   The combined voice of much of the world scientific
community in advocating preservation of Aldabra as a scientific reserve when it was
proposed to establish a large airbase there,was a major factor in securing the
decision to site the base at Diego Garcia (2; 3).   A scientific research station
was established in 1970 by the British Royal Society and Aldabra has since been
declared as a nature reserve.   The rail is legally protected from killing or
capture.

CONSERVATION MEASURES PROPOSED   Cats should be prevented from reaching all islands
from which they are still absent, and if their presence is confirmed should be
removed from Middle Island at the earliest possible moment (3).   Captive breeding
has been suggested as a means of maintaining a stock of this subspecies in the event
of extinction of the wild population (1).

REMARKS   This is the last remaining flightless bird of islands of the western
Indian Ocean.   D. c. abbotti is extinct on Assumption, Cosmoledo, and Astove, if
it was indeed that form that inhabited the latter two (4).   Nominate D. c. cuvieri
survives on Madagascar, where it is not at risk.

REFERENCES   1.   Penny, M.J. & Diamond, A.W. 1971.   The White-throated Rail
                   Dryolimnas cuvieri on Aldabra.   Phil. Trans. Roy. Soc. London
                   B260:   529-548.
              2.   Stoddart, D.R. 1968.   The Aldabra affair. Biol. Cons. 1: 62-69.
              3.   Stoddart, D.R. 1971.   Settlement, development and conservation
                   of Aldabra.   Phil. Trans. Roy. Soc. Lond. B. 260:   611-628.

HAWAIIAN COOT

Fulica americana alai Peale, 1848

Order GRUIFORMES   Family RALLIDAE

STATUS   Rare.   This coot is scarce in the Hawaiian Islands.   It has declined
because of destruction of its wetland habitat and possibly also through predation by
introduced mammals.

DISTRIBUTION   Recorded from all the main Hawaiian Islands except Lanai.   Its
present distribution is unchanged, but the coot now certainly occurs in fewer
localities on each island.   Among these Kanaha and Kealia Ponds, Maui, Menehune
Fish Pond and the Hanalei Valley, Kauai, and Kahuku Pond, but apparently no longer
Salt Lake and Kaelepulu Pond, on Oahu, are important (1; 2; 3).

POPULATION   In the 19th Century there were undoubtedly many more coot in Hawaii
than now, although estimates of the total population are lacking.   Flocks of 500-
600 birds were recorded (4; 5).   On Oahu as recently as 1958, 2002 were counted on
Salt Lake (6).   Annual censuses of coot throughout the Hawaiian Islands since 1969
produced figures ranging from 352 in 1972 (2) to 2369 in 1975 (7), with an average
of about 1,500 (1; 3).

HABITAT   Wetlands of all sorts, including fresh and brackish marshes, ponds,
irrigation ditches and flooded agricultural lands.   The extent of such habitats in
Hawaii has diminished significantly this century as a result of drainage for
cultivation and various other forms of development.   Another factor is that areas
surrounding wetlands are often infested by feral dogs, cats and mongooses, all of
which can be expected to prey on coot (1).   Thirdly, canals and drainage ditches
serving sugarcane plantations have sometimes been chemically cleared of filamentous
algae and the herbicides used may have poisoned the coots directly or through their
food plants (8).

CONSERVATION MEASURES TAKEN   Coot-hunting was prohibited in 1939 and the subspecies is now also fully protected from killing, capture or harrassment under the
U.S. Endangered Species Act of 1973.   Key areas of wetland habitat have either
been purchased (e.g Hanalei National Wildlife Refuge) or are in the process of being
acquired as refuges or sanctuaries.   Cooperative agreements between the U.S. Fish
and Wildlife Service and U.S. military authorities in Hawaii protect several
additional wetland areas where the coot occurs (2; 3).

CONSERVATION MEASURES PROPOSED   Additional wetland acquisition and preservation
(2; 3).

REMARKS   Three other subspecies in North America, Central America south to
Ecuador and the southern Caribbean are not at risk.

REFERENCES   1.   Berger, A.J. 1972.   Hawaiian Birdlife.   Honolulu:University
                    Press of Hawaii.
              2.   U.S. Dept. of Interior Fish and Wildlife Service, 1973.
                    Threatened Wildlife of the United States.   U.S. Fish Wildl.
                    Soc. Res. Pub. No. 114.
              3.   U.S. Bureau of Sport Fisheries and Wildlife and Hawaii Division
                    of Fish and Game, 1970.   Hawaii's endangered waterbirds.
              4.   Munro, G.C. 1960.   Birds of Hawaii.   Rutland:Bridgeway Press.

REFERENCES (cont.)

5. Schwartz, C.W. & Schwartz, E.R. 1952. The Hawaiian Coot.
   Auk 69: 446-449.
6. Udvardy, M.D.F. 1960. Movements and concentrations of the
   Hawaiian Coot on the island of Oahu. Elepaio 21: 20-22.
7. Whitten, H. 1975. Waterfowl count is up. Honolulu Star
   Bulletin, 30 August 1975, p. A-9. (reprinted in Elepaio 36:
   45).
8. Schwartz, C.W. & Schwartz, E.R. 1949. The Game Birds in
   Hawaii. Hawaii Board of Commissioners of Agriculture and
   Forestry.

HORNED COOT

Fulica cornuta Bonaparte, 1853

Order GRUIFORMES   Family RALLIDAE

STATUS   Rare.   Known from a few fresh water lakes in the high Andes of Chile, Bolivia and Argentina.   Although low in numbers, the species is not known to have declined.

DISTRIBUTION   Occurs in the puna zone above 3,050 m elevation in northern and central Chile (Tarapacá and Atacamá provinces), in south-western Bolivia, and in Jujuy, Salta, Catamarca and Tucumán provinces of Argentina (1-3).

POPULATION   Unknown, but believed to be quite small. On the 1 sq.km Santa Rosa Lake, at the southern end of Maricunga Salt Lake, in eastern Atacamá province, more than 100 were recorded in 1958, the largest known concentration, and 30 nests were found, not all of which were in use (1).

HABITAT   Fresh or slightly brackish lakes in the puna zone, supporting a growth of the waterweeds Ruppia filifolia and Myriophyllum sp., which are used for nest material (1; 4).

CONSERVATION MEASURES TAKEN   None known.

CONSERVATION MEASURES PROPOSED   None known.

REMARKS   The Giant Coot Fulica gigantea, which is partly sympatric with the Horned Coot but found at lower altitudes, is also an uncommon and local species, but possibly less so than the last-named (2).

REFERENCES   1. Johnson, A.W. 1965.   The Horned Coot, Fulica cornuta Bonaparte. Bull. Brit. Ornith. Club 85: 84-88.
2. Ripley, S.D. 1977.   Rails of the World.   Boston: Godine.
3. de Schauensee, R.M. 1966.   The Species of Birds of South America and their Distribution.   Narberth, Pa.: Livingston Publishing Co.
4. Ripley, S.D. 1957.   Notes on the Horned Coot, Fulica cornuta Bonaparte.   Postilla 30: 1-8.

MARIANAS GALLINULE

Gallinula chloropus guami Hartert, 1917

Order GALLIFORMES   Family RALLIDAE

STATUS   Rare.   The Marianas Gallinule is recorded in four of the Mariana Islands,
western Pacific, where its marshland habitat has been extensively drained.   It has
become rare only quite recently in parts of its range and its over-all status is not
adequately known.

DISTRIBUTION   Recorded from Pagan (48.4 sq. km), Saipan (121.7 sq. km), Tinian
(101.2 sq. km) and Guam (541 sq. km), Marianas.   In Saipan it has been found at
Lake Susupe, in Tinian at Lake Hagoi and Marpo Swamp and in Guam at Fena Lake
Reservoir, Agana Swamp, Abo Marsh, Atantano Marsh, a marsh east of Apra Harbor and
along the Ylig River, as well as on flooded agricultural lands (2; N. Drahos 1976,
pers. comm.).   It still occurs at Lake Hagoi (R. Owen 1975, pers. comm.) and Lake
Susupe (M. Bruce 1976, pers. comm.).

POPULATION   Considered abundant in Guam, Tinian and Saipan at least until 1945
(1; 3).   In 1974, only one bird was seen on a week's survey of Tinian, during which
a considerable time was spent at the two areas of habitat known to have been
frequented by the species (R. Owen 1975, pers. comm.).   In 1976, there were fewer
than 150 birds on Guam (N. Drahos 1976, pers. comm.).   The Pagan population is
unknown and only two were seen on Lake Susupe, Saipan in 1975 (M. Bruce 1976, pers.
comm.).

HABITAT   Wetlands, including reedbeds around fresh water lakes and along river
banks, marshes, rice paddies and taro patches (1).   Much wetland habitat has been
drained.   No wetlands are presently protected in the Marianas.

CONSERVATION MEASURES TAKEN   Fully protected by Guam law and listed on the Guam
Endangered Species list.   This list is yet to be incorporated into the Guam
Endangered Species Act of 1975.

CONSERVATION MEASURES PROPOSED   The subspecies has been recommended for inclusion
in the U.S. Trust Territories list of endangered species (R. Owen 1975, pers. comm.).

REMARKS   Of the 15 recognized subspecies distributed over most of the world only
this subspecies and G. c. sandvicensis, of Hawaii are known to be at risk.

REFERENCES   1.   Baker, R.H. 1951.   The avifauna of Micronesia, its origin,
                    evolution, and distribution.   Univ. Kansas Pubs. Mus. Nat.
                    Hist. 3(1): 1-359.
              2.   Strophlett, J.J. 1946.   Birds of Guam.   Auk 63: 534-540.
              3.   Marshall, J.T. 1949.   The endemic avifauna of Saipan, Tinian,
                    Guam and Palau.   Condor 51: 200-221.

HAWAIIAN GALLINULE

Gallinula chloropus sandvicensis Street, 1877

Order GRUIFORMES   Family RALLIDAE

STATUS   Endangered.   Limited to three islands in the Hawaiian Islands, where the
small surviving population is threatened by draining and filling of its wetland
habitat.   Draining of wetlands has drastically reduced the habitat available to
this subspecies in the recent past.   Predation by introduced rats, cats and
mongooses may also have been an important factor in decline of population (1; 2).

DISTRIBUTION   Formerly found on all main Hawaiian Islands except Lanai and
Niihau.   Presently occurs only on Kauai, Oahu and Molokai (1; 2).

POPULATION   Total population in the hundreds, mostly on Kauai.   Formerly far
more abundant (1; 2).

HABITAT   Freshwater ponds, marshes, irrigation ditches, reservoirs and taro
patches (2).

CONSERVATION MEASURES TAKEN   Protected by federal and state law from killing,
capture or harassment.   Purchase of important taro patch habitat in Halalei
Valley, Kauai, for a National Wildlife Refuge.   An attempted reintroduction of
this subspecies to Maui and Hawaii was not successful (1).

CONSERVATION MEASURES PROPOSED   Further purchases of wetlands by federal and
state governments.   Studies of population, life history and ecological requirements of the subspecies (1).

REMARKS   Subspecies has bred several times in captivity at Honolulu Zoo.   Of
the other 14 subspecies of this species, occurring on several islands and all
continents but Australia, only G. c. guami of the Mariana Islands is believed to
be at risk.

REFERENCES   1.   U.S. Department of Interior Bureau of Sport Fisheries and
                    Wildlife, 1973.   Threatened wildlife of the United States.
                    U.S. Bur. Sport Fish. Wildl. Res. Pub. 114
              2.   Berger, A.J. 1972.   Hawaiian Birdlife.   Honolulu:University
                    Press of Hawaii.

TAKAHE

Notornis mantelli Owen, 1848

Order GRUIFORMES   Family RALLIDAE

STATUS   Endangered.   Restricted to the Murchison Mountains, South Island, New
Zealand, where even in areas of most suitable habitat the species is only just
maintaining its numbers.   Its range today is not more than one-sixth of what it was
in the latter part of the 19th century.   Competition from introduced deer for food
and predation by introduced stoats are suspected of being the major factors in its
decline.

DISTRIBUTION   Towards the end of the 19th Century the species occupied about
4,000 sq. km of Fiordland in the relatively remote and rugged south-west corner of
South Island.   A population on North Island became extinct in pre-European times
and is known only from subfossil remains (1).   Today the Takahe is restricted to
approximately 650 sq. km of the Murchison Mountains west of Lake Te Anau and a small
adjacent area to the north (2; 3).

POPULATION   Never very abundant, the species today numbers about 100 pairs, with a
total population of about 250 (G. Williams 1976, pers. comm.).   Studies conducted
in two areas from 1972 to 1975 and in a third area since 1949 have shown that the
populations of the two areas are barely stable, while in the third area, Takahe
Valley, where the species was rediscovered in 1948, the population has suffered a
continuing decline which began in about 1966 (2; 3; 4; 5).

HABITAT   During most of the year the species occupies alpine snow tussock
(Chionochloa) grasslands.   Takahe rely heavily on bases of shoots and, when
available, seedheads of the tussock.   In winter when snow makes the tussock
unavailable, the birds move to adjacent beech (Nothofagus) forest where they feed
on grasses, herbs and fern rhizomes.   In some areas, such as Takahe Valley, the
forest understory has been depleted by deer (3).

CONSERVATION MEASURES TAKEN   The species is fully protected legally.   Its entire
range lies within Fiordland National Park.   Limited access to the Murchison
Mountain Restricted Area prevents undue disturbance of most of the population.
Research on the ecology of the species has been conducted for several years by
biologists of the New Zealand Wildlife Service and is still in process: at present
it covers an assessment of the impact on Takahe populations of introduced deer and
stoats, and qualitative studies of Takahe food.   The Wildlife Service has a captive
breeding program for this and several other endemic species at Mt. Bruce Native Bird
Reserve.   Fertile Takahe eggs have been laid each year since 1973, and several
chicks have hatched, but all have died shortly afterwards as a result of congenital
abnormalities (6; 7 G. Williams 1976, pers. comm.).

CONSERVATION MEASURES PROPOSED   Continued support of the excellent conservation
program undertaken by the New Zealand Wildlife Service for this species.   The
Wildlife Service has a new project for establishing a colony of Takahe on Maud
Island as an insurance policy for its survival and this is expected to be launched
in about 1978 (G. Williams 1976, pers. comm.).

REMARKS   Massive programs for control of deer have resulted in an improvement of
the critically important forest understory and tussock lands in the Takahe's range.
Only the longevity of the adults is saving this species at present.   A succession
of poor breeding seasons or harsh winters could at any time cause a further
deterioration in the status of the species (G. Williams 1976, pers. comm.).

REFERENCES 1. Williams, G.R. 1960. The Takahe (Notornis mantelli Owen, 1948): A general survey. Trans. Roy. Soc. N.Z.88: 235-258.
2. Mills, J.A. & Lavers, R.B., 1974. Preliminary results of research into the present status of Takahe (Notornis mantelli) in the Murchison Mountains. Notornis 21: 312-317.
3. Mills, J.A. 1974. Takahe. Wildlife - A review 5: 56-59.
4. Reid, B. 1969. Survival status of the Takahe, Notornis mantelli, of New Zealand. Bio. Cons. 1: 237-240.
5. Mills, J.A. 1973. Takahe research. Wildlife - A review 4: 24-27.
6. Roderick, C.D. 1973. Mt. Bruce Native Bird Reserve. Wildlife - A review 4: 43-46.
7. Roderick, C.D. 1974. Mt. Bruce Native Bird Reserve. Wildlife - A review 5: 60-68.

SAN CRISTOBAL MOUNTAIN RAIL

Pareudiastes sylvestris Mayr, 1933

Order GRUIFORMES   Family RALLIDAE

STATUS   Indeterminate.   Still known only from one specimen from San Cristobal
Island, Solomon Islands, which was taken by the Whitney South Sea Expedition in
1929 (1).   In 1953 it was said to be not uncommon in one locality on San Cristobal
(2).

DISTRIBUTION   The type specimen was collected at 580m elevation at Hunogahara, a
village in the mountains of central San Cristobal, Solomon Islands (1).   The
species is also known to inhabit valleys leading to the Naghasi Ridge, inland from
Ghoghe (2).

POPULATION   Only one was collected in 1929, despite efforts to secure additional
specimens (1).   Another single bird was seen in 1953 in an area where the local
inhabitants considered the species to be not uncommon (2).

HABITAT   Primeval forest, intermingled with patches of native cultivation and
secondary growth.   No standing water near the type locality.   Also said to occur
in rocky valleys below 425m elevation (1; 2).

CONSERVATION MEASURES TAKEN   None known.

CONSERVATION MEASURES PROPOSED   None known, but further efforts to establish the
status of the species are obviously necessary.

REFERENCES   1.   Mayr, E. 1933.   Birds collected during the Whitney South Sea
                      Expedition, XXII: Three new genera from Polynesia and Melanesia.
                      Amer. Mus. Novit. 590.
                2.   Cain, A.J. & Galbraith, I.C.J. 1956.   Field notes on birds
                      of the eastern Solomon Islands.   Ibis 98: 100-134.

LIGHT-FOOTED CLAPPER RAIL

Rallus longirostris levipes Bangs, 1899

Order GRUIFORMES   Family RALLIDAE

STATUS   Endangered.   A rail of coastal salt marshes of southern California and
Mexico.   Pressures to drain marshlands for development are intense in California.
The extent of this rail's habitat has already declined significantly and will
continue to do so unless extreme and expensive measures are taken.

DISTRIBUTION   The southern California coast from Santa Barbara County southward
to San Diego County, U.S.A., and the Pacific coast of Baja California, Mexico, to
Bahia de San Quintin.   Within this range, a linear distance of about 800 km, the
rail's distribution is highly discontinuous.   It presently occurs in 16 marshes
in California and at least 4 in Baja California. (1-3; 11; J. Aldrich 1977, pers.
comm.).   It is thought to have occurred in the past in almost all salt marshes
within its present range (4), many of which have been filled or drained or are now
polluted.

POPULATION   There has been a substantial decline, first noticed as early as
1915 (6).   A total population estimate of 400 in 1974 (2) has more recently been
revised downwards to 250 (1).   Tijuana Estuary just north of the U.S.-Mexico
border holds the most important concentration (75-85 birds) (7), followed by San
Diego Bay, Upper Newport Bay and Anaheim Bay each with 40-50; other occupied sites
in California have 10 or fewer birds and there is no information about numbers in
Baja California (1).

HABITAT   Saltmarsh, particularly with tall dense cordgrass Spartina foliosa and
also pickleweed Salicornia sp.   In 1971, out of an estimated original total of
10,500 ha of saltmarsh between Santa Barbara and the Mexican border, only 3440 ha
remained, much of which had been degraded by pollution, water diversion or
restriction of tidal flow (8), and this destruction of its habitat is clearly the
principal threat to the survival of this rail.

CONSERVATION MEASURES TAKEN   The subspecies has been given protection under the
U.S. Endangered Species Act, California law and the U.S./Mexico Migratory Bird
Treaty.   A Recovery Team, appointed by the U.S. Fish and Wildlife Service, has
completed the drafting of a Recovery Plan.

CONSERVATION MEASURES PROPOSED   The Recovery Plan proposes acquisition, at a
cost of several million dollars, of about 450 ha of saltmarsh in Tijuana Estuary,
San Diego Bay, Los Penasquitos Lagoon and Carpinteria marsh, involving the
restoration of tidal flow in the two last-mentioned and several other marshes; it
also aims at creating or restoring habitat not presently occupied by the rail and
investigating aspects of its ecology and management which would help to improve
its productivity in certain marshes (1).

REMARKS   Of 11 subspecies of the Clapper Rail found in coastal and other marshes
of North, Central and South America, R. l. obsoletus of west-central California
and R. l. yumanensis of the lower Colorado River and Salton Sea may also be or
have been at some risk because of restricted distribution and abundance.   However,
estimated numbers of the latter now exceed 1000 and its habitat is more extensive
today than at any time in its history (10; J. Aldrich 1977, pers. comm.); furthermore the complete legal protection accorded to it, including a requirement to take
its status into account in any federal or state projects affecting its habitat,

has appreciably reduced the threat to its survival, so that although listed and classified as rare in the previous edition of this Volume, it can now be safely omitted.

Some authors consider Rallus elegans of freshwater marshes to be conspecific with R. longirostris (5; 9).

REFERENCES
1. Wilbur, S.R., Jurek, R.M., Hein, R. & Collins, C.T. 1977. Light-footed Clapper Rail recovery plan. U.S. Fish and Wildlife Service.
2. Wilbur, S.R. 1974. The status of the Light-footed Clapper Rail. Amer. Birds 28: 868-870.
3. Wilbur, S.R. & Tomlinson, R.E. 1976. The literature of the western Clapper Rails. U.S. Fish Wildl. Service Spec. Sci. Rept. Wildl. 194.
4. Grinnell, J., Bryant, H.C. & Storer, T.I. 1918. The Game Birds of California. Berkeley: University of California Press.
5. Ripley, S.D. 1977. Rails of the World. Boston: Godine.
6. Grinnell, J. 1915. A distributional list of the birds of California. Pacific Coast Avifauna 11.
7. Jorgenson, P.D. 1975. Habitat preference of the Light-footed Clapper Rail in Tijuana Marsh, California. MSc. Thesis, San Diego State University, San Diego, California.
8. Speth, J.W. 1971. The status of coastal wetlands in southern California. Paper presented at annual meeting, Western Section, The Wildlife Society. 19 pp.
9. Meanley, B. 1965. King and Clapper Rails of Broadway Meadows. Delaware Conservationist winter issue: 3-7.
10. Ohmart, R.D. & Smith, R.W. 1973. North American Clapper Rails (Rallus longirostris) literature survey with special consideration being given to the past and current status of yumanensis. Report under U.S. Bureau of Reclamation Contract No. 14-06-300-2409.
11. Massey, B.W. 1977. Occurrence and nesting of the Least Tern and other endangered species in Baja California, Mexico. Western Birds 8: 67-70.

CALIFORNIA CLAPPER RAIL

Rallus longirostris obsoletus Ridgway, 1874

Order GRUIFORMES   Family RALLIDAE

STATUS   Vulnerable.   Now largely restricted to one major bay, on the U.S. west
coast, which is undergoing extensive land filling and development, so that much
of the marshland habitat has been polluted or denied the normal tidal flow
essential to the well-being of this species.

DISTRIBUTION   The former breeding range extended for about 670 km along the
coast of central California from Humboldt Bay, Humboldt County, south to Morro Bay,
San Luis Obispo County, in suitable saltmarsh habitats.   The majority of sites have
been deserted but the rail still breeds at Elkhorn Slough in Monterey Bay and,
most importantly, in South San Francisco Bay, though its range has become somewhat
contracted in recent years, and in San Pablo Bay, the north arm of San Francisco
Bay.   It is non-migratory but individuals have occasionally shown some tendency
to wander. (1-3; 6).

POPULATION   Once locally abundant but sharply reduced by commercial hunting
earlier this century.   However, by 1944, the rail's former abundance had been
regained in areas where there was still sufficient suitable habitat, although an
overall decline continued as the result of habitat losses.   In 1972, the number
in South San Francisco Bay was estimated at 2800, probably representing more than
half the total population, with smaller numbers at Corte Madera Marsh, Petaluma
Marsh, Tubbs Island and other marshes around the northern arm of San Francisco Bay.
Habitat destruction since 1972 has reduced these figures by an unknown amount and
in some areas there has also been a recent deterioration in breeding success. (1;
4; 5; 7; J. Aldrich 1977, pers. comm.).

HABITAT   Saltmarsh with a good cover of pickleweed Salicornia virginica,
cordgrass Spartina foliosa and also some gumweed Grindelia sp.   Many of the
saltmarshes of coastal California have been filled in for industrial and urban
development, those that are left being subject to an increasing threat of pollution.   Cessation of tidal flow as a result of construction activities has been
another reason for the abandonment of certain marshes by the rail.   However, some
of its remaining habitat has now been protected. (1; J. Aldrich 1977, pers. comm.).

CONSERVATION MEASURES TAKEN   This species is fully protected by the U.S. Migratory Bird Treaty Act and Endangered Species Act and by California law.   Part of its
habitat is included in the South San Francisco Bay National Wildlife Refuge and The
Nature Conservancy has recently purchased Tubbs Island in San Pablo Bay and Elkhorn
Slough, Monterey Bay, in order to protect additional critical areas of habitat.

CONSERVATION MEASURES PROPOSED   Reintroduction of San Francisco Bay stock to
Morro Bay was considered in 1972, but rejected because of uncertainty as to
whether any of the original Morro Bay population survived (S. Wilbur 1977, pers.
comm. to J. Aldrich).   The U.S. Fish and Wildlife Service proposes to acquire
further important areas of suitable habitat or develop conservation agreements with
their owners (8).

REMARKS   Of the other subspecies, Rallus longirostris levipes of coastal
southern California and Baja California is classified as endangered (see relevant

data sheet). <u>R. l. yumanensis</u> of the lower Colorado River and Salton Sea is at some risk because of its comparatively low numbers and threats to its habitat; but it is now more abundant and widespread than at any other time (9) and no longer justifies inclusion in the Red Data Book, although listed in the previous edition as 'rare and localized'. None of the other subspecies is known to be at risk.

This rail shares its saltmarsh habitat in South San Francisco Bay with a race of the song sparrow, <u>Melospiza melodia pusillula</u>, and in San Pablo Bay with a different race, <u>M. m. samuelis</u>, both of them calling for a careful eye to be kept on their status; and also with the saltmarsh harvest mouse <u>Reithrodontomys raviventris</u>, listed in Vol. 1 of the Red Data Book as 'endangered'.

<u>REFERENCES</u>
1. Wilbur, S.R. & Tomlinson, R.E. 1976. The literature of the western Clapper Rails. <u>U.S. Fish Wildl. Service Spec. Sci. Rept. Wildl.</u> 194.
2. Grinnell, J. & Miller, A.H. 1944. The distribution of the birds of California. <u>Pacific Coast Avifauna</u> 27.
3. Van Rossem, A.J. 1929. The status of some Pacific Coast Clapper Rails. <u>Condor</u> 31: 213-215.
4. Gill, R., Jr. 1972. South San Francisco Bay breeding bird survey. Calif. Dept. Fish Game Fed. Aid Wildl. Restor. Prog. W-54-R, Special Wildl. Investigation.
5. Gould, G. 1973. California rail survey, 1973. Calif. Dept. Fish Game Spec. Wildl. Investigation Job II-10.
6. Varoujean, D.E. 1972. A study of the California Clapper Rail in Elkhorn Slough. Calif. Dept. Fish Game Fed. Aid Wildl. Restor. Prog. W-54-R, Spec. Wildl. Investigation.
7. Zucca, J.H. 1954. A study of the California Clapper Rail. <u>Wasmann Journ. Biol.</u> 12: 135-153.
8. U.S. Bureau of Sport Fisheries and Wildlife. 1973. Threatened wildlife of the United States. <u>U.S. Bur. Sport Fish. Wildl. Res. Pub.</u> 114.
9. Ohmart, R.D. & Smith, R.W. 1973. North American Clapper Rails (<u>Rallus longirostris</u>) literature survey with special consideration being given to the past and current status of <u>yumanensis</u>. Report under U.S. Bureau of Reclamation Contract No. 14-06-300-2409.

GUAM RAIL

Rallus owstoni (Rothschild, 1895)

Order GALLIFORMES   Family RALLIDAE

STATUS   Vulnerable.   Endemic to Guam, Mariana Islands, Western Pacific, this
flightless rail has survived thanks to its secretiveness and its ability to adapt
to both woodlands and grasslands; but there are now indications of a recent
population decline.

DISTRIBUTION   Formerly widespread in the 541 sq. km of Guam (1).   There is no
evidence of any changes in its distribution.

POPULATION   Population censuses began in 1961.   Maximum monthly abundance of
birds observed per 100 miles of road from 1962 to 1971 averaged 151.3 in the north
and 72.3 in the south.   Since 1972 the average has fallen to 26.7 per 100 miles
in the north and 5.6 in the south, though a slight increase was noted in 1974 as
compared with 1973 (3).   The population tends to fluctuate with rainfall cycles (2),
but it is clear that a major decrease took place in 1971 or 1972, from which the
species has not yet recovered.

HABITAT   Upland grassy areas, forests and marshlands, comprising, in fact, most of
the habitats to be found on Guam.   The rail is captured by the inhabitants for food,
using dogs and snares.   Feral pigs and cats are widespread on Guam (1) and their
presence may contribute to, but does not fully explain, the very recent decline of a
species which had coped with these potential predators for more than a century.

CONSERVATION MEASURES TAKEN   With effect from 1976 the species may no longer be
hunted.   It has been placed on the Protected List of the government of Guam.

CONSERVATION MEASURES PROPOSED   No further measures are known to be under
consideration, but see below regarding the general need for status surveys.

REMARKS   The continued existence of a flightless rail on an oceanic island in the
presence of numerous predators is remarkable.   That it is common, or was so until
very recently, is miraculous.   Comprehensive status surveys are a basic conservation requirement for the endemic birds of Guam and the U.S. Trust Territories.

REFERENCES   1.   Baker, R.H. 1951.   The avifauna of Micronesia, its origin,
                   evolution, and distribution.   Univ. Kansas Pubs. Mus. Nat.
                   Hist. 3(1): 1-359.
              2.   Perez, G.S.A. 1968.   Notes on the breeding season of Guam Rails
                   (Rallus owstoni).   Micronesica 4(1): 133-135.
              3.   Guam Division of Fish and Wildlife. 1975.   Quail and rail life
                   history study.   Guam Fish and Wildlife Investigations
                   Project FW-2R-12, job W-3.

AUCKLAND ISLAND RAIL

Rallus pectoralis muelleri Rothschild, 1893

Order GRUIFORMES   Family RALLIDAE

STATUS   Indeterminate. Confined to one or possibly two small islands of the
Auckland Islands 500 km south of New Zealand, where its population is almost
certainly very small.

DISTRIBUTION   Known with certainty only from Adams Island (9,000 ha), but possibly
also occurs on Ewing Island (1), although none were seen or heard during a careful
search in 1972 (G. Williams 1976, pers. comm.).   Presumably occurred on all islands
of the Auckland group prior to the arrival and establishment of introduced mammals
in the last century.

POPULATION   Aside from the type specimen described in 1893, the subspecies is
known only from a bird captured in 1966 on Adams Island; it was the only one seen.
Rail-like birds were also sighted on Adams Island in 1942 and on Ewing Island in
1942 and 1962 (1), but no idea was obtained of their abundance.

HABITAT   Unknown.   The bird collected in 1966 was captured at a garbage dump in
scrub and tussock (1).   Introduced cats, black rats Rattus rattus, pigs and goats
are established on Auckland Island itself and some but not all the other islands of
the group.

CONSERVATION MEASURES TAKEN   The rail is protected by law and all the islands in
the Auckland group are Reserves for the Preservation of Flora and Fauna, with
access strictly controlled.

CONSERVATION MEASURES PROPOSED   The strictest possible supervision of visits to
Adams Island to prevent accidental introduction of predators.

REMARKS   About nine other subspecies of Rallus pectoralis are recognized.   They
have been found in Luzon, Flores, New Guinea, Australia and Tasmania, but not New
Zealand, and some are thought to be scarce or are known only from a few specimens.
But only this Auckland Islands subspecies is believed to be at risk.

REFERENCES   1.   Falla, R.A. 1967.   An Auckland Island rail.   Notornis
                      14: 107-113.
              2.   Williams, G.R. 1970.   Unpublished report of the Auckland Islands
                      expedition.   New Zealand Wildlife Service.

BARRED-WING RAIL

Rallus poecilopterus (Hartlaub, 1866)

Order GRUIFORMES   Family RALLIDAE

STATUS   Endangered.   On the basis of a sighting in 1973, this species is
resurrected to the ranks of the living, if only as an endangered species.   It was
thought that introduced mongooses and possibly rats and cats had caused its
extinction and they must still be considered as the major factors threatening its
survival.

DISTRIBUTION   Formerly occurred on Viti Levu and Ovalau, Fiji (1; 2), now only
known from the Nadrau Plateau, Viti Levu (D.T. Holyoak 1973, pers. comm.).

POPULATION   No estimate was ever made of the abundance or rarity of this species,
since it was shy and seldom seen.   It totally eluded the searches of the Whitney
South Sea Expedition in the 1920s (2).   The surviving population is equally
unknown, only a single bird having been observed in June 1973, the first in 83 years
(D.T. Holyoak 1973, pers. comm.).

HABITAT   Thick taro beds and swamps.   The 1973 bird was seen in an old taro patch
surrounded by secondary forest.

CONSERVATION MEASURES TAKEN   None known.

CONSERVATION MEASURES PROPOSED   None known.

REFERENCES   1.   Mayr, E. 1945.   Birds of the Southwest Pacific.   New York:
                   Macmillan Company.
              2.   Greenway, J.C., Jr. 1958.   Extinct and Vanishing Birds of the
                   World.   Amer. Comm. Internat. Wild Life Prot. Spec.'Pub. No. 13.

BOGOTA RAIL

Rallus semiplumbeus Sclater, 1856

Order GRUIFORMES   Family RALLIDAE

STATUS   Vulnerable. Of somewhat limited distribution, the populations of this
rail have been increasingly depleted by the drainage of wetlands and hunting in
the Bogotá savanna, Colombia.

DISTRIBUTION   The species is restricted to the Bogota savanna, at a mean
altitude of 2600 m in the eastern Andes, in Boyaca and Cundinamarca departments
(1). It is now known only from the marshes of Lake Tota and the Parque del
Florida near Bogotá (R. Ridgely 1977, pers. comm.).

POPULATION   Unknown. The species was considered not uncommon but locally
distributed in 1917 (2). A decline has undoubtedly followed the destruction of
numerous wetland areas within its circumscribed range (J. Hernandez 1974, pers.
comm. to M. Rylander).

HABITAT   Wetlands. Drainage of such areas on the Bogotá savanna has caused
serious problems for all the birds which use them for nesting or feeding,
including several species and subspecies endemic to the area. Hunting pressure
on the few remaining wetlands has intensified (J. Hernandez 1974, pers. comm. to
M. Rylander).

CONSERVATION MEASURES TAKEN   The municipal park in which the species is known
to occur should afford it some protection.

CONSERVATION MEASURES PROPOSED   None known.

REFERENCES   1. Ripley, S.D. 1977. Rails of the World. Boston: Godine.
              2. Chapman, F.M. 1917. The distribution of bird-life in
                  Colombia; a contribution to a biological survey of
                  South America. Bull. Amer. Mus. Nat. Hist. 36: 1-729.

LORD HOWE WOOD RAIL

Tricholimnas sylvestris (Sclater, 1869)

Order GRUIFORMES   Family RALLIDAE

STATUS   Endangered.   Restricted to the 13 sq. km of Lord Howe Island, 630 km from
the Australian coast in the south-west Pacific.   The population continues to
decline, being restricted to two mountain tops, where rats take many eggs and where
the vegetation is being altered by continual foraging of feral goats and pigs
(1; 2; 3; 4).

DISTRIBUTION   At the time of discovery of Lord Howe Island (1788) the species was
abundant, especially in the lowlands.   By 1908, it could only be found on the summit
plateaux and slopes of Mt. Lidgbird and Mt. Gower and in the intervening Erskine
Valley (1).   In 1969, it was confined to the two mountain top plateaux (less than
50 hectares), although individuals occasionally wandered somewhat lower (3).

POPULATION   Once abundant over the entire island, the species has become
increasingly rare.   The 1963 population estimate was between 150 and 200 pairs (2),
although more recent studies suggest the estimate was over-optimistic.   In 1969, 16
birds were counted on Mt. Gower and the population was described as being very low
(3).   In February 1974, there were 19 birds on Mt. Gover and one immature bird was
seen on Mt. Lidgbird.   There appears to be territorial room for no more than 9
pairs on Mt. Gower and perhaps three pairs on Mt. Lidgbird (4).

HABITAT   Formerly all habitats of Lord Howe Island (1).   Now only the moss
forest plateaux of the mountain tops (3).

CONSERVATION MEASURES TAKEN   The island was gazetted as an Ordinary Faunal
District in 1939.   A rat poisoning program is underway, even on the relatively
inaccessible top of Mount Gower.   A research program on the species is also in
progress (3).

CONSERVATION MEASURES PROPOSED   A campaign to exterminate goats, pigs and rats in
the summit area of Mount Gower, both to prevent further damage to the vegetation
and to stop the taking of this rail's eggs by rats, has been recommended (3).
National Park status for the area inhabited by the rail has also been advocated by
an Australian government survey team (5).

REMARKS   In view of the extinction of many island rails throughout the world by
introduced mammalian predators, it is remarkable that this species still survives,
even in its presently beleaguered state.   Its nearest relative was the extinct
New Caledonian Wood Rail T. lafresnayanus.

REFERENCES   1.   Hindwood, K.A. 1940.   The birds of Lord Howe Island.
                   Emu 40: 1-86.
              2.   McKean, J.L. & Hindwood, K.A. 1965.   Additional notes on the
                   birds of Lord Howe Island.   Emu 64: 79-97.
              3.   Disney, H.J. de S. & Smithers, C.N. 1972.   The distribution of
                   terrestrial and freshwater birds on Lord Howe Island, in
                   comparison with Norfolk Island.   Austral. Zool. 17: 1-11.
              4.   Disney, H.J. de S. 1974.   Woodhen.   Austral. Nat. Hist.
                   18(2): 70-73.
              5.   Recher, H.F. & Clark, S.S. 1974.   Exploitation vs. conservation.
                   Austral. Nat. Hist. 18(2): 74-77.

KAGU

Rhynochetos jubatus Verreaux and des Murs, 1860

Order GRUIFORMES   Family RHYNOCHETIDAE

STATUS   Endangered.   Increasing diminution of both range and numbers.   The most
important threats to this unique species are from introduced mammalian predators,
especially dogs, but also cats, pigs and rats; destruction of habitat from nickel
mining; and the trapping of the birds mainly for keeping as pets.

DISTRIBUTION   Known only from the island of New Caledonia, in which it was
formerly widespread.   It has become increasingly localized in those valleys of the
central mountain range least accessible to man (1; 2; 3; 4; 5).   In 1945, it was
still present in the northern mountains and in the mountains of the southern third
of the island (4).

POPULATION   No estimates have been made.   However, it is certain that the species
has been and still is declining, although perhaps at a slower rate recently (1; 2;
3; 4).

HABITAT   Dense forest and brush of river and stream valleys (2).   Extensive
forested areas have been laid waste by nickel mining and operations connected with
it, which continue unabated (H. Bregulla 1974, pers. comm.).

CONSERVATION MEASURES TAKEN   The species is protected by law.   Capture and export
can be authorized only exceptionally for scientific purposes (6).   The species is
listed in Appendix 1 of the 1973 Convention on International Trade in Endangered
Species of Wild Fauna and Flora.   A park proposed for the Rivière Bleue area, which
would have protected part of the Kagu's range, has not been established, but a
forest park is being developed near Nouméa, which will provide a semi-captive
breeding situation for five or six pairs.

CONSERVATION MEASURES PROPOSED   Larger reserves are needed, as are more rigorous
enforcement of the laws protecting the species and more conservation education.   A
system of permits and of close-ringing or permanent banding of kagus kept as pets
in local homesteads has been recommended as a first step toward a more comprehensive
and effective conservation program (H. Bregulla, pers. comm.; P. Rancurel 1974,
pers. comm.).

REMARKS   The Kagu is of great scientific as well as aesthetic value.   It
comprises a unique genus and family of birds.   Twelve were held in captivity in six
collections outside of New Caledonia in 1973, two of which had been bred in
captivity (7).   In addition a number of Kagus are kept in captivity in New
Caledonia and are said to breed readily, though the young frequently die (P. Rancurel, pers. comm.).

REFERENCES   1.   Fisher, J., Simon, N. & Vincent, J. 1969.   Wildlife in Danger.
                   New York:Viking Press; London:Collins.
              2.   Greenway, J.C. Jr. 1958.   Extinct and Vanishing Birds of the
                   World.   Amer. Comm. Internat. Wildlife Prot. Spec. Pub. No. 13.
              3.   Sarasin, F. 1913.   Die Voegel New-Caledoniens und der Loyalty
                   Inseln.   In Nova Caledonia, Zoology, Vol. 1: 1-78.
              4.   Warner, D.W. 1947.   The Ornithology of New Caledonia and the
                   Loyalty Islands.   Cornell Univ.: Ph.D. Thesis.
              5.   Warner, D.W. 1948.   The present status of the Kagu, Rhynochetos
                   jubatus, on New Caledonia.   Auk 65: 287-288.

6. Barrau, J. 1963. Present status of preservation of the Kagu
    Rhynochetos jubatus in New Caledonia. _Bull. ICBP_ 9: 90.
7. Duplaix-Hall, N. (ed.) 1974. Census of rare animals in
    captivity, 1973. _International Zoo Yearbook_ 14: 396-429.

GREAT INDIAN BUSTARD

Choriotis nigriceps (Vigors, 1831)

Order GRUIFORMES   Family OTIDIDAE

STATUS   Endangered.   Restricted to a small fraction of its former range in north-
western India, where in spite of legal protection it is hunted regularly for food
and where its grassland habitat meets with increasing disturbance from overgrazing
and expanding agriculture.

DISTRIBUTION   Formerly widespread in Pakistan from Punjab and Sind west of the
Indus across northern India in the Gangetic Plains to West Bengal and south through
Rajasthan, Gujarat, Madhya Pradesh and Orissa to the Deccan plateau and Tamil Nadu
(1).   It now occurs not at all or only sporadically over most of India and Pakistan
but is still to be found regularly in Rajasthan, in several districts of Gujarat,
especially Jamnagar District, near Gwalior in Madhya Pradesh (2) and in Ahmadnagar
District, Maharashtra (1).   It presently occupies only about 1.7 per cent of its
former range (3).

POPULATION   No early estimates were made, although it is clear that the species
was once far more numerous than it is today.   One hunter in Ahmadnagar District
alone shot 961 between 1809 and 1829 (1).   By 1971, no more than 1,000 Great Indian
Bustards were said to remain throughout the known range of the species (2), although
owing to its erratic seasonal movements and the vast extent of the open grasslands
needing to be investigated for the census, a more precise estimate was not practical.
The negative factors operating on the bustard populations have increased in
intensity and the total number today is doubtless well below that of 1971.

HABITAT   Grasslands interspersed with scrub or cultivated land in semi-desert
country (1).   The grasslands in question are all under heavy pressure from grazing
by domestic stock.   More cultivation has also encroached on the grassland and with
it has come increased disturbance by humans, although on some farms where this
bustard is not persecuted it has thrived.   Poaching by nomadic pastoralists and
others is, however, probably the most serious problem confronting this species (2).

CONSERVATION MEASURES TAKEN   This bustard is legally protected in every Indian
state in which it is known to occur, although in practice the task of providing the
wardens to carry out an effective patrol of the extensive habitat is impossible.
The species is listed in Appendix 2 of the 1973 Convention on International Trade in
Endangered Species of Wild Fauna and Flora.

CONSERVATION MEASURES PROPOSED   Several reserves, sanctuaries and other protected
areas have been recommended as the result of a survey of this species undertaken in
1971.   At the same time the strengthening of the warden force responsible for
protecting this species and giving it increased mobility were also suggested.
Another proposal is to breed this bustard in a captive or semi-captive state with a
view to eventually augmenting wild populations by the release of young birds (2).

REMARKS   Two Great Indian Bustards were in captivity in Mysore in 1974 (4).
Several have also been kept successfully in a private collection elsewhere in India
(5).

REFERENCES   1.   Ali, S. & Ripley, S.D. 1969.   Handbook of the Birds of India
               and Pakistan, Vol. 2.   Bombay, London, New York:Oxford
               University Press.
          2.   Dharmakumarsinhji, R.S. 1971.   Study of the Great Indian
               Bustard.   Final report to WWF, Morges, Switzerland, on
               Project 453.
          3.   Mukherjee, A.K. 1973.   Some examples of recent faunal
               impoverishment and regression.   In M.S. Mani (ed.) Ecology and
               Biogeography in India, pp. 330-368.   The Hague:Dr. W. Junk b.v.
          4.   Duplaix-Hall, N. 1975.   Census of rare animals in captivity,
               1974.   Internat. Zoo Yearbook 15: 397-405.
          5.   Fisher, J., Simon, N. & Vincent, J. 1969.   Wildlife in Danger.
               New York:Viking Press; London:Collins.

CHATHAM ISLAND OYSTERCATCHER

Haematopus chathamensis Hartert, 1927

Order CHARADRIIFORMES   Family HAEMATOPODIDAE

STATUS   Endangered.   Occurs only in the Chatham Islands, 800 km east of New
Zealand, where it is very scarce but apparently increasing slowly.   Increases on
two islands have been associated with the establishment of these islands as reserves
coupled with the reduction and ultimate removal of sheep from them.

DISTRIBUTION   The species has been recorded on Chatham, Pitt, South-East and
Mangere islands in the Chatham group (1).

POPULATION   The total population is about 50 birds, concentrated mainly on South
East (8 breeding pairs) and Mangere islands (1).

HABITAT   This oystercatcher, like others, spends most of its time on rocky
shorelines, but also occasionally feeds on sandy beaches (1).

CONSERVATION MEASURES TAKEN   Fully protected by law.   The two islands on which
the species is most abundant have recently been made Reserves for the Preservation
of Flora and Fauna.   The species has recently been the subject of taxonomic
research.

CONSERVATION MEASURES PROPOSED   Research on the habitat utilization and life
history of this species on South-East Island is now planned (G. Williams 1976,
pers. comm.).

REFERENCES   1.   Baker, A.J. 1973.   Distribution and numbers of New Zealand
oystercatchers.   Notornis 20: 128-144.

CANARIAN BLACK OYSTERCATCHER

Haematopus moquini meadewaldoi Bannerman, 1913

Order CHARADRIIFORMES

Family HAEMATOPODIDAE

STATUS   Endangered, if still extant. A sighting of this species in the Canary Islands in 1968 has renewed the hope that it is not yet extinct.

DISTRIBUTION   Canary Islands, where it has been recorded on Fuerteventura, Lanzarote, Lobos, Graciosa, Montãna Clara, Allegranza and probably Roque del Este and was said also to occur on Tenerife (1).   Doubts about its occurrence on Tenerife must now be weighed against a reported sighting on that island in 1968 (2).   It apparently disappeared from Graciosa, Montaña Clara and Allegranza about 1940, judging from reports of local inhabitants (3); its presumed extirpation on Fuerteventura and Lanzarote dates from early this century, although the only actual specimen from Fuerteventura was taken in 1890 (1).

POPULATION   This subspecies was always considered rare and its nest has never been found.   It was met with most frequently and presumably bred on Graciosa, where the last specimen was taken in 1913, and on Allegranza where parties of 2 or 3 were regularly encountered early in the century.   The 1968 sighting, about which there can be little doubt for the Black Oystercatcher cannot easily be confused with any other shorebird , has revived the possibility that a small population persists along an isolated stretch of shoreline somewhere in the Canaries. (1-3).

HABITAT   Sea-shores.

CONSERVATION MEASURES TAKEN   None known.

CONSERVATION MEASURES PROPOSED   Several searches for the subspecies have been made in the past, but it is clear that further efforts are needed to resolve the question of its status.

REMARKS   The nominate race of South Africa and Namibia is not at risk.

REFERENCES
1. Bannerman, D.A. 1963.   Birds of the Atlantic Islands. Vol. 1.   Edinburgh and London: Oliver and Boyd.
2. Bannerman, D. 1969.   A probable sight record of a Canarian Black Oystercatcher.   Ibis 111: 257.
3. Lovegrove, R. 1971.   B.O.U. supported expedition to the northeast Canary Islands.   Ibis 113: 269-272.

NEW ZEALAND SHORE PLOVER

Thinornis novaeseelandiae (Gmelin, 1789)

Order CHARADRIIFORMES   Family CHARADRIIDAE

STATUS   Endangered.   Now only known to survive on one small island in the Chatham
Islands, 800 kilometres east of New Zealand, where its numbers are small.

DISTRIBUTION   Formerly occurred in many coastal areas of North and South Islands,
New Zealand, as well as several islands of the Chatham group, but became extinct in
New Zealand proper by the end of the last century.   At about that same time, it was
likewise destroyed on Chatham, Pitt and Mangere in the Chatham Islands by introduced
cats.   For over 70 years it has been entirely confined to the small South-East
Island (220 ha) of the Chatham group (1).

POPULATION   Never particularly numerous, the Shore Plover was already considered
to be very rare by the 1880s.   In the South-East Island stronghold of the species,
the population was seriously depleted by commercial collectors between 1890 and 1910.
By 1937, the population was estimated at 70 pairs (2), and, more recently, 85 birds
were counted in 1968, 90 birds in 1970, 81 in 1973 (1) and 100 in 1974.   The last
census was based on color-banded birds (G. Williams 1976, pers. comm.).   There is a
suggestion that a slight decline has, still more recently, taken place, possibly due
to vigorous regeneration of vegetation since the removal of sheep in the 1950s.   In
1970, 15 adults were reintroduced to Mangere Island, but quickly homed to South-East.
Further reintroductions in 1972 and 1973 of partially wing-clipped adults and
juveniles proved equally unsuccessful (1; 3).

HABITAT   Mud flats, inlets and sand spits in New Zealand and rock wave-platforms
and salt meadows in the Chatham Islands (4).   Some coastal areas on South-East
Island once used by this species were close-cropped by sheep, but are now heavily
overgrown with rank vegetation (G. Williams 1976, pers. comm.).

CONSERVATION MEASURES TAKEN   Fully protected by law.   South-East Island was
declared a Reserve for the Preservation of Flora and Fauna in 1954.   Most cattle
and sheep were removed by 1959, the last few in 1961, by the New Zealand Wildlife
Service.   Reintroduction to predator-free Mangere Island has been attempted but has
not yet succeeded due to the birds' strong homing instinct (3; 5).   Research on the
habitat preferences or requirements of this plover is now in progress.

CONSERVATION MEASURES PROPOSED   Further attempts to reintroduce the species to
Mangere Island and the Star Keys should be made without jeopardizing the existing
population on South-East Island.   The reservation of the southern portion of Pitt
Island and proposed animal control might enable it to be re-established there
(G. Williams 1976, pers. comm.).

REMARKS   This species is the sole representative of its genus.   It is docile,
confiding and highly vulnerable to mammalian predation (5).

REFERENCES   1.   Merton, D.V. & Bell, B.D.   Undated manuscript.   Endemic birds
                     of the Chatham Islands.   New Zealand Wildlife Service.
               2.   Fleming, C.A. 1939.   Birds of the Chatham Islands.   Part 3,
                     The Shore Plover.   Emu 39: 1-15.
               3.   Bell, B.D. 1974.   Mangere Island.   Wildlife - A review 5:
                     31-34.

4. Falla, R.A., Sibson, R.B. & Turbott, E.G. 1967. <u>A Field Guide</u>
   <u>to the Birds of New Zealand and Outlying Islands</u>. Boston:
   Houghton Mifflin Co.; London: Collins.
5. Merton, D.V. & Phillips, R.E. in press. Current status of the
   New Zealand Shore Plover with notes on behaviour.

JAVANESE WATTLED LAPWING

Vanellus macropterus (Wagler, 1827)

Order CHARADRIIFORMES   Family CHARADRIIDAE

STATUS   Indeterminate. Once found on Sumatra, Java and Timor, but its present
distribution is not known. In the cultivated lowlands of these islands, where
this lapwing might be expected to occur, all species of birds have been seriously
depleted.

DISTRIBUTION   Java, and possibly Sumatra and Timor (1).   One was said to have
been collected on Timor in 1828 or 1829, and at that time the species was said to
migrate between Timor and Java (2).   A specimen and a clutch of eggs taken in the
same period were reputedly from Sumatra (3).   But there is some question of the
validity of these early records (G.F. Mees 1976, pers. comm.) and no trace of the
species has been found on Timor or Sumatra subsequently.   On Java it was collected
near Djakarta in 1872 (4; 5) and several perched on a ship's railing off the north
coast of Java shortly before 1885 (4).   It was also collected in the Tjitaroem
delta and at Tangerang, west of Djakarta, in the 1920s, although it was not found
during a two-month survey of the delta in 1949 (G.F. Mees 1976, pers. comm.).   The
most recent reports are from Meleman on the south coast of East Java in 1939 (6) and
there are no further clues to its present distribution.

POPULATION   No estimate has ever been made and there is no indication that the
species has been anything but rare during the last hundred years: if it still
exists, it is likely to be not only rare but in danger of extinction.   When last
observed in the 1920s and again in 1940, it was rated as local and by no means
common (6; 7; G.F. Mees, 1976, pers. comm.).

HABITAT   Open areas near fresh water ponds (4) and presumably also agricultural
lands.   All kinds of birds now tend to be scarce in the cultivated zones of Java,
being trapped and hunted mercilessly (D. Wells in litt. to K. Scriven, 1974).

CONSERVATION MEASURES TAKEN   None known.

CONSERVATION MEASURES PROPOSED   None known.

REMARKS   This species was known as Xiphidiopterus or Rogibyx tricolor, but has
recently been placed in Vanellus, necessitating a change also in its specific name
(7).

REFERENCES   1.   Kuroda, N. 1936.   The Birds of the Island of Java, Vol. 2.
                    Tokyo.
              2.   Temminck, C.J. and Meiffren Laugier, 1838.   Nouveau Recueil
                    de Planches Coloriées d'Oiseaux.   Vol. 5.
              3.   Schlegel, H. 1865.   Revue méthodique et critique des collections
                    déposées dans cet établissement, Tome IV, Cursores.   Muséum
                    d'Histoire Naturelle des Pays-Bas.
              4.   Vorderman, A.G. 1885.   Bataviasche Vogels, vi.   Natuurk.
                    Tijdschr. Nederl. Indie 44: 208-253.
              5.   Hoogerwerf, A. 1948.   Contribution to the knowledge of the
                    distribution of birds on the island of Java, with remarks on some
                    new birds.   Treubia 19: 83-137.
              6.   Kooiman, J.G. 1940. Mededeelingen over het voorkomen in Oost-
                    Java van enkele voor dit gewest nog niet in de literatuur
                    genoemde vogels.   Ardea 29: 98-108.
              7.   Bock, W.J. 1958.   A generic review of the plovers (Charadriinae,
                    Aves).   Bull. Mus. Comp. Zool. Harvard 118: 27-97.

NEW ZEALAND SNIPE

Coenocorypha aucklandica (Gray, 1845)

Order CHARADRIIFORMES   Family SCOLOPACIDAE

STATUS   Rare.   Five subspecies of aucklandica have been described, each confined
to an oceanic island south or south-east of New Zealand.   Four are relatively
common but vulnerable because of their restricted range, the fifth became extinct
in the last decade (1; 2; 3; 4).

DISTRIBUTION   C. a. aucklandica (Gray, 1845) was extirpated in Auckland Island
many years ago, but still occurs on nearby Ewing, Enderby, Disappointment and Adams
islands.   C. a. huegeli (Tristram, 1893) is known only from Snares Island.
C. a. meinertzhagenae Rothschild, 1927, occurs on Antipodes Island (1).   C. a.
pusilla (Buller, 1869) formerly occurred on Pitt, South East and Mangere islands of
the Chatham group, but was exterminated on Pitt and Mangere by introduced cats
before 1900.   Subfossil evidence indicates it once occurred on main Chatham Island
(G. Williams 1976, pers. comm.).   Following the disappearance of cats on Mangere,
it was recently successfully reintroduced there (2) and has apparently also
colonized the Star Keys, 8 km from South East Island (3).   C. a. iredalei
Rothschild, 1921, occurred on South Cape and Jacky Lee islands off Stewart Island,
where its subfossil bones have also been found (G. Williams 1976, pers. comm.).
It was exterminated on Jacky Lee by introduced Wekas Gallirallus australis scotti
earlier this century, and more rapidly on the South Cape islands when they were
overrun by black rats Rattus rattus in 1964 (3; 4).   Relocation of the subspecies
to nearby islets in that year was apparently unsuccessful and the suggestion that
the subspecies may still survive on the seldom visited Little Solander Island (4),
is considered unlikely (G. Williams 1976, pers. comm.).

POPULATION   The subspecies from the Auckland Islands, Snares and Antipodes islands
are all relatively common, although no precise population estimates have been made
(1).   The Chatham Islands subspecies numbers about 1,000 on South East Island and
the 23 reintroduced to Mangere in 1970, established themselves successfully and
multiplied rapidly (2); but the population increase has now tapered off, owing to
the dense growth of grass following removal of domestic stock in 1968 although it is
expected to start again as the forest cover regenerates (G. Williams 1976, pers.
comm.).

HABITAT   Forest and scrub floor leaf mould and grassy or heathy areas, so long as
these are free from mammalian predators and domestic stock; the snipe apparently
only thrive in their absence.

CONSERVATION MEASURES TAKEN   Fully protected by law.   All islands inhabited by
the species except the Star Keys in the Chatham Islands are Reserves for the
Preservation of Flora and Fauna.   Introduced mammals have been removed from both
South East and Mangere and the reintroduction of one of the subspecies into the
last-mentioned island has proved successful.

CONSERVATION MEASURES PROPOSED   Extreme care must continue to be taken to ensure
that predators, particularly rats, are not accidentally introduced into any of the
islands on which the snipe now occurs.

REFERENCES   1.   Bell, B.D. 1975.   The rare and endangered species of the New
                    Zealand region and the policies that exist for their management.
                    ICBP Bull. 12: 165-172.

2. Merton, D.W. & Bell, B.D. no date. Endemic birds of the Chatham Islands. New Zealand Wildlife Service unpublished ms.
3. Ellis, B.A. 1975. Rare and endangered New Zealand birds; the role of the Royal Forest and Bird Protection Society of New Zealand Inc. ICBP Bull. 12: 173-186.
4. Blackburn, A. 1965. Muttonbird Island diary. Notornis 12: 191-207.

ASIAN DOWITCHER

Limnodromus semipalmatus (Blyth, 1848)

Order CHARADRIIFORMES   Family SCOLOPACIDAE

STATUS   Rare.   Breeds in several small widely scattered areas across north-central Asia.   Migrates to South East Asia where it is considered very rare throughout its known wintering range.

DISTRIBUTION   Known to breed very locally in small colonies in the Baraba and Kulunda steppes in south-western Siberia, in the Argun River Valley in Transbaikalia, on the shores of Lake Orok-nor in Mongolia and possibly in adjacent river valleys, and near Tsitsihar in Manchuria.   Has been recorded on passage or wintering in Japan, along the China coast, Hong Kong, Indochina, Malaya, eastern India, Burma, Singapore and the Philippines (2; 3; 4; 5; 6; 7; M.A. Webster 1974, pers. comm.).

POPULATION   Not known precisely.   On its breeding grounds it is considered not numerous, nesting in colonies of 10 to 20 pairs; elsewhere it is very rare, there being only one or a very few records from most countries within its winter range. In 1965, a flock of 27 was observed at Kuala Gula, Malay Peninsula (6), which is the largest number recorded away from the breeding grounds.   Most observations are of one or two birds.

HABITAT   Breeds in wetlands, meadows, and grassy flood plains below 800 m elevation (1).   In winter presumably along mud flats and marshlands.

CONSERVATION MEASURES TAKEN   None known.

CONSERVATION MEASURES PROPOSED   It has been pointed out that under new legislation in Malaysia, this species and other rare shorebirds are classified as game birds (8).

REFERENCES   1.   Dementiev, G.P., Gladkov, N.A. & Spangenberg, E.P. 1951.
                     Birds of the Soviet Union, Vol. 3.   Trans. from Russian by
                     Israel Program for Scientific Translations, Jerusalem, 1969.
              2.   Ornithological Society of Japan, 1974.   Check-list of Japanese
                     Birds (5th Ed.).   Tokyo:Gakken Co.
              3.   La Touche, J.D.D. 1933.   A Handbook of the Birds of Eastern
                     China, Vol. 2, Part 4.   London:Taylor and Francis.
              4.   Vaurie, C. 1965.   Birds of the Palearctic Fauna.
                     Non-Passeriformes.   London:H.F. and G. Witherby.
              5.   Medway, G. & Nisbet, I.C.T. 1966.   Bird report:1964.
                     Malayan Nature Journ. 19:   160-194.
              6.   Medway, G. & Nisbet, I.C.T. 1967.   Bird report:1965.
                     Malayan Nature Journ. 20:   59-80.
              7.   Delacour, J. & Mayr, E. 1946.   Birds of the Philippines.
                     New York:MacMillan Co.
              8.   Wells, D.R. 1973.   Letter to Chairman.   ICBP Asian Section
                     News 4:   5-6.
              9.   Paige, J.P. 1965.   Field identification and winter range of the
                     Asian Dowitcher Limnodromus semipalmatus.   Ibis 107:   95-97.

ESKIMO CURLEW

Numenius borealis (J.R. Forster, 1772)

Order CHARADRIIFORMES   Family SCOLOPACIDAE

STATUS   Endangered.   This excessively rare species has never recovered its
former abundance, when immense numbers were shot on its northward migration.
Agricultural development of the prairies, on which it depended for food on
migration and during the northern winter, may have been partly to blame, and
climatic changes affecting its migrations could also have been a contributory
factor.

DISTRIBUTION   The breeding grounds were on the arctic tundra between the
Coppermine and Mackenzie rivers of the Mackenzie District, Northwest Territories,
Canada, and possibly also further west across Alaska to the Bering Sea.   The
species migrated south-eastwards to southern Labrador, Newfoundland and Nova
Scotia and thence directly across the sea to eastern South America and its winter
quarters from southern Brazil south through Paraguay and Uruguay to mid-Argentina
as far as the Chubut River and occasionally to Chile.   Migrants were sometimes
diverted by storms to Bermuda or the eastern United States coastline.   The return
migration traversed the north of Central America, the Gulf of Mexico and the
prairies of central United States and so back to Canada. (1-3).   No breeding or
wintering sites are at present known although there have been a few recent
observations of the species in the area of its former nesting grounds (G. Cooch
1977, pers. comm. to J. Aldrich) and since the 1950s there have been a handful of
records of specimens seen or collected on Barbados, the U.S. Gulf and east coasts,
and the west coast of James Bay, north-east Ontario (4-11).

POPULATION   In the 19th century the species was numbered in the millions at its
Labrador staging posts, but intensive shooting in the 1870s and 1880s, mainly in
the Mississippi Valley on the return migration but also in the fall in Labrador,
Newfoundland and New England, and in winter in Argentina, undoubtedly played a
major part in this curlew's decline (2; 12).   A recent theory suggests that
slight climatic changes caused both in the long term by a warmer cycle and in the
short term by volcanic activity, may have contributed to the decline by forcing
birds off course on migration and by adversely affecting reproductive success.
By the mid-1890s the species had all but disappeared (3) but recent sightings,
which have been reported about every other year, give grounds for cautious
optimism about its continuing existence.

HABITAT   Arctic tundra in the breeding season.   The pampas of Argentina
provided the main winter habitat and the tall grass prairies of the Mississippi
Valley that of north-bound migrants.   In late summer the species formed dense
concentrations on the Labrador coast to fatten on berries and small snails.   In
the latter half of the 19th century major agricultural development modified
millions of hectares of pampas and the tall grass prairie alike, which may well
have impaired the availability of the curlews' food. (1-3).   Thus an important
food item was the egg cases of the grasshoppers which decline so sharply in
abundance when prairie is brought under cultivation (J. Aldrich 1977, pers. comm.).

CONSERVATION MEASURES TAKEN   The Eskimo Curlew is protected from killing,
capture, or harassment in the United States and Canada.   It is listed in Appendix
1 of the 1973 Convention on International Trade in Endangered Species of Wild
Fauna and Flora.

CONSERVATION MEASURES PROPOSED   None known.

REMARKS   Not much can be done to improve the status of this species apart from ensuring careful protection of any seen on migration, continuing the search for their breeding grounds and keeping areas of former concentration under observation.   Some authors consider this species to be conspecific with N. minutus of central Siberia, which winters in South East Asia and Australasia (13).

REFERENCES   1.   Bent, A.C. 1929.   Life histories of North American shorebirds.   U.S. Nat. Mus. Bull. 146.
2.   Greenway, J.C., Jr. 1958.   Extinct and Vanishing Birds of the World.   Amer. Comm. Inter. Wildl. Prot. Spec. Pub. 13.
3.   Banks, R.C. 1977.   The decline and fall of the Eskimo Curlew, or why did the curlew go extaille?   Amer. Birds 31: 127-134.
4.   U.S. Fish and Wildlife Service, 1973.   Threatened wildlife of the United States.   U.S. Dept. of Interior Resource Pubs. 114.
5.   Emanuel, V.L. 1962.   Texans rediscover the near extinct Eskimo Curlew.   Audubon 64: 162-165.
6.   Weston, F.M. & Williams, E.A. 1965.   Recent records of the Eskimo Curlew.   Auk 82: 493-496.
7.   Wallace, G.J. et al. 1971.   Report of the Committee on Conservation, 1970-71.   Auk 88: 902-910.
8.   Lieftinck, J.E. 1968.   Report of an Eskimo Curlew from Texas Coast.   Bull. Tex. Ornith. Soc. 2: 28.
9.   Lahrman, F.W. 1972.   A rare observation of the Eskimo Curlew (on Padre Island, Texas).   Blue Jay 30: 87-88.
10.   Daniels, G.F. 1972.   Possible sight record of Eskimo Curlew on Martha's Vineyard, Mass.   Amer. Birds 26: 907-908.
11.   Hagar, J.A. & Anderson, K.S. 1977.   Sight record of Eskimo Curlew (Numenius borealis) on west coast of James Bay, Canada.   Amer. Birds 31: 135-136.
12.   Swenk, M.H. 1916.   The Eskimo Curlew and its disappearance. Smithsonian Inst. Report 1915: 325-340
13.   Dementiev, L.P. & Gladkov, N.A. (eds) 1951-52.   Birds of the Soviet Union, Vol. 3.   Translated from Russian. Jerusalem: Israel Program for Scientific Translations, 1969.

TUAMOTU SANDPIPER

Prosobonia (Aechmorhynchus) cancellatus (Gmelin, 1789)

Order CHARADRIIFORMES   Family SCOLOPACIDAE

STATUS   Vulnerable.   This species is confined to several small atolls in the
Tuamotu Archipelago, South Pacific, that are free from cats and rats.   Its
continued existence is dependent on the preservation of such predator-free atolls
(1; 2).

DISTRIBUTION   The type specimen came from Christmas Island, Line Islands, but the
species has been chiefly recorded in the Tuamotu archipelago and from the following
islands: Makaroa, Kamaka and Manui in the Mangareva or Gambier group; S. Marutea,
Maria, Tenaroa, Tenarunga, Maturei-Vavao in the Actaeon group; and Pukapuka, Raraka,
Pinaki, Fakarava, Tahanea, Rataka, Katiu, Kauehi, Tepoto and Tuanake in the main
Tuamotus.   Recent reports are from Maturei-Vavao, Rangiroa (a single bird, probably
a visitor), Pinaki, Marutea and Nakutavake (a new location).   No longer found on
Christmas Island, Makaroa, Kamaka or Manui, the sandpiper is suspected to have
vanished from several of the other islands also (1; 2; 3; 4; C. Jouanin in litt. to
F.B. Gill, 7 Feb. 1967).

POPULATION   Unknown.   May be relatively abundant on some islands without cats or
rats and in 1969 was reported to be moderately so on South Marutea and perhaps even
more common on Maturei-Vavao, but possibly no longer surviving on Pukapuka (6).

HABITAT   All habitats of the Tuamotu chain are visited but the sandpiper has been
most commonly found on stretches of bare gravel (1).

CONSERVATION MEASURES TAKEN   None.

CONSERVATION MEASURES PROPOSED   Total protection of atolls on which the species
still occurs, with special care taken to prevent the introduction of cats or rats.

REMARKS   Zusi and Jehl (1970) have synonymized Aechmorhynchus parvirostris Peale,
1848, which was the old name of the Tuamotu population, with A. cancellatus (Gmelin,
1789), the unique Christmas Island type, placing the species in the genus
Prosobonia along with P. leucoptera (Gmelin, 1789) of Tahiti (where it is now
extinct) and P. ellisi Sharpe, 1906, from Moorea, which is now synonymized with
P. leucoptera (5) and also extinct.

REFERENCES   1.   Greenway, J.C., Jr. 1958.   Extinct and Vanishing Birds of the
              World.   Amer. Comm. Internat. Wild Life Prot., Spec. Pub. No. 13.
          2.   Holyoak, D.T. 1973.   Notes on the birds of Rangiroa, Tuamotu
                Archipelago, and the surrounding ocean.   Bull. Brit. Orn.
                Club 93: 26-32.
          3.   Thibault, J.C. 1973.   Notes ornithologiques polynésiennes.   I.
                Les Iles Gambier.   Alauda 41: 111-119.
          4.   Bruner, P.L. 1972.   Birds of French Polynesia.   Honolulu:
                B.P. Bishop Museum.
          5.   Zusi, R.L. & Jehl, J.R. 1970.   The systematic relationships of
                Aechmorhynchus, Prosobonia, and Phegornis (Charadriiformes,
                Charadrii).   Auk 87: 760-780.
          6.   Lacan, F. & Mougin, J.-L. 1974.   Les oiseaux des Iles Gambier
                et de quelques atolls orientaux de l'archipel des Tuamotu
                (Océan Pacifique).   L'Oiseau et R.F.O. 44: 192-280.

NORDMANN'S OR SPOTTED GREENSHANK

Tringa guttifer (Nordmann, 1835)

Order CHARADRIIFORMES   Family SCOLOPACIDAE

STATUS   Indeterminate.   Breeds on southern Sakhalin Island, U.S.S.R., and
probably elsewhere in north-eastern Siberia.   Migrates south through eastern Asia
to winter very locally in South East Asia.   This species is among the least known
of the shorebirds or waders and is rare throughout its range; the reasons for this
rarity are unknown.

DISTRIBUTION   Confirmed as breeding on Sakhalin Island (1), but also may breed in
Kamchatka, the Bering Islands and along the coast of the Gulf of Okhotsk (2; 3).
Occurs widely but erratically on migration or in winter in the Amur and Ussuri
basins in eastern Siberia, Korea, Japan, China, Hong Kong, Hainan, Taiwan, Singapore,
Borneo, Malaya, Burma and possibly Assam and Bangladesh (3; M.A. Webster 1975, pers.
comm.).

POPULATION   No estimate of the total population has ever been made and it is clear
that the species is excessively rare throughout its range.   However, in its only
known breeding area on Sakhalin Island 50 to 60 were seen and it was considered not
uncommon (4).   Elsewhere, most reports are of one or two individuals, but in Korea
39 were observed in 1961 and 1962 (5), and up to 90 were thought to have been seen
at Kuala Gula, Malaya in 1964 (6).   Malaya is the only area where sightings might
be considered to be of regular occurrence.

HABITAT   Coastal mud flats and shallow lagoons, also swamps and wet meadows (2).

CONSERVATION MEASURES TAKEN   The species is protected in Japan as a Special Bird
for Protection (Y. Yamashina 1974, pers. comm.).

CONSERVATION MEASURES PROPOSED   None known.

REMARKS   The possibility of confusing this species with related species calls for
extreme care in identification.

REFERENCES   1.   Kuroda, N. 1936.   On a new breeding ground for Pseudototanus
                   guttifer.   Tori 9(43): 232-238.
              2.   Vaurie, C. 1965.   Birds of the Palearctic Fauna.   Non-
                   Passeriformes.   London:H.F. and G. Witherby.
              3.   Dementiev, G.P., Gladkov, N.A. & Spangenberg, E.P. 1951.
                   Birds of the Soviet Union, Vol. 3.   Trans. from Russian by
                   Israel Program for Scientific Translations, Jerusalem, 1968.
              4.   Austin, O.L., Jr. & Kuroda, N. 1953.   The birds of Japan: their
                   status and distribution.   Mus. Comp. Zool. Bull. (Harvard)
                   109(4): 279-627.
              5.   Fennell, C.M. & King, B. 1964.   New occurrences and recent
                   distributional records of Korean birds.   Condor 66: 239-246.
              6.   Medway, G. & Nisbet, I.C.T. 1966.   Bird report: 1964.
                   Malayan Nature Journal 19: 160-194.

HAWAIIAN STILT

Himantopus himantopus knudseni Stejneger, 1887

Order   CHARADRIIFORMES   Family   RECURVIROSTRIDAE

STATUS   Rare.   A low but stable population of this stilt occurs on several
islands in Hawaii.   Destruction of wetlands was the major cause of its
historical decline.

DISTRIBUTION   Found on Niihau, Kauai, Oahu, Maui, Molokai and Hawaii.   Movement
of birds between islands has been documented (1; 2).

POPULATION   The stilt was an abundant bird in wetlands of Hawaii last century,
but its population declined as wetland areas were drained.   By the 1940s a
scant 1,000 were estimated to survive (3).   State-wide censuses have been
conducted several times since 1968, and the results indicate that there is now a
relatively stable population of 1,300-1,500 birds, the majority being found on
Oahu and Maui (2).

HABITAT   Freshwater and brackish wetlands and flooded agricultural fields.
The extent of wetlands in Hawaii has diminished significantly this century.   For
example the 810ha Mana Swamp of Kauai, one of Hawaii's largest, was drained in the
1920s and is now under sugar cane cultivation (4), while the land used for rice
and taro cultivation has decreased from nearly 14,000 to a few hundred hectares
(5).   Although drainage continues to be a threat to the few remaining wetlands,
some notable areas have recently been protected.   Feral dogs, cats and mongooses
occur in the vicinity of the wetland areas and can be expected to prey on the
stilts from time to time.

CONSERVATION MEASURES TAKEN   The subspecies is fully protected by state and
federal law, particularly the U.S. Endangered Species Act of 1973.   Hunting of
stilts in Hawaii was prohibited in 1939.   Several key wetlands, including
portions of the Hanalei Valley on Kauai and Kealia Pond on Maui have become or
will shortly become U.S. National Wildlife Refuges.   Cooperative agreements
between the U.S. Fish and Wildlife Service and U.S. military installations in
Hawaii protect additional wetland areas where stilts occur (2).

CONSERVATION MEASURES PROPOSED   Acquisition of additional wetland areas has been
proposed by the U.S. Fish and Wildlife Service (2).

REMARKS   None of several other subspecies is believed at risk, although the
closely related New Zealand Black Stilt *Himantopus novaezealandiae* is endangered.

REFERENCES   1.   Berger, A.J. 1972.   *Hawaiian Birdlife*.   Honolulu:
                    University Press of Hawaii.
              2.   U.S. Dept. of Interior Bureau of Sport Fisheries and Wildlife,
                    1973.   Threatened Wildlife of the United States.   *U.S. Bur.*
                    Sport Fish. Wildl. Res. Pub. 114.
              3.   Schwartz, C.W. and Schwartz, E.R. 1949.   *The Game Birds in*
                    Hawaii.   Honolulu: Board of Commissioners of Agriculture
                    and Forestry.
              4.   Wenkam, R. 1967.   *Kauai and the Park Country of Hawaii*.
                    San Francisco: Sierra Club.
              5.   U.S. Dept. of Interior Fish and Wildlife Service, 1968.
                    Hawaii's endangered wildlife.   *U.S. Bur. Sport Fish. Wildl.*

BLACK STILT

Himantopus novaezealandiae Gould, 1841

Order CHARADRIIFORMES   Family RECURVIROSTRIDAE

STATUS   Endangered.   Restricted during its breeding season to one river valley in
New Zealand, where its population is very small and possibly decreasing.   The
valley is scheduled for development by a large hydroelectric and irrigation scheme
(1; 2).

DISTRIBUTION   Formerly widely distributed on both North and South islands, New
Zealand.   Breeding range now confined to the upper Waitaki River valley, an area of
7,000 sq. km and between 700 and 800 m in elevation on South Island (1; 2).   Both
adults and immatures are generally sedentary, although some juveniles or immatures
but considerably fewer adults do migrate to the North Island during winter (R.J.
Nilsson 1976, pers. comm.).

POPULATION   Formerly larger, although the species was never considered abundant.
It was always more numerous in South Island than North Island (4).   The present
population is estimated at 50 to 100 birds.   Hybridization with the Pied Stilt
Himantopus h. leucocephalus has been recorded (3; R.J. Nilsson, pers. comm.)., and
may become more frequent as Black Stilts become even less numerous and have difficulty in finding appropriate mates.   Although early observations in New Zealand
suggested that the two species bred well apart, recent Black Stilt nestings have
taken place within or very near Pied Stilt colonies (1; 3).   In the 1973-1974
breeding season only four Black Stilt juveniles reached the age of six months
(R.J. Nilsson 1976, pers. comm.).

HABITAT   This stilt breeds along dry stony watercourses and shingle river banks
inland, dispersing to feed in small parties along lake shores and lower river
valleys (R.J. Nilsson 1976, pers. comm.).

CONSERVATION MEASURES TAKEN   The species is fully protected by law.   Its
distribution and ecology is under study by the New Zealand Wildlife Service.

CONSERVATION MEASURES PROPOSED   The establishment of wildlife management reserves
in the upper Waitaki River valley, where this species still breeds, is now being
undertaken by the New Zealand Wildlife Service, and in 1976 was to be supplemented
by the construction of a number of artificial ponds (R.J. Nilsson 1976, pers. comm.).

REMARKS   The development of the Waitaki River for hydroelectric power and
irrigation has already resulted in the loss of some breeding and feeding habitat.
Future development may prove incompatible with the survival of this species.

REFERENCES   1.   Ellis, B.A. 1975.   Rare and endangered New Zealand birds: the
                     role of the Royal Forest and Bird Protection Society of New
                     Zealand Inc.   ICBP Bull. 12: 173-186.
              2.   Falla, R.A., Sibson, R.B. & Turbott, E.G. 1967.   A Field Guide
                     to the Birds of New Zealand and Outlying Islands.   Boston:
                     Houghton Mifflin; London:Collins.
              3.   Soper, M.F. 1967.   Some observations on Black Stilts.   Notornis
                     14: 8-10.
              4.   Oliver, W.R.B. 1955.   New Zealand Birds (2nd Ed.).
                     Wellington:A.H. and A.W. Reed.

AUDOUIN'S GULL

Larus audouinii Payraudeau, 1826

Order CHARADRIIFORMES   Family LARIDAE

STATUS   Rare.   Most of the few known breeding colonies of this species in the
Mediterranean are subject to harvesting of eggs and young and disturbance from
fishermen and tourists.

DISTRIBUTION   Although individual colonies may have been eliminated, the present
day range of the species is almost unchanged.   It breeds on the Islas Chafarinas
east of Melilla, Spanish Morocco, (and in the 19th century also on Isla da
Alboran, north of Melilla); formerly and possibly still on Nakl Island off the
Lebanon coast; on the Klidhes Islands off the north-eastern tip of Cyprus; on some
islands of the Turkish Aegean, northern Greek Sporades, Dodecanese and possibly
also Cyclades; Sardinia, Corsica, Elba, the Columbretes, off the Spanish coast
near Valencia, and the Balearics, where a colony on Pityusen was destroyed in 1970.
It used to nest on the Jeziret Jalita off the north-eastern coast of Tunisia and
may still do so, though a record from Kneis Island off the east coast near Sfax is
now rejected.   In autumn and winter it occurs in large numbers along the Mediterranean and Atlantic coasts of North Africa, although some remain in their
breeding areas (1-4; 10; 11; 14; H. Witt 1974, pers. comm.).

POPULATION   The only estimates are recent ones and there is no certain evidence
of a decline.   Estimates of a total of 800-1000 pairs in 1968 (12) and 600-800
pairs in 1976 (10) took no account of the Chafarinas population, which explains
the 1977 estimate of a total of about 1500 breeding pairs.   The largest colony in
the Chafarinas, contained 500 breeding pairs in 1956, only 270 in 1970, 200 in 1973,
but over 1,000 pairs in 1976, and has apparently shifted from island to island and
even to the Moroccan coast, depending upon the level of disturbance (2; 5; 6; 10).
The Nakl Island colony of 12-15 pairs, off Lebanon, is not known to have been
active for at least 40 years, but 18 birds were identified in the vicinity in 1973
(7).   Forty pairs bred on the Klidhes, off northern Cyprus, in 1973 (8), an
increase from 9 pairs in 1961 and 20-25 pairs in the late 1960s (9; 10).   Twenty-
five pairs bred on an island off the Turkish coast in 1973 and 28 pairs in 1974
(10).

    In the northern Sporades 20-30 pairs bred in 1973, and two colonies of 5 and 10
pairs, respectively, were in the Dodecanese or southern Sporades.   There were
estimated to be 50-150 breeding pairs off Sardinia in 1976 (13) and 40 pairs off
Corsica in 1974, a decline from 70 pairs in 1963 (1; H. Witt 1974, pers. comm.)
followed by a further decline to only about 5 pairs by 1977 (15).   Up to 20 pairs
may breed off Calpe on the east coast of Alicante.   45 pairs bred in 1974 on the
Columbretes, 10 pairs off Majorca in the Balearics in 1976, and 20 pairs off Ibiza
in 1969 (but only a single pair in 1970). (10; 14; H. Witt 1977, pers. comm. to
M. Bijleveld).

HABITAT   The species nests on south slopes of small low islands covered with
grass and low bushes, often in the company of larger numbers of Larus argentatus.
Many of these islets are subject to periodic disturbance by fishermen, egg
collectors, tourists and shepherds.

CONSERVATION MEASURES TAKEN   In 1974 a guard was posted to protect the Klidhes
colony off Cyprus, landing on the breeding islands being by permit only (8), but
there is no information about the situation since Cyprus became partitioned.   No
other Audouin's gull colonies are known to be protected.

CONSERVATION MEASURES PROPOSED   Protection of colonies during the breeding
season has been advocated as the best means of preventing the decline of this rare
species (1; 3; H. Witt 1974, pers. comm.). A WWF/IUCN Project (1413) has been
launched to promote establishment of reserves, protection of breeding colonies and
other measures.

REMARKS   The assistance of Dr. H. Witt and Dr. M. Bijleveld in supplying
information on this species is gratefully acknowledged.

REFERENCES   1.   de Bournonville, D. 1964.   Observations sur une importante
                   colonie de Goélands d'Audouin Larus audouini Payrandeau au
                   large de la Corse.   Le Gerfaut 54: 439-453.
             2.   Brosset, A. & Olier, A. 1966.   Les îles Chaffarines, lieu
                   de reproduction d'une importante colonie de Goélands d'Audouin,
                   Larus audouini.   Alauda 34: 187-190.
             3.   Watson, G.E. 1973.   Sea-bird colonies in the islands of the
                   Aegean Sea.   Nat. Geogr. Soc. Res. Repts. 1966 Projects,
                   299-305.
             4.   Smith, K.D. 1965.   On the birds of Morocco.   Ibis 107:
                   493-526.
             5.   Groh, G. 1970.   Beitrag zur Vogelwelt Nordwestafrikas.
                   Mitt. Pollichia 17: 144-156.
             6.   Bueno, J.M., Carbonell, M., de Juana, E., Perez-Mellado, V.,
                   Salvador, A. & Varela, J.M. undated.   A study of the
                   vertebrate fauna of the Chafarinas Islands (Spain), and the
                   breeding colony of the Audouin's Gull- Larus audouinii, Payr.
                   Unpublished report to WWF.
             7.   Tohme, G. & Neuschwander, J. 1974.   Nouvelles données sur
                   l'avifaune de la République Libanaise.   Alauda 42: 243-257.
             8.   Neophytou, P. undated.   Audouin's Gull - protection of
                   breeding colony.   Unpublished WWF report (project 1123).
             9.   Bannerman, D.A. & Bannerman, W.M. 1971.   Handbook of the
                   Birds of Cyprus and Migrants of the Middle East.   Edinburgh:
                   Oliver and Boyd.
            10.   Witt, H.-H. 1976.   Zur Biologie der Korallenmöwe, Larus
                   audouinii.   Bonn: Friedrich-Wilhelms-Universitat.
            11.   Etchécopar, R.D. & Hüe, F. 1964.   Les Oiseaux du Nord de
                   l'Afrique.   Paris: Editions N. Boubée.
            12.   Makatsch, W. 1968.   Beobachtungen an einem Brutplatz der
                   Korallenmöwe (Larus audouinii).   Journ. f. Ornith. 109: 43-56.
            13.   Schenk, H. 1976.   Analisi della situazione faunistica in
                   Sardegna: Uccelli e Mammiferi.   In Camerino (ed.) S.O.S. Fauna
                   - Animali in pericolo in Italia.
            14.   Pechuan, C. 1974.   La colonia de Larus audouinii de las Islas
                   Columbretes.   Ardeola 20: 358-359.
            15.   Thibault, J.-C. 1977.   Les oiseaux de mer nicheurs en Corse.
                   Parc Naturel Régional de Corse.

RELICT GULL

Larus relictus Lönnberg, 1931

Order CHARADRIIFORMES   Family LARIDAE

STATUS   Rare.   This little-known gull has been found on lakes in the Kazakh S.S.R.
and eastern Mongolia and has only recently been confirmed as a valid species rather
than a hybrid.

DISTRIBUTION   Known to breed on the Torey lakes, Transbaikalia (1; 2) and on Lake
Alakul, Kazakhstan, U.S.S.R. (3).   It may also breed on Lake Buyr Nor in eastern
Mongolia.   Specimens have now been obtained from several localities in Transbaikalia, the lower Etsin River in eastern Mongolia, coastlands of the Yellow Sea,
and in northern Vietnam, this last being a recovery of a bird banded on Lake Alakul
and possibly indicative of an important wintering ground (5).

POPULATION   The Relict Gull is undoubtedly a rare species, to judge from the very
few records since it was described in 1931, from a specimen taken on the Etsin
River in 1929.   The earliest breeding record was from Lake Zum Torey, where about
100 pairs were estimated to be nesting in 1965 (2).   Another colony on Lake Alakul
contained 120 breeding pairs between 1968, when it was discovered, and 1972, when it
shifted to a nearby site which has not been precisely located (2; 5).   There is no
evidence of a decline in the total population.

HABITAT   The species was first found nesting in a mixed colony of gulls and terns
on a terraced island at an altitude of 65 m above the level of the surrounding lake.
It has been collected at widely separated localities on rivers, lakes and sea coasts.
Its particular habitat requirements are still undetermined.

CONSERVATION MEASURES TAKEN   Listed in Appendix 1 of the 1973 Convention on
International Trade in Endangered Species of Wild Fauna and Flora, which implies
strict control, by States which have become party to the Convention, of any dealings
in specimens alive or dead.

CONSERVATION MEASURES PROPOSED   No additional measures are known to have been put
forward for consideration.

REMARKS   As recently as 1965, only the single original specimen was available and
was thought to be of hybrid origin (4).

REFERENCES   1.   Larionov, V.F. & Cheltsov-Byebutov, A.M. 1972.   The finding of
                     Larus relictus on the Toryeiski lakes (Zabaikal).   Ornitologiya
                     10:    277-279. (In Russian).
               2.   Stubbe, M. & Bolod, A. 1971.   Möwen und Seeschwalben (Laridae:
                     Aves) der Mongolei.   Mitt. Zool. Mus. Berlin 47:   51-62.
               3.   Auezov, E.M. 1971.   Taxonomic evaluation and systematic status
                     of the Relict Gull.   Z. Zhurn. 50:   235-242 (In Russian)
               4.   Vaurie, C. 1965.   The Birds of the Palearctic Fauna.   Non-
                     Passeriformes.   London:H.F. and G. Witherby.
               5.   Isenmann, P. 1977.   A propos de Larus relictus.   Alauda 45:
                     235-236.

CALIFORNIA LEAST TERN

Sterna albifrons browni Mearns, 1916

Order CHARADRIIFORMES   Family LARIDAE

STATUS   Endangered.   Destruction of the coastal beach and marsh habitats of this
tern in California has caused a major decline.   Rehabilitation will be expensive,
since human activities compete for most of the sites where the tern still occurs.

DISTRIBUTION   The subspecies breeds locally from San Francisco Bay, California,
U.S.A., south along the Pacific coast to Scammons Lagoon and probably as far as
the southern end of Baja California, Mexico.   It is to be found most frequently
in the stretch from southern Santa Barbara County to San Diego County, inclusive.
It is migratory, but the limits of its winter distribution are unknown; specimens
taken in Guatemala and Veracruz, Mexico, have been identified as of this subspecies. (1-3; 5; 11; S. Wilbur 1978, pers. comm.).

POPULATION   There has been a gradual but serious decline in this tern's former
abundance, beginning in the early 1900s and continuing to the present.   For
example in 1915, a 5 km stretch of beach in San Diego County held an estimated
1000 pairs (4), yet in 1973 a California-wide breeding population census estimated
the total at between 623 and 763 pairs (5).   Subsequent surveys in 1975, 1976 and
1977 have estimated 600 to 700 pairs located at about 20 sites. (6; 7; S. Wilbur
1977, pers. comm.).   The Mexican population is small: colonies of about 15 pairs
each occur south of Ensenada and at Bahia San Quintin, while the population further
south is not known but also believed to be small.   The largest extant colony (125
pairs in 1976) is in the Camp Pendleton U.S. Marine Corps Base, San Diego County
(7; 11).

HABITAT   Open expanses of sand, mud or dumped rubbish, near a lagoon or estuary,
including land fills, spoil banks and parking lots; also at one time sandy ocean
beaches, but all colonies in such situations have been abandoned due to human
activities, developments along the California coast,with the concomitant disturbance and pollution,having been the major cause of decline.   The tern is
nevertheless remarkably tolerant of human interference and now nests in highly
modified areas, but the absence of good feeding grounds in their vicinity may well
be a limiting factor, since the filling, pollution or restriction of tidal flow
in many lagoons and estuaries has certainly reduced the supply of fish (1).

CONSERVATION MEASURES TAKEN   This tern is fully protected by the U.S. Endangered
Species Act, by California law and under the U.S.-Mexico Migratory Bird Treaty,
and the U.S. Fish and Wildlife Service has appointed a recovery team to look after
it.   Protection has been given to several breeding sites, for example at Camp
Pendleton by the U.S. Marine Corps (8), and quite a few coastal marshes where the
subspecies occurs are California State ecological reserves.

CONSERVATION MEASURES PROPOSED   Acquisition, restoration or protection of some of
the more important coastal lagoons, estuaries and adjacent coastal wetlands will be
the main recommendation of the California Least Tern recovery team, but it will
also recommend that a number of additional nesting sites are protected and that
regular annual surveys are continued (S. Wilbur 1978, pers. comm.).

REMARKS   As many as 11 additional subspecies, distributed along coasts and major
river systems of all continents, have been variously recognized by authors.   Among
those which have declined are Sterna albifrons athalassos (doubtfully distinct from

<u>S. a. browni</u>) of inland rivers in the United States, the population of the U.S. Atlantic coast, <u>S. a. antillarum</u>, (9) and the nominate race <u>S. a. albifrons</u> of Great Britain and Ireland (10), in all cases due to human disturbance of breeding sites and deterioration of feeding habitat.

<u>REFERENCES</u>
1. Wilbur, S.R. 1974.   The literature of the California Least Tern.   U.S. Dept. Interior Bur. Sport Fish. Wildl. <u>Spec. Sci. Rept. Wildl.</u> 175.
2. Grinnell, J. & Miller, A. 1944.   The distribution of the birds of California.   <u>Pacific Coast Avifauna</u> 27: 608 pp.
3. Grinnell, J. 1928.   A distributional summation of the ornithology of Lower California.   <u>Univ. Cal. Pubs. Zool.</u> 32(1): 300 pp.
4. Sechrist, E.E. 1915.   Least Tern.   <u>Oologist</u> 32(1): 18.
5. Bender, K. 1973.   California Least Tern Census and Nesting Survey, 1973.   Cal. Dept. Fish Game Spec. Wildl. Investig. W-54-R Progress report.
6. Massey, B.W. 1975.   California Least Tern Census and Nesting Survey.   Unpublished report to California State Dept. of Fish and Game.
7. Jurek, R.M. (ed.) 1977.   California Least Tern Census and Nesting Survey, 1976.   Unpublished report to California State Dept. of Fish and Game.
8. Swickard, D.K. 1972.   Status of the Least Tern at Camp Pendleton, California.   <u>Calif. Birds</u> 3: 49-58.
9. Fisk, E.J. 1975.   Least Tern: beleagered, opportunistic and roof-nesting.   <u>Amer. Birds</u> 29(1): 15-16.
10. Cramp, S., Bourne, W.R.P. & Saunders, D. 1974.   <u>The Seabirds of Britain and Ireland</u>.   London & New York: Collins; Taplinger Publishing Co.
11. Massey, B.W. 1977.   Occurrence and nesting of the Least Tern and other endangered species in Baja California, Mexico. <u>Western Birds</u> 8: 67-70.

DAMARA TERN

Sterna balaenarum (Strickland, 1852)

Order CHARADRIIFORMES   Family LARIDAE

STATUS   Rare.   This south-west African tern has a very limited range, within
which it is quite scarce.   Disturbance to nest sites by off-road vehicles is a
potential threat, while development of coastal resorts has had adverse effects on
some of its feeding habitats.

DISTRIBUTION   Inshore waters and coasts of southern Africa from just east of
Cape Agulhas, South Africa, to Cabinda, Angola, during the breeding season, and
further north as far as Lagos, Nigeria, in the off-season.   The species nested
near Cape Town until the 1930s and perhaps later, but does so no longer.   Its
nesting sites are known to include gravel or stony plains up to 1 km or more from
the coast (1; 2).

POPULATION   Scarce throughout its range, this tern can be seen regularly only in
the area of Walvis Bay, South West Africa.   Several small nesting colonies,
totalling about 150 pairs, are known between Swakopmund and Cape Cross, and less
than 50 pairs along the much greater stretch of coast between Swakopmund and
Oranjemund, although total numbers are probably rather larger.   No decline has
yet been documented, but it may very likely have taken place, especially at the
southern end of the tern's range (1; 2).

HABITAT   The feeding grounds of the species are coastal waters, particularly of
bays, estuaries and lagoons, many of which have been altered by the dredging,
reclamation and pollution associated with housing and industrial development.
In addition, nesting sites have been disturbed by four-wheel drive or off-road
vehicles, particularly between Swakopmund and Walvis Bay where recreational use of
the coastline is locally intense. (1; 3).

CONSERVATION MEASURES TAKEN   The species is protected by nature conservation
ordinances in both South African and South West Africa/Namibia and also by the
South African Sea Birds and Seals Protection Act of 1973.   However, no section of
either breeding or feeding habitat receives protection although that of the former
is rendered difficult by the fact that nesting colonies are small and widely
dispersed.   Some degree of incidental protection is however afforded by the
restrictions on public access to nearly 1000 km of coastline between Oranjemund
and Swakopmund. (1; 2).

CONSERVATION MEASURES PROPOSED   Locate other breeding areas; determine more
exactly the total population size and trends; and assess more reliably the impact
of human disturbance on breeding colonies (1).

REMARKS   The ecology of this species resembles that of the Least Tern Sterna
albifrons, several populations of which, both in Europe and North America, are
under threat for very similar reasons.

REFERENCES   1.   Frost, P.G.H. & Shaughnessy, G. 1976.   Breeding adaptations
                      of the Damara Tern Sterna balaenarum.   Madoqua 9: 33-39.
               2.   Frost, P.G.H. & Johnson, P.G. 1977.   Report on survey of the
                      status of the Damara Tern Sterna balaenarum between Kleinzee
                      and Luderitz, December 1976.   Unpublished.
               3.   Rand, R.W. 1971.   Some hazards to seabirds.   In Proc. 3rd Pan-
                      African Ornith. Congress 1969.   Ostrich Suppl. No. 8: 515-520.

CHINESE CRESTED TERN

Sterna zimmermanni Reichenow, 1903

Order CHARADRIIFORMES   Family LARIDAE

STATUS   Indeterminate.   This tern of coastal China and South East Asia has not
been reported since 1937, and could be severely threatened or extinct.

DISTRIBUTION   Believed to breed on islands off the coast of Shantung Province and
to migrate south in winter.   Winter records exist from Foochow, the east coast of
peninsular Thailand, Sarawak, Halmahera, in the Moluccas, and the Philippines, but
none of them are at all recent (1).

POPULATION   Unknown.   The species has always been considered rare, although as
recently as 1937 a series of 21 birds was collected at Tsangkow near Tsingtao and
on Mukuantao islet just off the Shantung coast, where the species was believed to
breed.   But there have been no subsequent reports from this area or elsewhere in
its range (1).

HABITAT   Coastlines of East and South East Asia.

CONSERVATION MEASURES TAKEN   None known.   Terns and gulls are not protected in
the People's Republic of China.

CONSERVATION MEASURES PROPOSED   An investigation of the tern's status on its
presumed breeding grounds has been suggested as a prerequisite for its protection.

REMARKS   The important paper by G.F. Mees (1) on this species synonymizes Sterna
zimmermanni Reichenow, 1903, with S. bernsteini Schlegel, 1863, but usage favors the
new name.   He points out that it has been frequently overlooked or confused with
other terns because of inaccuracies in its description and the assumption by some
ornithologists that it was a local representative of the Crested Terns Sterna
bergii or S. bengalensis.

REFERENCES   1.   Mees, G.F. 1975.   Identiteit en Status van Sterna bernsteini
                    Schlegel.   Ardea 63: 78-86.

PALAU NICOBAR PIGEON

Caloenas nicobarica pelewensis Finsch, 1875

Order COLUMBIFORMES   Family COLUMBIDAE

STATUS   Endangered.   Recorded from four islands in the Palau group, south-west
Pacific, where it is very rare and under continued threat from hunters.

DISTRIBUTION   The Palau islands on which the species has been recorded are:
Babelthuap, (397 sq. km), Koror (9.3 sq. km), Ngercheu (2.6 sq. km) and Peleliu,
(12.6 sq. km) (1) and it has also been found on some of the many forested raised
coral islets (2).   A specimen was taken from one of these, Ngarmalk Island, in
1950 by P.J.R. Hill.   The present distribution of this bird is poorly known.

POPULATION   In 1870, this species was one of the least common birds in the Palaus
(3).   It was not recorded at all between 1880 and 1945, in which year single birds
were seen on Peleliu and Koror and five on Ngercheu (1).   A resident biologist in
the Palaus has stated it was much more abundant twenty years before than it was in
1975, although sightings were made six times in the last six months of 1975,
including once on highly populated Koror (R. Owen 1976, pers. comm.).

HABITAT   Forests, where it is most frequently seen perched in trees or flying
high overhead (1).   There is adequate forest in the Palaus, but access to
formerly seldom visited islands is now facilitated by the use of fast motorboats,
so that hunting pressure is thought to be more widespread (R. Owen 1975, pers.
comm.).

CONSERVATION MEASURES TAKEN   Protected from hunting in the Palaus by U.S. Trust
Territory law, but not by U.S. federal law.   Illegal hunting of this striking,
confiding species occurs during the two-month legal hunting season for the
Micronesian Pigeon Ducula oceanica.

CONSERVATION MEASURES PROPOSED   Recommended for inclusion in the U.S. Trust
Territories list of endangered species, which would give it protection under the
Trust Territories Endangered Species Act of 1975.

REMARKS   The nominate subspecies is widely distributed from the Nicobar Islands
through Malaysia to Melanesia and is not at risk.

REFERENCES   1.   Baker, R.H. 1951.   The avifauna of Micronesia, its origin,
                    evolution, and distribution.   Univ. Kansas Pubs. Mus. Nat.
                    Hist. 3(1): 1-359.
              2.   Mayr, E. 1945.   Birds of the Southwest Pacific.   New York:
                    MacMillan Co.
              3.   Finsch, O. 1875.   Zur Ornithologie der Südsee-Inseln, 1:
                    Die Vögel der Palau-Gruppe.   Journ. Mus. Godeffroy 8: 1-51.

PURPLE-WINGED GROUND-DOVE

Claravis godefrida (Temminck, 1811)

Order COLUMBIFORMES   Family COLUMBIDAE

STATUS   Vulnerable.   There have been major declines of this ground-dove in the
coastlands of south-eastern Brazil.   Its status elsewhere in its restricted range
is unknown, but suspected of suffering similar deterioration as a result of forest
destruction.

DISTRIBUTION   South-eastern Brazil, including southern part of Bahia state and
the states of Minas Gerais, Espírito Santo, Rio de Janeiro, São Paulo, Paraná and
Santa Catarina, also eastern Paraguay and possibly Misiones, Argentina (1).   In
the Serra do Mar, Rio de Janeiro, the species is nearing extinction (2).

POPULATION   Unknown.   It has sharply decreased in the coastal zone of south-east
Brazil, where flocks of 50 to 100 once occurred but it is now unusual to see as
many as 10, and the decline is presumed to apply throughout its range (2).   In
eastern Paraguay recent searches failed to find it and it is not represented in
local collections (R. Ridgely 1978, pers. comm.).

HABITAT   Tropical forests.   In south-eastern Brazil most such forest has been
destroyed and only relatively small relict patches remain.   It has been suggested
that the abundance of this species may be linked with the infrequent and irregular
setting of bamboo seeds, which are its preferred food (H. Sick 1976, pers. comm.).

CONSERVATION MEASURES TAKEN   Protected by Brazilian law.

CONSERVATION MEASURES PROPOSED   None known.

REMARKS   This species was often kept in captivity in the past, but has not been
represented in European or North American collections for some time (3).

REFERENCES   1.   de Schauensee, R.M. 1966.   The Species of Birds of South
                    America and their Distribution.   Narberth, Pa.:   Livingston
                    Publishing Co.
              2.   Sick, H. 1972.   A ameaça da avifauna brasileira.
                    In Espécies da Fauna Brasileira Ameaçadas de Extinção,
                    pp. 99-153.   Rio de Janeiro: Academia Brasileira de Ciências.
              3.   Delacour, J. 1959.   Wild Pigeons and Doves.   Fond du Lac,
                    Wisc.: All-Pets Books, Inc.

JAMAICAN PLAIN PIGEON

Columba inornata exigua (Ridgway, 1915)

Order COLUMBIFORMES   Family COLUMBIDAE

STATUS   Indeterminate.   There have been very few confirmed sightings of this
subspecies this century, in spite of large numbers of amateur and professional
observers who have studied the Jamaican avifauna.   This pigeon was apparently easy
prey for the numerous hunters on Jamaica, from whom most of the recent reports of
its occurrence do in fact come (1; A. Downer 1974, pers. comm.; D. Lack 1971, pers.
comm.).

DISTRIBUTION   Formerly widespread in Jamaica at all altitudes (2).   Its present
distribution is unknown, although some recent reports suggest that it may still be
found in the Blue Mountains and possibly in the John Crow Mountains (3; A. Downer,
pers. comm.; P. Lack 1974, pers. comm.).

POPULATION   By 1920, this pigeon was disappearing rapidly and believed to be
heading for extinction (4), but in 1952 several were shot near Old Harbour (1).
An ornithologist resident in Jamaica for ten months in 1970 and 1971, searched for
the pigeon repeatedly and made only doubtful sightings (P. Lack 1974, pers. comm.).
But a 1973 report suggested that it appears regularly in the foothills of the Blue
Mountains when fig (Ficus) trees are fruiting (3).

HABITAT   This always tended to be either rather open country or mangroves (2),
but now seems to be restricted to mountain rainforest, except when the pigeons make
forays to lowland fruit trees to feed (3; P. Lack 1974, pers. comm.).

CONSERVATION MEASURES TAKEN   Protected by law, under which shooting of this
pigeon is prohibited at all times; however, Jamaican hunting regulations have
sometimes been inadequately enforced (A. Downer 1974, pers. comm.).

CONSERVATION MEASURES PROPOSED   No suggestions are known to have been made.

REMARKS   The nominate race, C. i. inornata, is still locally common in Cuba and
Hispaniola, but another subspecies, C. i. wetmorei of Puerto Rico, is endangered.

REFERENCES   1.   Bond, J. 1956.   Check-list of Birds of the West Indies.
                    Philadelphia Acad. Nat. Sci.
              2.   Gosse, P.H. 1847.   The Birds of Jamaica.   London:John Van
                    Voorst.
              3.   Spence, S. 1973.   Plain or Blue Pigeon.   In Bird Notes,
                    Gosse Bird Club (Jamaica) Broadsheet 21: 21.
              4.   Bangs, O. & Kennard, K.H. 1920.   A list of the birds of Jamaica.
                    In The Handbook of Jamaica, 1920.   Kingston:Govt. Printing
                    Office.

PUERTO RICAN PLAIN PIGEON

Columba inornata wetmorei Peters, 1937

Order COLUMBIFORMES   Family COLUMBIDAE

STATUS   Endangered.   This subspecies was rediscovered in 1958, after having been
apparently extinct for more than thirty years.   It is now restricted to one
locality in the hills of east-central Puerto Rico, where the population is very
small and where habitat destruction and human interference (mainly in the form of
nest plundering, for the young birds or squabs) prevents population growth despite
the protected status of the pigeon (1; 2).

DISTRIBUTION   Formerly widespread over most of Puerto Rico.   Now known from the
immediate vicinity of Lago de Cidra, east-central Puerto Rico.   Two additional but
very small populations have been discovered quite recently between Cidra and Cayey
(2).

POPULATION   In January 1973, a careful survey by a team of observers revealed a
population of 45 to 102 birds.   This census was repeated in January 1974, when 41
to 68 birds were recorded (2).   At one time the Plain Pigeon was rated as common.

HABITAT   The pigeon nests in bamboo Bambusa vulgaris thickets and hardwood canyons
on the shores of Lago de Cidra and feeds arboreally on fruits and seeds, the royal
palm Roystonea borinquena providing the bulk of its food.   Stands of the nesting
and food trees are subject to continual destruction as more dwelling houses are
built in the limited area in which the pigeon still occurs (2).

CONSERVATION MEASURES TAKEN   The subspecies is legally protected by the Commonwealth of Puerto Rico and by the U.S. Federal government.   Hunting in the vicinity
of the Lago de Cidra has been prohibited since 1971.   A biologist with the Puerto
Rico Department of Natural Resources is conducting an intensive ecological study of
the pigeon and a recovery team, appointed by the U.S. Fish and Wildlife Service, is
at work on a plan for its rehabilitation.

CONSERVATION MEASURES PROPOSED   A massive program to protect nests of the subspecies from disturbance during the highly synchronous two or three weeks nesting
season would immediately increase annual production.   Protection of habitat from
further housing development and the planting of additional bamboo groves would
provide additional safeguards against extinction (2).

REMARKS   This subspecies lays only one egg per year and it is not replaced if the
egg (or the young bird) is taken or destroyed.   Of 18 nests found by a research
biologist in 1974, 15 failed, one as a direct result of rat predation, two from
disturbance by children at the base of the nest trees and the other twelve having
been raided by Puerto Ricans for squabs (2).   Of the two other subspecies, the
nominate, C. i. inornata is still locally common on Cuba and Hispaniola, and
C. i. exigua of Jamaica is of indeterminate status but certainly very rare.

REFERENCES   1.   Leopold, N.F. 1963.   Checklist of birds of Puerto Rico and the
                   Virgin Islands.   Univ. Puerto Rico Agric. Expt. Stn. Bull. 168.
              2.   Wiley, J.W. 1974.   Puerto Rico Island-Wide Columbid investiga-
                   tions, Quarterly Report, 1 January - 31 March 1974.   Puerto Rico
                   Dept. Nat. Res.

LAUREL PIGEON

Columba junoniae Hartert, 1916

Order COLUMBIFORMES   Family COLUMBIDAE

STATUS   Endangered.   Known from two of the Canary Islands, where it is ruth-
lessly hunted and where there is a steady deterioration in the quality and
quantity of forest.

DISTRIBUTION   Restricted to Gomera and Palma, Canary Islands (1).

POPULATION   At one time this species was fairly abundant, particularly on Gomera
where it now appears to be quite rare, rarer in fact than Columba trocaz, which is
now classified as vulnerable (see relevant data sheet): it was not, for example,
seen alive by the members of a 1948 expedition, although they were shown by a
hunter one that he had just bagged.   However, there was a probable sighting of at
least one bird on Gomera in 1957 (3) and at least two and possibly as many as eight
were seen in 1977 (A. van den Berg 1977, pers. comm.).   On Palma it was considered
not uncommon in 1949, on the eastern outer slopes of the Caldera at altitudes of
1220-1525 m, but no further sightings have been reported, although observations
made on two or three more recent visits to the island have been published (3; 4).

HABITAT   This pigeon shares what remains of the laurel forests with the endangered Columba trocaz, but it is also found in mixed pine-laurel shrub forest,
from which it used to descend to agricultural areas to feed on barley, flax and
cherries (1).   It breeds in crevices on precipitous rock faces.   On Palma the
pine belt is fairly extensive, stretching along eastern slopes at between 1200 and
1600 m elevation, but virgin laurel forests have almost entirely disappeared, as
indeed has laurel forest on Gomera (2).

CONSERVATION MEASURES TAKEN   Hunting of this species is subject to the same
hunting season control regulations as that of other gamebirds in the Canary
Islands.

CONSERVATION MEASURES PROPOSED   None known.

REMARKS   The Laurel Pigeon has occasionally been kept in European aviaries but it
is not known whether any are at present in captivity (5).

REFERENCES   1. Bannerman, D.A. 1963. Birds of the Atlantic Islands.
                  Vol. 1. Edinburgh and London: Oliver and Boyd.
              2. Cullen, J.M., Guiton, P.E., Horridge, G.A. & Peirson, J. 1952.
                  Birds on Palma and Gomera (Canary Islands). Ibis 94: 68-84.
              3. Knecht, S. 1960. Ein Beitrag zur Erforschung der kanarischen
                  Vogelwelt, insbesondere der Brutvögel, unter hauptsächlicher
                  Berücksichtigung der drei westlichen Inseln Teneriffa, Gomera
                  und La Palma. Anzeiger Ornith. Gesell. Bayern 5: 525-556.
              4. Morphy, M.J. 1965. Some birds of northeast La Palma,
                  Canary Islands, August-September 1963. Ibis 107: 97-100.
              5. Delacour, J. 1959. Wild Pigeons and Doves. Fond du Lac,
                  Wisconsin: All-Pets Books Inc.

AZORES WOOD PIGEON

Columba palumbus azorica Hartert, 1905

Order COLUMBIFORMES   Family COLUMBIDAE

STATUS   Rare.   Local, reduced seriously in abundance on several of the Azores,
but still persistently hunted.   Forest destruction has also contributed to the
parlous status of the subspecies.

DISTRIBUTION   This Wood Pigeon has been recorded from Pico, São Jorge, Santa
Maria, São Miguel, Graciosa, Terceira and Faial, i.e. all the main islands of the
Azores except Corvo (1).   It is uncertain whether it still occurs on some of them.

POPULATION   In 1903 the subspecies was commonest on São Jorge and Pico, but
small numbers were found on the other islands named above (1).   In 1960, extensive
search revealed only two on Pico, but reports from São Miguel in 1964 indicated
that there was still a modest population on that island.   There are no recent
reports of its status on São Jorge or any of the other islands from which it has
been recorded (2).

HABITAT   Woodlands, which on several of the islands have been reduced to small
patches.

CONSERVATION MEASURES TAKEN   On São Miguel there are four protected areas
totalling 4000 hectares, where shooting of the Wood Pigeon is prohibited.   Elsewhere up to ten may be shot on Sundays or holidays between August and January
(J.M. Alvarez Cabral 1977, pers. comm.).

CONSERVATION MEASURES PROPOSED   None known.

REMARKS   None of the four other subspecies of the Wood Pigeon, ranging over much
of the Palearctic, the Middle East and northern Africa is known to be at risk, but
C. p. maderensis of Madeira is now extinct, the last specimen having been taken in
1904.

REFERENCES   1.   Hartert, E. & Ogilvie-Grant, W.R. 1905.   On the birds of
                    the Azores.   Novit. Zool. 12: 80-128.
              2.   Bannerman, D.A. and W.M. 1966.   Birds of the Atlantic
                    Islands.   Vol. 3.   Edinburgh and London: Oliver and
                    Boyd.

LONG-TOED PIGEON

Columba trocaz trocaz Heineken, 1829

Columba trocaz bollii Godman, 1872

Order COLUMBIFORMES   Family COLUMBIDAE

STATUS   Vulnerable.   Its numbers have greatly declined on Madeira and on most
of the Canaries, where it once occurred.   It is still avidly hunted and its
laurel forest habitat has been seriously reduced.

DISTRIBUTION   The nominate race, C. t. trocaz is confined to Madeira, where at
least since 1850 it is only known to survive in the mountain forests of the north
side of the island, where however it remains fairly widespread.   The subspecies
C. t. bollii has been recorded in Grand Canary, Tenerife, Gomera and Palma, and
there is hearsay evidence of its occurrence on Hierro.   It was last seen on Grand
Canary in 1888, but no specimens from that island are known to exist and it must
surely have been extirpated.   On Tenerife a specimen was collected in 1956, and it
could conceivably turn up again.   It was seen with certainty on Gomera in 1949,
and was quite common within the limited area of suitable habitat there in 1977
(10 were seen in a period of 45 minutes; A. van den Berg 1977, pers. comm.).   On
Palma the last reliable record was in 1905, although probable sightings were made
in 1947, but not subsequently. (1-4).

POPULATION   The nominate subspecies on Madeira remains relatively secure,
although there has been a significant decline since the 1870s.   However, it was
still rated as fairly common in 1890 (5).   In 1960, 13 were seen on one outing (2)
and as recently as 1969, 33 were shot by hunters in one day and several were
observed on every foray into the mountain habitat (6).   This population appears to
be holding its own (P.A. Zino 1977, pers. comm.).   The subspecies C. t. bollii, on
the other hand, may have been extirpated on Tenerife, where it is certainly
excessively rare (7).   On Palma its status is in doubt, but it must clearly have
suffered a major decline, for none could be found in 1948.   Very numerous on
Gomera in 1888, it was becoming rare by 1949, although several were observed in
the El Cedro valley, and in 1957 there was one probable sighting. (3-5; 8).   A
laurel pigeon, most likely C. t. bollii, but possibly C. junoniae, was said on
good authority to have persisted on Hierro until 1948, when the last 8 birds were
shot (9).

HABITAT   Forest composed of laurel Laurus, tree-heath Erica, til Oreodaphne
(=Ocotea), viñatigo Persea and haya Myrica species, which is still extensive
between 750 and 1500 m elevations on the mountains of central and northern Madeira,
but has been seriously depleted in the Canaries.   On Grand Canary there are now
only a few relict patches, on Tenerife and Palma the forest is greatly reduced, and
on Gomera though still fairly widespread it has been degraded and modified by
selective felling for charcoal burning. (1; 2; 4; 7).   In Madeira numerous rats,
which are known to prey on eggs of this pigeon, are an additional adverse factor (6).

CONSERVATION MEASURES TAKEN   The pigeon has legal protection on Madeira and the
Canaries but only to the same extent as other gamebirds, which means that it
remains subject to strong hunting pressure, although on Madeira the shooting season
is limited to the period mid-September to November or December and only two days
per week.   On Madeira the laurel forests are carefully protected from exploitation
(1).

<u>CONSERVATION MEASURES PROPOSED</u>   Special protection on Madeira (6) and year-round protection on the Canaries have been advocated.

<u>REMARKS</u>   Some authors have considered the Madeiran and Canarian Long-toed Pigeons to be distinct species, but they are more usually treated as subspecies, although their complete geographical separation means that evidence of the real extent of their genetic isolation is wanting. <u>C</u>. <u>t</u>. <u>bollii</u> has been bred successfully in captivity (1).

<u>REFERENCES</u>

1. Bannerman, D.A. 1963. <u>Birds of the Atlantic Islands</u>, Vol. 1. Edinburgh and London: Oliver and Boyd.
2. Bannerman, D.A. and W.M. 1965. <u>Birds of the Atlantic Islands</u>, Vol. 2. Edinburgh and London: Oliver and Boyd.
3. Volsø, H. 1951. The breeding birds of the Canary Islands. 1. Introduction and synopsis of the species. <u>Vidensk. Medd. dansk naturh. Foren.</u> 113: 1-153.
4. Cullen, J.M., Guiton, P.E., Horridge, G.A. & Peirson, J. 1952. Birds on Palma and Gomera (Canary Islands). <u>Ibis</u> 94: 68-84.
5. Ogilvie-Grant, W.R. 1890. Notes on some birds obtained at Madeira, Deserta Grande and Porto Santo. <u>Ibis</u> (6)2: 438-445.
6. Zino, A. 1969. Observations sur <u>Columba</u> <u>trocaz</u>. <u>l'Oiseau et R.F.O.</u> 39: 261-264.
7. Mountfort, G. 1960. Notes on the birds of Tenerife. <u>Ibis</u> 102: 618-619.
8. Knecht, S. 1960. Ein Beitrag zur Erforschung der kanarischen Vogelwelt, insbesondere der Brutvögel, unter hauptsächlicher Berücksichtigung der drei westlichen Inseln Teneriffa, Gomera und La Palma. <u>Anzeiger Ornith. Gesell. Bayern</u> 5: 525-556.
9. Hemmingsen, A.M. 1963. Birds on Hierro and the relation of number of species, and of specific abundance and body weights, to island area. <u>Vidensk. Medd. dansk naturh. Foren.</u> 125: 207-236.

TOOTH-BILLED PIGEON

Didunculus strigirostris (Jardine, 1845)

Order COLUMBIFORMES   Family COLUMBIDAE

STATUS   Vulnerable.   Found on Upolu and Savai'i, Western Samoa, where it is
scarce and locally distributed.   Like all other Samoan pigeons, it is hunted
avidly throughout the year.   The species is restricted to undisturbed mature
forest and while a good deal of this remains, especially on Savai'i, the strong
demographic pressure on Upolu and systematic felling by a foreign lumber company on
Savai'i are resulting in extensive forest destruction.   Western Samoa has one of
the most rapid rates of human population increase in the world (1; 2).

DISTRIBUTION   Locally distributed in virgin forest between 300 and 1400 m
elevation on Upolu and Savai'i.   The clearing of forests in recent years for
coconut plantations, pastures for domestic animals, timber and fuel has brought
about a substantial reduction of areas suitable for this species (1; 2; 3).

POPULATION   The unique Tooth-billed Pigeon is still regularly seen in the primary
forests on Savai'i, but is scarcer on Upolu, where mainly restricted to the upper
end of a number of heavily forested valleys.   Never known to be numerous, its
population density in areas of mature forest is probably undiminished (1; 2; 3).
Some years ago one local hunter estimated that one of every ten or twelve pigeons
shot belonged to this species (N.T. Shelton in litt. to B.R. Cancell, 20 Feb. 1969).

HABITAT   Undisturbed mature forest.   The species is unable to adapt itself to
areas that have been cut, cleared or replanted with exotic species such as coconut
palms (1; 3).

CONSERVATION MEASURES TAKEN   Export of the Tooth-billed Pigeon from Western Samoa
is forbidden.

CONSERVATION MEASURES PROPOSED   Control of indiscriminate hunting by the promulga-
tion and enforcement of hunting regulations, including a close season during the
pigeon's breeding season.   Reafforestation of areas cleared by lumber companies.
Control of human population in keeping with the environmental constraints of the
islands.   Preservation of tracts of mature forest by the establishment of reserves
and, in particular, the creation of a reserve on Nu'ulua Island, offshore of Upolu,
which is free of cats (1; see also Remarks below).

REMARKS   Another Columbid species, the Samoan Friendly Ground Dove Gallicolumba
stairii stairii, which is very scarce and local in Western Samoa, is also regularly
found on Nu'ulua Island.   Preservation of this undisturbed islet as a sanctuary
would therefore protect both species and would have the additional advantage that
the islet also supports significant seabird populations and is a breeding place of
the green turtle (Chelonia mydas).

    Didunculus has been kept as a pet in Western Samoa.   In 1968 ten were sent to
the Berlin Zoo (2).   It is a species of special scientific interest, being the only
member of the subfamily Didunculinae and by some authorities being considered worthy
of being placed in a separate full family of the Columbiformes (4).

REFERENCES   1. Crossin, R.S. in prep. The birds of Samoa.
              2. Ziswiler, V. 1968.   Die Bedrohung der Landvogelfauna
                  sudwestpazifischer Inseln.   Final Report, World Wildlife
                  Fund Project No. 391.
              3. DuPont, J.E. 1972.   Notes from Western Samoa, including the
                  description of a new parrot-finch (Erythrura).   Wilson Bull.
                  84: 375-376.
              4. Burton, P.J.K. 1974.   Jaw and tongue features in
                  Psittaciformes and other orders with special reference to
                  the anatomy of the Tooth-billed Pigeon (Didunculus
                  strigirostris).   Journ. Zool. 174: 255-276.

CLOVEN-FEATHERED DOVE

Drepanoptila holosericea (Temminck, 1810)

Order COLUMBIFORMES   ·   Family COLUMBIDAE

STATUS   Vulnerable.   Decreasing in range and numbers on New Caledonia.   In spite of complete legal protection, this species is hunted widely and indiscriminately.

DISTRIBUTION   Once widespread in forested areas of New Caledonia and the offshore Ile des Pins, this dove has not been seen recently on the Ile des Pins and its range on the main island has been seriously reduced (1; 2).

POPULATION   No precise figures are available.   The species has decreased as a result of excessive hunting and some loss of habitat, although the total population is still considered to be in excess of 1000 birds (P. Rancurel 1974, pers. comm.). In 1944 and 1945 an ornithologist, searching the forests of New Caledonia for this species, found a total of only three (2).

HABITAT   Indigenous forests and also perhaps savanna woodlands (3) of New Caledonia.   Forests, originally covering much of the island, are now largely restricted to the mountains.   Wherever the more inaccessible parts of New Caledonia have been opened up by logging or by prospecting for or mining of nickel, hunting pressure has quickly eliminated this highly attractive dove.

CONSERVATION MEASURES TAKEN   The species is completely protected by law, but enforcement of the law is ineffective (H. Bregulla, pers. comm.; P. Rancurel, pers. comm.).

CONSERVATION MEASURES PROPOSED   The establishment of large forest reserves has been urged as essential (H. Bregulla 1974, pers. comm.).

REMARKS   The Cloven-feathered Dove is the sole representative of a genus unique to New Caledonia.   It has been kept in captivity on New Caledonia, but the prospects for captive breeding are poor (P. Rancurel, pers. comm.).

REFERENCES
1.   Sarasin, F. 1913.   Die Voegel New Caledoniens und der Loyalty Inseln.   Nova Caledonia, Zoology, 1: 1-78.
2.   Warner, D.W. 1947.   The Ornithology of New Caledonia and the Loyalty Islands.   Cornell Univ.: Ph.D. Thesis.
3.   Delacour, J. 1966.   Guide des oiseaux de la Nouvelle Calédonie. Neuchâtel (Switzerland: Delachaux and Niestlé).

SOCIETY ISLANDS PIGEON

Ducula aurorae (Peale, 1848)

Order COLUMBIFORMES   Family COLUMBIDAE

STATUS   Vulnerable.   Known only from Tahiti, Society Islands, and Makatea,
Tuamotu Archipelago.   It was thought to have been extirpated from Tahiti shortly
after 1921, and its rediscovery on Tahiti in July, 1972, was quite unexpected.
The population is extremely small and restricted to one valley.   On Makatea a
sizable population still survives.

DISTRIBUTION   On Tahiti, at least since the arrival of the first European visitors
at the end of the 18th Century, the species was reputed to have a very local
distribution.   It is now restricted to a section of the Papenoo Valley (1; 2).
On Makatea (28 sq. km) it is found in the wooded southern part of the island (J.-C.
Thibault 1974, pers. comm.).

POPULATION   It was already considered rare in Tahiti by 1904.   Members of the
Whitney South Sea Expedition collected three and observed a very few more during a
six-month stay in 1921 and it was thought to have become extinct on the island
shortly afterwards.   When rediscovered in 1972, the population was estimated at
about ten (1).   In the same year the Makatea population was estimated to be at
least 500 (J.-C. Thibault 1974, pers. comm.).   In the absence of any early
population estimates, the presumption is that the species was at one time more
numerous on both islands but to what extent is unknown.

HABITAT   Forests, especially of fruit-bearing species (1).   Following the
conclusion of phosphate rock mining in the northern half of Makatea the vegetation
is recovering rapidly, to the extent that it may once again provide suitable
habitat within a few more years.   With the departure of most of the workers
employed in the phosphate mining, the remaining largely indigenous population is
relatively small (3; J.-C. Thibault, 1974, pers. comm.).

CONSERVATION MEASURES TAKEN   Hunting of all birds was prohibited in French
Polynesia in 1967.   A nature reserve has been established in Papenoo Valley,
Tahiti.

CONSERVATION MEASURES PROPOSED   Establishment of extensive nature reserves in the
interior of Tahiti, coupled with efficient wardening to reduce the impact of hunting,
burning and over-grazing (1).

REMARKS   That this pigeon survived the period of intensive mining on Makatea
suggests that it is once more fairly secure, at least on that island, if not on
Tahiti.

REFERENCES   1.   Holyoak, D.T. 1974.   Les oiseaux des Îles de la Société.
                    L'Oiseau et R.F.O. 44: 1-27, 153-181.
              2.   Thibault, J.-C. No date.   Unpublished report to IUCN on status
                    of the avifauna of French Polynesia.
              3.   Douglas, G. 1969.   Draft check list of Pacific oceanic islands.
                    Micronesica 5(2): 327-463.

MARQUESAS PIGEON

Ducula galeata (Bonaparte, 1855)

Order COLUMBIFORMES   Family COLUMBIDAE

STATUS   Endangered.   Severely restricted in range and in population on Nukuhiva in the Marquesas Islands.   Although protected, it is still occasionally hunted for food because of its large size and tasty flesh.   Only its relatively isolated habitat prevents it from being hunted more frequently.   An international 'jetport' is proposed for Nukuhiva and would be constructed within a kilometre of the pigeon's range.   Meanwhile, its habitat is already deteriorating and decreasing gradually in size due to grazing by cattle, pigs and goats (1; 2; 3; 4).

DISTRIBUTION   Restricted to mountain ridges and valleys at the western end of Nukuhiva.   May have existed formerly on Fatuhiva, but its existence there was never proved (1) and there is no good evidence of any change in the distribution of the species.

POPULATION   The 1972 estimate was 90 $\pm$ 15 birds (1).   A subsequent estimate was 200 to 400 birds (5).

HABITAT   Narrow wooded valleys rising to the mountain ridge from 700 to 1300 m above sea level; the pigeon descends to lower levels on feeding forays (1).

CONSERVATION MEASURES TAKEN   Hunting of all birds in French Polynesia was prohibited in 1967.

CONSERVATION MEASURES PROPOSED   Strict enforcement of the hunting ban.   Establishment of reserve to protect habitat, including eradication of introduced grazing animals.   Relocation of proposed jetport at a much greater distance from the habitat of the pigeon (1; 5).

REMARKS   This species might well be amenable to captive breeding.   One was kept as a pet on Nukuhiva in 1972.   Lays only one egg (1).

REFERENCES   1.   Holyoak, D.T. 1975.   Les oiseaux des Îles Marquises.
                   L'Oiseau et R.F.O. 45: 207-233, 341-366.
             2.   Bruner, P.L. 1972.   Field Guide to the Birds of French Polynesia
                   Honolulu:B.P. Bishop Museum.
             3.   Holyoak, D.T. 1973.   Polynesian land birds face H-bombs and
                   malaria.   New Scientist 57(832): 288-290.
             4.   Holyoak, D.T. 1973.   Endangered land-birds in French Polynesia.
                   Biol. Cons. 5(3): 231-232.
             5.   Thibault, J.-C. no date.   Fragilité et protection de l'avifaune
                   en Polynésie Française.   Unpublished report to ICBP.

GIANT IMPERIAL PIGEON

Ducula goliath (G.R. Gray, 1859)

Order COLUMBIFORMES   Family COLUMBIDAE

STATUS   Vulnerable.   Restricted to montane forests of New Caledonia, where
hunting pressure on this large pigeon is intense.

DISTRIBUTION   Known only from New Caledonia and Ile des Pins, but there have been
no recent reports from the latter.   On the main island the species is now confined
to indigenous forests, and is found almost entirely on the mountains and in remote
valleys (1; 2).

POPULATION   No estimates have been made.   However, there is no doubt the species
has become increasingly scarce in recent years as the result of excessive hunting
(1; 2).

HABITAT   Primary forests of New Caledonia, now largely restricted to the
mountains, upper valleys and occasionally some lower valleys.   Many of these forest
habitats have been logged or cleared to make way for nickel mining.   Mining roads
and villages bring miners and their families into forestlands previously difficult
of access, which results in bringing ever increasing areas under intense hunting
pressure (2).

CONSERVATION MEASURES TAKEN   Hunting of this species is authorized between 15
March and 15 April at weekends between sunrise and 8 p.m.   Illegal hunting, outside
these limits, is considered to have been a major cause of the species' decline
(P. Rancurel 1974, pers. comm.).

CONSERVATION MEASURES PROPOSED   Strict enforcement of the hunting season.
Establishment of parks or reserves sufficiently large to maintain populations of
this large pigeon (H. Bregulla 1974, pers. comm.).   The breeding biology of the
species is under investigation, so that the effectiveness of the present hunting
season can be assessed scientifically (P. Rancurel 1974, pers. comm.).

REMARKS   Four Giant Imperial Pigeons are known to be in captivity outside of New
Caledonia (3).   Those held in the island itself have bred successfully, but
considerable difficulties have been encountered in raising the chicks (P. Rancurel
1974, pers. comm.).

REFERENCES   1.   Sarasin, F. 1913.   Die Vögel New-Caledoniens und der Loyalty
                   Inseln.   Nova Caledonia, Zoology 1: 1-78.
              2.   Warner, D.W. 1947.   The Ornithology of New Caledonia and the
                   Loyalty Islands.   Cornell Univ.: Ph.D. Thesis.
              3.   Duplaix-Hall, N. (ed.) 1975.   Census of rare animals in
                   captivity, 1974.   International Zoo Yearbook 15: 397-429.

RADAK MICRONESIAN PIGEON

Ducula oceanica ratakensis (Takatsukasa and Yamashina, 1932)

Order COLUMBIFORMES   Family COLUMBIDAE

STATUS   Indeterminate.   Known from two atolls in the Radak (eastern) Chain,
Marshall Islands, Central Pacific.   A recent report suggests it may have declined
on one atoll, while there is no specific report from the other of the current
status of this pigeon.   Predation by rats has been suggested as a cause of
reduction in the distribution and abundance of this species on one island.

DISTRIBUTION   Recorded from Arno (12 sq. km) and Wotje (8.2 sq. km) atolls (1).
On Arno in 1950 the pigeon was only found on the islands in the southern half of the
atoll, including Arno itself, Ine, Ijoen, Lomarin Malel, Kirage, Rakaru and Nameej,
and was absent from many apparently suitable localities (2).   In 1975, it was not
seen at all during a three week visit to Ine (D. Anderson 1975, pers. comm.).   Its
distribution in Wotje atoll is unknown.

POPULATION   The only indication of the population was obtained in Arno atoll in
1950, when the pigeon was considered abundant on Arno Island and parts of Ine and
Kirage islands, and one or two were seen or heard on the four other islands listed
above (1).   As also noted above, it seemed to have disappeared from Ine Island,
the largest of the atoll, by 1975 (D. Anderson loc. cit.).

HABITAT   Woodlands, especially coconut plantations.   There has been no diminution
of this habitat in the Marshalls, but rats occur regularly in the coconut trees in
which this species breeds.   The black rat Rattus rattus was introduced to Ine
Island prior to 1950, during the Japanese administration, and in 1950 Polynesian
rats Rattus exulans were noted as abundant on almost all islands of Arno atoll (2).
Both species are potential predators on eggs or young birds, the former more so
than the latter.

CONSERVATION MEASURES TAKEN   None known.

CONSERVATION MEASURES PROPOSED   None known.

REMARKS   This subspecies is doubtfully distinct from D. o. oceanica of Kusaie,
Caroline Islands, and Jaluit and Ailinglapalap in the Ralik (western) Chain of the
Marshalls (3).   D. o. teraokai of Truk, Caroline Islands, is classified as
endangered (see separate sheet), and still other subspecies from Palau and Ponape
are not considered to be at risk, in spite of having been heavily hunted during and
following World War II.

REFERENCES   1.   Baker, R.H. 1951.   The avifauna of Micronesia, its origin,
                   evolution, and distribution.   Univ. Kansas Pubs. Mus. Nat. Hist.
                   3(1): 1-359.
              2.   Marshall, J.T., Jr. 1951.   Vertebrate ecology of Arno Atoll,
                   Marshall Islands.   Atoll Res. Bull. 3.
              3.   Amadon, D. 1943.   The Whitney South Sea Expedition: Notes
                   on some non-passerine genera, 3.   Amer. Mus. Novit. 1237.

TRUK MICRONESIAN PIGEON

Ducula oceanica teraokai (Momiyama, 1922)

Order COLUMBIFORMES   Family COLUMBIDAE

STATUS   Endangered.   This pigeon has been found on Truk and possibly on two
others of the Caroline Islands, western Pacific.   Owing to over-hunting during
World War II and subsequently, it has become excessively rare on Truk and could not
be found during a week's survey of that island group in 1975.

DISTRIBUTION   Specimens are known only from the Truk Islands (95.8 sq. km), but
pigeons observed in the late nineteenth century on the Lukunor (2.8 sq. km) and
Nukuoro (1.7 sq. km) atolls a few hundred kilometres south-east of Truk were
believed to be of the same subspecies (1).   Prior to World War II, teraokai was
distributed throughout the high islands of Truk, but by the end of the war had
disappeared from most of them.   This was the result of intense hunting pressure
by the Japanese, who were short of food because of the blockade of Truk by American
forces.   By 1957, it was only left on Tol, the largest, and a few of the other high
islands (2).   In 1975, four of these islands, including Tol, were searched over a
period of a week and the subspecies was neither seen nor heard.   On Lukunor and
Nukuoro to the south-east the pigeon is thought to be extinct, visits to these
islands in the last ten years having failed to yield any new information of its
existence (R. Owen 1976, pers. comm.).

POPULATION   Prior to World War II this subspecies was widespread and presumably
common, but by the end of the war it had been markedly reduced in numbers.   In
1945, no birds could be found, but not all islands were visited (1); on further
visits between 1957 and 1960, very small populations were found on several islands,
the largest flocks being restricted to Tol Island (2); by 1975, none was seen or
heard in a week-long survey, although the local inhabitants stated that it was still
present but very scarce (R. Owen 1975, pers. comm.).

HABITAT   Dense forests on the mountains.   The species has rarely been encountered
in the lowlands.   The original forests of Truk have been severely depleted and
none of the remnants is as yet protected.

CONSERVATION MEASURES TAKEN   None known.

CONSERVATION MEASURES PROPOSED   The subspecies was recommended for inclusion in
the U.S. Trust Territories list of endangered species which was being compiled in
1975 (R. Owen, pers. comm.).   Species so listed are protected by the U.S. Trust
Territories Endangered Species Act of that year, which prohibits the taking of
endangered species, except by specified indigenous inhabitants for subsistence.
All listed birds and particularly those endemic to the U.S. Trust Territories are
urgently in need of basic conservation management.

REMARKS   This subspecies is doubtfully distinct from D. o. monacha of Palau and
Yap (3).   Other subspecies are found in the Marshalls and Ponape and other eastern
Carolines.   None are thought to be at risk, except for D. o. ratakensis of the
Radak Chain, Marshalls, which is of indeterminate status (see separate sheet).

REFERENCES   1.   Baker, R.H. 1951.   The avifauna of Micronesia, its origin,
                    evolution, and distribution.   <u>Univ. Kansas Pubs. Mus.
                    Nat. Hist.</u> 3(1): 1-359.
              2.   Brandt, J.H. 1962.   Nests and eggs of the birds of the
                    Truk Islands.   <u>Condor</u> 64: 416-437.
              3.   Amadon, D. 1943.   Birds collected during the Whitney
                    South Sea Expedition. 52.   Notes on some non-passerine
                    genera, 3.   <u>Amer. Mus. Novit.</u> 1237.

CHRISTMAS IMPERIAL PIGEON

Ducula whartoni (Sharpe, 1887)

Order COLUMBIFORMES   Family COLUMBIDAE

STATUS   Vulnerable. Restricted to Christmas Island, Indian Ocean, and avidly
hunted. This is another of the species that have suffered as the result of the
phosphate mining operations. Not only has part of its habitat been destroyed, but
the system of access roads throughout the island has deprived it of its natural
sanctuaries or areas in which it was out of reach of hunters.

DISTRIBUTION   Endemic to Christmas Island, Indian Ocean, where it is now found
almost exclusively on the inland plateau, although prior to the arrival of the main
body of settlers in 1897 it may have visited the shore terrace. It was introduced
to the Cocos Keeling Islands between 1885 and 1900 (1) and was still present there
in 1958 (2).

POPULATION   This species has shown a gradual decline from the time of its discovery late last century to the present. In 1887, it was considered very abundant
and still very common at the turn of the century. In 1904, it was said to have
decreased in numbers but to be still relatively plentiful. A further decline was
noticeable in 1932 (3) and by 1938-1940 it was less plentiful than in 1932, and the
suggestion was first made that it was on the way to extinction, although not in the
immediate future (1). Visits in 1965, 1972 and 1974 led to an estimate of fewer
than 100 pairs (4), but by 1977 it was by contrast considered to be widespread,
fairly common and increasing (J.B. Nelson, unpublished report).

HABITAT   Rainforest of the inland plateau. Access for hunters to all parts of
this habitat is believed to be one of the most serious consequences of mining
activities, in addition to actual habitat destruction in the course of removing high
grade phosphate from what, by 1994, is expected to comprise 30 per cent of the
island's surface. The mined area will be almost devoid of vegetation and have much
of the appearance of a moonscape, utterly unsuited to the pigeon or most other forms
of life.

CONSERVATION MEASURES TAKEN   A closed hunting season was first declared in 1904.
Total legal protection was given from 1930 to 1932, but enforcement proved
impossible and in 1933 was once again replaced by a 4-month close season (1).
Subsequently total protection was reintroduced but poaching continues to be a
serious problem (5). A Conservation Officer was appointed in 1975.

CONSERVATION MEASURES PROPOSED   Stricter enforcement of hunting regulations and
control of poaching have been recommended. The reserves which have been suggested
for safeguarding the habitat of Abbott's Booby Sula abbotti would also be of benefit
to Imperial Pigeon. Most of the present 3,000 human inhabitants of Christmas
Island are to be resettled elsewhere when mining activities come to an end in 1994
(5).

REMARKS   Some authors treat this pigeon as a subspecies of Ducula rosacea of the
Lesser Sundas, but the two are sufficiently distinct to be given specific rank (6).

REFERENCES   1.   Gibson-Hill, C.A. 1947.   Notes on the birds of Christmas
                   Island.   Bull. Raffles Mus. 18: 87-165.
              2.   Alfred, E.R. 1961.   Some birds of the Cocos-Keeling Islands.
                   Malay. Nature Journ. 15: 68-69.
              3.   Chasen, F.N. 1933.   Notes on the birds of Christmas Island,
                   Indian Ocean.   Bull. Raffles Mus. 8: 55-87.
              4.   Van Tets, G.F. 1976.   A report on the conservation of resident
                   birds on Christmas Island.   Bull. ICBP. 12: 238-242.
              5.   Australian House of Representatives Standing Committee on
                   Environment and Conservation, 1974.   Conservation of endangered
                   species on Christmas Island.   Canberra:Australian Government
                   Publishing Service.
              6.   Goodwin, D. 1960.   Taxonomy of the Genus Ducula.
                   Ibis 102: 526-535.

SOCIETY ISLANDS GROUND DOVE

Gallicolumba erythroptera (Gmelin, 1788)

Order COLUMBIFORMES   Family COLUMBIDAE

STATUS   Indeterminate.   Extirpated from Moorea and Tahiti, Society Islands, in
the mid-nineteenth century.   Status on several atolls in the Tuamotu archipelago
unknown, but presumably still occurs on several that remain free from introduced
cats and rats.

DISTRIBUTION   Formerly Moorea and Tahiti in the Society Islands, and Aratika,
Katiu, Maria, Tenararo, Vanavana, Tenarunga, Hiti, Hao and South Marutea in the
Tuamotus (1; 2; 3; D. Goodwin 1974, pers. comm.).   Reported in 1966 from Maturei-
Vavao at the eastern end of the Tuamotu chain and at the same time noted as
apparently absent from South Marutea, a short distance to the west and from Hao
much further to the west (3).   Believed extinct in Moorea and Tahiti and there are
no reports of its occurrence from other islands in the Tuamotus since 1922.

POPULATION   Known to have been quite large in the Society Islands, where now
extinct.   Nothing is known of this dove's present-day numbers, but it was said to
be not very numerous on Maturei-Vavao when found there in 1966 (3).

HABITAT   Dense original forest (4).

CONSERVATION MEASURES TAKEN   Hunting of all birds in French Polynesia was
prohibited in 1967.

CONSERVATION MEASURES PROPOSED   None known.

REFERENCES   1.   Murphy, R.C. 1924.   Birds collected during the Whitney South
                    Sea Expedition.   I. Amer. Mus. Novit. 115.
              2.   Goodwin, D. 1967.   Pigeons and Doves of the World.   London:
                    Trustees of the British Museum (Natural History).
              3.   Lacan, F. & Mougin, J.L. 1974.   Les oiseaux des Iles Gambier
                    et de quelques atolls orientaux de l'archipel des Tuamotu
                    (Océan Pacifique).   L'Oiseau et R.F.O. 44: 192-280.
              4.   du Pont, J.E. 1976.   South Pacific Birds.   Delaware Museum
                    of Natural History, Monograph series No. 3.

MARQUESAS GROUND DOVE

Gallicolumba rubescens (Vieillot, 1818)

Order COLUMBIFORMES   Family COLUMBIDAE

STATUS   Indeterminate. The well-separated Marquesan islets Hatutu and Fatuhuku
comprise the entire range of this species, and are the only ones in the entire
Marquesas group that enjoy freedom from introduced rats, cats, dogs or pigs.
Unfortunately, considerable French military activity began on Eiao, barely five
kilometres from Hatutu, soon after Eiao was given protected status in 1971,
bringing into question the reliability of the similar status of Hatutu.   If Hatutu
is used by military personnel from Eiao for recreational purposes, there would be a
much graver risk of predators and non-indigenous plants being accidentally or even
deliberately introduced (1; 2; 3).

DISTRIBUTION   Now restricted to Hatutu (18 sq. km) and Fatuhuku (1 sq. km).
Probably occurred in the past on the much larger island of Nukuhiva, from which the
type specimen was supposed to have come, about half way between Hatutu and Fatuhuku,
which are 250 km apart.   It could well have inhabited some or all of the other
islands also, though probably well before the first attempt at European colonization
in the 1840s (1).

POPULATION   In 1922, this dove was common on the two islands on which it still
occurs.   In 1960, several flocks of 10-25 birds each were to be seen on Hatutu
(B. Decker 1974, pers. comm.).   In 1975, 225 ± 25 were estimated to survive on
Hatutu (4).   There are no recent reports from Fatuhuku, but its very small size
and rocky terrain suggest that it could never have been numerous.

HABITAT   Bushy areas and on the ground under trees in small islands with a low
rainfall.

CONSERVATION MEASURES TAKEN   Hatutu and Fatuhuku were given protected status in
1971 (1; 4; 5).   Hunting of all birds in French Polynesia was prohibited in 1967.

CONSERVATION MEASURES PROPOSED   None known.

REMARKS   This species has bred successfully in captivity.   Two eggs comprise
the clutch (6).

REFERENCES   1. Holyoak, D.T. 1975.   Les oiseaux des Îles Marquises.
                  L'Oiseau et R.F.O. 45: 207-233, 341-366.
              2. Holyoak, D.T. 1973.   Polynesian land birds face H-bombs and
                  malaria. New Scientist 57(832): 288-290.
              3. Holyoak, D.T. 1973.   Endangered land birds in French Polynesia.
                  Biol. Cons. 5(3): 231-232.
              4. Thibault, J.-C. undated.   Fragilité et protection de l'avifaune
                  en Polynésie Française.   Unpublished report to ICBP.
              5. Decker, B.G. 1973.   Unique dry-island biota under official
                  protection in northwestern Marquesas Islands (Iles Marquises).
                  Biol. Cons. 5(1): 66-67.
              6. Gifford, E.W. 1925.   The Gray-hooded Quail Dove (Gallicolumba
                  rubescens) of the Marquesas Islands, in captivity.   Auk 42:
                  388-396.

CHATHAM ISLAND PIGEON

Hemiphaga novaeseelandiae chathamensis (Rothschild, 1891)

Order COLUMBIFORMES   Family COLUMBIDAE

───

STATUS   Critically endangered.   Restricted to portions of the two largest of the
Chatham Islands, 800 km east of New Zealand, where its population is critically low.
The woodlands on which the pigeon depends continue to deteriorate due to the
combined effects of heavy browsing by stock, strong winds and fire, although an
important area has been made into a reserve by the New Zealand government.   The
number of pigeons may have become so low as to make management of the area futile,
at least from the point of view of rehabilitating the pigeon.   Hunting and the
introduction of cats are also considered to have been factors contributing to its
decline (1).

DISTRIBUTION   Formerly widespread in forested portions of Chatham, Pitt and
Mangere islands in the Chatham group.   Now restricted to the wooded southern
extremity of Chatham and Pitt, and possibly already extinct on Pitt (1).

POPULATION   The Chatham Island Pigeon's decline started with the arrival of
European and Maori settlers in the 1830s.   It was quickly extirpated from Mangere,
but survived on Chatham and Pitt and was still to be found in the northern parts
of these islands as recently as 1960, although by that time its strongholds were
already confined to the south.   In 1968, biologists of the New Zealand Wildlife
Service spent 86 man-days on Pitt looking for the pigeon, but failed to see one, in
spite of insistence by the inhabitants that it still occurred.   Three were seen on
Chatham in 1968, but none could be found in November 1970.   The present population
is estimated to be below 25 birds (1).

HABITAT   Woodlands.

CONSERVATION MEASURES TAKEN   Protected by law since 1922, but was still being
hunted for food two decades later.   In 1974, the single most important remaining
block of woodland and scrub on Pitt Island, the "Glory Block", was purchased by the
New Zealand government.   About half of its 1,200 ha has been declared a Reserve
for the Preservation of Flora and Fauna and has been fenced; steps to rid it
completely of domestic livestock were initiated in 1974 (1; D. Merton, pers. comm.).

CONSERVATION MEASURES PROPOSED   Establishment of reserves on main Chatham Island
and enlargement of the newly created reserve on Pitt.   Relocation of pigeons on
predator-free South-East Island, where conditions appear suitable, has also been
suggested.   An attempt is to be made to control feral cats within the Pitt Island
reserve (G. Williams 1976, pers. comm.).

REMARKS   H. n. spadicea, the subspecies of this pigeon on Norfolk Island, became
extinct by about 1801, and an undescribed population from Raoul Island in the
Kermadec group was exterminated about 1870 by hunting and introduced cats (2).
The nominate H. n. novaeseelandiae of North and South Islands, New Zealand, is not
threatened.   The establishment of reserves on Chatham and Pitt Islands is long
overdue: their forests have deteriorated sadly and the population of endemic birds
that inhabit them may have been reduced beyond the point of recovery.

REFERENCES   1.   Merton, D.V. & Bell, B.D. undated.   Endemic birds of the
                            Chatham Islands.   New Zealand Wildlife Service: unpublished ms.
                     2.   Cheeseman, T.F. 1890.   On the birds of the Kermadec Islands.
                            Trans. N.Z. Inst. 23: 216-226.

TOLIMA DOVE

Leptotila conoveri Bond and de Schauensee, 1943

Order COLUMBIFORMES   Family COLUMBIDAE

STATUS   Indeterminate.   Very locally distributed in Colombia in an area where forest destruction has been particularly severe.

DISTRIBUTION   Eastern slopes of the Central Andes of Colombia in Tolima and Huila divisions, including the area of the headwaters of the Magdalena River. Localities from which specimens have been taken include Toche in Tolima and Isnaos, San Agustin and Belén in Huila. (1-3).

POPULATION   Unknown, but a decline is certain in the light of the extensive destruction of subtropical forests in Huila and Tolima.   This species could not be found during recent searches of its former haunts in the upper Magdalena valley (R. Ridgely 1978, pers. comm.).

HABITAT   Subtropical forest, including second growth.   Although none of the dove's habitat is protected, hope for its continued existence lies in its ability to adapt to secondary forest (3).

CONSERVATION MEASURES TAKEN   None known.

CONSERVATION MEASURES PROPOSED   ·None known.

REFERENCES   1.   de Schauensee, R.M. 1966.   The Species of Birds of South America and their Distribution.   Narberth, Pa.: Livingston Publishing Co.
2.   de Schauensee, R.M. 1949.   The birds of the Republic of Colombia.   Part 2.   Caldasia 5: 381-644.
3.   Bond, J. & de Schauensee, R.M. 1943.   A new species of dove of the genus Leptotila from Colombia.   Notulae Naturae 122.

GRENADA DOVE

Leptotila wellsi (Lawrence, 1884)

Order COLUMBIFORMES   Family COLUMBIDAE

STATUS   Indeterminate.   Thought to be very rare and localized on Grenada, Lesser
Antilles, West Indies.

DISTRIBUTION   Most records this century have come from the south-western coast of
Grenada at Beausejour, Fontenoy, Grand Anse, Point Salines and Glover's Island, and
also formerly, but no longer, on Green Island, off the north-eastern point (1; 2;
3; 4).   It has been suggested that the range of the species may have been reduced
through competition with the northward-spreading Violet-eared Dove Zenaida
auriculata (2).

POPULATION   No estimates have been made. The dove was thought to have been heard
calling near Point Salines in 1929 (2); two were collected between Grand Anse and
Point Salines in 1961 (4); and the species was still present in that area in 1963
(3).   In 1971 one was seen at Beausejour and at least 5 were seen or heard behind
Grand Anse (1).   The status of the species may not have changed much in the last
century (J. Bond 1975, pers. comm.).

HABITAT   Xerophytic scrublands receiving 750 to 1000 mm rainfall annually.
Several other species of doves occur in the same habitat (3).   The scrublands
around Grand Anse are being developed for holiday housing (D. Lack in litt. to
P. Barclay-Smith, 1971).

CONSERVATION MEASURES TAKEN   None known.

CONSERVATION MEASURES PROPOSED   It has been suggested that the National Trust of
Grenada should be persuaded to prevent building on some of the hilltops of the
dove's range (D. Lack in litt. to P. Barclay-Smith, 1971).

REMARKS   Either this species or the very similar L. verreauxi of tropical South
America bred in captivity between 1920 and 1925 (3).

REFERENCES   1.   Lack, D. & Lack, A. 1973.   Birds on Grenada.   Ibis 115:   53-59.
               2.   Bond, J. 1961.   Extinct and near extinct birds of the West
                    Indies.   Pan-American Section, ICBP, Res. Rep. No. 4.
               3.   Bond, J. 1963.   Eighth supplement to the Check-list of Birds
                    of the West Indies (1956).   Philadelphia Acad. Nat. Sci.
               4.   Schwartz, A. & Klinikowski, R.F. 1963.   Observations on West
                    Indian birds.   Proc. Acad. Nat. Sci. Phila. 115:   53-77.

PINK PIGEON

Nesoenas mayeri (Prévost, in Knip, 1843)

Order COLUMBIFORMES   Family COLUMBIDAE

STATUS   Critically endangered.   Very rare and restricted in range and declining.
It is threatened by habitat destruction as well as nest predation by introduced
mammals.   Still also occasionally shot by hunters.

DISTRIBUTION   Found only on the island of Mauritius in the Indian Ocean and never
known to have occurred elsewhere.   Restricted to indigenous montane evergreen
forest and scrub that occurs only in the south-western corner of the island, from
the Black River Gorges southward to the southern escarpment of the upland plateau
(especially around Mount Cocotte) and the Savanne Mountains.   The species formerly
occurred over most of the upland areas of Mauritius, although the area presently
occupied has always been known as its stronghold (1; 2; S. Temple 1976, pers. comm.).

POPULATION   Never particularly large, but certainly much greater than it has ever
been during the last half-century when the major decline took place (1; 2).   In
1974, the total population numbered 28-30 birds (2; 3) and by 1976 had decreased to
24 (D. McKelvey 1976, pers. comm.).

HABITAT   Limited almost exclusively to indigenous montane evergreen forest and
scrub, but exotic vegetation, especially the conifer Cryptomeria, intermingled
with or adjacent to native forests, is sometimes used for feeding, communal roosting
and nesting.   Macaque monkeys Macaca fascicularis and black rats Rattus rattus,
which have been introduced into Mauritius, are abundant throughout the habitat and
serious nest predators (1; 2; S. Temple 1976, pers. comm.).

CONSERVATION MEASURES TAKEN   Fully protected by laws forbidding the killing or
capture of native birds.   A portion of the bird's range in the south-western
corner of the island is included in officially declared reserves.   During 1972-
1976, ecological studies have been carried out to define the bird's status and
requirements (4).   In 1977, eleven birds were in captivity in Mauritius, including
one successfully reared by its parents, while another five had been taken to the
Jersey Wildlife Preservation Trust for captive breeding (D. McKelvey 1977, P. Trefry
1977, pers. comms.).

CONSERVATION MEASURES PROPOSED   Continued protection and management of the
remnant native forests is essential to the bird's survival.   A management plan for
a system of nature reserves and national parks has been submitted to the Mauritius
Government.   Protection of nest sites and control of macaque monkeys is necessary
to allow breeding success.   Eventual release of captive-bred pigeons in suitable
habitat on Mauritius and possibly nearby Réunion is anticipated (2; 5).

REMARKS   Pink Pigeons have been kept successfully in captivity in the past but
have not bred (6).   Because eating the flesh of this species is known to have
unpleasant effects at certain seasons, it is not hunted regularly (1).

REFERENCES   1.   Meinertzhagen, R. 1912.   On the birds of Mauritius.   Ibis
                    9(6): 82-108.
              2.   Temple, S.A., Staub, J.J.F. & Antoine, R. 1974.   Some background
                    information and recommendations on the preservation of the native
                    flora and fauna of Mauritius.   Unpublished report submitted to
                    the Mauritius Government.
              3.   Temple, S.A. 1974.   Wildlife in Mauritius today.   Oryx 12:
                    584-590.

4. Temple, S.A. 1975. <u>World Wildlife Yearbook</u> 1974-75, pp. 210-212. Morges: World Wildlife Fund.
5. Procter, J. & Salm, R. 1974. Conservation in Mauritius, 1974. Unpublished report submitted to the Mauritius Government.
6. Delacour, J. 1959. <u>Wild Pigeons and Doves</u>. Fond du Lac, Wisconsin: All-Pets Books, Inc.

RAPA FRUIT DOVE

Ptilinopus huttoni Finsch, 1874

Order COLUMBIFORMES   Family COLUMBIDAE

STATUS   Rare.   Restricted to the wooded hills of Rapa Island near the eastern end of the Austral or Tubuai Island chain; it is hunted regularly for food.

DISTRIBUTION   Rapa Island (54 sq. km).   The species is becoming increasingly restricted in range as forest continues to be destroyed (J.C. Thibault 1975, pers. comm.).

POPULATION   Possibly at one time somewhat larger, although there is no evidence of a decline.   At present estimated to be about 125 pairs (J.C. Thibault 1975, pers. comm.).

HABITAT   Wooded hills and valleys of the interior of Rapa Island.   The woodlands continue to be cleared and apparently no consideration is being given to the creation of reserves.   The browsing of introduced goats is also causing a good deal of damage to the forest (1).

CONSERVATION MEASURES TAKEN   All hunting of birds was prohibited in French Polynesia in 1967.   Apparently there is no enforcement of this prohibition on Rapa.

CONSERVATION MEASURES PROPOSED   None known.

REFERENCES   1.   Thibault, J.C. undated.   Fragilite et protection de l'avifaune en Polynésie Française.   Unpublished report to ICBP.

MARIANAS FRUIT DOVE

Ptilinopus roseicapillus (Lesson, 1831)

Order COLUMBIFORMES   Family COLUMBIDAE

STATUS   Vulnerable.   Restricted to four of the Mariana Islands, Western Pacific;
on at least two of them it is believed to have decreased substantially in abundance
quite recently.   Clearing of original forests and excessive hunting have probably
contributed to the decrease, although the fruit-dove is now no longer normally shot.

DISTRIBUTION   Recorded from Guam (541 sq. km), Rota (85.5 sq. km), Tinian (101.2
sq. km) and Saipan (121.7 sq. km) (1).   The present distribution of the species
is unchanged, except that a smaller portion of each island is now occupied.   On
Guam it is presently confined to the northern plateau area, near and below the
cliffline, whereas it once occurred throughout the island (N. Drahos 1976, pers.
comm.).

POPULATION   As recently as 1945, this dove was considered fairly numerous to
abundant on all four islands (1; 2), although a decrease on Guam had already been
noted (3).   Recent observers now estimate that fewer than 200 birds survive on
Guam (N. Drahos 1976, pers. comm.) and it is also quite rare on Tinian (R. Owen
1975, pers. comm.).

HABITAT   Forests, both original growth and second growth scrub on Guam, and on
Saipan also Casuarina trees (1).   On Tinian the species is restricted to the
remaining small area of original forest.   Original forest continues to be cleared
in the southern Marianas (R. Owen 1975, pers. comm.).

CONSERVATION MEASURES TAKEN   Listed on the Guam Endangered Species list, but this
list has not yet been incorporated into the Guam Endangered Species Act of 1975.

CONSERVATION MEASURES PROPOSED   The species was recommended for inclusion in the
U.S. Trust Territories list of endangered species which was being compiled in 1975
(R. Owen, pers. comm.).

REMARKS   This species is shot occasionally when encountered by hunters who are
after the introduced Philippines Turtle Dove, Streptopelia bitorquata.   A
comprehensive survey of this fruit-dove and other endemic birds of the U.S. Trust
Territories is long overdue.

REFERENCES   1.   Baker, R.H. 1951.   The avifauna of Micronesia, its origin,
                    evolution, and distribution.   Univ. Kansas Pubs. Mus. Nat.
                    Hist. 3(1):   1-359.
              2.   Marshall, J.T., Jr. 1949.   The endemic avifauna of Saipan,
                    Tinian, Guam and Palau.   Condor 51:   200-221.
              3.   Baker, R.H. 1947.   Size of bird populations at Guam,
                    Mariana Islands.   Condor 49:   124-125.

SEYCHELLES TURTLE DOVE

Streptopelia picturata rostrata (Bonaparte, 1855)

Order COLUMBIFORMES   Family COLUMBIDAE

STATUS   Endangered.   This well-marked Seychelles race of the Turtle Dove of the
islands of the western Indian Ocean is now extinct, for all practical purposes,
through genetic swamping by the introduced S. p. picturata from Madagascar.

DISTRIBUTION   Formerly occurred throughout the Seychelles, but as early as 1867,
it was eliminated from Mahé by S. p. picturata, which had been introduced a few
years previously (1).   By 1959, birds with the characteristic vinaceous head and
short wings of the endemic subspecies could only be found on Cousin and Cousine
islands, while on Marianne and Félicité there was still evidence of mixed populations (2).   By 1965, the population on Cousin appeared to be entirely mixed, while
individuals of the endemic race were very rare on Cousine (3).   By 1975, the
endemic race was considered extinct as a recognizable entity (4).

POPULATION   No population estimates have been made, but it is clear that the
decline of the Seychelles subspecies dates from the introduction of S. p. picturata
some time prior to 1867 (1).   The decline evidently continued gradually as each
island in the Seychelles was invaded by the introduced race.   By 1975, no pure
S. p. rostrata individuals were thought to remain (4).

HABITAT   Lowland forests and fairly open country (5).   Habitat loss or alteration
has not affected this subspecies.

CONSERVATION MEASURES TAKEN   None known.

CONSERVATION MEASURES PROPOSED   In 1959, selective control of the introduced race
on Cousin and Cousine was recommended as the only means of preserving the endemic
race (2).   The recommendation was not acted upon.

REFERENCES   1.   Newton, E. 1867.   On the land-birds of the Seychelles
                    Archipelago.   Ibis (2)3: 335-360.
              2.   Crook, J.H. 1960.   The present status of certain rare land
                    birds of the Seychelles Islands.   Seychelles Government
                    Bulletin.   5 pages.
              3.   Gaymer, R., Blackman, R.A.A., Dawson, P.G., Penny, M. & Penny,
                    C.M. 1969.   The endemic birds of Seychelles.   Ibis 111:
                    157-176.
              4.   Diamond, A.W. 1975.   Cousin Island Nature Reserve Management
                    Plan 1975-79.   London: ICBP.
              5.   Penny, M. 1974.   The Birds of Seychelles and the Outlying
                    Islands.   New York: Taplinger Publishing Co; London: Collins.

MOHELI GREEN PIGEON

Treron australis griveaudi Benson, 1960

Order COLUMBIFORMES   Family COLUMBIDAE

STATUS   Rare.   Restricted to montane forest on Moheli Island, Comoro group,
western Indian Ocean.   This subspecies is under constant pressure from local
hunters.

DISTRIBUTION   On Moheli this recently described subspecies is confined on the
north side of the island to evergreen forests at altitudes of over 300 m, which
occupy an area of less than 3,000 ha (1), but occurs much lower on the more forested
south side (A.S. Cheke 1977, pers. comm.).   Presumably it was more widespread
before the clearance of the forest at lower elevations (1).

POPULATION   No estimates have been made, but it was suggested that it was probably
not uncommon within its restricted range in 1958 (1); the situation was unchanged in
1975 (A.S. Cheke 1977, pers. comm.).

HABITAT   Evergreen forest along the main ridge of Moheli.   This forest has been
degraded by the planting of banana groves and other human activities, although less
so than the forest of the other main islands of the Comoro group.   Moheli, with an
area of 216 sq. km had in 1958 a human population density of 23 per sq. km, the
lowest in the Comores (1).

CONSERVATION MEASURES TAKEN   None known.

CONSERVATION MEASURES PROPOSED   None known.

REMARKS   The nominate and one other subspecies on Madagascar are not known to be
at risk and there are at least another eleven on the African mainland if the widely
held view that calva and delalandii are synonyms of australis, is accepted.

REFERENCES   1.   Benson, C.W. 1960.   The birds of the Comoro Islands.   Results
                    of the British Ornithologists' Union Centenary Expedition 1958.
                    Ibis 103b: 5-106.

RED-NECKED PARROT or JACQUOT

Amazona arausiaca P.L.S. Müller, 1766

Order PSITTACIFORMES   Family PSITTACIDAE

STATUS   Endangered.   Known from Dominica in the Lesser Antilles, West Indies.
A disastrous decline in the abundance of this species has resulted from continued
hunting pressure in spite of legal protection.

DISTRIBUTION   The species still occurs over the northern two-thirds of the island
of Dominica in the lowlands below 600 m elevation.   Formerly it was also found
regularly in the southern third where it is now only very occasional (1; 2; 3; 4;
5; 6).

POPULATION   There has been a catastrophic decline in the abundance of the Red-
necked Parrot during the past few decades and it is now excessively rare.   In 1975
the total population was estimated at 350 (5; 6).   Hunting is the major cause of
decline, although competition for nest sites and predation of eggs and young by
Pearly-eyed Thrashers Margarops fuscatus may limit reproductive success (6).

HABITAT   Lowland forests of Dominica, usually below 600 m elevation, including
coastal mangroves in certain seasons (1).   It has been suggested the presence of
this species in lowland forests may have the effect of restricting A. imperialis
to the mountain tops because of direct competition, presumably for nest sites and
food (J. Terborgh 1974, pers. comm.).   Mixed flocks of the two species have,
however, been observed and their decline has coincided.   A Canadian company
terminated a massive lumbering program in the lowland forests in 1972, although
not for conservation reasons.   The Dominican government has sought to re-sell
timber rights, but unsuccessfully.   The lowland forests of Dominica are still
among the most extensive and unaltered in the Caribbean, even though trails and new
roads now facilitate entry to many parts formerly considered inaccessible.
Individual trees of more valuable timber species have been extracted from some
remote areas, while piecemeal clearing of forest patches for charcoal production and
for small-scale agriculture continues to present a problem (6).

CONSERVATION MEASURES TAKEN   The species has legal protection, but unrelenting
hunting is widely practised and socially acceptable.   A national park has been
established in the southern part of the island, but it is uncertain whether this
species is still to be found within its boundaries.   A study of its breeding
biology and ecology and that of three other extant, endangered Amazon Parrots of the
Lesser Antilles, has been undertaken (1).

CONSERVATION MEASURES PROPOSED   Captive breeding has been suggested as a means of
preventing the extinction of the species (5).   Other proposals include further
research on distribution, interactions with thrashers and feeding ecology; more
effective control of hunting; creation of a Morne Diablotin National Park, in which
key roosting sites of the species are known to occur; conservation education; and
supervision of timber harvesting (6).

REMARKS   Owing to the fact that the Red-necked Parrot's main haunts are in more
accessible lowlands, it is in greater danger of extinction than the Imperial Parrot.
A determined program of conservation education is needed to convince Dominicans
that their unique parrots should be given protection rather than hunted to
extinction.   The species has not bred in captivity, although eight captive
specimens in the island and two more elsewhere were reported in 1972.

REFERENCES   1.   Nichols, H.A.J. 1974.   Proposal to World Wildlife Fund for
                  study of the four Lesser Antillean Amazon Parrots.
             2.   Kepler, C.B. 1973.   West Indian Parrots.   In N. Sitwell (ed.)
                  Animal Life '73: The world conservation yearbook, pp. 62-67.
                  Danbury Press.
             3.   Forshaw, J. 1973.   Parrots of the World.   Garden City:
                  Doubleday and Co.; Melbourne: Lansdowne Press.
             4.   Snyder, N.F.R. 1973.   Unpublished report dated 12 October, to
                  the Director, Patuxent Wildlife Research Center, U.S. Fish and
                  Wildlife Service.
             5.   Nichols, H.A.J. 1976.   Parrot watching in the Caribbean.
                  SAFE Newsletter 6:   1-8.
             6.   Nichols, H.A.J., Nichols, C.A., Van Vliet, G.B. & Gray, G.S.
                  1976.   Endangered Amazons of Dominica: the Imperial and
                  Arausiaca Parrots.   Unpublished report.

RED-TAILED PARROT

Amazona brasiliensis (Linnaeus, 1758)

Order PSITTACIFORMES   Family PSITTACIDAE

STATUS   Endangered.   This parrot is one of the several endangered species that
occur only in south-eastern Brazil, where forest destruction has been so extensive.

DISTRIBUTION   Recorded from south-east São Paulo, Santa Catarina and Rio Grande
do Sul states of Brazil.   Its present distribution is not precisely known, but it
no longer inhabits substantial portions of its former range and most of the recent
records are from Santa Catarina. (1-3).   Its occurrence in Rio Grande do Sul is
based solely on an old sight record (W. Belton 1975 in litt. to R. Ridgely).   The
last record from São Paulo was in 1972, when young were taken from a nest (H. Sick
1977, pers. comm.).

POPULATION   Unknown, but certainly becoming increasingly sparse (3).

HABITAT   Primary forest, of which only meagre tracts remain within the range of
this species, the extensive forests that once covered south-east Brazil having
been largely destroyed and none of the relict patches being protected (R. Ridgely
1978, pers. comm.).   The species does in fact also occur, together with the
vulnerable Red-spectacled Parrot, Amazona pretrei, in stands of Araucaria pines (1).

CONSERVATION MEASURES TAKEN   The species is protected by Brazilian law, but like
many others can still be acquired for a suitable sum through the cage-bird trade.

CONSERVATION MEASURES PROPOSED   None known.

REMARKS   This species is closely related to and has been considered conspecific
with Amazona rhodocorytha (4), which replaces it to the north, along the eastern
coast of Brazil, and which has also suffered from loss of habitat: there have been
no recent records of it and its survival could well be equally at risk.

REFERENCES   1.   Sick, H. 1969.   Aves brasileiras ameaçadas de extinção e
                      noções gerais de conservação de aves no Brasil.   An. Acad.
                      Brasil. Ciênc. 41 (Supl.): 205-229.
               2.   de Schauensee, R.M. 1966.   The Species of Birds of South
                      America and their Distribution.   Narberth, Pa.: Livingston
                      Publishing Co.
               3.   Forshaw, J.M. 1973.   Parrots of the World.   Garden City,
                      N.Y.: Doubleday and Co.
               4.   Camargo, H.F. de A. 1962.   Sobre as raças geográficas
                      brasileiras de Amazona brasiliensis (L., 1758) (Aves,
                      Psittacidae).   Papeis Dept. Zool. S. Paulo 15: 67-77.

ST. VINCENT PARROT

Amazona guildingii Vigors, 1836

Order PSITTACIFORMES   Family PSITTACIDAE

STATUS   Endangered.   Found only on St. Vincent, Lesser Antilles, West Indies.
The population is now quite small and probably still declining.   It is confined to
several valleys along the mountainous backbone of the island.   The species is
hunted illegally, and significant numbers of young are captured each year for the
pet trade (1; 2; 3; 4).

DISTRIBUTION   Most of the forested mountain slopes and valleys of St. Vincent
between Soufrière in the north and Grande Bonhomme in the south.   Formerly somewhat
more widespread, as the forests extended farther into the lowlands.   The potential
breeding area encompasses about 30 sq. km, although portions of this are unsuitable
because of extraction of most of the large timber (1; 3; 4).

POPULATION   Once very much larger, the population was estimated at 300 to 450
individuals in 1974.   In a normal year about 30 to 40 young birds are captured for
the pet trade.   In 1974, almost no young were reared because of unusually heavy
rains during the breeding season (1; 5).

HABITAT   Humid forests on St. Vincent between 350 and 600 m above sea level.
Large mature trees with cavities are utilized for nesting.   These are most apt to
be found towards the heads of sheltered valleys.   Although trees continue to be
felled on the forest periphery in a desultory manner, the forests are largely
government-owned and relatively secure (I.A.E. Kirby 1974, pers. comm.).

CONSERVATION MEASURES TAKEN   The species is protected by law, although hunting
and robbing of nests continue to take place virtually unchecked.   One hunter
claimed to have killed about 20 in one valley in 1971.   A study of the breeding
biology and ecology of the species is under way (3; I.A.E. Kirby 1974, pers. comm.).

CONSERVATION MEASURES PROPOSED   Reafforestation of some cleared areas is planned
by the St. Vincent government, utilizing indigenous trees important to parrots
rather than the customary exotics.   Delegation of adequate powers to enforce
wildlife ordinances to police and forest officers with a view to reducing the
illegal shooting and capture of parrots and protecting government forest land from
further encroachment.   Establishment of inviolate forest reserves to protect
watersheds and ensure sufficient habitat for this and other endemic species
(1; I.A.E. Kirby pers. comm.).

REMARKS   The St. Vincent Parrot bred in captivity for the first time in 1972 (6).
In addition to 28 captive birds seen on St. Vincent in 1973 (H.A.J. Nichols 1974,
pers. comm.), 16 are known to be held in Barbados, 28 in the United States and 4 in
Europe.

REFERENCES   1.   Nichols, H.A.J. 1974.   Proposal to World Wildlife Fund for
                    study of four Lesser Antillean Amazon Parrots.
              2.   Kepler, C.B. 1973.   West Indian Parrots.   In N. Sitwell (ed.)
                    Animal Life '73: The world conservation yearbook, pp. 62-67.
                    Danbury Press.
              3.   Snyder, N.F.R. 1973.   Unpublished report dated 12 October to
                    the Director, Patuxent Wildlife Research Center, U.S. Fish and
                    Wildlife Service.

4. Andrle, R.F. & Andrle, P.R. 1975. Report on the status and conservation of the Whistling Warbler on St. Vincent, West Indies, with additional observations on the St. Vincent Parrot and Rufous-throated Solitaire. ICBP Bull. 12: 245-251.

5. Nichols, H.A.J. 1974. Report on St. Vincent Parrot research. S.A.F.E. Newsletter No. 2.

6. Berry, R.J. 1974. Successful breeding of the St. Vincent Parrot Amazona guildingii at Houston Zoo. Int. Zoo Yearbook 14: 96-97.

IMPERIAL PARROT or SISSEROU

Amazona imperialis Richmond, 1899

Order PSITTACIFORMES   Family PSITTACIDAE

STATUS   Endangered.   Known only from Dominica, Lesser Antilles, West Indies,
where it is confined to two areas of mountain rain forest.   Hunting of this
gregarious species, by local inhabitants for the pot and by visitors from neighbouring islands for sport, is the most serious threat to this species.   Hunting of
parrots, although illegal, is socially acceptable and widely practised in the
island.

DISTRIBUTION   Montane forest, at altitudes above 450 m and now only in higher
forested portions of Morne Diablotin in the north of Dominica and Morne Anglais in
the south.   Formerly the species probably also occurred at higher elevations on
other mountains (1; 2; 3; 4).

POPULATION   The Imperial Parrot has always been considered a scarce species and is
now very rare indeed.   The Morne Diablotin population was estimated at 30 to 50
in 1973, and that of Morne Anglais was thought to be of a similar order of magnitude (3; J. Terborgh, 1974, pers. comm.).   In 1976, however, surveys revealed a
total population of about 150, of which only about 8 remain in the vicinity of
Morne Anglais (4).

HABITAT   Dwarf rainforest above 450 m dominated by Clusia thickets (1; 3; 4).
It has been suggested that A. imperialis is excluded from the remainder of
Dominica's extensive forests as a result of competition with the Red-necked Parrot
A. arausiaca (J. Terborgh 1974, pers. comm.), although the decline of both has been
simultaneous.   Large-scale logging programs of Dominican forests have been
attempted in the past and may be re-negotiated in the future, but as imperialis
occupies higher, less accessible areas it should be less affected than arausiaca.
General forest deterioration is, however, brought about by selective extraction of
valuable timber species and by clearing of patches for agriculture and charcoal
production (4).

CONSERVATION MEASURES TAKEN   The species is protected from hunting and capture by
law, but law enforcement is not very effective.   A national park has been established, which may protect the small remnant population on Morne Anglais.   An
advisor from the Canadian Nature Federation has worked with the Dominican Government
for two years on the legal and legislative groundwork for a park system, and
training government staff to manage it.   An investigation of the breeding biology
and ecology of this and the three other extant but endangered Lesser Antillean
Amazona species, has been undertaken (1; 4).

CONSERVATION MEASURES PROPOSED   Captive breeding of the species as a means of
preventing its extinction (5).   Other recommendations include further research on
distribution, interaction with thrashers Margarops, and feeding ecology; the
establishment of a Morne Diablotin National Park; more effective control of hunting;
conservation education in the schools; and careful supervision of logging (4).

REMARKS   In spite of the relative security of the damp, inhospitable habitat of
this parrot, it will not be safe until a program of conservation education at all
levels convinces Dominicans of the parrot's rarity and uniqueness, and that it is
worth taking pains to protect it by preventing needless shooting.   The species has
been kept in captivity (including three in Dominica in 1975), but has not yet bred
successfully.

REFERENCES   1.   Nichols, H.A.J. 1974.   Proposal to World Wildlife Fund for
                  study of the four Lesser Antillean Amazon Parrots.
             2.   Kepler, C.B. 1973.   West Indian Parrots.   In N. Sitwell (ed.)
                  Animal Life '73: The world conservation yearbook, pp. 62-67
                  Danbury Press.
             3.   Snyder, N.F.R. 1973.   Unpublished report dated 12 October to
                  the Director, Patuxent Wildlife Research Center, U.S. Fish
                  and Wildlife Service.
             4.   Nichols, H.A.J., Nichols, C.A., Van Vliet, G.B. & Gray, G.S.
                  1976.   Endangered Amazons of Dominica: the Imperial and
                  Arausiaca Parrots.   Unpublished report.
             5.   Nichols, H.A.J. 1976.   Parrot watching in the Caribbean.
                  SAFE Newsletter 6: 1-8.

BAHAMAS PARROT

Amazona leucocephala bahamensis (Bryant, 1867)

Order PSITTACIFORMES   Family PSITTACIDAE

STATUS   Rare.   Still occurs in low numbers on two of the Bahama Islands where it
is locally distributed.   Logging of forests, hunting and trapping have caused its
recent decline.   In the more distant but historic past, the subspecies was far more
extensively distributed (1; 2).

DISTRIBUTION   Formerly known from Inagua, Abaco, Acklin's, Fortune and Long
islands and in the recent geologic past from Crooked and New Providence, Bahama
Islands.   It has been extinct on Fortune and Long for many years, and has
disappeared from Acklin's Island since the 1940s.   It now occurs on Abaco, where
all recent sightings but one have been from the southern end of the island (3;
J. Patterson 1973, pers. comm.).   It is fairly widely distributed at the northern
end of Inagua (2; A. Sprunt IV 1974, pers. comm.).

POPULATION   Once common on all the islands within its historical range, the
species now reaches maximum abundance on Inagua where the population is estimated to
be 400-500 birds and is thought to be stable (A. Sprunt IV 1974, pers. comm.).
Several sightings of flocks of 10 to 100 birds have been made on Abaco, and one
experienced hunter claims to have seen 400-500 at one time (3; J. Patterson,
H.F. Mayfield 1973, pers. comm.).   A more recent, conservative estimate of 275
birds has been made for the Abaco population (A. and C. Kepler, and N. Snyder 1977,
pers. comm.).   None have been found on several recent visits to Acklin's Island.

HABITAT   Native broadleaf woodland, and on Abaco, at least while breeding, pine
woodlands.   The pine woodlands of Abaco were harvested a decade ago, to unknown
effect.   Cats may prey on the parrot, which sometimes nests in limestone rock
cavities (3).

CONSERVATION MEASURES TAKEN   Legal protection.   Listed on Appendix 1 of the 1973
Convention on International Trade in Endangered Species of Wild Fauna and Flora.
A reserve on Inagua, in which this parrot occurs, is administered by the Bahamas
National Trust.   An educational program sponsored by the National Trust has
generated an awareness of its protected status.

CONSERVATION MEASURES PROPOSED   No additional measures are known to have been
suggested.

REMARKS   A. l. leucocephala from Cuba and the Isle of Pines is still relatively
common.   A. l. caymanensis is uncommon and possibly declining on Grand Cayman.
A. l. hesterna is moderately common on Cayman Brac but has been absent for many
years from Little Cayman (R. Noegel 1977, pers. comm. to D. Bruning).   Although the
Bahamas Parrot has been kept in captivity in the past, it has never bred and no
captive specimens are known to survive in 1977.

REFERENCES   1.   Bond, J. 1956.   Check-list of Birds of the West Indies
                    Philadelphia Acad. Nat. Sci.
              2.   Fisher, J., Simon, N. & Vincent, J. 1969.   Wildlife in
                    Danger.   New York: Viking Press; London: Collins.
              3.   King, W.B. 1976. The Bahama Parrot. Bahamas Naturalist,
                    Summer Number 28-30.

CAYMAN BRAC PARROT

Amazona leucocephala hesterna Bangs, 1916

Order PSITTACIFORMES   Family PSITTACIDAE

STATUS   Rare.   Confined to one of the Cayman Islands, Caribbean Sea, where its
population is low.

DISTRIBUTION   Once included both Cayman Brac (c. 52 sq. km) and Little Cayman
(1).   But this parrot is no longer to be found on Little Cayman and has not been
known there within the living memory of most of its inhabitants, although in point
of fact the last record apparently dates back to as recently as 1911 (2).   On
Cayman Brac it occurs along the central ridge, whence the birds frequently make
feeding forays into cultivated land near the coast (3).

POPULATION   There are no early estimates.   Visits lasting several months in
1975 and 1976 revealed a maximum population of about 130 birds (4).   There is no
evidence of decline, but development plans for Cayman Brac make it likely that one
will soon take place.   The population of Little Cayman is unlikely ever to have
been large in view of the shortage of suitable habitat (3).

HABITAT   Dry forest of the ridge top plateau on Cayman Brac, also nearby
agricultural holdings.   A newly constructed road runs the length of the ridge and
will permit house construction on the ridgetop.   A plan for an oil refinery on
Little Cayman could result in additional development on Cayman Brac (3).

CONSERVATION MEASURES TAKEN   The species is listed in Appendix 1 of the 1973
Convention on International Trade in Endangered Species of Wild Fauna and Flora.

CONSERVATION MEASURES PROPOSED   None known.

REMARKS   Six of this subspecies are currently in captivity in Florida and another
5 on Cayman Brac.   The inhabitants of Cayman Brac keep several other parrots
captive, including 8 of the subspecies A. l. caymanensis from Grand Cayman (150 km
distant).   These quite often escape or are set free, with the result that there is
a real threat of hybridization or of other parrot species establishing themselves
and becoming competitors with A. l. hesterna (3).   One other subspecies of
A. leucocephala, A. l. bahamensis from the Bahamas, is sufficiently reduced in
population to be considered rare and included in this Volume, but the subspecies of
Grand Cayman and Cuba are not yet at risk, although the Grand Cayman population is
probably relatively low.

REFERENCES   1.   Bond, J. 1956.   Check-list of Birds of the West Indies.
                   4th ed. Philadelphia: Acad. Nat. Sci.
              2.   Bangs, O. 1916.   A collection of birds from the Cayman
                   Islands.   Harvard Bull. Mus. Comp. Zool. 60: 303-320.
              3.   Noegel, R. 1976.   The Cayman Brac Amazon Parrot.
                   Avicult. Mag. 82: 202-209.
              4.   Noegel, R. 1977.   Captive breeding of Amazona leucocephala
                   leucocephala and subspecies.   Unpublished ms, 8 pp.

RED-SPECTACLED PARROT

Amazona pretrei (Temminck, 1830)

Order PSITTACIFORMES   Family PSITTACIDAE

STATUS   Vulnerable.   Declining in abundance as a result of forest destruction
and formerly also of hunting.   It is especially vulnerable in winter when what
may be the entire population of the species congregates in one forest patch.

DISTRIBUTION   South-eastern Brazil in southern São Paulo and Rio Grande do Sul,
in adjacent Misiones, Argentina, and also possibly in northern Uruguay.   It
probably no longer occurs in São Paulo, is absent from much of Rio Grande do Sul,
which nevertheless remains its present stronghold, and is of uncertain status in
Argentina and Uruguay (1).   Major seasonal movements have been noted (2).

POPULATION   There is evidence of a serious decline, especially towards the end
of the 19th century when hundreds were shot in the hope of winging a few for the
cage-bird trade.   It was once common in south-eastern Brazil, but is now scarce
and decidedly local (2; 3).   In 1971, numbers at its only known winter roost in
Rio Grande do Sul were put at between 10,000 and 30,000 (1), but fell to 5,000 in
1972, after part of the roost had been destroyed by logging (W. Belton 1974, pers.
comm.).   In 1976, the roost was deserted, for reasons unknown (J. Thomé 1976,
pers. comm.), but a flock of about 2,000 began roosting in a Podocarpus lamberti
grove, a few km away from the original site (H. Sick 1977, pers. comm.).

HABITAT   Araucaria forests.   This type of forest has been cleared over extensive
areas of south-eastern Brazil.

CONSERVATION MEASURES TAKEN   The Araucaria grove used in the past by this parrot
for winter roosting, has been protected by the Brazilian Government as a reserve
and the bird itself like most other native species in Brazil nominally enjoys legal
protection.   It is listed in Appendix 1 of the 1973 Convention on International
Trade in Endangered Species of Wild Fauna and Flora.

CONSERVATION MEASURES PROPOSED   The Rio Grande do Sul state government has
proposed a research and conservation project for the species (J. Thomé 1976, pers.
comm.).

REMARKS   The Red-spectacled Parrot is closely related to the Tucuman or Alder
Parrot, Amazona tucumana of northern Argentina, and they are treated as conspecific
by some authors (3; 4).   Both have apparently been recorded in Misiones province,
but it is not clear if they occur or breed sympatrically, although their habitats,
at least, are said to be very different (R. Ridgely 1978, pers. comm.).

REFERENCES   1.   Forshaw, J. 1973.   Parrots of the World.   Garden City,
                   N.Y.: Doubleday and Co.
              2.   Sick, H. 1968.   Vogelwanderungen im kontinentalen Sudamerika.
                   Vogelwarte 24: 217-243.
              3.   Sick, H. 1969.   Aves brasileiras ameaçadas de extinção e
                   noções gerais de conservação de aves no Brasil.   An. Acad.
                   Brasil. Ciênc. 41 (Supl.): 205-229.
              4.   Peters, J.L. 1961.   Check-list of Birds of the World,
                   Vol. 3.   Cambridge: Harvard University Press.

ST. LUCIA PARROT

Amazona versicolor (P.L.S. Müller, 1776)

Order PSITTACIFORMES   Family PSITTACIDAE

STATUS   Endangered.   Restricted to the central mountain forests of St. Lucia,
West Indies, where its numbers continue to dwindle as the result of illegal hunting
and the encroachments of agriculture at the periphery of the forest, causing a
gradual diminution of its habitat.   Forestry projects utilizing exotic timber
species have also made large areas of former habitat unsuitable (1; 2; 3; 4).

DISTRIBUTION   Confined to St. Lucia, where the range formerly included all the
forested slopes of the island, but now restricted to between 50 and 65 sq. km of
forest between Barre de l'Isle and Grand Magasin, east of Morne Gimie (1; 2; 3; 4).

POPULATION   An estimate of 125 birds was made in 1975 (6).   The species was
formerly considered to be far more abundant than it is today.   In 1969, it was
estimated that 40 were still being shot annually (3).   The species is still
declining and the traditional causes of decline are still operating unabated (1; 4).

HABITAT   Indigenous mountain forest.   The species nests in cavities in certain
mature trees, especially the gommier Dacryodes.   The continued presence of trees
old and large enough to have formed cavities may be an essential factor in the
species' survival (1).

CONSERVATION MEASURES TAKEN   Legal protection; but hunting of this species
continues unabated as a result of inadequate enforcement.   A study of the breeding
biology of this parrot and other endangered Lesser Antillean Amazons, in conjunction
with a long-term captive breeding project, is under way (5).

CONSERVATION MEASURES PROPOSED   Establishment of a strict nature reserve in the
area of Morne Gimie is under consideration by the St. Lucia government.   Increased
power for forest wardens, including the power to search a hunter's bag, is essential
for the control of illegal hunting of this species (1; 2; 3; 4).

REMARKS   Although the St. Lucia Parrot has not bred in captivity, there is every
reason to believe it would do so under proper conditions.   In 1976 there were at
least 6 birds in captivity outside St. Lucia.

REFERENCES   1.   Snyder, N.F.R. 1973.   Unpublished report dated 12 October to
                    the Director, Patuxent Wildlife Research Center, U.S. Fish and
                    Wildlife Service.
              2.   Diamond, A.W. 1973.   Habitats and feeding stations of St. Lucia
                    forest birds.   Ibis 115: 313-329.
              3.   Wingate, D.B. 1969.   A summary of the status of the St. Lucia
                    Parrot Amazona versicolor and other rare native birds of St.
                    Lucia based on a survey of the island from April 22 to May 15,
                    1969, conducted under a grant from the International Committee
                    for Bird Protection.   Unpublished report.
              4.   Kepler, C.B. 1973.   West Indian Parrots.   In N. Sitwell (ed.)
                    Animal Life '73: The World Conservation Yearbook, pp. 62-67.
                    Danbury Press.
              5.   Nichols, H.A.J. 1974.   Proposal to World Wildlife Fund for study
                    of the four Lesser Antillean Amazon Parrots.
              6.   Nichols, H.A.J. 1976.   Parrot watching in the Caribbean.
                    SAFE Newsletter 6: 1-8.

PUERTO RICAN PARROT

Amazona vittata (Boddaert, 1783)

Order PSITTACIFORMES   Family PSITTACIDAE

STATUS   Critically endangered.   Restricted to portions of one forest at the
eastern end of Puerto Rico, West Indies.   The population is now among the lowest of
any species of bird for which accurate figures are known, and most of the factors
responsible for its decline still pertain.   An intensive program of research and
management has been under way since 1969.   It is slightly reassuring that since
1971 the population in the wild has remained stable, while during the same period a
nucleus has been obtained for captive breeding.

DISTRIBUTION   Formerly occurred throughout forested portions of Puerto Rico.   A
subspecies inhabiting nearby Culebra Island became extinct last century.   Since
1930, restricted to Luquillo Experimental Forest at the north-eastern end of Puerto
Rico.   More recently the parrot has been confined to about 2,000 ha of the 11,200
ha forest, comprising the upper portions of the Mamayes and Espiritu Santo river
drainages.   Individual parrots may still rarely wander into lower forests or farm
land adjacent to Luquillo Forest (1; 2; C. Kepler and N. Snyder 1975, pers. comm.).

POPULATION   In the 19th century this species was common on Puerto Rico, but by
1912 only small populations could be found.   A census conducted between 1953 and
1956 established that a flock of about 200 birds survived in the Luquillo Forest,
which probably constituted most of the population at that time.   By 1962 the
largest flock that could be found during a census was 13 birds (1).   In 1969,
scarcely 20 birds remained in the total population, and between 1971 and 1974 the
wild population stayed at 14-16 birds; 3, 3, 6 and 8 birds fledged in each of the
years 1973 to 1976; in 1977 only 3 pairs bred (C. Kepler and N. Snyder 1975, 1977,
pers. comm.).

HABITAT   Forest, both montane and lowland, also mangroves.   The greatest decline
in numbers of this species took place as the lowland forests of Puerto Rico were
cleared last century and the early part of this century.   Presently less than one
per cent of Puerto Rico's land area is unaltered by man and the range of the parrot
may now well be in marginal or submarginal habitat.   The heavy rainfall in the
montane rainforest where the parrot still occurs has recently been responsible for
mortality of adult birds: nest holes in large Colorado (Cyrilla) trees frequently
flood or the trees themselves are blown down by storms.   The lack of suitable nest
holes may presently be a limiting factor in reproduction.   The Pearly-eyed Thrasher
Margarops fuscatus, which has become abundant on Puerto Rico only recently, competes
for nest sites and preys on eggs or young parrots.   Red-tailed Hawks Buteo
jamaicensis prey on adult and juvenile birds.   Rats are also known to prey on nest
contents.   Parrot chicks are often infested with bot fly warbles, which can be
fatal if the warbles become too numerous (C. Kepler and N. Snyder 1975, pers. comm.).

CONSERVATION MEASURES TAKEN   Fully protected by Puerto Rico Commonwealth and U.S.
Federal law, the species is entirely confined within the boundaries of a U.S.
national forest.   Biologists of the U.S. Fish and Wildlife Service have studied
the species intensively since 1969.   Predator control programs have been conducted.
Manipulation of nest cavities has effectively discouraged predation of nest contents
by thrashers.   A program of captive breeding is under way.   Presently there are
three birds at Patuxent Wildlife Research Center in Maryland, U.S.A., and seven in
captivity in Luquillo Forest.   No breeding has taken place yet in captivity,

although prospects for success are hopeful. Many chicks used to be taken illegally from nests in the wild for sale as cage birds, but by 1970 the practice was believed to have been effectively stopped (N. Snyder 1975, 1977, pers. comm.).

CONSERVATION MEASURES PROPOSED   Continuation of the research and conservation programs.   Continuation of captive breeding program for eventual restocking of areas within former range of species, although an attempt in the 1940s to restock the Toro Negro area in the island's center ended in failure (2).   Assessment of possible threats to the population through competition or hybridization with Hispaniola Parrots A. ventralis which are now established in lowland Puerto Rico. Control of Red-tailed Hawks in the valleys where the parrots are breeding has also been suggested (N. Snyder 1975, 1977, pers. comm.).

REMARKS   The careful and imaginative research and conservation activities undertaken to halt the decline of this species at the last possible moment are witness to the dedication of the biologists and administrators responsible.   Their work has shown that a complex of factors may act in concert to depress a population but that with patience and determination comes understanding and a measure of success.

REFERENCES   1.   Forshaw, J. 1973.   Parrots of the World.   Garden City, N.Y.:
                  Doubleday and Co.; Melbourne: Lansdowne Press.
              2.   U.S. Fish and Wildlife Service, 1973.   Threatened Wildlife
                  of the United States.   U.S. Bur. Sport Fish. Wildl. Res.
                  Pub. 114.

GLAUCOUS MACAW

Anodorhynchus glaucus (Vieillot, 1816)

Order PSITTACIFORMES   Family PSITTACIDAE

STATUS   Endangered, if indeed the species still exists.   There have been no
recent records and inhabitants in the areas where it was known to occur appear
to have no knowledge of it.

DISTRIBUTION   Paraguay, northern Argentina in Misiones and Corrientes provinces
(from which two of the few specimens are derived) and formerly south-eastern
Brazil; possibly also Artigas department in north-western Uruguay.   Nothing is
known of its present distribution.   In the 19th century it was most often
recorded along the lower Paraguay, Paraná and Uruguay rivers. (1-3; R. Ridgely
1978, pers. comm.).

POPULATION   Unknown, but likely to be very low, if indeed the species is still
extant in the wild.   Bird dealers of Asunción, Paraguay, have been quite unable
to obtain any specimens for at least three decades.

HABITAT   Subtropical forest.   Little of such forest survives in south-eastern
Brazil, but there are still some fairly extensive tracts within this macaw's
former range, for example in south-eastern Paraguay and north-eastern Argentina.
It may have been especially associated with gallery forest, which would have made
it vulnerable to hunting, but a good deal of gallery forest is relatively intact
and other likely hunting targets such as the curassows, Crax spp., have managed
to survive in it (R. Ridgely 1978, pers. comm.).

CONSERVATION MEASURES TAKEN   Listed in Appendix 1 of the 1973 Convention on
International Trade in Endangered Species of Wild Fauna and Flora.   Protected by
law in Brazil.

CONSERVATION MEASURES PROPOSED   None known.

REFERENCES   1.   Forshaw, J.M. 1973.   Parrots of the World.   Garden City,
                    N.Y.: Doubleday and Co.
              2.   de Schauensee, R.M. 1966.   The Species of Birds of South
                    America and their Distribution.   Narberth, Pa.: Livingston
                    Publishing Co.
              3.   Sick, H. 1969.   Aves brasileiras ameaçadas de extinção e
                    noções gerais de conservação de aves no Brasil.   An. Acad.
                    Brasil. Ciênc. 41 (Supl.):   205-229.

LEAR'S or INDIGO MACAW

Anodorhynchus leari Bonaparte, 1856

Order PSITTACIFORMES   Family PSITTACIDAE

STATUS   Endangered.   The haunts of this little-known but striking macaw were
discovered for the first time in 1978.   The great demand for it among aviculturists
constitutes the most serious threat to its continuing existence.

DISTRIBUTION   This enigmatic species has hitherto been known only from captive
birds.   A captive bird in 1950 was said to come from Juazeiro on the São
Francisco River, which here forms the northern border of Bahia state with
Pernambuco, but that immediate vicinity is unsuited to macaws and if Juazeiro were
really the provenance of the specimen, it must surely have been transported there,
perhaps along the São Francisco river (R. Ridgely 1978, pers. comm.).   Late in
1978, the breeding locality of this macaw was discovered in a tightly circumscribed
and virtually inaccessible part of Bahia state (H. Sick 1979, pers. comm.).

POPULATION   The recently discovered population of this macaw is said to be quite
small (H. Sick 1979, pers. comm.).

HABITAT   Precise details are not yet available other than that the area where
these macaws were recently discovered was very dry and desertlike.

CONSERVATION MEASURES TAKEN   The species is listed in Appendix 1 of the 1973
Convention on International Trade in Endangered Species of Wild Fauna and Flora
and has legal protection in Brazil.   Quite unexpectedly this macaw was discovered
to inhabit an existing ecological reserve, which should give it some additional
protection.

CONSERVATION MEASURES PROPOSED   Expansion of the boundaries of the ecological
reserve inhabited by this species, with the aim of protecting a larger part of its
population (H. Sick 1979, pers. comm.).

REMARKS   It has been suggested that Lear's Macaw is of hybrid origin, the result
of crosses between A. glaucus and A. hyacinthinus (3), but this view can now be
discounted following the discovery of a wild population.   In 1978 there were said
to be 4 Indigo Macaws in captivity in Europe (G. Smith 1978, pers. comm.).

REFERENCES   1.   Forshaw, J.M. 1973.   Parrots of the World.   Garden City,
                   N.Y.: Doubleday and Co.
              2.   Pinto, O.M. de O. 1950.   Miscelânea ornitologica, V.
                   Papeis Dept. Zool. São Paulo 9: 361-365.
              3.   Voous, K.H. 1965.   Specimens of Lear's Macaw in the
                   Zoological Museum of Amsterdam.   l'Oiseau et R.F.O.
                   35 (no. special): 153-155.

GUAYAQUIL GREAT GREEN MACAW

Ara ambigua guayaquilensis Chapman, 1925

Order PSITTACIFORMES   Family PSITTACIDAE

STATUS   Indeterminate.   This subspecies of the Great Green Macaw now occurs
very locally in Ecuador, where its decline is attributable to forest destruction
and probably also to being hunted for food and for the cage bird trade.

DISTRIBUTION   Known only from lowland western Ecuador, particularly the hills
near Guayaquil (1).   Its precise range has not yet been determined, but may now
be restricted to the Chongon Hills, north-west of Guayaquil, whence the type
specimen came (R. Ridgely 1977, pers. comm.).

POPULATION   No estimate has been attempted, but this subspecies is believed to
be now quite rare (R. Ridgely 1977, pers. comm.), although it was rated as not
uncommon in the Chongon Hills in 1926 (1) and was recorded in small numbers in the
same locality in July 1978 (R. Ridgely 1978, pers. comm.).

HABITAT   Lowland forest and adjacent clearings.   Much of this forest has been
felled in Ecuador, but there is still a substantial amount in the Chongon Hills,
despite the fact that in 1978 it was beginning to be invaded by settlers, following
the building of roads for selective extraction of timber (R. Ridgely 1978, pers.
comm.).

CONSERVATION MEASURES TAKEN   None known.

CONSERVATION MEASURES PROPOSED   Legal protection for this macaw has been
recommended to the Ecuadorian government (R. Ridgely 1977, pers. comm.).

REMARKS   The subspecies is apparently segregated geographically from the
nominate race of southern Middle America south to the valley of the Dagua river,
which enters the sea near Buenaventura in south-western Colombia (2).   The latter
has declined seriously in parts of its range, but still occurs in reasonably
secure numbers in certain localities, notably in Nicaragua and Darién, Panama (3).

REFERENCES   1.   Chapman, F.M. 1926.   The distribution of bird-life in
                    Ecuador: a contribution to a study of the origin of
                    Andean bird-life.   Bull. Amer. Mus. Nat. Hist. 55.
              2.   de Schauensee, R.M. 1949.   The birds of the Republic of
                    Colombia.   Segundo entrega: Accipitridae-Picidae.
                    Caldasia 23: 381-644.
              3.   Ridgely, R. 1976.   Macaw status survey.   World Wildlife
                    Fund, U.S. Appeal, Project 61.   Unpublished report.

WAGLER'S or CANINDE MACAW

Ara caninde (Wagler, 1832)

Order PSITTACIFORMES   Family PSITTACIDAE

STATUS   Indeterminate. Presumably occurs in south central South America, but
there are no recent records from the wild and the provenance of the very few birds
that have appeared in captivity in the last few years is in doubt.

DISTRIBUTION   Reputedly south-eastern Bolivia, Paraguay and north-western
Argentina, but recent enquiries in this region lead to the conclusion that this
macaw no longer occurs in Paraguay, if it ever actually did (R. Ridgely 1978,
pers. comm.). It is now most likely to be found in south-eastern Bolivia, where
confusion with the closely related Blue-and-yellow Macaw Ara ararauna is likely,
and in north-western Argentina (1; 2; Ridgely 1978, pers. comm.; see also under
REMARKS).

POPULATION   Unknown. Judging by the very few reports of this macaw and its
great scarcity in captive collections, it is likely to be quite rare. A sighting
of a pair of either this macaw or the Blue-and-yellow Macaw in Salta province,
Argentina, in the late 1940s is the most recent report within the presumed range
of the former (G. Hoy 1977, pers. comm. to R. Ridgely).

HABITAT   Probably dry deciduous forest, of which substantial and largely
undisturbed areas still exist in north-western Argentina and south-eastern
Bolivia (R. Ridgely 1978, pers. comm.).

CONSERVATION MEASURES TAKEN   None known.

CONSERVATION MEASURES PROPOSED   None known.

REMARKS   The taxonomic relationship between this macaw and the more common and
widespread Blue-and-yellow Macaw A. ararauna is in doubt. A. caninde is
frequently considered to be a subspecies of the latter, replacing it at the south-
western margin of its range. Some have speculated that A. caninde is a localized
age class of A. ararauna, but this seems most unlikely. In fact, the tendency of
macaws to form species pairs, e.g. Ara militaris with ambigua and A. macao with
chloroptera, suggests that treatment of A. caninde and ararauna as separate
species, conceivably overlapping in Bolivia, should not be discounted.

Only one A. caninde is presently said to be in captivity, in the United States;
another died recently at a German Zoo.

REFERENCES   1.   de Schauensee, R.M. 1966. The Species of Birds of South
                    America and their Distribution. Narberth, Pa.: Livingston
                    Publishing Co.
              2.   Forshaw, J.M. 1973. Parrots of the World. Garden City,
                    N.Y.: Doubleday and Co.

GOLDEN PARAKEET

Aratinga guarouba (Gmelin, 1788)

Order PSITTACIFORMES   Family PSITTACIDAE

STATUS   Vulnerable.   Occurs only in one circumscribed area of northern South
America and much in demand for the cage bird trade.   Forest destruction has also
become a problem which threatens its survival.

DISTRIBUTION   Northern Brazil from the Xingu River, Pará, to north-western
Maranhão (1; 2).

POPULATION   No population estimates have been made, but the parakeet was already
becoming rare by 1946 (3).   Increasingly rapid destruction of its forest habitat
has undoubtedly contributed to its further decline (R. Ridgely 1978, pers. comm.).

HABITAT   Tropical rainforest.   None of this within the parakeet's range
receives any kind of protection, and meanwhile development and colonization of
extensive areas recently cleared of forest continues at a rapid pace (R. Ridgely
1978, pers. comm.).

CONSERVATION MEASURES TAKEN   The species is listed in Appendix 1 of the 1973
Convention on International Trade in Endangered Species of Wild Fauna and Flora.
It has legal protection in Brazil, but specimens can still be readily acquired
through what is now the illicit trade in captive birds.

CONSERVATION MEASURES PROPOSED   None known.

REMARKS   This parakeet has bred in captivity on a number of occasions and
its dramatic coloration make it one of the most highly coveted species for
parrot fanciers (4).

REFERENCES   1.   de Schauensee, R.M. 1966.   The Species of Birds of South
                    America and their Distribution.   Narberth, Pa.: Livingston
                    Publishing Co.
              2.   Forshaw, J.M. 1973.   Parrots of the World.   Garden City,
                    N.Y.: Doubleday and Co.
              3.   Pinto, O.M. de O. 1946.   Aves brasileiras da família dos
                    papagaios.   Relat. Inst. Bot. São Paulo: 126-129.
              4.   Low, R. 1972.   The Parrots of South America.   London:
                    John Gifford Ltd.

RUFOUS-FRONTED PARAKEET

Bolborhynchus ferrugineifrons (Lawrence, 1880)

Order PSITTACIFORMES   Family PSITTACIDAE

STATUS   Indeterminate.   Found only in a limited area of the Colombian Andes,
but there have been no records since the 1950s.   Forest destruction may pose a
serious threat to this species.

DISTRIBUTION   The species has been recorded in Colombia from the Tolima and
Cauca divisions in the central part of the central Andes (1; 2).   Its present
distribution is unknown.

POPULATION   No information is available on the population of this species.   It
was last collected in 1955, north of Purace volcano in the Cauca division of
Colombia, since when there have been no reliable records, although recent sightings
of a parakeet in high-altitude scrubland surrounding Mt. Nevada del Ruiz, on the
Tolima/Caldas boundary, may be referable to this species (R. Ridgely 1977, pers.
comm.).

HABITAT   Temperate páramo scrub on mountain slopes of the central Andes, up to
an elevation of 3,750 m (1).   This parakeet also occurs in scrub forest, which,
in the area where the species is known to have occurred, has been reduced to small
isolated patches (R. Ridgely 1977, pers. comm.).

CONSERVATION MEASURES TAKEN   None known.

CONSERVATION MEASURES PROPOSED   None known.

REFERENCES   1.   Forshaw, J.M. 1973.   Parrots of the World.   Garden City,
                     N.Y.: Doubleday and Co.
              2.   de Schauensee, R.M. 1970.   A Guide to the Birds of South
                     America.   Wynnewood, Pa.: Livingston Publishing Co.

SEYCHELLES LESSER VASA PARROT

Coracopsis nigra barklyi E. Newton, 1867

Order PSITTACIFORMES   Family PSITTACIDAE

STATUS   Endangered.   Although this parrot is quite conspicuous in one valley in
the Seychelles, it is largely restricted to that valley and its population is very
small.   Were it not for the protection at present afforded by its habitat, it
might well be considered among the most endangered birds of the world.

DISTRIBUTION   Known only from Praslin (67 sq. km), Seychelles Archipelago, where
it was reported from several localities in 1865 (1), but by 1939 had become confined
to a small area of hills in the eastern half of the island (2).   Most recent
observations of the parrot have been in and around the Vallée de Mai, except for its
occasional feeding forays to nearby fruit trees (3; 4; 5).   An early record of the
subspecies from Marianne is considered doubtful (6).   A study in 1976 showed that
about 70 per cent of the population were roosting in the Vallée de Mai, but some
six additional patches of indigenous forest nearby were also found to be used for
roosting and may possibly provide some nesting sites.

POPULATION   No early estimates were made.   In 1939, the parrot was common within
its limited range (2) and was even considered a pest in the recent past, flocks of
as many as 50 birds or more being said to raid fruit trees in neighbouring areas of
cultivation (5).   In 1965, a census revealed a certain total of 17 birds and an
estimate of 30 to 50 for the entire population (4).   Since then the population may
have become rather more stable thanks to protection of the small area of remaining
habitat; a synchronized count by members of an expedition to the island in 1976
suggested a total of 90 ± 20 (7).

HABITAT   Forests dominated by endemic Seychelles palms, among which Verschaffeltia
splendida, although rather scarce, is a key food plant for the parrot.   These
forests once covered several of the islands, but were destroyed by continual cutting
and burning.   The parrot's decline undoubtedly coincided with the reduction of the
palm forest area on Praslin to its present limits in the Vallée de Mai and on
adjacent hillsides in the east centre of the island.   The valley has the finest
remaining stand of the remarkable Coco-de-mer Lodoicea maldivica, which is now
carefully protected, and the continuous succession of fruiting palms is no doubt
responsible for the present concentration of the parrots in the vicinity.   Fruit
trees are now being planted in the valley to make it still more attractive to them
(4; 5).

CONSERVATION MEASURES TAKEN   Listed in Appendix 2 of the 1973 Convention on
International Trade in Endangered Species of Wild Fauna and Flora.   Legal
protection in the Seychelles from shooting or capture.   A Nature Reserve has been
established in the upper section of the Vallée de Mai and the number of introduced
fruit trees has been supplemented by further plantings.

CONSERVATION MEASURES PROPOSED   National Park status has been suggested for the
Vallée de Mai Nature Reserve and the surrounding slopes (8).   A proposal to
provide nest-boxes, although approved in principle (4), was still awaiting
implementation in November 1976.   A policy of leaving dead (introduced) Albizia
and Acacia trees standing, after ring-barking them, has also been suggested as a
method of providing additional nest-sites (7), there being little doubt that
shortage of such sites is at present the principal limiting factor.

<u>REMARKS</u>   Monitoring and provision of nest-boxes should be continued and some attention should perhaps be paid to the possibility of competition for nest sites from the introduced mynah <u>Acridotheres</u> <u>tristis</u> and, if this proves to be the case, to methods of dealing with the problem.

<u>REFERENCES</u>   1.   Newton, E. 1867.   On the land-birds of the Seychelles Archipelago.   <u>Ibis</u> (2)3:   335-360.

2.   Vesey-Fitzgerald, D. 1940.   The birds of the Seychelles, Pt. 1. <u>Ibis</u> (14)4:   480-489.

3.   Crook, J.H. 1960.   The present status of certain rare land birds of the Seychelles Islands.   Seychelles Government Bulletin, 5 pages.

4.   Penny, M. 1968.   Endemic birds of the Seychelles.   <u>Oryx</u> 9: 267-275.

5.   Penny, M. 1974.   <u>The Birds of Seychelles and the Outlying Islands</u>.   New York: Taplinger Publishing Co.; London: Collins.

6.   Forshaw, J. 1973.   <u>Parrots of the World</u>.   Garden City, New York: Doubleday and Co.;   Melbourne: Lansdowne Press.

7.   Evans, P.G.H. 1977.   Aberdeen University Expedition to Praslin, Seychelles, 1976.   Preliminary Report (cyclostyled).

8.   Seychelles Government, 1971.   Conservation policy in the Seychelles.   Seychelles Government Printer.

SPIX'S or LITTLE BLUE MACAW

Cyanopsitta spixii (Wagler, 1832)

Order PSITTACIFORMES   Family PSITTACIDAE

STATUS   Vulnerable.   Although there are several examples of this attractive
macaw in captivity, virtually nothing is known of its status in the wild.   In
contrast to the majority of South American parrots which face devastating habitat
destruction, excessive capture for the cage bird trade is the most serious threat
to this species.

DISTRIBUTION   Confined to the area of east central Brazil, which includes
southern Piauí, north-western Bahia, southern Maranhão and eastern Goiás (1; 2;
R. Ridgely 1978, pers. comm.).   The sighting of 3 in 1975, in north-western
Bahia, is the only recent record by an ornithologist of the species in the wild
(H. Sick 1976, pers. comm.).

POPULATION   Unknown, although no doubt quite small.   Several of the specimens
offered for sale in the last few years have been aviary-reared, the offspring of
a captive pair that bred several times in São Paulo, but recently died.   Only
wild-caught birds are at present being offered for sale in Brazil (3; H. Sick
1977, R. Ridgely 1978, pers. comms).

HABITAT   Buriti palm groves and adjacent caatinga woodland.   Suitable habitat
is local and rather scattered, but not seriously threatened with destruction (4;
R. Ridgely 1978, pers. comm.).

CONSERVATION MEASURES TAKEN   The species is listed in Appendix 1 of the 1973
Convention on International Trade in Endangered Species of Wild Fauna and Flora
and protected by law in Brazil, but nevertheless still occasionally but illicitly
finds its way onto the market in the pet trade.

CONSERVATION MEASURES PROPOSED   None known.

REMARKS   This species has only rarely been bred in captivity.   Because most
captive specimens are in private hands, there has been no comprehensive program
to ensure that they are paired and housed under conditions conducive to breeding.
Thirteen were in captivity in Europe in 1978 (G. Smith 1978, pers. comm.).

REFERENCES   1.   de Schauensee, R.M. 1966.   The Species of Birds of South
                    America and their Distribution.   Narberth, Pa.: Livingston
                    Publishing Co.
              2.   Forshaw, J.M. 1973.   Parrots of the World.   Garden City,
                    N.Y.: Doubleday and Co.
              3.   Sick, H. 1969.   Aves brasileiras ameaçadas de extinção e
                    noções gerais de conservação de aves no Brasil.   An. Acad.
                    Brasil. Ciênc. 41 (Supl.): 205-229.
              4.   de Schauensee, R.M. 1970.   A Guide to the Birds of South
                    America.   Wynnewood, Pa.: Livingston Publishing Co.

CHATHAM ISLAND YELLOW-CROWNED or FORBES'S PARAKEET

Cyanoramphus auriceps forbesi Rothschild, 1893

Order PSITTACIFORMES   Family PSITTACIDAE

STATUS   Endangered.   Restricted to one very small island in the Chatham Islands,
800 kilometres east of New Zealand.   The subspecies is beginning to recolonize a
second island but is unfortunately hybridizing with a closely related species.
The scrub woodland on the small island which is its stronghold is gradually
receding (1).

DISTRIBUTION   Formerly occurred on Mangere (112 ha) and Little Mangere (16 ha)
Islands, some birds migrating seasonally to Pitt Island, 2.5 km distant. Following
deforestation of Mangere the subspecies was restricted to Little Mangere, except for
occasional stragglers (1), but since the removal of sheep and consequent revegetation has now begun to recolonize the larger island, where, however, some
hybridization with the Chatham Island Red-crowned Parakeet Cyanoramphus novaezelandiae chathamensis has taken place (1).

POPULATION   Apparently quite large in the 19th century within its limited range.
In 1937 the population, which by then was restricted to Little Mangere, was
estimated at over 100 birds (2) and a similar figure was arrived at in 1961.   But
subsequent censuses in 1968 and 1973 suggested that the earlier ones may have been
optimistic and the present population is estimated at no more than 20-30 (1).

HABITAT   Low scrubby forest, occupying only about 4 ha of the summit area of
Little Mangere.   In the 1960s muttonbirders visited this otherwise nearly
inaccessible island by helicopter to hunt shearwaters, causing considerable damage
to the vegetation.   Although there are now no helicopters left in the Chatham
Islands, a succession of dry seasons, wind and storms, and the constant loosening of
the soil substrate by a high density of burrowing petrels, has continued to bring
about a gradual deterioration of the scrub cover (1).

CONSERVATION MEASURES TAKEN   The subspecies has been given full legal protection.
Mangere Island, where it was once most abundant, was purchased recently by the New
Zealand government and made a Reserve for the Preservation of Flora and Fauna in
1967.   The remaining sheep were removed in the following year and the New Zealand
Wildlife Service is making strenuous efforts to speed regeneration of scrub forest
(1).

CONSERVATION MEASURES PROPOSED   The Wildlife Service has attempted to secure
Little Mangere as a reserve, but its Maori owners insist on retaining their
muttonbirding rights, although this activity, which has in the past resulted in
widespread damage to the island vegetation, is now illegal throughout the Chatham
group.   Negotiations are currently deadlocked, but a resolution of the problem is
essential, if the future of the two endangered taxa surviving on this small island
is to be assured.   The further threat of hybridization of the population now
establishing itself on the larger Mangere Island needs to be constantly monitored
and, if necessary, dealt with by management practices that would favour it at the
expense of the Red-crowned Parakeet, which already has a satisfactory centre of
abundance not far away on South-East Island (D. Merton 1974, pers. comm.).

REMARKS   The nominate race C. a. auriceps is fairly common on North, South and
several offshore islands of New Zealand.

REFERENCES   1.   Merton, D.V. & Bell, B.D., date not ascertained.   Endemic birds
                 of the Chatham Islands.   New Zealand Wildlife Service:
                 unpublished manuscript.
             2.   Fleming, C.A. 1939.   Birds of the Chatham Islands, Part 2.
                 Emu 38:   492-509.

ORANGE-FRONTED PARAKEET

Cyanoramphus malherbi Souancé, 1857

Order PSITTACIFORMES   Family PSITTACIDAE

STATUS   Endangered.   Known with certainty only from South Island, New Zealand.
This parakeet has been reported only six times this century, most recently in 1965.

DISTRIBUTION   Formerly reported from Fiordland to Marlborough, South Island, New
Zealand.   There is a record of a single specimen collected on Stewart Island.
Early references to the occurrence of this species in North Island and its offshore
islands as well as 400 km south of South Island in the Auckland group, are now
considered questionable.   In general, its South Island range was considered to be
much the same as that of the Yellow-crowned Parakeet (1; 2).

POPULATION   Never as large as that of the Yellow-crowned Parakeet Cyanoramphus
a. auriceps or of the Red-crowned Parakeet Cyanoramphus n. novaezelandiae, the
population of this parakeet crashed in the 1890s as did those of the other two, its
sharp decline having been preceded by a build-up in numbers, especially around
orchards.   Since 1900, there have been records from only six localities, three of
them substantiated by specimens and all but one at the north end of South Island (1),
and the species has shown none of the same signs of recovery as its two congeners.

HABITAT   Although this parakeet acquired an early reputation for occurring in
alpine habitats, most of the 19th century reports of its presence were from
altitudes of 600 m to 750 m, occasionally even lower, in heavily forested hills and
mountains.   It was rarely if ever seen outside this zone, which it shared with the
Yellow-crowned Parakeet (1; 2).

CONSERVATION MEASURES TAKEN   The species has been given full legal protection.

CONSERVATION MEASURES PROPOSED   Continuing efforts to establish the existence and
status of the species.

REMARKS   It has quite recently been pointed out that differences in measurements
between this species and the Yellow-crowned Parakeet are not statistically significant, that colour differences between the two are explicable in terms of simple
genetic control of the extent and intensity of carotenoid pigmentation, that there
are no recorded differences in habitat preference, voice, food or distribution, and
that Orange-fronted Parakeets have been most often seen in the company of flocks of
the Yellow-crowned species.   All of this suggests that the Orange-fronted Parakeet
is merely a colour-morph of the Yellow-crowned Parakeet, although this conclusion
has not received wide acceptance.   Because of the obvious present rarity of
Orange-fronted Parakeets, there may never be an opportunity to obtain direct
evidence bearing on the problem, namely through observation of mixed pairs and their
offspring (3).

REFERENCES   1.   Harrison, M. 1970.   The Orange-fronted Parakeet Cyanoramphus
                     malherbi.   Notornis 17:   115-125.
              2.   Falla, R.A., Sibson, R.B., & Turbott, E.G. 1967.   A Field Guide
                     to the Birds of New Zealand and Outlying Islands.   Boston:
                     Houghton Mifflin Co.; London: Collins.
              3.   Holyoak, D.T. 1974.   Cyanoramphus malherbi, is it a colour
                     morph of C. auriceps?   Bull. Brit. Orn. Club 94(1): 4-9.

NORFOLK ISLAND PARAKEET

Cyanoramphus novaezelandiae cookii (G.R. Gray, 1859)

Order PSITTACIFORMES   Family PSITTACIDAE

STATUS   Endangered.   Occurs only on Norfolk Island, South West Pacific, where it
is restricted in range and very low in numbers.   It may be in the process of being
displaced by the introduced Rosella Platycercus elegans, with which it probably
competes for nest sites.   Many were shot, especially in the 19th century, when
raiding fruit trees in agricultural areas.

DISTRIBUTION   Once very common over most of the 35 sq. km of Norfolk Island (1),
this parakeet has been largely restricted since 1908 to the indigenous forest, of
which the last remaining area, estimated at a scant 405 hectares around Mount Pitt
and Mount Bates, now constitutes a forest reserve (2; 3; 4; 5; G. Mees 1974, pers.
comm.).

POPULATION   Had declined to not more than 20 individuals in January 1969 (G. Mees
1974, pers. comm.), having been considered very scarce as long ago as 1908 (5).

HABITAT   Now to a large extent the single patch of rainforest at the north-
western end of the island.   But the parakeet is still known to visit gardens when
trees are fruiting and also occurs in Eucalyptus plantations adjacent to the
indigenous forest (2; 4).

CONSERVATION MEASURES TAKEN   Although the parakeet is apparently accorded legal
protection, a licence to shoot it is still obtainable and nothing has been done to
stop the lumbering program which affects the Mount Pitt forest reserve or virtually
the entire range of the subspecies (1).

CONSERVATION MEASURES PROPOSED   Upgrading the Mount Pitt forest reserve to
National Park status, with adequate funds for fencing, to prevent further degradation of the forest by cattle, and complete and effective exclusion of any more
roads or trails through the forested area (1).   Scientific assessment of
competitive interactions between this parakeet and the Rosella, leading possibly to
control of the latter species.

REMARKS   Several other subspecies of novaezelandiae are still to be found in New
Zealand, the Antipodes, Kermadec and Chatham Islands, and in New Caledonia.   None
of them is known to be at risk, but two other subspecies, C. n. erythrotis of
Macquarie Island and C. n. subflavescens of Lord Howe Island have become extinct
(6).

REFERENCES   1.   Turner, J.S., Smithers, C.N. & Hoogland, R.D. 1968.   The
                    Conservation of Norfolk Island.   Austral. Cons. Found.
                    Special Pub. No. 1.
              2.   Smithers, C.N. & Disney, H.J. de S. 1969.   The distribution of
                    terrestrial and freshwater birds on Norfolk Island.   Austral.
                    Zool. 15: 127-140.
              3.   Disney, H.J. de S. & Smithers, C.N. 1972.   The distribution of
                    terrestrial and freshwater birds on Lord Howe Island, in
                    comparison with Norfolk Island.   Austral. Zool. 17: 1-11.

4. Wakelin, H. 1968.   Some notes on the birds of Norfolk Island.
    Notornis 15: 156-176.
5. Hull, A.F.B. 1909.   The birds of Lord Howe and Norfolk Islands.
    Proc. Linn. Soc. N.S.W. 34: 636-693.
6. Forshaw, J.M. 1973.   Parrots of the World.   Garden City;
    Doubleday and Co.; Melbourne: Lansdowne Press.

UVEA HORNED PARAKEET

Eunymphicus cornutus uvaeensis (Layard and Layard, 1882)

Order PSITTACIFORMES   Family PSITTACIDAE

STATUS   Endangered.   Restricted to Uvea, Loyalty Islands.   The population is
very low, and the woodlands on which the subspecies depend are being steadily
reduced in area.   Attempts to transplant the subspecies to other islands have so
far failed.

DISTRIBUTION   Formerly occurred throughout the forests of Uvea Atoll, Loyalty
Islands, South West Pacific (1).   Now concentrated in the wooded areas of St.
Joseph District, between Cap Rossel and Cap Escarpé (H. Bregulla 1974, pers. comm.).

POPULATION   Presumably far larger when the parrot ranged over most of Uvea and in
1939 the population was estimated at about 1000 birds (1).   The most recent
estimate (H. Bregulla 1974, pers. comm.) was 200 birds at the very most.

HABITAT   Mature, indigenous forests, especially those in which Kauri pines
(Agathis sp.) are present (1).   Unfortunately much of this habitat has been
destroyed by fire (2).

CONSERVATION MEASURES TAKEN   Legal protection has been accorded to the parakeet
and its export from Uvea controlled.   There have been two attempts to transplant
it to Lifou, the next largest island of the chain - 100 birds in 1925 and 14 birds
in 1963 -, but neither was successful, possibly because the transplanted birds
were able to fly back the 60 km to Uvea (3; H. Bregulla 1974, pers. comm.).   The
species is listed in Appendix 2 of the 1973 Convention on International Trade in
Endangered Species of Wild Fauna and Flora.

CONSERVATION MEASURES PROPOSED   Conservation of remaining indigenous forest on
Uvea.   An educational campaign aimed at stopping the capture of birds for pets and
export.   Further attempts at transplanting, preferably aviary-raised birds, to
other islands with suitable habitat (H. Bregulla 1974, pers. comm.).

REMARKS   The nominate race E. c. cornutus is still fairly common in the indigenous
forests, secondary growth and savanna-type woodland of New Caledonia, but could also
become endangered unless sufficiently large forest reserves are established and
suitably maintained (3; 4).

REFERENCES   1.   Warner, D.W. 1947.   The Ornithology of New Caledonia and the
                   Loyalty Islands.   Cornell Univ.: Ph.D. Thesis.
              2.   Douglas, G. 1969.   Draft check list of Pacific oceanic islands.
                   Micronesica 5: 327-463.
              3.   Delacour, J. 1966.   Guide des Oiseaux de la Nouvelle Calédonie
                   et ses Dépendances.   Neuchâtel: Delachaux et Niestlé.

NIGHT PARROT

Geopsittacus occidentalis Gould, 1861

Order PSITTACIFORMES   Family PSITTACIDAE

STATUS   Indeterminate.   Existence uncertain.   Formerly occurred over a wide
area of the interior of Australia; the most recent record confirmed by a specimen
is dated 1912.   However, there have been recent unconfirmed sightings and some
authorities consider it likely this secretive, nocturnal species will one day be
rediscovered somewhere in the vast expanses of its habitat, although others are
convinced that it is extinct (1; 2; 3).

DISTRIBUTION   Sightings of the Night Parrot were made during the 19th century in
the arid interior of every mainland Australian state, though in widely separated
locations.   The only 20th century specimen, already mentioned, came from Nichol
Spring, Western Australia and the recent unconfirmed sightings are from Western and
South Australia - the region in which it is most likely to survive, if at all (1;
2; 3; 4).

POPULATION   The Night Parrot was described as uncommon by explorers in the
interior of the Australian continent toward the end of the last century.   It may
have declined because of deterioration of its habitat due to grazing and because of
predation by introduced rats and cats, but these two factors are unlikely to have
been solely responsible for its extinction or near-extinction over such a vast
area (1; 3; 4).

HABITAT   Associated with spinifex (_Triodia_) grasslands and also samphire
(_Salicornia_) flats.   It is said to burrow under spinifex tussocks and to feed
primarily on spinifex seeds.   There are still thousands of square miles of
spinifex grassland virtually unvisited by man in central Australia (1).

CONSERVATION MEASURES TAKEN   The species has been protected by law since 1937 (3).
Several large national parks have recently been established in the interior of
Australia, in places where this species might be expected to occur (J.M. Forshaw
1974, pers. comm.).   Listed in Appendix 1 of the 1973 Convention on International
Trade in Endangered Species of Wild Fauna and Flora.

CONSERVATION MEASURES PROPOSED   None known.

REMARKS   In the 19th century one or two specimens are known to have been kept in
captivity, but never for more than a few months and there is no authentic record
of captive breeding (3).

REFERENCES   1.   Forshaw, J.M. 1969.   _Australian Parrots_.   Melbourne: Lansdowne
                   Press.
              2.   Forshaw, J.M. 1973.   _Parrots of the World_.   Garden City:
                   Doubleday and Co.;   Melbourne: Lansdowne Press.
              3.   Fisher, J., Simon, N. & Vincent, J. 1969.   _Wildlife in Danger_.
                   New York: Viking Press;   London: Collins.
              4.   Greenway, J.C., Jr. 1958.   _Extinct and Vanishing Birds of the
                   World_.   American Committee for International Wildlife
                   Protection, Special Publication No. 13.

INDIGO-WINGED PARROT

Hapalopsittaca amazonina fuertisi (Chapman, 1912)

Order PSITTACIFORMES   Family PSITTACIDAE

STATUS   Indeterminate.   There are no recent records of this little known bird
of temperate zone forest in the central Andes of Colombia.   Everywhere within its
known range, forest destruction has been extensive.

DISTRIBUTION   Recorded only from Laguneta (3,100 m) and Santa Isabel (3,800 m)
in the temperate zone of the central Andes of Colombia, in the Caldas division (1).
No information is available about its present distribution.

POPULATION   Unknown.   There have been no records since 1911, when seven specimens were collected (1).

HABITAT   Temperate forest, destruction of which in the area where this subspecies
has been found, is widespread and thorough (R. Ridgely 1977, pers. comm.).

CONSERVATION MEASURES TAKEN   None known.

CONSERVATION MEASURES PROPOSED   None known.

REMARKS   None of the three other subspecies of H. amazonina, described from
subtropical and temperate Venezuela, Colombia and Ecuador (3) are known to be at
risk, but nor are they known to be secure.   H. a. fuertisi has been treated as
a full species by some authors (1; 2).

REFERENCES   1. Chapman, F.M. 1912.   Diagnoses of apparently new Colombian
                  birds.   Bull. Amer. Mus. Nat. Hist. 31: 139-166.
              2. Peters, J.L. 1937.   Check-list of Birds of the World.
                  Vol. III. Cambridge: Harvard University Press.
              3. Forshaw, J.M. 1973.   Parrots of the World.   Garden City,
                  N.Y.: Doubleday and Co.

ORANGE-BELLIED PARAKEET

Neophema chrysogaster (Latham, 1790)

Order PSITTACIFORMES   Family PSITTACIDAE

STATUS   Rare.   Restricted to Tasmania and adjacent coasts of south-eastern
Australia.   The main breeding locality is not known but is thought to be in western
Tasmania.   The reasons for the rarity of this species are poorly understood (1; 2).

DISTRIBUTION   Occurs in Tasmania, in South Australia east of St. Vincent Gulf and
in Victoria west of Port Phillip Bay.   It was also known from near Sydney, New
South Wales, around the turn of the century, but not recorded there before or since.
The species is presently considered to be resident along the west coast of Tasmania
and also to breed in south-eastern South Australia.   Birds are absent from Victoria
between November and March, apparently flying over to Tasmania to breed (1; 2).

POPULATION   It is not entirely certain that any great decline in numbers has taken
place.   Early accounts of the abundance of the species in Tasmania and south-
eastern Australia probably reflect short-lived irruptions, following specially
successful breeding seasons, and this may also account for the population that
appeared briefly in New South Wales.   No precise population estimates have been
quoted, but the species is everywhere considered to be very rare and possibly fewer
than 2000 now exist (J.M. Forshaw 1974, pers. comm.).

HABITAT   Coastal areas, including grassland, light scrub, pastures, sand dunes,
tidal flats and swamplands (1).

CONSERVATION MEASURES TAKEN   The species has been given legal protection and is
also listed in Appendix 1 of the 1973 Convention on International Trade in
Endangered Species of Wild Fauna and Flora.

CONSERVATION MEASURES PROPOSED   None known.

REMARKS   The Orange-bellied Parakeet has only rarely been kept in captivity and
appears never to have been bred successfully.   Two subspecies have been named, the
nominate N. c. chrysogaster from Tasmania and N. c. mab from mainland Australia, but
they are now regarded as identical.   Assessment of its status is complicated by the
difficulty of separating this species in the field from the very similar Blue-
winged Parakeet Neophema chrysostoma (1).

REFERENCES   1.   Forshaw, J.M. 1969.   Australian Parrots.   Melbourne: Lansdowne
                   Press.
              2.   Forshaw, J.M. 1973.   Parrots of the World.   Garden City:
                   Doubleday and Co.;   Melbourne: Lansdowne Press.

TURQUOISE PARAKEET

Neophema pulchella (Shaw, 1792)

Order PSITTACIFORMES   Family PSITTACIDAE

STATUS   Recovering and out of danger, although still rather rare. Occurs over a
fairly wide area in south-eastern Australia. Land clearance associated with human
settlement, trapping, predation by feral cats, and disease have been suggested as
reasons for its decline at the turn of the century (1).

DISTRIBUTION   Formerly occurred from the Suttor River district of Queensland,
150 km south of Townsville, south through parts of New South Wales to the vicinity
of Melbourne, Victoria. In the early 1900s thought to have disappeared from most
of its known range, and, in fact, considered extinct in New South Wales and Victoria.
It is now found locally in south-eastern Queensland, eastern New South Wales and
northern Victoria (1; 2).

POPULATION   In the 19th century the Turquoise Parrot was considered to be quite
abundant in some places, but its numbers decreased drastically and by 1917 it was
supposedly extinct over most of its range. Since 1940, however, it has been
sighted with increasing frequency, and is now found in a number of localities,
although the population is still considered to be divided into a number of discrete
and discontinuous subpopulations (1).

HABITAT   Open forests and wooded grasslands on mountain slopes and ridges, and
along watercourses. The critical element appears to be the combination of forest
and grassland (1).

CONSERVATION MEASURES TAKEN   The species has been given legal protection. The
establishment of national parks, such as Warrumbungle National Park in New South
Wales, has provided conditions under which it apparently thrives (1).

CONSERVATION MEASURES PROPOSED   Preservation of additional tracts of suitable
habitat (1).

REMARKS   The Turquoise Parakeet is among the most common and successful of cage
birds in Australia, and numbers of them are found in zoos and private collections
elsewhere. These captive populations are now self-sustaining (1; 2).

REFERENCES   1.   Forshaw, J.M. 1969. Australian Parrots. Melbourne: Lansdowne
                    Press.
              2.   Fisher, J., Simon, N. & Vincent, J. 1969. Wildlife in Danger.
                    New York: Viking Press; London: Collins.

SPLENDID or SCARLET-CHESTED PARAKEET

Neophema splendida (Gould, 1841)

Order PSITTACIFORMES   Family PSITTACIDAE

STATUS   Rare.   Occurs very locally in the interior of Australia and has
apparently always been a rare species.   There have been several spectacular
irruptions, the most recent in 1966, but they should not be taken as an indication
of any general trend of increase.   This parakeet is highly prized as a cage bird
and excessive trapping might, in view of its rarity, pose a threat to its survival
at any time (1).

DISTRIBUTION   Interior of Australia and particularly the interior of South
Australia, but also reported sporadically from south-eastern Western Australia.
There have been records from as far east as New South Wales, from north-western
Victoria, and from as far north as the south of Northern Territory.   There is no
evidence of any significant change in distribution since the species was first
discovered (1; 2).

POPULATION   No estimates are known to have been made of what has always been
considered quite a rare species.   It is usually seen in pairs or small groups of
up to about ten, but during its very infrequent irruptions may gather in flocks of
up to a hundred (1).

HABITAT   Mallee, scrubland and saltbush (Atriplex) or spinifex (Triodia) plains
(1).

CONSERVATION MEASURES TAKEN   The species has been given legal protection and
should also benefit from the recent establishment of several large national parks
in the interior of Australia.   Listed in Appendix 1 of the 1973 Convention on
International Trade in Endangered Species of Wild Fauna and Flora.

CONSERVATION MEASURES PROPOSED   None known.

REMARKS   The Splendid Parakeet is well established in captivity in Australia and
other continents.   Captive populations are self-sustaining (1; 2).

REFERENCES   1.   Forshaw, J.M. 1969.   Australian Parrots.   Melbourne: Lansdowne
                   Press.
              2.   Fisher, J., Simon, N. & Vincent, J. 1969.   Wildlife in Danger.
                   New York: Viking Press; London: Collins.

YELLOW-EARED CONURE

Ognorhynchus icterotis (Massena and Souancé, 1854)

Order PSITTACIFORMES   Family PSITTACIDAE

STATUS   Vulnerable.   Sparsely distributed in Colombia and Ecuador.   There has
been a substantial decline in areas where the species was formerly most abundant,
as a result of extensive forest destruction.

DISTRIBUTION   Recorded from several localities in the eastern, central and
western Andes of Colombia, and the adjacent Imbabura and Pichincha provinces of
northern Ecuador (1; 2).   Recent sightings in Colombia have been confined to the
Purace and Cueva de los Guacharos National Parks.   The majority of sites where
the species once occurred, such as the Moscopan area of Cauca division, are now
largely deforested.   There are no longer any places in Ecuador where it is
presently known to survive, although several specimens have been collected in
recent years in Carchi province, which borders on Colombia (R. Ridgely 1977, 1978,
pers. comms).

POPULATION   Unknown.   In 1917, this species was still considered to be common
in Colombia (3), but by 1956 it had apparently become scarce (4) and now, two
decades later, no substantial population is known to exist anywhere.   A pair was
seen in the Purace National Park in May 1976, and very small numbers were seen
occasionally and irregularly during 1975, in the Cuevo de los Guacharos National
Park (R. Ridgely 1977, pers. comm.).

HABITAT   Subtropical and temperate forest, usually between 2,500 and 3,200 m
elevation.   The species has been noted as breeding in colonies in stands of
Wax Palms Ceroxylon sp. (3).   Destruction of forests, particularly at more
accessible lower elevations, has been extensive, and Ceroxylon alpinum and
quindieunse, two wax palms with which this parrot has been associated, are
themselves now considered vulnerable or endangered due to lack of regeneration (6).

CONSERVATION MEASURES TAKEN   The species occurs sparingly in two National Parks
in Colombia and therefore enjoys some measure of protection.

CONSERVATION MEASURES PROPOSED   A National Park has been proposed in the Nevado
del Huila area, to the south-east of Cali, in which this species might be expected
still to occur.

REMARKS   At least one example is in captivity, in a private collection in
England (5).   The Golden-plumed Conure Leptopsittaca branickii, locally
distributed in temperate zone forest of Colombia, south-west Ecuador and central
Peru, may occur in some of the same localities as L. icterotis: it is poorly
known and may also be at risk.

REFERENCES   1.   de Schauensee, R.M. 1949.   The birds of the Republic of
                   Colombia.   Segundo entrega, Accipitridae-Picidae.
                   Caldasia 5: 381-644.
              2.   Forshaw, J.M. 1973.   Parrots of the World.   Garden City,
                   N.Y.: Doubleday and Co.
              3.   Chapman, F.M. 1917.   The distribution of bird-life in
                   Colombia: a contribution to a biological survey of South
                   America.   Bull. Amer. Mus. Nat. Hist. 36: 1-729.

4. Lehmann, F.C. 1957.   Contribuciones al estudio de la fauna de Colombia, XII.   _Noved. Colomb._ 3:   101-156.
5. Smith, G.A. 1977.   Notes on some species of parrot in captivity.   _Avicult. Mag._ 83:   21-27.
6. Moore, H.E. Jr. 1977.   Endangerment at the specific and generic levels in palms.   In Prance, G.T. and Elias, T.S. (eds) _Extinction is Forever_, pp. 267-282.   New York: New York Botanical Garden.

WESTERN GROUND PARROT

Pezoporus wallicus flaviventris North, 1911

Order PSITTACIFORMES   Family PSITTACIDAE

STATUS   Endangered.   Restricted to a small stretch of coastline in south-western
Australia, where it is rare and has declined seriously (1; 2).

DISTRIBUTION   Formerly more widespread along the south-western coastline of
Western Australia north to Geraldton.   Presently known only from the two widely
separated localities of Irwin's Inlet and Cheyne Beach (1; 2).

POPULATION   The subspecies was formerly more common, although never abundant, but
the population declined towards the end of the 19th century and by 1913 it had been
thought to be extinct until small numbers were found at Irwin's Inlet and Wilson's
Inlet.   The size of the population known to survive at Irwin's Inlet and Cheyne
Beach is unknown: four were seen at the former locality in 1952, and the birds
have recently twice been seen at the latter site, about 100 km east of Albany (1).

HABITAT   Coastal plain grasslands, wet flats and swamps.   Extensive tracts of the
coastal grasslands have been cleared and burned and the wetlands have been drained,
which may have contributed to the disappearance of this subspecies from most of its
former range (2).

CONSERVATION MEASURES TAKEN   The subspecies has been given legal protection.

CONSERVATION MEASURES PROPOSED   None known.

REMARKS   Of the two other subspecies, P. w. wallicus is restricted in distribution
and population to the east coast of Australia and classified as vulnerable, while
P. w. leachi from Tasmania is supposed to be still moderately common (but see
Remarks under nominate wallicus, the account of which follows).

REFERENCES   1.   Fisher, J., Simon, N. & Vincent, J. 1969.   Wildlife in Danger.
                    New York: Viking Press; London: Collins.
              2.   Forshaw, J.M. 1969.   Australian Parrots.   Melbourne: Lansdowne
                    Press.

EASTERN GROUND PARROT

Pezoporus wallicus wallicus (Kerr, 1792)

Order PSITTACIFORMES   Family PSITTACIDAE

STATUS   Vulnerable.   Localized in a number of small, discontinuous heathlands on
the east coast of Australia.   Proper management of these heathlands is essential
for the continued survival of the subspecies (1; 2).

DISTRIBUTION   In the 19th century the subspecies was known from Noosa and Frazer
Island, Queensland, south along the coastal plain through New South Wales and
Victoria and west to south-eastern South Australia, where it occurred on the
Adelaide plains and in the southern Flinders Ranges.   It is presently considered
to have been extirpated from South Australia and nearly so from Queensland, although
at least one important breeding area remains at Cooloola.   Its range in Victoria
and New South Wales is considerably reduced, though it is still present in a number
of locations (1; 2; 3).

POPULATION   No estimates have been made but it is clear there has been a
continuing population decline, for which the development of the eastern coastal
plain, with its now substantial human population, was largely responsible.   The
subspecies is now split into a mosaic of tiny subpopulations (1; 2).

HABITAT   Formerly coastal heath, grassland and swamp, as well as montane heaths in
the immediate hinterland of the coast.   Today the coastal plain has been extensively developed and much of the swampland drained, with the result that coastal and
montane heathlands are the only portion of the former range which are still widely
occupied.   The largest heathland area occupied by Ground Parrots in New South
Wales extends over about 7,000 hectares; most are considerably smaller.   The total
of all the heathland in the state is only 834 sq. km (1).   Mining of mineral sands
is now a threat to some of the still occupied sites (J.M. Forshaw 1974, pers. comm.).

CONSERVATION MEASURES TAKEN   The subspecies has been given legal protection and is
also found in a number of nature reserves and national parks in Queensland, New
South Wales and Victoria.   Its ecological requirements are under study, with an eye
to management of the heathlands by controlled burning, thus maintaining a heath
cover of appropriate age and density (1).

CONSERVATION MEASURES PROPOSED   No additional measures are known to have been or
be under consideration.

REMARKS   Of the two other subspecies, which are questionably distinct, P. w.
flaviventris of south-western Australia is considered to be critically endangered.
P. w. leachi of Tasmania is apparently common (4), but further and up to date
confirmation of this would be desirable.

REFERENCES   1.   Forshaw, J.M. 1969.   Australian Parrots.   Melbourne: Lansdowne
                    Press.
               2.   Forshaw, J.M., Fullager, P.J. & Groves, R.H. 1975.   In Wheeler,
                    W.R. Report on rare and endangered species of birds from the
                    Australian mainland and from Tasmania.   ICBP Bull. 12: 159-164.
               3.   Fisher, J., Simon, N. & Vincent, J. 1969.   Wildlife in Danger.
                    New York: Viking Press; London: Collins.
               4.   Hinsby, K.B. 1948.   Notes on the Ground Parrot.   Emu 47:
                    313-314.

GOLDEN-SHOULDERED PARAKEET

Psephotus chrysopterygius chrysopterygius Gould, 1857

Order PSITTACIFORMES   Family PSITTACIDAE

STATUS   Rare and localized.   Restricted to a large segment of Cape York
Peninsula, Queensland, Australia, but nowhere common.   Continuing illegal capture
of this species for parrot fanciers poses a serious threat to its small population.

DISTRIBUTION   Southern portion of the Cape York Peninsula, where it occurs in
three extensive tracts in the interior and along the east coast of the Gulf of
Carpentaria, from Normanton north to the Watson River, totalling some 2 million
hectares in area.   It is no longer present in the south-western part of its
historical range (1).

POPULATION   No accurate census of this subspecies has ever been attempted, in
view of its remote range, its spotty distribution within that range, and its
nomadic habit.   It is most abundant in woodland near Musgrave (1), where the
population has been estimated as 'less than 250 birds', not a very precise figure
but still conveying quite a good idea of order of magnitude (H.J. Lavery, 1974,
pers. comm.).   Recent surveys have suggested that it may in fact not be much less
numerous now than it ever was (2).

HABITAT   Semi-arid savannah woodland, with well-distributed termitaria, in which
the bird nests; also mangroves.   Grass and herb seeds are its principal food (1).
There is no shortage of such food or nest sites within its present range, even
though portions of it are swept by fires and are being subjected increasingly to
grazing by domestic livestock (2; J. M. Forshaw 1974, pers. comm.).

CONSERVATION MEASURES TAKEN   The Fauna Conservation Act of 1974 lists this
parakeet as a Permanently Protected Species, illegal possession of which can incur
a fine of up to $3000.   The Queensland Fauna Conservation Branch is conducting
systematic surveys of its habitat (2).   It is also listed in Appendix 1 of the 1973
Convention on International Trade in Endangered Species of Wild Fauna and Flora.

CONSERVATION MEASURES PROPOSED   Continued study of the species to determine the
causes of its rarity.   Continued patrolling with a view to apprehending illegal
trappers.

REMARKS   Captive stocks of this subspecies are to be found in Australia and the
United States and frequent success has been achieved with breeding it in captivity.
The current price for a pair is several times the maximum fine which can be levied
in Australia from anyone found to be in illegal possession of them (3; H.J. Lavery
1974, pers. comm.).

REFERENCES   1.   Forshaw, J.M. 1969.   Australian Parrots.   Melbourne: Lansdowne
                   Press.
              2.   Lavery, H.J. & Weaver, C.M. 1975.   In Wheeler, W.R.   Report on
                   rare and endangered species of birds from the Australian mainland
                   and from Tasmania.   ICBP Bull. 12: 159-164.
              3.   Fisher, J., Simon, N. & Vincent, J. 1969.   Wildlife in Danger.
                   New York: Viking Press; London: Collins.

HOODED PARAKEET

Psephotus *chrysopterygius* *dissimilis* Collet, 1898

Order PSITTACIFORMES   Family PSITTACIDAE

STATUS   Rare.   Occurs in the Melville Peninsula, Northern Territory, Australia.
It has a small population but is highly prized as a cagebird, so that illegal
capture could pose a threat to its survival (1; H.J. Lavery 1974, pers. comm.).

DISTRIBUTION   The Arnhem Land Plateau on the Melville Peninsula from the South
Alligator River and Pine Creek, south-east to the Macarthur River and the south-
western shores of the Gulf of Carpentaria.   Not known to have changed (1).

POPULATION   No estimate of the population has been made.   This parakeet is
considered always to have been rare and locally distributed, its centre of
abundance in the Pine Creek area (1).

HABITAT   Dry open forest and spinifex (*Triodia*) grassland where termitaria, in
which this parakeet breeds, are widespread.   Feeds mainly on grass seeds.   There
is no shortage of food or nest sites within its range (1).

CONSERVATION MEASURES TAKEN   The species has been given legal protection and the
Kakadu National Park protects a portion of its range in the South Alligator River
basin (H.J. Lavery 1974, pers. comm.).   Listed in Appendix 1 of the 1973
Convention on International Trade in Endangered Species of Wild Fauna and Flora.

CONSERVATION MEASURES PROPOSED   None known.

REMARKS   In 1974, the number of this subspecies in captivity in zoos in Australia,
the United States and Europe was 48, of which 43 were known to have been captive
bred (2).   In addition, an unknown number are held in private collections in
several continents.   Wild caught individuals command a remarkably high price,
which encourages illegal capture.

REFERENCES   1.   Forshaw, J.M. 1969.   Australian Parrots.   Melbourne:Lansdowne
                    Press.
              2.   Duplaix-Hall, N. (ed.) 1975.   Census of rare animals in
                    captivity, 1974.   International Zoo Yearbook 15: 397-429.

PARADISE or BEAUTIFUL PARAKEET

Psephotus pulcherrimus (Gould, 1845)

Order PSITTACIFORMES   Family PSITTACIDAE

STATUS   Endangered, if indeed the species still exists.   Known from southern
Queensland and northern New South Wales, Australia, but the last confirmed
observation of the species was in 1927.   Nonetheless, there have been recent
unconfirmed sightings in Queensland which suggest that it may yet be rediscovered
(1; H.J. Lavery 1974, pers. comm.).

DISTRIBUTION   Formerly distributed sporadically from Archer River and Rockhampton,
Queensland, south and inland into northern New South Wales.   There is the distinct
possibility that the northernmost records of this species were the result of confusion with the Golden-shouldered Parakeet P. chrysopterygius (J.M. Forshaw 1974,
pers. comm.).   Present distribution unknown, although reports of its presence recur
along the Queensland coast (1; H.J. Lavery 1974, pers. comm.).

POPULATION   This parakeet was locally common, but generally scarce, until the end
of the 19th century.   At the turn of the century a succession of drought years,
coinciding with an expansion of livestock grazing, may have been the cause of the
decline from which it never recovered.   Capture for parrot fanciers has also been
suggested as contributing to the decline.   If the species survives, it may be a
matter of only a few individuals (1; 2; H.J. Lavery 1974, pers. comm.).

HABITAT   Open savannah woodland and scrubby grasslands with well-distributed
termitaria, which this parakeet like other Psephotus species used as its nesting-
place, its favored food, the seeds of grasses and herbs, also being similar (1).

CONSERVATION MEASURES TAKEN   The species is permanently protected in Queensland
(H.J. Lavery 1974, pers. comm.) and listed in Appendix 1 of the 1973 Convention on
International Trade in Endangered Species of Wild Fauna and Flora.

CONSERVATION MEASURES PROPOSED   None known.

REMARKS   The Paradise Parakeet was highly prized as a cage bird at the end of the
last century, but was a more delicate and demanding species than some of its
congeners.   It is unlikely that any remain in private collections (1; 2).

REFERENCES   1.   Forshaw, J.M. 1969.   Australian Parrots.   Melbourne: Lansdowne
                   Press.
              2.   Fisher, J., Simon, N. & Vincent, J. 1969.   Wildlife in Danger.
                   New York: Viking Press; London: Collins.

MAURITIUS PARAKEET

Psittacula echo (A. and E. Newton, 1876)

Order PSITTACIFORMES   Family PSITTACIDAE

STATUS   Endangered. Very rare and restricted in range; declining slowly in
numbers and now seriously threatened with extinction. The main threats are habitat
destruction, competition for nest sites from introduced birds, and nest predation by
introduced mammals.

DISTRIBUTION   Confined to the island of Mauritius in the Indian Ocean and never
recorded elsewhere. Occurs now only in restricted areas of forest habitat
(especially the Macabé Forest) surrounding the Black River Gorges in the south-west
of the island, and has done so since at least 1911 (1; 2).

POPULATION   The species is believed at one time to have been very common in
Mauritius, but had already become rare and local by 1911 or earlier (1). Its
total population was estimated at 40-50 individuals in 1975 (3; S. Temple 1976,
pers. comm.), and about the same in 1977 (D. McKelvey pers. comm.).

HABITAT   Mature indigenous montane evergreen forest, which provides suitable
nesting and roosting sites in large forest trees and original native food plants
(1; 2). The extent of such forest is now put at no more than 1,822 ha, about one
per cent of the amount that existed in 1753. The parakeet has also now to compete
for nest sites with introduced parakeets Psittacula krameri and mynahs Acridotheres
tristis, and suffers frequent nest predation from introduced macaques Macaca
fascicularis, black rats Rattus rattus and possibly other species (2; 3).

CONSERVATION MEASURES TAKEN   The species is fully protected by laws forbidding the
killing or capture of native birds and a large portion of its range is within
officially declared reserves. Ecological studies to determine the bird's status
and requirements were begun in 1972 and have continued up to the present (4).
In 1974 several specimens were captured for propagation in a local aviary, but have
proved difficult to maintain and no success has yet been reported with the survivors.

CONSERVATION MEASURES PROPOSED   Continued protection and management of the
remnant native forests is essential for this bird's survival. A management plan
for a system of nature reserves and national parks has been submitted to the
Mauritius Government (5). Control of introduced competitors and nest predators
may be necessary. Eventual release of captive-produced parakeets into suitable
habitat on Mauritius, and possibly also Réunion, is anticipated (S. Temple 1976,
pers. comm.).

REMARKS   Captive propagation should succeed as most species of Psittacula breed
freely in captivity. The Mauritius Parakeet has been considered a subspecies of
the Ring-necked Parakeet Psittacula krameri which is widespread in India and Africa.
However, recent evidence indicates that there is no interbreeding where the two
occur together on Mauritius; their behavior and appearance forms are in fact
somewhat different (6; S. Temple 1976, pers. comm.).

REFERENCES   1. Meinertzhagen, R. 1912. On the birds of Mauritius. Ibis
                  9(6): 82-108.
              2. Temple, S.A., Staub, J.J.F. & Antoine, R. 1974. Some background
                  information and recommendations on the preservation of the native
                  flora and fauna of Mauritius. Unpublished report submitted to
                  the Mauritius Government.

3. Temple, S.A. 1974.   Wildlife in Mauritius today.   <u>Oryx</u> 12: 584-590.
4. Temple, S.A. 1975.   Report in World Wildlife Yearbook, 1974-75, pp. 210-212.   Morges: World Wildlife Fund.
5. Procter, J. & Salm, R. 1974.   Conservation in Mauritius, 1974. Unpublished report to the Mauritius Government.
6. Forshaw, J. 1973.   <u>Parrots of the World</u>.   Garden City, New York: Doubleday and Co.;   Melbourne: Lansdowne Press.

OCHRE-MARKED PARAKEET or BLUE-THROATED CONURE

Pyrrhura cruentata (Wied, 1820)

Order PSITTACIFORMES   Family PSITTACIDAE

STATUS   Rare. Occurs in a circumscribed area in south-eastern Brazil, where forest destruction has certainly contributed to its rarity.

DISTRIBUTION   South-eastern Brazil from southern Bahia and Minas Gerais states, through Espírito Santo and Rio de Janeiro, to north-eastern São Paulo (1; 2). It is now very locally distributed in this area, with known populations only in the Sooretama Reserve and Klabin Farm, Rio Doce valley, both in Espírito Santo, in the Monte Pascoal National Park, Bahia, and in the Rio Doce State Park, Minas Gerais (R. Ridgely 1978, pers. comm.).

POPULATION   In 1935, P. cruentata was described as locally common (2) and it remains so, except that it now occurs in far fewer areas. It is more common at Sooretama and on Klabin Farm, rather less so at Monte Pascoal (R. Ridgely 1978, pers. comm.).

HABITAT   Principally primary forest, which in south-eastern Brazil has been mostly cleared, only relict patches remaining (4). One such patch in Espírito Santo where this species is known to occur, is in the forested portion (4,000 ha) of the privately-owned Klabin Farm.   Recently, however, this parakeet has been seen in flocks in cacao plantations in southern Bahia and, if it can adapt to and breed successfully in this man-altered habitat, concern for its future will be reduced (R. Ridgely 1978, pers. comm.).

CONSERVATION MEASURES TAKEN   Listed as endangered by the United States government, and thus may not be imported or held in the U.S.A. without a special permit for scientific or captive propagation purposes.   Brazilian law protects this and most other native birds.   Its occurrence in one national park, a state park and a well-protected reserve ensure some additional protection.

CONSERVATION MEASURES PROPOSED   None known.

REMARKS   A slightly smaller parakeet, *Pyrrhura leucotis leucotis* of south-eastern Brazil, has very similar ecological requirements to those of P. cruentata and is likewise becoming rare (R. Ridgely 1978, pers. comm.).

REFERENCES   1.   de Schauensee, R.M. 1966. The Species of Birds of South America and their Distribution. Narberth, Pa.: Livingston Publishing Co.
2.   Forshaw, J.M. 1973. Parrots of the World. Garden City, N.Y.: Doubleday and Co.
3.   Pinto, O.M. de O. 1935. Aves da Bahia. Rev. Mus. Paul. 19: 1-325.
4.   Sick, H. 1972. A ameaça da avifauna brasileira.   In Espécies da Fauna Brasileira Ameaçadas de Extinção, pp. 99-153. Rio de Janeiro: Academia Brasileira de Ciências.

THICK-BILLED PARROT

Rhynchopsitta pachyrhyncha pachyrhyncha (Swainson, 1827)

Order PSITTACIFORMES   Family PSITTACIDAE

STATUS   Vulnerable. Restricted to north-western Mexico and decreasing in
numbers due to logging of its pine forest habitat, to shooting and to being
captured for the pet trade.

DISTRIBUTION   Formerly occurred regularly in the Sierra Madre Occidental of
Mexico from Chihuahua and eastern Sonora south to Michoacan; during irruptions it
ranged northwards to southern Arizona and south-western New Mexico and south-
eastwards to Veracruz, in the more distant past also reaching northern Arizona.
It no longer occurs at the northern and southern extremities of this range. The
mountains of southern Chihuahua, western Durango and eastern Sinaloa remain its
stronghold, though it probably tends to move to the more southerly parts of its
range in winter (1; 2).

POPULATION   This subspecies was formerly quite common. For example, in the
autumn of 1917 up to 1500 invaded the Chiricahua Mountains of southern Arizona (3)
and large flocks of 100 or more were at one time commonplace. But few flocks of
this size have been seen in the last 15 years (1), although in 1964 a flock of 200
was reported on the Sinaloa-Durango border (R. Crossin 1974, pers. comm.). In the
1970s the only large flocks that have been reported were in southern Jalisco, where
it is apparently present only in winter. A sizable breeding population has,
however, recently been located along the Chihuahua-Sonora border (V. Emanuel 1977,
pers. comm.). No estimates of the total population have ever been made, but it is
clear that there has been a serious decline, for while the number of bird-watchers
in northern Mexico has increased, the number of sightings of this species has
markedly decreased.

HABITAT   Pine forests. The mature montane pine forests of the Sierra Madre
Occidental continue to be logged, although in many places on a selective basis.
Unfortunately, the largest pines which provide the preferred nesting and feeding
places also attract the lumberman's axe. While habitat destruction is thus the
most serious problem affecting the species, easier access to the pinewoods has
also meant that more of the parrots are shot or taken as pets. No part of their
habitat is at present protected by a reserve.

CONSERVATION MEASURES TAKEN   This subspecies has been listed in Appendix 1 of
the 1973 Convention on International Trade in Endangered Species of Wild Fauna and
Flora. It is also protected by law in Mexico, but in practice such laws are
unenforceable in the remote areas where it still occurs.

CONSERVATION MEASURES PROPOSED   None known beyond the as yet unheeded plea that
portions of the pine forests should be protected from logging by suitable
reservations (4).

REMARKS   In 1975, 76 Thick-billed Parrots were known to be held in captivity in
24 collections, of which 10 (13.2 per cent) were captive bred (5).

REFERENCES   1.   Forshaw, J.M. 1973.   <u>Parrots of the World</u>.   Garden City: Doubleday and Co.; Melbourne: Lansdowne Press.

2.   Schnell, G.D., Weske, J.S. & Hellack, J.J. 1974.   Recent observations of Thick-billed Parrots in Jalisco.   <u>Wilson Bull</u>. 86: 464-465.

3.   Wetmore, A. 1935.   The Thick-billed Parrot in southern Arizona.   <u>Condor</u> 37: 18-21.

4.   Monson, G. 1965.   A pessimistic view - the Thick-billed Parrot.   <u>Audubon Field Notes</u> 19: 389.

5.   Olney, P.J.S., ed., 1976.   Census of rare animals in captivity, 1975.   <u>Internat. Zoo. Yearbook</u> 16: 411-446.

MAROON-FRONTED PARROT

Rhynchopsitta pachyrhyncha terrisi Moore, 1947

Order PSITTACIFORMES   Family PSITTACIDAE

STATUS   Endangered.   Known from a small area in north-eastern Mexico, where the
montane pine forests, on which it depends, continue to be logged.   It is
undoubtedly also shot for food and caught for caging, although habitat destruction
is a far more important factor in its decline.

DISTRIBUTION   Confined to a section of the Sierra Madre Oriental in Mexico, including the Cerro Potosi of west-central Nuevo Leon, the adjacent southern Coahuila
area near Saltillo and San Antonio de las Alazanas, and, still further south, the
Sierra de Guatemala near Gomez Farias in Tamaulipas State (1; 2; 3; 6).   In short,
the subspecies ranges from north to south along about 400 km of the Sierra Madre
Oriental.

POPULATION   A decline is presumed, although no estimates are available for the
population as a whole.   The subspecies has always been considered as relatively
rare.   In 1958, flocks totalling over 600 birds were seen at Las Vacas near
Saltillo and also commonly near San Antonio de las Alazanas (4), and in 1975 a
flock of 120 was recorded in the same general area (7).   In 1977, roosts near
Saltillo held 900-1200 birds (6).   More than 60 were seen on the Cerro Potosi in
1975 (3) and about 80 were counted in 1977 near Gomez Farias at the southern end of
their range (6).   The total population is believed to be of the order of 2000 (3;
6).

HABITAT   Montane pine forest usually at an altitude exceeding 1500 m.   These
forests cover a far smaller area in the Sierra Madre Oriental than they do in the
Sierra Madre Occidental.   There has been extensive logging throughout the area,
particularly of the largest trees, which provide the biggest cone crop and which the
parrots depend upon for food and for nest cavities (1).   Some encouragement may be
found in the fact that some recent sightings have been made in areas that have been
greatly disturbed by logging (3).   Forest fires are also considered to be a serious
threat to the habitat of major segments of the population (6).

CONSERVATION MEASURES TAKEN   The subspecies has been listed in Appendix 1 of the
1973 Convention on International Trade in Endangered Species of Wild Fauna and
Flora.   It also has local legal protection, but in the remote areas where it now
survives, the law cannot be effectively enforced.   No reserves have yet been
established to protect the tracts of mature pinewood which are essential for the
well-being of this parrot.

CONSERVATION MEASURES PROPOSED   No additional recommendations for the better
protection of this subspecies are known to have been put forward.

REMARKS   The nominate subspecies is also at risk, but is somewhat more widespread
and numerous in the Sierra Madre Occidental of north-western Mexico.   Some authors
treat the two as separate species (5).   All captive examples are believed to belong
to the nominate race.

REFERENCES   1.   Forshaw, J.M. 1973.   Parrots of the World.   Garden City:
                  Doubleday and Co.;   Melbourne: Lansdowne Press.
             2.   Robins, C.R. & Heed, W.B. 1951.·. · Bird notes from La Joya de
                  Salas, Tamaulipas.   Wilson Bull. 63: 263-270.
             3.   Ridgely, R. 1976.   Macaw status survey.   World Wildlife Fund,
                  U.S. Appeal Project 61.   Unpublished interim report.
             4.   Ely, C.A. 1962.   The birds of southeastern Coahuila, Mexico.
                  Condor 64: 34-39.
             5.   Hardy, J.W. 1967.   Rhynchopsitta terrisi is probably a valid
                  species: a reassessment.   Condor 69: 527-528.
             6.   Lanning, D.V. & Lawson, P.W. 1977.   Observations of the Maroon-
                  fronted Parrot, Rhynchopsitta terrisi, in northeastern Mexico:
                  1976-1977.   Chihuahuan Desert Research Institute: unpublished
                  report.
             7.   Kincaid, E. 1976.   Mesa de las Tablas, Coahuila, Mexico,
                  Christmas Bird Count.   Amer. Birds 30: 623.

KAKAPO

Strigops habroptilus Gray, 1845

Order PSITTACIFORMES   Family PSITTACIDAE

STATUS   Critically endangered.   A long-term historical decline probably began
with the arrival of Maoris on New Zealand about 950 A.D.   Its rate accelerated
following European settlement, and the species is now on the edge of extinction.
It can no longer be found in its former haunts including Fiordland, South Island,
once its stronghold.   A last chance program to transfer birds to competitor-and
predator-free islands has resulted in initial success, but whether the relocated
birds will develop into a self-sustaining population remains to be seen.   A small
but probably viable population has, however, very recently been rediscovered on
Stewart Island.

DISTRIBUTION   Formerly widespread though local in North, South and Stewart Islands,
New Zealand.   Its alleged former occurrence in the Chatham Islands, 800 km to the
east, now seems doubtful.   It became extinct on North Island by 1930 (1).   In
South Island, reliable reports during the last two decades have come only from the
Milford and Transit watersheds of Fiordland.   Between 1974 and 1976, attempts to
locate the species by its characteristic signs and the replaying of its taped calls
revealed that it had all but vanished from these two localities also, except for a
few isolated birds in valleys in the Milford area.   Three of these were captured
and moved to Maud Island in the Marlborough Sounds (2; D. Merton 1976, pers. comm.).
The Stewart Island population was presumed extinct by 1951, but in 1976 was
rediscovered in an isolated 11 by 5 km area in the south-east (D. Merton 1977, pers.
comm.).

POPULATION   The species was widespread and common on the west coast of South
Island until early this century.   It is sensitive to disturbance of any sort, and
was apparently on the decrease on North Island and eastern South Island prior to
the arrival of European settlers in New Zealand early in the 19th century (1).
By 1960 the population was estimated to be under 200 birds, and in 1961 had dropped
to less than 100 (3; 4).   The present population is not known precisely but no
doubt still below 100.   On South Island the location of only 10 birds is known, 7
in the Milford area and 3 on Maud Island, all except perhaps one of them males
(2; D. Merton 1976, pers. comm.).   In 1976, evidence of 30 Kakapo, which gives
grounds for hoping that a stable population will be proved to exist, was found in
south-eastern Stewart Island (D. Merton 1977, pers. comm.).

HABITAT   In the past, climax Podocarpus and Nothofagus forests (1), but in recent
times most often near forest margins in sub-alpine scrub and tussock, scrub
regenerating on avalanche scree, and borders of flood channels of mountain streams
(5).   Over three-quarters of New Zealand's indigenous forests have been cleared
since human habitation began some 1,000 years ago (3).   Moreover, the Kakapo's
last strongholds in the Milford area have been infiltrated by predators such as rats
and stoats, and, more recently, by Australian brush-tailed possums, deer and
chamois, which may compete with it for food (2).   Fortunately stoats, which are
possibly the most serious predator, have not become established on Stewart Island.

CONSERVATION MEASURES TAKEN   The species has been given full legal protection and
the area where it still occurs on South Island is within the boundaries of Fiordland National Park.   Five birds were captured in 1961 and one in 1967 for a
captive breeding program, but all proved to be males and the last of them died in
1968.   Two birds, hopefully a male and a female, were captured in March 1974 and

translocated to Maud Island in the Marlborough Sounds, a third bird being added in March 1975. They have remained in good condition and have established territories, but no breeding has yet occurred (2).

CONSERVATION MEASURES PROPOSED   The New Zealand Wildlife Service will continue its efforts to locate and monitor surviving birds in Fiordland and Stewart Island. It is proposed to transfer additional birds from Fiordland to Maud Island in an attempt to establish a viable breeding population in isolation from most of the alien influences which are active elsewhere, and where management is practicable (G. Williams 1976, pers. comm.).

REMARKS   In view of the extremely precarious status of the species and the fact that it is the sole representative of a distinctive subfamily, the Strigopinae, of the Psittacidae, the New Zealand Wildlife Service attaches the highest priority to preservation of the Kakapo (6).

REFERENCES   1. Williams, G.R. 1956.   The Kakapo (Strigops habroptilus, Gray). A review and re-appraisal of a near-extinct species. Notornis 7: 29-56.
2. Merton, D.V. 1975.   Kakapo.   Wildlife - A review 6: 39-51.
3. Fisher, J., Simon, N. & Vincent, J. 1969.   Wildlife in Danger. New York: Viking Press; London: Collins.
4. Forshaw, J.M. 1973.   Parrots of the World.   Garden City: Doubleday and Co.; Melbourne: Lansdowne Press.
5. Atkinson, I.A.E. & Merton, D.V. in prep.   Habitat of the Kakapo (Strigops habroptilus, Gray) in the Esperance Valley, Fiordland. J. Roy. Soc. N.Z.
6. Bell, B.D. 1975.   The rare and endangered species of the New Zealand region and the policies that exist for their management. ICBP Bull. 12: 165-172.

BROWN-BACKED or BLACK-EARED PARROTLET

Touit melanonota (Wied, 1818)

Order PSITTACIFORMES   Family PSITTACIDAE

STATUS   Rare. This parrotlet is restricted in distribution to south-eastern
Brazil, where it is now quite rare as the result of extensive forest destruction.

DISTRIBUTION   South-eastern Brazil from southern Bahia, through Espírito Santo
and Rio de Janeiro, to southern São Paulo. Recorded recently from Guanabara near
the city of Rio de Janeiro and also sighted in the Floresta da Tijuca reserve, Rio
de Janeiro, and elsewhere in the Serra do Mar, for example the Serra das Orgãos
National Park (1; 2; R. Ridgely 1978, pers. comm.).

POPULATION   The species was once common in the coastal forests of São Paulo
state, but is now rated as rare both there and also in all other parts of its
range (3). However, several sightings during the 1970s have raised hopes that it
may not be quite as rare as has been feared (1).

HABITAT   Montane forests in the coastal zone. This type of primary forest has
been seriously depleted within the range of this species.

CONSERVATION MEASURES TAKEN   Its occurrence in one reserve and one national park
in Rio de Janeiro state afford it some measure of protection in addition to the
legal protection which it nominally enjoys throughout Brazil.

CONSERVATION MEASURES PROPOSED   None known.

REMARKS   Several other members of the genus Touit, e.g. T. stictoptera, are rare
or poorly known. Their habit of keeping themselves inconspicuous, high in the
forest canopy, may however partly account for this presumption of rarity (R. Ridgely
1978, pers. comm.). The species is not known to be in captivity (2).

REFERENCES   1.   Sick, H. 1969. Aves brasileiras ameaçadas de extinção
                    e noções gerais de conservação de aves no Brasil. An. Acad.
                    Brasil. Ciênc. 41 (Supl.): 205-229.
               2.   Forshaw, J.M. 1973. Parrots of the World. Garden City,
                    N.Y.: Doubleday and Co.
               3.   Pinto, O.M. de O. 1946. Aves brasileiras da família
                    dos papagaios. Relat. Inst. Bot. São Paulo: 126-129.

GOLDEN-TAILED PARROTLET

Touit surda (Kuhl, 1820)

Order PSITTACIFORMES   Family PSITTACIDAE

STATUS   Indeterminate. This little-known parrotlet of the coastal forests of
eastern Brazil is likely to be at risk as a result of extensive habitat destruction
within its range.

DISTRIBUTION   Eastern Brazil near Recife, Pernambuco state (T. s. ruficauda), and
from southern Bahia south to Minas Gerais, Espírito Santo and Rio de Janeiro and
possibly to southern Goiás and São Paulo (T. s. surda). Present distribution is
not known to differ from this, although very large portions of its range are no
longer suitable for this species.

POPULATION   Unknown. Due to forest destruction numbers have seriously declined
(H. Sick 1977, pers. comm.).

HABITAT   Coastal forest and adjacent montane forest, both of which have been
extensively cleared in eastern Brazil, leaving only a sparse mosaic of relict
patches.

CONSERVATION MEASURES TAKEN   Protected by Brazilian law, this parrotlet may also
derive some protection from its probable occurrence in Monte Pascoal National Park,
south-eastern Bahia state (R. Ridgely 1978, pers. comm.).

CONSERVATION MEASURES PROPOSED   None known.

REMARKS   The validity of the northern race T. s. ruficauda has been questioned.
T. melanonota, also of eastern Brazil but more restricted to montane situations,
is believed to be at risk and classified as 'rare' (see relevant data sheet).

REFERENCES   1. Forshaw, J.M. 1973. Parrots of the World. Garden City,
                  N.Y.: Doubleday and Co.
              2. de Schauensee, R.M. 1966. The Species of Birds of South
                  America and their Distribution. Narberth, Pa.: Livingston
                  Publishing Co.

TAHITI LORIKEET

Vini peruviana (P.L.S. Müller, 1776)

Order PSITTACIFORMES   Family PSITTACIDAE

STATUS   Rare. Extirpated from most of its former range, including all of the
larger Society Islands in which it was recorded, and now surviving only in some of
the islands of the Tuamotu Archipelago and two in the Society group, on the
periphery of its former range. It was apparently introduced by Polynesians to
Aitutaki, Cook Islands, where it is now plentiful. Its disappearance from Tahiti,
Moorea and Bora Bora came shortly after the introduction of the harrier Circus
aeruginosus, which is known to prey on birds and may have preyed on the lorikeet
(1; 2). It has been suggested that its recent disappearance from Niau in the
Tuamotus coincided with the introduction of a mosquito (Culinoides) which is a
vector of avian malaria (J.-C. Thibault 1974, pers. comm.). If this is so, the
spread of this mosquito to other islands in the lorikeet's range poses a major
threat to its existence.

DISTRIBUTION   Once included Tahiti, Moorea, Bora Bora, Huahine, Mehetia, Mopelia,
and Scilly in the Society Islands, and Rangiroa, Tikehau, Niau, Kaukura, Ahii,
Aratua and Apataki in the Tuamotus,as well as Aitutaki, Cook Islands, where it was
probably introduced. The lorikeet was extirpated from Tahiti and Moorea at the
turn of the century, and from Bora Bora and most other Society islands in the 1920s.
It survives on Scilly and Bellingshausen (a new location) in the Society Islands, on
Rangiroa and apparently on other Tuamotu atolls, and on Aitutaki, Cook Islands
(1; 2; 3; 4; J.-C. Thibault, 1974, pers. comm.).

POPULATION   The species is presumed to have been formerly widespread and abundant
in the Society Islands. Present day figures are 100-200 on Rangiroa (43 sq. km)
(3), 350-400 pairs on Scilly (350 ha) and possibly a like number on Bellingshausen
(233 ha) (2); small flocks are said to occur on several other Tuamotu atolls and the
species is plentiful on Aitutaki (18 sq. km) (D. Holyoak 1973, pers. comm.).

HABITAT   Coconut groves and, less frequently, stands of other trees (1).

CONSERVATION MEASURES TAKEN   The species is protected by law in Rangiroa and also
in the Society Islands, where hunting or killing it is strictly prohibited.

CONSERVATION MEASURES PROPOSED   Creation of a sanctuary to give complete protection on the Rangiroa islets where the lorikeet is found (3). Legal protection
for the species in the Cook Islands (5). Fumigation of aircraft flying to islands
where the species still occurs, to prevent introduction of mosquitos (1).

REMARKS   The occurrence of the lorikeet on Bellingshausen, which has never been
visited by an ornithologist, has been confirmed by the identification in Papeete of
captive birds brought from that island. Successful captive breeding of the
species is reported (2; J.-C. Thibault, 1974, pers. comm.).

REFERENCES   1.   Holyoak, D.T. 1974. Les oiseaux des Îles de la Société.
                    L'Oiseau et R.F.O. 44: 1-27, 153-181.
              2.   Thibault, J.-C. 1974. Le Peuplement Avien des Iles de la
                    Société (Polynésie). Papeete: Mus. Nat. Hist. Natur. Antenne
                    de Tahiti.

3. Bruner, P.L. 1972. The Birds of French Polynesia.
    Honolulu: B.P. Bishop Museum.
4. Thibault, J.-C. undated. Report to IUCN on status of birds of
    French Polynesia. Unpublished mimeo.
5. Holyoak, D. 1973. Suggestions for the conservation of birds
    and other wildlife in the Cook Islands. Unpublished report.

ULTRAMARINE LORIKEET

Vini ultramarina (Kuhl, 1820)

Order PSITTACIFORMES   Family PSITTACIDAE

STATUS   Rare.   Restricted to two of the Marquesas Islands and introduced to a
third.   Deterioration of the native forests caused by the grazing of introduced
mammals poses a long-term threat to its survival.   The forests have decreased in
size 60 to 90 per cent in the last 50 years (1; 2; 3).

DISTRIBUTION   Once even more widespread, the lorikeet is still widely distributed
in about a dozen valleys in Uapou (104 sq. km), but on Nukuhiva (337 sq. km) it is
restricted to a few valleys at the north-western end, near which the construction of
a jetport has been proposed.   On Uahuka (78 sq. km) the lorikeet was introduced
several decades ago and it appears to be restricted to two or three valleys (1; 2).

POPULATION   Common on Uapou, the lorikeet can be seen frequently in small groups
of up to six individuals.   The population was estimated at 300 ± 50 pairs in 1975
(4).   On Nukuhiva a population of about 70 individuals is thinly spread in high
valleys and ridges at the north-western end.   A 1975 estimate for Uahuka, where the
lorikeet is not very common was 225 ± 25 pairs (4).

HABITAT   Montane forest at altitudes of 700 to 1000 m.   Banana plantations and
mango trees at lower levels are frequented seasonally for feeding.

CONSERVATION MEASURES TAKEN   Introduction to the third island of the group,
Uahuka, where it successfully established itself and has survived for several
decades.   The lorikeet was given protection by a law enacted in 1936, and in French
Polynesia generally, hunting of all birds was prohibited in 1967.

CONSERVATION MEASURES PROPOSED   Establishment of mountain reserves and control of
introduced grazing mammals.   Fumigation of airplanes to prevent spread of the
mosquito vector of avian malaria (1; 3).

REMARKS   Clutch size is two (in captivity) (1).

REFERENCES   1.   Holyoak, D.T. 1975.   Les oiseaux des Îles Marquises.
                   L'Oiseau et R.F.O. 45: 207-233, 341-366.
              2.   Thibault, J.-C. 1973.   Notes ornithologiques polynésiennes.
                   II. Les Iles Marquises.   Alauda 41: 301-316.
              3.   Holyoak, D.T. 1973.   Polynesian land birds face H-bombs and
                   malaria.   New Scientist 57: 288-290.
              4.   Thibault, J.-C.   Undated.   Fragilité et protection de
                   l'avifaune en Polynésie Française.   Unpublished report to the
                   ICBP.

ZANZIBAR RED-CRESTED LOURIE

Tauraco fischeri zanzibaricus (Pakenham, 1937)

Order CUCULIFORMES   Family MUSOPHAGIDAE

STATUS   Rare. This subspecies is restricted to one small forest in Zanzibar,
off the East African coast, where its habitat is subjected to encroachment by
woodcutters and gatherers.

DISTRIBUTION   Limited to the Jozani Forest, an area situated 35 km south-east of
Zanzibar Town, Tanzania, and estimated to be between 2 and 10 sq. km in extent,
depending upon the amount of saline swamp forest and coastal evergreen bush
reckoned as being within its borders (1; 2).

POPULATION   Unknown, but certainly small; in 1939 the lourie was judged to be
very uncommon even in the heart of its exiguous range (1) and on two visits to the
forest of 6 and 7 hours duration, in 1936 and 1950 respectively, its calls were
never once heard (R.H.W. Pakenham 1977, pers. comm.), although it was heard
calling in 1956 and this appears to be the last report of its presence (2).
An expedition to Zanzibar in 1972, by the Oxford University Exploration Club,
failed to find it.

HABITAT   Humid forest, the whole of it divided into rectangles by woodcutters'
paths. Cutting and felling continue, but at a relatively slow pace, and as this
part of Zanzibar island is thinly populated, some forest may persist for many
years, although the possibility of progressive destruction cannot be discounted.
Meanwhile, the Jozani Forest is believed to be still without any formal legal
protection (R.H.W. Pakenham 1977, pers. comm.).

CONSERVATION MEASURES TAKEN   The Jozani Forest has been a forest reserve since
1960, but little has been done for many years to make this effective. However,
it was reported in 1977 that some conservation and management measures have now
been initiated (3).

CONSERVATION MEASURES PROPOSED   None known.

REMARKS   The nominate race of this lourie occurs in coastal districts of East
Africa and is not at risk.

REFERENCES   1. Pakenham, R.H.W. 1939. Field notes on the birds of
                  Zanzibar and Pemba. Ibis (14)3: 522-554.
              2. Pakenham, R.H.W. 1959. Field notes on the birds of
                  Zanzibar and Pemba. Ibis 101: 245-247.
              3. Thornback, J. (comp.) 1979. The Zanzibar Red Colobus.
                  In Red Data Book, Vol. 1, revised edition. Morges: IUCN.

SOUTH-EASTERN RUFOUS-VENTED GROUND-CUCKOO

Neomorphus geoffroyi dulcis Snethlage, 1927

Order CUCULIFORMES   Family CUCULIDAE

STATUS   Endangered.   Never numerous, this extremely shy species is among the first to disappear if its primary forest habitat is disturbed and,in south-eastern Brazil where it occurs, most of such forest has been destroyed.

DISTRIBUTION   South-eastern Brazil:- in southern Bahia, where it has been recorded from the Rio Jaguaribe, Rio Belmonte and Serra do Palhão; Espírito Santo at Lagoa Juparanã on the Rio São José, a tributary of Rio Doce; and Minas Gerais, on the Rio Matipos and Rio Suçui, also tributaries of the Rio Doce; there is a questionable record from Cantagallo, Rio de Janeiro.   It is not known to be present at any of these sites today nor have there been any recent reports of it elsewhere (1; H. Sick 1977, R. Ridgely 1978, pers. comms).

POPULATION   Certainly very low, if it still survives.   Although widespread, it was never rated as common, even before the felling of so much of the primary forests of the region.

HABITAT   Primary forest, which in south-eastern Brazil is now restricted to small relict patches (2; 3).   There is no evidence of its presence in the two most likely remnants of this habitat, in Sooretama Reserve, Espírito Santo, and Monte Pascoal National Park, Bahia (R. Ridgely 1978, pers. comm.).

CONSERVATION MEASURES TAKEN   The subspecies is protected under Brazilian law.

CONSERVATION MEASURES PROPOSED   None known.

REMARKS   Of the five other subspecies described from tropical forests of Middle and South America, only one is known to be at risk, namely N. g. maximiliani, which replaces N. g. dulcis just to the north of the latter's former range in Bahia (see relevant data sheet).

REFERENCES   1.   Peters, J.L. 1940.   Check-list of Birds of the World. Vol. 4.   Cambridge: Harvard Univ. Press.
                2.   Sick, H. 1949.   Beobachtungen an dem brasilianischen Bodenkuckuck Neomorphus geoffroyi dulcis Snethlage. In E. Mayr and E. Schuz (eds) Ornithologie als Biologische Wissenschaft, pp. 220-239.   Heidelberg: Carl Winter-Universitätsverlag.
                3.   Sick, H. 1972.   A ameaça da avifauna brasileira.   In Espécies da Fauna Brasileira Ameaçadas de Extinção, pp. 99-153. Rio de Janeiro: Academia Brasileira de Ciências.

BAHIA RUFOUS-VENTED GROUND-CUCKOO

Neomorphus geoffroyi maximiliani Pinto, 1962

Order CUCULIFORMES   Family CUCULIDAE

STATUS   Indeterminate. This rare, shy, terrestrial cuckoo requires undisturbed primary forest, which in south-eastern Brazil is now severely limited in extent.

DISTRIBUTION   This subspecies has only been recorded in the vicinity of its type locality, the Rio Gongogi, a tributary of the Rio das Contas, Bahia, Brazil.

POPULATION   Unknown, but likely to be extremely small.   There are no records since 1932, when the type specimen of this subspecies was collected.

HABITAT   Primary forest.   The ground-cuckoo is particularly sensitive to disturbance of the primeval forest which it frequents and is one of the first species to vanish when forest destruction takes place, as it has done on an extensive scale in south-eastern Brazil.

CONSERVATION MEASURES TAKEN   The subspecies is protected by law in Brazil, but no protection has been given to its habitat.

CONSERVATION MEASURES PROPOSED   None known.

REMARKS   *N. g. dulcis*, which formerly, at least, was found directly to the south of the range of *N. g. maximiliani*, is also at serious risk (see relevant data sheet).   The four other subspecies, distributed over the tropical forests of Middle and South America, are not known to be threatened.

REFERENCES   1.   Pinto, O. 1962.   Miscelânea ornitologica, VII: Notas sobre a variação geográfica nas populações brasileiras de *Neomorphus geoffroyi*, com a descrição de uma subspécie nova. Depto. Zool. São Paulo: Papeis Avulsos 15: 299-300.

MADAGASCAR THICK-BILLED CUCKOO

Pachycoccyx audeberti audeberti (Schlegel, 1879)

Order CUCULIFORMES   Family CUCULIDAE

STATUS   Indeterminate.   This little known species, unique to Madagascar, has not
been reported in more than 40 years.

DISTRIBUTION   Recorded from near Mananara on the south-western shores of Antongil
Bay (1), the Rogez Forest between Perinet and Brickaville (3), and Sihanaka Forest
(1); nothing more has been learned of its present distribution if it still exists.

POPULATION   This species has always been considered very rare.   The most recent
reports date from the 1930s and only five specimens have ever been collected (1).

HABITAT   The humid forest zone of eastern Madagascar (1).   The extent of the
forests has been steadily diminished this century through clearing for agriculture,
reforestation utilizing exotic pines and eucalypts, and annual burning of adjacent
areas of cultivation with little or no attempt at keeping the fires under control
(2).   It has also been suggested that disappearance of this cuckoo may be connected
with a diminution of the species which it is believed to parasitise, the Vanga
Leptopterus chaberti (3).

CONSERVATION MEASURES TAKEN   None known.

CONSERVATION MEASURES PROPOSED   Full legal protection for most of the endemic
birds of Madagascar has been recommended (K. Curry-Lindahl in litt. to
G. Ramanantsoavina, Director, Service des Eaux et Forêts, Chasse et Pêche, Jan.
1973).

REMARKS   Of the two other subspecies described from continental Africa, validus,
which occupies the greater part of a range extending from Togoland to the
Transvaal, and the doubtfully distinct canescens further to the south, are
apparently not at risk.

REFERENCES   1.   Milon, P., Petter, J.-J., & Randrianasolo, G. 1973.
                   Faune de Madagascar, 35: Oiseaux.   Tananarive and Paris:
                   ORSTOM and CNRS.
              2.   McNulty, F. 1975.   Madagascar's endangered wildlife.
                   Defenders of Wildlife 50: 92-134.
              3.   Benson, C.W., Colebrook-Robjent, J.F.R. & Williams, A. 1976-77.
                   Contribution à l'ornithologie de Madagascar.   L'Oiseau et R.F.O.
                   46(3): 218.

SOUMAGNE'S OWL

Tyto soumagnei (A. Grandidier, 1878)

Order STRIGIFORMES   Family TYTONIDAE

STATUS   Endangered.   This very rare owl is confined to the forests of Madagascar and the reasons for its extreme scarcity are unknown.

DISTRIBUTION   The eastern humid forest zone, including Sihanaka Forest and the Masoala Peninsula (1; 2).   The only recent sighting was in Fierenana district, about 65 km north of Perinet (A. Forbes-Watson 1974, pers. comm.).

POPULATION   Always considered rare, this owl was last collected in 1930; it was thought possibly to have become extinct but an unconfirmed sighting was made in 1973.

HABITAT   Humid forest.   The specific requirements of this rare species are not known but there is no doubt that the continuing decline in the extent of the humid forest on Madagascar must affect it adversely.   The decline is the combined result of clearing for subsistence agriculture, repeated burning of adjacent grasslands and reafforestation projects that utilize exotic eucalypts and pines (3).

CONSERVATION MEASURES TAKEN   All birds of prey, including this species, were stipulated as in need of total protection under the 1968 African Convention for the Conservation of Nature and Natural Resources, which the Malagasy Government signed and ratified.   However, no specific legal protection has as yet been extended to Soumagne's Owl.

CONSERVATION MEASURES PROPOSED   Legal protection for most endemic birds of Madagascar has again been recommended (K. Curry-Lindahl in litt. to G. Ramanant-soavina, Jan. 1973).

REMARKS   The 1973 sighting of this rather small very rufous version of a Barn Owl Tyto alba was made deep in the forest about a day's walk from the nearest motorable road, and is considered quite reliable (A. Forbes-Watson, 1977, pers. comm.).

REFERENCES   1.   Rand, A.L. 1936.   The distribution and habits of Madagascar
                     birds.   Bull. Amer. Mus. Nat. Hist. 72(5): 143-499.
              2.   Milon, P., Petter, J.-J., & Randrianasolo, G. 1973.   Faune de
                     Madagascar, 35: Oiseaux.   Tananarive and Paris: ORSTOM and
                     CNRS.
              3.   McNulty, F. 1975.   Madagascar's endangered wildlife.
                     Defenders of Wildlife 50(2): 92-134.

TOBAGO STRIPED OWL

Asio clamator oberi (E.H. Kelso, 1936)

Order STRIGIFORMES   Family STRIGIDAE

STATUS   Rare.   Known only from the forests of the island of Tobago, north-east
of Trinidad.   Thanks to a provision in local legislation, which permits the
elimination of so-called 'pests', this very scarce subspecies is virtually
unprotected.

DISTRIBUTION   Confined to the forests of Tobago (1).

POPULATION   Not known precisely, since the species as a whole is strictly
nocturnal.   Although this subspecies is said to be locally common, it has been
seen only occasionally since its discovery in 1936, most recently in 1971 at
Grafton Estate (1).

HABITAT   Both primary and secondary forest, mostly in the lowlands.   Although
three-quarters of Tobago's forest has been cleared for agriculture, it is estimated
that about 75 sq. km remain wooded.

CONSERVATION MEASURES TAKEN   The owl has been given legal protection, but this
has effectively been cancelled out by recent authorization of a "pest control"
program (R. ffrench 1974, pers. comm.).

CONSERVATION MEASURES PROPOSED   None known but enforcement of legal protection by
specific exclusion of the owl from the 'pest' category, would be an obvious first
step.

REMARKS   Other subspecies occur from Mexico south to Argentina and Uruguay and
are not known to be at risk.

REFERENCES   1.   ffrench, R. 1973.   A Guide to the Birds of Trinidad and Tobago.
                      Wynnewood, Pa.: Livingston Publishing Co.

PONAPE SHORT-EARED OWL

Asio flammeus ponapensis Mayr, 1933

Order STRIGIFORMES   Family STRIGIDAE

STATUS   Rare.   Restricted to Ponape, Caroline Islands, Western Pacific, where it
has a very small but apparently stable population.   No decline is believed to have
taken place.

DISTRIBUTION   Known only from Ponape (334 sq. km), Caroline Islands, where it is
restricted to the open grasslands (1).   Presumed records of this subspecies from
Kusaie (2) and the Marianas (1; 4) are doubtless referable to the nominate A. f.
flammeus, well known as a wanderer to more tropical parts of the Pacific basin from
the Holarctic.

POPULATION   In 1930 the population was estimated to be at least two dozen (1).
A more careful appraisal, made in 1956, yielded an estimate of about 50 birds (3).
No significant change is thought to have taken place since then, even though only a
single example was seen in the course of a week's survey of Ponape in 1975 (R. Owen
1975, pers. comm.).

HABITAT   Open grasslands, both in the lowlands and in forest clearings on the
mountains (3).

CONSERVATION MEASURES TAKEN   None known.

CONSERVATION MEASURES PROPOSED   This subspecies has been recommended for inclusion
in the U.S. Trust Territories list of endangered species (R. Owen 1975, pers. comm.).

REMARKS   There are 9 subspecies, one other of which, A. f. portoricensis from
Puerto Rico, was classified as very rare in the previous edition and is still
considered rare, although reports suggest its population has recently increased.

REFERENCES   1.   Baker, R.H. 1951.   The avifauna of Micronesia, its origin,
                     evolution, and distribution.   Univ. Kansas Pubs. Mus.
                     Nat. Hist. 3(1): 1-359.
              2.   Kelso, L. 1938.   An addition to the range of the Short-eared
                     Owl. Oologist 60: 138.
              3.   Marshall, J.T., Jr. 1962.   Predation and natural selection.
                     In T.I. Storer, ed., Pacific Island rat ecology. B.P. Bishop
                     Mus. Bull. 225.
              4.   Ornithological Society of Japan, 1958.   A Hand-list of
                     Japanese Birds.   Fourth and revised edition.   Tokyo: Yamashina
                     Inst. for Ornith.

FOREST LITTLE OWL

Athene blewitti (Hume, 1873)

Order STRIGIFORMES   Family STRIGIDAE

STATUS   Indeterminate.   The continued existence of this little known owl is
tentatively confirmed by a recently published photograph, supposedly of the species,
taken in 1968.

DISTRIBUTION   Occurred from near Mandvi, on the Tapti River 220 km north of
Bombay, eastward to Sambalpur, Orissa (1; 2).   Most recently reported from near
Nagpur, Madhya Pradesh.   It could not be found in the forested areas near the
Mahanadi River in Orissa, toward the eastern end of its presumed range, in 1975 (3).

POPULATION   Unknown.   Only six specimens have been collected, the last of them
north of Bombay in 1914 (1).   The owl was believed to be extinct until an
individual attributed to this species was photographed in 1968.   It is certainly
very rare (3).

HABITAT   Moist tropical and subtropical deciduous woodlands in the foothills of
the Satpura range (1).

CONSERVATION MEASURES TAKEN   A search for this species was made in 1975 and 1976,
to no avail (3).

CONSERVATION MEASURES PROPOSED   None known, but there is an obvious necessity for
further field investigations to establish the status of the species.

REMARKS   This owl is similar in appearance to and partly sympatric with the
Spotted Little Owl Athene brama.   The latter has a longer wing and tail, but
shorter bill and legs.   The Forest Little Owl also differs in that it on the whole
lacks the spotting on the crown and nuchal collar diagnostic of the commoner
species (3).

REFERENCES   1.   Ali, S. & Ripley, S.D. 1969.   Handbook of the Birds of
                   India and Pakistan.   Vol. 3.   Bombay, London, New York:
                   Oxford Univ. Press.
              2.   Burton, J.A., ed., 1973.   Owls of the World.   New York: Dutton;
                   European edition: Peter Lowe.
              3.   Ripley, S.D. in press.   Reconsideration of Athene blewitti
                   (Hume).   Journ. Bombay Nat. Hist. Soc.

NDUK EAGLE OWL

Bubo poensis vosseleri Fraser, 1853

Order STRIGIFORMES   Family STRIGIDAE

STATUS   Rare.   Known only from one area of mountain forest in Tanzania, this owl is now threatened by forest destruction.

DISTRIBUTION   The Usambara Mountains, north-eastern Tanzania.   The forest area of this range was estimated to be no more than 1300 sq. km, and must now be substantially less.   All recent specimens of the owl have come from the Amani area, East Usambaras, but it is reported to have been heard recently near the Ambangulu Estate and in the Mazumbai Forest Reserve, West Usambaras; also an owl which might possibly have been of this species was observed recently in the Nguru Mountains, some 200 km to the south-west of the Usambaras (4).

POPULATION   This poorly known forest-dwelling owl has been recorded on only nine occasions.   Its population, never considered large, has declined as a result of forest destruction to certainly less than 200 individuals (4; S. Stuart 1977, pers. comm.).

HABITAT   Evergreen montane forest.   In the Usambaras this biotope has suffered considerably, particularly between 1880 and 1935, from clearing for subsistence farming and also, more recently, for tea and cardamom cultivation.   In a 195 sq. km area near Amani, 49 percent was forested in 1954, but only 38 percent remained undisturbed in 1977.   However, several young owls of this subspecies have been found on the ground in areas cleared for cardamom plantations, suggesting that undisturbed forest may not be essential for its survival (4).

CONSERVATION MEASURES TAKEN   None known.

CONSERVATION MEASURES PROPOSED   Specific areas in the Usambaras have been recommended to the Tanzanian government for protection as nature reserves (S. Stuart 1977, pers. comm.).

REMARKS   The Usambara population of this owl is quite distinctive in its appearance and calls from the nominate B. p. poensis of northern Congo and West Africa, about 1500 km distant, and has been treated by several authors as a separate species.   Three specimens are in captivity in London, England (3).

REFERENCES   1.   Hall, B.P. & Moreau, R.E. 196?.   A study of the rare birds of Africa.   Bull. Brit. Mus. (Nat. Hist.) Zool. 8(7): 315-378.
              2.   Brown, L. et al. Undated.   A report on threatened bird species in East Africa.   East African Wildlife Society, mimeo, 12 pp.
              3.   Olney, P.J.S. (ed.) 1977.   Census of rare animals in captivity 1976.   Internat. Zoo Yearbook 17: 333-371.
              4.   Stuart, S.N. & Hutton, J.M. (eds) 1977.   The avifauna of the East Usambara Mountains, Tanzania.   Cambridge University.

NORFOLK BOOBOOK OWL

Ninox novaeseelandiae undulata (Latham, 1801)

Order STRIGIFORMES   Family STRIGIDAE

STATUS   Indeterminate. This subspecies is described as having declined in
abundance on Norfolk Island, south-west Pacific, primarily as the result of a lack
of nest sites.

DISTRIBUTION   Known only from Norfolk Island (35 sq. km). Formerly, before the
arrival of Pitcairn Islanders on Norfolk in 1856, it undoubtedly occurred throughout
this then extensively forested island. Its present distribution has not been
precisely ascertained, but it is believed to be unchanged since 1909, when it was
restricted to the gullies surrounding Mount Pitt (1; 2; 3; 4).

POPULATION   No estimates appear to have been made, although the subspecies is
considered to have undergone a serious decline and now has an extremely low
population level. It was neither seen nor heard when a party of biologists made
a visit to the island in 1968, but local naturalists still claim that they hear the
bird's call regularly (1; 2).

HABITAT   Forest patches, particularly of hardwoods, cavities in which are utilized
for nesting. The only extensive forested area (405 ha within the Mount Pitt
reserve) continues to suffer degradation from lumbering and cattle grazing. The
shortage of mature hardwood trees with suitable cavities to provide nest sites is
considered the most important limiting factor (2).

CONSERVATION MEASURES TAKEN   None known.

CONSERVATION MEASURES PROPOSED   The bulk of the remaining habitat would be
protected by the creation of a Mount Pitt National Park, provided it was accompanied
by adequate fencing of forested areas to prevent their further degradation by cattle
and provided that complete protection was given from the construction and intrusion
of additional roads or trails. Suggestions to this end were submitted in 1968,
but up to 1976 no consequent action had been taken by the Australian government.

REMARKS   None of the 13 other extant subspecies of this owl, which ranges from
New Zealand through Australia to the Lesser Sunda Islands, is believed to be at risk
but one subspecies, _N. n. albaria_ from Lord Howe Island, is extinct.

REFERENCES   1.   Smithers, C.N. & Disney, H.J. de S. 1969.   The distribution of
                    terrestrial and freshwater birds on Norfolk Island.   _Austral._
                    Zool. 15: 127-140.
              2.   Turner, J.S., Smithers, C.N. & Hoogland, R.D. 1968.   The
                    conservation of Norfolk Island.   _Austral. Cons. Found. Special_
                    Pub. No. 1.
              3.   Disney, H.J. de S. & Smithers, C.N. 1972.   The distribution of
                    terrestrial and freshwater birds on Lord Howe Island, in
                    comparison with Norfolk Island.   _Austral. Zool._ 17: 1-11.
              4.   Hull, A.F.B. 1909.   The birds of Lord Howe and Norfolk Islands.
                    Proc. Linn. Soc. N.S.W. 34: 636-693.

CHRISTMAS ISLAND OWL

Ninox squamipila natalis Lister, 1888

Order STRIGIFORMES   Family STRIGIDAE

STATUS   Rare.   Restricted to Christmas Island, Indian Ocean, and quite scarce.
Mining of Christmas Island for phosphate poses a threat to this as to other endemic
forms.

DISTRIBUTION   Known only from Christmas Island, Indian Ocean, where it is evenly
distributed throughout, including the inland plateau and shore terrace (1).

POPULATION   In 1938-1940 this subspecies was considered not particularly rare (1),
but population estimates of less than 100 were made on visits by biologists to the
island in 1965, 1972 and 1974 (2).   There could well have been a decline in the
number of the owls as a result of the destruction of parts of its forest habitat by
phosphate mining, but there is no adequate documentation to prove it.

HABITAT   Forest.   By 1994, when phosphate mining is due to have been completed,
at least 30 per cent of the surface of Christmas Island will have been cleared of
vegetation by the mining operations (3).   However, a substantial area of forest
should survive, unless mining of a lower grade of phosphate than is presently
planned to be taken, is unexpectedly decided upon.

CONSERVATION MEASURES TAKEN   Legally protected from killing or capture.

CONSERVATION MEASURES PROPOSED   Forest areas recommended for protection as
habitat for Abbott's Booby Sula abbotti, would also benefit this owl and, in the
long term, the proposed revegetation of mined areas, might recreate suitable
conditions.   The evacuation of most of the 3,000 human residents of Christmas
Island, planned to take place at the end of mining operations, should also assist
conservation of this and other species (3).

REMARKS   Four other subspecies of squamipila are recognized, all from East Indian
islands.   None are believed to be at risk.

REFERENCES   1. Gibson-Hill, C.A. 1947.   Notes on the birds of Christmas Island.
                  Bull. Raffles Mus. 18:   87-165.
              2. Van Tets, G.F. 1976.   A report on the conservation of resident
                  birds on Christmas Island.   Bull. ICBP 12: 238-242.
              3. Australian House of Representatives Standing Committee on
                  Environment and Conservation, 1974.   Conservation of endangered
                  species on Christmas Island.   Canberra: Australian Government
                  Publishing Service.

LANYU SCOPS OWL

Otus elegans botelensis Kuroda, 1928

Order STRIGIFORMES   Family STRIGIDAE

STATUS   Endangered.   A forest owl, restricted to one island off Taiwan, where
the native forest has been almost wholly replaced by an introduced coarse grass.

DISTRIBUTION   Lanyu (also known as Hung-T'ou Hsü, Orchid Island or Botel Tobago:
7x12 km), 29 km off the south-east coast of Taiwan (1).   In 1969, the owl was
found at the northern end of the island on both slopes of the forested central
ridge (S. Severinghaus 1977, pers. comm.), but in 1973, the remaining forest
patches of the central ridge were searched in vain for it, although it was still
present in at least one wooded canyon (J.T. Marshall 1977, pers. comm.).

POPULATION   As recently as 1969, this subspecies was considered to be fairly
common (S. Severinghaus 1977, pers. comm.) but, as mentioned above, it could no
longer be found along the central ridge in 1973, although about 10 males were heard
calling in one canyon (J.T. Marshall 1977, pers. comm.).

HABITAT   Forest, which on Lanyu has been almost entirely destroyed, its
regeneration being largely inhibited by an invasion of lalang grass, Imperata
cylindrica.   The island has been extensively developed for tourism and although
isolated pairs of the scops owl are apparently able to survive in tiny relict
clumps of forest vegetation, it is unlikely that they can do so in the long term.

CONSERVATION MEASURES TAKEN   The subspecies was given legal protection in 1974.

CONSERVATION MEASURES PROPOSED   None known.

REMARKS   There are two other subspecies of Otus elegans, in the Ryukyu and the
Daito Islands, the status of which is not presently known.

REFERENCES   1.   Marshall, J.T., Jr. 1978.   Systematics of smaller
                    Asian night birds.   Amer. Ornith. Union Ornith. Monographs, 25.

SEYCHELLES OWL

Otus insularis (Tristram, 1880)

Order STRIGIFORMES   Family STRIGIDAE

STATUS   Rare.   Although this species is quite rare and is restricted to only one
island in the Seychelles, it is not known to be in any immediate danger of
extinction.

DISTRIBUTION   Known only from Mahé Island, Seychelles Archipelago, despite
occasional suggestions that it may yet be found on Praslin and Félicité (1).   On
Mahé it has recently been observed or heard in several localities, all above 300 m
elevation (2; 3; C.J. Feare 1974, pers. comm.).

POPULATION   From 1906 to 1959 this species was believed to be extinct, although a
specimen taken in 1940 was subsequently discovered (1).   An estimate of no more
than 20 birds in 1965 (3) has proved somewhat pessimistic, for there are now known
to be at least 80 pairs and there could be possibly twice that number (J. Watson
in litt. to J.T. Marshall, 1977).   The owl probably suffered its major decline as
a result of the destruction by fire and felling of the greater part of the
Seychelles forests, which followed the arrival of settlers in the middle of the
18th century.

HABITAT   Forest, both high primary rainforest and secondary forest, though there
is a possibility that nest-sites may be situated in clefts and cavities at ground
level or not far above it (J. Watson pers. comm.).   Destruction of forests in the
Seychelles is now complete except in specifically protected areas or in areas too
remote or steep for felling operations or cultivation.   Since 1950, over 800 ha
have been re-afforested on Mahé and the target is a total of 1,220 ha, which should
be sufficient to meet local needs for forest products (4).

CONSERVATION MEASURES TAKEN   None known, except for the reafforestation program
just mentioned.

CONSERVATION MEASURES PROPOSED   Protection of portions of the owl's habitat would
be covered by the suggested creation of a Morne Seychellois National Park (4).

REMARKS   The readiness of this owl to respond to the playing of tape-recordings of
its call has greatly facilitated the determination of its status.

REFERENCES   1.   Penny, M. 1974.   The Birds of Seychelles and the Outlying
                      Islands.   New York: Taplinger Publishing Co.
                2.   Loustau-Lalanne, P. 1962.   Land birds of the granitic islands
                      of the Seychelles.   Seychelles Soc. Occ. Pub., 1.
                3.   Gaymer, R., Blackman, R.A.A., Dawson, P.G., Penny, M. & Penny,
                      C.M. 1969.   The endemic birds of Seychelles.   Ibis 111:
                      157-176.
                4.   Seychelles Government. 1971.   Conservation policy in the
                      Seychelles.   Government Printer.

MORDEN'S SCOPS OWL

Otus ireneae Ripley, 1966

Order STRIGIFORMES   Family STRIGIDAE

STATUS   Rare.   Confined to one forested area in East Africa, portions of which
have been destroyed since this owl's discovery.   The threat of additional forest
destruction remains.

DISTRIBUTION   The Arabuko-Sokoke forest near Kilifi, eastern Kenya.   The owl is
patchily distributed within the forest and in the decade 1956-1966 the extent of
the forest was halved (1; 2).   However, an area of some 360 sq. km remains, in
which the owl is still to be found in all but the most impoverished habitats (4).

POPULATION   Formerly thought to number a few scores but to be reasonably common
in those parts of the forest where it occurred (3).   A more recent estimate puts
the population at 1300-1500 pairs in what is left of the forest (4).   Nevertheless
there has undoubtedly been a decline as a result of the habitat destruction of
recent years, which has included the area from which the type specimen came in
1965 (2).

HABITAT   Lowland forest.   The Arabuko-Sokoke forest, a composite of several
distinct forest types varying with elevation and soil characteristics, is the
northernmost of the eastern coastal forests of south and east Africa.   It has been
subjected to clearing for agriculture and for forestry (involving the planting of
exotic species, which now occupy about 3 percent of the forest area) and is also
suffering from deterioration attributable to the constant gathering of wood (2;
4; 5).

CONSERVATION MEASURES TAKEN   This owl is protected by Kenya law.   Within the
400 sq. km of the Arabuko-Sokoke Forest Reserve, one nature reserve of 40 sq. km,
in which no disturbance is allowed, has so far been established.

CONSERVATION MEASURES PROPOSED   Recommendations include the reservation of an
additional 20 sq. km as nature reserve and the protection of sizeable tracts of
each of the three main types of habitats of importance to this and other threatened
bird species of the forest.   It has also been suggested that an area of 200 sq. km
surrounding the proposed nature reserve should be kept for traditional utilizat:on
only (4; P. Britton 1977, pers. comm.).

REFERENCES   1.   Ripley, S.D. 1966.   A notable owlet from Kenya.
                   Ibis 108: 136-137.
              2.   Ripley, S.D. & Bond, G.M. 1971.   Systematic notes on a
                   collection of birds from Kenya.   Smithsonian Contrib.
                   Zool. 111.
              3.   Brown, L.H. et al. Undated.   A report on threatened bird
                   species in East Africa.   East African Wildlife Society.
                   Mimeo, 12 pp.
              4.   Britton, P.L. 1976.   Primary forestland destruction now
                   critical.   Africana 5(12): i-ii.
              5.   Turner, D.A. 1977.   Status and distribution of the
                   East African endemic species.   Scopus 1: 2-11.

PAPUAN SCOPS OWL

Otus magicus beccarii (Salvadori, 1875)

Order STRIGIFORMES   Family STRIGIDAE

STATUS   Indeterminate. Known from one island off Irian Jaya, north-western
New Guinea, much of which is now occupied by settlers. As a result, little
remains of the undisturbed forest which this owl evidently requires.

DISTRIBUTION   Biak Island (32 x 104 km), situated off the mouth of Teluk
Cendrawasih (formerly Geelvink Bay), on the northern coast of Irian Jaya,
Indonesia (1-5).

POPULATION   Unknown. Only three specimens have been taken, the last in 1937 (2).
In 1973, an ornithologist spent 7 days on Biak searching exclusively for this owl
and finding only one pair (J.T. Marshall 1977, pers. comm.).

HABITAT   Biak Island was still largely covered by primary forest in 1937, and
the haunt of the pair of these owls collected that year was in deep forest on
Korido, the smaller of the two oblong sections of Biak, which are connected by a
low swampy isthmus (1; S.D. Ripley 1977, pers. comm.). By 1973, much of this
forest had been cut over, at least within a 16 km radius of the island's airport,
which is situated on the larger eastern segment of the island. A very considerable part of the land is now devoted to cultivation and to the housing of local
inhabitants and Indonesian military personnel, with a single patch of swampy
forest, backing onto wooded limestone cliffs, representing the only relatively
undisturbed forested area seen in 7 days of searching. This was the place in
which a single pair of these owls was found (J.T. Marshall 1977, pers. comm.).

CONSERVATION MEASURES TAKEN   None known.

CONSERVATION MEASURES PROPOSED   None known.

REMARKS   This owl has also been considered to be a full species by some authors
(1; 4; 5) and, by one author, a subspecies of _Otus manadensis_ (3).

REFERENCES   1.   Mayr, E. & de Schauensee, R.M. 1939. Zoological
                   results of the Denison-Crockett Expedition to the South
                   Pacific for the Academy of Natural Sciences of Philadelphia,
                   1937-1938, Part 1: The birds of the island of Biak.
                   Proc. Acad. Nat. Sci. Philadelphia 91: 1-37.
              2.   Marshall, J.T., Jr., 1978. Systematics of smaller Asian
                   nightbirds. Amer. Ornith. Union Ornith. Monogr. No. 25.
              3.   Burton, J.A. 1973. Owls of the World. New York & London:
                   E.P. Dutton; Peter Lowe.
              4.   Peters, J.L. 1940. Check-list of Birds of the World.
                   Vol. IV. Cambridge: Harvard University Press.
              5.   Rand, A.L. & Gilliard, E.T. 1968. Handbook of New Guinea
                   Birds. Garden City, N.Y.: Natural History Press.

VIRGIN ISLANDS SCREECH OWL

Otus nudipes newtoni (Lawrence, 1860)

Order STRIGIFORMES   Family STRIGIDAE

STATUS   Rare.   Known from four islands in the Caribbean, three of which are in
the Virgin Islands; but very rarely recorded.   Forests on three of the four islands
are being cut continually to provide more land for a burgeoning human population.

DISTRIBUTION   Specimen-supported records are confined to St. Croix, St. Thomas,
and St. John, American Virgin Islands, and Vieques off the east end of Puerto Rico
(1).   The last known occasion on which the call of this owl was heard was on 25
November 1966 in the Caledonia Valley of St. Croix (2).   Shortly before this the
call of an owl, almost certainly of this subspecies, was heard on 7 November 1966,
in the summit forest of Sage Mountain, Tortola, British Virgin Islands (2).

POPULATION   This subspecies is not known to have ever been particularly numerous
and the present population is certainly very low.   A maximum of 25 birds has been
estimated (G.A. Seaman 1973, pers. comm.).   Recent attempts to hear its call at
night on Vieques, St. Croix and St. John have proved fruitless (3; C.B. Kepler,
H. Raffaele 1973, pers. comm.).

HABITAT   Dry woodland.   The most extensive woodland in the Virgin Islands is on
St. John, and this is one of the areas where repeated attempts to find the owl have
been unsuccessful (3).

CONSERVATION MEASURES TAKEN   Legal protection.   Most of the extensive forests of
St. John are preserved within a National Park.   The summit area of Sage Mountain
on Tortola is treated as a forest reserve.

CONSERVATION MEASURES PROPOSED   Continuation of efforts to locate a population of
the Screech Owl (3).

REMARKS   The nominate subspecies on Puerto Rico is local and uncommon but in no
danger of extinction (C.B. Kepler 1973, pers. comm.).

REFERENCES   1.   Bond, J. 1956.   Check-list of Birds of the West Indies.
                     Philadelphia Acad. Nat. Sci.
               2.   Bond, J. 1967.   Twelfth supplement to the Check-list of Birds
                     of the West Indies (1956).   Philadelphia Acad. Nat. Sci.
               3.   U.S. Fish and Wildlife Service Office of Endangered Species and
                     International Activities, 1973.   Threatened Wildlife of the
                     United States.   U.S. Dept. of Interior Resource Pub. 114.

ANJOUAN SCOPS OWL

Otus rutilus capnodes (Gurney, 1889)

Order STRIGIFORMES   Family STRIGIDAE

STATUS   Endangered, if in fact it still survives.   Known only from Anjouan Island,
Comoro group, western Indian Ocean, it was not found during an extensive investigation of the Anjouan avifauna in 1958 and was therefore thought to be already
extinct at that time.   No subsequent information to the contrary has come to hand.

DISTRIBUTION   Presumably restricted to the forests of Anjouan which by 1958 had
been reduced to two patches of 7,000 ha and 2,000 ha respectively, along the central
ridge of the island.   In spite of frequent search of these areas during the full
month's survey in 1958, the owl was not found (1).   In the 19th century, when
forest covered much of Anjouan, it was apparently widespread.

POPULATION   Exceedingly small, if any,-since no trace of the owl has been
discovered in recent searches.   By contrast, between 1884 and 1897, at least 31
specimens were collected and the owl was undoubtedly reasonably common at the time;
however, a collector who visited Anjouan in 1906 and 1907 apparently failed to
obtain it (1).

HABITAT   Evergreen forest.   This on Anjouan has been severely degraded by felling
for replacement by banana plantations and other human activities, aggravated by the
effects of cyclones.   Soil erosion of the forested slopes had become a serious
problem by 1958.   The fact remains, however, that the species is still quite
common in secondary forest on other islands in the Comoros, so that it has been
suggested that over-collecting rather than habitat destruction may have caused the
possible extinction of the Anjouan subspecies (1).

CONSERVATION MEASURES TAKEN   None known.

CONSERVATION MEASURES PROPOSED   None known.

REMARKS   Three other subspecies, on Grand Comoro and Mayotte in the Comoros and on
Madagascar, are not known to be at risk.   The status of Otus pembaensis, which is
restricted to Pemba island, Tanzania, and which is also sometimes considered a
subspecies of O. rutilus (1), has not recently been determined.

REFERENCES   1.   Benson, C.W. 1960.   The birds of the Comoro Islands: Results
                    of the British Ornithologists' Union Centenary Expedition 1958.
                    Ibis 103b: 5-106.

PUERTO RICAN WHIPPOORWILL

Caprimulgus noctitherus (Wetmore, 1919)

Order CAPRIMULGIFORMES   Family CAPRIMULGIDAE

STATUS   Rare.   Known from three small areas on or near the south coast of Puerto
Rico, West Indies.   The introduced mongoose undoubtedly preys on this ground-
nesting species, as do other introduced predators.   Moreover, the future of its
habitat is made precarious by the intense pressure on unsettled land, especially
along the coast, from the ever-growing human population of the island.

DISTRIBUTION   At the turn of the century, the species inhabited the forests of
the limestone zone along both the north and south coasts of Puerto Rico, its range
extending inland to the edges of the Cordillera Central in suitable habitat.   It
presently inhabits 2,300 ha of Guanica Commonwealth Forest, about 400 ha of Susua
Commonwealth Forest, and about 500 ha in the Guayanilla Hills, all in the southern
half of the island and representing about 3 per cent of its probable historical
distribution (1).

POPULATION   The species was thought to be extinct from about 1911 until 1961, when
it was rediscovered.   Recent censuses show about 400 breeding pairs in Guanica
Forest, about 30 pairs in Susua Forest and roughly 50 pairs in the Guayanilla Hills
(1).

HABITAT   Dry forest, on limestone soils, of semi-deciduous hardwood tree species,
with a canopy up to 5 m height, and especially those areas which have no grass or
brush at ground level.   The nightjar seems to prefer extremely dry areas which are
entirely without any standing water and seldom visited by mongooses (1).   It should
survive indefinitely as long as this habitat is assured complete protection.

CONSERVATION MEASURES TAKEN   Fully protected by Puerto Rico Commonwealth and U.S.
Federal law.   Two of the three areas in which the species presently occurs are
Commonwealth Forests, which provides some measure of habitat protection.   Nevertheless, in the recent past, other areas designated as Commonwealth Forest have been
given over to development for heavy industry and there have been similar threats to
the integrity of Guanica Forest, on which 80 per cent of the extant population of
the nightjar now depends.   These threats took the form of a proposed copper smelter
adjacent to and upwind from the forest, sanitary landfill proposals for parts of the
forest, and a project for an international jetport less than 10 km away.   However,
as the result of pleas by conservation interests, the smelting plant was eventually
relocated elsewhere (1).

CONSERVATION MEASURES PROPOSED   Stricter protection for the three areas in which
the species occurs, especially for the presently quite unprotected site in
Guayanilla Hills (1; 2).   Continued study of the distribution and ecology of the
species (2).

REFERENCES   1.   Kepler, C.B. & Kepler, A.K. 1972.   The distribution and ecology
                    of the Puerto Rican Whip-poor-will, an endangered species.
                    The Living Bird 11: 207-239.
              2.   U.S. Fish and Wildlife Service. 1973.   Threatened Wildlife of
                    the United States.   U.S. Bur. Sport Fish. Wildl. Res. Pub. 114.

BLACK INCA

Coeligena prunellei (Bourcier, 1843)

Order APODIFORMES   Family TROCHILIDAE

STATUS   Indeterminate.   This poorly known Colombian hummingbird has been only
rarely recorded during the last forty years, although other members of its genus
are relatively conspicuous and easily observed.   Destruction of forests is the
probable cause of its apparent disappearance.

DISTRIBUTION   The Cundinamarca, Boyacá and Santander divisions of central
Colombia.   Most existing specimens were collected in the 19th century and labelled
"Bogotá", implying localities anywhere in central Colombia but presumably on the
western slopes of the Eastern Andes.   Specimens are also known to have been taken
at Facatativá, La Vega, Pedropalo, Albán, Guaduas and Yacopi in Cundinamarca (1-3)
and 150 km to the north-east at Virolin, Santander division (3 specimens at U.S.
Nat. Mus. collected in 1943).   A sighting was made in 1974 at Bojacá, not very
far from Facatativá (J. Hernandez 1977, pers. comm. to R. Ridgely).   In 1978, the
species was again encountered in Boyacá, at an altitude of 2,300-2,500 m on the
slopes of Cerro Carare, 9 km ESE of Togui and about 200 km NE of Bogotá (B.K. &
D.W. Snow 1979, pers. comm. to H.F.I. Elliott).

POPULATION   Unknown, but a serious decline must have taken place, for although a
number of specimens were collected in the 19th century, there have been very few
reports of this hummingbird in recent years.   It was, however, quite common in
the forest on Cerro Carare in 1978, with a total population, to judge from the
extent of forest remaining, that must have run into many hundreds (B.K. & D.W. Snow
1979, pers. comm. to H.F.I. Elliott).

HABITAT   Subtropical and temperate forest.   The forest of the western slopes of
the Eastern Andes has been seriously depleted and none of what is left within this
hummingbird's range has been given protection.

CONSERVATION MEASURES TAKEN   None known.

CONSERVATION MEASURES PROPOSED   None known, although the reservation of at least
part of the forest in which the species has recently been observed in fair numbers,
would seem desirable.

REFERENCES   1.   de Schauensee, R.M. 1966.   The Species of Birds of South
                   America and their Distribution.   Narberth, Pa.: Livingston
                   Publishing Co.
              2.   de Schauensee, R.M. 1949.   The birds of the Republic of
                   Colombia. Part 2.   Caldasia 5: 381-644.
              3.   Olivares, A. 1969.   Aves de Cundinamarca.   Bogota:
                   Univ. Nac. Colombia.

CHILEAN WOODSTAR

Eulidia yarrellii (Bourcier, 1847)

Order APODIFORMES   Family TROCHILIDAE

STATUS   Endangered.   The species had an extremely restricted distribution in
Chile and is now becoming exceedingly rare from unknown causes.

DISTRIBUTION   This species is now found only in Tarapacá, the northernmost
province of Chile, where it is restricted to the city of Arica, adjacent suburbs
in the Azapa valley and the neighbouring Lluta valley; individual birds, possibly
vagrants, have been seen at Chupicilca in Camarones valley, 70 km south of the
Azapa valley, and also, well inland and a further 130 km south, at Mamiña.   Many
years ago a specimen was collected at Cobija on the northern coast of Antofagasta
province. (1; 2).

POPULATION   The species was considered common to abundant within its restricted
range between 1935 and 1948, but had become much scarcer by 1971; between April
1972 and July 1973 an ornithologist resident in the Azapa valley encountered it
only three times (1).

HABITAT   Urban gardens and agricultural areas, which are presumably a surrogate
for the original vegetation of the valleys where this species occurs.   The only
suitable habitat is in fact confined to several narrow fertile valleys which are
surrounded by sere and inhospitable desert.   The species is said to be
occasionally attracted in considerable numbers to certain flowering trees in the
city of Arica (1).

CONSERVATION MEASURES TAKEN   None known.

CONSERVATION MEASURES PROPOSED   None known.

REMARKS   In 1943, in Arica, this species was more abundant than the Oasis
Hummingbird Rhodopis vesper (3), but Rhodopis, which is half as large again as
Eulidia, is now by far the commoner (1).

REFERENCES   1. McFarlane, R.W. 1975.   The status of certain birds in
                   northern Chile.   Bull. ICBP 12: 300-309.
               2. Johnson, A.W. 1967.   The Birds of Chile and Adjacent
                   Regions of Argentina, Bolivia and Peru.   Buenos Aires:
                   Platt Establecimientos Gráficos S.A.
               3. Philippi, B.R.A., Johnson, A.W. & Goodall, J.D. 1944.
                   Expedición ornitológica al norte de Chile.   Bol. Mus.
                   Nac. Hist. Nat. Santiago 22: 65-120.

HOOK-BILLED HERMIT

Glaucis dohrnii (Bourcier and Mulsant, 1852)

Order APODIFORMES   Family TROCHILIDAE

STATUS   Endangered. Presently known only from two areas of primary forest in south-eastern Brazil, one of which is a national park.

DISTRIBUTION   Formerly occurred in eastern Brazil from southern Bahia to Rio de Janeiro (1).   In 1939, the total size of its range was estimated at 35,000 sq. km (2), but by 1967, it could still be found in an area of only about 100 sq. km (3). It is found today in a 4,000 ha forest tract of Klabin Farm, an estate near Conceição da Barra and close to the border of Espírito Santo with Bahia (3) and was also detected in 1977 in the Monte Pascoal National Park (22,500 ha) of south-eastern Bahia (R. Ridgely 1978, pers. comm.).

POPULATION   There are no early estimates, although clearly this species was once vastly more abundant than it is today.   In 1976, the Klabin Farm population was put at about 20 (4) and in 1977, at Monte Pascoal, it was rated as uncommon (R. Ridgely 1978, pers. comm.).

HABITAT   The forest belt in the region originally occupied by this species was 50 km wide, stretching from the Bahian plateau nearly to the Atlantic coast.   Now only relict patches of uncut forest remain and the rest of the countryside is devoted to cattle and to a lesser extent to cacao culture.

CONSERVATION MEASURES TAKEN   The species is listed in Appendix 1 of the 1973 Convention on International Trade in Endangered Species of Wild Fauna and Flora, protected by law in Brazil and included in the Brazilian list of endangered species.   Its occurrence in one national park gives it a little added protection.

CONSERVATION MEASURES PROPOSED   The establishment of a special reserve for this species has been advocated.

REMARKS   The Hook-billed Hermit shares the Klabin Farm forest with several other endangered species of birds, including two newly described hummingbirds, two cotingas, and a piping guan (see relevant data sheets).

REFERENCES   1.   de Schauensee, R.M. 1966. The Species of Birds of South America and their Distribution.   Narberth, Pa.: Livingston Publishing Co.
2.   Sick, H. 1972.   A ameaça da avifauna brasileira.   In Espécies da Fauna Brasileira Ameaçados de Extinção, pp. 99-153. Rio de Janeiro: Academia Brasileira de Ciências.
3.   Ruschi, A. 1967.   Beija-flores raros ou ameaçadas de extinção.   Bol. Mus. Biol. Mello Leitão, proteção a natureza, 29.
4.   Ruschi, A. 1976.   Areas ideais para as reservas florestais e biológicas.   Bol. Mus. Biol. Mello Leitão No. Especial: 139-141.

KLABIN FARM LONG-TAILED HERMIT

Phaethornis margarettae Ruschi, 1972

Order APODIFORMES   Family TROCHILIDAE

STATUS   Endangered.   Recently discovered and known with certainty only from one forest tract in Brazil.

DISTRIBUTION   This hermit has been collected only in the 4,000 ha area of forest on Klabin Farm, Conceição da Barra, Espírito Santo, Brazil, but a hermit, in all likelihood of this species, was observed in 1977 in Sooretama Reserve, Espírito Santo (R. Ridgely 1978, pers. comm.).

POPULATION   Unknown, although likely to be small in view of the very limited area presently occupied.   At one time, before the greater part of the primary forest in Espírito Santo had been cut, the species was no doubt more widespread and numerous.

HABITAT   Primary rainforest.   In Espírito Santo, after decades of forest clearing, only two tracts of this habitat remain: Sooretama Reserve, 24,000 ha, and the Klabin Farm forest, 4,000 ha.   This species is known with certainty only from the latter, which is in private ownership (R. Ridgely 1978, pers. comm.).

CONSERVATION MEASURES TAKEN   The species is protected by law in Brazil.

CONSERVATION MEASURES PROPOSED   None known.

REMARKS   Eight other threatened species or subspecies of birds occur on Klabin Farm, a concentration almost certainly unequalled anywhere else in the world.

REFERENCES   1.   Ruschi, A. 1972.   Uma nova espécie de Beija-Flor do E.
                        E. Santo.   Bol. Mus. Biol. Mello Leitão, Ser. Zool., 35.
              2.   Ruschi, A. 1976.   Aves que estão em vias de ectinção
                        e se encontram eclusivamente no território do estado do
                        Espírito Santo, em floresta virgem pertencentes aos
                        Irmãos Klabin.   Bol. Mus. Biol. Mello Leitão, Num.
                        Especial: 118.

BLACK-BILLED HERMIT

Phaethornis nigrirostris Ruschi, 1973

Order APODIFORMES   Family TROCHILIDAE

STATUS   Rare.   Restricted to primary forest in one reserve in south-eastern Brazil.

DISTRIBUTION   Known only from the type locality, Nova Lombardia, Municipia de Santa Teresa, 50 km north-west of Vitória in Espírito Santo, Brazil (1).

POPULATION   Unknown, but likely to be very small in view of the restricted range of the species.   In the Nova Lombardia Reserve it is outnumbered by another hermit P. eurynome (R. Ridgely 1978, pers. comm.).

HABITAT   Primary forest at about 950 m elevation.   The extent of primary forest in Espírito Santo is seriously reduced and there are now no more than a few local patches.

CONSERVATION MEASURES TAKEN   The species has legal protection in Brazil and its occurrence in the Nova Lombardia (4,350 ha) Reserve, administered by the Instituto Brasileiro de Desenvolvimento Florestal of the Brazilian government, gives it some additional protection.

CONSERVATION MEASURES PROPOSED   None known.

REFERENCES   1.   Ruschi, A. 1973.   Uma nova espécie de Beija-flor do E.E. Santo.   Bol. Mus. Biol. Mello Leitão, Ser. Zool., 36.

BLACK BARBTHROAT

Threnetes grzimeki Ruschi, 1973

Order APODIFORMES   Family TROCHILIDAE

STATUS   Endangered.   Discovered in 1972, this hummingbird is known only from
two areas in south-eastern Brazil.

DISTRIBUTION   Occurs only in the Sooretama Reserve (24,000 ha) and in the
forested section of Klabin Farm (4,000 ha), Conceição da Barra, both in the state
of Espírito Santo, Brazil (1).

POPULATION   Unknown, although certainly quite small.   Only four specimens are
known to have been collected.   Presumably, before the great part of the forests
of Espírito Santo had been felled, this species would have been far more widespread
but it is now decidedly sparse even in the neighbourhood of its type locality (1).

HABITAT   Primary rainforest, now, in Espírito Santo, restricted to two areas;
all the rest, probably amounting to millions of hectares, has been cleared.

CONSERVATION MEASURES TAKEN   The species is protected by law in Brazil.   In
addition, the current protection of the two areas to which it is apparently
restricted, can be rated as excellent (R. Ridgely 1977, pers. comm.).

CONSERVATION MEASURES PROPOSED   None known.

REMARKS   Eight other threatened species or subspecies of birds occur at Klabin
Farm (2), which is probably a greater concentration than is to be found in any
area of comparable size elsewhere in the world.

REFERENCES   1.   Ruschi, A. 1973.   Uma nova espécie de Threnetes (Aves,
                    Trochilidae): Threnetes grzimeki sp. n. Bol. Mus. Biol.
                    Mello Leitão, Ser. Zool., 37.
              2.   Ruschi, A. 1976.   Aves que estão em vias de extinção e
                    se encontram eclusivamente no território do estado do
                    Espírito Santo, em floresta virgem pertencentes aos
                    Irmãos Klabin.   Bol. Mus. Biol. Mello Leitão., Num.
                    Espécial: 118.

RESPLENDENT QUETZAL

Pharomacrus mocinno mocinno de la Llave, 1832

Pharomacrus mocinno costaricensis Cabanis, 1869

Order TROGONIFORMES   Family TROGONIDAE

STATUS   Vulnerable.   Although still common in remote areas of Central America
this species has declined seriously throughout its range as a result of the
extensive destruction of its cloud forest habitat and of the hunting and capture
of birds for local use or trade.   Very little of the remaining cloud forest
receives legal or effective protection.

DISTRIBUTION   The nominate subspecies ranges from the highlands of Oaxaca and
Chiapas, Mexico (1; A. Gardner 1973, pers. comm.), south and east: through central
Guatemala, particularly in Alta Verapaz and the Sierra de las Minas (2; 3); locally
in Honduras on the Montana de Pijol, the Cerro Santa Barbara and in other areas(4);
in El Salvador, by 1954, only at Los Esesmiles y Miramundo toward the border of
Honduras, though once more widespread (5); possibly still in the 12 sq. km
Montecristo forest on the Honduras/Guatemalan border (6); and as far as Nicaragua,
where it is locally distributed in the few areas of cloud forest in highlands above
1300 m (7).   The subspecies P. m. costaricensis occurs in Costa Rica from the
Cordillera Central to the northern Talamanca Cordillera, in the mountains of
Cartago Province and in the Cordillera de Tilarán (8); in Panama it is found in the
mountains of eastern and western Chiriqui, Bocas del Toro and Veraguas, particularly
on Volcan Baru and above Cerro Punta and Boquete, (9; 10).   Throughout this
extensive range it is now very rarely found in accessible forest or at elevations
below 1500 m and the total area it inhabits is continually decreasing.

POPULATION   Although the species is still common in remote areas, it has
seriously decreased in numbers in the past few decades in all accessible parts of
its range and is now most abundant in Honduras and Costa Rica (11).   Its decline
is perhaps most marked in southern Mexico, although even there it is still
certainly present in suitably remote areas.
    Capture for the pet trade may have a local impact on populations, for example
in 1973, a dealer in Costa Rica claimed to have exported 100 adult quetzals
(N. Smith 1974, pers. comm.).

HABITAT   Cloud forest above 1300 m, although the species does occasionally
wander into partially cleared areas or pastures adjacent to the forest.   Cloud
forest has been extensively felled or thinned in Central America for coffee
plantations, shifting subsistence agriculture and cattle grazing (12; 13).
Very little of the once vast stretches of cloud forest has ever received protection.

CONSERVATION MEASURES TAKEN   The species is listed in Appendix 1 of the
Convention on International Trade in Endangered Species of Wild Fauna and Flora.
It is legally protected in Mexico, Guatemala, Costa Rica and Panama, although
enforcement is virtually impossible in the remote areas where this species is
mostly found.   It has been designated as the National Bird of Guatemala, although
the consequent notoriety tends to result in its regular appearance in captivity
rather than to provide added protection.   Areas of cloud forest habitat that
receive some protection include 10,000 ha of federal land at El Triunfo, Mexico,
administered by the Chiapas Institute of Natural History; the Monteverde Cloud
Forest Reserve in Costa Rica, maintained by the Tropical Science Center; two
private reserves in Guatemala (14); and, lastly, Volcan Poas National Park and the
newly established Cerro Cirripo National Park in Costa Rica (R. Ridgely 1978, pers.
comm.).

CONSERVATION MEASURES PROPOSED   The creation of a national park at Volcan Baru, Panama, was recommended to the Panama government by IUCN, FAO and UNDP in 1973 (15); it still remains unfulfilled,so the forested slopes continue to be denuded. (R. Ridgely 1978, pers. comm.).

REMARKS   Pharomachrus antisianus of northern South America has sometimes been considered a subspecies of P. mocinno.   The Quetzal is often kept in captivity but is not known to have been bred successfully.   This species, which is familiar to people around the world because of its dramatic appearance and its cultural significance, is no more threatened than a number of other cloud forest species of Central America.   It has been selected for inclusion mainly to draw attention to the need for additional protection of a habitat type that is constantly under attack and becoming increasingly scarce.

REFERENCES   1.   Alvarez del Toro, M. 1964.   Lista de las Aves de Chiapas. Tuxtla Gutierrez: Instituto de Ciencias y Artes de Chiapas.
2.   Land, H.C. 1970.   Birds of Guatemala.   Wynnewood, Pa.: Livingston Publishing Co.
3.   Bowes, A.L. & Allen, D.G. 1969.   Biology and conservation of the Quetzal.   Biol. Cons. 1:   297-306.
4.   Monroe, B.L. Jr. 1968.   A distributional survey of the birds of Honduras.   Amer. Ornith. Union Ornith. Monog. 7.
5.   Rand, A.L. & Traylor, M.A. 1954.   Manual de las Aves de El Salvador.   San Salvador: Univ. de El Salvador.
6.   Daugherty, H.E. 1973.   The Montecristo cloud-forest of El Salvador - a chance for protection.   Biol. Cons. 5:   227-230.
7.   Howell, T.R. 1970.   Avifauna in Nicaragua.   In H.K. Buechner and J.H. Buechner (eds) The Avifauna of Northern Latin America: A Symposium Held at the Smithsonian Institution 13-15 April 1966, pp. 58-61.   Smithsonian Contrib. Zool. 26.
8.   Slud, P. 1964.   The birds of Costa Rica.   Bull. Amer. Mus. Nat. Hist. 128:   1-430.
9.   Wetmore, A. 1968.   The Birds of the Republic of Panama. Part 2.   Washington: Smithsonian Inst. Press.
10.   Ridgely, R. 1976.   A Guide to the Birds of Panama. Princeton: Princeton Univ. Press.
11.   Monroe, B.L. Jr. 1970.   Effects of habitat changes on population levels of the avifauna in Honduras.   In H.K. Buechner and J.H. Buechner (eds) The Avifauna of Northern Latin America, pp. 38-41.   Smithsonian Contrib. Zool. 26.
12.   Budowski, G. 1968.   La influencia humana en la vegetación natural de montañas tropicales americanas.   Colloquium Geogr. 9:   157-162.
13.   Veblen, T.T. 1976.   The urgent need for forest conservation in highland Guatemala.   Biol. Cons. 9:   141-154.
14.   La Bastille, A. 1973.   Establishment of a Quetzal cloud-forest reserve in Guatemala.   Biol. Cons. 5:   60-62.
15.   La Bastille, A. 1974.   First proposed national park for Panama.   Biol. Cons. 6:   102-105.

GUAM MICRONESIAN KINGFISHER

Halcyon cinnamomina cinnamomina Swainson, 1821

Order CORACIIFORMES   Family ALCEDINIDAE

STATUS   Endangered.   Restricted to Guam, Mariana Islands, Western Pacific Ocean,
where it has declined seriously in recent years and is now quite rare.

DISTRIBUTION   Known only from Guam (541 sq. km), where it is widely dispersed in
the forest and along the forest edge (1; 2).

POPULATION   This, the nominate race of the species, was considered common on Guam
as recently as 1945.   At that date, it comprised 1.2 per cent of all birds
observed along the island's roadways, even though it had inconspicuous habits (3).
Its decline in abundance has taken place within the last few years and by 1976 the
population was estimated to be not more than 150 pairs (N. Drahos 1976, pers. comm.).

HABITAT   Forest and forest edge (1).   In recent years, the extent of forest on
Guam has decreased as the pace of human development of the island has increased.

CONSERVATION MEASURES TAKEN   The subspecies is listed on Guam's Endangered
Species list, but this has not yet been incorporated in the Guam Endangered Species
Act of 1975.

CONSERVATION MEASURES PROPOSED   None known.

REMARKS   Two other subspecies of the Micronesian Kingfisher have been described,
from the Palaus and from Ponape, at either end of the Caroline Islands.   Neither
is believed to be presently at risk.

REFERENCES   1.   Baker, R.H. 1951.   The avifauna of Micronesia, its origin,
                    evolution and distribution.   Univ. Kansas Pubs. Mus.
                    Nat. Hist. 3(1): 1-359.
              2.   Guam Division of Fish and Wildlife. 1975.   Habitat appraisal
                    and study of exotics for Guam.   Guam Fish and Wildlife
                    Investigations, Project FW-2R-12, job W-5.
              3.   Baker, R.H. 1947.   Size of bird populations on Guam, Mariana
                    Islands.   Condor 49: 124-125.

CROSSLEY'S GROUND ROLLER

Atelornis crossleyi Sharpe, 1875

Order CORACIIFORMES   Family CORACIIDAE

STATUS   Rare.   This species has only been found in a few localities in the
eastern forests of Madagascar.   Its forest habitat continues to decline in extent.

DISTRIBUTION   Recorded in the humid forests of eastern Madagascar from Andapa
south to Fanovana (1).   Specific localities include the Sihanaka forest (2), Didy
85 km inland from Tamatave and, farther north, Marojejy and the Tsaratanana massif
(3).

POPULATION   No estimate has been made, but this ground roller has been considered
rare since at least 1930 (1; 2).   It apparently is rather common only in the
vicinity of Didy (3) and was considered to be very scarce at Marojejy in 1958 (4).

HABITAT   Dense humid forest at altitudes of between 800 and 1800 m (2).   The
forests of Madagascar are being destroyed at an accelerating rate by clearance for
agricultural purposes, replacement by plantations of exotic pines and eucalypts,
and fires, from repeated burning of adjacent areas, spreading into the forest itself
(5).

CONSERVATION MEASURES TAKEN   No specific legal protection has been extended to
this species, but part of its known habitat is protected in two localities by the
Tsaratanana and Marojejy nature reserves.

CONSERVATION MEASURES PROPOSED   The protection by law of this and most other
endemic birds of Madagascar has been advocated to the Malagasy Government (K. Curry-
Lindahl in litt. to G. Ramanantsoavina, Director, Service des Eaux et Forêts,
Chasse et Pêche, Jan. 1973).

REFERENCES   1.   Lavauden, L. 1937.   Supplement au Vol 12 - Oiseaux.   In A. and
                   G. Grandidier, Histoire Physique, Naturelle et Politique de
                   Madagascar.   Paris: Société d'Editions Géographiques, Maritimes
                   et Coloniales.
              2.   Rand, A.L. 1936.   The distribution and habits of Madagascar
                   birds.   Bull. Amer. Mus. Nat. Hist. 72: 143-499.
              3.   Milon, P., Petter, J.-J. & Randrianasolo, G. 1973.   Faune de
                   Madagascar 35: Oiseaux.   Tananarive and Paris: ORSTOM and CNRS.
              4.   Grivaud, P. 1961.   Un mission entomologique au Marojejy.
                   Le Naturaliste Malgache 12: 43-55.
              5.   Curry-Lindahl, K. 1975.   Man in Madagascar.   Defenders of
                   Wildlife 50(2): 164-169.

PITTA-LIKE GROUND ROLLER

Atelornis pittoides (Lafresnaye, 1834)

Order CORACIIFORMES   Family CORACIIDAE

STATUS   Rare.   Known from several localities on Madagascar and common only in
one, this species inhabits the dense forest which is being cleared gradually but
inexorably.

DISTRIBUTION   Restricted to north and central parts of the humid forest of
eastern Madagascar, south to Fanovana and north-west to Maromandia and Mt. d'Ambre
(1).   It has also been recorded from Andringitra, Sihanaka forest, Masoala
peninsula, the Anosyennes chain, Mandraka and Didy (2).

POPULATION   No estimate has been made.   This ground roller has been described as
common on Mt. d'Ambre in the far north of Madagascar and rather less so near
Mandraka and Didy, but rare elsewhere (2).   There may well have been a decline in
its total population as the result of continuing destruction of Madagascar's
forests, although this has not been fully documented.

HABITAT   Dense moist forest above 400 m altitude.   Forests now only cover 10 per
cent of the surface of Madagascar, and their destruction continues.   It is largely
caused by clearing for subsistence agriculture, replacement of indigenous species
by plantations of exotic pines and eucalypts, and uncontrolled burning of adjacent
grasslands.

CONSERVATION MEASURES TAKEN   Part of the habitat of this species is now within
the Mt. d'Ambre National Park.

CONSERVATION MEASURES PROPOSED   Most endemic bird species have been recommended to
the Malagasy government as worthy of legal protection (K. Curry-Lindahl in litt. to
G. Ramanantsoavina, Director, Service des Eaux et Forêts, Chasse et Pêche, Jan.
1973).

REFERENCES   1.   Lavauden, L. 1937.   Supplément au Vol. 12 - Oiseaux.   In
                    A. and G. Grandidier, Histoire Physique, Naturelle et Politique
                    de Madagascar.   Paris: Société d'Editions Géographiques,
                    Maritimes et Coloniales.
               2.   Milon, P., Petter, J.-J. & Randrianasolo, G. 1973.   Faune de
                    Madagascar, 35: Oiseaux.   Tananarive and Paris: ORSTOM and
                    CNRS.

SHORT-LEGGED GROUND ROLLER

Brachypteracias leptosomus (Lesson, 1833)

Order CORACIIFORMES   Family CORACIIDAE

STATUS   Rare.   Restricted to certain parts of the humid forests of Madagascar,
and nowhere common.   As a ground-dwelling species it is vulnerable to predation,
while the extent of its forest habitat continues to diminish.

DISTRIBUTION   Known only from the wettest areas of humid forest in the northern
and central portions of eastern Madagascar (1; 2).   Its precise distribution
within this area has not been determined.

POPULATION   While no population estimate has ever been attempted, this species
was already considered to be uncommon by 1930 (2) and was described as 'rather rare'
in 1973 (1).

HABITAT   Dense shady moist forest with a ground cover of small saplings (2).
Only 10 per cent of Madagascar's original forests survives and is being further
reduced annually as a result of forestry projects to replace them with exotic pine
or eucalypt plantations, clearing for subsistence agriculture, and the repeated and
uncontrolled burning of adjacent grasslands (3).   The amount of original habitat
of this species now remaining has not been calculated but must be very limited.

CONSERVATION MEASURES TAKEN   None known.

CONSERVATION MEASURES PROPOSED   A recommendation has been made to the Malagasy
government that this species and almost all other endemic birds of Madagascar
be legally protected (K. Curry-Lindahl in litt. to G. Ramanantsoavina, Director,
Service des Eaux et Forêts, Chasse et Pêche, Jan. 1973).

REFERENCES   1.   Milon, P., Petter, J.-J. & Randrianasolo, G. 1973.   Faune de
                    Madagascar, 35: Oiseaux.   Tananarive and Paris: ORSTOM and
                    CNRS.
              2.   Rand, A.L. 1936.   The distribution and habits of Madagascar
                    birds.   Bull. Amer. Mus. Nat. Hist. 72: 143-499.
              3.   Curry-Lindahl, K. 1975.   Man in Madagascar.   Defenders of
                    Wildlife 50(2): 92-134.

SCALED GROUND ROLLER

Brachypteracias squamigera Lafresnaye, 1838

Order CORACIIFORMES   Family CORACIIDAE

STATUS   Rare.   Restricted in distribution to certain areas of the eastern
Madagascar forests, and nowhere common.   What is left of this forest continues to
diminish as do the forests throughout the island.

DISTRIBUTION   Known only from the central and northern portions of the humid
forest zone of the east coast, this ground roller is very locally distributed from
sea level to 1800 m elevation between the Sihanaka Forest and Andapa (1).

POPULATION   No estimate has ever been made, but apparently the species has always
been rare and was certainly so by 1930 (1).   Its cryptic coloration makes it
especially difficult to census, but it has been described as rarer than its close
relative B. leptosomus, which has an identical distribution (2).

HABITAT   Dense shady moist evergreen forest with sparse ground cover.   Native
forest of all kinds in Madagascar is still being destroyed and at an accelerating
rate, through clearing for subsistence agriculture, replacement by exotic tree
species, and as a result of forest fires often initiated by grass burning.   Only
about 10 per cent of the original forest is now left (3).

CONSERVATION MEASURES TAKEN   None known.

CONSERVATION MEASURES PROPOSED   This species and most other endemic birds of
Madagascar have been recommended to the Malagasy government for complete legal
protection (K. Curry-Lindahl in litt. to G. Ramanantsoavina, Director, Service des
Eaux et Forêts, Chasse et Pêche, Jan. 1973).

REFERENCES   1.   Rand, A.L. 1936.   The distribution and habits of Madagascar
                    birds.   Bull. Amer. Mus. Nat. Hist. 72: 143-499.
              2.   Milon, P., Petter, J.-J. & Randrianasolo, G. 1973.   Faune de
                    Madagascar, 35: Oiseaux.   Tananarive and Paris: ORSTOM and
                    CNRS.
              3.   Curry-Lindahl, K. 1975.   Man in Madagascar.   Defenders of
                    Wildlife 50(2): 164-169.

CEYLON BROAD-BILLED ROLLER

Eurystomus orientalis irisi Deraniyagala, 1951

Order CORACIIFORMES   Family CORACIIDAE

STATUS   Indeterminate.   This race, if it still exists and does in fact breed in
Sri Lanka, is the rarest and most threatened of any bird in the island.

DISTRIBUTION   Known in the 19th century from a very few localities in the southern
half of Sri Lanka, including Maha-Oya, Kuruwita, Pasdun Korale, Gillymally, the
vicinity of Kandy and of Kadugannawa, and Lemastota.   Its present distribution is
completely unknown.   The only record since 1900 is of a pair collected in 1950 at
Maha-Oya (2).

POPULATION   By 1880 this bird was already considered the rarest in Ceylon (1).
There is still some question whether it is or ever was a breeding bird of what is
now Sri Lanka or whether the remarkably few that have been seen or collected were
no more than migrants or vagrants from continental India.   However, the pair
collected in 1950 in the south-eastern lowlands was about to breed (2), while some
of the others recorded were thought to be investigating possible nesting-holes.
The complete lack of records during the 60 years prior to 1950 and for the 25 years
which have subsequently elapsed, raises serious doubts about the continued
existence of this subspecies, which was differentiated from that of Kerala in south
India solely by its smaller size.

HABITAT   Extensive primary forest (1; 2).   Such forests in Sri Lanka are
disappearing at a rate of just over one per cent per year, but primary rainforest,
where this roller would be most likely to be found, is being destroyed considerably
faster.   Only 1300 sq. km of it remained in 1976 (3).

CONSERVATION MEASURES TAKEN   The species has been given legal protection from
killing or capture.

CONSERVATION MEASURES PROPOSED   None known.

REMARKS   The collecting in 1950 of what may prove to be the last pair of this
subspecies known to man for a museum collection was an inexcusably selfish act.
Of the 11 other subspecies that have been described from the Indian sub-continent
and most of east and south-east Asia and Australasia, none is believed to be at
present at risk.

REFERENCES   1.   Legge, W.V. 1880.   A History of the Birds of Ceylon.   London.
              2.   Henry, G.M. 1955.   A Guide to the Birds of Ceylon.   London:
                   Oxford University Press.
              3.   Wigesinge, L.C.A. de S. 1972.   The role of forestry in the
                   development of Ceylon's land resources.   Proc. 27th Annual
                   Session Ceylon A.A.S. Pt. 2: 179-198.

LONG-TAILED GROUND ROLLER

Uratelornis chimaera W. Rothschild, 1895

Order CORACIIFORMES   Family CORACIIDAE

STATUS   Vulnerable.   Restricted in distribution and now quite rare, this ground
roller is still decreasing in numbers, due largely to habitat destruction.

DISTRIBUTION   Found only in south-western Madagascar between the Mangoky River
and the Fiherenana River, just north of Tuléar, and between sea level and 80 m
(1; 2).

POPULATION   As recently as 1929, this species was fairly common (3), but its
population has seriously declined.   A transect survey has revealed that no more
than 500 pairs at most exist: the actual number is thought to be nearer 250 pairs,
with an 80 per cent degree of probability (1).

HABITAT   Brushland of the flat sandy sub-desert coast.   The vegetation of this
region is suffering rapid degradation (1).   None of the habitat of this remarkable
species is within a protected area.

CONSERVATION MEASURES TAKEN   None known.

CONSERVATION MEASURES PROPOSED   This species and most other endemic birds of
Madagascar have been recommended for legal protection (K. Curry-Lindahl in litt. to
G. Ramanantsoavina, Director, Service des Eaux et Forêts, Chasse et Pêche, Jan.
1973).   The response of the Malagasy authorities is awaited.

REFERENCES   1.   Milon, P., Petter, J.-J. & Randrianasolo, G. 1973.   Faune de
                     Madagascar, 35: Oiseaux.   Tananarive and Paris: ORSTOM and
                     CNRS.
               2.   Appert, O. 1968.   Zur Brutbiologie der Erdracke Uratelornis
                     chimaera Rothschild.   Journ. f. Ornith. 109: 264-275.
               3.   Rand, A.L. 1936.   The distribution and habits of Madagascar
                     birds.   Bull. Amer. Mus. Nat. Hist. 72: 143-499.

HELMETED HORNBILL

Rhinoplax vigil (J.R. Forster, 1781)

Order CORACIIFORMES   Family BUCEROTIDAE

STATUS   Indeterminate.   Widespread in South East Asia, but persecuted wherever
it is found.   Its forest habitat is also being destroyed at an accelerating rate.

DISTRIBUTION   Formerly throughout the Malay Peninsula, from extreme southern
Burma through peninsular Thailand to Malaysia, and onwards to Borneo and Sumatra
(1; 2).   Not known to differ today, except that vast areas within this distribution no longer have the forest canopy essential for the survival of this species.

POPULATION   Unknown.   The species may still be relatively abundant in remote
forested areas, but such areas are becoming increasingly rare and, where forests
have become accessible, the hornbill has declined.   It is hunted for food, for its
feathers, and particularly for its bony casque which is in international demand as
material for carving (3; 4).

HABITAT   Closed canopy forests in lowlands and in hills up to 1500 m in altitude
(2).   In Sumatra, these have been extensively cleared for agriculture and in
Borneo, virtually the entire island, including several existing national parks, has
been let out on contract to lumbermen.   All primary forest in Sabah, except in the
Mt. Kinabalu and Pulau Gaya National Parks, is scheduled to be cut by 1980, and in
Kalimantan, under existing schedules, will be felled by 1995 (W. Meijer 1976, pers.
comm.).

CONSERVATION MEASURES TAKEN   The species is listed in Appendix 1 of the 1973
Convention on International Trade in Endangered Species of Wild Fauna and Flora
and is legally protected in Indonesia and Malaysia, despite which hunting pressure
on it continues to be heavy, at least in some parts of its range.

CONSERVATION MEASURES PROPOSED   None additional known.

REMARKS   The threats to this species also apply, although perhaps less intensively, to other large hornbills of South East Asia, in particular the Rhinoceros
Hornbill Buceros rhinoceros, which is however rather more numerous (3; 4).

REFERENCES   1.   Medway, Lord & Wells, D.R. 1976.   The Birds of the Malay
                      Peninsula, Vol. 5.   London: H.F. and G. Witherby Ltd.
                2.   King, B.F., Woodcock, M. & Dickinson, E.C. 1975.   A Field
                      Guide to the Birds of South-east Asia.   London: Collins;
                      Boston: Houghton Mifflin Co.
                3.   Harrisson, T.H. 1951.   Humans and hornbills in Borneo.
                      Sarawak Mus. Journ. 3 (new series):   400-413.
                4.   Smythies, B.E. 1968.   The Birds of Borneo. 2nd Ed.
                      Edinburgh: Oliver and Boyd.

TOUCAN BARBET

Semnornis ramphastinus (Jardine, 1855)

Order PICIFORMES   Family CAPITONIDAE

STATUS   Vulnerable.   Locally distributed in north-western South America.   The demand for this barbet as a cage bird threatens it throughout its restricted range.

DISTRIBUTION   Foothills of the Western Andes in Colombia (Valle, southern Cauca and western Narino) and in north-western Ecuador (1-3).

POPULATION   Unknown, but certainly declining in all accessible parts of this barbet's range.   In 1977, it was found to be not uncommon locally around Barbacoas, in west central Narino division, Colombia, but is now very scarce further north, around Cali, in the Valle division (R. Ridgely 1977, pers. comm.).   It was still fairly common in north-western Ecuador in 1978 (R. Ridgely 1978, pers. comm.).

HABITAT   Forests of the upper tropical and subtropical zones.   There is still a fair amount of suitable habitat for this barbet, but little of it is effectively protected and the species is very susceptible to trapping, even in only marginally accessible areas.

CONSERVATION MEASURES TAKEN   Portions of the habitat protected in Los Farallones National Park and along the Rio Anchicaya valley, where the forest is protected in order to stop runoff and consequent silt damage to two hydroelectric installations.

CONSERVATION MEASURES PROPOSED   ·The proposed Cotacachi-Cayapas ecological reserve in north-western Ecuador will protect an additional area of the barbet's habitat.

REMARKS   Two subspecies have been described, the nominate from Ecuador and S. r. caucae from Colombia: they are equally at risk.   The species is one of several in northern South America, including the Red Siskin, Spinus cucullatus, the two Cocks-of-the-Rock, Rupicola spp., and the Long-wattled Umbrellabird, Cephalopterus pendiguler, threatened more by direct persecution than by habitat destruction.

REFERENCES   1.   de Schauensee, R.M. 1966.   The Species of Birds of South America and their Distribution.   Narberth, Pa.: Livingston Publishing Co.
              2.   Gyldenstolpe, N. 1941.   On some new or rare birds chiefly from southwestern Colombia.   Arkiv f. Zool. 33A(6):   1-17.
              3.   de Schauensee, R.M. 1949.   The birds of the Republic of Colombia.   Part 2.   Caldasia 5:   381-644.

NGOYE GREEN BARBET

Stactolaema olivacea woodwardi Shelley, 1895

Order PICIFORMES   Family CAPITONIDAE

STATUS   Rare.   Restricted to one forest in South Africa.

DISTRIBUTION   Confined to the 3,000 ha Ngoye Forest near Eshowe, Zululand, Natal, and not known to have occurred elsewhere (1).

POPULATION   On the basis of an estimated density of 37 of these barbets per 100 hectares, the total population in the Ngoye Forest is believed to be of the order of 1000 (I. Garland pers. comm. to J. Cooper, 1977).   They may well have been more numerous when the coastal forests were more extensive, but no decline has been noticed in recent years.

HABITAT   Coastal evergreen forest, of which only a few somewhat degraded stands remain in Zululand (1).   The Ngoye Forest suffers from a certain amount of illegal woodcutting, but not enough to threaten its integrity (J. Cooper and P. Frost 1977, pers. comms).

CONSERVATION MEASURES TAKEN   The Ngoye Forest, formerly a state forest, was recently handed over to the Kwazulu government and it appears likely that its protection will be maintained or even improved.

CONSERVATION MEASURES PROPOSED   None additional known.

REMARKS   Of the three other subspecies, the nominate race of the coastal lowland forests of Kenya and Tanzania and S. o. rungweensis of south-western Tanzania and northern Malawi are reasonably widespread; S. o. belcheri, known only from Thyolo mountain (7.8 sq. km) in southern Malawi and Namuli mountain in northern Mozambique, has a very small and subdivided range, but has been considered as quite common within it; however forest destruction poses a constant threat (2-4).

REFERENCES   1.   Clancey, P.A. 1964.   The Birds of Natal and Zululand.
                    Edinburgh and London: Oliver and Boyd.
              2.   Vincent, J. 1935.   The birds of northern Portuguese East
                    Africa.   Comprising a list of, and observations on, the
                    collections made during the British Museum Expedition of
                    1931-1932. Part VI.   Ibis (13)5: 1-37.
              3.   Benson, C.W. & F.M. 1977.   The Birds of Malawi.   Limbe,
                    Malawi: Montfort Press.
              4.   Benson, C.W. 1948.   A new race of barbet from south-western
                    Tanganyika Territory and northern Nyasaland.   Bull. Brit.
                    Ornith. Club. 68: 144-145.

IMPERIAL WOODPECKER

Campephilus imperialis (Gould, 1832)

Order PICIFORMES   Family PICIDAE

STATUS   Endangered, if in fact still extant.   There have been no confirmed
reports of the species from its pine-forested mountain habitat in north-western
Mexico since 1958.   Its precarious status is attributed to shooting and, to a
lesser extent, to the harvesting of mature pines.

DISTRIBUTION   The species formerly ranged through the Sierra Madre Occidental
in the Mexican states of Sonora, Chihuahua, Durango, Zacatecas, Jalisco and
Michoacan (1).   Whether it now occurs in any part of that range is unknown,
although it has been suggested that it may yet be found in remote areas of
Zacatecas and Durango and there are recent unconfirmed reports from south-western
Chihuahua (R. Clement 1977, pers. comm.) and from the Sonora-Chihuahua border (2;
V. Emanuel 1977, pers. comm.).

POPULATION   Estimated in 1964 to be at a density of one pair per 25 sq. km in
suitable habitat (1).   The species cannot be said to have been abundant at any
time, although it was surely more so than today.   The last substantiated record
appears to have been in 1958 (2) and if a population survives, it must be
exceedingly small.

HABITAT   Mature pine-oak forest above 2,000 m in the north and 2,500 m in the
south.   The pines of the Sierra Madre are being continually felled without regard
for preservation of representative samples large enough to support a population of
this woodpecker.   However, most timber extraction is fairly selective and cut
areas still contain many large trees.   Unfortunately, shooting of all sizeable
wildlife, including this species, invariably follows the construction of new
logging roads, leading to the conclusion that hunting has been a more important
factor than habitat destruction in decimating the woodpecker population. (1).

CONSERVATION MEASURES TAKEN   The species is listed in Appendix 1 of the 1973
Convention on International Trade in Endangered Species of Wild Fauna and Flora
and is protected from killing or capture by Mexican law although it would be
unrealistic to expect effective enforcement in the remote habitats which it
favoured.   An extensive search for it was made in 1962. (1).

CONSERVATION MEASURES PROPOSED   None known.

REFERENCES   1.   Tanner, J.T. 1964.   The decline and present status of
                       the Imperial Woodpecker of Mexico.   Auk 81: 74-81.
                 2.   Plimpton, G. 1977.   Un gran pedazo de carne.
                       Audubon 79(6): 10-25.

CUBAN IVORY-BILLED WOODPECKER

Campephilus principalis bairdii Cassin, 1863

Order PICIFORMES   Family PICIDAE

STATUS   Critically endangered.   A very small population still survives in the
pine forests at the eastern end of Cuba, but whether sufficient forest remains to
maintain it is questionable.   Much of the destruction of old-growth forest
occurred early in the present century to make way for sugar cane, and the major
decline of this subspecies probably dates from this period.   Shooting has also no
doubt contributed to its decline (1; 2).

DISTRIBUTION   This woodpecker is thought to have occurred at one time in suitable
habitat over much of Cuba, although reliable records exist only from the Pinar del
Rio, Matanzas, Las Villas and Oriente Provinces, and since 1900 only from the last-
named (1).   As far as is known it now only occurs in or near the Cupeyal reserve,
south of Moa in Oriente Province (1; 2).

POPULATION   Undoubtedly more common once, although no precise figures are
available, this subspecies has been very rare for the last several decades; in 1956
a population of only 12 or 13 was estimated to survive in Oriente Province (1).
More recent sightings include 2 south of Cupeyal in late 1967, a female north-west
of Cupeyal in February 1968 (3), a female at Yateras in May 1972, and a female at
Monte Cristo near Cupeyal in November 1973 (L.S. Varona 1974, pers. comm.).
Certainly no more than 8 pairs still exist and more probably fewer than 6 pairs
(O.H. Garrido 1974, pers. comm.).

HABITAT   Mixed pine and hardwood forests on lateritic soils.   Feeding occurs on
both types of tree, but roosting and nesting takes place almost entirely in cavities
in mature pines.   The woodpecker is now confined to montane forests, though it
formerly also frequented the lowlands (1).

CONSERVATION MEASURES TAKEN   Forest reservations have been established at Cupeyal
and Jaguani under the auspices of the Academy of Sciences since 1963.   Each of the
reservations is wardened, and no further exploitation of the timber is being
permitted, although much of the larger timber has already been removed (1; 2).

CONSERVATION MEASURES PROPOSED   No additional measures are known to be under
consideration.

REMARKS   The nominate subspecies in the south-eastern United States is perhaps
even rarer and more endangered.

REFERENCES   1.   Lamb, G.R. 1957.   The Ivory-billed Woodpecker in Cuba.
                         Pan-American Section, ICBP, Research Report No. 1.
              2.   Fisher, J., Simon, N. & Vincent, J. 1969.   Wildlife in Danger.
                         New York: Viking Press; London: Collins.
              3.   Bond, J. 1968.   Thirteenth Supplement to the Check-list of Birds
                         of the West Indies (1956).   Philadelphia Acad. Nat. Sci.

AMERICAN IVORY-BILLED WOODPECKER

Campephilus principalis principalis (Linnaeus, 1758)

Order PICIFORMES   Family PICIDAE

STATUS   Endangered.   Unconfirmed sightings or tape recordings of this woodpecker's characteristic call, every few years, reinforce hopes of its continued
existence, but the specific locations of such occurrences are unknown or are not
being publicized and few specific programs are aimed directly at this woodpecker's
conservation.   The exact date of its extinction, whether already passed or in the
future, is unlikely to be ascertainable.

DISTRIBUTION   The south-eastern United States from south-east North Carolina,
southern Kentucky, Illinois, Missouri, Arkansas and Oklahoma to the coast of the
Gulf of Mexico and the Florida peninsula.   The woodpecker had disappeared from
the northern and western extremities of its range before 1885, between 1885 and
1900 from most of Missouri, Arkansas, Mississippi and Alabama, and by 1930 from
most of Florida, eastern Texas and Louisiana (1).   Unconfirmed reports suggest
that isolated populations or possibly only vagrant individuals survived until the
1960s and 1970s in scattered localities such as the Big Thicket in south-eastern
Texas, Atchafalaya Swamp in Louisiana, Santee Swamp in South Carolina, and
possibly in Florida (2-7).

POPULATION   Always considered rare or local throughout its range, the maximum
recorded density for this woodpecker was one pair per 16 sq. km.   Over most of its
range the greatest decline took place in the late 19th century and between 1900 and
1915 in the more remote swamps at the heart of its range.   In 1941, only 24, in 5
scattered localities, were believed to survive and by 1948 the last known population of any size, in the 311 sq. km Singer Tract in Louisiana (which had numbered
18 birds in 1934) disappeared following the clearing of the tract for soybean
culture (1; 2; 6).   Accurate assessments can no longer be made, for any sightings
are greeted with scepticism or go unreported (8).   Possible confusion with the
more abundant Pileated Woodpecker Dryocopus pileatus, compounded by an overzealous
desire on the part of many people to see what has become an increasingly fabulous
bird, also confounds objective appraisal; but it nevertheless seems likely that a
few individual birds may still exist.

HABITAT   Mature bottomland hardwood swamp forest; also at least occasionally
pinewoods and second growth forest.   Most of the virgin swamp forest of the south-
eastern U.S. had been cut by 1915, though some of the more remote of such areas
were still undisturbed in the 1930s; today only a few small mature blocks of swamp
forest remain.   Forest destruction was thus clearly the major cause of the woodpecker's decline, though commercial collectors pursued it with great persistence
around the turn of the century and were undoubtedly responsible for eliminating
particular populations (1).   The future of the bird depends on whether it is able
to adapt itself to second-growth forest and increasing human disturbance.

CONSERVATION MEASURES TAKEN   This woodpecker is fully protected by the U.S.
Endangered Species Act and by state law in several states.   Portions of the Big
Thicket in Texas, now a mosaic of forest and cultivation, were protected in 1974
by the creation of the 342 sq. km Big Thicket National Preserve.   Habitat management designed to favour it has been practised in two sections of a U.S. National
Wildlife Refuge in Florida, and numerous small areas of what might be considered
suitable habitat are located on U.S. federal or state land, which gives them a
greater or lesser degree of protection.   A 525 ha area of swamp forest on the
Apalachicola River in northern Florida was made a sanctuary in 1950, but the
woodpeckers eventually disappeared from the area.

<u>CONSERVATION MEASURES PROPOSED</u>   Effective conservation may no longer be practicable, in view of the woodpecker's requirement of immense areas of mature forest.   It has been suggested that the only measure likely to help it, would be the reservation of quite large tracts of fairly mature forest, within which the management aim for particular areas would be to provide a constant supply of recently dead trees, such as the woodpecker usually chooses when searching for food.   Meanwhile, any reported sightings of the bird should be confirmed by experienced observers and likely areas surveyed to ascertain if it is present (1; 2; 9).

<u>REMARKS</u>   The other subspecies, <u>C</u>. <u>p</u>. <u>bairdii</u> of Cuba is equally in danger of extinction, the last reported sighting having been in 1973 (see relevant data sheet).

<u>REFERENCES</u>   1.   Tanner, J.T. 1942.   The Ivory-billed Woodpecker.   <u>National Audubon Society Research Report</u> 1.
2.   Dennis, J.V. 1977.   Untitled manuscript on the Ivory-billed Woodpecker.
3.   Agey, H.N. & Heinzmann, G.M. 1971.   The Ivory-billed Woodpecker found in central Florida.   <u>Florida Nat</u>. 44: 46-47, 64.
4.   Stewart, J.R., Jr. 1971.   Central Southern Region. <u>Amer. Birds</u> 25: 865-869.
5.   Hamilton, R.B. 1975.   Central Southern Region. <u>Amer. Birds</u> 29: 700-705.
6.   Fisher, J., Simon, N. & Vincent, J. 1969.   <u>Wildlife in Danger</u>.   New York: Viking Press; London: Collins.
7.   American Ornithologists' Union.   1971   Report of the Committee on Conservation, 1970-71.   <u>Auk</u> 88: 902-910.
8.   American Ornithologists' Union. 1975.   Report of the Committee on Conservation, 1974-75.   <u>Auk</u> 92(4, Suppl.): 1B-16B.
9.   U.S. Dept. of Interior Bureau of Sport Fisheries and Wildlife. 1973.   Threatened wildlife of the United States. <u>U.S. Bur. Sport. Fish. Wildl. Res. Pub</u>. 114.

OWSTON'S WHITE-BACKED WOODPECKER

Dendrocopos leucotos owstoni (Ogawa, 1905)

Order PICIFORMES   Family PICIDAE

STATUS   Rare.   Restricted to one island in the Ryukyu chain, south of Japan,
where it is scarce and faced with increasing destruction of its habitat.

DISTRIBUTION   Known only from Amami-oshima in the northern Ryukyu Islands, where
it inhabits primary evergreen forests.   Its distribution is therefore becoming
increasingly restricted as the forest continues to be cleared (1).

POPULATION   No early estimate.   Twenty-five years ago the species was, however,
described as common (2).   In 1973, line censuses showed that of 17,597 ha of
forested land on Amami-oshima, 5,300 ha provided suitable habitat for this woodpecker.   An observed density of 0.1 birds per hectare yielded an estimated total
of 500 birds for the whole island (1).

HABITAT   Primary evergreen forest.   This is not protected on Amami-oshima and
continues to be cleared.   Since the 1973 estimate of 5,300 ha of suitable habitat
was made, there has been further extensive clearing (Y. Yamashina 1974, pers. comm.).

CONSERVATION MEASURES TAKEN   Designated a Natural Monument and a Special Bird for
Protection in 1973.

CONSERVATION MEASURES PROPOSED   The full protection of a portion of the forest
habitat of this subspecies is essential for its survival (Y. Yamashina 1974, pers.
comm.).

REMARKS   Eight other subspecies are recognized and widely distributed over
temperate Eurasia.   None of them is known to be at risk.

REFERENCES   1.   Yamashina Inst. for Ornith. 1975.   Save these Birds.
                   Tokyo: The Kasumikaikan. (In Japanese).
              2.   Hachisuka, M. & Udagawa, T. 1953.   Contribution to the
                   ornithology of the Ryukyu Islands.   Quart. J. Taiwan Mus.
                   6:   141-279.

HELMETED WOODPECKER

Dryocopus galeatus (Temminck, 1822)

Order PICIFORMES   Family PICIDAE

STATUS   Indeterminate.   There have been no records of this poorly known South
American woodpecker for 20 years.   Its habitat has suffered extensive clearing.

DISTRIBUTION   Recorded from the states of São Paulo, Paraná and Rio Grande do
Sul, Brazil, from Paraguay, and from Misiones province, Argentina (1).   Its
present distribution is unknown and despite several searches, it has not been
found in Brazil, since last recorded near Porto Camargo on the Paraná river, about
100 km from the Paraguayan border, in 1954 (H. Sick 1977, pers. comm.).   It was
also recorded in the 1950s in Misiones, north-eastern Argentina (2; L. Short 1977,
pers. comm.).

POPULATION   Unknown.   The species may well be in grave danger of extinction.
Fewer than 20 specimens have been taken for scientific collections (L. Short 1977,
pers. comm.).

HABITAT   Lowland subtropical forest and possibly other habitats.   The lowland
forests of south-eastern Brazil, Paraguay and north-eastern Argentina have been
seriously depleted as a result of clearance for agriculture and livestock ranching;
but there are still substantial forested areas in parts of this woodpecker's range,
notably in Paraguay (R. Ridgely 1978, pers. comm.).

CONSERVATION MEASURES TAKEN   None known.

CONSERVATION MEASURES PROPOSED   None known.

REMARKS   This is the world's least known species of woodpecker (L. Short 1977,
pers. comm.).

REFERENCES   1.   de Schauensee, R.M. 1966.   The Species of Birds of South
                     America and their Distribution.   Narberth, Pa.: Livingston
                     Publishing Co.
               2.   Short, L. In prep.   Woodpeckers of the World.

TRISTRAM'S WOODPECKER

Dryocopus javensis richardsi Tristram, 1879

Order PICIFORMES   Family PICIDAE

STATUS   Endangered.   Close to extinction but still persisting in a few localities
in central Korea.

DISTRIBUTION   Formerly included a much more extensive area of central and southern
Korea (1) and also the twin islands of Tsushima in the Korean Strait between Korea
and Japan.   It was last collected on Tsushima in 1920 and has not been seen there
subsequently (2).   It still occurs in one or two localities in the Kyonggi Do and
Kangwon Do provinces of northern South Korea, particularly at Solak Mount (3; 4; 5)
and Kwangneung (Won Pyong-Oh in litt. to S.D.Ripley, 1976).   It had earlier been
reported breeding in Kumnung and Kwangnung at least up to the outbreak of the Korean
War in 1950 and more recently on Songri Mount, Chungchong province; but searches of
these areas between 1955 and 1961 failed to find any trace of the bird (6).   In
southern North Korea it still occurs in several areas including Kaesong district and
Rinsan, Pyongsan and Pyongchon counties (7).

POPULATION   Although this woodpecker never seems to have been very abundant in
historic times, given the large area of habitat required to maintain a single pair
and the extensive destruction of forests over a very long period, there can be no
doubt that its population has suffered a serious decline.   On Tsushima fourteen or
fifteen specimens were taken and it has been suggested that scientific collecting
was responsible for its extirpation (2).   Its present population in South Korea,
where it is only known from two areas, is uncertain but must be very small (3; 4).
In North Korea a 1969 estimate put the total at something over 40 pairs (7).

HABITAT   Mature forests of pine, fir, Cryptomeria, oak and camphor (2).   A
preference for chestnut trees for nesting has been noted in the north (7).   Much of
the mature forest throughout the range of the woodpecker has suffered severe damage
from logging, road-building and from the ravages of war.

CONSERVATION MEASURES TAKEN   This subspecies is listed in Appendix 1 of the 1973
Convention on International Trade in Endangered Species of Wild Fauna and Flora.
In South Korea it was designated National Treasure No. 11 in 1933 and Natural
Monument No. 197 in 1968, and some of its habitat is protected in Kwangnung National
Park, Solak Mount Nature Reserve and Kwangneung Forest Natural Monument.   Hunting is
prohibited on Songri Mount (3; 6).   In North Korea recently discovered breeding
sites have been decreed as conserved areas: for example, the Rinsan Tristram's
Woodpecker Reserve (8).

CONSERVATION MEASURES PROPOSED   No additional measures are known to be under
consideration.

REMARKS   The number of other subspecies recognized by various authors varies from
5 to 14 and their range extends over much of southern Asia.   None of them are known
to be at risk presently.

REFERENCES   1.   Austin, O.L., Jr. 1948.   The birds of Korea.   Bull. Mus. Comp.
                         Zool. Harvard 101: 1-301.
                  2.   Austin, O.L., Jr. & Kuroda, N. 1953.   The birds of Japan; their
                         status and distribution.   Bull. Mus. Comp. Zool. Harvard 109:
                         280-637.

3. Won Pyong-Oh, 1974.   Bird Treasures (Natural Monuments) in Korea. (In Korean).

4. Won Pyong-Oh, 1975.   Rare and endangered species of birds and mammals in Korea.   The Conservation of Nature and Natural Resources, 9. (In Korean).

5. Won Pyong-Oh, 1967.   The present status of some threatened and rare birds in Korea, 1962-1966.   ICBP Bull. 10:   109-113.

6. Won Pyong-Oh, 1963.   The urgent problem of bird protection in Korea with special suggestions for habitat improvement and wildlife management.   ICBP Bull. 9:   121-129.

7. Pak Won-Hyong, 1969.   Korean Nature 3: 4-5.

8. Anon. 1975.   Nature of the fatherland conserved in All People's Movement under the Wise Guidance of the Great Leader.   Korean Nature 3: photo insert.

GRAND BAHAMA RED-BELLIED WOODPECKER

Melanerpes superciliaris bahamensis (Cory, 1892)

Order PICIFORMES   Family PICIDAE

STATUS   Indeterminate.   Restricted to one island in the Bahamas, West Indies.
Suspected to be seriously reduced in number and in danger of extinction because of
land clearing and cutting of pine forests.

DISTRIBUTION   Confined to Grand Bahama Island (1,373 sq. km) at the north-
western extremity of the Bahama Island chain, in which it was formerly more
widespread.   There are no recent first-hand reports of its present distribution
on Grand Bahama (1; A. Sprunt IV 1973, pers. comm.).

POPULATION   Several observers have recently looked for this woodpecker on Grand
Bahama but without success, although in one case the search extended over seven
months in 1968 and 1969 (J.T. Emlen 1973, pers. comm.).   A second-hand report of
a sighting of the subspecies about seven years ago is the only evidence available
of its continued existence (A. Sprunt IV 1973, pers. comm.).

HABITAT   Native hardwood coppice, but also pines and coconut palms.   The
pinewoods of Grand Bahama have been extensively cut and another new threat to the
woodpecker's survival is a recent invasion and overwintering on Grand Bahama by
starlings Sturnus vulgaris, which would compete for nest cavities if they became a
resident population.   Much of the clearing of woodland on Grand Bahama has been
for housing developments.

CONSERVATION MEASURES TAKEN   None known.

CONSERVATION MEASURES PROPOSED   None known.

REMARKS   Of the four other subspecies, those from Isle of Pines, Cuba, and from
Grand Cayman Island are apparently common and at no particular risk; M. s. blakei
(Ridgway, 1886) of Great Abaco, also at the north-western end of the Bahaman chain,
is widely distributed on that island and, although included in the previous
edition of this volume, can now be safely omitted (2); and M. s. nyeanus (Ridgway,
1886) of San Salvador island, lying to the north-east of the central part of the
archipelago, is rare and at moderate risk (see relevant data sheet).

REFERENCES   1.   Bond, J. 1969.   Fourteenth supplement to the Check-list
                    of Birds of the West Indies (1956).   Phila. Acad. Nat. Sci.
              2.   King, W.B. et al.(in press).   Noteworthy ornithological
                    records from Abaco, Bahamas.   Amer. Birds.

SAN SALVADOR RED-BELLIED WOODPECKER

Melanerpes superciliaris nyeanus (Ridgway, 1886)

Order PICIFORMES   Family PICIDAE

STATUS   Rare.   Restricted to one of the Bahama Islands, West Indies, where its population is small.

DISTRIBUTION   San Salvador or Watling Island (163 sq. km), situated north-east of the central part of the Bahama Island chain.   It was formerly spread all over the island but is now only found at the northern end (J. Bond 1974, pers. comm.).

POPULATION   Island inhabitants consider that this subspecies was once more numerous, but that it had become very scarce by 1965, only two being seen by a visitor in December of that year (1).   However, subsequent visits which have been made annually since 1973, revealed a secure population of about 100 to 160 pairs established in territories, and there is a slight chance that a second sizeable population exists (2).

HABITAT   Hardwood coppice.

CONSERVATION MEASURES TAKEN   None known.

CONSERVATION MEASURES PROPOSED   None known.

REMARKS   Of the four other subspecies, those of the Isle of Pines, Cuba, and of Grand Cayman Island are apparently common and not at risk; _M. s. blakei_ (Ridgway, 1886), although included in the previous edition of this Volume, is now apparently common and widely distributed on Great Abaco, at the north-western end of the Bahaman chain(3) and has therefore been omitted; and the status of _M. s. bahamensis_ (Cory, 1892) of Grand Bahama is uncertain, although it is believed to be at some risk (see relevant data sheet).

REFERENCES   1.   Paulson, D.R. 1966.   New records of birds from the Bahama Islands.   Phila. Acad. Nat. Sci., Not. Nat., 394.
              2.   Miller, J.R. 1978.   Notes on birds of San Salvador Island (Watling), the Bahamas.   Auk 95: 281-287.
              3.   King, W.B. et al. (in press).   Noteworthy ornithological records from Abaco, Bahamas.   Amer. Birds.

RED-COCKADED WOODPECKER

Picoides borealis (Vieillot, 1807)

Order PICIFORMES   Family PICIDAE

STATUS   Vulnerable. Resident in mature pine forests of the south-eastern
United States, where it is rare and locally distributed. Although legally
protected it is declining in numbers due to forestry management practices that
eliminate pine stands more than 60 years old.

DISTRIBUTION   Recorded from Oklahoma, S. Missouri, Kentucky, Virginia and
Maryland, south to the Gulf Coast states and Florida, and the present distribution
is much the same, although the species no longer occurs in Missouri, and populations in peripheral areas are now extirpated or severely depleted (1; 2; 8).

POPULATION   Considered abundant within historic times. A 1971 estimate was of
3,000 to 10,000 birds distributed in 2,500 colonies of up to 8 birds each, but
recent information suggests that this may have been an overestimate. Northern
Florida and South Carolina now have the largest remaining populations. These
woodpeckers are becoming increasingly separated into a mosaic of genetically
isolated subpopulations. Between 1971 and 1975, a sample of 312 colonies under
study had declined by 13 percent to 271. (1; 2; 7; 8).

HABITAT   Restricted to stands of mature conifers, usually 80 years or more old,
generally with a low or open understory maintained by periodic fire. Nest or
roost cavities are mostly in trees infested by redheart, Fomes pini. Individual
colonies have home ranges of up to 80 ha. Most privately owned forest land is
harvested on cycles of 45 years or less and out of the 10.4 million ha of pine
forest within the range of this species, only 9 percent is in public ownership.
Furthermore, although 75 percent of its existing population is on U.S. National
Forest land, much of this is managed on too short a rotation to promote the long
term survival of the woodpecker colonies. Trees with cavities and diseased or
defective trees of potential use to the woodpecker are often removed, fire is
frequently excluded or improperly used, and the pesticide Mirex, favoured in the
south-eastern U.S. to control fire-ants, Solenopsis saevissima, may cause direct
reproductive failure in the woodpeckers or deplete their food supply. (2-6; 8).

CONSERVATION MEASURES TAKEN   The species has protection under the U.S. Endangered
Species Act of 1973, and the U.S. Fish and Wildlife Service has appointed a
recovery team, which has drafted a recovery plan. Federal and some State forestry
agencies have initiated a policy of saving some large pine trees infected with
redheart in areas where this woodpecker is known to occur. The U.S. Forest
Service's management plans for the promotion of the welfare of the species, include
further limitations on the size of clear-cut blocks, increasing the length of
rotation, selective logging in areas inhabited by woodpeckers, leaving some dead or
dying trees, and restricting all activities in some areas which have substantial
woodpecker populations.

CONSERVATION MEASURES PROPOSED   A coordinated forest management plan for federal,
state and private landowners, to ensure the conservation of the species; tax
incentives to persuade private landowners to leave mature woodland unharvested;
where timber harvesting cannot be avoided, promotion of selective logging or clear-
cutting in the smallest possible units, to provide maximum age diversity of
forests; reintroduction of the woodpecker into parts of its former range which once
more become suitable; periodical survey of the status of its population; and
establishment and maintenance of corridors of suitable habitat, along highways, in
parks and on other public lands, to permit gene flow between the populations (8).

<u>REMARKS</u>   Two subspecies have been named, but they are weakly differentiated, representing in effect a clinal increase in wing and tail length from south to north and with increasing distance from the coast (9).

<u>REFERENCES</u>
1. U.S. Bureau of Sport Fisheries and Wildlife, 1973. Threatened Wildlife of the United States. <u>U.S. Bureau Sport Fish. Wildl. Res. Pub.</u> 114.
2. Jackson, J.A. 1971. The evolution, taxonomy, distribution, past populations, and current status of the Red-cockaded Woodpecker. In R.L. Thompson (ed.) <u>The Ecology and Management of the Red-cockaded Woodpecker.</u> U.S. Bureau of Sport Fisheries and Wildlife and Tall Timbers Research Station.
3. Czuhai, E. 1971. Synoptic review of forest resource and use within the range of the Red-cockaded Woodpecker. In R.L. Thompson (ed.) <u>The Ecology and Management of the Red-cockaded Woodpecker.</u> U.S. Bureau of Sport Fisheries and Wildlife and Tall Timbers Research Station.
4. Beland, J.M. 1971. Timber management practices for Red-cockaded Woodpeckers on federal lands. In R.L. Thompson (ed.) <u>The Ecology and Management of the Red-cockaded Woodpecker.</u> U.S. Bureau of Sport Fisheries and Wildlife and Tall Timbers Research Station.
5. Thompson, R.L. & Baker, W.W. 1971. A survey of Red-cockaded Woodpecker habitat requirements. In R.L. Thompson (ed.) <u>The Ecology and Management of the Red-cockaded Woodpecker.</u> U.S. Bureau of Sport Fisheries and Wildlife and Tall Timbers Research Station.
6. Beckett, T.A., III, 1974. Habitat acreage requirements of the Red-cockaded Woodpecker. <u>EBBA News</u> 37: 3-7.
7. Jackson, J.A. 1976. Red-cockaded Woodpeckers and red heart disease of pines. <u>Auk</u> 94: 160-163.
8. Thompson, R.L. 1976. Change in status of Red-cockaded Woodpecker colonies. <u>Wilson Bull.</u> 88: 491-492.
9. Jackson, J.A., Baker, W.W., Carter, V., Cherry, T. & Hopkins, M.L. 1976. Recovery plan for the Red-cockaded Woodpecker, preliminary draft. U.S. Fish and Wildlife Service.
10. Mengel, R.M. & Jackson, J.A. 1977. Geographic variation of the Red-cockaded Woodpecker. <u>Condor</u> 79: 349-355.

INOUYE'S THREE-TOED WOODPECKER

Picoides tridactylus inouyei Yamashina, 1943

Order PICIFORMES   Family PICIDAE

STATUS   Rare.   Restricted to a portion of the montane forest of Hokkaido, Japan, where it has been seen only a very few times and where the forest itself is being steadily felled.

DISTRIBUTION   Known only from Mitsumata in the Daisetsu Mountains, Tokachi Prefecture, Central Hokkaido. There is no evidence that it has ever been more widely distributed (1).

POPULATION   This subspecies is known from three specimens and several additional sightings.   No estimate of its population has ever been made, but it is reported to be apparently rare (Y. Yamashina 1974, pers. comm.).

HABITAT   Montane coniferous forest comprised of Picea jezoensis and Abies sachalinensis; also mixed coniferous-deciduous forest.   The forests in question are being progressively cleared (Y. Yamashina 1974, pers. comm.).

CONSERVATION MEASURES TAKEN   Designated a Special Bird for Protection in 1972. Much of the range of this subspecies lies within Daisetsuzan National Park, but this has not prevented the continuance of forest-clearing within the park boundaries.

CONSERVATION MEASURES PROPOSED   None known.

REMARKS   Eleven other subspecies are recognized and range throughout mountains or higher latitudes of Eurasia and North America.   None of them are thought to be at risk.

REFERENCES   1.   Austin, O.L., Jr. & Kuroda, N. 1953.   The birds of Japan: their status and distribution. Harvard Mus. Comp. Zool. Bull. 109(4): 279-637.

TAKATSUKASA'S GREEN WOODPECKER

Picus awokera takatsukasae Kuroda, 1921

Order PICIFORMES   Family PICIDAE

STATUS   Rare.   Restricted to two of the Ryukyu Islands south of Japan, where
destruction of primary forests is responsible for the decline in its population.

DISTRIBUTION   The range of this subspecies within the northern Ryukyu Islands of
Yakushima and Tanegashima coincides exactly with the extent of surviving primary
forest between 500 and 1,700 m elevation (1).

POPULATION   Unknown but believed to have seriously declined in recent years.   In
1970 a few of these woodpeckers were observed on Yakushima (2) and in 1973 similarly
small numbers on Tanegashima (Y. Yamashina 1974, pers. comm.).

HABITAT   Primary forest.   On Tanegashima this has been almost completely
destroyed and on Yakushima it continues to be felled at top speed (1).   On neither
of the islands has any of the forest been given protected status.

CONSERVATION MEASURES TAKEN   None known.

CONSERVATION MEASURES PROPOSED   Protection of a remnant of the primary forest on
Yakushima has been strongly recommended (Y. Yamashina 1974, pers. comm.).

REMARKS   The two other subspecies of awokera, in southern Japan, are not known to
be in any danger.

REFERENCES   1.   Yamashina Inst. for Ornith. ed. 1975.   Save these Birds.
                    Tokyo: The Kasumikaikan. (In Japanese).

OKINAWA WOODPECKER

Sapheopipo noguchii (Seebohm, 1887)

Order PICIFORMES   Family PICIDAE

STATUS   Endangered.   Restricted to a small portion of Okinawa, Ryukyu Islands, to
the south of Japan, where its population is now small and fragmented.   Woodcutting
continues to remove still more of its already much reduced woodland habitat.
Uncontrolled fires and replacement of native forest by exotic tree plantations are
other contributing factors in this habitat destruction (1).

DISTRIBUTION   The woodpecker was apparently always confined to the forested hills
of the northern half of Okinawa.   It now occurs, or recently occurred, within an
area of no more than 1500 ha on Yonaha, Nashime, Ibu, Hedo and Igu mountains (1).

POPULATION   Since 1920, this species has always been considered very rare.   By
1941 its population was believed to have fallen below 100 (2) and by 1973 it was
estimated that not less than 20 pairs and certainly no more than 60 pairs survived,
the larger figure being described as optimistic (1).

HABITAT   Moist broad-leaved evergreen forests, primarily undisturbed first growth;
second growth forest is, however, to some extent utilized for foraging.   The
undisturbed forest is now only to be found in scattered patches in secondary forest,
clearings and plantations; it is constantly under threat from woodcutting for fuel
and timber, burning during the summer, and clearing for additional plantations (1).

CONSERVATION MEASURES TAKEN   In 1973 this species was declared a Natural Monument
and a Special Bird for Protection.   A 7 hectare nature reserve has been established
on Yonaha Mountain, inhabited by two or possibly three pairs of the woodpeckers.
Areas on Ibu and Nashime mountains are protected by the Ryukyu Forestry Department,
but they are unfenced and protection appears to be nominal.   Much of the forest has
been utilized by the U.S. Marines, who maintain a base on Okinawa, although jurisdiction over the island has recently reverted to Japan; at least, however, the
Marine Corps activities in the forested area have tended to discourage tree-cutting
by the local inhabitants (1).

CONSERVATION MEASURES PROPOSED   It has been pointed out that there is no
comprehensive plan for the conservation of this unique species.   Of over-riding
importance is the establishment of strict forest reserves to prevent further erosion
of the already greatly diminished and fragmented primary forest habitat (1;
Y. Yamashina 1974, pers. comm.).

REMARKS   This woodpecker is the sole representative of a unique genus.

REFERENCES   1.   Short, L.L. 1973.   Habits, relationships, and conservation of
                   the Okinawa Woodpecker.   Wilson Bull. 85: 5-20.
              2.   Hachisuka, M. & Udagawa, T. 1953.   Contribution to the
                   ornithology of the Ryukyu Islands.   Q. Journ. Taiwan Mus.
                   6(3-4): 141-279.

TRINIDAD STRAIGHT-BILLED WOODCREEPER

Xiphorhynchus picus altirostris (Leotaud, 1866)

Order PASSERIFORMES   Family DENDROCOLAPTIDAE

STATUS   Rare.   Known at present from one mangrove swamp on Trinidad where it is
seldom seen.

DISTRIBUTION   Formerly widespread in mangrove swamps on Trinidad, but recently
observed only in the Caroni Swamp (6,885 ha).   It may, however, still occur in
other small areas of mangrove on Trinidad. (1; 2).

POPULATION   Not known precisely, but this subspecies has been observed or
collected only a few times since its discovery, and there is but one breeding
record.   Due to the fact that it is confined to dense mangrove swamps it is
unlikely an accurate population estimate can be made (1; R. ffrench 1974, pers.
comm.).

HABITAT   Dense mangrove swamps.

CONSERVATION MEASURES TAKEN   Portions of the Caroni Swamp are protected as a
wildlife sanctuary.   The subspecies is protected by law, but is in any case
unlikely to be hunted (R. ffrench 1974, pers. comm.).

CONSERVATION MEASURES PROPOSED   None known.

REMARKS   The nominate race ranges from Panama south to the Guianas, Peru,
northern Bolivia and the Amazon region and Bahia state in Brazil (3); it is not
thought to be at risk.

REFERENCES   1.   ffrench, R. 1973.   A Guide to the Birds of Trinidad
                      and Tobago.   Wynnewood, Pa.: Livingston Publishing Co.
               2.   Herklots, G.A.C. 1961.   The Birds of Trinidad and
                      Tobago.   London: Collins.
               3.   de Schauensee, R.M. 1970.   A Guide to the Birds of
                      South America.   Wynnewood, Pa.: Livingston Publishing
                      Co.; Edinburgh: Oliver and Boyd.

NARROW-BILLED ANTWREN

Formicivora iheringi Hellmayr, 1909

Order PASSERIFORMES   Family FORMICARIIDAE

STATUS   Vulnerable.   Of very restricted distribution in one state of Brazil, where its woodland habitat is unprotected and is being progressively cleared.

DISTRIBUTION   Interior of south-eastern Bahia, Brazil (1).

POPULATION   Unknown, but surely decreasing as its habitat dwindles.   This antwren is found in the same woodlands as another vulnerable species, the Slender Antbird Rhopornis ardesiaca (q.v.), but in localities where they were seen in 1977, it appeared to be the less numerous of the two (R. Ridgely 1978, pers. comm.).

HABITAT   Dry ridge woodlands, particularly where terrestrial bromeliads occur. This habitat is rapidly being cleared in south-eastern Bahia to provide pasture for cattle and it has been estimated that little will remain within 30 years (E. Willis 1975, pers. comm.).

CONSERVATION MEASURES TAKEN   The species is protected by Brazilian law, but no portion of its habitat is at present safeguarded.

CONSERVATION MEASURES PROPOSED   None known.

REFERENCES   1.   de Schauensee, R.M. 1966.   The Species of Birds of South America and their Distribution.   Narberth, Pa.: Livingston Publishing Co.

MOUSTACHED ANTPITTA

Grallaria alleni Chapman, 1912

Order PASSERIFORMES   Family FORMICARIIDAE

STATUS   Indeterminate.   Only known from the type specimen from Colombia.
Forest destruction is likely to threaten this antpitta, if in fact it still exists.
Antpittas are secretive and difficult to observe, so that it is possible this
species may survive undetected in an uncut patch of forest.

DISTRIBUTION   The type was collected in 1911 at Salento in the Caldas division
of Colombia, on the western slope of the central Andes (1-3).

POPULATION   Unknown.

HABITAT   The type locality was in subtropical forest at an altitude of 2,100 m.
None of the forest in this area is protected and the extent of forest on the
western slope of the central Andes has been seriously reduced since the antpitta
was described.   How far such forest destruction may have directly affected it, is
unknown.

CONSERVATION MEASURES TAKEN   None known.

CONSERVATION MEASURES PROPOSED   None known.

REMARKS   Two additional antpittas from the same general area which may also be
threatened by forest destruction are the Brown-banded Antpitta Grallaria milleri
and the Bicolored Antpitta Grallaria rufocinerea.   The latter has also been
collected in the Antioquia and Cauca divisions (J. Hernandez 1977, pers. comm. to
R. Ridgely).

REFERENCES   1.   de Schauensee, R.M. 1966.   The Species of Birds of South
                      America and their Distribution.   Narberth, Pa.: Livingston
                      Publishing Co.
               2.   de Schauensee, R.M. 1950.   The birds of the Republic of
                      Colombia. Part 3.   Caldasia 5: 645-871.
               3.   Chapman, F.M. 1912.   Diagnoses of apparently new Colombian
                      birds.   Bull. Amer. Mus. Nat. Hist. 31: 139-166.

TRINIDAD SCALED ANTPITTA

Grallaria guatimalensis aripoensis (Hellmayr and Seilern, 1912)

Order PASSERIFORMES   Family FORMICARIIDAE

STATUS   Very rare.   Restricted to the northern mountains of Trinidad, where
this subspecies was last recorded in 1925.

DISTRIBUTION   Confined to the Northern Range of Trinidad.   The subspecies was
discovered in 1912 on Cerro del Aripo and subsequently observed in the nearby
region of the upper Oropuche river in 1925 (1; 2).

POPULATION   Unknown.   The discoverer of the subspecies collected 17 specimens
in 1912; two were seen in 1925.   Hunters familiar with the area concerned are
inclined to believe that it may still exist (1; R. ffrench 1974, pers. comm.).

HABITAT   Rainforest.   The forests of the Northern Range of Trinidad have been
reduced in extent by clearing for timber and agriculture, but a substantial
forested area (in excess of 130 sq. km) is still left (R. ffrench 1974, pers.comm.).

CONSERVATION MEASURES TAKEN   This antpitta has been given full legal protection.

CONSERVATION MEASURES PROPOSED   None known.

REMARKS   Seven other subspecies range from Mexico south to Ecuador, Peru and
northern Brazil and are not known to be at risk.

REFERENCES   1.   ffrench, R. 1973.   A Guide to the Birds of Trinidad and
                    Tobago.   Wynnewood, Pa.: Livingston Publishing Co.
              2.   Herklots, G.A.C. 1961.   The Birds of Trinidad and Tobago.
                    London: Collins.

BROWN-BANDED ANTPITTA

Grallaria milleri Chapman, 1912

Order PASSERIFORMES   Family FORMICARIIDAE

STATUS   Indeterminate.   This Colombian antpitta has not been seen since the year the type was collected.   Much of its habitat has now been destroyed.

DISTRIBUTION   Recorded only from Laguneta in the Caldas division of Colombia, between 2,700 and 3,100 m elevation on the western slope of the central Andes (1-3).

POPULATION   Unknown.   Seven specimens were collected in 1911 (3), which suggests it may have been locally common at that time.   There are no other records.

HABITAT   Presumably forest of the temperate zone.   None of this habitat in the area concerned has been protected and large portions of it have been destroyed (R. Ridgely 1978, pers. comm.).

CONSERVATION MEASURES TAKEN   None known.

CONSERVATION MEASURES PROPOSED   None known.

REMARKS   The status of the Moustached Antpitta Grallaria alleni, also recorded in the Caldas division, causes similar concern, and the Bicolored Antpitta Grallaria rufocinerea, collected at Santa Elena in Antioquia, as well as at Salento and Laguneta, Caldas, may also be at risk as the result of habitat destruction; but two specimens of it were recently captured in the Purace National Park, Cauca division, and constitute a considerable southward extension of its range (J. Hernandez 1977, pers. comm. to R. Ridgely).

REFERENCES   1.   de Schauensee, R.M. 1961.   The Species of Birds of South America and their Distribution.   Narberth, Pa.: Livingston Publishing Co.
              2.   de Schauensee, R.M. 1950.   The birds of the Republic of Colombia.   Caldasia 5: 645-871.
              3.   Chapman, F.M. 1912.   Diagnoses of apparently new Colombian birds.   Bull. Amer. Mus. Nat. Hist. 31: 139-166.

BLACK-HOODED ANTWREN

Myrmotherula erythronotos (Hartlaub, 1852)

Order PASSERIFORMES   Family FORMICARIIDAE

STATUS   Endangered, if in fact it still exists.   This poorly known antwren has
been found in two areas in south-eastern Brazil, where forest destruction has been
extensive.

DISTRIBUTION   The species was originally described from a specimen collected near
Nova Friburgo, between Rio de Janeiro and Campos, in Rio de Janeiro state, but has
not been reported from this area for many years (1).   In 1953, it was listed as
occurring further to the north, in Espírito Santo (2), but this has never been
confirmed (H. Sick 1977, pers. comm.).

POPULATION   Unknown, but likely to be very small if still extant.

HABITAT   Tropical forest, presumably primary but possibly also secondary.
Deforestation in the type locality of the species is almost complete and the
position is not much better in Espírito Santo (3).

CONSERVATION MEASURES TAKEN   The species is legally protected in Brazil, but
none of its habitat is known to be protected.

CONSERVATION MEASURES PROPOSED   None known.

REMARKS   The species was included in the previous edition of this volume under
the name of Red-rumped Ant-Thrush.

REFERENCES   1.   de Schauensee, R.M. 1966.   The Species of Birds of South
                    America and their Distribution.   Narberth, Pa.: Livingston
                    Publishing Co.
              2.   Ruschi, A. 1953.   Lista das aves do Estado do Espírito
                    Santo.   Bol. Mus. Biol. Santa Teresa 1953(11): 1-21.
              3.   Sick, H. 1969.   Aves brasileira ameaçadas de extinção e
                    noções gerais de conservação de aves no Brasil.   An. Acad.
                    Brasil. Ciênc. 41(Supl.): 205-229.

FRINGE-BACKED FIRE-EYE

Pyriglena atra (Swainson, 1825)

Order PASSERIFORMES   Family FORMICARIIDAE

STATUS   Endangered.   Locally distributed in eastern Brazil where extensive
destruction of its habitat threatens this and several other species of the
coastal tropical forest.

DISTRIBUTION   The species has only been recorded from Piranga and Santo Amaro,
in the vicinity of Salvador, southern Bahia, Brazil (1) and it is likely that its
range has been greatly reduced by the clearing of forest for development.   It has
never been reported from anywhere south of the Rio Paraguaçu and is now only known
in a locality a few kilometres to the north of Salvador along the Atlantic coast
(E. Willis 1975, pers. comm.).

POPULATION   Unknown.   In 1968, two small populations of this species were found
near Santo Amaro, separated by a road through the forest (2), and it was again found
and studied in that area in 1974 (E. Willis 1975, pers. comm.).

HABITAT   Primary but slightly disturbed coastal tropical forest, most of which
in this part of Bahia has now disappeared.   For example, the forest near Santo
Amaro, where it was found in 1968 and 1974, was reduced to small patches by 1977.
The whole area north of Salvador, where this species might survive, is heavily
populated and government programs for industrial, agricultural and pastoral
expansion are certain to involve the continuing destruction of the few remaining
forest tracts (E. Willis 1975, R. Ridgely 1978, pers. comms).

CONSERVATION MEASURES TAKEN   Brazilian law protects this and most other bird
species.

CONSERVATION MEASURES PROPOSED   A biological reserve for this species and other
constituents of the coastal biota has been recommended but so far no action has
been taken (E. Willis 1975, 1978, pers. comms).

REMARKS   This species has been considered by some authorities to be conspecific
with P. leucoptera (including P. leuconota), a superspecies widespread in tropical
and subtropical South American forests (3; 4).   P. leucoptera replaces P. atra
south of the Rio Paraguaçu (E. Willis 1975, pers. comm.).

REFERENCES   1.   de Schauensee, R.M. 1966.   The Species of Birds of South
                    America and their Distribution.   Narberth, Pa.: Livingston
                    Publishing Co.
              2.   Sick, H. 1972.   A ameaça da avifauna brasileira.   In
                    Espécies da Fauna Brasileira Ameaçadas de Extinção, pp. 99-153.
                    Rio de Janeiro: Academia Brasileira de Ciências.
              3.   Pinto, O.M. de O. 1938.   Catálogo das aves do Brasil, pt. 1.
                    Rev. Mus. Paulista 23: 1-566.
              4.   Zimmer, J.T. 1931.   Studies of Peruvian birds, II.
                    Amer. Mus. Novit. 509.

SLENDER ANTBIRD

Rhopornis ardesiaca Wied, 1831

Order PASSERIFORMES   Family FORMICARIIDAE

STATUS   Vulnerable.   This forest bird has been recorded in four localities in
eastern Brazil where forest destruction has been extensive.

DISTRIBUTION   So far as is known, confined to Ituaçu, Boa Nova, Jequie and the
vicinity of Irajuba, in the interior of south-eastern Bahia, Brazil (1).   The
species may possibly also occur to the south of Boa Nova toward Vitória de
Conquista and further inland from Ituaçu (E. Willis 1975, pers. comm.).

POPULATION   Only four specimens of this antbird are known, but in 1974 and 1977
it was found without difficulty within its restricted habitat (E. Willis 1975,
R. Ridgely 1977, pers. comms).

HABITAT   Dry forest of the coastal ridge of Bahia, particularly where terrestrial
bromeliads are common.   Only a limited amount of this habitat now remains and it
is still being cleared to create pasture for cattle, so that very little is likely
to be left in another 30 years (E. Willis 1975, pers. comm.).

CONSERVATION MEASURES TAKEN   The species is protected by law in Brazil.

CONSERVATION MEASURES PROPOSED   None known.

REFERENCES   1.   de Schauensee, R.M. 1966.   The Species of Birds of South
                    America and their Distribution.   Narberth, Pa.: Livingston
                    Publishing Co.
               2.   Sick, H. 1972.   A ameaça da avifauna brasileira.   In
                    Espécies da Fauna Brasileira Ameaçadas de Extinção, pp. 99-153.
                    Rio de Janeiro: Academia Brasileira de Ciências.

STRESEMANN'S BRISTLEFRONT

Merulaxis stresemanni Sick, 1960

Order PASSERIFORMES   Family RHINOCRYPTIDAE

STATUS   Indeterminate.   Known only from two specimens collected in the coastal
zone of eastern Brazil.

DISTRIBUTION   The type specimen was collected in the vicinity of Salvador, Bahia
state, between 1831 and 1838, and the second specimen in the same state near
Ilheus, about 250 km south of Salvador along the Atlantic coast (1).

POPULATION   Unknown.   There have been no reports of this species for over 30
years (H. Sick 1977, pers. comm.) and a brief search in 1977, the first for a long
time, failed to detect it (R. Ridgely 1978, pers. comm.).

HABITAT   Coastal forest, which in eastern Brazil has largely been cleared for
agricultural and other development resulting from an expanding human population.

CONSERVATION MEASURES TAKEN   Brazilian law protects this species but not its
habitat.

CONSERVATION MEASURES PROPOSED   None known.

REFERENCES   1.   Sick, H. 1960.   Zur Systematik und Biologie der
                    Burzelstelzer (Rhinocryptidae) speziell Brasiliens.
                    Jour. f. Ornith. 101: 141-174.

BRASILIA TAPACULO

Scytalopus novacapitalis Sick, 1958

Order PASSERIFORMES   Family RHINOCRYPTIDAE

STATUS   Indeterminate.   Known only from the immediate area of Brasília, the
capital of Brazil, where the new city has replaced the forest habitat of this
species.

DISTRIBUTION   Brasília, D.F. (formerly eastern Goiás), Brazil.

POPULATION   Three specimens were collected, all in 1957; there have been no
subsequent records (H. Sick 1977, pers. comm.).

HABITAT   Perennially flooded dense thickets of lianas, underbrush and inter-
twined fallen palm fronds surmounted by a gallery forest of Euterpe and Blechnum
palms.   At the type locality of this species this habitat has been replaced by
the city of Brasília; but there may well be other similar areas within the millions
of square kilometres of the Brazilian plateau, although in none of those so far
investigated has this tapaculo been found (1).

CONSERVATION MEASURES TAKEN   Protected by Brazilian law.

CONSERVATION MEASURES PROPOSED   None known.

REMARKS   Described in 1958 as a subspecies of S. indigoticus but subsequently
considered by the describer as a valid species (1).

REFERENCES   1.   Sick, H. 1960.   Zur Systematik und Biologie der
                   Burzelstelzer (Rhinocryptidae) speziell Brasiliens.
                   Journ. f. Ornith. 101: 141-174.
              2.   de Schauensee, R.M. 1966.   The Species of Birds of South
                   America and their Distribution.   Narberth, Pa.: Livingston
                   Publishing Co.

KINGLET CALYPTURA

Calyptura cristata (Vieillot, 1818)

Order PASSERIFORMES   Family COTINGIDAE

STATUS   Indeterminate.   A little-known species of south-eastern Brazil, where
most of its primary forest home has been felled and where like other species
dependent on this habitat it is therefore likely to be at serious risk.

DISTRIBUTION   The type locality of the species was near Nova Friburgo, Rio de
Janeiro state, about half way between the state capital and the city of Campos;
it has also been listed as occurring in Espírito Santo (1; 2), but the record has
not been properly confirmed (H. Sick 1977, pers. comm.).

POPULATION   Unknown.   This species has very seldom been reported and is likely
to be near extinction, if indeed a population of it still exists.

HABITAT   Primary coastal forest of south-eastern Brazil, a habitat which has in
fact been largely destroyed, with only a few relict patches remaining: this is
particularly so around Nova Friburgo, where deforestation is nearly complete (3).

CONSERVATION MEASURES TAKEN   The species has legal protection in Brazil and some
5,000 ha of its habitat are safeguarded within the Serra das Orgãos National Park;
unfortunately it is not known to occur within the park boundaries (R. Ridgely 1978,
pers. comm.).

CONSERVATION MEASURES PROPOSED   None known.

REFERENCES   1.   de Schauensee, R.M. 1966.   The Species of Birds of South
                    America and their Distribution.   Narberth, Pa.: Livingston
                    Publishing Co.
              2.   Ruschi, A. 1953.   Lista das aves do Estado do Espírito
                    Santo.   Bol. Mus. Biol. Santa Teresa 1953(11): 1-21.
              3.   Sick, H. 1972.   A ameaça da avifauna brasileira.
                    In Espécies da Fauna Brasileira Ameaçadas de Extinção,
                    pp. 99-153.   Rio de Janeiro: Academia Brasileira de
                    Ciências.

LONG-WATTLED UMBRELLABIRD

Cephalopterus penduliger Sclater, 1859

Order PASSERIFORMES   Family COTINGIDAE

STATUS   Vulnerable. Of somewhat limited distribution, this bizarre cotinga
from north-western South America is avidly hunted for the cage-bird trade and is
also large enough to be shot for food.   As new areas of primary forest are
opened up, it is one of the first species to disappear.

DISTRIBUTION   Western Colombia on the seaward slopes of the western Andes and
extending south into western Ecuador (1).

POPULATION   No estimates have been made.   This always seems to be a scarce
bird, even in suitably remote habitat, and is quickly extirpated in any area close
to human settlement.   There is still, however, a considerable amount of remote
and little-disturbed forest within its range, where its abundance should be at
about normal or natural levels (R. Ridgely 1978, pers. comm.).

HABITAT   Montane tropical and subtropical forest, which has often been seriously
depleted, but in parts of the range of the Umbrellabird is still fairly considerable.

CONSERVATION MEASURES TAKEN   Small numbers of this cotinga occur in the
Archicaya valley in the Valle division of Colombia, where the watershed is protected for the purposes of hydro-electric development.   No other area of its
habitat presently receives any form of protection (S. Hilty 1978, pers. comm. to
R. Ridgely).

CONSERVATION MEASURES PROPOSED   None known.

REMARKS   This species, along with C. glabricollis of Costa Rica and Panama, has
sometimes been treated as a subspecies of C. ornatus (2).   C. glabricollis is at
some risk as forests are cleared and human access to once remote areas becomes
possible; but C. ornatus of central South America is not at present threatened
(R. Ridgely 1978, pers. comm.).

REFERENCES   1.   de Schauensee, R.M. 1966.   The Species of Birds of South
                   America and their Distribution.   Narberth, Pa.: Livingston
                   Publishing Co.
              2.   Hellmayr, C.E. 1929.   Catalogue of birds of the Americas,
                   Part VI.   Field Mus. Nat. Hist. Pub. 266.

BANDED COTINGA

Cotinga maculata (Muller, 1776)

Order PASSERIFORMES   Family COTINGIDAE

STATUS   Vulnerable.   Seriously reduced in abundance and distribution in south-eastern Brazil as the result of forest destruction.

DISTRIBUTION   This cotinga has been recorded fairly widely in south-eastern Brazil, from southern Bahia state through Espírito Santo to Rio de Janeiro and adjacent Minas Gerais (1), but no longer occurs in many parts of this range.   It was found in 1970 in the 4,000 ha forested area of Fazenda Klabin or Klabin Farm near Conceição de Barra in Espírito Santo state (2), and in 1977 in the Sooretama Reserve (24,000 ha), also in Espírito Santo (R. Ridgely 1978, pers. comm.).

POPULATION   Unknown but unquestionably very much reduced.

HABITAT   Primary tropical forest.   Only relict patches of this habitat, which at one time extended over most of the coastlands of south-eastern Brazil, are now left (2).

CONSERVATION MEASURES TAKEN   The species is listed in Appendix 1 of the 1973 Convention on International Trade in Endangered Species of Wild Fauna and Flora and has formal protection under Brazilian law.

CONSERVATION MEASURES PROPOSED   None known.

REMARKS   This species is closely related to C. cotinga, which is widely distributed in northern South America, and may be conspecific with it.

REFERENCES   1.   de Schauensee, R.M. 1966.   The Species of Birds of South America and their Distribution.   Narberth, Pa.: Livingston Publishing Co.
              2.   Sick, H. 1972.   A ameaça da avifauna brasileira.   In Espécies da Fauna Brasileira Ameaçadas de Extinção, pp. 99-153. Rio de Janeiro: Academia Brasileira de Ciências.

MARCGRAVE'S BEARDED BELLBIRD

Procnias averano averano Hermann, 1783

Order PASSERIFORMES   Family COTINGIDAE

STATUS   Vulnerable. Occurs in small disjunct populations in two northern
Brazilian states, its decline being attributable to forest destruction and
trapping for the cage-bird trade.

DISTRIBUTION   Recorded in north-eastern Brazil from Maranhão to Alagoas, but no
longer present in Piaui, Ceará (where it was last collected in 1941), Rio Grande
do Norte, Paraiba or Pernambuco (except possibly in the south-eastern corner and
on Itamaracá Island, where it was found in 1939). In 1924 and 1925, it was
recorded at Tranqueira and Grajaú in Maranhão (1-3) and, again in that state, in
1973, 1976 and 1977 (H. Sick 1977, R. Ridgely 1978, pers. comms). In Alagoas
state it occurs at São Miguel dos Campos and in forest patches near Porto Calvo
close to the Pernambuco border (1).

POPULATION   No early estimates exist, although it is safe to assume that this
subspecies was once far more numerous than it is today. In 1971, the estimate
for the state of Alagoas was about 250 birds, on the basis that the size of each
territory averages about 30 ha (1). The bellbird is commoner in Maranhão, since
this state still has much more forest than Alagoas (H. Sick 1977, pers. comm.).

HABITAT   Coastal rainforest, which in north-eastern Brazil has been seriously
reduced in extent: no areas of this habitat, on which the subspecies entirely
depends, have been given any form of protection.

CONSERVATION MEASURES TAKEN   None known.

CONSERVATION MEASURES PROPOSED   None known.

REMARKS   Another subspecies, P. a. carnobarba, is widespread in north-western
South America and Trinidad, and not at risk. The species as a whole is one of the
best known South American cage-birds.

REFERENCES   1. Coimbra-Filho, A.F. 1971. Tres formas da avifauna do
                  nordeste do Brasil ameaçadas de extinção: Tinamus solitarius
                  pernambucensis Berla, 1946, Mitu m. mitu (Linnaeus, 1766) e
                  Procnias a. averano (Hermann, 1783) (Aves-Tinamidae, Cracidae,
                  Cotingidae). Rev. Brasil. Biol. 31: 239-247.
              2. Pinto, O.M. de O. 1940. Aves de Pernambuco. São Paulo
                  Arq. Zool. 1: 219-282.
              3. Hellmayr, C.E. 1929. A contribution to the ornithology
                  of northeastern Brazil. Field Mus. Nat. Hist. Pubs. Zool.
                  series 12: 235-501.

WHITE-WINGED COTINGA

Xipholena atropurpurea (Wied, 1820)

Order PASSERIFORMES   Family COTINGIDAE

STATUS   Vulnerable. Forest destruction in eastern Brazil has proceeded to the
point where this and many other species which are restricted to primary forest, are
at serious risk.

DISTRIBUTION   Eastern Brazil from Paraiba south along the Atlantic coast to Rio
de Janeiro (1), but through much of this range suitable habitat for the species no
longer exists. It is known to occur in the Sooretama Reserve (24,000 ha) and on
the forestland of Klabin Farm (4,000 ha), both in Espírito Santo state, and in the
Monte Pascoal National Park (22,500 ha) in south-eastern Bahia (R. Ridgely 1978,
pers. comm.).

POPULATION   Unknown but certainly seriously reduced.

HABITAT   Primary tropical forest, of which very few areas remain along Brazil's
eastern coast; most have been clear felled and those that remain form a mosaic of
relict patches with areas of agricultural, pastoral or other development (2).

CONSERVATION MEASURES TAKEN   The species is listed in Appendix 1 of the 1973
Convention on International Trade in Endangered Species of Wild Fauna and Flora.
Part of this cotinga's habitat is protected in one national reserve and one
national park.

CONSERVATION MEASURES PROPOSED   None known.

REMARKS   This species has been kept in captivity and on one occasion a captive
bird is known to have laid an egg but it broke almost immediately (3).

REFERENCES   1.   de Schauensee, R.M. 1966. The Species of Birds of South
                    America and their Distribution. Narberth, Pa.: Livingston
                    Publishing Co.
              2.   Sick, H. 1972. A ameaça da avifauna brasileira. In
                    Espécies da Fauna Brasileira Ameaçadas de Extinção, pp. 99-153.
                    Rio de Janeiro: Academia Brasileira de Ciências.
              3.   Snow, D.W. 1977. Waltzing cotingas. Animal Kingdom 80(4):
                    13-18.

BOGOTA BEARDED TACHURI

Polystictus pectoralis bogotensis (Chapman, 1915)

Order PASSERIFORMES   Family TYRANNIDAE

STATUS   Indeterminate. Known only from two localities in Colombia and not
reported for over 50 years.

DISTRIBUTION   Recorded from the marshes of Suba, in the Bogotá savanna of the
Cundinamarca division, eastern Andes, and from Pavas, La Cumbre, in the Valle
division, western Andes, Colombia (1; 2).

POPULATION   Unknown, although likely to be small if still extant.

HABITAT   Temperate zone marshes.

CONSERVATION MEASURES TAKEN   None known.

CONSERVATION MEASURES PROPOSED   None known.

REMARKS   The two other subspecies in South America which have been recognized,
are not known to be at risk. It is surprising there are no recent records of this
tyrant-flycatcher and the cause of its rarity is unknown.

REFERENCES   1.   Cory, C.B. & Hellmayr, C.E. 1927. Catalogue of birds of the
                    Americas and the adjacent islands in Field Museum of Natural
                    History, Part V, Tyrannidae.   Field Museum of Natural History
                    Pub. 242.
              2.   Chapman, F.M. 1917. The distribution of bird life in Colombia;
                    a contribution to a biological survey of South America.
                    Bull. Amer. Mus. Nat. Hist. 36: 1-729.

GURNEY'S PITTA

Pitta gurneyi Hume, 1875

Order PASSERIFORMES   Family PITTIDAE

STATUS   Indeterminate.   Restricted to lowland forests of peninsular Thailand
and adjacent Burma.   The forest over much of its range has been cut.

DISTRIBUTION   This species occupies a limited stretch of less than 500 km in the
north-western section of the Malay Peninsula from Trang and Junk Zeylon island
north to Koh Lak, an island on the west coast of the Isthmus of Kra in Thailand,
and to Tenasserim, in southern Burma (1).   Its present distribution is not known
to differ, although there are believed to be large areas of former habitat which
no longer support the species (D. Wells in litt. to K. Scriven, 1974).

POPULATION   No estimate has been made.   It was considered relatively common
throughout much of its limited range half a century ago (1).   It is now scarce
over much of its range in Thailand.   Its status in Burma is unknown (D. Wells
in litt. to K. Scriven, 1974).

HABITAT   Primary lowland evergreen forests below 915 m elevation (2).   In
Thailand these lowland forests have suffered extensive clearing.

CONSERVATION MEASURES TAKEN   None known.

CONSERVATION MEASURES PROPOSED   None known.

REFERENCES   1.   Chasen, F.N. 1939.   The Birds of the Malay Peninsula, Vol. 4.
                   London: H.F. and G. Witherby.
              2.   King, B.F., Woodcock, M. & Dickinson, E.C. 1975.   A Field
                   Guide to the Birds of South-East Asia.   Boston: Houghton
                   Mifflin Co.; London: Collins.

NEW ZEALAND BUSH WREN

Xenicus longipes (Gmelin, 1789)

Order PASSERIFORMES   Family ACANTHISITTIDAE

STATUS   Critically endangered.   At least two of the three subspecies of this
Bush Wren, comprising a species unique to New Zealand, are extinct, having fallen
prey to introduced predators.   It is not known with certainty whether the third
subspecies still exists.

DISTRIBUTION   X. l. stokesi Gray 1862, North Island Bush Wren, was known from
the southern and central portions of the island.   The last, unconfirmed, reports
were from the Lake Waikaremoana area in the Huiarau Range near Gisborne in 1949
and 1955 (1; 2).   X. l. longipes (Gmelin, 1789), the South Island Bush Wren, was
formerly widespread throughout the forests, but is now greatly reduced: recent
unconfirmed sightings have all come from Fiordland, where it may still exist (2; 3).
X. l. variabilis Stead, 1937, Stead's Bush Wren, was known from Stewart Island and
several outliers: it was last reported on Stewart Island in 1951, but flourished
on Big South Cape Island off the south-west coast until 1963; but black rats,
Rattus rattus, which had been accidentally introduced some time prior to that year
finally exterminated it by 1965 (2-5).   A last-ditch relocation of birds to nearby
Kaimohu Islet (8 ha) was attempted, but failed, and the subspecies is now extinct
(G. Williams 1976, pers. comm.).

POPULATION   All subspecies were formerly fairly common, but rapidly declined
following the introduction of predatory mammals by European settlers.   No precise
population figures are known for the South Island bird; if it exists it must be
reduced to the last few individuals.   Nine Stead's Bush Wrens were captured on
Big South Cape Island in 1964, by the New Zealand Wildlife Service, when it was
apparent that rats were about to cause the subspecies' extinction; three died but
the remaining six were relocated on Kaimohu Islet where four were seen in 1965, two
in 1967, and possibly two again in March 1972 (3; D. Merton 1974, pers. comm.).
None could be found in 1976 when a thorough search was made (G. Williams 1976,
pers. comm.).

HABITAT   Restricted to the lower strata of heavy forest on the three main islands
and to the indigenous coastal scrub association in Big South Cape Island, where it
was most frequently observed creeping amongst dense foliage near the ground (6;
G. Williams 1976, pers. comm.).

CONSERVATION MEASURES TAKEN   Fully protected by law.   The New Zealand Wildlife
Service unsuccessfully attempted a last-ditch relocation of Stead's Bush Wren.

CONSERVATION MEASURES PROPOSED   Follow-up on any recent reported sightings of the
species in an attempt to find a viable population.

REMARKS   The related Stephen Island Wren X. lyalli, found only on Stephen Island
(150 ha), was swiftly exterminated by a single domestic cat in 1894.

REFERENCES   1.   Edgar, A.T. 1949.   Winter notes on New Zealand birds.
                    N.Z. Bird Notes 3: 170-174.
              2.   Ornithological Society of New Zealand, 1970.   Annotated
                    Checklist of the Birds of New Zealand Including the Birds of
                    the Ross Dependency.   Wellington: A.H. and A.W. Reed.

3. Ellis, B.A. 1975. Rare and endangered New Zealand birds: the role of the Royal Forest and Bird Protection Society of New Zealand Inc. ICBP Bull. 12: 173-186.

4. Williams, G.R. 1962. Extinction and the land and freshwater-inhabiting birds of New Zealand. Notornis 10: 15-32.

5. Blackburn, A. 1965. Muttonbird Islands diary. Notornis 12: 191-207.

6. Oliver, W.R.B. 1955. New Zealand Birds, 2nd Ed. Wellington: A.H. and A.W. Reed.

SMALL-BILLED WATTLED SUNBIRD

Neodrepanis hypoxantha Salomonsen, 1933

Order PASSERIFORMES   Family PHILEPITTIDAE

STATUS   Indeterminate. This Madagascar endemic is known only from about ten
specimens collected between 1879 and 1925.

DISTRIBUTION   The type locality is a forest east of Tananarive (1).   The species
was also collected to the south of Tananarive at Andrangoloaka, east of Ansirabe,
and in Sianaka Forest.   It has been suggested that there is a chance that the
species may once more be found in the forests east of Ankazobe (2) or in the
Fierenana district north of Perinet (A. Forbes-Watson 1974, pers. comm.).

POPULATION   Only 11 specimens are known (5-7).   The species has always been
considered very rare.

HABITAT   Humid forest.   Only 10 percent of Madagascar's forests remain, and
these are being constantly depleted (3).

CONSERVATION MEASURES TAKEN   None known.

CONSERVATION MEASURES PROPOSED   It has been recommended that most of Madagascar's
endemic avifauna should receive legal protection (K. Curry-Lindahl in litt. to
G. Ramanantsoavina, Director, Service des Eaux et Forêts, Chasse et Pêche,
Jan. 1973).

REMARKS   This species is considered to be a subspecies of N. coruscans Sharpe,
1875, by some authors (4).   The similarity between the two makes field confirmation of the continued existence of N. hypoxantha more difficult.

REFERENCES   1. Greenway, J.C. Jr. 1958.   Extinct and Vanishing Birds of
                  the World.   Amer. Comm. Internat. Wildlife Prot. Spec. Pub. 13.
              2. Lavauden, L. 1937.   Oiseaux.   In A. and G. Grandidier (eds)
                  Histoire physique, naturelle et politique de Madagascar,
                  Vol. 12.   Paris.
              3. Curry-Lindahl, K. 1975.   Man in Madagascar.   Defenders of
                  Wildlife 50: 164-169.
              4. Milon, P., Petter, J.-J. & Randrianasolo, G. 1973.
                  Faune de Madagascar, 35: Oiseaux.   Tananarive and Paris:
                  ORSTOM and CNRS.
              5. Benson, C.W. 1971.   The Cambridge collection from the
                  Malagasy Region, Part II.   Bull. Brit. Orn. Club. 91: 1-7.
              6. Salomonsen, F. 1965.   Notes on the sunbird-asitys
                  (Neodrepanis).   Oiseau 35 suppl.: 103-111.
              7. Benson, C.W. 1974.   Another specimen of Neodrepanis hypoxantha.
                  Bull. Brit. Ornith. Club. 94: 141-143.

NOISY SCRUB-BIRD

Atrichornis clamosus (Gould, 1844)

Order PASSERIFORMES   Family ATRICHORNITHIDAE

STATUS   Endangered by virtue of its critically low population restricted to one
small area, although at present the population does not appear to be decreasing
and visits to the area where it occurs are carefully controlled.   The species was
considered to have become extinct in 1889, but was rediscovered in 1961.

DISTRIBUTION   Described in 1842 from Drakesbrook, south of Perth, Western
Australia, and subsequently found along the south-western coast of Australia at
Margaret River, Augusta, Torbay and Albany, and 50 km inland from Albany as far as
Mt. Barker.   In 1961, it was rediscovered 40 km east of Albany on a small headland
around Mt. Gardner at Two Peoples Bay (1).

POPULATION   No estimate was made prior to the presumed extinction of the species
in 1889, although it was noted that the bird was most numerous in the Albany area.
The number of breeding pairs recorded in what is now the only known breeding area
has varied from 40 to 45 between 1970 and 1974, and the population is thought to
be stable (1; 2).

HABITAT   The species is presently confined to areas of eucalypts where steep,
damp and densely vegetated gullies drain seawards; to shallow drier gullies
draining inland; and also to stunted eucalypts in the heath between these gullies.
Formerly occurred in wetter parts of jarrah-marri forest (Eucalyptus marginata -
E. calophylla) where bullich (E. megacarpa), tea-tree (Leptosperma sp.) and rushes
(Lepidosperma spp.) were plentiful.   This forest has been cleared and burned
repeatedly by man, and a prolonged drought at the end of the nineteenth century and
the introduction of cats further weakened the precarious status of the Scrub-bird
(1; 2; G.T. Smith 1975, pers. comm.).

CONSERVATION MEASURES TAKEN   The species is fully protected by law.   A Class A
reserve of 5,508 ha has been established around the area where it occurs.   A
strict management plan restricts visits to a portion of the reserve by visitors on
foot only; the rest is out of bounds for visitors.   A ranger is permanently
stationed on the reserve.   Present management calls for exclusion of fires,
although the long-term survival of the species may in fact require selective
burning of the gullies to maintain appropriate habitat.   A town site of 405 ha,
initially planned for a portion of the reserve, has been relocated (1; G.T. Smith
1975, pers. comm.).   Listed in Appendix 1 of the 1973 Convention on International
Trade in Endangered Species of Wild Fauna and Flora.

CONSERVATION MEASURES PROPOSED   In the future a small group of birds may be
translocated to another suitable area (G.T. Smith 1975, pers. comm.).

REMARKS   Permission was obtained in 1975 to collect two young birds for aviary
studies but there is little hope of breeding the species in captivity (G.T. Smith
1975, pers. comm.) and no success in this respect has been reported.

REFERENCES   1.   Smith, G.T. & Robinson, F.N. 1976.   The Noisy Scrub-Bird:-
                   an interim report.   Emu 76: 37-42.
              2.   Smith, G.T. 1974.   Ecological and behavioural comparisons
                   between the Atrichornithidae and Menuridae.   Canberra:
                   Proc. 16th Int. Ornith. Congr.: pp. 125-136.

RUFOUS SCRUB-BIRD

Atrichornis rufescens (Ramsay, 1866)

Order PASSERIFORMES   Family ATRICHORNITHIDAE

STATUS   Rare and localized.   Historically greatly reduced in abundance and
range.   However, there is no indication of further decline at present and the
several localities where this species now occurs are all within national parks.

DISTRIBUTION   Formerly considered to be restricted to the Macpherson Range on
the Queensland-New South Wales border in eastern Australia and, further south, to
the Clarence and Richmond river areas (1).   It is now known to be distributed more
widely, although very locally, from just south of Brisbane well into New South
Wales.   It is found in Mt. Barney National Park and Lamington National Park in
Queensland and in Gibraltar Range, New England, Dorrigo and Barrington Tops
National Parks in New South Wales (G.T. Smith 1975, pers. comm.).

POPULATION   Thought to be relatively common in the Clarence and Richmond river
areas prior to large scale clearing of the forest for agriculture.   Although no
estimate exists for the species as a whole, it is significant that no more than 10
territories are known from any locality.   Rugged terrain, dense vegetation,
dispersed territories and infrequent vocalizations of males make estimation of
numbers difficult.   At present no decline is thought to be taking place (G.T.
Smith 1975, pers. comm.).

HABITAT   Nothofagus forest, edges of subtropical rainforest and wet sclerophyll
forest with a dense scrub layer.   The habitat of this species was largely
destroyed by clearing by man, while a severe drought last century probably also
contributed to its deterioration.   The remaining areas of suitable habitat are
quite small (G.T. Smith 1975, pers. comm.).

CONSERVATION MEASURES TAKEN   Fully protected by law.   All known populations are
within the borders of national parks.

CONSERVATION MEASURES PROPOSED   It is suggested that logging may be required in
the long term to increase sunlight locally and promote dense scrub growth, which
the species requires (G.T. Smith 1975, pers. comm.).

REMARKS   The race A. r. jacksoni White is no longer considered valid.

REFERENCES   1.   Greenway, J.C. Jr. 1958.   Extinct and Vanishing Birds
                    of the World.   Amer. Comm. Int. Wildl. Prot. Spec.
                    Pub. No. 13.

RAZO LARK

Alauda razae (Boyd Alexander, 1898)

Order PASSERIFORMES   Family ALAUDIDAE

STATUS   Rare.   Restricted to one small island in the Cape Verde archipelago,
where it is subject to marked population fluctuations.   The threat that rats
could find their way onto the island is ever present and, if it happened, this
ground-nesting bird would quickly disappear.

DISTRIBUTION   The lark is found only on Razo (more correctly spelt Raso), an
island with an area of 4.9 sq. km in the Windward group of the Cape Verde Islands,
where it keeps mainly to the central plateau which is less than 100 hectares in
extent (1; 2).

POPULATION   At times the species is abundant within its exiguous range (3), but
prolonged drought can apparently discourage breeding.   Thus in 1962, it was
abundant, but in 1965, following three years of poor rainfall, the population had
dropped below 50 pairs and in 1968 was down to less than 40 pairs (2).

HABITAT   A flat plain of decomposing lava and volcanic tuff, with a sparse
cover of herbs and low scrub.   The relative desiccation of the island's vegetation
results from a highly variable local rainfall (2).

CONSERVATION MEASURES TAKEN   None known.

CONSERVATION MEASURES PROPOSED   Recommendations have been made to the Portuguese
authorities that Razo should be established as a nature sanctuary for the protection of this lark and of the skink Macroscincus coctei, and that the endemic
species of the Cape Verdes, including the lark, should be fully protected by law
(4).

REMARKS   This bird, which is still often referred to as the Raza Lark, has been
variously placed in the short-toed lark genera, Spizocorys and Calandrella, and
even to a genus on its own, Razocorys, but is now usually regarded as an aberrant
skylark.

REFERENCES   1.   Bannerman, D.A. & W.M. 1968.   History of the Birds of the
                    Cape Verde Islands.   Edinburgh: Oliver and Boyd.
              2.   de Naurois, R. 1969.   Notes brèves sur l'avifaune de
                    l'archipel du Cap-Vert.   Faunistique, endémisme, ecologie.
                    Bull. Inst. Fond. Afr. Noire 31 (ser. A): 143-218.
              3.   Bourne, W.R.P. 1955.   The birds of the Cape Verde
                    Islands.   Ibis 97: 508-556.
              4.   de Naurois, R. 1964.   Les oiseaux des Îles du Cap-Vert.
                    Garcia de Orta (Lisboa) 12: 609-620.

JAMAICA GOLDEN SWALLOW

Kalochelidon euchrysea euchrysea (Gosse, 1847)

Order PASSERIFORMES   Family HIRUNDINIDAE

STATUS   Indeterminate.   This subspecies may well be critically endangered, since
it is now known from only a single locality in Jamaica, West Indies, and the causes
of its decline are not understood, although it has been suggested that competition
by the introduced Starling Sturnus vulgaris may have been significant (1).

DISTRIBUTION   Formerly more widespread, although apparently always restricted to
the mountainous interior of Jamaica (5).   By 1936, the swallow was restricted to
the Cockpit Country in the western third of Jamaica (2) and recently it has been
observed only in the vicinity of Ram Goat Cave in the Cockpit Country (3; 4;
P. Lack, A. Downer, R. Sutton 1974, pers. comms).

POPULATION   No estimate has been made, although the swallow was at one time quite
numerous (2).   Since the mid-1960s it has been observed only a few times, usually
one or two individuals, once several and once, in June 1969, 12 birds (3; 4;
P. Lack, A. Downer, R. Sutton 1974, pers. comms).   The population may be close to
extinction.

HABITAT   Dry, wooded limestone hills; formerly also in moist high montane forest
(2).

CONSERVATION MEASURES TAKEN   Protected by law.

CONSERVATION MEASURES PROPOSED   None known.   Provision and monitoring of nest
boxes might be a simple management technique applicable to the situation if
competition by starlings for nesting cavities is an important factor.

REMARKS   The other subspecies, K. e. sclateri of Hispaniola, is local but not
uncommon.

REFERENCES   1.   Bond, J. 1961.   Extinct and near extinct birds of the West
                  Indies.   Pan-American Section, ICBP, Res. Rept. No. 4.
             2.   Bond, J. 1936.   Birds of the West Indies.   Philadelphia
                  Acad. Nat. Sci.
             3.   Downer, A. & Sutton, R. 1972.   Birds of the Cockpit Country.
                  Gosse Bird Club (Jamaica) Broadsheet 19:   12-14.
             4.   Sutton, R. 1973.   Golden Swallow.   In Bird Notes.
                  Gosse Bird Club (Jamaica) Broadsheet 21:   21.
             5.   Bangs, O. & Kennard, K.H. 1920.   A list of the birds of
                  Jamaica.   In The Handbook of Jamaica, 1920.   Kingston:
                  Govt. Printing Office.

WHITE-EYED RIVER MARTIN

Pseudochelidon sirintarae Kitti, 1968

Order PASSERIFORMES   Family HIRUNDINIDAE

STATUS   Indeterminate.   Known only from one lake in Thailand, where it occurs
in winter in small numbers.   The location of its breeding area, the size of its
population and its distribution at other seasons are all unknown.

DISTRIBUTION   This distinctive species was recently discovered in winter on Lake
Boraphet (25,000 ha), Nakhon Sawan Province, central Thailand (1).   Where it goes
to during the remainder of the year has not yet been discovered.

POPULATION   Unknown but certainly small.   Ten specimens were collected in 1968,
the only ones found in among the thousands of birds gathered in the reed beds of
Lake Boraphet (1).   Two were subsequently found in 1972 (J. McNeely 1976, pers.
comm.) and six were seen in 1977, all on Lake Boraphet (2).

HABITAT   Between November and February this martin visits reed beds in a large
shallow marshy lake at night to roost.   Professional bird catchers trap large
numbers of swallows and other birds in these reed beds.   Habitat preferences of
the species by day and during the rest of the year are unknown.   It has been
suggested that it may breed in holes in river banks in Thailand or possibly in
China (1; 2).

CONSERVATION MEASURES TAKEN   Listed in Appendix 2 of the 1973 Convention on
International Trade in Endangered Species of Wild Fauna and Flora.   Legally
protected in Thailand from capture or hunting.

CONSERVATION MEASURES PROPOSED   Location of the nesting place of this martin has
been suggested as a first step towards its conservation (1).   Other measures that
would improve its status include reduction or elimination of bird trapping on Lake
Boraphet and the establishment of the lake as a wildlife sanctuary (2).

REMARKS   The nearest relative of this species and only other member of the
swallow sub-family Pseudochelidoninae is P. eurystomina from the Zaire River,
west-central Africa, 10,000 km distant.

REFERENCES   1.   Kitti, T. 1968.   A new martin of the genus Pseudochelidon
                    from Thailand.   Thai Nat. Sci. Papers Fauna Series 1: 1-10.
               2.   King, B. & Kanwanich, S. 1978.   First wild sighting of
                    the White-eyed River-Martin Pseudochelidon sirintarae.
                    Biol. Cons. 13: 183-185.

SOKOKE PIPIT

Anthus sokokensis Van Someren, 1921

Order PASSERIFORMES   Family MOTACILLIDAE

STATUS   Rare.   Known from three small areas in East Africa, this unique forest-dwelling pipit is exceedingly rare.   Its forest habitat is threatened with destruction.

DISTRIBUTION   Recorded in south-eastern Kenya, from the Arabuko-Sokoke and Gedi forests, and in Tanzania, from scrub forest at Moa on the coast near the Usambara mountains, 160 km south of the Kenyan locality, and in the Pugu Forest, 200 km farther south, west of Dar-es-Salaam, although not found recently in the two Tanzanian localities.   The coastal forests of eastern Africa were far more extensive in recent historical times, which suggests that this pipit's distribution might once have been continuous or nearly so (1; 6).

POPULATION   Unknown.   In 1940, it was apparently rare in the Pugu Forest (2) and there are no more recent records.   Between 1964 and 1966, 14 specimens were taken in the Arabuko-Sokoke Forest in localities which by 1971 had been more or less completely cleared (3).   However, investigations during the past few years have shown that this pipit is widespread and can be regularly observed and that it occurs in all but the most impoverished habitats (5; P. Britton 1977, pers. comm.).

HABITAT   Edges and clearings of lowland coastal forest in East Africa.   The extent of this forest has been seriously depleted, the area, for example, covered by the Arabuko-Sokoke Forest having been halved between 1956 and 1966 (3).   By 1977, however, a total of 360 sq. km of this forest still remained and there is room for cautious optimism that much of this will survive for the foreseeable future.

CONSERVATION MEASURES TAKEN   The species is protected by Kenya law.   Within the 400 sq. km Arabuko —Sokoke Forest Reserve, a 40 sq. km block has been designated as a nature reserve, in which no disturbance is allowed (P. Britton 1977, pers. comm.).

CONSERVATION MEASURES PROPOSED   Enlargement of the nature reserve to 60 sq. km, in order to safeguard an adequate tract of each of the three habitats in which the endemic coastal forest birds are found (P. Britton 1977, pers. comm.).   It has also been suggested that the Kenya Forestry Department should modify its policy of replacing indigenous forest with exotic timber species (4).

REMARKS   Morden's Scops Owl Otus ireneae, Clarke's Weaver Ploceus golandi and the Amani Sunbird Anthreptes pallidigaster are the three other species, wholly or largely confined to the Arabuko-Sokoke Forest, which are included in this volume (see relevant data sheets).

REFERENCES   1.   Hall, B.P. & Moreau, R.E. 1962.   A study of the rare birds of Africa.   Bull. Brit. Mus. (Nat. Hist.) Zool. 8(7): 313-378.
             2.   Moreau, R.E. 1940.   Distributional notes on East African birds. Ibis (14)4: 454-463.
             3.   Ripley, S.D. & Bond, G.M. 1971.   Systematic notes on a collection of birds from Kenya.   Smithsonian Contrib. Zool. 111

4. Brown, L.H. et al. Undated.   A report on threatened bird
    species in East Africa.   East African Wildlife Society.
    Mimeo, 12 pp.
5. Britton, P.L. 1976.   Primary forestland destruction now
    critical.   Africana 5(12): i-ii.
6. Turner, D.A. 1977.   Status and distribution of the East
    African endemic species.   Scopus 1: 2-11.

REUNION CUCKOO-SHRIKE

Coracina newtoni (Pollen, 1866)

Order PASSERIFORMES   Family CAMPEPHAGIDAE

STATUS   Rare.   Occurs in a restricted area of forest in the north of Réunion
Island, Indian Ocean, where its population is small.   The secretive nature of this
species has in the recent past caused it to be frequently overlooked, hence
reports of its impending extinction.   There are extensive forested areas on
Réunion which have not yet been carefully surveyed, where this species might be
expected to occur (A.S. Cheke 1974, pers. comm.).

DISTRIBUTION   There has been no consensus in the past on the extent of this
Cuckoo-shrike's distribution.   It was recorded from the "hauts de St. Benoit" (1),
also near St. Philippe, and from Le Volcan above the gorges of the Rivière de
l'Est, and it may still occur in these places today.   However, it is now thought
that the forests of the Plaine des Chicots and the Plaine d'Affouches, whence it
was originally described last century, constitute the epicentre of its distribution.   This area comprises about 10 sq. km, although suitable habitat not yet
investigated may cover another 100 sq. km (A.S. Cheke 1974, pers. comm.).

POPULATION   Early reports throw little light on the size of the population. The
most recent ones have suggested that as few as 10 pairs survive and that the
species is in danger of extinction (1; 2), but in 1974 several pairs and some
single birds were seen in 3½ days of observation, an estimate of a minimum of 125
pairs was made, and it was considered that 300 pairs or more might exist
(A.S. Cheke 1974, pers. comm.).

HABITAT   Indigenous mixed forest between 1200 and 1700 m elevation and forest
dominated by Acacia heterophylla between 1600 and 1900 m; also tree heath at
higher elevations.   Plantations of Cryptomeria have replaced some of these
forests, while others are "deer reserves".   The presence of introduced deer is
having adverse effects on regeneration of the natural forest (A.S. Cheke 1974,
pers. comm.).

CONSERVATION MEASURES TAKEN   Legally protected from capture, but in practice
birds are regularly trapped for food, by bird-liming.

CONSERVATION MEASURES PROPOSED   The threat to the habitat of this species from
plantations of exotic trees and from deer, and the need for nature reserves, have
been pointed out recently in a report submitted to the Director of Forests on
Réunion (A.S. Cheke, pers. comm.).

REFERENCES   1.   Milon, P. 1951.   Notes sur l'avifaune actuelle de l'île
                   de la Réunion.   La Terre et la Vie 98: 129-177.
              2.   Berlioz, J. 1946.   Oiseaux de la Réunion.   Faune de l'Empire
                   Français, IV.   Paris: Librairie La Rose.

MAURITIUS CUCKOO-SHRIKE

Coracina typica (Hartlaub, 1865)

Order PASSERIFORMES   Family CAMPEPHAGIDAE

STATUS   Vulnerable.   Uncommon and restricted in range but not immediately
threatened with extinction.   The main threats seem to be habitat destruction and
nest predation by introduced birds and mammals.

DISTRIBUTION   Found only on the island of Mauritius in the Indian Ocean and
never known to occur elsewhere.   Restricted to the indigenous montane evergreen
forests in the south-western corner of the island from Montagne Bris Fer southward
to the southern escarpment of the upland plateau and the Savanne Mountains.
Formerly more widespread when upland forests were more extensive (1; 2; S. Temple
1976, pers. comm.).

POPULATION   Said to have once been plentiful but accurate information on its
historical abundance is lacking (1).   Its total population now numbers about
100 pairs, which may be near the carrying capacity of the occupied habitat (2;
S. Temple 1976, pers. comm.).

HABITAT   Limited almost exclusively to indigenous montane evergreen forest and
scrub, but very occasionally exotic second growth vegetation adjacent to native
forest (S. Temple 1976, pers. comm.).   Indigenous vegetation has been reduced to
the point where it now covers only about five percent of Mauritius (3).   Nest
predation by introduced bulbuls Pycnonotus jocosus, mynahs Acridotheres tristis,
macaque monkeys Macaca irus and rats Rattus rattus and R. norvegicus pose a serious
threat (S. Temple 1976, pers. comm.).

CONSERVATION MEASURES TAKEN   Fully protected by laws forbidding the killing or
capture of native birds.   A large portion of the bird's range in the south-western
corner of the island is on officially declared reserves.   During 1972-1975,
ecological studies were carried out to define the bird's status and requirements
(4).

CONSERVATION MEASURES PROPOSED   Continued protection and management of the
remnant areas of indigenous evergreen forest are essential for this bird's
survival.   A management plan for a system of nature reserves and national parks
has been submitted to the Mauritius Government (5).   The Cuckoo-shrike could be
reintroduced into suitable unoccupied habitat in the Bambou Mountain Range in the
east-central region of the island (S. Temple 1976, pers. comm.).

REMARKS   Six pairs of this species were transported to the Jersey Wildlife
Preservation Trust in 1976, with a view to possible captive breeding (G. Durrell
1976, pers. comm.).

REFERENCES   1.   Meinertzhagen, R. 1912.   On the birds of Mauritius.
                     Ibis (9)6: 82-108.
              2.   Temple, S.A., Staub, J.J.F. & Antoine, R. 1974.   Some
                     background information and recommendations on the
                     preservation of the native flora and fauna of Mauritius.
                     Unpublished report submitted to the Mauritius Government.

3. Temple, S.A. 1974.   Wildlife in Mauritius today.
    Oryx, 12: 584-590.
4. Temple, S.A. 1975.   In World Wildlife Yearbook,
    1974-75.   Morges:World Wildlife Fund.   Pp. 210-212.
5. Procter, J. & Salm, R. 1974.   Conservation in Mauritius.
    Unpublished report to Mauritius Government.

SAN CLEMENTE LOGGERHEAD SHRIKE

Lanius ludovicianus mearnsi Ridgway, 1903

Order PASSERIFORMES   Family LANIIDAE

STATUS   Endangered.   This highly distinctive subspecies is restricted to one
island off the Californian coast which has been mostly denuded of vegetation by
introduced free-ranging livestock.

DISTRIBUTION   The subspecies occurs only on San Clemente Island (34 km long by
between 2.4 and 6.4 km wide), the southernmost of the Channel Islands, lying 80 km
south-west of the California mainland, between Los Angeles and San Diego, and 34 km
south of Santa Catalina, the nearest island.   It was once distributed throughout
the island, but is now decidedly local (1-5).

POPULATION   This Loggerhead Shrike was described in the 19th century as fairly
common, to the extent that 2 or 3 could be seen on an hour's walk and, certainly
at one time, several pairs might breed in a single canyon (2-5).   In 1974, no
more than 16 individuals were observed, during the periods 1-5 and 8-9 May, when
all the best bird habitats in the island were visited (1).   The percentage of
immature birds was noted to be about 36 compared with 50 percent in mainland
populations, suggesting poorer reproductive success in this island form (2).

HABITAT   Dense brushy vegetation, which is now very much restricted to the steep
sides of canyons.   There has been virtually no regeneration of brush or trees
since at least 1934.   Goats were introduced by 1827, sheep prior to 1877 and
feral pigs in 1957.   Between 1877 and 1933, fences restricted the movements of
livestock, but in 1934 jurisdiction over the island passed to the U.S. Navy from a
private livestock ranch, and all control of livestock ceased until 1973, when an
active but inadequate goat removal program began (1).

CONSERVATION MEASURES TAKEN   Protected by U.S. Federal and California State law.
Listed as endangered by the U.S. government in 1977. The goat removal program,
begun in 1973, has been based on the profit motive rather than aimed at eradication.

CONSERVATION MEASURES PROPOSED   Creation of a goat-proof fence bisecting San
Clemente, coupled with removal of goats from certain key areas, followed by
additional fencing, as a short-term means of promoting regeneration of vegetation
(1).

REMARKS   Ten other subspecies, covering much of southern Canada, the United
States and Mexico, including other islands in the Channel Islands, are not at risk.

REFERENCES   1.   Stewart, R.M., Smail, J., Clow, W.C. & Henderson, R.P. 1974.
                   The status of the Song Sparrow and Bewick's Wren on San
                   Clemente Island and Santa Barbara Island, California.
                   Point Reyes Bird Observatory unpublished report to the
                   U.S. Fish and Wildlife Service Office of Endangered Species.
              2.   Miller, A.H. 1931.   Systematic revision and natural history
                   of the American shrikes (Lanius).   Univ. Calif. Pub. Zool.
                   38: 11-242.
              3.   Grinnell, J. 1897.   Report on the birds recorded during a
                   visit to the islands of Santa Barbara, San Nicolas, and San
                   Clemente, in the spring of 1897.   Pasadena Acad. Sci. Pub.
                   1: 1-21.

4. Linton, C.B. 1908. Notes from San Clemente Island.
    Condor 10: 82-86.
5. Howell, A.B. 1917. Birds of the islands off the coast of
    southern California. Pacific Coast Avifauna 12.

BLACK-CAPPED BUSH-SHRIKE

Malaconotus alius Friedmann, 1927

Order PASSERIFORMES   Family LANIIDAE

STATUS   Endangered.   Restricted to a small area of mountain forest in Tanzania.
Recent searches for this bush-shrike have not been successful.

DISTRIBUTION   The species has only been recorded in the Uluguru Mountain forests
between 1525 m and 1830 m elevation and in an area of probably less than 260 sq.
km (1).

POPULATION   No estimate has been made.   This bush-shrike is said to be elusive
and shy and several expeditions to the Uluguru Mountains, for example in 1964 and
1972, have failed to observe it.   It was last recorded in 1952.   If it still
exists, it must surely be in very low numbers, so much so in fact that further
collection of scientific specimens should not be permitted (2-4; S. Stuart,
R. Stjernstedt, 1977, C. Mann 1978, pers. comms).

HABITAT   Canopy forest.   There has apparently been a good deal of felling of
this forest in the Ulugurus, but current information is poor, since access to the
Ulugurus has been restricted by various military activities and, until fairly
recently, in connection with the construction of the Tanzam railway.   Forest on
the western slopes of the Ulugurus begins abruptly above the cultivation line at
an altitude of 1830 m.   The eastern slopes are more difficult of access and much
less disturbed.

CONSERVATION MEASURES TAKEN   Part of the summit area of the Ulugurus is included
in a forest reserve, which gives some measure of protection to the wildlife.

CONSERVATION MEASURES PROPOSED   An expedition to the mountain forests of Tanzania
in 1977 to study endangered birds was unable to visit the habitat of this species,
so an up to date assessment of its status combined with establishment of appropriate
strict nature reserves would be an obvious first step in assuring its conservation.

REMARKS   Other species more or less entirely restricted to the Ulugurus are
Scepomycter winifredi and Nectarinia loveridgei but as long as a reasonable amount
of forest remains, they should not be at risk.

REFERENCES   1.   Hall, B.P. & Moreau, R.E. 1962.   A study of the rare birds
                    of Africa.   Bull. Brit. Mus.(Nat. Hist.) Zool. 8(7):   315-378.
               2.   Brown, L. et al.   Undated.   A report on threatened bird
                    species in East Africa.   East African Wildlife Society.
                    Mimeo, 12 pp.
               3.   Friedmann, H. & Stager, K.E. 1964.   Results of the 1964
                    Cheney Tanganyikan Expedition.   Ornithology.   Contrib. in Sci.
                    84: 1-50.
               4.   Turner, D.A. 1977.   Status and distribution of the East African
                    endemic species.   Scopus 1:   2-11.

KUPE MOUNTAIN BUSH-SHRIKE

Malaconotus kupeensis (Serle, 1951)

Order PASSERIFORMES   Family LANIIDAE

STATUS   Rare.   Restricted to one mountainside in west Africa, where it
apparently is not at all common.

DISTRIBUTION   The species is only known from the isolated Kupé Mountain, Kumba
Division, Cameroun, about 100 km north of Cameroun Mountain, where its total range
is no more than 21 sq. km (1; 2).

POPULATION   Unknown, but thought to be less than 2,000 (2).   The fact that
several unsuccessful searches were made for this bush-shrike between 1949, when the
type was collected, and 1951, when it was next seen, suggests that it is by no
means common.   Two birds, of which one, the type, was collected, were seen in 1949
and in 1951 a party of 3 was encountered (1).

HABITAT   Primary rainforest at an altitude of 1375 m.   There are no reports of
imminent destruction to forests on the steep slopes of Kupé Mountain.

CONSERVATION MEASURES TAKEN   None known.

CONSERVATION MEASURES PROPOSED   None known.

REMARKS   This very distinctive bush-shrike has been placed by some authors in
the genus Telophorus (= Chlorophoneus) and in many respects appears to be
intermediate between species in that genus and Malaconotus species.

REFERENCES   1.   Serle, W. 1951.   A new species of Shrike and a new race of
                   Apalis from West Africa.   Bull. Brit. Ornith. Club 71: 41-43.
              2.   Hall, B.P. & Moreau, R.E. 1962.   A study of the rare birds
                   of Africa.   Bull. Brit. Mus. (Nat. Hist.) Zool. 8(7): 313-378.

BERNIER'S VANGA

Oriolia bernieri Geoffroy Saint-Hilaire, 1838

Order PASSERIFORMES   Family VANGIDAE

STATUS   Indeterminate.   Occurs in eastern Madagascar where its present range
is not precisely known.   It is believed to be rare and its forest habitat is
gradually being destroyed.

DISTRIBUTION   This species is distributed widely in the forests of eastern
Madagascar between 500 and 1000 m elevation.   It was originally discovered near
Vondrozo, inland from Farafangana in south-east Madagascar, and in 1929-30 found
again in several localities in the north-east, since when very little additional
information on its distribution has been obtained.

POPULATION   No estimate has been made apart from the conclusion that the species
must be rather rare.   The 1929-30 expedition collected 9 specimens and saw
several others (1) and much more recently, in 1972, a specimen was taken near
Marojezy, also in the north-east about 70 km NW of Antalaha (3).

HABITAT   Dense humid forest, where this bird has been observed in or near the
tree tops (1).   The forests of Madagascar have been seriously depleted during
this century and as a result of clearing for agriculture, of reforestation with
exotic pines and eucalypts, and of burning, the process is continuing, so that now
only about 10 percent of the island remains forested (2).

CONSERVATION MEASURES TAKEN   None known.

CONSERVATION MEASURES PROPOSED   This and many other endemic species of Madagascar
have been commended to the Malagasy government for legal protection (K. Curry-
Lindahl in litt. to G. Ramanantsoavina, Director, Service des Eaux et Forêts,
Chasse et Pêche, Jan. 1973).

REFERENCES   1.   Rand, A.L. 1936.   The distribution and habits of Madagascar
                    birds.   Bull. Amer. Mus. Nat. Hist. 72: 143-499.
              2.   Curry-Lindahl, K. 1975.   Man in Madagascar.   Defenders of
                    Wildlife 50(2):   164-169.
              3.   Benson, C.W. Colebrook-Robjent, J.F.R. & Williams, A. 1977.
                    Contribution a l'ornithologie de Madagascar.   L'Oiseau et
                    R.F.O. 47:   41-64.

VAN DAM'S VANGA

Xenopirostris damii (Schlegel, 1866)

Order PASSERIFORMES   Family VANGIDAE

STATUS   Endangered.   Now occurs in only one forest on Madagascar, where it is
scarce.   Forest destruction has seriously reduced the area in which this species
could well have been found.

DISTRIBUTION   This vanga was discovered on the mainland at the north-western tip
of Madagascar, in the vicinity of Nossi Bé island, but since the turn of the
century has only been recorded near Ankarafantsika, some 400 km further south,
south-east of Majunga (1; 2).

POPULATION   Never known to be anything but rare, the species was rediscovered in
1928 (1) and again in 1969.   Four birds were seen in 1971 (2).   In the light of
these few observations, the population is presumed to be quite small.

HABITAT   Deciduous forests of the dry savannah region (1).   Clearance of this
type of forest like others in Madagascar shows no signs of slowing down.

CONSERVATION MEASURES TAKEN   The species presently occurs within Ankarafantsika
Nature Reserve but is not legally protected.

CONSERVATION MEASURES PROPOSED   Most of the endemic birds of Madagascar have
been recommended for complete legal protection (K. Curry-Lindahl in litt. to
G. Ramanantsoavina, Director, Service des Eaux et Forêts, Chasse et Pêche, Jan.
1973).

REMARKS   1.   Rand, A.L. 1936.   The distribution and habits of Madagascar
                  birds.   Bull. Amer. Mus. Nat. Hist. 72(5): 143-499.
           2.   Forbes-Watson, A.D., Turner, D.A. & Keith, G.S. 1973.
                 Report on bird preservation in Madagascar, Pt. 3, Appendix 1.
                 Unpublished report submitted to ICBP.

POLLEN'S VANGA

Xenopirostris polleni (Schlegel, 1868)

Order PASSERIFORMES   Family VANGIDAE

STATUS   Endangered.   Very locally distributed on Madagascar, and presently
confined to one small patch of forest.   Neither the species nor its habitat is
protected.

DISTRIBUTION   This species is restricted to the eastern humid forests of
Madagascar.   It has been collected in the Sianaka and Tsarafidy Forests, north of
Fianarontsoa in Ambohimahasoa district (1), but recently only reported from
Sianaka Forest (2).   One is thought to have been seen in 1972 at Marojezy in the
far distant north-east of Madagascar (3).

POPULATION   No estimates have been made, but it is clear that this species was
more numerous when it was more widespread.   It is now very rare.   Two were seen
in 1971, in addition to the possible sighting, previously mentioned, of a single
bird in 1972 (2; 3).

HABITAT   Humid forests.   The apparent decline in abundance of this species is
doubtless due to the extensive destruction of forests in the eastern highlands
which has gone on since the beginning of the century (2).

CONSERVATION MEASURES TAKEN   None known.

CONSERVATION MEASURES PROPOSED   Most of the endemic birds of Madagascar have
been recommended for legal protection (K. Curry-Lindahl in litt. to G. Ramanantsoavina, Director, Service des Eaux et Forêts, Chasse et Pêche, Jan. 1973).

REMARKS   The remarkable similarity between the immature of this vanga and Tylas
eduardi, another vanga with which it overlaps in range, makes identification in
the field difficult (3).

REFERENCES   1.   Milon, P., Petter, J.-J. & Randrianasolo, G. 1973.
                   Faune de Madagascar, 35: Oiseaux.   Tananarive and Paris:
                   ORSTOM and CNRS.
              2.   Forbes-Watson, A.D., Turner, D.A. & Keith, G.S.   Bird
                   preservation in Madagascar.   Report submitted to ICBP.
              3.   Benson, C.W., Colebrook-Robjent, J.F.R. & Williams, A. 1977.
                   Contribution à l'ornithologie de Madagascar.   L'Oiseau et
                   R.F.O. 47: 41-64.

RUFOUS-THROATED DIPPER

Cinclus schultzi Cabanis, 1882

Order PASSERIFORMES   Family CINCLIDAE

STATUS   Indeterminate.   Restricted to the Andes of north-western Argentina and
rare.   Watercourse diversion and pollution threaten portions of its habitat.

DISTRIBUTION   Argentine provinces of Jujuy, Salta, Tucumán and Catamarca. It is
unclear why the distribution of this dipper is so circumscribed: there is an
abundance of seemingly suitable dipper habitat in the Andes to the south of its
known range.

POPULATION   Decidedly sparse.   An ornithologist resident in Salta province has
seen this species only a very few times in the past 30 years (G. Hoy 1977, pers.
comm. to R. Ridgely) and it has not been encountered on any recent searches of the
areas where it has been recorded (R. Ridgely 1978, pers. comm.).

HABITAT   Andean streams in the subtropical zone.   This dipper occurs in a
relatively dry region where there are only a limited number of constantly flowing
streams.   Several of these have been tapped or diverted for irrigation, while
others are grossly polluted (R. Ridgely 1978, pers. comm.).

CONSERVATION MEASURES TAKEN   None known.

CONSERVATION MEASURES PROPOSED   None known.

REFERENCES   1.   de Schauensee, R.M. 1966.   The Species of Birds of South
                   America and their Distribution.   Narberth, Pa.: Livingston
                   Publishing Co.

APOLINAR'S MARSH-WREN

Cistothorus apolinari Chapman, 1914

Order PASSERIFORMES   Family TROGLODYTIDAE

STATUS   Vulnerable.   Restricted to one area of marshland on an Andean plateau.
Progressive drainage of its habitat poses a continuing threat to its survival.

DISTRIBUTION   Known to comprise the Suba marshes of the Bogotá plateau, Colombia
(1-3; J. Hernandez 1974, pers. comm. to M. Rylander), with recent records mainly
coming from the Parque del Florida and the shores of Lake Tota (R. Ridgely 1978,
pers. comm.).

POPULATION   Unknown.   The species appears to be most plentiful in swampy areas
of the Parque del Florida, a suburban park of the city of Bogotá, and is
substantially less so at Lake Tota despite the fact that suitable habitat there,
along the lakeshore, is far more extensive (R. Ridgely 1978, pers. comm.).

HABITAT   Marshland of the temperate zone in Colombia.   Many of the Bogotá
plateau wetlands formerly frequented by this marsh-wren have been drained and, as
a result of the human population pressure, the process is likely to continue.
None of the remaining wetlands have been included in a reserve or otherwise
effectively safeguarded.

CONSERVATION MEASURES TAKEN   None known.   The suburban park in which this wren
occurs does not provide adequate protection of its habitat.

CONSERVATION MEASURES PROPOSED   None known.

REMARKS   A wren inhabiting the Alnus scrub of the Andean slopes and bogs above
Bogotá was assumed to belong to this species (1; 3; J. Hernandez 1974, pers. comm.
to M. Rylander), but is now believed to be a form of the Grass Wren C. platensis
(R. Ridgely 1978, pers. comm.).
    Other birds of the Bogotá plateau and the Cundinamarca and Boyacá highlands at
risk from wetland drainage include the Colombian Grebe Podiceps andinus, Bogotá
Least Bittern Ixobrychus exilis bogotensis, Borrero's Cinnamon Teal Anas cyanoptera
borreroi, Bogotá Rail Rallus semiplumbeus and Bogotá Spot-flanked Gallinule
Porhyriops melanops bogotensis (J. Hernandez 1974, pers. comm. to M. Rylander;
J.I. Borrero 1974, pers. comm.).   Only the two full species, grebe and rail, have
like Apolinar's Marsh-wren been included in this volume, as particularly deserving
attention, but conservation of adequate samples of their habitat would help to
ensure the survival of numerous other interesting and valuable species and subspecies.

REFERENCES   1.   de Schauensee, R.M. 1966.   The Species of Birds of South
                   America and their Distribution.   Narberth, Pa.: Livingston
                   Publishing Co.
              2.   de Schauensee, R.M. 1964.   The Birds of Colombia.   Narberth
                   Pa.: Livingston Publishing Co.
              3.   de Schauensee, R.M. 1950.   The birds of the Republic of
                   Colombia. Part 3.   Caldasia 5: 645-871.

ZAPATA WREN

Ferminia cerverai Barbour, 1926

Order PASSERIFORMES   Family TROGLODYTIDAE

STATUS   Rare and localized.   The wren occurs in part of one area of swampland.
It is therefore at risk because of the ease with which its habitat could be
destroyed by draining, even though at present no such drainage scheme is under
consideration.

DISTRIBUTION   Confined to the section of Zapata Swamp in Las Villas Province,
Cuba, where an area of only about 13 sq. km, near Santo Tomas, is known to have
been frequented by this wren (1).

POPULATION   No estimate has been made, but its restricted distribution makes it
unlikely that the population can be at all large, although at one time the wren
was considered common enough (1; 2).   However, in October 1955 the species could
not be found in a search of the Santo Tomas area (G. Watson 1976, pers. comm.) and
the last definite record dates back to April 1935, when a few were heard singing
(2).

HABITAT   The dense bayberry or bog myrtle (Myrica sp.) zone of the Zapata Swamp.
Small portions of the swamp have been drained but there is no immediate threat to
the integrity of the habitat as a whole (O. Garrido 1974, pers. comm.).

CONSERVATION MEASURES TAKEN   None known.

CONSERVATION MEASURES PROPOSED   None known.

REMARKS   The future of two other birds included in this Volume, the Zapata Rail
Cyanolimnas cerverai and the nominate race of the Zapata Sparrow Torreornis
inexpectata inexpectata (q.v.), is equally dependent on the preservation of the
Zapata Swamp.

REFERENCES   1.   Bond, J. 1956.   Check-list of Birds of the West Indies.
                    Philadelphia Acad. Nat. Sci.
               2.   Bond, J. 1973.   Eighteenth supplement to the Check-list
                    of Birds of the West Indies (1956).   Philadelphia
                    Acad. Nat. Sci.

GUADELOUPE WREN

Troglodytes aedon guadeloupensis (Cory, 1886)

Order PASSERIFORMES   Family TROGLODYTIDAE

STATUS   Endangered.   Restricted to the mountain forests of Guadeloupe, Lesser
Antilles, West Indies, where it was rediscovered in 1969 after having been
considered extinct since 1914 (1; 2).   Introduced rats, cats and mongooses and
hunting of all bird species on the island have been responsible for the decline
of this subspecies and doubtless will continue to threaten it.

DISTRIBUTION   The mountains of Guadeloupe.   The mountain forests of this island
remain extensive and the wren might be expected to occur more widely than
previously thought.

POPULATION   Three singing males were observed when the wren was rediscovered in
1969 (1).   It was formerly more widespread in the island, occurring even around
settled areas.   No estimate was ever made of the total population.

HABITAT   Mountain forests with high rainfall.

CONSERVATION MEASURES TAKEN   None known.

CONSERVATION MEASURES PROPOSED   None known.

REMARKS   *T. a. martinicensis* of Martinique became extinct last century; *T. a.
mesoleucus* of St. Lucia is endangered and close to extinction; and *T. a. musicus*
of St. Vincent has recovered somewhat from near extinction.   Twenty-six
additional subspecies have been named, covering most of the American continents
and several neighbouring islands.   No others are thought to be threatened.

REFERENCES   1.   Roché, J.C. 1969.   Unpublished report to Paris Museum
                    of Natural History.
              2.   Bond, J. 1950.   Check-list of Birds of the West Indies.
                    Philadelphia Acad. Nat. Sci.

ST. LUCIA WREN

Troglodytes aedon mesoleucus (Sclater, 1876)

Order PASSERIFORMES   Family TROGLODYTIDAE

STATUS   Critically endangered.   Apparently restricted to a single small valley
on St. Lucia, Lesser Antilles, West Indies.   Although the decline of this and
other Caribbean subspecies of the House Wren has been attributed to predation by
the introduced mongoose Herpestes auropunctatus, it has been pointed out that the
species thrives on other Caribbean islands where the mongoose is present.   Rats
Rattus sp. and the boa constrictor Constrictor orophias have also been named as
potential predators of the wren on St. Lucia, although the latter has been
considered a predator on mongooses and therefore a potential benefactor to this
subspecies.

DISTRIBUTION   Formerly distributed more widely on St. Lucia, but restricted for
two decades to two valleys on the windward eastern coast, Le Marquis and Grand
Anse; in the last few years it has only been seen in the latter (1–3).

POPULATION   Once apparently fairly numerous, although good estimates are
lacking.   In the past 20 years it has been considered very rare even in the two
valleys from which it was known.   A survey in 1969 failed to find any sign of it
(4) and the most recent record is of one wren heard but not seen in May 1971, in
the tangle of trees fringing Grand Anse beach (J. Gulledge 1974, pers. comm.).

HABITAT   Dry lowland scrub forest, especially thickets and tangles (1).   A
subdivision development has been started in the Grand Anse area which may destroy
the wren's habitat in the last remaining place where it is known to occur
(J. Gulledge 1974, pers. comm.).

CONSERVATION MEASURES TAKEN   None known.

CONSERVATION MEASURES PROPOSED   None known.

REMARKS   It seems likely this subspecies will be extinct by the end of this
decade, if indeed it is not so already.   Of the seven Lesser Antillean subspecies
of the House Wren, T. a. martinicensis from Martinique became extinct last century;
T. a. guadeloupensis from Guadeloupe was also considered extinct, since 1914, until
rediscovered in 1969; T. a. musicus of St. Vincent is relatively common now,
having recovered from near extinction to a population peak in 1963; and the other
three subspecies from Tobago, Grenada and Dominica are still common.

REFERENCES   1.   Diamond, A.W. 1973.   Habitats and feeding stations of
                    St. Lucia forest birds.   Ibis 115:   313–329.
              2.   Fisher, J., Simon, N. & Vincent, J. 1969.   Wildlife
                    in Danger.   New York:Viking Press; London:Collins.
              3.   Greenway, J.C. Jr. 1958.   Extinct and Vanishing Birds of
                    the World.   Amer. Comm. Int. Wild Life Prot. Special
                    Pub. No. 13.
              4.   Wingate, D.B. 1969.   A summary of the status of the
                    St. Lucia Parrot Amazona versicolor and other rare native
                    birds of St. Lucia based on a survey of the island from
                    April 22 to May 15, 1969, conducted under a grant from the
                    International Committee for Bird Protection.   Unpublished
                    report.

FAIR ISLE WREN

Troglodytes troglodytes fridariensis Williamson, 1951

Order PASSERIFORMES   Family TROGLODYTIDAE

STATUS   Rare.   Inhabits one of the Shetland Islands, north of Scotland; its
total population is small but apparently steady.

DISTRIBUTION   Confined to Fair Isle (850 ha), the southernmost of the Shetlands
(1).

POPULATION   Numbers of this wren have remained stable at about 40 pairs since a
census was carried out in 1950 (1).   The most recent complete census was as long
ago as 1956, but there appears to have been no significant change since that time
(P.J. Sellar 1977, pers. comm. to S. Cramp), the 1978 estimate based on singing
males being about 30 pairs (2).

HABITAT   This subspecies is mainly confined to cliffs and rocks along or close to
the rugged Fair Isle coastline (1).   The ample cover and abundant food supply of
this habitat apparently enable the wren to survive in the frequently tempestuous
weather conditions.

CONSERVATION MEASURES TAKEN   Fair Isle, which has been owned and managed by the
National Trust for Scotland since 1954, is a renowned sanctuary with a resident
warden appointed by the Fair Isle Observatory Trust.   The island's breeding birds
are well cared for, the wren being among those which are also protected by law.

CONSERVATION MEASURES PROPOSED   No recommendations for additional measures have
been reported.

REMARKS   Of approximately 35 subspecies of this wren, distributed over most of
the Holarctic, including a number of islands, only this subspecies is at sufficient
risk in view of its very small population to warrant inclusion in the Red Data
Book.   T. t. hirtensis of the St. Kilda group, west of Scotland, listed as rare in
the previous edition of the Red Data Book, has a larger and, subject to slight
fluctuations, stable population of around 230 pairs distributed between the four
main islands of the group (3; P.J. Sellar 1977, pers. comm. to S. Cramp), which
suggests that any threat to its survival must be appreciably less than that to the
Fair Isle Wren.   T. t. alascensis of the Pribilof and Komandorski islands in the
Bering Sea was also listed in the previous edition but is now known to be
sufficiently abundant not to be considered at risk (4).

REFERENCES   1.   Williamson, K. 1951.   The wrens of Fair Isle.   Ibis 93:
                    599-601.
              2.   Waterston, G. & Arnott, J. (eds) 1979.   Fair Isle Bird
                    Observatory Report, No. 31 for 1978.   Edinburgh: Fair Isle Bird
                    Observatory Trust.
              3.   Armstrong, E.A. 1953.   The history, behavior, and breeding
                    biology of the St. Kilda Wren.   Auk 70: 127-150.
              4.   King, W.B. et al. 1976.   Report of the American Ornithologists'
                    Union Committee on Conservation 1975-76.   Auk 93(4, suppl.):
                    1DD-19DD.

MARTINIQUE TREMBLER

Cinclocerthia ruficauda gutturalis (Lafresnaye, 1843)

Order PASSERIFORMES   Family MIMIDAE

STATUS   Endangered.   Now restricted to woodlands of the southern half of
Martinique, Lesser Antilles, where only a few pairs are thought to survive.

DISTRIBUTION   Formerly widespread in the island forests, but the diminution of
its range was noted as early as 1878 (1; 2).   In the 1950s it could be found only
behind Trois-Ilets, at the base of the Pitons du Carbet, Colson and La Médaille
(3; 4), and by 1964 only in woodlands near Trois-Ilets (1).

POPULATION   In the 19th century considered to be quite large, although it was
already decreasing in 1878.   By 1950, the Trembler was stated to be very rare (2),
by 1964 only a very few pairs could be found and, later that same year, it had
disappeared altogether (3).   There have been no subsequent reports of this
subspecies.

HABITAT   Woodlands.   Much of Martinique's woodland has been cleared for sugar
cane culture.   Introduced mongooses and rats are present in the greater part of
the island and may well prey on the Trembler.

CONSERVATION MEASURES TAKEN   None known.   The subspecies has no legal protection
and recently hunters and children shooting at it with slings or catapults may well
have had a negative impact on the already reduced population (1).

CONSERVATION MEASURES PROPOSED   Repeated representations have been made to have
the Trembler protected, coupled with clear warnings that failure to do so would
hasten its extinction on Martinique (1).

REMARKS   Five other subspecies of the Trembler occur on islands of the Lesser
Antilles; their status is thought to be still relatively secure.

REFERENCES   1.   Fisher, J., Simon, N. & Vincent, J. 1969.   Wildlife in
                     Danger.   New York: Viking Press; London: Collins.
              2.   Bond, J. 1950.   Check-list of Birds of the West Indies.
                     Philadelphia Academy of Natural Sciences.
              3.   Bond, J. 1956.   Check-list of Birds of the West Indies.
                     Philadelphia Academy of Natural Sciences.
              4.   Pinchon, R. 1963.   Faune des Antilles Françaises:
                     Les Oiseaux.   Fort-de-France.

CHARLES MOCKINGBIRD

Nesomimus trifasciatus trifasciatus (Gould, 1837)

Order PASSERIFORMES   Family MIMIDAE

STATUS   Rare.   Restricted to two of the smaller of the Galapagos Islands,
Ecuador, where its population is very low but apparently stable.

DISTRIBUTION   Now confined, in the Galapagos, to Gardner islet, about 10 km off
the south-east coast of Floreana (Santa Maria or Charles) Island, and to Champion
islet, which is much nearer the Floreana coast, the combined area of the two islets
being 88 ha (1).   It also at one time occurred on Floreana Island itself, but has
not been reported from there since Darwin's visit in 1835; indeed the specimens
collected at that time could just as well have come from Champion as from the
Floreana mainland (2; 5).

POPULATION   In 1966, the total population of mockingbirds on the two islets was
estimated to be no more than 150 individuals (3).   No recent change in numbers
has been noted (Tj. DeVries 1974, pers. comm.).   Mockingbirds were reported to be
quite common on Floreana in 1813, a quarter of a century before this species was
described (4).

HABITAT   Presumably all varieties of habitat on the very small islands which now
constitute the last refuge of this mockingbird are utilized.   Its extirpation from
Floreana is blamed on cats and dogs although these potential predators are present
on islands where other subspecies of N. trifasciatus still survive (2; 5).

CONSERVATION MEASURES TAKEN   The subspecies is protected by law and the islets on
which it lives are included in the Galapagos National Park, which should give some
added protection.

CONSERVATION MEASURES PROPOSED   None known.

REMARKS   Eight other subspecies, distributed among most of the Galapagos Islands,
are not at risk.   They have been grouped by some authors into four separate
species (1).

REFERENCES   1.   Harris, M.P. 1974.   A Field Guide to the Birds of Galapagos.
                    New York: Taplinger Publishing Co.; London: Collins.
              2.   Swarth, H.S. 1931.   The avifauna of the Galapagos Islands.
                    Cal. Acad. Sci. Occ. Papers 18.
              3.   Harris, M.P. 1968.   Egg-eating by Galapagos Mockingbirds.
                    Condor 70: 269-270.
              4.   Beebe, W. 1924.   Galapagos-World's End.   New York: Putnam.
              5.   Harris, M.P. 1973.   The Galapagos avifauna.   Condor 75:
                    265-278.

MARTINIQUE WHITE-BREASTED THRASHER

Ramphocinclus brachyurus brachyurus (Vieillot, 1818)

Order PASSERIFORMES   Family MIMIDAE

STATUS   Endangered.   Now restricted to one peninsula on the windward coast of
Martinique, West Indies.   Neither the bird nor its habitat are protected.   This
largely terrestrial species probably falls frequent prey to introduced rats
Rattus sp. and mongooses Herpestes auropunctatus.   The Fer-de-lance Bothrops
lanceolatus is absent from the peninsula on which it is found.

DISTRIBUTION   Last century the subspecies was widespread over much of Martinique.
It was thought to have become extinct by the turn of the century until rediscovered
in 1950 on the Caravelle Peninsula, on the north-east side of the island, to which
it now appears to be restricted (1-4).

POPULATION   Formerly considered not uncommon, it became very rare by the end of
the 19th century.   A small population was rediscovered on the Caravelle Peninsula
in 1950 (1).   The subspecies was last reported in 1966, but no thorough search
for it has been made recently (2).   No population figures have been given, but
there is no doubt its numbers are very low.

HABITAT   Scrubby dry woodlands without an understory but with an abundant leaf
litter in which this species searches for food (5).   The Fer-de-lance snake is
absent from Caravelle Peninsula, but what effect the snake's absence or the
peninsula's aridity may have on rat and mongoose populations and consequently on
the distribution and abundance of this largely terrestrial thrasher, is uncertain.

CONSERVATION MEASURES TAKEN   None known.   Hunting of birds, large or small, is
a favorite pastime on Martinique.

CONSERVATION MEASURES PROPOSED   None known, although many come to mind, such as
legal protection for the bird and its habitat.

REMARKS   R. b. sanctaeluciae of the north-eastern coast of St. Lucia, is
similarly endangered.   The two are the only representatives of this unique West
Indian genus.

REFERENCES   1. Fisher, J., Simon, N. & Vincent, J. 1969.   Wildlife in
                   Danger.   New York:Viking Press.
              2. Bond, J. 1966.   Eleventh supplement to the Check-list of
                   Birds of the West Indies (1956). Philadelphia Acad. Nat. Sci.
              3. Bond, J. 1961.   Extinct and near extinct birds of the
                   West Indies.   Pan American Section, ICBP: Research
                   Rep't. No. 4.
              4. Pinchon, R. 1963.   Faune des Antilles Françaises:
                   Les Oiseaux.   Fort-de-France.
              5. Diamond, A.W. 1973.   Habitats and feeding stations of
                   St. Lucia forest birds.   Ibis 115: 313-329.

ST. LUCIA WHITE-BREASTED THRASHER

Ramphocinclus brachyurus sanctaeluciae Cory, 1887

Order PASSERIFORMES   Family MIMIDAE

STATUS   Endangered.   Restricted to a portion of the windward coast of St. Lucia,
West Indies, where it has a very small population.   The future of this subspecies
depends upon protection of the scrub forest in the valleys in which it occurs.
Introduced rats Rattus sp. and mongooses Herpestes auropunctatus may have
contributed to its continued decline.   It may not be a coincidence that the
distribution of this largely terrestrial subspecies coincides with the area where
mongooses are least common and where the Fer-de-lance Bothrops lanceolatus is
abundant (1-4).

DISTRIBUTION   Once widespread, the species has been confined to valleys of the
north-east coast since 1927, with the exception of a pair observed near Castries on
the north-west coast in 1951 (3; 4).   A survey in 1971, revealed it was restricted
to five ravines between Louvet and Grand Anse, a distance of less than 8 km,
ranging inland no more than 1.5 km (3).

POPULATION   Considered to have been fairly numerous last century, but by 1927
already quite rare (2).   In 1971, no more than 75 pairs were believed to survive
(3).

HABITAT   Low scrub woodland in ravine bottoms, with a dense stand of thin tree
trunks, no understory and abundant leaf litter (1).   Subdivision developments
have been started at Louvet and Grand Anse, at the southern and northern ends of
the range of the species, and are likely to destroy part of the remaining habitat
(3).

CONSERVATION MEASURES TAKEN   The entire present distribution of this subspecies
lies within a forest reserve, which gives the woodland habitat some protection but
only on paper for, in practice, there are continual encroachments, apparently
without causing concern in the Forestry Department which is responsible for
administration of the area (3; J. Gulledge 1974, pers. comm.).

CONSERVATION MEASURES PROPOSED   Preservation of remaining habitat.   It has been
suggested that the physical requirements of the species could be easily replicated
in captivity and that there may be a potential for captive breeding (J. Gulledge
1974, pers. comm.).

REMARKS   The nominate subspecies is restricted to one peninsula on Martinique and
also classified as endangered.   These two subspecies comprise the entire genus.

REFERENCES   1.   Diamond, A.W. 1973.   Habitats and feeding stations of
                   St. Lucia forest birds.   Ibis 115: 313-329.
              2.   Fisher, J., Simon, N. & Vincent, J. 1969.   Wildlife in
                   Danger.   New York:Viking Press; London:Collins.
              3.   Gulledge, J. (no date).   Notes on the White-breasted
                   Thrasher (Ramphocinclus brachyurus) of St. Lucia, West
                   Indies.   Unpublished ms.
              4.   Bond, J. 1967.   Twelfth supplement to the Checklist of
                   Birds of the West Indies (1956).   Philadelphia Acad.
                   Nat. Sci.

USAMBARA ROBIN-CHAT

Alethe montana Sclater and Moreau, 1933

Order PASSERIFORMES

Family MUSCICAPIDAE

Subfamily TURDINAE

STATUS   Rare.   Entirely restricted to part of a single East African mountain
forest which is suffering from continual felling and clearing of its mature tracts
for the purpose of tea-planting and other agricultural uses.

DISTRIBUTION   Confined to the West Usambara Mountains, near Shume and Mazumbai,
where this species occupies an area of no more than 260 sq. km in size and possibly
as small as 26 sq. km (1; 2).   However, the most recent studies suggest it may
range more widely in suitable habitat in the West Usambaras than had previously
been thought and, in 1966, a specimen was collected for the first time in the East
Usambaras (4; S. Stuart 1978, pers. comm.), which is again more suggestive of
wider range than of vagrancy.

POPULATION   Unknown, but believed to be small and certainly less than a thousand
(S. Stuart 1978, pers. comm.).   Six were collected in 1962 (2) but recent visits
to the forest in 1977 produced only a single sighting (D. Turner 1977, pers.comm.).

HABITAT   Mature evergreen cloud-forest at altitudes between 1675 and 2,450 m
(1; 2).   Forest cover of this category in the Usambaras is being replaced by
subsistence agriculture and tea and cardamom plantations.   Cardamom is grown in
the shade of mature forest trees but its cultivation involves clearing the forest
floor of the undergrowth to which this terrestrial species is almost entirely
confined (4; 5).   It was suggested in 1974 that the stands of dense, undisturbed
primary forest on which it thus depends might well be virtually eliminated by the
end of the decade (3).

CONSERVATION MEASURES TAKEN   None known.

CONSERVATION MEASURES PROPOSED   Mapping of what is left of the primary forest
in the Usambaras and of the precise distribution within this habitat of the robin-
chat and species dependent upon it, with a view to the selection and establishment
of some reserves (S. Stuart 1978, pers. comm.).

REMARKS   This species is very closely related to another Tanzanian robin-chat,
A. lowei, which is known only from the Uwemba and Mdando forests, about 20 and 50
km, respectively, south of Njombe, in the Livingstone Mountains, and from forest
patches on the Uzungwa Plateau, in the vicinity of Dabaga and about 50 km SSE of
Iringa.   A. lowei is also quite rare and locally distributed but not as gravely
threatened as A. montana by forest destruction (S. Stuart 1978, D. Turner 1977,
pers. comms).   The two forms have been considered conspecific by some authors
and others have placed them variously in the genera Dessonornis, Erithacus or
Dryocichloides (2; 6).

REFERENCES   1.   Hall, B.P. & Moreau, R.E. 1962.   A study of the rare
                   birds of Africa.   Bull. Brit. Mus. (Nat. Hist.) Zool. 8: 313-378
              2.   Ripley, S.D. & Heinrich, G.H. 1966.   Comments on the avifauna
                   of Tanzania, part I.   Postilla 96: 20-22.
              3.   White, G.B. 1974.   Rarest eagle owl in trouble.   Oryx 12:
                   484-486.

4. Stuart, S.N. & Hutton, J.M. (eds).   Report dated 1977.
    The avifauna of the East Usambara Mountains, Tanzania.
    Cambridge University.
5. Turner, D.A. 1977.   Status and distribution of the
    East African endemic species.   Scopus 1:   2-11.
6. Hall, B.P. & Moreau, R.E. 1970.   An Atlas of Speciation
    in African Passerine Birds, map 143.   London: British
    Museum (Nat. Hist.).

ST. LUCIA FOREST THRUSH

Cichlherminia _lherminieri_ _sanctaeluciae_ (Sclater, 1880)

Order PASSERIFORMES   Family MUSCICAPIDAE

                                              Subfamily TURDINAE

STATUS   Endangered.   This subspecies is very locally distributed on St. Lucia,
West Indies, and its population is very low.   The wooded ravines in which it is
now found are gradually being cleared, but are apparently still free from the
mongoose _Herpestes_ _auropunctatus_, an introduced species which is now established
elsewhere in the island (1; J. Gulledge 1974, pers. comm.).

DISTRIBUTION   In the 19th century the thrush was widespread in the forests of St.
Lucia, but is now thought to be restricted to La Sorcière and La Chaloupe ravines on
the north-eastern side of the island; it might possibly still survive elsewhere in
patches of humid forest, but the present evidence does not support this (1;
J. Gulledge 1974, pers. comm.).

POPULATION   The subspecies was formerly quite common but a marked decline has
taken place since the turn of the century.   An extensive survey of the island in
1969 failed to record it (2), but there have been subsequent sightings by two
observers, although one of them only saw the bird once during three months of field
research in La Sorcière Valley (1; J. Gulledge 1974, pers. comm.).   No recent
population estimate has been made, but numbers are believed to be very low.

HABITAT   Known to have comprised both moist and semi-arid forests, but now
apparently restricted to the latter (1).   The nest is built close to the ground,
and it may well have been vulnerable to introduced rats and mongooses.   In the
existing very limited range of the subspecies the mongoose is absent and the Fer-de-
lance _Bothrops_ _lanceolatus_ still plentiful (J. Gulledge 1974, pers. comm.).

CONSERVATION MEASURES TAKEN   None known.

CONSERVATION MEASURES PROPOSED   Protection of the habitat by stricter enforcement
of restrictions on tree felling in the forest reserves within which the present
range of the subspecies is included (J. Gulledge 1974, pers. comm.).

REMARKS   Other subspecies include C. l. _lherminieri_ of Guadeloupe, which is
apparently rather more plentiful, although recent reports are lacking, and C. l.
lawrencei of Monserrat and C. l. _dominicensis_ of Dominica, both of which are
thriving in the absence in these two islands of any introduced mongooses.

REFERENCES   1.   Diamond, A.W. 1973.   Habitats and feeding stations of St. Lucia
                    forest birds.   _Ibis_ 115: 313-329.
              2.   Wingate, D.B. undated.   A summary of the status of the St. Lucia
                    Parrot _Amazona_ _versicolor_ and other rare native birds of St.
                    Lucia based on a survey of the island from April 22 to May 15,
                    1969, conducted under a grant from the International Committee
                    for Bird Protection.   Unpublished report.

SEYCHELLES MAGPIE ROBIN

Copsychus sechellarum Newton, 1865

Order PASSERIFORMES   Family MUSCICAPIDAE

                                                        Subfamily TURDINAE

STATUS   Endangered.   Very rare and restricted to one small island in the
Seychelles Archipelago, where it is preyed upon by cats, which were reduced in
numbers but not eliminated by a recent control program.   Competition or nest
predation from introduced birds may also have contributed to the species' decline.

DISTRIBUTION   Recorded from Marianne, Félicité, La Digue, Praslin, Aride, Frigate
and, possibly, Mahé in the Seychelles (1; 2).   Introduced last century to Alphonse
in the southern Amirantes, where it survived for at least 60 years.   Disappeared
long ago from Félicité, La Digue and Praslin, in the 1930s from Marianne and Aride
(3) and by about 1960 from Alphonse.   It is now present only on Frigate (2 sq. km),
where it is commonest on the two flat coastal plateaux but also occurs on the hills
(2; 4; 8).

POPULATION   Although this species must have been fairly common prior to the
introduction of predatory mammals to the archipelago, it was already rather scarce
by the time it was first described in 1865 (1).   It was definitely rare by 1939
(2) and is now among the rarest species in the world.   In 1959, only 10 pairs
could be found on Frigate (5) and in 1965 a survey of the island yielded
simultaneous sightings of 8 birds and an estimated population of 15 (6).   The
figures for similar counts in 1967 and 1970, were respectively 15 birds seen and an
estimated total of 20 (2) and 16 birds seen and an estimated total of 25 (7).   In
1960, more than 80 cats had been killed on Frigate by the Seychelles Dept. of
Agriculture (2) and a continuing decline in the Magpie-Robin population may have
been arrested and hopefully reversed by this timely control program.   The most
recent estimate (J. Watson 1977) is 12 known pairs, with 15 attendant youngsters
(July) dropping to 12 (August), and a possibility of an additional 2-3 undiscovered
pairs, a grand total of at most about 40 individual birds.

HABITAT   Pterocarpus and Artocarpus (breadfruit) groves, cashew, citrus and
coffee plantations, vegetable gardens and vicinity of houses, occasionally coastal
coconut plantations provide the habitats used by the robin on Frigate, to which
island it is now confined (4) and which no longer supports any significant
indigenous vegetation.   Mynahs Acridotheres tristis have become established on the
island, especially in the low-lying plateau areas.   Edward Newton suggested, more
than a century ago, that competition between this species and Mynahs may have been
responsible for its decline (1).   On the other hand, absence of rats may be one
important reason for its survival on Frigate.

CONSERVATION MEASURES TAKEN   Protected by law from hunting or capture.   The then
owner of Frigate Island was responsible for the successful campaign to reduce the
number of cats carried out in 1960.

CONSERVATION MEASURES PROPOSED   Continued vigilance against inadvertent introduction of rats is essential (2); and the interactions between this species and
introduced Mynahs, Cattle Egrets Bubulcus ibis and Barn Owls Tyto alba (if any)
could usefully receive further attention, though preliminary conclusions from
current studies (8) suggest that food availability may be the critical factor.
Bounty payments for elimination of cats have been effective in the past (4) and
should if necessary be continued.

REMARKS   The future of this tame, ground-feeding species is precarious at best. Relocation of pairs to suitable predator-free islands, if such exist or could be recreated, should be a matter of high priority and current studies suggest that there may be a surplus of immature birds which could be utilized for this purpose (8).   Although plans for constructing a harbour on Frigate to accommodate vessels from Mahé have been laid aside, there is always a risk that rats will sooner or later find their way ashore.

REFERENCES   1.   Newton, E. 1867.   On the land-birds of the Seychelles Archipelago.   Ibis 2(3):   335-360.

2.   Penny, M. 1968.   Endemic birds of the Seychelles. Oryx 9:   267-275.

3.   Vesey-Fitzgerald, D. 1940.   The birds of the Seychelles. I. Ibis (14)4:   480-489.

4.   Diamond, Dr. A.W. and Mrs. 1973.   Report on a visit to Frigate Island, L'Îlot, and St. Marie.   Unpublished report to ICBP.

5.   Crook, J.H. 1960.   The present status of certain rare land birds of the Seychelles Islands.   Unnumbered Seychelles Government Bulletin; 5 pages.

6.   Dawson, P.G. 1965.   Bristol University Seychelles Expedition, 6. Frigate, home of the Magpie-Robin.   Animals 7:   520-522.

7.   Procter, J. 1970.   Conservation in the Seychelles.   Report of the Conservation Advisor 1970.   Seychelles Government Printer.

8.   Watson, J. 1977.   The Seychelles Magpie-Robin (Copsychus seychellarum).   (sic) Unpublished progress report No. 1 to ICBP, dated 19 August 1977.

SOUTHERN RYUKYU ROBIN

Erithacus komodori subrufa (Kuroda, 1923)

Order PASSERIFORMES   Family MUSCICAPIDAE

                                             Subfamily TURDINAE

STATUS   Endangered.   Restricted to the three southernmost Ryukyu islands, south-
west of Japan, where it is very rare, if it still exists; it has not been seen in
recent years.   Destruction of its forest habitat has been extensive and no doubt
mainly responsible for the threat to its existence.

DISTRIBUTION   Recorded from Ishigaki, Iriomote and Yonakuni islands (1), at the
southern extremity of the Ryukyu Retto, 120-250 km east of northern Taiwan.

POPULATION   Not precisely known; the subspecies must presumably at one time have
been more common, but has long been considered very rare and not observed at all in
recent years (Y. Yamashina 1974, pers. comm.).

HABITAT   Broad-leaved evergreen forests, especially bordering mountain streams.
Such forests in the Ryukyus are being cleared at an alarming rate and none of this
robin's habitat is presently protected (Y. Yamashina 1974, pers. comm.).

CONSERVATION MEASURES TAKEN   The subspecies was designated as a Natural Monument
in Japan in 1970 and a Special Bird for Protection in 1973.

CONSERVATION MEASURES PROPOSED   Protection of forest habitats in the Ryukyus is
urgently needed (Y. Yamashina 1974, pers. comm.).

REMARKS   There are two other subspecies, one in the central Ryukyus and one in the
northern Ryukyus, of which the latter is considered to be relatively common, the
former uncommon but not yet rare.   Additional but as yet subspecifically
undetermined populations have recently been found on Tokashiki in the central
Ryukyus and on the Daito Islands, 300 km east of Okinawa (Y. Yamashina 1974, pers.
comm.).

REFERENCES   1.   Ornithological Society of Japan, 1974.   Check-list of Japanese
              Birds.   Fifth (revised) Edition.   Tokyo: Gakken Co.

DAPPLED MOUNTAIN-ROBIN

Modulatrix orostruthus orostruthus (Vincent, 1933)

Modulatrix orostruthus amani (Sclater and Moreau, 1935)

Order PASSERIFORMES   Family MUSCICAPIDAE

                                             Subfamily TURDINAE

STATUS   Endangered.   The range in eastern Africa of both the subspecies is
exceedingly restricted and the existence of both is threatened by forest
destruction.

DISTRIBUTION   M. o. orostruthus is known from the type specimen collected in 1932
in montane forest at 1465 m elevation on the Namuli massif in northern Mozambique.
A second bird was seen at the time.   There are no subsequent records (1; 2).
    M. o. amani occurs in montane forest in the East Usambara mountains of north-
eastern Tanzania, 1150 km north of Namuli.   The area of forest in which it is
found does not now exceed 50 sq. km, though at the beginning of the century it was
more extensive and presumably the range of the robin was also larger (2; 3; 6;
S. Stuart 1977, pers. comm.).

POPULATION   The population of the nominate subspecies is unknown, but if extant
is likely to be very small indeed.   Specimens of the northern race were collected
in 1935 (1), in 1962 (4), and in 1963 and 1966 (2), and it has always been considered
rare (5):   a 1977 estimate of the population put the number at between 85 and 200,
based on a study in which four were found to be occupying 1.6 sq. km of suitable
habitat (S. Stuart 1977, pers. comm.).

HABITAT   Forest floor of montane evergreen cloud-forest (2; 4).   Much of this
forest in the East Usambaras has been cleared for agricultural purposes in recent
years.

CONSERVATION MEASURES TAKEN   None known.

CONSERVATION MEASURES PROPOSED   Protection of certain key tracts of montane
forest has been recommended (S. Stuart 1977, pers. comm.).

REMARKS   When discovered and for many years subsequently (as in the previous
edition of this Volume of the Red Data Book) the species was placed in the genus
Phyllastrephus (Pycnonotidae) but a reappraisal in 1975 showed it to be a thrush
rather than a bulbul (3).

REFERENCES   1.   Vincent, J. 1935.   The birds of northern Portuguese East
                   Africa.   Comprising a list of, and observations on, the
                   collections made during the British Museum Expedition of
                   1931-32, Part VII.   Ibis (13)5: 355-397.
              2.   Fisher, J., Simon, N. & Vincent, J. 1969.   Wildlife in
                   Danger.   New York: Viking Press; London: Collins.
              3.   Benson, C.W. & Stuart Irwin, M.P. 1975.   The systematic
                   position of Phyllastrephus orostruthus and Phyllastrephus
                   xanthophrys, two species incorrectly placed in the family
                   Pycnonotidae (Aves).   Arnoldia 7: 1-10.

4. Ripley, S.D. & Heinrich, G. 1966.   Comments on the
    avifauna of Tanzania, I.   Yale Peabody Museum _Postilla_ 96:
    1-45.
5. Moreau, R.E. & W.M. 1937.   Biological and other notes on
    some East African birds, Part II.   _Ibis_ (14)1:   321-345.
6. Stuart, S.N. & Hutton, J.M. (eds) 1977.   The avifauna of
    the East Usambara Mountains, Tanzania.   Cambridge University
    expedition report.

ST. VINCENT SOLITAIRE

Myadestes genibarbis sibilans Lawrence 1878

Order PASSERIFORMES

Family MUSCICAPIDAE

Subfamily TURDINAE

STATUS   Rare.   The St. Vincent race of the Rufous-throated Solitaire, a species known from several islands in the West Indies, is sparsely distributed in a few narrow densely-wooded valleys.   The reasons for its rarity are not understood. Although introduced mongooses Herpestes auropunctatus and rats Rattus sp. may prey on it, these mammals are also present on other islands where it is more common. Furthermore, on St. Vincent it is neither hunted for food nor trapped for the cage bird trade (1; 2; 3; I.A.E. Kirby 1974, pers. comm.).

DISTRIBUTION   There is no evidence that this solitaire has ever been more widespread than at present.   It is found chiefly in the southern part of the central mountain chain of St. Vincent in suitable ravines and valleys.   It used to be found on the Soufrière in the north, was absent from that area for a time following the 1902 eruption, but is now apparently recolonizing it (1).

POPULATION   No estimates have been made.   The subspecies is considered to be uncommon and sparsely distributed (1; 2) and only a few have been seen or heard during recent surveys in the island.

HABITAT   Densely vegetated ravines and gorges, and steep slopes of narrow valleys between 400 and 950 m elevation.   This habitat is not at present under any particular threat except possibly from forest clearing at its lower end (1).   The solitaire nests on steep banks or declivities (3).

CONSERVATION MEASURES TAKEN   Legal protection has been extended to the subspecies.

CONSERVATION MEASURES PROPOSED   Preservation of suitable forest in inviolate reserves with adequate wardening (1).

REMARKS   Other subspecies on Jamaica, Hispaniola, Dominica, Martinique and St. Lucia are all commoner than the St. Vincent one (4), although M. g. sanctaeluciae of St. Lucia has been described as 'relatively scarce' compared with the Dominica population (5).

REFERENCES   1.   Andrle, R.F. & Andrle, P.R. 1975.   Report on the status and conservation of the Whistling Warbler on St. Vincent, West Indies, with additional observations on the St. Vincent Parrot and Rufous-throated Solitaire.   ICBP Bull. 12: 245-251.
2.   Lack, D., Lack, E., Lack, P. & Lack, A. 1973.   Birds on St. Vincent.   Ibis 115: 46-52.
3.   Bond, J. 1961.   Extinct and near extinct birds of the West Indies.   Pan American Section, ICBP, Res. Rept. No. 4
4.   Bond, J. 1956.   Check list of Birds of the West Indies. Philadelphia Acad. Nat. Sci.
5.   Wingate, D. 1969.   A summary of the status of the St. Lucia Parrot Amazona versicolor and other rare native birds of St. Lucia based on a survey of the island from April 22 to May 15, 1969, conducted under a grant from the International Committee for Bird Protection.   Unpublished report.

TRISTAN STARCHY

Nesocichla eremita eremita Gould, 1855

Order PASSERIFORMES   Family MUSCICAPIDAE

                                              Subfamily TURDINAE

STATUS   Rare.   Locally distributed on Tristan da Cunha, south Atlantic, where
it persists in low numbers in spite of predation by cats and rats Rattus rattus.

DISTRIBUTION   The subspecies has a wide but localized distribution on Tristan da
Cunha (95 sq. km), a few pairs nesting not far above sea level but the majority
only from about 300 m to 1200 m up the mountain slopes and in the gulches; the
summit area, rising to the 2,060 m peak, and in the case of this subspecies the
seashores also, are probably very seldom visited by it (1-4).

POPULATION   The subspecies was said to have dwindled on Tristan, following the
introduction of predators and herbivores, and was at one time thought to have
become extinct soon after 1922; but in 1937 a small though apparently stable
population was discovered (1).   In 1952, its numbers were put at between 200 and
400 (H.F.I. Elliott 1963, pers. comm. to J. Vincent) but may have been over-
estimated, unless there has been a substantial subsequent decline, as a more recent
(1974) count suggested a total of no more than 40-60 pairs (4).

HABITAT   Grassy moorland, fern bush and woodland glades below the 1200 m contour.
Every one of about 30 sheltered gulches around the island probably supports at
least a pair of these thrushes, and others are established along shallower drainage
lines with dense vegetation and also in the conifer and apple plantation at the
foot of the sheltered eastern flank of the island.   Damage to the original forest
by introduced goats (finally eliminated in the 1950s) is unlikely to have affected
the Starchy, but there is no doubt that it frequently falls victim to predation by
feral cats and black rats Rattus rattus, the latter accidentally introduced in 1882.
(2-4).

CONSERVATION MEASURES TAKEN   Feral goats were finally eliminated in 1951.   For
human health reasons, domestic cats were destroyed in 1974, which had the added
advantage of removing the reservoir for the replenishment of the feral cat
population, estimated at no more than 40 individuals at that time.   A bounty
payment for the destruction of feral cats was introduced simultaneously (4).

CONSERVATION MEASURES PROPOSED   None known.

REMARKS   The Starchy subspecies of Inaccessible Island, N. e. gordoni, and of
Nightingale Island, N. e. procax, are both relatively abundant and at no greater
risk than any other largely terrestrial birds inhabiting rat and cat free islands.
Although included in the previous edition of this Volume they have thus been
omitted, despite the fact that it is feared to be only a matter of time before rats
become established on other islands of the Tristan group (4).

REFERENCES   1.   Hagen, Y. 1952.   Birds of Tristan da Cunha.   Oslo: Norske
                   Videnskaps-Akademi.
              2.   Elliott, H.F.I. 1957.   A contribution to the ornithology of
                   the Tristan da Cunha group.   Ibis 99: 545-586.
              3.   Wace, N.M. & Holdgate, M.W. 1976.   Man and Nature in the
                   Tristan da Cunha Islands.   Morges: IUCN, Monograph No. 6.
              4.   Richardson, M.E. 1975.   Aspects of the ornithology of the
                   Tristan da Cunha group.   Unpublished ms.

KAUAI THRUSH

Phaeornis obscurus myadestina   Stejneger, 1887

Order   PASSERIFORMES   Family   MUSCICAPIDAE
                                              Subfamily   TURDINAE

STATUS   Endangered.   Restricted to the Alaka'i Swamp region of Kauai,
Hawaiian Islands, where it has become increasingly rare in the past several
years.   The extent of undisturbed rain forest, which this species apparently
requires, continues to decrease.   A power and irrigation dam is proposed at
the margin of the Alaka'i Swamp.   Pigs are abundant in the Alaka'i forest,
and their rooting prepares the way for aggressive exotic plants (1; 2).
Introduced avian diseases may be the cause of the major decline of this species (3)

DISTRIBUTION   Occurs only in the Alaka'i Swamp Forest Reserve, Kauai, Hawaiian
Islands (1; 2).

POPULATION   Formerly more numerous.   Reported to have been the most abundant
songbird in Kauai forests at the end of the last century.   Present numbers not
known, but they are certainly low, and there has been a decrease even in the
past decade (1; 2).

HABITAT   Undisturbed native rain forest, formerly from near sea level to the
mountain tops, presently restricted to the Alaka'i Swamp, elevation 1,220 m to
perhaps 1,375 m (1; 2).

CONSERVATION MEASURES TAKEN   Protected by federal and state law from killing,
capture or harassment.   The State of Hawaii has established the 4,050 ha Alaka'i
Swamp Wilderness Preserve.   Survey of population, life history and ecology of
species begun (1).

CONSERVATION MEASURES PROPOSED   Control of introduced pigs, grazing animals
and exotic vegetation in Alaka'i Swamp Preserve.   Quarantine on all imported
birds to prevent introduction of additional bird diseases.   Prohibit import
of birds that could further threaten species through competition (1).

REMARKS   P. o. oahensis from Oahu and P. o. lanaiensis from Lanai are both
extinct.   P. o. obscurus from Hawaii is still relatively common.   P. o. rutha
from Molokai is severely endangered.

REFERENCES   1.   U.S. Dept. of Interior Bureau of Sport Fisheries and
                    Wildlife, 1973.   Threatened Wildlife of the United States.
                    U.S. Bur. Sport Fish. Wildl. Res. Pub. 114.
              2.   Berger, A.J. 1972.   Hawaiian Birdlife.   Honolulu:
                    University Press of Hawaii.
              3.   Warner, R.E. 1968.   The role of introduced diseases in
                    the extinction of the endemic Hawaiian avifauna.
                    Condor 70: 101-120.

MOLOKAI THRUSH

Phaeornis obscurus rutha   (W.A. Bryan, 1908)

Order   PASSERIFORMES   Family   MUSCICAPIDAE
                                         Subfamily TURDINAE

STATUS   Endangered.   Known from the small remaining area of native rain
forest on the mountain ridge of Molokai, Hawaiian Islands.   Thought to have
been extinct for several decades until rediscovered in 1963 (1).   The forests
of Molokai have been severely depleted by introduced animals including cattle,
goats and axis deer.   Introduced predators include rats, cats and mongooses
(2; 3).   Avian diseases, against which at least some of the native birds show
no immunity, have been proved to be present (4).

DISTRIBUTION   Restricted to native rain forest in the area of Puu Haha, central
Molokai, Hawaiian Islands (1).

POPULATION   Two were seen in 1963 (1).   No subsequent observations have been
reported (2; 3).

HABITAT   Undisturbed mountain rain forest.

CONSERVATION MEASURES TAKEN   Protected by federal and state law.

CONSERVATION MEASURES PROPOSED   Survey to determine if subspecies still exists.
Creation of sanctuary in area of last sightings.   Control of introduced birds
and mammals in proposed sanctuary (2).

REMARKS   P. o. oahensis from Oahu and P. o. lanaiensis from Lanai are both
extinct.   P. o. obscurus from Hawaii is still relatively common.   P. o.
myadestina from Kauai is endangered.

REFERENCES   1.   Pekelo, N., Jr. 1963.   Nature notes from Molokai.
                  Elepaio 24: 17-18.
             2.   U.S. Dept. of Interior Bureau of Sport Fisheries and
                  Wildlife, 1973.   Threatened Wildlife of the United States.
                  U.S. Bur. Sport Fish. Wildl. Res. Pub. 114.
             3.   Berger, A.J. 1972.   Hawaiian Birdlife.   Honolulu:
                  University Press of Hawaii.
             4.   Warner, R.E. 1968.   The role of introduced diseases
                  in the extinction of the endemic Hawaiian avifauna.
                  Condor 70: 101-120.

PUAIOHI or SMALL KAUAI THRUSH

Phaeornis palmeri Rothschild, 1893

Order   PASSERIFORMES   Family   MUSCICAPIDAE
                                               Subfamily TURDINAE

STATUS   Endangered.   Confined to a small portion of the Alaka'i Swamp,
Kauai, Hawaiian Islands.   Not known to have ever been widespread or numerous.
The species occurs in a remote area of relatively undisturbed rain forest.
The introduction of exotic plants, competing bird species, vectors of avian
diseases, grazing and predatory mammals, are possible threats which could lead
to the extinction of this species (1; 2; 3; 4).

DISTRIBUTION   Known only from the undisturbed rain forests of the Alaka'i
Swamp plateau at 1,220 m elevation on Kauai, Hawaiian Islands.   The former
distribution of the species is unknown, but was probably somewhat more extended,
when the area of rain forest was larger (1; 2; 3).

POPULATION   Unknown but probably very low.   Fifteen were seen and two
collected in an extensive survey in 1960 (3).   Observed subsequently several
times but apparently always in the same locality.   It was considered rare at
the time of its discovery.

HABITAT   Undisturbed montane rain forest at about 1,220 m above sea level.

CONSERVATION MEASURES TAKEN   Protected by federal and state law.   The state
of Hawaii has established a 4,050 hectare Alaka'i Swamp Wilderness Preserve
which includes the entire range of this species.   Surveys of status of species
have been undertaken.

CONSERVATION MEASURES PROPOSED   Continued survey of the distribution,
population and ecology of the species.   Control of introduced mammals and
plants within the Alaka'i Swamp Preserve (1).

REMARKS   A female has been in captivity at the Honolulu Zoo since 1968.

REFERENCES   1.   U.S. Dept. of Interior Bureau of Sport Fisheries and
                   Wildlife, 1973.   Threatened Wildlife of the United States.
                   U.S. Bur. Sport Fish. Wildl. Res. Pub. 114
              2.   Berger, A.J. 1972.   Hawaiian Birdlife.   Honolulu:
                   University Press of Hawaii.
              3.   Richardson, F. and Bowles, J. 1964.   A survey of the birds
                   of Kauai, Hawaii.   B.P. Bishop Museum Bull. 227.
              4.   Warner, R.E. 1968.   The role of introduced diseases in the
                   extinction of the endemic Hawaiian avifauna.   Condor
                   70: 101-120.

GREY-HEADED BLACKBIRD

Turdus poliocephalus poliocephalus Latham, 1801

Order PASSERIFORMES   Family MUSCICAPIDAE

                                               Subfamily TURDINAE

STATUS   Endangered.   Occurs on Norfolk Island, south-west Pacific, where it is
becoming increasingly local, with a small and declining population, due to
destruction of its habitat, competition with the widespread introduced European
Blackbird Turdus merula, and presumably also predation by rats (G. Mees 1974, pers.
comm.).   Rats apparently proliferated after 1951, when the island's cat population
was depleted by cat distemper (2; 3).

DISTRIBUTION   Known only from Norfolk Island where it once occurred over most of
the 35 sq. km of the island (4), but is now confined to the 405 hectares of
indigenous forest remaining in the Mount Pitt reserve.   In 1962 it was found
throughout this forest but by January 1969 in only two localities (G. Mees 1974,
pers. comm.).

POPULATION   The numbers of this subspecies, which was once common in a variety of
habitats, are now severely depleted.   The 1962 estimate of about 100 birds had to
be revised to certainly less than half that number in January 1969 (G. Mees 1974,
pers. comm.).

HABITAT   Formerly all wooded areas in the island, including stands of exotic
trees (4), but now only the indigenous rainforest, where this Grey-headed Blackbird
is apparently able to compete more effectively with the European Blackbird (1).

CONSERVATION MEASURES TAKEN   Protected from shooting, except under licence.   The
Mount Pitt reserve, to which the subspecies is now restricted, is still subject to
lumbering (2).

CONSERVATION MEASURES PROPOSED   National Park status has been recommended for the
Mount Pitt reserve, and, if accorded, the area would be fenced to keep cattle out,
lumbering would cease, and no more roads or trails would be built (2).   More
research is needed to determine the actual extent of competition between this
subspecies and the European Blackbird, and whether control of the introduced bird
in the reserve is desirable.   It has also been suggested that a rat-poisoning
campaign should be launched (2), but this would probably be impractical on an
island as large as Norfolk Island.

REMARKS   This, the nominate subspecies, is one of 50 subspecies scattered through
many of the islands of the south-west Pacific.   Three other subspecies are extinct:
T. p. vinitinctus of Lord Howe Island, T. p. pritzbueri of Lifu Island and T. p.
mareensis of Mare Island (Lifu and Mare being the two largest of the Loyalty
Islands).

REFERENCES   1.   Smithers, C.N. & Disney, H.J. de S. 1969.   The distribution of
                    terrestrial and freshwater birds on Norfolk Island.   Austral.
                    Zool. 15: 127-140.
              2.   Turner, J.S., Smithers, C.N. & Hoogland, R.D. 1968.   The
                    conservation of Norfolk Island.   Austral. Cons. Found. Special
                    Pub. No. 1.

3. Disney, H.J. de S. & Smithers, C.N. 1972. The distribution of terrestrial and freshwater birds on Lord Howe Island, in comparison with Norfolk Island. Austral. Zool. 17: 1-11.
4. Hull, A.F.B. 1909. The birds of Lord Howe and Norfolk Islands. Proc. Linn. Soc. N.S.W. 34: 636-693.

AMAMI GROUND THRUSH

Zoothera dauma major (Ogawa, 1905)

Order PASSERIFORMES   Family MUSCICAPIDAE

                                       Subfamily TURDINAE

STATUS   Indeterminate. Restricted to one island in the Ryukyu Archipelago,
south-west of Japan, where it is thought to be rare and where its forest habitat is
being cleared.

DISTRIBUTION   Known only from Amami-oshima, northern Ryukyu Islands.

POPULATION   No precise figures are available, although this subspecies has been
described as extremely rare (Y. Yamashina 1974, pers. comm.).   None were collected
during an expedition to Amami-oshima in 1922 (1), but about thirty years later its
song is reported to have been heard (2).   Another subspecies, Z. d. aurea of
western Asia, winters on Amami-oshima, so that field identification of the endemic
subspecies is possible only in summer (3).

HABITAT   Broad-leaved evergreen forest. This forest is unprotected on Amami-
oshima and is being felled (Y. Yamashina 1974, pers. comm.).

CONSERVATION MEASURES TAKEN   Designated a Special Bird for Protection in Japan in
1972.

CONSERVATION MEASURES PROPOSED   None known.

REMARKS   Fifteen additional subspecies have been recognized, ranging from the
extreme east of Europe to eastern Siberia, Korea, Japan and south through China,
the Philippines, Indo-China, Malaysia and the Indian sub-continent to Indonesia,
New Guinea, the Solomons and eastern Australia.   None of them are thought to be at
risk.

REFERENCES   1.   Kuroda, N. 1925.   Avifauna of the Riu Kiu Islands and the
                    Vicinity.   Tokyo.
              2.   Hachisuka, M. & Udagawa, T. 1953.   Contribution to the
                    ornithology of the Ryukyu Islands.   Q. Journ. Taiwan Mus.
                    6(3-4): 141-279.
              3.   Yamashina Institute for Ornithology, 1975.   Save These Birds.
                    Tokyo: The Kasumikaikan.   (In Japanese).

WESTERN WHIPBIRD

Psophodes nigrogularis Gould, 1844

Order PASSERIFORMES   Family MUSCICAPIDAE

                                             Subfamily ORTHONYCHINAE

STATUS   Out of danger.   Recent reports have shown the distribution of all three
subspecies comprising this species to be more extensive than previously thought.
Furthermore, portions of the habitat of two of them are safeguarded in National
Parks, and the creation of another National Park which would cover much of the area
where the third subspecies occurs, is under consideration (1).

DISTRIBUTION   P. n. nigrogularis Gould, 1844, was formerly more widespread in
South and Western Australia.   It occurs presently in the Eyre Peninsula, South
Australia, from Coffin Bay to the Lincoln National Park, and in five areas in
Western Australia, two of which are National Parks.
     P. n. pondalowiensis Condon, 1966, occurs from south of Pondalowie Bay north to
Royston Head at the south-western end of the Yorke Peninsula, South Australia, and
is presumed to be the subspecies present on nearby Kangaroo Island.
     P. n. leucogaster Howe and Ross, 1933, is no longer known in the area from which
it was described near Peebinga, 230 km due east of Adelaide, South Australia, but
it has been rediscovered near Comet Bore, further to the south, and also near the
South Australia/Victoria border, and its range has recently been found to extend
up to 60 km into Victoria (1; 2; R.F. Brown 1974, pers. comm.).

POPULATION   Only leucogaster is now considered to be rare, the other two
subspecies moderately common (R.F. Brown 1974, pers. comm.).   No precise figures
are available or likely to become so, due to the secretive nature of the species.

HABITAT   Dense undergrowth in heath or mallee country.   This habitat is vulnerable to the ravages of bushfires, but its extent is now known to be sufficient to
ensure that no single bushfire would affect the entire habitat of any of the
subspecies (R.F. Brown 1974, pers. comm.).

CONSERVATION MEASURES TAKEN   Protected by law.   Several National Parks have
recently been established which protect some of the range of the species and
proposals have been made for adding to them.   The species is listed in Appendix 1
of the 1973 Convention on International Trade in Endangered Species of Wild Fauna
and Flora.

CONSERVATION MEASURES PROPOSED   Establishment of a National Park in western
Victoria to protect the habitat of P. n. leucogaster (R.F. Brown 1974, pers. comm.).

REMARKS   The status of all three subspecies in 1966 was described in the previous
edition of this Volume as 'very rare and localized'.

REFERENCES   1.   Condon, H.T. 1969.   A Handlist of the Birds of South Australia.
                     Adelaide: South Australian Ornithological Association.
               2.   Serventy, D.L. & Whittell, H.M. 1976.   Birds of Western
                     Australia, 5th ed.   Perth: University of Western Australia
                     Press.

LOWER YANGTZE KIANG CROW-TIT

Paradoxornis heudei heudei David, 1872

Order PASSERIFORMES

Family MUSCICAPIDAE

Subfamily PANURINAE

STATUS   Indeterminate. Very restricted in distribution in China and unreported
for many years. The reed beds that comprise its entire habitat are harvested
regularly and extensively.

DISTRIBUTION   Known only from 500 sq. km of reed beds along the lower Yangtze
Kiang River between Nanking and Chinkiang, a distance of 110 km (1).

POPULATION   Unknown. It is certainly not large, if indeed it still exists.

HABITAT   Reed beds. The reeds are harvested in January each year, forcing the
birds to concentrate in the few uncut areas, in what is one of the most heavily
populated parts of the world, until new reeds emerge in late spring (1).

CONSERVATION MEASURES TAKEN   None known.

CONSERVATION MEASURES PROPOSED   Protection from cutting of some sections of the
reed beds was recommended as long ago as 1914, but whether anything was ever done
about it is not known (1).

REMARKS   In 1973, a form of Paradoxornis was collected on the shores of Lake
Khanka, Ussuriland, USSR, which has now been determined to be conspecific with the
form from the lower Yangtze Kiang. It has been named P. h. polivanovi Stepanyan,
1974, and is a more or less common breeding bird of the Khanka lakeshore (A. Ivanov
in litt. to S.D. Ripley, 1974).

REFERENCES   1.   Lynes, H. 1914. Some notes on the habits and distribution
of Paradoxornis heudei David. Ibis (10)2: 177-185.

WHITE-NECKED PICATHARTES

Picathartes gymnocephalus (Temminck, 1825)

Order PASSERIFORMES   Family MUSCICAPIDAE

                                       Subfamily PICATHARTINAE

STATUS   Vulnerable. This picathartes, or rock-fowl as it is sometimes called,
occurs very locally in West Africa and is in great demand by zoos and private
collections.   The wild population may be large enough to withstand constant
depletion by trappers but this has yet to be proved.

DISTRIBUTION   Reported to include the high forests of Guinea, Sierra Leone,
Ghana, Togoland and Liberia.   No changes have been documented, although the
species no longer occurs in some of the areas in that range and, on the other hand,
should eventually be found in intervening forestlands in the Ivory Coast, where it
has not yet been recorded. (1; 2; 10).

POPULATION   Unknown and there is no evidence of a decline, although one is
suspected.   The species nests colonially in rock caves, on the walls of which it
builds nests of mud and fibrous plant materials.   One Ghanaian colony observed in
1963 contained 13 nests, only 5 of which contained eggs or young (3); and only 2
out of a group of 5 nests were in use at another colony found in Sierra Leone some
years earlier, in 1950, when it was said to be widespread in that country and not
to have suffered any serious reduction in numbers (4).   No less than 30 colonies
have in fact been found in Sierra Leone recently, between the Moho and Moa rivers,
while in south central Ghana it has been found in several localities along the
length of the Kwahu escarpment and to the south and south-west of it, at Bodweseanwo
and at Fumso, and the known population is of the order of 200-300 pairs (10;
L. Grimes 1977, pers. comm.).

HABITAT   High primary and secondary rainforest, within which the breeding-places
of the species are restricted to areas with rocky cliffs or caves, to the walls of
which the nest is attached.   The habit of nesting colonially in sometimes readily
identifiable sites renders it vulnerable to collecting.   In parts of its range it
has been eliminated locally by total clearing of the forest, but moderate
disturbance or exploitation of the forest cover, even in the immediate vicinity of
its nesting caves, seems to be tolerated (1; 3; 4; 10).

CONSERVATION MEASURES TAKEN   The species is listed in Appendix 1 of the 1973
Convention on International Trade in Endangered Species of Wild Fauna and Flora,
which was ratified by Ghana in 1977.   It is also protected by Ghanaian law and
several of the areas in which it is known to occur lie within forest reserves.

CONSERVATION MEASURES PROPOSED   No measures, in other countries in which the
species occurs, are known to be under consideration.

REMARKS   The White-necked Picathartes is well represented in several of the
world's major zoos.   In the decade 1967-1976, the captive population in from 12 to
15 of these collections ranged between 38 and 68, but the species has bred
successfully only at Amsterdam zoo (once) and Frankfurt zoo (twice) (5-7).
    The systematic position of the genus Picathartes has been subject to much debate.
Several recent authors suggest its affinities are with the babblers Timaliinae (8;
9).

REFERENCES   1.   Bannerman, D.A. 1948.   The Birds of Tropical West Africa.
                  Vol. 6.   London: Crown Agents for the Colonies.
             2.   Hall, B.P. & Moreau, R.E. 1970.   An Atlas of Speciation
                  in African Passerine Birds.   London: Trustees of the
                  British Museum (Natural History).
             3.   Grimes, L. 1964.   Some notes on the breeding of Picathartes
                  gymnocephalus in Ghana.   Ibis 106: 258-260.
             4.   Glanville, R.R. 1954.   Picathartes gymnocephalus in Sierra
                  Leone.   Ibis 96: 481-484.
             5.   Data compiled from censuses of rare animals in captivity.
                  International Zoo Yearbook, 1967-1976, Vols. 8-17.
             6.   Faust, I. 1970.   Brut und Aufzucht einer Weisshals-
                  Stelzenkrahe (Picathartes gymnocephalus Temminck) im
                  Zoologischen Garten Frankfurt am Main.   Der Zoologische
                  Garten 38(1-2): 30-36.
             7.   Dekker, D. 1971-72.   Weisshals-Stelzenkrahen (Picathartes
                  gymnocephalus).   Zeitschrift des Kölner Zoo 4: 155-161.
             8.   Delacour, J. & Amadon, D. 1951.   The systematic position
                  of Picathartes.   Ibis 93: 60-62.
             9.   Sibley, C.G. 1973.   The relationships of Picathartes.
                  Bull. Brit. Ornitn. Club 93: 23-25.
            10.   Grimes L. & Darku, K. 1968.   Some recent breeding records
                  of Picathartes gymnocephalus in Ghana and notes on its
                  distribution in West Africa.   Ibis 110: 93-99.

GREY-NECKED PICATHARTES

Picathartes oreas Reichenow, 1899

Order PASSERIFORMES

Family MUSCICAPIDAE

Subfamily PICATHARTINAE

STATUS   Vulnerable.   Quite locally distributed in West Africa, this picathartes
or rock-fowl is highly vulnerable to collectors because of its habit of nesting
colonially on rock faces, the location of many of which is known.

DISTRIBUTION   Mainly within Cameroon, where it has been found along a 320 km
stretch of coast and inland for distances up to 150 km and at altitudes up to
2,135 m; in the total area of about 18,000 sq. km, the occurrences of the species
are very sporadic (1-6; 12).   In 1963, it was also discovered at six cave sites
in Gabon (10; 11).

POPULATION   Unknown, but thought to be small and possibly declining as the result
of incessant attempts to capture the species wherever it is found.   In one area
near the headwaters of the Cross River, Cameroon, 10 colonies were discovered
between 1949 and 1951, separated from one another by a walking time of 15 minutes
to 3 hours; each comprised 4 to 8 nests, not all in use (7).   In 1964, the largest
known colony in Gabon numbered 10 birds.

HABITAT   High primary and secondary rainforest from sea level to mountain top,
provided that rocky areas and cliffs are present (3; 4; 7).   So far as is known,
forest destruction is not a contributory factor in the concern felt about the
status of this species, for it appears to spend much of its time in caves or the
adjacent tangle of thick leafy vegetation (10).

CONSERVATION MEASURES TAKEN   The species is listed in Appendix 1 of the 1973
Convention on International Trade in Endangered Species of Wild Fauna and Flora,
to which neither Cameroon nor Gabon has yet become a party.

CONSERVATION MEASURES PROPOSED   None known.

REMARKS   This picathartes has always been rarer in captive collections than its
congener 1100 km to the west.   In the decade 1967-1976, a maximum of 11 birds was
reported to be in captivity in 3 collections (in 1970 and 1972), but by 1976 this
number had dwindled to 3, all at Frankfurt Zoo, which alone has had success in
breeding the species (8; 9).   For comments on the systematic position of the genus
Picathartes see the Remarks section of the data sheet for Picathartes gymnocephalus.

REFERENCES   1.   Hall, B.P. & Moreau, R.E. 1962.   A study of the rare birds
                    of Africa.   Bull. Brit. Mus. (Nat. Hist.) Zool. 8:   313-378.
              2.   Good, A.I. 1953.   The Birds of French Cameroon.   Part II.
                    Mem. Inst. Français Afr. Noire, Sci. Nat. 3.
              3.   Bannerman, D.A. 1948, 1951.   The Birds of Tropical West
                    Africa, Vols. 6 and 8.   London: Crown Agents for the Colonies.
              4.   Webb, C.S. 1949.   Some notes on the Grey-necked Picathartes
                    (Picathartes oreas).   Avicult. Mag. 55: 149-154.
              5.   Serle, W. 1954.   A second contribution to the ornithology
                    of the British Cameroons.   Ibis 96: 47-80.
              6.   Serle, W. 1965.   A third contribution to the ornithology
                    of the British Cameroons.   Ibis 107: 230-246.

7. Serle, W. 1952. The affinities of the Genus Picathartes Lesson. Bull. Brit. Ornith. Club 72: 2-6.

8. Summarized from censuses of Rare Animals in Captivity. International Zoo Yearbook, 1967-1976, Vols. 8-17.

9. Duplaix-Hall, N. (ed.) 1972. Species of wild animals bred in captivity during 1971. Internat. Zoo Yearbook 13: 281-346.

10. Brosset, A. 1965. La biologie de Picathartes oreas. Biologia Gabonica 1: 101-115.

11. Brosset, A. 1965. Un oiseau africain troglophile: Picathartes oreas. Annal. Spéléol. 2): 425-429.

12. Kreffer, C. 1953. Quelques observations sur le Picathartes oreas Rchw. l'Oiseau et R.F.O. 23: 142-144.

EIAO POLYNESIAN WARBLER

Acrocephalus caffer aquilonis (Murphy and Mathews, 1928)

Order PASSERIFORMES   Family MUSCICAPIDAE

                                          Subfamily SYLVIINAE

STATUS   Endangered. This subspecies is restricted to Eiao Island in the
Marquesas, which was recently the site of intensive French military activity, when
it was proposed as a nuclear testing site to replace the Tuamotu Archipelago.   This
activity began in 1971, only months after Eiao had been given protected status.

DISTRIBUTION   Restricted to Eiao Island (52 sq. km), Marquesas Islands.

POPULATION   The warbler was apparently common in 1922, when the Whitney South Sea
Expedition collected a number of specimens (1).   Three more were collected in two
days in 1929 and it was still present but in small numbers in 1968 (1).

HABITAT   Other races of the species occupy a variety of habitats possessing trees
or tall bushes, ranging from cultivated areas to dense forest.   On Eiao, by 1960,
only scraps of woodland remained and, after many years of grazing by introduced
sheep and swine, it was described as "a barren gullied desert of rock and orange
clay", where runoff after rainstorms reddens the surrounding sea (3).

CONSERVATION MEASURES TAKEN   Eiao was given protected status in 1971, but this
was almost immediately modified to permit the French military activities referred to
above (3; 4).

CONSERVATION MEASURES PROPOSED   Restoration of full protected status and removal
of sheep and pigs from the island (5).

REMARKS   This subspecies is one of the eight described from all the larger
Marquesas Islands.   All of the others that have recently been surveyed are still
rated as common.   Should nuclear testing take place on Eiao, A. c. postremus on
Hatutu, which is only 3 km away, would also be vulnerable.

REFERENCES   1.   Holyoak, D.T. 1975.   Les oiseaux des Îles Marquises.
                    L'Oiseau et R.F.O. 45: 207-233, 341-366.
              2.   Fisher, A.K. & Wetmore, A. 1931.   Report on birds recorded by
                    the Pinchot Expedition of 1929 to the Caribbean and Pacific.
                    Proc. U.S. Nat. Mus. 79(10): 1-66.
              3.   Decker, B.G. 1973.   Unique dry-island biota under official
                    protection in northwestern Marquesas Islands (Iles Marquises).
                    Biol. Cons. 5(1): 66-67.
              4.   Holyoak, D.T. 1973.   Polynesian landbirds face H-bombs and
                    malaria.   New Scientist 57: 288-290.
              5.   Thibault, J.-C. undated.   Fragilité et protection de l'avifaune
                    en Polynésie Française.   Unpublished report to ICBP.

MOOREA POLYNESIAN WARBLER

Acrocephalus caffer longirostris (Gmelin, 1789)

Order PASSERIFORMES   Family MUSCICAPIDAE

                                              Subfamily SYLVIINAE

_____

STATUS   Endangered.   Found only on Moorea in the Society Islands, where it was
scarce and local in 1921; two recent searches for it resulted in sightings of only
two individuals and two pairs respectively (1; 2).   This subspecies and other
endemic birds of the Society Islands, have newly become exposed to vectors of avian
malaria.   It has been shown that lack of immunity to this disease may have caused
the extinction of several species in the Hawaiian Islands (3).

DISTRIBUTION   Now very local on Moorea (132 sq. km), Society Islands, though
once comparatively widespread and common (1).

POPULATION   Three specimens of this warbler were collected in 1921 by the
Whitney South Sea Expedition, when it was already considered rather scarce and
confined to only a few areas.   In 1972 a search revealed only two individuals,
3 km apart (1) and in 1973 two pairs were found (2).   The total population is
unknown, but must be very small.

HABITAT   Apparently confined to native montane forests on Moorea at elevations of
between 800 and 900 m.   Some other subspecies, e.g. the nominate A. c. caffer on
Tahiti, display a wider choice of habitat, occurring also in introduced vegetation
and at lower elevations (1).

CONSERVATION MEASURES TAKEN   Legal protection from killing or hunting has been
extended to this subspecies.

CONSERVATION MEASURES PROPOSED   Further surveys to determine the distribution and
size of the surviving population.

REMARKS   Out of the ten subspecies described from the Society and Marquesas
Islands, only this, A. c. postremus of Hatutu and A. c. aquilonis of Eiao are
known to be at risk.

REFERENCES   1.   Holyoak, D.T. 1974.   Les oiseaux des îles de la Société.
                    L'Oiseau et R.F.O. 44: 1-27, 153-181.
              2.   Thibault, J.-C. 1974.   Le Peuplement Avien des Iles de la
                    Société (Polynésie).   Papeete; Mus. Nat. Hist. Natur. Antenne
                    de Tahiti.
              3.   Warner, R.E. 1968.   The role of introduced diseases in the
                    extinction of the endemic Hawaiian avifauna.   Condor 70:
                    101-120.

HATUTU POLYNESIAN WARBLER

Acrocephalus caffer postremus (Murphy and Mathews, 1928)

Order PASSERIFORMES   Family MUSCICAPIDAE

                                              Subfamily SYLVIINAE

STATUS   Rare.   Restricted to one small island in the Marquesas, South Pacific,
where its population is quite small.

DISTRIBUTION   Known only from Hatutu (18 sq. km), Marquesas Islands.

POPULATION   This subspecies was common on Hatutu in 1922, when first discovered,
although in keeping with the small size of the island its numbers could not have
been large (1).   In 1975, the total population was estimated to be 40 ± 10 pairs
(2).

HABITAT   Hatutu is among the least altered of the Marquesas islands and was
probably never permanently inhabited by humans.   It is unique among the high
islands of the group in having only one introduced mammal, Rattus exulans, and it
also has several plant species rare or lacking on the others (2; 3).

CONSERVATION MEASURES TAKEN   Hatutu was given protected status in 1971, as was
Eiao Island, 3 km distant.   However, shortly afterwards the latter became the
scene of intensive human activity related to the preparation of an alternative
nuclear test site to the one previously used by French military forces in the
Tuamotus.   A considerable potential threat to Hatutu's intact biota is posed not
only by nuclear explosions but also by the destruction of biota or introduction of
exotic plant or animal species by visitors from Eiao (4).

CONSERVATION MEASURES PROPOSED   None known.

REMARKS   Of ten subspecies in the Society and Marquesas Islands, only this,
A. c. aquilonis of Eiao and A. c. longirostris of Moorea are believed to be at risk.

REFERENCES   1.   Holyoak, D.T. 1975.   Les oiseaux des îles Marquises.
                   L'Oiseau et R.F.O. 45:   207-233, 341-366.
              2.   Thibault, J.-C. undated.   Fragilité et protection de
                   l'avifaune en Polynésie Française.   Unpublished report to ICBP.
              3.   Decker, B.G. 1973.   Unique dry-island biota under official
                   protection in northwestern Marquesas Islands (Iles Marquises).
                   Biol. Cons. 5:   66-67.
              4.   Holyoak, D.T. 1973.   Polynesian landbirds face H-bombs and
                   malaria.   New Scientist 57:   288-290.

NIHOA MILLERBIRD

Acrocephalus familiaris kingi (Wetmore, 1924)

Order   PASSERIFORMES   Family   MUSCICAPIDAE
                                          Subfamily   SYLVIINAE

STATUS   Rare. Restricted to Nihoa Island (0.64 sq. km), north-western
Hawaiian Islands, where a small population exists.   Severe alteration of
vegetation, introduction of predators such as cats or rats, might rapidly cause
the extinction of this subspecies (1; 2; 3).

DISTRIBUTION   Endemic to Nihoa Island, north-western Hawaiian Islands.

POPULATION   Not known to have declined significantly since its discovery.
Recent censuses suggest the population fluctuates from year to year between 200
and 600 individuals.   A census in July 1973 yielded an estimate of 200 birds
(4; 5).

HABITAT   Chenopodium and Sida shrubs over most of Nihoa Island (2; 4).

CONSERVATION MEASURES TAKEN   Nihoa Island is part of the Hawaiian Islands
National Wildlife Refuge.   Landings on the island are only by permit.   The
subspecies is protected by federal and state law.   The U.S. Fish and Wildlife
Service conducts annual censuses of this subspecies (1; 4).

CONSERVATION MEASURES PROPOSED   Increase patrol of Hawaiian Islands National
Wildlife Refuge to prevent unauthorized landings which could result in introduction
of pest plants and predators such as cats and rats.   Introduction of this
subspecies to nearby Necker Island is suggested as a last-resort measure in case
of severe population decline (1; 2; 3).

REMARKS   This is the only remaining extant subspecies.   The other subspecies,
A. f. familiaris of Laysan Island, was extirpated by 1923 as the result of
destruction of Laysan's vegetation by introduced European rabbits (Oryctolagus
cuniculus).

REFERENCES   1.   U.S. Dept. of Interior Bureau of Sport Fisheries and Wildlife,
                   1973.   Threatened Wildlife of the United States.   U.S. Bur.
                   Sport Fish. Wildl. Res. Pub. 114.
              2.   Berger, A.J. 1972.   Hawaiian Birdlife.   Honolulu: University
                   Press of Hawaii.
              3.   King, W.B. 1973.   Conservation status of birds of central
                   Pacific islands.   Wilson Bull. 85: 89-103.
              4.   U.S. Fish and Wildlife Service.   Kailua, Hawaii:
                   unpublished reports.
              5.   Clapp, R.B., Kridler, E. and Fleet, R.R., in press.   The
                   natural history of Nihoa Island, Northwestern Hawaiian Islands.
                   Atoll Research Bull. 207.

RODRIGUES BRUSH WARBLER

Bebrornis rodericana (Newton, 1865)

Order PASSERIFORMES   Family MUSCICAPIDAE

                                       Subfamily SYLVIINAE

STATUS   Endangered.   Confined to a small portion of Rodrigues Island in the
Mascarenes.   The total population of this species is very small and is not yet
protected.

DISTRIBUTION   When discovered in the middle of the 19th century, this species
was presumably distributed throughout Rodrigues, and as recently as 1957 a visit
resulted in the collection of four specimens (1).   Yet in 1958 and 1963 it could
not be found (2), although subsequent visitors in 1964 and 1971 and 1972 reported
that it was extant but very local (3; 4).   In 1974, a thorough survey showed that
half the surviving population was based in the La Source-Cascade Pigeon valley on
the slopes of Mt. Lubin, and the remainder in other valleys radiating from the same
mountain.   It was also reported to have disappeared only quite recently from the
Sygangue and Grande Montagne areas.   The present range occupies less than 2.5 sq.
km (1).

POPULATION   Although considered common last century, the warbler has declined
during the present century to a critical level.   The 1974 investigation revealed
only 24 sites in which it was still present and of these only 10 were definitely
occupied by pairs.   It is, however, an inconspicuous bird and a few sites may have
been overlooked.   The total population was estimated at between 20 and 25 pairs
(1).

HABITAT   Thickets dominated by jamrose (Eugenia jambos), preferably with small
glades or clearings, at an altitude of 240 to 420 m.   Most of the indigenous
vegetation of Rodrigues had been cleared by the turn of the century and jamrose
planting reached a peak by 1910, by which time the warbler must already have become
adapted to it.   However, a major clearance of jamrose took place in the 1960s,
which no doubt greatly reduced and fragmented the warbler population.   Recent
conservation of vegetation by the Forest Department for watershed protection has
unintentionally contributed to an increase in the extent of suitable habitat for the
warbler, but is offset by the great demand for firewood from the island's growing
human population, which results in continuing clearing of thickets and disturbance
of the species (1).

CONSERVATION MEASURES TAKEN   Much of the remaining habitat of the species
receives some protection as a "mountain reserve" and additional areas of potential
habitat have recently been created by new Forestry Department plantations (1).

CONSERVATION MEASURES PROPOSED   Declaration of Cascade Pigeon as a nature reserve
and legal protection of the warbler from killing or disturbance was under consideration in 1975, but the relevant legislation was still awaiting enactment in
February 1977.   Specific modification of the forest management program to take
account of the requirements of this and other endemic species in the island's fauna
has been recommended.

REMARKS   Frequent cyclones on Rodrigues have apparently reduced the population of this species to perhaps one-half of what the existing habitat could support.   Thus, some areas recently shown to be without brush warblers might well be recolonized if the population can be built up (1).

REFERENCES   1.   Cheke, A.S. 1974.   Report on Rodrigues.   Brit. Ornith. Union Mascarene Islands Expedition.   Ibis (in prep.).
          2.   Vinson, J. 1964.   Quelques remarques sur l'Ile Rodrigue et sur sa faune terrestre.   Proc. Roy. Soc. Arts and Sci. Mauritius 2(3):   263-277.
          3.   Gill, F.B. 1967.   Birds of Rodriguez Island (Indian Ocean).   Ibis 109:   383-390.
          4.   Staub, F. 1973.   Birds of Rodrigues Island.   Proc. Roy. Soc. Arts and Sci. Mauritius 4(1):   17-59.

SEYCHELLES BRUSH WARBLER

Bebrornis sechellensis (Oustalet, 1877)

Order PASSERIFORMES   Family MUSCICAPIDAE

                                   Subfamily SYLVIINAE

_____

STATUS   Out of immediate danger, although still rare.   This warbler is restricted
to one small island in the Seychelles and 15 years ago was among the world's rarest
birds but is now relatively common.   This follows the management of the island as
a nature sanctuary and the associated recovery of much of its natural vegetation.

DISTRIBUTION   Known only from the Seychelles Islands, where it was recorded on
Marianne and Cousin, although it disappeared from the former with clearance of the
forest during the 19th century (1).   It is now almost confined to Cousin Island
(27 ha), although in 1960 it was introduced to Cousine where it was subsequently
seen from time to time (2; 6) but not recently (M. Garnett 1977, pers. comm.).

POPULATION   At the time of its discovery on Marianne in the 1870s that island was
being cleared and it was not seen subsequently (1; 2).   At about the same date it
was reported as rare on Cousin (1) and still had that status as recently as 1938
(3).   But in 1959, 30 birds were counted (4) and in 1965 it was estimated that
about 50 adults were present (5).   By 1970, the number on the island was estimated
to be 85 (2), and numbers have continued to increase encouragingly under ICBP
management: in January 1975, they were estimated at 250 to 300, with about 120
pairs holding territories (6).

HABITAT   Dense scrub and mangrove swamp (2).   Since 1968, when ICBP acquired
Cousin Island, extensive woodland scrub has grown up under the coconut groves which
have covered much of the island since early in the century.   The coconuts have
been gathered, thus inhibiting regeneration, with the result that the understory of
native shrubs and trees which had been removed by former owners is once more
developing (6).

CONSERVATION MEASURES TAKEN   The species is legally protected from hunting or
capture.   Cousin Island was approved as a Strict Nature Reserve by the Seychelles
Government in 1975, having been managed as a nature reserve since 1968 by ICBP.
As stated above the native vegetation on which the warbler depends has been
actively encouraged, based on the continuing study of its social behaviour and
ecological requirements begun in 1968.   The only introduced predator present on
the island is the Barn Owl Tyto alba which is regularly controlled but which
periodically re-invades Cousin from nearby Praslin (6).

CONSERVATION MEASURES PROPOSED   Maintenance of research and vegetation management
in the interests of this species.   Continuation of the control of Barn Owls and of
measures designed to exclude other predators, especially rats and cats (6).

REMARKS   Establishment of the warbler on another island is an important long-term
safeguard that should receive serious consideration.

REFERENCES 1. Oustalet, M.E. 1878.   Etude sur la faune ornithologique des
                îles Seychelles.   Bull. Soc. philomath. Paris (7)2: 161-206.
            2. Penny, M. 1974.   The Birds of Seychelles and the Outlying
                Islands.   New York: Taplinger Publishing Co.; London: Collins.
            3. Vesey-Fitzgerald, D. 1940.   The birds of the Seychelles. 1.
                Ibis (14)4: 480-489.
            4. Crook, J.H. 1960.   The present status of certain rare land
                birds of the Seychelles Islands.   Unnumbered Seychelles
                Government Bulletin; 5 pages.
            5. Penny, M. 1967.   A new sanctuary in the Seychelles.   Oryx 9:
                214-216.
            6. Diamond, A.W. 1975.   Cousin Island Nature Reserve Management
                Plan 1975-1979.   London: ICBP.

JAPANESE MARSH WARBLER

Megalurus pryeri pryeri Seebohm, 1884

Order PASSERIFORMES

Family MUSCICAPIDAE

Subfamily SYLVIINAE

STATUS   Rare.   Restricted to parts of two prefectures on Honshu, Japan, where it is local and scarce.   Formerly threatened by extensive use of nets for bird catching for the markets, but now mainly at risk because of its very local distribution and the lack of protection of its habitat.

DISTRIBUTION   Formerly occurred near Tokyo and around Suruga Bay, Honshu (1). In 1936, the subspecies was found breeding at Gamoh, Miyagi Prefecture, and in 1937 suspected of breeding in Shizuoka Prefecture.   Presently restricted to Mutsu-Ogawabara and Juusan-ko, Aomori Prefecture, and Hachiro-gata, Akita Prefecture, at the northern end of Honshu.   Winters in Ibaraki Prefecture, farther south in Honshu (Y. Yamashina 1974, pers. comm.).

POPULATION   Little is known of former abundance of this subspecies, but it has always been considered rare.   In 1973, the population at Juusan-ko was estimated at 100 pairs (3) but no estimates are available for the two other known breeding localities.

HABITAT   Reed beds along rivers and coastal marshes.   The marshes where this subspecies is most often found are unprotected and vulnerable to exploitation (Y. Yamashina 1974, pers. comm.).

CONSERVATION MEASURES TAKEN   In 1972 this species was designated a Special Bird for Protection in Japan.

CONSERVATION MEASURES PROPOSED   Preservation of the breeding marshes, which is considered to be much the most important factor in securing the future existence of this subspecies (Y. Yamashina 1974, pers. comm.).

REMARKS   Another subspecies M. p. sinensis has been encountered only on migration and is little known but probably breeds in Manchuria, although its nest has not been discovered.   It migrates south through Hopei probably to winter in the Yangtze River Valley (4).

REFERENCES   1.   Austin, O.L. Jr. & Kuroda, N. 1953.   The birds of Japan: their status and distribution.   Harvard Mus. Comp. Zool. Bull. 109(4):   279-637.
2.   Ornithological Society of Japan, 1974.   Check-list of Japanese Birds.   Fifth (revised) Edition.   Tokyo: Gakken Co.
3.   Ohyagi, A. 1973.   Observations on the breeding of the Japanese Marsh-Warbler.   Yacho 38: 4-8.   (In Japanese).
4.   Vaurie, C. 1959.   Birds of the Palearctic Fauna.   Passeriformes. London: H.F. and G. Witherby.

ALDABRA BRUSH WARBLER

Nesillas aldabranus Benson and Penny, 1968

Order PASSERIFORMES   Family MUSCICAPIDAE

                                               Subfamily SYLVIINAE

STATUS   Rare.   Confined to Aldabra Atoll, western Indian Ocean.

DISTRIBUTION   The species has only been detected in the western two kilometres
of Middle Island, Aldabra.   Within this area it is restricted to the strip of
extremely dense mixed scrub, on average less than 100 metres deep, along the north
coast and there is no evidence that it ever penetrates further inland.   Even
within the dense scrub its distribution is discontinuous.   Because the vegetation
is so thick, the rest of the western nine kilometres of Middle Island has not been
studied closely and it is possible that the Brush Warbler may occur elsewhere in
that area; but extensive searches indicate that it is unlikely to occur in other
parts of Aldabra, with the possible exception of the dense scrub in the south-west
corner of South Island.

POPULATION   By extrapolation from the results of studies of the species in the
westernmost two kilometres of Middle Island scrub, it has been calculated that the
total population probably would not exceed 25 individuals even if habitat as
suitable for the Brush Warbler as that in which it has so far been found, continues
to be a feature of the remainder of the western 9 km of the island (1).   It would
need the discovery of the Brush Warbler in some other part of Aldabra before any
higher figure could be justified.

HABITAT   Contrary to previous ideas on the subject (2; 3), the habitat of the
Brush Warbler, by virtue of a combination of factors each of which on its own is
not unique in the atoll, is demonstrably distinct from anything to be found
elsewhere (1).   These factors are:

    (i) extremely tall, dense, closed-canopy mixed scrub with,
         by Aldabran standards, a considerable leaf litter/soil layer;
   (ii) large, dense stands of almost pure Pandanus;
  (iii) a marked abundance of Dracaena reflexa, a plant generally
         uncommon on Aldabra, which has an associated insect fauna much
         utilized by the Brush Warbler; and
   (iv) the absence of the giant tortoises Testudo gigantea and feral
         goats Capra hircus that, elsewhere on Aldabra, probably play a
         significant role in opening up dense mixed scrub and in scattering
         the layer of litter which is of considerable importance to the
         Brush Warbler for foraging purposes.

    The combination of these factors, particularly the first two, is probably
critical.
    Environmental changes in the recent past, due to slight climatic shifts and/or
the introduction of goats and rats, may also have contributed to the restriction
of the Brush Warbler to its present limited area; rats, in particular, have a
devastating effect on the breeding success of small Aldabran land birds and, for
the time being at least, eradication of this pest does not seem feasible (R. Prys-
Jones 1977, pers. comm.).

CONSERVATION MEASURES TAKEN   Aldabra's reprieve from development as an air base
was partly due to protests on scientific and conservation grounds.   A research
station was established on the atoll by the Royal Society (U.K.) in 1970 and is due
to be transferred to new management in 1980.   Aldabra is now a nature reserve and
the Brush Warbler is legally protected.

CONSERVATION MEASURES PROPOSED   The only further appropriate conservation
measure would appear to be total protection of the dense scrub in the western half
of Middle Island.   In particular, no east-west paths should be cut which might
tend to allow goats or tortoises from the eastern half of the island to infiltrate
any intervening geological or vegetational barriers.   Further exploration of the
area should only be facilitated by narrow north-south traces running inland from
the sea or lagoon coasts (R. Prys-Jones 1977, pers. comm.).

REMARKS   This sheet was prepared with the generous cooperation of Dr R.P. Prys-
Jones.

REFERENCES   1.   Prys-Jones, R.P. (in press).   Ecology and conservation of
                    the Aldabran Brush Warbler Nesillas aldabranus.   Phil. Trans.
                    Roy. Soc. Lond. B.
              2.   Benson, C.W. & Penny, M.J. 1968.   A new species of warbler
                    from the Aldabra Atoll.   Bull. Brit. Ornith. Club 88: 102-108.
              3.   Benson, C.W. & Penny, M.J. 1971.   The land birds of Aldabra.
                    Phil. Trans. Roy. Soc. Lond. B 260:   417-527.

GUADALUPE KINGLET

Regulus calendula obscura Ridgway, 1876

Order PASSERIFORMES   Family MUSCICAPIDAE

                                          Subfamily SYLVIINAE

STATUS   Indeterminate. Said to be quite localized on Guadalupe Island, Mexico,
the biggest threat to it probably being habitat destruction by goats.

DISTRIBUTION   This subspecies is indigenous to Guadalupe Island, 250 km west of
central Baja California, Mexico, where it is restricted to a grove of cypress
trees on the ridge top at 1200 m elevation. In 1886, it also inhabited a second
cypress grove and an area of pines further north along the ridge, but by 1906 it
only survived at the major cypress grove site (1; 2). In 1973, it was once again
seen in the pinewood area (E. N. Mirsky 1977, pers. comm.).

POPULATION   No estimate has been made, but there can be little doubt that the
decline of the subspecies has been directly related to the decrease in the area
covered by cypress. The last report of this kinglet, made in 1973, was of the
sighting of 8 over a period of 17 days (E.N. Mirsky 1977, pers. comm.).

HABITAT   Cypress Cupressus guadalupensis and pine Pinus radiata-oak Quercus
tomentella groves. These continue to be reduced in area, as all young plants are
browsed off by goats, and no regeneration has taken place for a century. Cats,
which were formerly abundant and responsible for the extinction of several species,
are now rare (3; 4), but in any case they would have had little or no impact on a
bird like the kinglet.

CONSERVATION MEASURES TAKEN   Guadalupe Island has been a sanctuary since 1924.
In 1971, thousands of goats were removed (J. Jehl 1977, pers. comm.), but unless
the program of elimination is persevered with until total success is achieved, it
will have been quite futile as, even when reduced by thousands, a goat population
is capable of rapid recovery.

CONSERVATION MEASURES PROPOSED   None additional known.

REMARKS   Despite the destruction by goats of much of the vegetation of Guadalupe
several endemic birds survive in adequate numbers, including a kestrel Falco
sparverius guadalupensis (questionably distinct from the adjacent continental form),
a house finch Carpodacus mexicanus amplus, a junco Junco hyemalis insularis, and a
rock wren Salpinctes obsoletus guadeloupensis (3; 4; E.N. Mirsky 1977, pers. comm.).
On the other hand, the Guadalupe Storm Petrel Oceanodroma macrodactyla, Guadalupe
Caracara Caracara lutosa, Guadalupe Flicker Colaptes auratus rufipileus, Guadalupe
Bewick's Wren Thryomanes bewickii brevicauda and Guadalupe Rufous-sided Towhee
Pipilo erythrophthalmus consobrinus are extinct. The other subspecies of the
kinglet Regulus calendula, which range over much of North America, are not at risk.

REFERENCES   1. Bryant, W.E. 1887. Additions to the ornithology of
                  Guadalupe Island. Bull. Cal. Acad. Sci. 2: 269-318.
              2. Thayer, J.E. & Bangs, O. 1908. The present state of the
                  ornis of Guadaloupe Island. Condor 10: 101-106.
              3. Howell, T.R. & Cade, T.S. 1954. The birds of Guadalupe
                  Island in 1953. Condor 56: 283-294.
              4. Jehl, J.R., Jr. 1972. On the cold trail of an extinct
                  petrel. Pac. Discovery 25(6): 24-29.

LONG-LEGGED WARBLER

Trichocichla rufa Reichenow, 1891

Order PASSERIFORMES   Family MUSCICAPIDAE

                                              Subfamily SYLVIINAE

_____

STATUS   Endangered.   This species known only from Fiji was described from 3
specimens taken in 1890; an additional specimen was taken in 1894 (1) but there
were no further records until it was observed in 1967 and again in 1973 (2).   The
Whitney South Sea Expedition failed to find it in 1928 and it was thought to have
been extirminated by introduced mongooses and possibly rats and cats (3).   These
predators undoubtedly still threaten its existence, but the quite recent discovery
of a second population slightly increases hopes for its chances of survival.

DISTRIBUTION   What is now recognized as the nominate form was described from Viti
Levu, Fiji, and is now only known from the ridgetops of Namosi District in that
island (2).   In 1974 a new subspecies T. r. cluniei was discovered on the southern
slopes of the Delanacau mountains in west-central Vanua Levu (1).

POPULATION   Unknown.   Since its discovery the species appears never to have been
common, for none were recorded after 1894 until 1967, when one was believed seen
(H. Bregulla 1974, pers. comm.) and again in July 1973, when two were seen (2).
However, the fact that there is a native Fijian name for the species (Manu Kalo)
suggests that it must once have been more widespread and plentiful than has been
thought.   Only one individual of the recently described new subspecies was
collected, but a second bird was seen 3 km distant from the collection site (1).

HABITAT   Dense scrub associated with mountain forests (1; 2).   Despite continuing
widespread logging and reafforestation with exotic species, there is still a
considerable area of the scrub habitat favoured by the species.

CONSERVATION MEASURES TAKEN   None known.

CONSERVATION MEASURES PROPOSED   None known.

REFERENCES   1.   Kinsky, F.C. 1975.   A new subspecies of the Long-legged Warbler
                   Trichocichla rufa Reichenow, from Vanua Levu, Fiji.   Bull.
                   B.O.C. 95: 98-101.
              2.   Holyoak, D. undated.   Notes on the birds of Viti Levu and
                   Taveuni, Fiji.   Unpublished manuscript.
              3.   Mayr, E. 1945.   Birds of the Southwest Pacific.   New York:
                   Macmillan Company.

EYREAN GRASS WREN

Amytornis goyderi (Gould, 1875)

Order PASSERIFORMES

Family MUSCICAPIDAE

Subfamily MALURINAE

STATUS   Indeterminate. This species was found in numbers in 1976, in the
sandhills of the Simpson Desert in the extreme north-east of South Australia, but
its reputation for ephemeral appearances was reinforced when, in the following
year, the habitat was found to be seriously deteriorated and the grass wrens
largely gone.   Prior to 1976, it had only been recorded at the time of its
discovery in 1874, in 1931 and in 1961 (1).

DISTRIBUTION   The vicinity of water holes near the Macumba River which flows
after rare heavy rains into the north-west corner of Lake Eyre.   The 1961 record
was made at Christmas Waterhole, in the same general area of the north-east to
north centre of South Australia and about 40 km north of Lake Eyre (2), and those
in 1976 were made between Poepel's Corner and Eyre Creek over a distance of 64 km,
and also, further to the north-east, near Birdsville, just over the Queensland
border (J. Forshaw 1977, pers. comm.).

POPULATION   Unknown.   Two specimens were taken in 1874 and only a pair with a
nest containing two young seem to have been seen in 1961.   On the other hand, in
1976, this grass wren was abundant in both the areas where it was found; in 1977
it had vanished from the neighbourhood of Birdsville, but there was still a remnant
population near Poepel's Corner, of which 4 were netted and photographed
(J. Forshaw 1977, pers. comm.).

HABITAT   Spinifex (Triodia) grasslands, and also canegrass and the legume
Swainsona growing on sandhills.   The vegetation in which this enigmatic species
was found in 1976 had died back when revisited in 1977.   Predation by feral cats
has been suggested as a cause of the rarity of this species, but no proof of this
has been forthcoming (2; 3).

CONSERVATION MEASURES TAKEN   The species is listed in Appendix 1 of the 1973
Convention on International Trade in Endangered Species of Wild Fauna and Flora
and also protected by Australian law.   A portion of its habitat lies within the
Simpson Desert National Park.

CONSERVATION MEASURES PROPOSED   None known.

REMARKS   Two of the birds captured and photographed in 1977 were brought back to
the Taronga Zoo in Sydney.

REFERENCES   1.   Cayley, N.W. 1968.   What Bird is That?, 5th Ed.   Sydney:
                    Angus and Robertson.
              2.   Fisher, J., Simon, N. & Vincent, J. 1969.   Wildlife in
                    Danger.   New York: Viking Press; London: Collins.
              3.   Campbell, A.J. 1923.   The long-lost Eyrean Grass Wren.
                    Emu 23: 81.

CODFISH ISLAND FERNBIRD

Bowdleria punctata wilsoni Stead, 1937

Order PASSERIFORMES   Family MUSCICAPIDAE

                                         Subfamily MALURINAE

STATUS   Endangered.   Restricted to one island off the coast of Stewart Island,
New Zealand, where it has a very small, unstable population.   Modification of
habitat, by an introduced herbivore, and predation are thought to be the causes of
its decline.

DISTRIBUTION   Occurs only on Codfish Island (1,480 hectares), off the north-west
coast of Stewart Island, New Zealand, and separated from it by a 3 km wide strait
(1).

POPULATION   Not long ago, in 1966, this fernbird was considered to be relatively
safe (1), but more recent estimates indicate a gradually declining population,
currently put at a scant 100 birds (2).   Its absence from parts of Codfish Island
in which it formerly occurred is corroborative evidence of a decline.

HABITAT   Mainly low scrub (1).   The vegetation of Codfish Island is being
modified by the introduced Australian brush-tailed possum Trichosurus vulpecula.
The Weka Gallirallus australis scotti and the Polynesian rat Rattus exulans, which
have also found their way to the island, are believed to prey on the fernbirds or
their eggs (3; D. Merton 1974, pers. comm.).

CONSERVATION MEASURES TAKEN   Protected by law.   Codfish Island is a Scenic
Reserve, entry to which is subject to certain restrictions.

CONSERVATION MEASURES PROPOSED   The New Zealand Wildlife Service will attempt to
eliminate Wekas from Codfish Island and to study the effects of the introduced
possum on the vegetation of the island (D. Merton 1974, pers. comm.).

REMARKS   Other subspecies of the Fernbird include B. p. vealae from North Island
and B. p. punctata from South Island, B. p. stewartiana from Stewart Island and
B. p. caudata from Snares Island, all of them relatively common; and B. p.
rufescens of the Chatham Islands, extinct since 1900.

REFERENCES   1.   Blackburn, A. 1967.   Nesting of the Codfish Island Fernbird.
                  Notornis 14: 62-66.
             2.   Bell, B.D. 1975.   The rare and endangered species of the
                  New Zealand region and the policies that exist for their
                  management.   ICBP Bull. 12: 165-172.
             3.   Ellis, B.A. 1975.   Rare and endangered New Zealand birds:
                  the role of the Royal Forest and Bird Protection Society
                  of New Zealand Inc.   ICBP Bull. 12: 173-186.

WESTERN BRISTLEBIRD

Dasyornis brachypterus longirostris Gould, 1840

Order PASSERIFORMES   Family MUSCICAPIDAE

                                        Subfamily MALURINAE

STATUS   Rare and very local. Restricted to a small area in south-western
Western Australia. Its habitat is now reasonably secure from devastating fires,
but its very small population continues to give cause for concern.

DISTRIBUTION   The subspecies was discovered along the Swan River near Perth,
Western Australia in 1839, where it was not seen subsequently. It occurred in
the King George Sound Area around Albany until the 1880s and near Wilson Inlet up
to 1914, when a bush fire destroyed the colony there, at which point it was
thought to be extinct. However, in 1945 it was rediscovered at Two Peoples Bay
near Albany and in the 1960s found to be present also in the nearby Waychinicup-
Mt. Manypeaks area. (1; 2).

POPULATION   No early estimates were made, but ever since it was discovered this
subspecies has always been considered to be rare. At present the only known
population, in the vicinity of Two Peoples Bay, is estimated at about 50 pairs
(G.T. Smith 1975, pers. comm.).

HABITAT   Wet coastal heathland. Large areas of this habitat have been brought
under cultivation or burned repeatedly in order to convert them into pasture for
livestock. Fortunately, the heathland at Two Peoples Bay is now fully protected,
and the range of the subspecies in the Waychinicup-Mt. Manypeaks area is
sufficiently large and divided up by bare granite outcrops and swamps to make it
unlikely that the whole of it would be burned in any one fire (G.T. Smith 1975,
pers. comm.).

CONSERVATION MEASURES TAKEN   A 5,508 ha Class A reserve is shared by this
subspecies and the Noisy Scrub-bird Atrichornis clamosus at Two Peoples Bay.
Access to the reserve is restricted to people on foot and to only one sector.
A proposed town site within the reserve's boundaries has been relocated elsewhere
(G.T. Smith 1975, pers. comm.). The species is listed in Appendix 1 of the 1973
Convention on International Trade in Endangered Species of Wild Fauna and Flora.

CONSERVATION MEASURES PROPOSED   None additional known.

REMARKS   The nominate race of this bristlebird is locally distributed in eastern
Victoria, New South Wales and south-eastern Queensland but not at risk.

REFERENCES   1. Fisher, J., Simon, N. & Vincent, J. 1969. Wildlife in
                 Danger. New York: Viking Press; London: Collins.
             2. Serventy, D.L. & Whittell, H.M. 1976. Birds of Western
                 Australia, 5th ed. Perth: University of Western Australia Press.

WESTERN RUFOUS BRISTLEBIRD

Dasyornis broadbenti littoralis (Milligan, 1902)

Order PASSERIFORMES   Family MUSCICAPIDAE

                                          Subfamily MALURINAE

STATUS   Endangered, if in fact the subspecies is still extant. It is known
from two coastal localities in the extreme south-west of Western Australia, where
searches for it since 1940 have not proven successful.

DISTRIBUTION   The subspecies was described from Ellensbrook, Western Australia,
and has also been recorded at Cape Naturaliste, a range of less than 50 km of
coastline.   It was last observed in 1940, in coastal thickets west of Mammoth
Cave, and recent searches for it have been in vain (1; G.T. Smith 1975, pers.
comm.).

POPULATION   Unknown, but if the subspecies survives it must certainly be in very
small numbers.   It was last collected in 1906 and last observed in 1940 (1), and
it is probable that its decline predates its discovery and description in 1902.

HABITAT   The most recent observations of the subspecies were made in dense
coastal thicket, but it is not certain this is identical to the habitat in which
it was originally found.   The coastal scrub of south-westernmost Western Australia
has been repeatedly and extensively cleared or burned by man, so that optimum
habitat for this bristlebird may no longer exist (G.T. Smith 1975, pers. comm.).

CONSERVATION MEASURES TAKEN   The species is protected by law, but none of its
presumed habitat is protected.   It has been listed in Appendix 1 of the 1973
Convention on International Trade in Endangered Species of Wild Fauna and Flora.

CONSERVATION MEASURES PROPOSED   None known.

REMARKS   The nominate race, which is found along the coasts of South Australia
and Victoria, is comparatively common and not at risk.

REFERENCES   1.   Serventy, D.L. & Whittell, H.M. 1976.   Birds of
                    Western Australia, 5th ed.   Perth: University of
                    Western Australia Press.

FANOVANA NEWTONIA

Newtonia fanovanae Gyldenstolpe, 1933

Order PASSERIFORMES   Family MUSCICAPIDAE

                                            Subfamily MUSCICAPINAE

STATUS   Indeterminate.   Only one specimen of this endemic Madagascar species
has been collected.   Nothing further is known of it.

DISTRIBUTION   The type specimen was collected in Fanovana forest, which is
traversed by the Tananarive-Tamatave railway, in the central zone of the humid
forest region of eastern Madagascar (1).

POPULATION   Unknown; there are no records of this species other than the type
which was collected in 1931 (2).

HABITAT   Dense humid forest.   The extent of the indigenous forests of
Madagascar continues to decline.

CONSERVATION MEASURES TAKEN   None known.

CONSERVATION MEASURES PROPOSED   Legal protection for most endemic birds has been
recommended to the Malagasy government (K. Curry-Lindahl in litt. to G. Ramanantsoavina, Director, Service des Eaux et Forêts, Chasse et Pêche, Jan. 1973).

REMARKS   It has been suggested that N. fanovanae might be conspecific with the
more widespread and abundant N. brunneicauda, although it is admitted to be the
most distinctive of these small flycatchers (3).

REFERENCES   1.   Rand, A.L. 1936.   The distribution and habits of Madagascar
                    birds.   Bull. Amer. Mus. Nat. Hist. 72: 143-499.
              2.   Gyldenstolpe, N. 1933.   A remarkable new flycatcher from
                    Madagascar.   Arkiv f. Zool. 25B(2): 1-3.
              3.   Milon, P., Petter, J.-J. & Randrianasolo, G. 1973.
                    Faune de Madagascar, Pt. 25 Oiseaux.   Tananarive and
                    Paris: ORSTOM and CNRS.

CHATHAM ISLAND BLACK ROBIN

Petroica traversi (Buller, 1872)

Order PASSERIFORMES   Family MUSCICAPIDAE

                                       Subfamily MUSCICAPINAE

STATUS   Critically endangered. Restricted to one small island in the Chatham
Islands, 800 kilometres east of New Zealand, having been recently transferred from
a smaller island on which the patch of its scrub forest habitat had seriously
deteriorated. This robin presently has the smallest population of any bird
species for which precise figures are known. The future of this precarious
population hangs in the balance.

DISTRIBUTION   Formerly occurred on Chatham, Pitt, Mangere and Little Mangere
islands of the Chatham group, but disappeared from Chatham and Pitt before 1871
and from Mangere when cats were introduced late in the 19th century. It survived
solely on the 16 hectares of Little Mangere (1; 2), until the entire population
was translocated to Mangere in 1976 and 1977 (7).

POPULATION   At one time more widespread and abundant, although early estimates
are lacking. Surveys in 1937 (3) and 1961 (1) suggested a population of 20-35
pairs on Little Mangere. Censuses since 1973, after the entire population had
been color-banded, revealed much lower figures: a total of 6 pairs and 4 unpaired
males in.1973 (4); 4 pairs and 1 unmated bird in 1975; 4 pairs and 3 sub-adults
in early 1976 (J. Flack 1976, pers. comm.), but by late 1976, when the translocation began, only 2 pairs and 3 unpaired males remaining. In 1977, following
successful transfer to a small but rapidly regenerating patch of scrub forest on
Mangere, one female was produced and one male died, and the population then
consisted of 3 pairs and 1 unpaired male (7).

HABITAT   ⁴Low scrub forest. The scrub on Little Mangere (4 ha in extent)
deteriorated from a succession of dry seasons, wind and storms, compounded by the
effects of burrowing by the island's large and highly concentrated petrel
population. Muttonbirders, using helicopters to make illegal harvests of petrels
on Little Mangere in the 1960s, also caused some scrub destruction and, incident-
ally, increased the danger of plant or animal pests being introduced (1; 2). The
patch of scrub forest on Mangere to which the population has been moved is very
small but healthy and supports a rich leaf litter and ample insect food (7).

CONSERVATION MEASURES TAKEN   The species is protected by law. . Mangere Island
was made a Reserve for the Preservation of Flora and Fauna in 1967. Sheep were
removed in 1968 and grassland is gradually being replaced by scrub. The New
Zealand Wildlife Service has undertaken an ambitious revegetation program on
Mangere to speed the recovery of the island as robin habitat (2; 5).
    The related New Zealand Robin P. australis has been the subject of intensive
study by the Wildlife Service, which has provided an insight into problems
associated with the management of the Black Robin and its habitat (6). The
entire surviving population of the robin on Little Mangere was captured and
translocated over a two-year period, 1976 and 1977, to what is believed to be a
healthier patch of its habitat, and one which the species formerly occupied, on
Mangere (7).

CONSERVATION MEASURES PROPOSED   Negotiations between the New Zealand government
and the Maori owners of Little Mangere Island for making the island a reserve
have for the time being broken down because the owners insist on being given
muttonbirding rights, this activity having been made illegal in the Chatham
Islands as a whole.   It would nevertheless be highly desirable for Little Mangere
Island to be made a reserve and for negotiations to be resumed towards that end
(1; 2; 4).

REMARKS   The total population of seven robins surviving on Little Mangere
towards the end of 1976, undoubtedly made the species extremely vulnerable,
subject as it was not only to the vagaries of nature and human interference with
its habitat, but also to possible instability as a result of an inherent lack of
genetic variability.   In these circumstances, the New Zealand Wildlife Service's
translocation of the entire remnant of a species, when it became apparent that
time was running out for it on the only island where it still survived, was a
bold, imaginative and quite unprecedented conservation action.

REFERENCES   1.   Merton, D.V. & Bell, B.D. undated.   Endemic birds of the
Chatham Islands.   New Zealand Wildlife Service.   Unpublished
ms.
2.   Flack, J.A.D. 1975.   The Chatham Island Black Robin,
extinction or survival?   Bull. ICBP 12: 146-150.
3.   Fleming, C.A. 1939.   Birds of the Chatham Islands, Part 2.
Emu 38: 492-509.
4.   Flack, J.A.D. 1974.   Chatham Island Black Robin.   Wildlife -
A review 5: 25-31.
5.   Bell, B.D. 1974.   Mangere Island.   Wildlife - A review 5:
31-34.
6.   Flack, J.A.D. 1973.   Robin research - a progress report.
Wildlife - A review 4: 28-36.
7.   Morris, R.B. 1977.   Black Robin transfers.   Wildlife -
A review 8: 44-48.

TRUK MONARCH

Metabolus rugensis (Hombron and Jacquinot, 1841)

Order   PASSERIFORMES   Family   MUSCICAPIDAE

                                         Subfamily   MONARCHINAE

STATUS   Rare.   Endemic to the Truk group, Caroline Islands, Western Pacific,
where it is far from common, although apparently it is still rather more so than
when it was at its lowest level in 1945.

DISTRIBUTION   The species has been recorded on Moen, Fefan, Fanan, Tol, Dublon,
Udot and Uman islands of the Truk group, the total land surface of which is 95.8
sq. km (1; 2).   Its present distribution is not known with certainty, but is not
believed to be different (R. Owen 1975, pers. comm.).

POPULATION   No estimates have been made.   The species was apparently not
uncommon until World War II, during which it must have suffered a considerable
setback, for in 1945 an observer was unable to find it on the several islands he
visited, which roused concern about its possible extinction (1).   However, by
1957 it had recovered to the point where it was considered to be once again rather
well distributed (2).   By 1975, it was nevertheless still rated as quite rare,
only 4 or 5 having been seen altogether, on the 4 islands of Moen, Uman, Udot and
Tol (R. Owen 1975, pers. comm.).   The striking white plumage, shrill call and
confiding nature of the species make it conspicuous and hence unlikely to be
overlooked (2).

HABITAT   Original forest of the mountain tops, but also the mixture of breadfruit
and coconut groves which now constitutes the dominant vegetation of the high
volcanic islands where the species is found.   The amount of original forest,
still the preferred habitat, is now much reduced (R. Owen 1975, pers. comm.).

CONSERVATION MEASURES TAKEN   The species is now on the U.S. Trust Territories
list of endangered species.

CONSERVATION MEASURES PROPOSED   None known.

REMARKS   This species is the sole representative of the genus Metabolus.
Its single egg clutch gives it a low reproductive potential and renders it more
vulnerable (2).   Status surveys and conservation action on behalf of this and
other endemic birds of the U.S. Trust Territories is long overdue.

REFERENCES   1.   Baker, R.H. 1951.   The avifauna of Micronesia, its
                   origin, evolution and distribution.   Univ. Kansas Pubs.
                   Mus. Nat. Hist. 3(1): 359 pp.
              2.   Brandt, J.H. 1962.   Nests and eggs of the birds of the
                   Truk Islands.   Condor 64: 416-437.

RAROTONGA FLYCATCHER

Pomarea dimidiata (Hartlaub and Finsch, 1871)

Order PASSERIFORMES   Family MUSCICAPIDAE

                                             Subfamily MONARCHINAE

STATUS   Vulnerable.   The species occurs only in the higher valleys of Rarotonga
Island, Cook Islands.   The extent of the forest in which it is found, is
constantly diminishing as a result of lumbering and clearing (1).

DISTRIBUTION   Restricted to forested hillsides, usually bordering higher valleys,
in the 66.8 sq. km island of Rarotonga, where it was at one time more widespread.

POPULATION   The total population was estimated at 50-100 individuals in 1973 (1)
and the flycatcher was still extant in 1976, when one bird thought to belong to
this species was observed.   It has been regarded as rare since at least 1899 (2).

HABITAT   Forest on the slopes of hills and valleys at higher altitudes (1).

CONSERVATION MEASURES TAKEN   A survey of the status of the birds of the Cook
Islands was carried out in 1973.

CONSERVATION MEASURES PROPOSED   Establishment, in the mountain forests, of
reserves or parks totalling two or three thousand hectares in area, in order to
protect this habitat from further deterioration (1).

REFERENCES   1.   Holyoak, D.T. 1973.   Report to the Premier, Cook Islands.
                    Unpublished.
               2.   Turbott, E.G. 1977.   Rarotongan birds with notes on
                    land bird status.   Notornis 24: 149-157.

EIAO FLYCATCHER

Pomarea iphis fluxa Murphy and Mathews, 1928

Order PASSERIFORMES   Family MUSCICAPIDAE

                                              Subfamily MONARCHINAE

STATUS   Indeterminate. Not reported from Eiao, Marquesas Islands, since its
discovery half a century ago.

DISTRIBUTION   Restricted to the 52 sq. km island of Eiao in the Marquesas (1-3).

POPULATION   In 1922 members of the Whitney South Sea Expedition collected 12
specimens of this subspecies on Eiao and it was considered fairly common within
the restricted area of forest at that time (2). It was not seen on a two-day
visit to the island in 1929 (4) or during a three-hour visit in 1975, but it may
well still survive (3).

HABITAT   Forest, which was never extensive on Eiao; only scraps remain today.
There are more than a thousand sheep and several hundred pigs on the island and
they have contributed to the severe degradation of its vegetation. Rats of
unknown species and domestic fowls are also present, although at present the
island has no human inhabitants (3; 7).

CONSERVATION MEASURES TAKEN   Hunting of all bird species in French Polynesia
was prohibited in 1967. Eiao was accorded protected status in 1971, but soon
afterwards became the scene of intense military activity as an alternative site
to islands in the Tuamotus for the French nuclear testing program (5; 6).

CONSERVATION MEASURES PROPOSED   Elimination of sheep and pigs from Eiao has been
recommended to the Service de l'Economie Rurale of the Society Islands (3).

REMARKS   The population of the nominate race of this species on Uahuka, P. i.
iphis, is still relatively large, having been estimated in 1975 at 900 ± 100
pairs (3).

REFERENCES   1. Murphy, R.C. & Mathews, G.M. 1928. Birds collected during
                  the Whitney South Sea Expedition, V. Amer. Mus. Novit. 337.
              2. Holyoak, D.T. 1975. Les oiseaux des Îles Marquises.
                  l'Oiseau et R.F.O. 45: 207-233, 341-366.
              3. Thibault, J.-C. Undated. Fragilité et protection de
                  l'avifaune en Polynésie Francaise. Report to ICBP.
              4. Fisher, A.K. & Wetmore, A. 1931. Report on birds recorded
                  by the Pinchot Expedition of 1929 to the Caribbean and
                  Pacific. Proc. U.S. Nat. Mus. 79(10): 1-66.
              5. Holyoak, D.T. 1973. Polynesian land birds face H-bombs
                  and malaria. New Scientist 57: 288-290.
              6. Decker, B.F. 1973. Unique dry-island biota under official
                  protection in northwestern Marquesas Islands (Iles Marquises).
                  Biol. Cons. 5: 66-67.
              7. Holyoak, D.T. & Thibault, J.-C. 1977. Habitats, morphologie
                  et interactions écologiques des oiseaux insectivores de
                  Polynésie Orientale. l'Oiseau et R.F.O. 47: 115-147.

HIVAOA FLYCATCHER

Pomarea mendozae mendozae (Hartlaub, 1854)

Order PASSERIFORMES   Family MUSCICAPIDAE

                                        Subfamily MONARCHINAE

STATUS   Endangered. Recorded from two of the Marquesas Islands, South Pacific,
but now barely surviving on one.   The precise reasons for its decline are unknown
but are probably related to the introduction of several browsing mammals and the
considerable effect they have had on the native vegetation.

DISTRIBUTION   At one time included Tahuata (52 sq. km) and Hivaoa (241 sq. km) in
the Marquesas Islands (1), but now only the latter supports a residual population
(J.-C. Thibault 1975, pers. comm.).

POPULATION   The subspecies was considered fairly common in 1922 (1) but was not
seen during brief surveys of Hivaoa in 1929 (2) or 1958 (3).   In 1975, it was
definitely no longer present on Tahuata and no more than a few pairs were thought
to survive on Hivaoa (J.-C. Thibault 1975, pers. comm.).

HABITAT   Wooded valleys, those at lower elevations having probably been
particularly favoured by the species in the past.   The forests of the Marquesas
have suffered degradation as a result of overgrazing by introduced cattle, sheep,
goats and pigs, and efforts to bring this under control have not been systematic
or effectual (1; 6; 7).

CONSERVATION MEASURES TAKEN   A careful survey of the avifauna of the Marquesas
Islands has recently been undertaken.

CONSERVATION MEASURES PROPOSED   The control of introduced mammals has been
advocated as essential if the remaining forested areas of the Marquesas are to be
saved (1; 6).

REMARKS   Three other subspecies of this flycatcher occur in the Marquesas:
P. m. nukuhivae, now possibly extinct on Nukuhiva; P. m. motanensis, which was
quite common (300 ± 50 pairs) on Mohotani in 1975; and P. m. mira which has been
reported as present in most valleys of Uapou, with a population of about 150 ± 50
pairs (4; 6).

REFERENCES   1. Holyoak, D.T. 1975.   Les oiseaux des Iles Marquises.
                  l'Oiseau et R.F.O. 45: 207-233, 341-366.
              2. Fisher, A.K. & Wetmore, A. 1931.   Report on birds collected
                  by the Pinchot Expedition of 1929 to the Caribbean and Pacific.
                  Proc. U.S. Nat. Mus. 79(10): 1-66.
              3. King, J.E. 1958.   Some observations on the birds of Tahiti
                  and the Marquesas Islands.   Elepaio 19: 14-17.
              4. Sachet, M.H., Schafer, P.A. & Thibault, J.-C. 1975.
                  Mohotani: une île protégée aux Marquises.   Bull. Soc. Etudes
                  Océan. 16: 557-568.
              5. Thibault, J.-C. 1973.   Notes ornithologiques polynésiennes.
                  II, Les Iles Marquises.   Alauda 41: 301-316.
              6. Thibault, J.-C.   Undated report to ICBP.   Fragilité et
                  protection de l'avifaune en Polynésie Française.
              7. Holyoak, D.T. & Thibault, J.-C. 1977.   Habitats, morphologie
                  et interactions écologiques des oiseaux insectivores de
                  Polynésie Orientale.   l'Oiseau et R.F.O. 47: 115-147.

UAPOU FLYCATCHER

Pomarea mendozae mira Murphy and Mathews, 1928

Order PASSERIFORMES   Family MUSCICAPIDAE

                                            Subfamily MONARCHINAE

STATUS   Rare. Restricted to one island in the Marquesas Islands, South Pacific, this subspecies is still fairly wide-ranging there but has a small population, which has declined in the past half century.

DISTRIBUTION   This subspecies is known only from the island of Uapou, in the Marquesas, which has an area of 104 sq. km (1; 2).

POPULATION   There are grounds for believing that there has been a decline in population of this subspecies between the time of its discovery in 1922, although no precise indication of its numbers was given, and 1975 when a total of 150 ± 50 pairs was estimated to be present (1).

HABITAT   Wooded valleys and now only the upper reaches at fairly high elevations (1; 2; 5). Most of the forests in the Marquesas have suffered severe degradation as a result of grazing, browsing and trampling by abundant wild cattle, goats and pigs.   All these forms of domestic stock are to be found on Uapou and the wood-lands which once covered 90 percent of the island now cover only about 15 percent (3).

CONSERVATION MEASURES TAKEN   Hunting of birds was prohibited in French Polynesia in 1967.

CONSERVATION MEASURES PROPOSED   Hohoi valley, an area seldom visited by the human inhabitants of Uapou, which supports a population of this subspecies and other endemic birds, has been recommended to the government of French Polynesia as a suitable site for a protected area or reserve (1; 2).

REMARKS   The three other subspecies of this flycatcher in the Marquesas are: P. m. mendozae of Hivaoa and Tahuata (now absent from the latter and very rare on the former); P. m. nukuhivae of Nukuhiva (possibly extinct) (1-3); and P. m. motanensis, which is common (300 ± 50 pairs) on Mohotani (3; 4).

REFERENCES   1.   Thibault, J.-C. Undated.   Fragilité et protection de
                    l'avifaune en Polynésie Française.   Report to ICBP.
              2.   Thibault, J.-C. 1973.   Notes ornithologiques polynésiennes.
                    II. Les Iles Marquises.   Alauda 41: 301-316.
              3.   Holyoak, D.T. 1975.   Les oiseaux des îles Marquises.
                    l'Oiseau et R.F.O. 45: 207-233, 341-366.
              4.   Sachet, M.H., Schafer, P.A. & Thibault, J.-C. 1975.
                    Mohotani: une île protégée aux Marquises.   Bull. Soc. Etudes
                    Océan. 16: 557-568.
              5.   Holyoak, D.T. & Thibault, J.-C. 1977.   Habitats, morphologie
                    et interactions écologiques des oiseaux insectivores de
                    Polynésie Orientale.   l'Oiseau et R.F.O. 47: 115-147.

NUKUHIVA FLYCATCHER

Pomarea mendozae nukuhivae Murphy and Mathews, 1928

Order PASSERIFORMES   Family MUSCICAPIDAE

                                            Subfamily MONARCHINAE

STATUS   Endangered, probably extinct.   In 1922 this subspecies was considered
scarce on Nukuhiva, Marquesas Islands, and it could not be found during a careful
search in 1972.

DISTRIBUTION   Formerly presumably more widespread on Nukuhiva.   In 1922
restricted to valleys at the western end of the island, where if it still exists
it would be most likely to be found (1-3).

POPULATION   The species was already scarce and very localized in 1922 and three
weeks of searching in 1972 produced no sighting (3), although the local inhabitants
stated that they had seen it several years previously (4).

HABITAT   Wooded valleys in which, in the past, the subspecies was probably more
abundant at lower elevations (3; 7).   Excessive browsing by feral goats and
grazing by cattle have seriously degraded these forested areas (4).

CONSERVATION MEASURES TAKEN   A thorough if fruitless search for this subspecies
was made in 1972 (3).   Hunting of birds had been prohibited in 1967 throughout
French Polynesia.

CONSERVATION MEASURES PROPOSED   None known.

REMARKS   The three other subspecies in the Marquesas are: P. m. mendozae of
Hivaoa and Tahuata, P. m. motanensis of Mohotani and P. m. mira of Uapou.   The
first has now disappeared from Tahuata and is very rare on Hivaoa (4); the second
was the most abundant bird breeding on Mohotani in 1975 (300 ± 50 pairs); and the
third is still present in most valleys of Uapou, with a population of about 150 ±
50 pairs (4; 5).   The first and the third are included in this volume.

REFERENCES   1.   Murphy, R.C. & Mathews, G.M. 1928.   Birds collected during
                    the Whitney South Sea Expedition.   V. Amer. Mus. Novit. 337.
              2.   Holyoak, D.T. 1973.   Polynesian land birds face H-bombs
                    and malaria.   New Scientist 57: 288-290.
              3.   Holyoak, D.T. 1975.   Les oiseaux des Îles Marquises.
                    l'Oiseau et R.F.O. 45: 207-233, 341-366.
              4.   Thibault, J.-C. Undated.   Fragilité et protection de l'avifaune
                    en Polynésie Francaise.   Report to ICBP.
              5.   Sachet, M.H., Schafer, P.A. & Thibault, J.-C. 1975.
                    Mohotani: une Île protégée aux Marquises.   Bull. Soc.
                    Etudes Océan. 16: 557-568.
              6.   Thibault, J.-C. 1973.   Notes ornithologique polynésiennes.
                    II. Les Iles Marquises.   Alauda 41: 301-316.
              7.   Holyoak, D.T. & Thibault, J.-C. 1977.   Habitats, morphologie
                    et interactions écologiques des oiseaux insectivores de
                    Polynésie Orientale.   l'Oiseau et R.F.O. 47: 115-147.

TAHITI FLYCATCHER

Pomarea nigra nigra (Sparrman, 1786)

Order PASSERIFORMES   Family MUSCICAPIDAE

                                       Subfamily MONARCHINAE

STATUS   Endangered.   Recent sightings of this subspecies confirm its continued
existence on Tahiti, Society Islands.   The causes of the decline of this and other
endemic land birds of these islands are poorly understood.

DISTRIBUTION   Restricted to Tahiti, Society Islands, where this subspecies is
very locally distributed in the inland forests (1).   It was recently found to be
still present in the mountains behind Papeete, on Mt. Marau (2).

POPULATION   The subspecies has been considered very rare since the beginning of
this century.   About 20 specimens were collected in 1920 and 1921 by the Whitney
South Sea Expedition (1), two sightings were made in 1937 (S.D. Ripley 1974, pers.
comm.) and one was seen after much searching in 1972 (1).   Still more recently a
population of several dozen pairs was found (2; 3).

HABITAT   Montane forest in valleys of the interior on Tahiti, at elevations of
between 700 and 950 m (4).

CONSERVATION MEASURES TAKEN   The subspecies is protected by law from killing or
capture.

CONSERVATION MEASURES PROPOSED   Additional surveys to determine distribution and
population size of this subspecies (2).   Mt. Marau is in the process of being made
into a reserve (3).

REMARKS   Pomarea n. tabuensis from Tongatabu, Tonga Islands, became extinct in
1773.   The other subspecies of this species, P. n. pomarea, which was included in
the previous edition of the Red Data Book, was confined to Maupiti, Society Islands,
where the unique type was collected in 1823.   A recent survey confirmed its
extinction and the local inhabitants no longer have a name for the species in their
language (2).

REFERENCES   1.   Holyoak, D.T. 1974.   Les oiseaux des Îles de la Societé.
                   l'Oiseau et R.F.O. 44: 1–27, 153–181.
              2.   Thibault, J.-C. 1974.   Le Peuplement Avien des Iles de
                   la Société (Polynésie).   Papeete: Mus. Nat. Hist. Natur.
                   Antenne de Tahiti.
              3.   Thibault, J.-C. Undated.   Fragilité et protection de
                   l'avifaune en Polynésie Française.   Report to ICBP.
              4.   Holyoak, D.T. & Thibault, J.-C. 1977.   Habitats, morphologie
                   et interactions écologiques des oiseaux insectivores de
                   Polynésie Orientale.   l'Oiseau et R.F.O. 47: 115–147.

MAURITIUS PARADISE FLYCATCHER or COQ DE BOIS

Terpsiphone bourbonnensis desolata (Salomonsen, 1933)

Order PASSERIFORMES   Family MUSCICAPIDAE

                                                     Subfamily MONARCHINAE

STATUS   Rare.   Uncommon and restricted in range but not immediately endangered.
The main threats to the subspecies seem to be habitat destruction as well as nest
predation by introduced birds and mammals and, because of its extreme tameness,
human persecution.

DISTRIBUTION   Confined to the island of Mauritius in the Indian Ocean, where it
extends along the east coast from Roches Noires south to the Bambou Mountain Range
(in native forests and isolated patches of second growth exotics); along the south
coast in several wooded river valleys from Savannah west to Baie du Cap; in the
montane evergreen forests from the Savanne Mountains and the southern scarp of the
upland plateau north to Montagne du Rempart; and in the Moka Mountain Range (1;
S. Temple 1976, pers. comm.).   The subspecies formerly ranged throughout the
forests of Mauritius.

POPULATION   At one time abundant both in forests and in gardens (2), the subspecies is now much less common and is somewhat locally distributed, although the
total population still numbers in the thousands (1; S. Temple 1976, pers. comm.).

HABITAT   Indigenous montane evergreen forest, also undisturbed patches of second
growth exotics and orchards.   The flycatcher is most often seen in river valleys
or in wet areas where insects abound (1; S. Temple 1976, pers. comm.).

CONSERVATION MEASURES TAKEN   The subspecies is fully protected by a law which
forbids the killing or capture of native birds.   A large portion of its range in
the south-western corner of the island is within officially declared reserves.
Ecological studies were carried out over the period 1972-1975 for the purpose of
determining the bird's status and requirements (3).

CONSERVATION MEASURES PROPOSED   Continued protection and management of the
remnant areas of indigenous evergreen forest are essential for the Paradise
Flycatcher's survival.   In 1974, a management plan for a system of nature reserves
and national parks was submitted to the Mauritius Government (4).

REMARKS   These flycatchers could well exist in many other regions of the island
but ignorant persecution inhibits their spread to any area close to human
activities.   The nominate subspecies, T. b. bourbonnensis of Réunion, is not at
risk, although,when the species as a whole was included in the previous edition of
the Red Data Book, it was described as depleted.

REFERENCES   1.   Newton, R. 1958.   Ornithological notes on Mauritius and
                    the Cargados Carajos Archipelago.   Proc. Roy. Soc. Arts
                    Sci. Mauritius 2: 39-71.
              2.   Meinertzhagen, R. 1912.   On the birds of Mauritius.
                    Ibis (9)6: 82-108.
              3.   Temple, S. 1975.   World Wildlife Yearbook, 1974-75, pp.
                    210-212.   Morges: World Wildlife Fund.
              4.   Procter, J. & Salm, R. 1974.   Conservation in Mauritius, 1974.
                    Unpublished IUCN Report to the Mauritius Government.

SEYCHELLES BLACK PARADISE FLYCATCHER

Terpsiphone corvina (Newton, 1867)

Order PASSERIFORMES   Family MUSCICAPIDAE

                                        Subfamily MONARCHINAE

STATUS   Endangered.   Restricted to a portion of one island in the Seychelles
Archipelago, where its numbers are very low.   It is a tame species and often nests
near human habitation, where in the past it has suffered seriously from disturbance.
But recent efforts in conservation education have generated an attitude of steward-
ship from which it has profited.

DISTRIBUTION   Restricted to the Seychelles, the species has been recorded from
Praslin, Marianne, Curieuse, Felicité and La Digue, but is now confined to La
Digue (1), having last been recorded on Marianne in 1892 (1), on Curieuse in 1906
and Felicité in 1936 (2).   A single bird and a recently built nest were found at
Baie St. Anne on Praslin in 1977 (10).   On La Digue it mainly nests on the lowland
plateau along the west coast (an area of 162 ha), but moves farther up the hill-
sides at other times (1; 8).   Individual pairs also breed at Anse Severe, Grand
Anse and Anse Gaulettes (10).

POPULATION   No early estimates were made, but the population has probably
declined in proportion to the number of islands inhabited.   In 1959 it was said to
be plentiful on La Digue (4); by 1965 only 28 birds could be found (5) and in 1969,
29 were counted, but the total population was estimated at 45 to 50 (8).   The
estimate had risen to 50 to 80 in 1971, the increase no doubt attributable to the
combination of a conservation education campaign on La Digue and a 1 rupee fine and
confiscation of weapon imposed on children threatening the flycatchers with
catapults or slingshots (3), and remained at about the same level, 25-35 pairs, in
1977 (10).

HABITAT   Lowland forest, which has been destroyed on most islands, but some of
which survives on La Digue and is to be secured through legal protection (6).
Terminalia and Calophyllum trees are favoured by the birds for nesting and the
proximity of a water source appears to be essential and the limiting factor (9; 10).

CONSERVATION MEASURES TAKEN   The species is protected by law from hunting or
capture and a warden is employed by the Seychelles Government and ICBP to supervise
its conservation on La Digue.   The inclusion of conservation education in the
syllabus of local schools has been effective in reducing disturbance to the
species (3).

CONSERVATION MEASURES PROPOSED   It has been suggested that La Digue should be
declared an Area of Outstanding Natural Beauty and that the habitat of the Black
Paradise Flycatcher on the west coast should become a Special Reserve (6).
Recommendations arising from a year-long study of the flycatcher under the
auspices of ICBP in 1977-78, will probably include conservation and management of
portions of the western plateau (9).

REMARKS   La Digue is the most densely populated of the Seychelles and the flycatcher frequently nests near human habitation or along paths, but it is apparently
undisturbed by and tolerant of nearby human activity (7).

<u>REFERENCES</u>

1. Penny, M. 1968.   Endemic birds of the Seychelles.
    <u>Oryx</u> 9:   267-275.
2. Penny, M. 1974.   <u>The Birds of Seychelles and the</u>
    <u>Outlying Islands</u>.   New York: Taplinger Publishing Co.;
    London: Collins.
3. Beamish, Sir Tufton, 1972.   The Paradise Flycatcher,
    Seychelles.   <u>Biol. Cons</u>. 4:   311-313.
4. Crook, J.H. 1960.   The present status of certain rare
    land birds of the Seychelles Islands.   Seychelles
    Government Bulletin. 5 pp.
5. Gaymer, R., Blackman, R.A.A., Dawson, P.G., Penny, M.
    & Penny, C.M. 1969.   The endemic birds of Seychelles.
    <u>Ibis</u> 111:   157-176.
6. Seychelles Government, 1971.   Conservation policy in the
    Seychelles.   Seychelles Government Printer.
7. Fraser, W. 1972.   Notes on <u>Terpsiphone</u> <u>corvina</u>.
    <u>Ibis</u> 114:   399-401.
8. Fayan, M. 1970.   The plight of the Paradise Flycatcher.
    <u>Journ. Seychelles Soc</u>. 7:   8-11.
9. Watson, J. 1977.   Annual report to World Wildlife Fund,
    Project No. 1590.
10. Watson, J. 1977.   The Seychelles Paradise-Flycatcher
    (<u>Terpsiphone</u> <u>corvina</u>).   Progress Report No. 2 to ICBP.

KABYLIAN NUTHATCH

Sitta ledanti Vielliard, 1976

Order PASSERIFORMES   Family SITTIDAE

STATUS   Rare. First described in 1975, when a tiny population was discovered in
a relict stand of conifers on the top of a mountain ridge in Algeria.

DISTRIBUTION   Known only from the summit ridge and shaded valleys between 1400
and 2,000 m elevation, of Djebel Babor, Little Kabylie range, Algeria, about 20 km
south of the Mediterranean Gulf of Bejaia (formerly Bougie). It has not been
found on Tababor, the neighboring mountain ridge, 3-4 km to the north, although it
may once have occurred there. (1-6).

POPULATION   Nine or 10 pairs occupied the ridge top or about one pair per 4 ha
of the oak-fir forest, and it was estimated that there were an additional 10-12
pairs in portions of the oak-cedar-wooded valleys, at the lower density of about
one pair per 10 ha. The total population is thus thought to be about 20 pairs
(6).

HABITAT   The 4 km long ridge and shaded valleys of Djebel Babor are covered by a
remarkable relict forest, about 1200 ha in extent, dominated by the oak Quercus
faginea, the endemic Algerian fir Abies numidica and Atlas cedar Cedrus atlantica.
This nuthatch occurs most abundantly in mixed forest, almost never in pure stands
of cedar (6). The climate is cold and humid, with precipitation mainly in the
form of heavy winter snowfall. Other endemic species of the Djebel Babor include
a number of plants and at least one insect. The relict forest suffers from over-
browsing by goats and cattle during the summer months, regeneration being
insufficient to replace losses from this cause and from winter storm damage (5).

CONSERVATION MEASURES TAKEN   Djebel Babor has been made into a national park, as
the result of the petitions of ornithologists and conservation organizations for
protection to be accorded to this newly discovered species (4).

CONSERVATION MEASURES PROPOSED   Promotion of forest regeneration by effectively
preventing the browsing of the forest by domestic livestock (5).

REFERENCES   1. Vielliard, J. 1976. La Sittelle Kabyle. Alauda 44: 351-352.
              2. Vielliard, J. 1976. Un nouveau témoin relictuel de la
                  spéciation dans la zone mediterranéanne: Sitta ledanti
                  (Aves: Sittidae). Comptes Rendues Acad. Sci. 283D: 1193-1195.
              3. Burnier, E. 1976. Une nouvelle espèce de l'avifaune
                  paléarctique: la sittelle Kabyle Sitta ledanti. Nos Oiseaux
                  33(8): 337-340.
              4. Géroudet, P. 1976. A propos de Sittelle kabyle. Nos Oiseaux
                  33(8): 340-342.
              5. Vielliard, J. 1978. Le Djebel Babor et sa Sittelle Sitta
                  ledanti Vielliard 1976. Alauda 46: 1-42.
              6. Ledant, J.-P. & Jacobs, P. 1977. La Sittelle Kabyle (Sitta
                  ledanti): données nouvelles sur la biologie. Aves 14:
                  233-242.

AMANI SUNBIRD

Anthreptes pallidigaster Sclater and Moreau, 1935

Order PASSERIFORMES   Family NECTARINIIDAE

STATUS   Rare.   Confined to two forested areas in East Africa, and rare in each.
Forest destruction constitutes the principal threat to this species.

DISTRIBUTION   This sunbird has been recorded in two widely separated localities:
evergreen forest up to 900 m elevation in the East Usambara Mountains, north-
eastern Tanzania, where its habitat covers no more than 78 sq. km (1; S. Stuart
1977, pers. comm.); and, 320 km to the north, the lowland Arabuko-Sokoke Forest,
Kilifi District, Kenya, where it occupies no more than about 70 sq. km of Brachystegia woodland (1; 2; 6).   In both areas forest destruction has caused a
reduction in its range (3).   The local movements of the species are still not
clearly understood (4; S. Stuart 1977, pers. comm.).

POPULATION   Unknown, but likely to be low.   In 1977, flocks of up to 18 were
observed near Amani, East Usambaras (5).

HABITAT   This sunbird is primarily a bird of lowland forests and is found only
in the forests of the lower slopes and foothills of the East Usambaras.   This type
of forest has been and doubtless always will be more prone to destruction and at a
more rapid rate than true montane forest (S. Stuart, P. Britton 1977, pers. comms).
In a 195 sq. km area around Amani, 49 percent was forested in 1954, but only 38
percent still consisted of undisturbed forest in 1977 (5).

CONSERVATION MEASURES TAKEN   Legal protection has been given to the species in
Kenya.   Within the 400 sq. km of the Arabuko-Sokoke Forest Reserve, a 40 sq. km
tract, which contains part of the habitat of this species, is a nature reserve in
which no disturbance is permitted (2).

CONSERVATION MEASURES PROPOSED   Enlargement of the nature reserve within the
Arabuko-Sokoke Forest Reserve to 60 sq. km has been recommended: it would then
include representative samples of each of the forest types essential to the
endangered bird species of the forest (P. Britton 1977, pers. comm.).   Portions of
the Usambara Mountain forests have similarly been recommended to the Tanzanian
government for protection as nature reserves (S. Stuart 1977, pers. comm.).

REFERENCES   1.   Hall, B.P. & Moreau, R.E. 1962.   A study of the rare birds
                   of Africa.   Bull. Brit. Mus.(Nat. Hist.)Zool. 8(7):   315-378.
              2.   Britton, P.L. 1976.   Primary forestland destruction now
                   critical.   Africana 5(12):   i-ii.
              3.   Brown, L. Undated.   A report on threatened bird species in
                   East Africa.   East African Wildlife Society.
              4.   Moreau, R.E. & W.M. 1937.   Biological and other notes on
                   some East African birds, Part II.   Ibis (14)1:   321-345.
              5.   Stuart, S.N. & Hutton, J.M. (eds) 1977.   The avifauna of the
                   East Usambara Mountains, Tanzania.   Cambridge University
                   expedition report.
              6.   Turner, D.A. 1977.   Status and distribution of the East African
                   endemic birds.   Scopus 1:   2-11.

PONAPE GREATER WHITE-EYE

Rukia longirostra (Takatsukasa and Yamashina, 1931)

Order PASSERIFORMES   Family ZOSTEROPIDAE

STATUS   Rare.   Confined to Ponape, Caroline Islands, Western Pacific, where its
population is very small.   The causes of its rarity are unknown.

DISTRIBUTION   Ponape Island (334 sq. km), where nothing much is known about the
distribution of this species, except that it occurs locally in the mountains of
the interior (1; 2).

POPULATION   No estimates have been attempted, but all who have sought this
species agree it is rare, although few were dissuaded by its rarity from collecting
as many specimens as they could.   Since World War II, one of four observed was
collected in 1948 (1), two were collected in 1956 (2) and in 1975 it was seen on
several occasions during a week's survey (R. Owen 1975, pers. comm.).   There is
no indication of a decline.

HABITAT   Primary and secondary forest on hills and mountains.   In 1931, seven
were collected in a single flowering gum-tree at 610 m elevation (1).   Although
there is still a considerable amount of forest on Ponape, none of it is protected.

CONSERVATION MEASURES TAKEN   Protected under the U.S. Endangered Species Act of
1973 and also included in the U.S. Trust Territories list of endangered species.

CONSERVATION MEASURES PROPOSED   None additional known.

REMARKS   While it appears this species is marginally more numerous than its
congeners R. oleaginea of Yap and R. ruki of Truk, it is still at serious risk.
Status surveys and habitat protection for the many endemic birds of the U.S. Trust
Territories are long overdue.   This species was included in the previous edition
of the Red Data Book under the name of Rukia sanfordi (Mayr 1931), but Takatsukasa
and Yamashina's name has priority.

REFERENCES   1.   Baker, R.D. 1951.   The avifauna of Micronesia, its origin,
                    evolution and distribution, pp. 334 and 335.   Univ. Kansas
                    Pubs. Mus. Nat. Hist. 3(1):   359 pp.
              2.   Mees, G.F. 1969.   A systematic review of the Indo-
                    Australian Zosteropidae (Part III).   Zool. Verh. 102.

TRUK GREATER WHITE-EYE

Rukia ruki (Hartert, 1897)

Order PASSERIFORMES   Family ZOSTEROPIDAE

STATUS   Endangered.   Apparently restricted to one island of the Truk group in
the Caroline Islands, Western Pacific, where it is very local.   There is no
evidence of a decline in this species, yet its total numbers must be very low
indeed.

DISTRIBUTION   This white-eye has only been observed or collected near the top of
Mt. Winibot on the 34.2 sq. km Tol Island, in the Truk group (1; 2).

POPULATION   Not known precisely, but certainly very small.   Presumably it has
always been so, for collectors who spent 14 months on Truk in the early 1870s (1)
and 2½ years there between 1957 and 1960 (3) failed to find it.   That the species
still exists was last confirmed by a sighting of 3 individuals in 1975, when a
week's survey of the Truk archipelago was undertaken (R. Owen 1975, pers. comm.).
Previous to that, there had been no report of the species since before World War II.

HABITAT   Primary forest of mountain tops, of very limited extent in the Truk
islands and in no way protected.   It still, however, occurs on several of the high
islands of the group but apparently only the small (12 ha) patch of forest
remaining on Mt. Winibot, which dominates Tol, the largest and highest of the
Truk islands, provides a home for this species (1; 3).

CONSERVATION MEASURES TAKEN   The Truk Greater White-eye is on the U.S. Trust
Territories list of endangered species.   This means that it is protected by the
U.S. Trust Territories Endangered Species Act of 1975, which prohibits the taking
or killing of endangered species.

CONSERVATION MEASURES PROPOSED   The top 100 m of Mt. Winibot has been recommended
as a conservation area (4).

REMARKS   It is deplorable that the habitat of what is one of the world's rarest
species is presently unprotected; comprehensive surveys and prompt conservation
action are needed if this and other endemic birds of the U.S. Trust Territories
are to have any chance of survival.   There are three relict species in the genus
Rukia, each confined to an island group in the Western Pacific and all sufficiently
rare to be regarded as at some risk, though only R. ruki from Truk and R. longirostra from Ponape are presently listed in this volume; the Yap R. oleaginea
remains fairly common (H.D. Pratt 1978, pers. comm.) and does not yet call for
inclusion.

REFERENCES   1.   Mees, G.F. 1969.   A systematic review of the Indo-Australian
                    Zosteropidae (Part III).   Zool. Verh. 102.
              2.   Baker, R.H. 1951.   The avifauna of Micronesia, its origin,
                    evolution and distribution, pp. 334 and 335.   Univ. Kansas
                    Pubs. Mus. Nat. Hist., 3(1):   359 pp.
              3.   Brandt, J.H. 1962.   Nests and eggs of the birds of the Truk
                    Islands.   Condor 64:   416-437.
              4.   Douglas, G. 1969.   Draft check list of Pacific Ocean islands.
                    Micronesica 5:   327-463.

WHITE-BREASTED SILVER-EYE

Zosterops albogularis Gould, 1837

Order PASSERIFORMES   Family ZOSTEROPIDAE

STATUS   Critically endangered.   Occurs on Norfolk Island (35 sq. km) in the
south-west Pacific Ocean, where it is restricted to the small remaining area of
indigenous forest.   The population is very small, on the verge of extinction.

DISTRIBUTION   Apparently always confined to the indigenous rainforest on Norfolk
Island, which once covered most of the island.   It is now restricted to the 405
remaining hectares in the Mount Pitt reserve, where it is very rare and local (1;
G. Mees 1974, pers. comm.).

POPULATION   This species has apparently never been common (1).   In 1962 it was
seen three times, possibly three different birds; in 1968 a pair was seen (2); and
in 1969 single birds were seen on two occasions.   The records in 1962 and 1969
were made during the course of two-week-long surveys specifically directed towards
this species and its two congeners on Norfolk Island.   An estimate of "considerably
less than 50 individuals" in 1962 is now viewed as correct but possibly over-
optimistic (1; G. Mees 1974, pers. comm.).

HABITAT   The Silver-eye is only known to have frequented the indigenous forest,
all of which except for one area of 405 hectares is badly degraded from its natural
state (3).

CONSERVATION MEASURES TAKEN   The species is protected from shooting except under
licence and now only occurs in the Mt. Pitt reserve, where however some lumbering
still takes place (3).

CONSERVATION MEASURES PROPOSED   A National Park in the Mt. Pitt reserve has been
proposed, but even if the recommendation were implemented immediately, it is
doubtful whether it will save this species from extinction, although at least it
would not speed the process.

REMARKS   This species is of considerable scientific interest as representing the
earliest of three successive colonizations of Norfolk Island by white-eyes, of
which the most recent may only have taken place after the greater part of the
native forest had been cleared.   Interactions between the three congeners may have
caused the decline and apparently impending demise of Z. albogularis, but predation
by rats may also have been a contributory factor.

REFERENCES   1.   Mees, G.F. 1969.   A systematic review of the Indo-Australian
                    Zosteropidae (Part III).   Zool. Verh. 102, p. 120.
              2.   Smithers, C.N. & Disney, H.J. de S. 1969.   The distribution
                    of terrestrial and freshwater birds on Norfolk Island.
                    Austral. Zool. 15:   127-140.
              3.   Turner, J.S., Smithers, C.N. & Hoogland, R.D. 1968.
                    The conservation of Norfolk Island.   Austral. Cons.
                    Found. Special Pub. No. 1.

ROTA BRIDLED WHITE-EYE

Zosterops conspicillata rotensis Takatsukasa and Yamashina, 1931

Order PASSERIFORMES   Family ZOSTEROPIDAE

STATUS   Indeterminate.   Restricted to one island in the Marianas, western
Pacific, where, according to a recent report, it has become much reduced in
abundance during the last three decades.

DISTRIBUTION   The island of Rota (85 sq. km) in the Mariana group.   The past
distribution of the subspecies on Rota is unknown, but by 1976 it appeared to be
restricted to patches of forest on the Sabana Plateau and was entirely absent from
lowland areas (1).

POPULATION   In 1946 this white-eye was numerous on Rota (2) but by 1976 it had
become rare and local, although an estimate based on six days of observations
suggested that the total population might be of the order of several hundred.

HABITAT   In 1976, the subspecies was found only in the scrubby Pandanus woods of
the upland plateau, where extensive clearing for agriculture has taken place.
However, Rota still supports a substantial native forest cover compared with the
other southern Mariana islands.   It has been suggested that the introduced Black
Drongo Dicrurus macrocercus, which is now common, particularly in the lowlands, may
be partly responsible for the decline of the white-eye.

CONSERVATION MEASURES TAKEN   None known.

CONSERVATION MEASURES PROPOSED   An investigation of the causes of decline of
the subspecies (1).

REMARKS   Five other subspecies, found in Palau, the Caroline Islands and other
islands of the southern Marianas, are not at risk.

REFERENCES   1.   Pratt, H.D., Berrett, D.G. & Bruner, P.L. 1976.
                   Observations on the birds of the southern Marianas.
                   Unpublished ms.
              2.   Baker, R.H. 1951.   The avifauna of Micronesia, its origin,
                   evolution and distribution.   Univ. Kansas Pubs. Nat. Hist.,
                   3(1): 359 pp.

GIZO WHITE-EYE

Zosterops luteirostris luteirostris Hartert, 1904

Order PASSERIFORMES   Family ZOSTEROPIDAE

STATUS   Endangered.   Restricted to one small island in the Solomons, south-west
Pacific, on which its forest habitat has suffered extensive destruction.

DISTRIBUTION   Gizo Island (35 sq. km), central Solomon Islands.

POPULATION   This subspecies was presumably once common and widespread on Gizo,
although no estimate of its numbers exists.   Eighteen specimens were collected in
1927 and 1928 (1).   In 1974, following the destruction of much of the forest on
the island, only a few parties of white-eyes could be found (J. Diamond 1977, pers.
comm. to S.D. Ripley).

HABITAT   Lowland forest.   Prior to 1974, most of this forest on Gizo had been
chopped down, or killed off by poisoning, by the Solomon Islands' Forestry
Department (J. Diamond 1977, pers. comm. to S.D. Ripley).

CONSERVATION MEASURES TAKEN   None known.

CONSERVATION MEASURES PROPOSED   None known.

REMARKS   The other subspecies Z. l. splendida of nearby Ganonga Island is not
known to be at risk.   Some authors have treated luteirostris as a subspecies of
Z. rendovae, others, while retaining it as a distinct species, do not recognize
splendida as a separable subspecies (2).

REFERENCES   1.   Murphy, R.C. 1929.   Birds collected during the Whitney
                    South Sea Expedition. IX. Zosteropidae from the Solomon
                    Islands.   Amer. Mus. Novit. 365.
              2.   Mees, G.F. 1961.   A systematic review of the Indo-Pacific
                    Zosteropidae (Part II).   Zool. Verh. 50.

SEYCHELLES WHITE-EYE

Zosterops modesta Newton, 1867

Order PASSERIFORMES   Family ZOSTEROPIDAE

STATUS   Rare.   Restricted to one island of the Seychelles archipelago where it
is locally distributed in small numbers.

DISTRIBUTION   This white-eye is only found on Mahé, the main island of the
Seychelles, where it largely keeps to rainforest above 300 m elevation, but very
occasionally ventures as low as 170 m (1).   Its distribution is not known to have
ever been different from what it is today.

POPULATION   No estimates appear to have been made and there is no clear indication of a population decline.   In its limited habitat it was seen not infrequently
by ornithologists in 1867 (2), 1906 (3), 1936 (4), 1965 (5), 1973 (1) and probably in
every year since then, though in the past there were long intervals when no birds
were reported.

HABITAT   Mixed secondary rainforest (1).   Most of the primary forest on Mahé was
destroyed by fire in the 1850s (2), but the amount of secondary forest is now
increasing as the result of reforestation (6).

CONSERVATION MEASURES TAKEN   The species is protected by law from hunting or
capture.

CONSERVATION MEASURES PROPOSED   Parts of the habitat will be protected in the
proposed Morne Seychellois National Park (7).

REMARKS   Another white-eye Zosterops mayottensis semiflava became extinct on
Marianne, Seychelles, in 1888, due to forest destruction.

REFERENCES   1. Feare, C.J. 1975.   Observations on the Seychelles White-eye
                  Zosterops modesta.   Auk 92: 615-618.
              2. Newton, E. 1867.   On the land-birds of the Seychelles
                  Archipelago.   Ibis(2)3: 335-360.
              3. Nicoll, M.J. 1906.   On the birds collected and observed
                  during the voyage of the "Valhalla" R.Y.S. from November
                  1905 to May 1906.   Ibis (8)6: 666-712.
              4. Vesey-Fitzgerald, D. 1940.   The birds of the Seychelles. I.
                  Ibis (14)4: 480-489.
              5. Gaymer, R., Blackman, R.A.A., Dawson, P.G., Penny, M. &
                  Penny, C.M. 1969.   The endemic birds of Seychelles.   Ibis
                  111: 157-176.
              6. Procter, J. 1970.   Conservation in the Seychelles: Report of
                  the Conservation Advisor, 1970.   Seychelles Government Printer.
              7. Seychelles Government, 1971.   Conservation Policy in the
                  Seychelles.   Seychelles Government Printer.

MAURITIUS WHITE-EYE

Zosterops olivacea chloronothos (Vieiliot, 1817)

Order PASSERIFORMES   Family ZOSTEROPIDAE

STATUS   Vulnerable. Rare and restricted in range. Although its total
population still probably numbers in the thousands, it is declining steadily due
mainly to habitat destruction.

DISTRIBUTION   Confined entirely to the island of Mauritius, Indian Ocean. The
subspecies has never been known to occur elsewhere. It is somewhat nomadic, in
its search for seasonal sources of nectar, ranging from the river valleys draining
the southern escarpment of the island northward to Curepipe and the Midlands region
between the Mare aux Vacoas in the east and the Tamarin Falls Reservoir in the
west. It was formerly distributed throughout the upland plateaus. (S. Temple
1976, pers. comm.).

POPULATION   No doubt this white-eye was at one time common and numerous, but by
1911 it was already considered to be rare (1). Substantial numbers, probably over
a thousand, survive but the total population continues to decline as the result
of the persistent clearing of indigenous forest (S. Temple 1976, pers. comm.).

HABITAT   During the nesting season largely limited to indigenous montane evergreen forest and scrub. But white-eyes often wander into exotic vegetation,
especially along watercourses, in search of nectar and, occasionally, into larger
suburban gardens (2). Destruction of indigenous forest is unceasing and in 1974
only 1,822 ha remained or about one percent of the area covered by forest two
centuries earlier (3).

CONSERVATION MEASURES TAKEN   The subspecies is fully protected by laws forbidding
the killing or capture of native birds. A large portion of its range in the
south-western corner of the island is within officially declared reserves. In the
period 1972-1975, ecological studies of the bird were undertaken for the purpose of
defining its status and requirements.

CONSERVATION MEASURES PROPOSED   It is essential that protection and management of
the remnant areas of indigenous evergreen forest should be maintained if this
white-eye is to survive. A management plan for a system of nature reserves and
national parks has been submitted to the Mauritius Government (4). The Mauritius
Forestry Service is embarking on a program of planting nectar-producing native
flowers along roadways, which should particularly benefit white-eyes.

REMARKS   The nominate subspecies, which is found in Réunion, is not at risk.

REFERENCES   1. Meinertzhagen, R. 1912. On the birds of Mauritius.
                  Ibis (9)6: 82-108.
              2. Gill, F.B. 1971. Ecology and evolution of the sympatric
                  Mascarene white-eyes, Zosterops borbonica and Zosterops
                  olivacea. Auk 88: 35-60.
              3. Temple, S.A. 1974. Wildlife in Mauritius today. Oryx
                  12(5): 584-590.
              4. Procter, J. & Salm, R. 1974. Conservation in Mauritius.
                  Unpublished report to I.U.C.N.

MUKOJIMA BONIN HONEYEATER

Apalopteron familiare familiare (Kittlitz, 1831)

Order PASSERIFORMES   Family MELIPHAGIDAE

STATUS   Endangered.   Restricted to two, possibly three, of the Bonin Islands,
south of Japan, and now possibly extinct.

DISTRIBUTION   Known from Mukojima (3.5 sq. km), Nakodojima (1.9 sq. km) and
formerly possibly on Chichijima (23.6 sq. km), Bonin Islands.   The honey-eater
now found on Chichijima is A. f. hahasima from the Hahajima group, the most
southerly of the Bonins, whence it was introduced by man (Y. Yamashina 1974, pers.
comm.).

POPULATION   In 1968 and 1969, biologists working in the Bonin Islands were unable
to find this subspecies anywhere in its recorded range, though it was subsequently
sighted by a team from Tokyo Metropolitan University (1).

HABITAT   Subtropical forest and scrub comprised primarily of Leucaena, Pandanus
and Hibiscus.   Much of the Bonin Island forest has been cleared to make room for
a growing tourist industry and none of it is protected.

CONSERVATION MEASURES TAKEN   The species was designated a Natural Monument in
1969 and a Special Bird for Protection in 1972.

CONSERVATION MEASURES PROPOSED   Attention has been drawn to the urgent need to
protect representative portions of the native forest of the Bonin Islands.

REMARKS   The other subspecies, A. f. hahasima of the Hahajima group at the
southern end of the Bonin island chain, was seen in 1969 on at least two of the
four islands of that group and was reasonably numerous on one of them (Y. Yamashina
1974, pers. comm.).

REFERENCES   1.   Yamashina Inst. for Ornith. (ed.) 1975.   Save these Birds.
                    Tokyo: The Kasumikaikan.   In Japanese.

HELMETED HONEYEATER

Meliphaga melanops cassidix (Gould, 1867)

Order PASSERIFORMES   Family MELIPHAGIDAE

STATUS   Endangered. Very locally distributed in Victoria, Australia, and total
population small.   Habitat alteration in portions of its range is preventing any
build-up in numbers or expansion of range.   It also has to face direct competition
from the Bell Miner Manorina melanophrys for food, whilst fire is a constant threat
to its habitat.   Adjudged to be one of Australia's most threatened birds. (1; 2).

DISTRIBUTION   Formerly comprised a large area in South Gippsland, south-eastern
Victoria.   Now restricted to riparian woodland along three creeks in the Yellingbo
District, the total area being estimated at about 259 sq. km (1; 2).

POPULATION   Presumed to have been larger when the range of the subspecies was
more extensive.   The first census was undertaken in 1963 and produced an estimate
of 300 birds.   The figure for 1967 was 170, for 1973 only 70 and for 1974 slightly
up again to 100.   In one area, at least, the breeding season of 1973-1974 was
encouragingly successful (1; 2).

HABITAT   Riparian eucalypt woodland.   This honeyeater seldom occurs more than a
mile from the creeks which run through the heart of the area it now occupies.
Wherever it has been found breeding in woodland cleared of underbrush it has
invariably declined; whereas colonies occurring in unaltered habitat appear to be
stable (1; 2).

CONSERVATION MEASURES TAKEN   Protected by law.   The Victoria Department of
Conservation has set aside 2 million dollars to purchase 208 hectares of the
habitat of this honeyeater in the vicinity of the existing 166 hectare Yellingbo
Fauna Reserve.   The installation of water pipelines which is planned by the
Victoria Board of Works will be undertaken outside the breeding season (1).   The
Helmeted Honeyeater is listed in Appendix 1 of the 1973 Convention on International
Trade in Endangered Species of Wild Fauna and Flora.

CONSERVATION MEASURES PROPOSED   Australian Commonwealth participation in habitat
acquisition (2).

REMARKS   The Victoria Bird Observers' Club has been responsible for gathering
information on this honeyeater and has spearheaded conservation efforts on its
behalf.   Recent work on its relationships indicate that it is best regarded as
one of four subspecies of M. melanops and not, as in the previous edition of this
Volume, as a separate species (3).   The other three subspecies are not known to be
at risk.

REFERENCES   1. Buckingham, R. 1975.   In W.R. Wheeler's Report on rare and
                  endangered species of birds from the Australian mainland and
                  from Tasmania.   ICBP Bull. 12: 159-164.
              2. Wheeler, W.R. 1974. Helmeted Honeyeater.   Gould League
                  of Victoria, Survival 2: 40-41.
              3. Crome, F.H.J. 1973.   The relationship of the Helmeted and
                  Yellow-tufted Honeyeaters.   Emu 73: 12-18.

KAUAI 'O'O or 'O'O'A'A

Moho braccatus (Cassin, 1885)

Order PASSERIFORMES   Family MELIPHAGIDAE

STATUS   Endangered. Occurs only in a small portion of the Alaka'i Swamp on
Kauai. It was thought to be extinct until rediscovered in 1960 (1). Other
members of the genus were taken in large numbers, for their colorful yellow
plumes, by native Hawaiians, but the relatively inconspicuous plumage of this
species saved it from wholesale exploitation. Its restriction to undisturbed
rainforest suggests that it is intolerant of habitat alteration, so continual
deterioration of the rainforest brought about by introduced herbivores and
encroachment by aggressive exotic plants is a serious threat to its survival.
Other adverse factors are the predators and potential avian competitors which have
also been introduced (1-3) and, very probably, susceptibility to introduced avian
diseases (4).

DISTRIBUTION   Restricted to the Alaka'i Swamp, Kauai, Hawaiian Islands, between
the upper Koaie River and Mt. Waialeale, at an altitude of 1,150 to 1, 375 m (1-3).

POPULATION   The species was common in the 19th century, for many years considered
extinct, following a precipitous decline in the first decades of the 20th century,
and rediscovered in 1960, when one was collected and twelve were observed (1).
Nests were found in 1971, 1972 (when six birds were seen) and 1973 (2), but the
present population is very small indeed, possibly as few as only 2 birds (5; 6).

HABITAT   Undisturbed montane rainforest. Even in remote areas these forests are
increasingly infiltrated by exotic plants and birds. The black rat Rattus rattus,
which is quite capable of climbing trees, occurs throughout the forested region (3).

CONSERVATION MEASURES TAKEN   The species is protected by federal and state law.
The State of Hawaii has established the 4,050 hectare Alaka'i Swamp Wilderness
Preserve, which includes the entire present range of this species. Programs to
control introduced plants have been undertaken but have proven ineffectual. The
population, distribution and ecology of the 'O'o are under study (2).

CONSERVATION MEASURES PROPOSED   Effective control of introduced plants and
grazing animals in the Alaka'i Swamp Preserve. Continuation of the detailed
studies of this species (2).

REMARKS   The Kauai 'O'o is the sole surviving member of a genus which included
species from Hawaii (M. nobilis), Molokai (M. bishopi) and Oahu (M. apicalis).

REFERENCES   1.   Richardson, F. & Bowles, J. 1964.   A survey of the birds of
                   Kauai, Hawaii. B.P. Bishop Museum Bull. 227.
              2.   U.S. Dept. of Interior Bureau of Sport Fisheries and Wildlife,
                   1973. Threatened Wildlife of the United States. U.S.
                   Bur. Sport Fish. Wildl. Res. Pub. 114.
              3.   Berger, A.J. 1972. Hawaiian Birdlife. Honolulu: University
                   Press of Hawaii.
              4.   Warner, R.E. 1968.   The role of introduced diseases in the
                   extinction of the endemic Hawaiian avifauna. Condor 70:
                   101-120.
              5.   Haley, D. 1975.   The last 'O'o. Defenders 50: 476-479.
              6.   Hart, A.D. 1976.   Field notes from Kauai, May 26-June 2,
                   1976, Part I. Elepaio 37: 28-29.

STITCHBIRD

Notiomystis cincta (Du Bus, 1839)

Order PASSERIFORMES   Family MELIPHAGIDAE

STATUS   Vulnerable. Presently restricted to one island off North Island, New Zealand, where its population is small but apparently stable. Factors suggested as causes of its decline and extirpation from North Island, include predation by introduced mammals, disease and collecting.

DISTRIBUTION   The species formerly occurred throughout North Island, Great and Little Barrier islands, and Kapiti island, New Zealand. It was extirpated from North Island by the end of the 19th century and today only survives on Little Barrier (3,056 ha), where it is well distributed over most of the island (1-3).

POPULATION   At the time of the arrival of European settlers early in the 19th century, the species was common, but by 1872 it had become rare in the northern half of North Island, though still comparatively common to the south. By 1888, it was exceedingly rare everywhere in North Island and shortly afterwards died out (4; 5). The population on Little Barrier was reduced almost to zero at about the same time, but subsequently recovered and is now apparently stable at about 200 pairs, in spite of the presence on the island of a large number of feral cats (1). Seasonally, the cats prey heavily on Cook's Petrels Pterodroma c. cookii and Black Petrels Procellaria parkinsoni, which may take pressure off the Stitchbird population, at least for a part of each year, while for the rest of the year the cats' main prey is the Polynesian rat Rattus exulans (D. Merton 1974, pers. comm.).

HABITAT   Indigenous forest, which everywhere in New Zealand has been invaded by introduced mustelids, cats and rats.

CONSERVATION MEASURES TAKEN   The species has legal protection and Little Barrier Island was made a Reserve for Protection of Flora and Fauna in 1890. A cat control campaign on the island has been launched by the New Zealand Wildlife Service but has not yet proved fully effective (D. Merton 1974, pers. comm.).

CONSERVATION MEASURES PROPOSED   The New Zealand Wildlife Service had plans for the translocation of some Stitchbirds to Hen Island (484 hectares) in 1978 but whether they have been implemented and with what success is not yet known. The Service also proposes to launch a more ambitious cat eradication program on Little Barrier Island, which, if successful, will ensure the future of this species and of two petrels, as well as providing a large island refuge on which other endangered New Zealand birds could also perhaps be released (D. Merton 1974, pers. comm.).

REMARKS   Two pairs of Stitchbirds were taken into captivity in 1969, but all died within two years. One pair had attempted to breed but the female died from a bee sting. (G. Williams 1976, pers. comm.).

REFERENCES   1. Gravatt, D.J. 1971. Aspects of habitat use by New Zealand honeyeaters with reference to other forest species. Emu 71: 65-72.
              2. Crook, I.G. 1974. Forest surveys. Wildlife- A review 5: 49-56.
              3. Crook, I.G. & Best, H.A. undated. Distribution of honeyeaters (Meliphagidae) on Little Barrier Island. New Zealand Wildlife Service Fauna Survey Unit Report Series, 1. Unpublished.

4. Falla, R.A., Sibson, R.B. & Turbott, E.G. 1970.
    A Field Guide to the Birds of New Zealand and Outlying
    Islands, 2nd Ed. Boston: Houghton Mifflin Co.; London: Collins.
5. Oliver, W.R.B. 1955.   New Zealand Birds, 2nd Ed.
    Wellington: A.H. and A.W. Reed.

CAPE SABLE SEASIDE SPARROW

Ammodramus maritimus mirabilis (Howell, 1919)

Order PASSERIFORMES   Family EMBERIZIDAE

                                        Subfamily EMBERIZINAE

STATUS   Rare.   Restricted to certain seasonally flooded prairies at the southern
end of the Florida peninsula, U.S.A.   The total population is small and, at least
in portions of its range, unstable.   Habitat alteration through invasion of the
prairies by brush and exotic tree species is believed to be the greatest long-term
threat to the subspecies.

DISTRIBUTION   Southernmost Florida from Cape Sable, north-west along coastal
prairies for a distance of 25 km, to southern Big Cypress Swamp near Carnestown
(an area of about 180 sq. km) and also the prairie dominated by Muhlenbergia grass
immediately to the north-east of Cape Sable around Taylor Slough.   The latter
supports 95 percent of the Seaside Sparrow population and is estimated to be
between about 88 ha to 128 sq. km in extent.   The larger western section of the
range is now occupied very thinly or only sporadically by the subspecies (1-3).

POPULATION   In 1935 the Cape Sable population was very nearly wiped out by a
hurricane, which had resulted in the whole of its habitat being flooded (3), but
in 1970 four singing males were once more found to be present, though the number
had dropped to only a single male in 1975 (1; 2).   The Big Cypress Swamp population was considered to be substantial in 1955, when as many as 56 were seen in a
day (3), but more recent surveys show it to have declined.   For example, at
Ochopee-Turner River, where at least 27 were located in 1970, only 2 were found in
1975.   The Taylor Slough population was discovered in 1972: it contained an
estimated 1,900 to 2,800 birds in 1975, clearly the most important population of
the subspecies (1; 2).

HABITAT   On Cape Sable formerly prairie dominated by Spartina, most of which has
however now been replaced by more salt-tolerant forbs, as the sea gradually
invades the Cape area.   The Big Cypress population inhabits mainly Spartina and
Cladium prairie.   The rapid vegetational succession in this area, which is subject
to temporary interruption by fire, sometimes in two or more years running, and
possibly also to permanent interruption as a result of increasing invasion by salt
water, tends to bring about frequent decline or extirpation of colonies.   The
Taylor Slough prairie is dominated by Muhlenbergia or Cladium and is usually
flooded during summer and fall.   Fires are frequent, and may be essential in
maintaining suitably structured prairie for the subspecies; certainly there is
generally a peak in its population 2 or 3 years after a fire, although man-made
fires prior to the breeding season tend to affect larger areas than the lightning-
caused fires after the breeding season and can destroy whole colonies of the
sparrow, particularly when they occur in successive years.   Fires help prevent
invasion of the prairie by vigorous exotic trees, chiefly Casuarina, Melaleuca and
Schinus (1; 2).

CONSERVATION MEASURES TAKEN   The subspecies is fully protected from capture,
killing or harassment under the 1973 Endangered Species Act of the U.S.   Most of
its habitat lies within the boundaries of Everglades National Park.   Its distribution and ecological requirements have been the subject of considerable research.

CONSERVATION MEASURES PROPOSED   Exotic plants, which pose the greatest threat to
the integrity of the Muhlenbergia prairie of Taylor Slough, should be eliminated in
areas occupied by the subspecies: periodic, controlled burning should be undertaken to perpetuate the prairie and to promote its suitable structure (2).
Unprotected habitat in the Ochopee area, now open to human disturbance and possible
development, should be purchased and added to the nearby national park (4).

REMARKS   Of eight other subspecies found along the east coast of North America,
A. m. nigrescens, which is restricted to coastal marshes near Titusville, Florida,
is at serious risk and A. m. pelonota, of north-eastern Florida, is local, reduced
in number and needs careful watching; the remaining subspecies are not believed to
be at risk.   The previous edition treated mirabilis as a full species and assigned
it to the genus Ammospiza.

REFERENCES   1.   Werner, H.W. 1976.   Distribution, habitat and origin
                    of the Cape Sable Seaside Sparrow.   Gainesville: Univ.
                    South Florida.   Unpublished Master's thesis.
              2.   Werner, H.W. 1975.   The biology of the Cape Sable
                    Sparrow.   Everglades National Park publication. 215 pp.
              3.   Stimson, L.A. 1956.   The Cape Sable Seaside Sparrow:
                    its former and present distribution.   Auk 73: 489-502.
              4.   U.S. Bureau of Sport Fisheries and Wildlife, 1973.
                    Threatened wildlife of the United States.   U.S. Bur. Sport
                    Fish. Wildl. Res. Pub. 114.

DUSKY SEASIDE SPARROW

Ammodramus maritimus nigrescens (Ridgway, 1873)

Order PASSERIFORMES   Family EMBERIZIDAE

                                         Subfamily EMBERIZINAE

STATUS   Endangered. With a very restricted distribution in certain salt
marshes on Florida's east coast, this subspecies is now very low in numbers as the
result of mosquito control and waterfowl enhancement measures in the marshes,
alienation of some of the habitat for development, and occasional destructive
wildfires.

DISTRIBUTION   Salt marshes bordering a section of the Indian River, the waterway
inside the extensive barrier islands along the Florida east coast. Within this
area the subspecies has been found on northern Merritt Island from Banana Creek
to Dummitt Creek and to the west of the Indian River, in the St. Johns River
marshes, in the vicinity of Titusville from State Highway 46 south to State
Highway 520. The area which it inhabits has dwindled and it is now all but
extirpated from Merritt Island, while the St. Johns River marshes site has been
reduced to a strip 32 by 5 km, of which it actually occupies less than 2,500 ha.
The Merritt Island site, prior to the 1956 impoundment of the salt marsh, was
about 2,430 ha. (1; 2).

POPULATION   The subspecies was relatively common last century within its limited
range, but several of its populations had declined by 1957 (3; 4). The Merritt
Island population, before the impoundment, totalled about 2,000 pairs, but by
1963 had declined to 70 pairs, by 1968 to about 29 pairs and since 1975 to only
1 or 2 pairs. The St. Johns River population was estimated to be about 894 pairs
in 1968, but has subsequently somewhat declined (1; 2; 5). On a 1,620 ha wildlife refuge, of which 102 ha was preferred habitat, the population declined from
144 pairs in 1968 to 110 in 1972 and to 54 in 1973, the major decline coming as
the result of two destructive fires (5). A census throughout the entire range of
the subspecies in 1977, revealed a further decline: 29 singing males were counted,
but many of these may not have been paired (H. Kale 1977, pers. comm.).

HABITAT   Salt marsh between 3 and 4.6 m above sea level, dominated by bunchgrass
Spartina bakerii. In 1956, about 2,500 ha of this habitat on Merritt Island was
impounded for mosquito control and waterfowl enhancement; the resulting freshwater inundation seriously reduced Spartina bakerii in the area.   Intentional
breaching of certain of the impoundment dikes has brought about some recovery of
the Spartina in two impoundment areas, but their sparrow population had apparently
been extirpated and the areas have not yet been reoccupied by the subspecies.   In
the St. Johns River marshes a considerable amount of habitat has been lost, even
since 1968, through housing development, highway construction and drainage to
improve pastures, which tends to promote the invasion of grasslands by woody
shrubs (1; 2; 6).

CONSERVATION MEASURES TAKEN   The subspecies is fully protected by the U.S.
Endangered Species Act (1973) from capture, killing or harassment.   Parts of its
habitat are located within the Merritt Island and the St. Johns National Wildlife
Refuges.   Some of the former is now managed to maintain at least a remnant
population of the sparrow and management of the St. Johns refuge includes provision
of fire lanes and a program of controlled burning also aimed at maintaining
suitable habitat.   A research biologist is employed by the U.S. Fish and Wildlife
Service to study and manage the subspecies and a recovery team appointed by the
Fish and Wildlife Service is preparing a recovery plan (2; 5).

CONSERVATION MEASURES PROPOSED   The Dusky Seaside Sparrow Recovery Plan will, when issued, contain a broad list of recommendations for management and acquisition of suitable habitat.

REMARKS   The Cape Sable Seaside Sparrow A. m. mirabilis of the southern tip of Florida is likewise at risk because of its rarity.   Another of the 9 races, A. m. pelonota of the north-eastern Florida coast, has a restricted distribution but is not sufficiently at risk to warrant inclusion in this volume; the remainder, distributed along the Atlantic and Gulf of Mexico coasts, are not at risk.   The previous edition of the Red Data Book treated nigrescens as a full species and assigned it to the genus Ammospiza.

REFERENCES   1.   Sharp, B. 1970.   A population estimate of the Dusky Seaside Sparrow.   Wilson Bull. 158-166.
             2.   Kale, H.W., II. 1977.   Endangered species: Dusky Seaside Sparrow.   Florida Naturalist 50(1):   16-21.
             3.   Chapman, F.M. 1899.   The distribution and relationships of Ammodramus maritimus and its allies.   Auk 16:   1-12.
             4.   Trost, C.H. 1968.   Ammospiza nigrescens (Ridgway) Dusky Seaside Sparrow.   In A.C. Bent (O.L. Austin ed.), Life Histories of North American Cardinals, Grosbeaks, Buntings, Towhees, Finches, Sparrows and Allies. U.S. Nat. Mus. Bull. 237: 849-859.
             5.   Baker, J.L. 1974.   Preliminary studies of the Dusky Seaside Sparrow on the St. Johns National Wildlife Refuge.   Proc. Ann. Conf. SE Assoc. Game Fish Comm. 27: 207-214.
             6.   Sharp, B. 1969.   Conservation of the Dusky Seaside Sparrow on Merritt Island, Florida.   Biol. Cons. 1: 175-176.

SAN CLEMENTE SAGE SPARROW

Amphispiza belli clementeae Ridgway, 1898

Order PASSERIFORMES   Family EMBERIZIDAE

                                              Subfamily EMBERIZINAE

STATUS   Endangered. Endemic to San Clemente, Channel Islands, off the coast of
southern California, United States. Now quite restricted in distribution even on
this small (34 km long by 2.4 to 6.4 km wide) island and continuing to decline
because of excessive grazing by introduced goats. A goat control program is
underway, but is not yet demonstrably effective.

DISTRIBUTION   Confined to San Clemente where in 1974 it was mostly to be found on
the lower west terrace between points Leo and Evelyn. Formerly it ranged throughout the mesa lands of the island (1).

POPULATION   In 1917 this subspecies was considered to be common (2), but a
census in 1974 yielded a count of only 7 adults and 37 juveniles, which was
interpreted as representing between 20 and 30 adults of breeding age (1).

HABITAT   Shrubs and grasses. Overgrazing by goats, introduced at some time
prior to 1827 has seriously degraded the vegetation of San Clemente. From 1877
to 1933 large numbers of sheep were kept on the island as well, but sheep ranching
ended in 1934 when the island came under jurisdiction of the U.S. Navy. In 1974,
however, there were still an estimated 6,000 to 10,000 goats on the island.
Until 1934, sheep and goats were restricted by fences; subsequently they roamed
freely. In 1957 feral swine were introduced as well. These pigs but no goats
were noted in the area inhabited by the Sage Sparrow in 1974. Almost no
regeneration of shrubs or trees has taken place since 1934 (1).

CONSERVATION MEASURES TAKEN   In 1973, the U.S. Navy launched a goat control
program on San Clemente. Although up to 5,000 goats were removed the first year,
the productivity of feral goats is probably sufficiently great to nullify the
effects of this action (1). The Sage Sparrow is fully protected under the U.S.
Migratory Bird Treaty Act and in 1977 was listed on the U.S. Secretary of Interior's
List of Endangered Species; it is also protected by California state law. A preliminary survey of its status was carried out in 1974.

CONSERVATION MEASURES PROPOSED   A system of fencing has been recommended, to
restrict goats to the southern portion of the island, and it would at least permit
the vegetation at the northern end of the island to begin to recover while the
goat control program continues to be implemented (1).

REMARKS   Four other subspecies of A. belli occur in the western United States
and Mexico; none of them is known to be at risk.

REFERENCES   1. Stewart, R.M., Smail, J., Clow, W.C. & Henderson, R.P. 1974.
                  The status of the Song Sparrow and Bewick's Wren on San
                  Clemente Island and Santa Barbara Island, California. Report
                  to the U.S. Fish and Wildlife Service Office of Endangered
                  Species.
              2. Howell, A.B. 1917. Birds of the islands off the coast of
                  southern California. Pac. Coast Avif. 12.

MANGROVE FINCH

Camarhynchus heliobates (Snodgrass and Heller, 1901)

Order PASSERIFORMES   Family EMBERIZIDAE

                                         Subfamily EMBERIZINAE

STATUS   Rare.   Restricted to small portions of two of the Galapagos Islands,
Ecuador.

DISTRIBUTION   Confined to dense mangroves on the eastern coast of Fernandina
Island and the western coast of Isabela Island; also one locality on the south-
eastern coast of Isabela, where one was recorded in 1971 (1).   Potentially
suitable habitat totals about 500 ha, although the species does not inhabit the
whole of it.   It no longer occurs at Punta Espinoza, its northernmost recorded
station on Fernandina, but one was seen at Punta Mangle in 1971 (1; 2).

POPULATION   Very small, although no change has been reported.   In 1974 there
were an estimated 100 to 200 birds (Tj. DeVries 1974, pers. comm.).   A density
of 1 to 2 pairs per hectare was recorded in 1962 at Punta Tortuga, Isabela (2).

HABITAT   Dense mangrove swamp.

CONSERVATION MEASURES TAKEN   Protected by law.

CONSERVATION MEASURES PROPOSED   None known.

REFERENCES   1.   Harris, M.P. 1973.   The Galapagos avifauna.
                   Condor 75: 265-278.
             2.   Curio, E. & Kramer, P. 1964.   Vom Mangrovefinken
                   (Cactospiza heliobates Snodgrass and Heller).
                   Zeitschrift f. Tierpsych. 21: 223-234.

FLOREANA LARGE GROUND FINCH

Geospiza magnirostris magnirostris Gould, 1837

Order PASSERIFORMES

Family EMBERIZIDAE

Subfamily EMBERIZINAE

STATUS   Indeterminate.   Restricted to one island of the Galapagos, Ecuador,
where its status is obscure; only one specimen has been taken since Darwin
collected the type series in 1835.

DISTRIBUTION   Floreana Island, Galapagos.

POPULATION   Unknown.   The subspecies may be extinct for, aside from a specimen
which was collected on Floreana in 1957, it has been unrecorded since 1835 (1).
Darwin's specimens do not have original labels, so there will always be a measure
of uncertainty as to the locality from which his type series came.   They and,
presumably, the 1957 specimen from Floreana have slightly longer bills than any of
the specimens of G. magnirostris from other islands in the archipelago (2).
If the nominate race is still extant on Floreana it must be very rare indeed (3).

HABITAT   Arid and transition zones, to judge from the habitat preferences of the
other subspecies, G. m. strenua.

CONSERVATION MEASURES TAKEN   The subspecies has been given legal protection.

CONSERVATION MEASURES PROPOSED   None known.

REMARKS   The subspecies G. m. strenua, which has been recorded from several of
the larger Galapagos islands, is not at risk although it may have disappeared from
one or two of the islands where it once occurred (3).

REFERENCES   1.   Bowman, R.I. 1961.   Morphological differentiation and
                       adaptation in the Galapagos Finches.   Univ. Calif. Pubs.
                       Zool. 58.
              2.   Swarth, H.S. 1931.   The avifauna of the Galapagos Islands.
                       Occ. Papers Cal. Acad. Sci. 18.
              3.   Harris, M.P. 1973.   The Galapagos avifauna.   Condor 75:
                       265-278.

AMAK SONG SPARROW

Melospiza melodia amaka Gabrielson and Lincoln, 1951

Order PASSERIFORMES   Family EMBERIZIDAE

                                      Subfamily EMBERIZINAE

STATUS   Endangered, if still extant.   The island in the Aleutians from which
this subspecies of the Song Sparrow was described has been overrun by introduced
foxes, which may have caused its extinction.

DISTRIBUTION   Confined to the Aleutian islet of Amak, which lies 24 km to the
north of the western tip of the Alaska Peninsula.   Like other Song Sparrows of
the Aleutians it is only found along the seashore (1; 2).

POPULATION   No estimate has been made.   The type specimen was selected from a
series taken in 1925.   Visits to Amak on 5 July 1973 and later in July or early in
August of the same year produced no records of this sparrow, despite searching, and
it may well be extinct (3; G.V. Byrd 1975, pers. comm.).

HABITAT   Beaches of a rocky island, where this sparrow inhabits vegetation just
above high tide line.   It may have been preyed upon by the Arctic foxes Alopex
lagopus which have been released and established themselves on Amak.

CONSERVATION MEASURES TAKEN   The subspecies is protected by U.S. law.

CONSERVATION MEASURES PROPOSED   None known; a thorough search of Amak for the
subspecies is clearly called for.

REMARKS   Thirty-one subspecies of the Song Sparrow are recognized, of which a few
have very local and small populations, e.g. M. m. pusillula of a portion of San
Francisco Bay, but except for M. m. amaka none are believed to be at serious risk,
although quite recently the subspecies M. m. graminea of Santa Barbara Island,
California, became extinct.   M. m. amaka is said to be very similar to M. m.
maxima of the far western Aleutians, in spite of its proximity to mainland Alaska.
It is effectively isolated from M. m. sanaka of the Alaska Peninsula, the mainland
coastal areas nearest Amak Island having no suitable habitat for Song Sparrows (1).

REFERENCES   1.   Gabrielson, I.N. & Lincoln, F.C. 1951.   The races of
                    Song Sparrows in Alaska.   Condor 53: 250-255.
              2.   Murie, O.J. 1959.   Fauna of the Aleutian Islands and
                    Alaska Peninsula.   U.S. Fish and Wildlife Service
                    North American Fauna 61.
              3.   American Ornithologists' Union, 1975.   Report of the
                    Committee on Conservation.   Auk 92 (4 Suppl): 1B-16B.

GROSBEAK BUNTING or BIG-BILLED TRISTAN CANARY

Nesospiza wilkinsi wilkinsi Lowe, 1923

Nesospiza wilkinsi dunnei Hagen, 1952

Order PASSERIFORMES

Family EMBERIZIDAE

Subfamily EMBERIZINAE

STATUS   Rare.   Each subspecies is restricted to one island in the Tristan da
Cunha group, south Atlantic.   Both depend on a type of habitat which has a very
limited distribution and both have very small populations.

DISTRIBUTION   The nominate race N. w. wilkinsi occurs on Nightingale Island
(2.2 sq. km) and N. w. dunnei on Inaccessible Island (16 sq. km), both islands
being about 40 km south-west of the main island of Tristan da Cunha.   The species
is, however, entirely dependent on Phylica woodland, of which only relatively
small patches remain on each of the two islands (1-3).

POPULATION   In 1952 the N. wilkinsi population on Nightingale Island was
estimated to be between 70 and 120 and the Inaccessible population between 40 and
90 or rather smaller despite the much larger size of the island, the extent of
Phylica woodland being substantially less (2).   The Nightingale population
remained at about 30 pairs in 1974 (3).   Both populations are thought to be about
as abundant as the habitat can support.

HABITAT   Woodlands of Phylica arborea, which may at one time have occupied up to
twice their present area, the Grosbeak populations then probably being
commensurately larger.   On Inaccessible introduced cattle and especially pigs
and sheep could have caused some destruction of the Phylica woods, but all domestic
livestock had died out or been removed by the 1960s (4).   Woods on both islands are
subject to some storm damage.   About a hectare of the estimated 20 hectares of
Phylica on Nightingale was unwittingly destroyed in 1974 during otherwise beneficial and at least temporarily successful efforts to control New Zealand Flax,
Phormium tenax, an aggressive invasive plant originally introduced to the island
by man (3).   The black rats Rattus rattus and feral cats which infest Tristan have
not yet effected a lodgement on either island.

CONSERVATION MEASURES TAKEN   None specifically, but the islanders are now well
aware of the dangers of introducing potential pest species and take care to avoid
doing so.   The removal of domestic stock from Inaccessible was partly dictated by
conservation considerations (H.F.I. Elliott, 1979, pers. comm.).

CONSERVATION MEASURES PROPOSED   None under immediate consideration but the
possibility of establishing a national park or reserve on part or all of
Inaccessible has often been suggested and may be looked into by an expedition to
the island in 1979/80 (H.F.I. Elliott, 1979, pers. comm.).

REMARKS   In spite of their small populations the two races of Big-billed Tristan
'Canaries' or Buntings do not appear to be at serious risk, the major threats being
the introduction of predators and deterioration of Phylica woodland.   The closely
related Small-billed Bunting, Nesospiza acunhae of Inaccessible, Nightingale and
formerly Tristan da Cunha, was listed in the previous edition of the Red Data Book,
but is reported to be sufficiently numerous and widespread on the islands where it
survives, not to be at risk; introduction of predators to either island would of
course change this picture drastically.

REFERENCES
1. Hagen, Y. 1952. Birds of Tristan da Cunha. Oslo: Norske Videnskaps-Akademi.
2. Elliott, H.F.I. 1957. A contribution to the ornithology of the Tristan da Cunha group. Ibis 99: 545-586.
3. Richardson, M.E. 1978. Aspects of the ornithology of the Tristan da Cunha group. Unpublished ms.
4. Wace, N.M. & Holdgate, M.W. 1976. Man and Nature in the Tristan da Cunha Islands. Morges: IUCN Monograph No. 6.

ZAPATA SPARROW

Torreornis inexpectata inexpectata Barbour and Peters, 1927

Torreornis inexpectata sigmani Spence and Smith, 1961

Order PASSERIFORMES   Family EMBERIZIDAE

                                              Subfamily EMBERIZINAE

___

STATUS   Rare and very local.   Each subspecies is known from a single locality
in Cuba.   Disturbance of the habitat within the circumscribed ranges of either
subspecies might quickly result in extinction.

DISTRIBUTION   The nominate race is known to occur only in the Santo Tomas sector
of the Zapata Swamp, Las Villas Province, Cuba.   T. i. sigmani is found in a
small patch of desert scrub near Baitiquiri in the coastlands about 40 km east of
Guantánamo, Oriente Province. (1-4).

POPULATION   No estimates have been made, but there is no indication that the
numbers of either subspecies have declined, although in both cases they are quite
small (O.H. Garrido 1974, pers. comm.).   The nominate race has occasionally been
observed in small flocks (3).

HABITAT   In the Zapata Swamp shrubby areas on higher ground, a nest having been
found in sawgrass tussock (1; 4); also along an old marine terrace covered with
acacia, cacti and a tangle of shrubs and vines at the base of a cliff.   The area
where T. i. sigmani occurs has been described as typical of the arid south Oriente
coast (2), so that it is by no means clear why it should apparently be restricted
to one very small area.

CONSERVATION MEASURES TAKEN   None known.

CONSERVATION MEASURES PROPOSED   None known.

REMARKS   The future of the nominate subspecies, and also of the Zapata Rail
Cyanolimnas cerverai and the Zapata Wren Ferminia cerverai, is dependent on the
preservation of the Zapata Swamp sector in which all three are found.   Proposals
to drain large portions of this swamp have not yet been implemented (O.H. Garrido
1974, pers. comm.).   Recently it has been reported that another population of
sparrows closely related to this species has been discovered on Isla Coco, off the
north coast of Camaguey Province, about 150 km east of the Zapata locality
(O. Garrido 1975, pers. comm.).

REFERENCES   1.   Bond, J. 1973.   Eighteenth supplement to the Checklist of
                   Birds of the West Indies (1956).   Philadelphia Acad.
                   Nat. Sci.
              2.   Schwartz, A. & Klinikowski, R.F. 1963.   Observations of
                   West Indian birds.   Proc. Acad. Nat. Sci. Philadelphia 115:
                   53-77.
              3.   Ripley, S.D. & Watson, G.E., 3rd, 1956.   Cuban bird
                   notes.   Postilla 26: 1-6.
              4.   Bond, J. 1961.   Birds of the West Indies.   Boston:
                   Houghton Mifflin Co.; London: Collins.

CHERRY-THROATED TANAGER

Nemosia rourei Cabanis, 1870

Order PASSERIFORMES

Family EMBERIZIDAE

Subfamily THRAUPINAE

STATUS   Endangered.   Unrecorded for more than a century, this tanager of south-eastern Brazil must be close to extinction, if it still exists.

DISTRIBUTION   This distinctive species is known only from the type specimen collected in 1870 near Muriahié, on the north bank of the rio Paraíba do Sul in Rio de Janeiro state (1; H. Sick 1977, pers. comm.).

POPULATION   It is doubtful if this species still exists, since the state of Rio de Janeiro has been well explored ornithologically.

HABITAT   Presumably forest, for the Muriahié region was only lightly developed when the type specimen was collected (2).

CONSERVATION MEASURES TAKEN   Protected by Brazilian law.

CONSERVATION MEASURES PROPOSED   None known.

REFERENCES   1.   de Schauensee, R.M. 1966.   The Species of Birds of South America and their Distribution.   Narberth, Pa.: Livingston Publishing Co.
2.   Cabanis, J. 1870.   Ueber eine neue brasilische Nemosie oder Wald-Tangare, Nemosia rourei nov. spec. Journ. f. Ornith. 18: 459-460.

AZURE-RUMPED TANAGER

Tangara cabanisi (Sclater, 1868)

Order PASSERIFORMES   Family EMBERIZIDAE

                                              Subfamily THRAUPINAE

STATUS   Indeterminate. The species has a very restricted distribution in
Mexico and Guatemala and is poorly known. Its cloud forest habitat continues to
be cleared for agriculture.

DISTRIBUTION   Known only from southern Chiapas, Mexico, and from the extension
of the highlands in western Guatemala (1; 2).

POPULATION   Unknown. Until recently there were only three records of the
species, one in 1937 from Mt. Ovando to the north of and overlooking Escuintla,
Chiapas (3), one in 1943 at 600 m elevation apparently in the vicinity of
Cacahoatan, Chiapas (6), and the third, the type specimen collected more than a
century ago, at Costa Cuca near Quezaltenango, western Guatemala, this still being
the only evidence of its occurrence in Guatemala. However, between 1972 and 1977
there were several sightings at El Triunfo, north-east of Mapastepec, Chiapas,
the largest being a flock of 16 in 1974 (5; 6; T. Parker 1974, pers. comm.).

HABITAT   Cloud forest of the Sierra Madre in south-eastern Chiapas and south-
western Guatemala. Much of this forest has been destroyed for coffee plantations
and cattle grazing and the habitat requirements of this tanager are now only to be
found in patches along the higher ridges. The type specimen was said to have been
collected in arid lowlands in Guatemala, but all recent observations have been made
at altitudes of between 1200 and 1500 m in humid evergreen broadleaf forest,
particularly in clearings where second-growth fruiting shrubs were abundant (6).

CONSERVATION MEASURES TAKEN   A reserve of 10,000 ha is maintained on federal
land at El Triunfo by the Institute of National History of Chiapas (M. Alvarez del
Toro 1973, pers. comm.).

CONSERVATION MEASURES PROPOSED   None known.

REMARKS   The reasons for the apparent rarity of this species are unknown.
Admittedly, however, there are still considerable areas of cloud forest on the
Mexico-Guatemala border which have not been thoroughly searched and could be a
refuge of this tanager. The closely related Gray-and-gold Tanager T. palmeri
of extreme north-western South America and adjacent eastern Panama is also poorly
known and vulnerable to forest destruction, although it has been suggested that
both species may temporarily profit from the proliferation of second-growth
fruiting shrubs following deforestation (6).

REFERENCES   1.   Parker, T.A.III, Hilty, S. & Robbins, M. 1976.   Birds of
                    El Triunfo Cloud Forest, Mexico, with notes on the Horned
                    Guan and other species.   Amer. Birds 30: 779-782.
              2.   Griscom, L. 1932.   The distribution of bird life in
                    Guatemala.   Bull. Amer. Mus. Nat. Hist. 64: 439pp.
              3.   Blake, E.R. 1953.   Birds of Mexico.   Chicago: Univ. of
                    Chicago Press.
              4.   Sclater, P.L. 1868.   On a recently discovered tanager of
                    the genus Calliste.   Ibis (new series) 4: 71-72.

5.   Cantwell, R. 1978.   Bird thou never wert.
     Sports Illustrated Feb. 13: 56–66.
6.   Hilty, S.L. & Simon, D. 1977.   The Azure-rumped
     Tanager in Mexico with comparative remarks on the
     Gray-and-gold Tanager.   Auk 94: 605–606.

SEVEN-COLORED TANAGER

Tangara fastuosa (Lesson, 1831)

Order PASSERIFORMES   Family EMBERIZIDAE

                                         Subfamily THRAUPINAE

_____

STATUS   Vulnerable.   Restricted to a portion of the east coast of Brazil where
it has declined markedly in abundance in the past 30 years.   It is highly sought
after as a cage bird.   Forest destruction has also contributed to its decline.

DISTRIBUTION   Eastern Brazil in Pernambuco state, where there are records from
Macuca, Quipapá, Cabo and the Mercês region, and in Alagoas state from Quebrangulo.
(1-3).

POPULATION   This species was considered very common in parts of Pernambuco
30 years ago, when it was captured in numbers for the pet trade.   Since that time
it has seriously diminished but is still avidly sought after as a cage bird (4).

HABITAT   Tropical coastal forest of eastern Brazil.   The greater part of this
forest has been destroyed (4).

CONSERVATION MEASURES TAKEN   The species is protected by law in Brazil, but like
almost any other Brazilian bird is available at a price through the still thriving
though illegal pet trade.

CONSERVATION MEASURES PROPOSED   None known.

REFERENCES   1.   de Schauensee, R.M. 1966.   The Species of Birds of
                    South America and their Distribution.   Narberth, Pa.:
                    Livingston Publishing Co.
              2.   Pinto, O.M. de O. & de Camargo, E.A., 1961.
                    Resultados ornitológicos de quatro recentes expedições
                    do Departamento de Zoologia ao Nordeste do Brasil,
                    com a descrição de seis novas subespécies.
                    Archiv. Zool. São Paulo 9: 193-284.
              3.   Berla, H.F. 1946.   Lista das aves colecionadas em
                    Pernambuco, com a descrição de uma subespécie n.,
                    de um alótipo fêmea e notas de campo.   Bol. Mus. Nac.
                    Rio de Janeiro, Zool. 65.
              4.   Sick, H. 1972.   A ameaça da avifauna brasileira.
                    In Espécies da Fauna Brasileira Ameaçadas de Extinção,
                    pp. 99-153.   Rio de Janeiro: Academia Brasileira de
                    Ciências.

KIRTLAND'S WARBLER

Dendroica kirtlandii (Baird, 1852)

Order PASSERIFORMES   Family PARULIDAE

STATUS   Endangered.   Breeding distribution severely restricted.   The extent of
suitable young, regrowth pine forests has been greatly reduced this century and
the invasion of the forests by a brood parasite against which the warbler has not
yet developed defences, has seriously impaired breeding success.   Although, local
elimination of the parasite and pineland management aimed at producing more stands
of appropriate age have apparently halted the long downward trend in the warbler's
populations, it is still uncertain whether the slight gains noted annually since
1974 mark the beginning of a real recovery.

DISTRIBUTION   In historical times the breeding range of this warbler has been
restricted to an area of 136 x 160 km in thirteen adjacent counties of northern
lower Michigan, U.S.A.   The actual area occupied by the species fell from 4860 ha
in 1957 to 1620-2430 ha (largely in 3 counties) in 1976.   It has occasionally been
found elsewhere during the breeding season, e.g. in southern Ontario in 1977, but
breeding, although suspected, has not been proved.   Migrates in winter to the
Bahamas, where it has been observed on nearly all the larger islands, and it has
been recorded in spring and fall in various states between Michigan and the
Bahamas and in a few states somewhat off the direct route.   Exceptional sightings
were of an adult male and a second bird, possibly an immature, on the Gulf coast of
Veracruz state, Mexico, in November 1977. (1-7).

POPULATION   Probably at its peak between 1870 and 1900, when the jack pine Pinus
banksiana forests of the warbler's breeding range were most subject to fire and
lumbering: the fact that 66 out of 71 specimens from the Bahamas were obtained
during this period supports this view.   In 1951, the first census of the breeding
population gave a total of about 500 pairs (1); the 1961 census showed that while
the number of pairs had been maintained the production of young per pair had
decreased (8); and the third, 1971, census, indicated a decline to 201 pairs.
Brown-headed Cowbirds Molothrus ater invaded the warbler's habitat for the first
time in the 1870s, and parasitized 67 percent of a sample of 140 nests between
1963 and 1971 (9), compared with only 24 percent of 29 nests between 1931 and 1955
(10).   Removal of cowbirds from breeding areas began in 1972, following several
years of experimentation (12); it has recently reduced parasitisim to below 5
percent of the nests sampled (2; 13).   Numbers of singing males (and hence pairs)
recorded each spring since 1972 have been 200, 216, 167, 179, 200 and 219 (2; 11).
Productivity, following upon cowbird elimination, has exceeded 4 young per nest, a
rate higher than for any other North American warbler (2).   The few recent
observations of the species in its Bahama wintering grounds suggest wide dispersal
over the archipelago.

HABITAT   Jack pine stands between 8 and 22 years old on well-drained sandy soil
('Grayling sands'), with low undergrowth and scattered clearings (1; 3).   Only at
the southernmost edge of the extensive jack pine forests of North America are there
substantial areas where soil and undergrowth conditions are suitable for this
ground nesting warbler, which may well account for its remarkably narrow breeding
range (1).   Since the mid-1950s, stands of suitable age have decreased from a
maximum of 7500 ha to less than 2000 ha as the result of fire control; plans now
call for the rotational management of an additional 50,600 ha by burning, cutting
and planting, which should provide about 15,000 ha of suitable habitat for the
future expansion of the warbler population (2; 3).   In the Bahamas the species has
most often been noted in broadleaved scrub, of which there is no shortage, but
there are also a few records from pine forests in the three northern islands; the
pines have been extensively cut over since the mid-1950s but are regrowing in most
places (2; 6; 15).

<u>CONSERVATION MEASURES TAKEN</u>   Fully protected by the U.S. Endangered Species Act
of 1973 and by Michigan state law.   Protected in Canada by the U.S.-Canada
Migratory Bird Treaty and by the Ontario Endangered Species Act.   Protected by law
in the Bahamas.   The U.S. Fish and Wildlife Service has appointed a recovery team,
which has prepared a recovery plan (3).   In 1957, the Michigan Dept. of Natural
Resources established three 10 sq. km tracts as reserves for this warbler.   In
1961, 1620 ha of the Huron National Forest were designated as a Kirtland's Warbler
Management Area by the U.S. Forest Service (14).   Research has been coordinated
by a committee set up by the Michigan Audubon Society since 1963, and more recently
by the Recovery Team.   Removal by the use of baited traps of Brown-headed Cowbirds
from the warbler's breeding range, was begun in 1972 and has virtually eliminated
the threat presented by cowbird brood parasitism to the production of young
warblers (2; 3; 12).   Studies of this productivity date from the 1930s and annual
censuses of the species from 1971.   State and federal agencies, universities, and
private companies and organizations have collaborated in management by fire,
cutting and planting to produce an increasing amount of optimal habitat.   Several
searches for this warbler have been undertaken in its winter quarters. (3; 6; 15).

<u>CONSERVATION MEASURES PROPOSED</u>   Continuation of existing programs, particularly
the enlargement of suitable habitat by a further 15,000 ha.   This should be
sufficient to support a population of over 1000 pairs.   A suggestion has been
made, but perhaps unnecessarily, that the warbler should be introduced to new
areas by using other warblers as foster parents (3).

<u>REMARKS</u>   The requirements of this species are now well enough understood and
the programs for its welfare seem adequate; subject to availability of funds,
improvement of its status should therefore be assured.

<u>REFERENCES</u>   1.   Mayfield, H. 1960.   <u>The Kirtland's Warbler</u>.   Cranbrook
                        Institute of Science.
               2.   American Ornithologists' Union, 1977.   Report of the Committee
                     on Conservation 1976-77.   <u>Auk</u> 94(4, Suppl.): 1DD-19DD.
               3.   Kirtland's Warbler Recovery Team, 1976.   Kirtland's Warbler
                     Recovery Plan.   U.S. Fish and Wildlife Service.
               4.   Ontario Ministry of Natural Resources, 1977.   Rare Warbler
                     added to endangered list.   News release of 6 September.
               5.   Clench, M.H. 1973.   The fall migration route of Kirtland's
                     Warbler.   <u>Wilson Bull</u>. 85: 417-428.
               6.   Radabaugh, B.E. 1974.   Kirtland's Warbler and its Bahama
                     wintering grounds.   <u>Wilson Bull</u>. 86: 374-383.
               7.   Lane, J. 1975.   Kirtland's Warbler in Mexico.   <u>Amer. Birds</u>
                     29: 144.
               8.   Mayfield, H.F. 1962.   1961 decennial census of the Kirtland's
                     Warbler.   <u>Auk</u> 79: 173-182.
               9.   Mayfield, H.F. 1972.   Third decennial census of Kirtland's
                     Warbler.   <u>Auk</u> 89: 263-268.
              10.   Walkinshaw, L.H. 1972.   Kirtland's Warbler--endangered.
                     <u>Amer. Birds</u> 26: 3-9.
              11.   Mayfield, H.F. 1975.   The numbers of Kirtland's Warblers.
                     <u>Jack-pine Warbler</u> 53: 39-47.
              12.   Shake, W.F. & Mattsson, J.P. 1975.   Three years of cowbird
                     control: an effort to save the Kirtland's Warbler.   <u>Jack-pine
                     Warbler</u> 53: 48-53.
              13.   Anderson, W.L. & Storer, R.W. 1976.   Factors influencing
                     Kirtland's Warbler nesting success.   <u>Jack-pine Warbler</u> 54:
                     105-115.
              14.   Mayfield, H.F. 1963.   Establishment of preserves for the
                     Kirtland's Warbler in the state and national forests of
                     Michigan.   <u>Wilson Bull</u>. 75: 216-220.
              15.   Mayfield, H.F. 1972.   Winter habitat of Kirtland's Warbler.
                     <u>Wilson Bull</u>. 84: 347-349.

BARBADOS YELLOW WARBLER

Dendroica petechia petechia (Linnaeus, 1766)

Order PASSERIFORMES   Family PARULIDAE

STATUS   Endangered.   Rare, local, and possibly still decreasing on Barbados,
West Indies.   Clearing of mangroves and nest parasitism by the Shiny Cowbird
Molothrus bonariensis have caused the grave deterioration in its status (1).

DISTRIBUTION   The subspecies was widespread in Barbados and to be seen in urban
gardens as recently as 1926.   Since that date, there has been a steady reduction
in its range (1) and it is now known from only five small areas on the west coast
and two slightly larger areas on the south and south-east coasts (J. Sheppard in
litt. to T. Lovejoy, 1976).

POPULATION   Formerly abundant, but since 1916, when the Shiny Cowbird became
established, increasingly small (1).   There are now no more than 30-40 pairs of
the warbler, segregated in several small mangrove swamps or manchineel (Hippomane)
groves.   The largest sub-population comprises six pairs in an area of 12-16
hectares (J. Sheppard in litt. to T. Lovejoy, 1976).

HABITAT   Once this warbler occurred in most habitats on Barbados but with the
arrival in the island of the Shiny Cowbird, which apparently parasitizes its nests,
the warbler retreated from the more open habitats favoured by the cowbird and is
now only to be found in the very few remaining areas of mangrove.   The west coast,
which formerly had substantial areas of mangrove, has now been almost entirely
'developed'.

CONSERVATION MEASURES TAKEN   None known.

CONSERVATION MEASURES PROPOSED   None known.

REMARKS   There are seven other subspecies of the Yellow Warbler, breeding from
Alaska to Florida and Mexico; none of them are believed to be at risk.

REFERENCE   1.   Bond, J. 1961.   Extinct and near extinct birds of
                   the West Indies.   Pan-American Section, ICBP,
                   Res. Rep. No. 4.

NEW PROVIDENCE BAHAMA YELLOWTHROAT

Geothlypis rostrata rostrata Bryant, 1867

Order PASSERIFORMES   Family PARULIDAE

STATUS   Indeterminate.   Restricted to one island in the Bahamas, West Indies.
A scarcity of recent records, in spite of considerable search for the subspecies,
suggests it may be seriously threatened.   Overdevelopment of its island home is
the suggested cause of decline.

DISTRIBUTION   Occurs only on New Providence, the most heavily populated of the
Bahamas, where it has been found recently only on the ridge to the south of Lake
Cunningham and in the area of St. Augustine's Monastery toward the eastern end of
the island (1).

POPULATION   This subspecies has become quite scarce since the mid-1950s.   Most
specimens were collected toward the end of last century.   It was seen and heard
several times in 1949, and there have apparently been occasional sightings more
recently, although two ornithologists failed to find it during extensive searches
in the past 15 years. (1-4).

HABITAT   Hardwood coppice and scrub.   Although substantial areas of hardwoods
on New Providence have been replaced by housing, there should still be sufficient
to sustain a reasonable population of this subspecies.   It tends to spend a good
deal of its time on the ground so may frequently fall victim to feral cats and
rats.

CONSERVATION MEASURES TAKEN   None known.

CONSERVATION MEASURES PROPOSED   None known.

REMARKS   The nominate race has in past taxonomic treatment been held to include
the abundant Yellowthroat population from the much larger island of Andros, but
Andros specimens have recently been shown to be morphologically separable and
have been distinguished at a subspecific level from those of New Providence (4).
Another subspecies, G. r. coryi, has not been observed recently on Eleuthera
island and may be at risk there, but it also occurs on nearby Cat island where it
is not uncommon.   Two other subspecies, from Grand Bahama and Abaco, are not at
risk.   The Bahamas populations of G. rostrata have been combined with G. trichas
of continental North America by one author (5).

REFERENCES   1.   Brudenell-Bruce, P.G.C. 1975.   The Birds of the Bahamas.
                     New York: Taplinger Publishing Co.
              2.   Bond, J. 1971.   Sixteenth supplement to the Check-list of
                     Birds of the West Indies (1956).   Philadelphia Acad. Nat. Sci.
              3.   Bond, J. 1976.   Twentieth supplement to the Check-list of
                     Birds of the West Indies (1956).   Philadelphia Acad. Nat. Sci.
              4.   Schwartz, A. 1970.   Subspecific variation in two species of
                     Antillian birds. Quart. Jour. Florida Acad. Sci. 33: 221-236.
              5.   Phillips, A.R. 1961.   Notas sistematicas sobre aves
                     mexicanas. 1.   Anales Inst. Biol. Mexico 32: 333-381.

SEMPER'S WARBLER

Leucopeza semperi Sclater, 1876

Order PASSERIFORMES   Family PARULIDAE

STATUS   Endangered.   Restricted to St. Lucia, Lesser Antilles, West Indies.
A warbler of the forest understory, probably nesting on or near the ground, it
may well have fallen easy prey to the introduced mongoose Herpestes auropunctatus.

DISTRIBUTION   Formerly throughout the mountain forests of St. Lucia, but of five
records of the species in the last forty years one was from Louvet on the windward
eastern coast while all the others were from the Barre de l'Ile ridge separating
the windward and leeward halves of the island, between Piton Flore and Piton
Canarie (1; 2).

POPULATION   No precise figures are available.   The last specimen was taken in
1934 on the summit of Piton Flore.   It has been seen or heard subsequently in
1947, 1961, possibly 1962 (1; 2) and most recently 1972, when a pair was observed
by several people at close range at Barre de l'Ile on the road between Castries
and Dennery (C.R. Mason 1974, pers. comm.).   The negative reports of those who
have spent a considerable time searching for this species suggest it must be very
rare indeed.

HABITAT   Undergrowth of mountain forests (1; 2).

CONSERVATION MEASURES TAKEN   None known.

CONSERVATION MEASURES PROPOSED   None known.

REMARKS   This species is clearly the rarest of the thirteen species of wood
warblers endemic to islands of the Caribbean.

REFERENCES   1.   Fisher, J., Simon, N. & Vincent, J. 1969.   Wildlife in
                    Danger.   New York: Viking Press; London: Collins.
              2.   Bond, J. 1961.   Extinct and near extinct birds of the
                    West Indies.   Pan-American Section, ICBP, Res. Rept. No. 4.

BACHMAN'S WARBLER

Vermivora bachmanii (Audubon, 1833)

Order PASSERIFORMES   Family PARULIDAE

STATUS   Endangered. This species is nearing if it has not yet quite reached
extinction. Unconfirmed sightings at the rate of about one a year may be of
isolated prospecting individuals rather than indicative of resident populations,
not one of which is at present known. Habitat destruction in the restricted
breeding area and/or the wintering area of the species, is thought to have been
responsible for its decline. It is North America's rarest songbird.

DISTRIBUTION   Nesting has been recorded in Missouri, Arkansas, Kentucky,
Alabama and South Carolina. The species has also been recorded in Florida,
Georgia, Louisiana, Mississippi, North Carolina, Virginia, Oklahoma and Indiana.
It migrates south through Florida to Cuba and the Isle of Pines and has also been
recorded at Cay Sal, Bahamas (1; 2). Its present distribution is virtually
unknown. Sightings, mostly unconfirmed, have been made in the 1970s in Cameron
Parish, Louisiana (3) and in I'On Swamp near Charleston, South Carolina (15;
J. Shuler 1977, pers. comm.).

POPULATION   This warbler was locally quite common until the turn of the century.
In March of the years 1886 to 1888, 38 were collected at Lake Ponchartrain,
Louisiana (1); in March 1890, 46 were collected along a 113 km stretch of the
Suwannee River in northern Florida and about 50 were noted in a single 5 ha area
in one day (4) and in March of 1892 and of 1893, another 50 were collected in the
same general area (5). In July and August of the years 1887 to 1889 some 150 to
200 were seen at Key West, Florida, and 58 collected. By contrast, only 2 have
been seen in Florida since 1949 (6). In Cuba several specimens were taken last
century, although there is evidence of increasing scarcity as early as 1893 (7),
but none have been taken since 1942 and the last sighting was in 1964 (6). In
I'On Swamp, South Carolina, 32 nests were found between 1906 and 1918, although
the species was already rare and very locally distributed (8-10). Twenty-two
pairs were located in two swamps in Kentucky in 1906 (11). The last nest was
found in Alabama in 1937. Since 1950 there have been no more than 6 sightings
in any year, none in some years, mostly toward the northern limits of distribution
and apparently not indicative of breeding populations (6).

HABITAT   Mature deciduous bottomland swamp forest, within which and on the edge
of which nests have been found in thickets, primarily of Arundinaria cane (9; 10).
Migrants were recorded in similar habitats in the 19th century (4). It has been
suggested that the species had a preference for nesting in areas of bottomland
forest that had been locally disturbed (16). Mature forest of this type has been
extensively exploited for lumber and the sloughs drained for agriculture throughout
the south-eastern United States, particularly in the decades around the turn of the
century when the major decline of Bachman's Warbler took place. In Cuba one 19th
century collector noted that the species had disappeared following the cutting of
the mahagua Hibiscus tiliaceus (7) and the turn of the century witnessed the large
scale clearing of Cuban lowland forests to make way for sugarcane plantations and
other agricultural uses.

CONSERVATION MEASURES TAKEN   The species is protected by law from killing,
capture or harassment in the United States under the Migratory Bird Treaty Act of
1965, the U.S. Endangered Species Act of 1973 and the laws of the individual
states in which it has occurred. I'On Swamp in South Carolina, where the species
was observed in 1975-1977, lies partly within Francis Marion National Forest and a
contract for a 5-year survey of the species in this swamp was placed by the U.S.
Forest Service in 1974.

CONSERVATION MEASURES PROPOSED   Protection of mature bottomland swamp forest in the Francis Marion National Forest sector of I'On Swamp for a trial 10-year period and active management of selected areas with the aim of establishing forest conditions similar to those which existed in the 1920s, when most of the nests of this warbler were found.   Investigation of other areas where breeding populations might be found, possibly assisted by the offer of rewards to induce more of the multitude of keen amateur bird-watchers in the United States to participate (14).

REMARKS   The large numbers of this species collected in the last century is not thought to have had any lasting effect on its populations at that time.   On the other hand, the suggestion that its numbers declined from purely natural causes unconnected with human activities (6) does not seem very plausible.

REFERENCES   1.   Sprunt, A. Jr. 1957.   Bachman's Warbler Vermivora bachmanii. In Griscom, L., Sprunt, A. Jr. et al.   The Warblers of America.   New York: Devin-Adair.
2.   Bond, J. 1956.   Check-list of Birds of the West Indies. Philadelphia Acad. Nat. Sci.
3.   Imhof, T.A. 1973.   Central Southern Region.   American Birds 27: 782-785.
4.   Brewster, W. 1891.   Notes on Bachman's Warbler (Helminthophila bachmani).   Auk 8: 149-157.
5.   Wayne, A.T. 1893.   Additional notes on the birds of the Suwanee River.   Auk 10: 336-338.
6.   Stevenson, H.M. 1972.   The recent history of Bachman's Warbler.   Wilson Bull. 84: 344-347.
7.   Gundlach, J. 1895.   Ornitologia Cubana.   Havana: La Moderna.
8.   Sprunt, A. Jr. & Chamberlain, E.B. 1949.   South Carolina Bird Life.   Columbia: Univ. South Carolina Press.
9.   Wayne, A.T. 1907.   The nest and eggs of Bachman's Warbler, Helminthophila bachmani, (Aud.), taken near Charleston, South Carolina.   Auk 24: 43-48.
10.   Shuler, J. 1977.   Bachman's Warbler habitat.   Chat 41: 19-23.
11.   Embody, G.C. 1907.   Bachman's Warbler breeding in Logan County, Kentucky.   Auk 24: 41-42.
12.   Hamel, P., Hooper, R.G. & Wright, L.M. 1976.   Where is Reverend Bachman's Warbler?   South Carolina Wildlife, March-April: 9-13.
13.   Hamel, P.B. 1976.   Searches for Bachman's Warblers in I'On Swamp, South Carolina.   Unpublished report to U.S. Forest Service.
14.   Evenden, F.G., Marshall, D.B. & Zeedyk, W.D. 1977.   Revised final report of the Bachman's Warbler Panel.   Unpublished.
15.   Shuler, J. 1977.   Three recent sight records of Bachman's Warbler.   Chat 41: 11-12.
16.   Hooper, R.G. & Hamel, P.E. 1977.   Nesting habitat of Bachman's Warbler - a review.   Wilson Bull. 89: 373-379.

MAUI NUKUPU'U

Hemignathus lucidus affinis Rothschild, 1893

Order   PASSERIFORMES   Family   DREPANIDIDAE

STATUS   Endangered.   Rediscovered high on the windward slopes of Haleakala
volcano, Maui, Hawaiian Islands, in August 1967, after having been considered
extinct since 1896.   It is restricted to one large valley and the adjacent
ridgetops (1; 2; 3).   The valley is considered among the least altered from its
natural state of Hawaii's many forested valleys.   Nonetheless, rats are present
throughout the valley as are introduced birds and plants (4).   Susceptibility to
avian diseases may have been a primary cause of the species' decline, for it was
already considered uncommon by the 1890s (5).

DISTRIBUTION   Known only from the north-east slope of Haleakala volcano, Maui,
Hawaiian Islands, the subspecies is apparently restricted at present to the upper
portions, above 1,675 m elevation, of Kipahulu Valley, and the adjacent ridgetops
(1; 2; 3).

POPULATION   Four were seen during the course of an expedition in Kipahulu Valley
in 1967 (3).   Others were seen in 1972 and 1973 in the same general area (6;
T.L.C. Casey 1974, pers. comm.).   The total population is not known, but it is
thought to be very small.   It should be pointed out, however, that conditions
for observing birds in Hawaii's rain forests are often poor, and the remote
valleys in which this and other rare honeycreepers still occur are visited only
very infrequently.

HABITAT   Undisturbed rain forest.   Even the least disturbed of Hawaii's rain
forests show some infiltration of non-native plants and animals.   For example,
the black rat Rattus rattus is widespread throughout mid- and upper-elevation
forests in Kipahulu Valley (4).

CONSERVATION MEASURES TAKEN   Protected by federal and state law from killing,
capture or harassment.   A biological survey of Kipahulu Valley was undertaken in
1967.   Portions of the valley were purchased by The Nature Conservancy and, in
conjunction with gifts of land, the entire valley is now included within the
boundaries of Haleakala National Park (4).   Access to the valley is restricted.

CONSERVATION MEASURES PROPOSED   Continued restriction of entry into Kipahulu
Valley to minimize further spread of introduced plants and animals (1).   Extension
of U.S. federal government jurisdiction to include portions of the Upper Hana and
Koolau Forest Reserves inhabited by this and other endangered Hawaiian honeycreepers.

REMARKS   The race H. l. lucidus from Oahu is extinct, and the Kauai race
H. l. hanapepe is near extinction.

REFERENCES   1.   U.S. Dept. of Interior Bureau of Sport Fisheries and Wildlife,
                    1973.   Threatened Wildlife of the United States.   U.S. Bur.
                    Sport Fish. Wildl. Res. Pub. 114.
              2.   Berger, A.J. 1972.   Hawaiian Birdlife.   Honolulu: University
                    Press of Hawaii.
              3.   Banko, W.E. 1968.   Rediscovery of Maui Nukupuu, Hemignathus
                    lucidus affinis, and sighting of Maui Parrotbill, Pseudonestor
                    xanthophrys, Kipahulu Valley, Maui, Hawaii.   Condor
                    70: 265-266.

4. Warner, R.E. (ed.) 1967.   Scientific report of the Kipahulu Valley Expedition.   Unpublished report.
5. Warner, R.E. 1968.   The role of introduced diseases in the extinction of the endemic Hawaiian avifauna.   <u>Condor</u> 70: 101-120.
6. Jacobi, J.D. and Casey, T. 1974.   New species of bird discovered on Maui, Hawaii.   <u>Elepaio</u> 34: 83-84.

KAUAI NUKUPU'U

Hemignathus lucidus hanapepe Wilson, 1889

Order PASSERIFORMES   Family DREPANIDIDAE

STATUS   Endangered. Restricted to a small portion of the Alaka'i Swamp, Kauai,
Hawaiian Islands, if it still exists. It was considered rare and local in the
1890s, and was not reported again until 1960. Since then it has rarely been seen,
despite repeated systematic searches in most parts of the Alaka'i Swamp forest (1;
2; 3; 4).

DISTRIBUTION   Records of this subspecies are confined to the upper Hanapepe Valley
and the Alaka'i Swamp, Kauai, Hawaiian Islands. It has been observed only three
or four times this century, always in the upper Koaie Stream Valley in the Alaka'i
Swamp (3).

POPULATION   Since the 1890s, when it was already rated as rare, the only sightings
have been of two in 1960, two in 1961 and three in 1964 (2). Although extensive
searches have been conducted in the area where it was found in the 1960s, it has
only been observed again once in 1972 and once in 1974 (4).

HABITAT   Undisturbed rainforest. Even the most remote portions of the Alaka'i
Swamp show indications of infiltration by exotic species. Rats and several
introduced birds occur throughout the swamp and invasive plants have become
established in many places, especially where human visitors are frequent (2).

CONSERVATION MEASURES TAKEN   The subspecies is protected by federal and state law.
The State of Hawaii has established a 4,050 hectare Alaka'i Swamp Wilderness
Preserve which includes the range of this subspecies. Surveys have been undertaken
to determine its distribution with greater precision.

CONSERVATION MEASURES PROPOSED   A major program to control the exotic plants
invading the swamp, since the existing programs have not proved adequate. Further
efforts to survey the recorded range of the subspecies and determine if it still
exists (1).

REMARKS   The nominate race H. l. lucidus of Oahu is extinct and H. l. affinis
of Maui is rated as endangered, having been rediscovered in 1967.

REFERENCES   1. U.S. Dept. of Interior Bureau of Sport Fisheries and Wildlife,
                  1973. Threatened wildlife of the United States. U.S. Bur.
                  Sport Fish. Wildl. Res. Pub. 114.
              2. Berger, A.J. 1972. Hawaiian Birdlife. Honolulu: University
                  Press of Hawaii.
              3. Richardson, F. & Bowles, J. 1964. A survey of the birds of
                  Kauai, Hawaii. B.P. Bishop Museum Bull. 227.
              4. Haley, D. 1975. The last Oo. Defenders 50: 476-479.

KAUAI 'AKIALOA

Hemignathus obscurus procerus   Cabanis, 1889

Order   PASSERIFORMES   Family   DREPANIDIDAE

STATUS   Critically endangered, possibly extinct.   Last seen in 1965, in
undisturbed rain forest in the upper Koaie Stream drainage of Alaka'i Swamp,
Kauai, Hawaiian Islands (1).   Specimens collected in 1891 were noted as having
sores on their feet and heads, evidence of the effects of avain diseases to which
many members of the Hawaiian honeycreeper family appear to have strong susceptibility (2).   Much of Kauai's forest has been grazed by cattle, goats or pigs,
and introduced predators, including arboreal rats, are present throughout, as
are several introduced birds and plants (3; 4).

DISTRIBUTION   In the 1800s considered widespread, occurring throughout the
native forests of Kauai.   If the species still exists it is to be found in the
upper Koaie Stream drainage of Alaka'i Swamp at an elevation of about 1,220 m.
All sightings in the 1960s came from this area (3; 4).

POPULATION   Formerly considered to be common.   A drastic decline took place
in the early decades of this century.   Two were seen in 1960; one of these was
collected (5).   One individual was seen in 1965 (1).   None have been seen
subsequently in spite of extensive systematic searches (3).

HABITAT   Formerly found throughout native forest on Kauai.   Observed most
recently in the relatively undisturbed rain forest of Alaka'i Swamp (4).

CONSERVATION MEASURES TAKEN   Protected by federal and state law.   The State of
Hawaii has established a 4,050 hectare Alaka'i Swamp Wilderness Preserve, which
includes the entire recent range of the species.   Repeated searches for the
species have been undertaken.

CONSERVATION MEASURES PROPOSED   Control of exotic plants and animals in the
Alaka'i Swamp Preserve (3).

REMARKS   Races of H. obscurus occurred on Oahu (ellisianus), Lanai (lanaiensis),
and Hawaii (obscurus).   All of these are extinct.

REFERENCES   1.   Huber, L.N. 1966.   Alaka'i Swamp, Kauai, March 1965.
                  Elepaio 26: 71.
             2.   Warner, R.E. 1968.   The role of introduced diseases in the
                  extinction of the endemic Hawaiian avifauna.   Condor
                  70: 101-120.
             3.   U.S. Dept. of Interior Bureau of Sport Fisheries and Wildlife.
                  1973.   Threatened Wildlife of the United States.   U.S. Bur.
                  Sport Fish. Wildl. Res. Pub. 114.
             4.   Berger, A.J. 1972.   Hawaiian Birdlife.   Honolulu: University
                  Press of Hawaii.
             5.   Richardson, F. and Bowles, J. 1964.   A survey of the birds of
                  Kauai, Hawaii.   B.P. Bishop Museum, Bull., 227.

'AKIAPOLA'AU

Hemignathus wilsoni (Rothschild, 1893)

Order PASSERIFORMES   Family DREPANIDIDAE

STATUS   Endangered.   Formerly widespread and common on the island of Hawaii.
Presently reduced to relict populations in two or three areas of native forest.
Deterioration of the native forests has been a major cause of its decline (1; 2).
Additional likely causes include the introduction of vectors of avian diseases (3),
introduced predators, especially arboreal rats, and possible competition of exotic
species of birds which have also been introduced (2).

DISTRIBUTION   Formerly found in all upland forests on the island of Hawaii, down
to 500 m elevation in Hilo District and to 1,050 m in Kona District (2).   Now
restricted to portions of the Kilauea Forest Reserve and adjacent land of Keauhou,
the western slope of Mauna Kea, the Kau forest, and at about 2,000 m in the Olaa
Forest Reserve, Puna District, where the species has also been sighted in the last
few years.   In addition, individual birds have been seen recently in the Kohala
Mountains and on Mt. Hualalai (5; 6; 7; W. Banko 1974, pers. comm.).

POPULATION   The species was considered to be common at the turn of the century,
but has since declined very markedly in abundance (1; 2).   Recent observations
are more a reflection of greater observation-effort than of an increase in
population.   In December 1972, 30 were observed on one day in or near the Kilauea
Forest Reserve, an area which at present supports the most substantial population
(5).   Surveys in 1976 in Kau District indicated that numbers may still be in the
low hundreds (8).   The total population is not known, but it is considered to be
low and will doubtless continue to decline as the forests to which the species is
restricted age and die (2).

HABITAT   Occurred formerly in all types of native forest, but with a preference
for those dominated by koa Acacia, mamane Sophora and naio Myoporum.   Presently
found in koa-'ohi'a Metrosideros forests in Kau District, in the koa forests of
Kilauea Forest Reserve between 1,525 m and 1,830 m elevation, and in the mamane-
naio forest on the west slope of Mauna Kea above 2,000 m elevation.   The last
mentioned is at an advanced stage of maturity, ground cover is sparse and erosion
severe due to overgrazing by goats and sheep and rooting of pigs, so that little
regeneration is taking place (2; 4; 5; 8).

CONSERVATION MEASURES TAKEN   The species is protected by federal and state law
from killing, capture or harassment.

CONSERVATION MEASURES PROPOSED   Management of Kaohe and Mauna Kea State Game
Management Areas for preservation of endangered species rather than as habitat for
sheep and goats and game birds.   Relinquishment of large privately held lands in
Kilauea Forest Reserve to private conservation organizations or the U.S. federal
government for management.   An aggressive policy of pig control is also needed (2).

REMARKS   Since 1960 attention has been repeatedly drawn by conservationists to
the problems of the mamane-naio forests on the flank of Mauna Kea and their failure
to regenerate due to excessive sheep and goat grazing (4), but so far with little
reaction from the State of Hawaii Department of Land and Natural Resources which is
responsible for looking after most of these forests.

REFERENCES 1. U.S. Dept. of Interior Bureau of Sport Fisheries and Wildlife.
                1973. Threatened wildlife of the United States. U.S. Bur.
                Sport Fish. Wildl. Res. Pub. 114.
            2. Berger, A.J. 1972. Hawaiian Birdlife. Honolulu: University
                Press of Hawaii.
            3. Warner, R.E. 1968. The role of introduced diseases in the
                extinction of the endemic Hawaiian avifauna. Condor 70:
                101-120.
            4. Warner, R.E. 1960. A forest dies on Mauna Kea. Pacific
                Discovery 14(5): 6-14.
            5. Van Riper, C., III. 1973. Island of Hawaii land bird distribu-
                tion and abundance. Elepaio 34: 1-3.
            6. Gagné, W.C. 1973. Highlights of the 1972 Volcano, Hawaii,
                Christmas Count. Elepaio 33: 88-90.
            7. Jacobi, J.D. 1974. 'Akiapola'au and its remaining habitat.
                Elepaio 34: 74-76.
            8. U.S. Fish and Wildlife Service, 1976. Kau Forest bird study -
                Hawaii. Unpublished report.

PALILA

Loxioides (Psittirostra) bailleui (Oustalet, 1877)

Order PASSERIFORMES   Family DREPANIDIDAE

STATUS   Endangered.   Restricted to the high-elevation park-like forests of
Mauna Kea, Hawaii, where it is rare, local and decreasing.

DISTRIBUTION   In the 1890s this species occurred in suitable habitat, between
1,220 m and 1,830 m elevation, in Kona and Hamakua Districts, and above 1,985 m
to the tree line on the slopes of Mauna Kea, Hilo District, Hawaii.   It is now
only to be found on the western slope of Mauna Kea (1; 2; 3).

POPULATION   In the 19th century the species was considered to be abundant,
although locally distributed.   It now survives only in the mamane (Sophora)-
naio (Myoporum) forest of Mauna Kea.   In 1966, a minimum of 100 birds in this
habitat along one mile of road was estimated to be present and a subsequent
estimate of the population in 1975 gave a total of 1400 birds; this was based on
two censuses in which numerous observers participated and over 200 birds were
counted (C. Van Riper 1975, J.M. Scott 1977, pers. comms.).

HABITAT   The species is dependent on the mamane tree for its existence, although
it is no longer present in the mid-elevation mamane forests of Hamakua and Kona
districts.   The high-elevation mamane-naio forest of Mauna Kea nearly encircles
the volcano between 1,830 m and 2,745 m elevation, and the Palila is now restricted
to a portion of this forest belt.   A substantial part of it, including Kaohe and
Mauna Kea Game Management Areas, is managed for hunting by the Hawaii State
Division of Fish and Game.   Maintenance of populations of game species at levels
high enough to satisfy hunters has resulted in severe overgrazing, erosion and
absence of forest regeneration over wide areas.   The upper tree limit has
receded more than 150 m in recent years (2; 4).

CONSERVATION MEASURES TAKEN   The species is protected by federal and state
laws from killing, capture or harassment.   A study of its ecology is being
undertaken.

CONSERVATION MEASURES PROPOSED   As long ago as 1960, the destructive management
of the Mauna Kea mamane-naio forest solely in the interests of maintaining high
populations of game was openly criticized (4).   No modification of this management
objective has been apparent despite the repeated, urgent and anxious pleas from
conservationists.   Construction of a system of sheep and goat exclosures and the
elimination of populations of grazing mammals are urgently required to promote
regeneration of what is in effect a dying forest (1; 2; 3).   The forest areas
now leased by the State of Hawaii to private cattle ranches as range-land should
be incorporated into the Hawaii forest reserve system and managed with preservation
of this species in mind.

REMARKS   If the Palila continues to decline it will be essentially because of
human carelessness and neglect.

REFERENCES   1.   U.S. Dept. of Interior Bureau of Sport Fisheries and
Wildlife, 1973.   Threatened Wildlife of the United States.
U.S. Bur. Sport Fish. Wildl. Res. Pub. 114.
2.   Berger, A.J. 1972.   Hawaiian Birdlife.   Honolulu:
University Press of Hawaii.
3.   Van Riper, C., III. 1973.   Unpublished progress report to
ICBP on Palila research.
4.   Warner, R.E. 1960.   A forest dies on Mauna Kea.
Pacific Discovery 13: 6-14.

HAWAII 'AKEPA

Loxops coccinea coccinea (Gmelin, 1789)

Order PASSERIFORMES   Family DREPANIDIDAE

STATUS   Vulnerable. General deterioration of native forests due to introduced
grazing animals and wholesale infiltration by arboreal rats, exotic birds, which
may compete with native species, and vectors of avian diseases, from which the
Hawaiian honeycreepers appear to have little immunity, are all thought to be
contributory causes of its decline (1; 2; 3).

DISTRIBUTION   This subspecies of 'Akepa has been recorded in historic times from
all native forests of Hawaii Island, but is now no longer to be found in the great
majority of them.   Its largest concentrations survive in the Kilauea Forest
Reserve, adjacent Keauhou and in parts of Kau District.   One or two have also
recently been reported from the west slopes of Mauna Kea and from Hualalai (1; 2;
4; 5).

POPULATION   Considered abundant in certain forests on Hawaii up until towards the
end of the 19th century, the subspecies declined in number shortly thereafter.
Recent sightings include about 12 seen in April 1971, in Kau District, and 13 seen
in December 1972, in the Kilauea Forest Reserve (4; 5).   The present population is
unknown, but surveys in 1976 in Kau District suggested that somewhere between 4,000
and 8,000 is the likely figure (6).

HABITAT   There are records of this subspecies from all types of native forest on
Hawaii, but it is now most frequently associated with koa (Acacia koa) woodlands
and less frequently with rainforest dominated by 'ohi'a (Metrosideros collina) (1).

CONSERVATION MEASURES TAKEN   Legal protection from killing, capture or harassment
has been given to this 'Akepa at both federal and state levels.

CONSERVATION MEASURES PROPOSED   Placing of the large, privately-owned portions of
the upper or Keauhou sector of Kilauea Forest Reserve under the management of
private conservation organizations or of the U.S. federal government, followed by
an aggressive program to control pigs and goats.   Pig rooting and browsing by
feral goats have combined to prevent regeneration of the native tree species in the
habitat on which the 'Akepa totally depends.   Research into its distribution,
population and ecology needs also to be continued (1; 2).

REMARKS   Of the other subspecies L. c. ochracea of Maui is excessively rare,
L. c. rufa of Oahu already extinct, but L. c. caeruleirostris of Kauai is still
fairly common.

REFERENCES   1.   U.S. Dept. of Interior Bureau of Sport Fisheries and Wildlife,
                    1973.   Threatened Wildlife of the United States.   U.S. Bur.
                    Sport Fish. Wildl. Res. Pub. 114.
               2.   Berger, A.J. 1972.   Hawaiian Birdlife.   Honolulu:University
                    Press of Hawaii.
               3.   Warner, R.E. 1968.   The role of introduced diseases in the
                    extinction of the endemic Hawaiian avifauna.   Condor 70:
                    101-120.

REFERENCES (cont.)

4. Van Riper, C., III. 1973. Island of Hawaii land bird distribution and abundance. _Elepaio_ 34: 1-3.
5. Gagne, W.C. 1973. Highlights of the 1972 Volcano, Hawaii, Christmas Count. _Elepaio_ 33: 88-90.
6. U.S. Fish and Wildlife Service, 1976. Kau Forest bird study - Hawaii. Unpublished report.

MAUI 'AKEPA

Loxops coccinea ochracea Rothschild, 1893

Order PASSERIFORMES

Family DREPANIDIDAE

STATUS   Critically endangered - approaching extinction.   Infiltration of Hawaiian
native forests by introduced mammals, including arboreal rats, by exotic birds that
may compete with native species, and by vectors of avian diseases, from which the
Hawaiian honeycreepers apparently have little immunity, are all likely contributory
causes of its decline (1; 2; 3).

DISTRIBUTION   The earlier distribution of this subspecies was never clearly
defined but it was known to occur in the rainforest on the north-eastern slopes of
Haleakala volcano, Maui, Hawaii (1; 2).   It is now only very occasionally reported
from the edge of the rainforest below Puu Alaea at 2,075 m (W. Banko 1974, pers.
comm.) and from the nearby ridge to the north-west of Kipahulu Valley, at altitudes
of between 2,045 m and 2,135 m, on the north-eastern shoulder of Haleakala (W.Banko
and T. Casey 1974, pers. comms.).

POPULATION   There are no precise indications of the former population of this
subspecies, except that in the 19th century it was thought to be relatively common.
In the present century, the only reports are of sightings of single birds in
November 1970, June 1972 and July 1973, and an earlier one, in November 1950, of an
unspecified but small number of others which might have belonged to this subspecies
(W. Banko and T. Casey, pers. comms.).   The Kipahulu Valley Expedition of 1967
failed to find it.

HABITAT   Undisturbed native rainforest dominated by 'ohi'a (Metrosideros).
Formerly also in koa (Acacia koa) woodlands.   There are still substantial amounts
of relatively undisturbed rainforest on the north-eastern slopes of Haleakala
volcano (4; 2).

CONSERVATION MEASURES TAKEN   The subspecies is protected by federal and state
laws from killing, capture or harassment.   The most recent sightings of it were
made on a ridge above Kipahulu Valley which is now included within the boundaries
of Haleakala National Park.

CONSERVATION MEASURES PROPOSED   Extension of U.S. federal government control over
a larger portion of the Upper Hana and Koolau Forest Reserves.   Careful regulation
of visits to the entire area.

REMARKS   The nominate race on Hawaii, L. c. coccinea, rates as vulnerable and the
Oahu L. c. rufa is extinct, but the Kauai L. c. caeruleirostris is still relatively
common.

REFERENCES   1.   U.S. Dept. of Interior Bureau of Sport Fisheries and Wildlife,
                     1973.   Threatened wildlife of the United States.   U.S. Bur.
                     Sport Fish. Wildl. Res. Pub. 114.
              2.   Berger, A.J. 1972.   Hawaiian Birdlife.   Honolulu: University
                     Press of Hawaii.
              3.   Warner, R.E. 1968.   The role of introduced diseases in the
                     extinction of the endemic Hawaiian avifauna.   Condor 70:
                     101-120.
              4.   Casey, T. 1973.   Excerpts from the Preliminary Report on the
                     Bird Life in Waihoi Valley, Maui, 1972.   Elepaio 34: 46-50.

PO'O ULI

Melamprosops phaeosoma   Casey and Jacobi, 1974

Order   PASSERIFORMES   Family   DREPANIDIDAE

STATUS   Rare and localized.   Discovered in 1973, in remote forests on the
north-eastern slopes of Haleakala volcano, Maui.   The species is very restricted
geographically and is rare throughout its known range (1).

DISTRIBUTION   Known only from the upper Koolau Forest Reserve on the north-
eastern flanks of Haleakala volcano, Maui, between 1,585 and 2,045 m elevation,
bounded on the south by the north wall of Kipahulu Valley and on the west by Puu
Alaea cinder cone.

POPULATION   Not known precisely, although considered to be very small.   The
species has been observed only a handful of times since its discovery.   A
maximum of five has been seen on any one day (T. Casey 1974, pers. comm.).

HABITAT   Wet, high elevation 'ohi'a (Metrosideros) forest.   The north-eastern
slope of Haleakala volcano supports extensive tracts of some of the least
altered native rain forest habitat remaining in the Hawaiian Islands.   Nonetheless
this forest has been invaded by feral pigs, two species of rats, mongooses, several
species of introduced songbirds, and many exotic plants.

CONSERVATION MEASURES TAKEN   Protected by federal law from killing, capture or
harassment.

CONSERVATION MEASURES PROPOSED   The upper Koolau Forest Reserve should be
administered by the U.S. federal government and visits to the area should be
strictly controlled.

REMARKS   The U.S. Department of Interior's Endangered Wildlife Program has
created a position for a biologist on Maui, whose work will involve research on
this and other endangered species on that island.

REFERENCES   1.   Casey, T.L.C. and Jacobi, J.D. 1974.   A new genus and
                     species of bird from the island of Maui, Hawaii
                     (Passeriformes: Drepanididae).   B.P. Bishop Museum Occas.
                     Papers 24 (12): 216-226.

CRESTED HONEYCREEPER

Palmeria dolei (Wilson, 1891)

Order   PASSERIFORMES   Family   DREPANIDIDAE

STATUS   Vulnerable.   Confined to the upper elevation rain forest of the north
and east sides of Haleakala volcano, Maui, Hawaiian Islands, where it has always
been considered local and uncommon; formerly also occurred on Molokai.   Although
the species has been sighted several times recently from several localities on
Haleakala, and where it occurs is conspicuous, its very narrow altitudinal range
and obviously small total population give cause for continuing concern.   The
introduction of arboreal rats, avian diseases, and exotic birds which may compete
with this species, are possible causes of its decline.   On Molokai, the forests
have suffered serious degradation (1; 2).

DISTRIBUTION   Known from the rain forests of Maui and Molokai, Hawaiian Islands.
The species was last observed on Molokai in 1907.   It is restricted on Maui to
the upper north and east slopes of Haleakala volcano between 1,800 and 2,150 m,
and has never been found much below 1,525 m.   Recent sightings are from the
forest below Puu Alaea on the north slope, the Kipahulu Valley and the ridges to
the south and north of it, especially in the vicinity of Wai Anapanapa on the
east slope of Haleakala volcano (1; 2; 3; 4).

POPULATION   The Crested Honeycreeper was never known to be particularly common.
Its present population is small, but exact numbers are not known (1; 2).

HABITAT   High-elevation rain forest, dominated by 'ohi'a (Metrosideros);
apparently seen frequently in association with trees and shrubs of the genus
Pelea (3).   Although this habitat is difficult of access to humans, introduced
pigs, birds and arboreal rats are regularly present.

CONSERVATION MEASURES TAKEN   Protected by federal and state law.   Kipahulu
Valley is within the boundaries of Haleakala National Park.   Access to Kipahulu
Valley is restricted by the U.S. National Park Service.

CONSERVATION MEASURES PROPOSED   Extension of U.S. federal government jurisdiction to include entire present range of species.

REFERENCES   1.   U.S. Dept. of Interior Bureau of Sport Fisheries and
                     Wildlife, 1973.   Threatened Wildlife of the United States.
                     U.S. Bur. Sport Fish. Wildl. Res. Pub. 114.
              2.   Berger, A.J. 1972.   Hawaiian Birdlife.   Honolulu: University
                     Press of Hawaii.
              3.   Warner, R.E., (ed.) 1967.   Scientific report of the Kipahulu
                     Valley Expedition.   Unpub. report submitted to The Nature
                     Conservancy.
              4.   Matthiessen, P.   1970.   Kipahulu from cinders to the sea.
                     Audubon 72(3):   11-23.

KAUAI CREEPER

Paroreomyza (Loxops) maculata bairdi (Stejneger, 1887)

Order PASSERIFORMES   Family DREPANIDIDAE

STATUS   Rare. Restricted to high elevation rainforest of the Alaka'i Swamp,
Kauai, Hawaii, where it is known to be less numerous than in former times.

DISTRIBUTION   Once widespread throughout the forest of Kauai, the subspecies is
presently confined to the central core of the Alaka'i Swamp (1; 2).

POPULATION   This subspecies was abundant at the end of the nineteenth century and
is still relatively common today, but only within the circumscribed area of least
disturbed rainforest in Alaka'i Swamp. At least 375 were seen in this small
portion of the swamp in 1960 and the present population must still be sizable (1; 2).

HABITAT   Montane rainforest of the Alaka'i Swamp on Kauai at an altitude of over
1,145 m. The dominant tree is the 'ohi'a (Metrosideros). The forests of Kauai
have been degraded by overgrazing from introduced mammals and the infiltration of
exotic plants. The Creeper may also suffer from the competition of introduced
songbirds and, like other Drepanidids, probably has little resistance to avian
diseases, while its nest may be vulnerable to introduced arboreal rats (1; 2; 3; 4).
No doubt all these factors have contributed to its decimation.

CONSERVATION MEASURES TAKEN   The subspecies is protected by state law. Most of
its range is included within the 4,050 ha Alaka'i Swamp Wilderness Preserve,
recently established by the State of Hawaii.

CONSERVATION MEASURES PROPOSED   A proposed dam and reservoir at the edge of the
Alaka'i Swamp would flood about 405 hectares of valuable habitat for native birds.
Abandonment of the plans for the reservoir has been strongly advocated by
conservation organizations; the Kauai Creeper is certainly a subspecies whose
future might be jeopardized by any activities threatening the ecological integrity
of the Alaka'i Swamp (1).

REMARKS   Of the other subspecies, nominate P. m. maculata of Oahu and P. m.
flammea of Molokai are both endangered, while P. m. montana of Lanai is extinct.
Only P. m. newtoni of Maui is still fairly widespread and common. P. m. mana
on Hawaii is now rather uncommon and local.

REFERENCES   1. Berger, A.J. 1972. Hawaiian Birdlife. Honolulu:University
                  Press of Hawaii.
              2. Richardson, F. & Bowles, J. 1964. A survey of the birds of
                  Kauai, Hawaii. B.P. Bishop Museum Bull. 227.
              3. Warner, R.E. 1968. The role of introduced diseases in the
                  extinction of the endemic Hawaiian avifauna. Condor 70:
                  101-120.
              4. Eddinger, C.R. 1970. A study of the breeding behavior of four
                  species of Hawaiian Honeycreepers (Drepanididae). Unpub. Ph.D.
                  thesis. Honolulu:University of Hawaii.

MOLOKAI CREEPER

Paroreomyza (Loxops) maculata flammea (Wilson, 1889)

Order PASSERIFORMES   Family DREPANIDIDAE

STATUS   Critically endangered - possibly extinct.   Thought to have been extinct
between 1949 and 1961 when rediscovered, but has not been seen since 1963.

DISTRIBUTION   In the 19th century this subspecies ranged widely in the native
forests of Molokai, Hawaiian Islands (1; 2).   It declined rapidly and disappeared
early in the present century, but was rediscovered along the Papaala Cliffs and
the Waikolu plateau of the central Molokai mountains (3).

POPULATION   The Creeper was considered abundant in the last century and still
common as late as 1907, but thereafter there was a catastrophic drop in its numbers
(2), so much so that it was assumed to have been extinct for some years when two
were sighted in 1961, three the following year and one more in 1963 (3).   It has
not been reported subsequently.   If a population still exists it is undoubtedly
very small.

HABITAT   Formerly throughout the Molokai forests.   Recent sightings have been
restricted to low dense 'ohi'a (Metrosideros) rainforest of the central mountain
ridge.   Molokai's forests have suffered severe reductions in area as the result of
grazing by goats, pigs, cattle and, more recently, axis deer, all of them
introduced to the island.   Occupation of the remaining forest by introduced birds,
which may compete with native species, by arboreal predators and by vectors of
avian diseases, from which Hawaiian honeycreepers appear to have limited immunity,
have probably all contributed to the decline of this now extremely rare subspecies.

CONSERVATION MEASURES TAKEN   Protection under federal and state laws from killing,
capture or harassment.

CONSERVATION MEASURES PROPOSED   Creation of a sanctuary along the forested
ridgetops and upper valleys of central Molokai, accompanied by intensive efforts to
control introduced grazing animals (1).

REMARKS   Of the other subspecies, P. m. bairdi of Kauai is fairly common but
local, P. m. maculata of Oahu nearly extinct, P. m. montana of Lanai certainly
extinct, P. m. newtoni of Maui fairly widespread and common, and P. maculata mana
of Hawaii uncommon and local.

REFERENCES   1.   U.S. Dept. of Interior Bureau of Sport Fisheries and Wildlife,
                    1973.   Threatened Wildlife of the United States.   U.S. Bur.
                    Sport Fish. Wildl. Res. Pub. 114.
              2.   Berger, A.J. 1972.   Hawaiian Birdlife.   Honolulu:University
                    Press of Hawaii.
              3.   Pekelo, N., Jr. 1963.   Some notes from Molokai.   Elepaio
                    23: 64.

OAHU CREEPER

Paroreomyza (Loxops) maculata maculata (Cabanis, 1850)

Order PASSERIFORMES   Family DREPANIDIDAE

STATUS   Endangered. This subspecies is difficult to distinguish in the field
from the comparatively common Oahu Amakihi Viridonia (Loxops) virens chloris, and
even the most experienced observers in Hawaii are cautious about making a positive
identification.   As in the case of other honeycreepers, destruction of much of the
native forest, introduction of predators, including arboreal rats, and of exotic
songbirds which may compete with native species, and introduction of vectors of
avian diseases from which most Hawaiian honeycreepers apparently have little
immunity, have been quoted as probable causes of decline (1; 2).

DISTRIBUTION   Widespread last century in the indigenous forests on the Waianae
and Koolau Mountain ranges of Oahu, Hawaii, this creeper has been most often
sighted in recent years along the upper ridges and adjacent high valleys of the
Koolau range, and on the flanks of Mt. Kaala in the Waianae range (1; 2; 3).

POPULATION   The creeper was formerly considered to be a common bird on Oahu. Its
present population is not known but considered to be very low in the light of the
small number of sightings in the Koolau range in 1973, 1974 and 1976, a single
probable sighting on Mt. Kaala in the Waianae range in December 1972, and the
sporadic sightings of earlier years (2; 3; 4; 5).

HABITAT   Formerly· many native forest areas on Oahu, but now confined to 'ohi'a
(Metrosideros) forest above 610 m elevation (1; 2).

CONSERVATION MEASURES TAKEN   Protection under federal and state laws from killing,
capture or harassment.

CONSERVATION MEASURES PROPOSED   Preservation and restoration of large tracts of
mature native forest on Oahu as refuges for endemic species.   Further research
into the population, distribution and life history of the subspecies (1).

REMARKS   Of the five other subspecies of this creeper, P. m. montana of Lanai is
extinct, P. m. flammea of Molokai critically endangered and the remaining three
uncommon to fairly common on their respective islands.

REFERENCES   1. U.S. Dept. of Interior Bureau of Sport Fisheries and Wildlife,
                  1973.   Threatened Wildlife of the United States.   U.S. Bur.
                  Sport Fish. Wildl. Res. Pub. 114.
              2. Berger, A.J. 1972.   Hawaiian Birdlife.   Honolulu: University
                  Press of Hawaii.
              3. Reports of recent sightings of this subspecies, taken from the
                  minutes of meetings or reports of trips of the Hawaiian Audubon
                  Society, dated 11 December 1972, 15 January 1973, 10 June 1973
                  and 18 June 1973, and reprinted in Elepaio 33 and 34.
              4. Wilson, E. 1974.   Field notes: Oahu Creeper on the Poamoho
                  Trail.   Elepaio 35: 31.
              5. Pyle, R.L. 1976.   The 1975 Honolulu Christmas Bird Count.
                  Elepaio 36: 92-94.

MAUI PARROTBILL

Pseudonestor xanthophrys Rothschild, 1893

Order   PASSERIFORMES   Family   DREPANIDIDAE

STATUS   Vulnerable. The forests of Maui, like all Hawaiian rain forests, are
infiltrated by introduced pigs, arboreal rats that are liable to prey on songbirds,
exotic birds that may compete with native species, and avian diseases. All of
these factors may have been contributory causes of the decline of this species
(1; 2).

DISTRIBUTION   In the 19th century known to be very local in the koa (Acacia
koa) forests at about 1,525 m elevation on the north-west slopes of Haleakala
volcano, Maui, Hawaiian Islands (1; 2). Found this century above 1,525 m in
'ohi'a (Metrosideros) forests of the north and east slopes of Haleakala, from
just north-west of Puu Alaea to the Wai Anapanapa area and upper Kipahulu Valley
(3; 4; 5; T. Casey 1974, pers. comm.).

POPULATION   Considered to be rare before 1900 (2). Sighted this century on
several occasions, in areas several miles distant from the 19th century localities
in which the species no longer is present (2; 3; 4; 5). No population estimate,
but in 1973 it was seen "in surprisingly high numbers" (5), as many as 9 on one
day (5, T. Casey 1974, pers. comm.).

HABITAT   Known last century from koa forests at 1,525 m on the north-western
slopes of Haleakala Crater. Found this century only in 'ohi'a forests above
1,525 m elevation. These forests are relatively intact and extensive on Maui (2).

CONSERVATION MEASURES TAKEN   Protected by federal and state law from killing,
capture or harassment. Kipahulu Valley lies within the boundaries of Haleakala
National Park. Visits to Kipahulu Valley are restricted by the U.S. National
Park Service.

CONSERVATION MEASURES PROPOSED   Extension of U.S. federal government jurisdiction
to include the high montane rain forest areas inhabited by this and other
endangered Hawaiian honeycreepers. Strict control of visits to this area.

REMARKS   The forests to the north-east of Haleakala volcano on Maui are probably
one of the two most important remaining forest habitats in the Hawaiian Islands.

REFERENCES   1.   U.S. Dept. of Interior Bureau of Sport Fisheries and Wildlife,
                    1973.   Threatened Wildlife of the United States.   U.S. Bur.
                    Sport Fish. Wildl. Res. Pub. 114.
              2.   Berger, A.J. 1972.   Hawaiian Birdlife. Honolulu: University
                    Press of Hawaii.
              3.   Richards, L.P. and Baldwin, P.H. 1953.   Recent records of some
                    Hawaiian honeycreepers.   Condor 55: 221-222.
              4.   Banko, W.E. 1968.   Rediscovery of Maui Nukupuu, Hemignathus
                    lucidus affinis, and sighting of Maui Parrotbill, Pseudonestor
                    xanthophrys, Kipahulu Valley, Maui, Hawaii.   Condor
                    70: 265-266.
              5.   Jacobi, J.D. and Casey, T. 1974.   New species of bird
                    discovered on Maui, Hawaii.   Elepaio 34: 83-84.

'O'U

Psittirostra psittacea (Gmelin, 1789)

Order PASSERIFORMES   Family DREPANIDIDAE

STATUS   Endangered.   The native forests of the Hawaiian Islands have been
degraded in the past century to a shadow of their former extent and quality.
They have been invaded by introduced grazing animals, terrestrial and arboreal
predators on native birds, avian disease from which the Hawaiian honeycreepers
apparently have little immunity (1) and exotic birds that may compete with native
species.   All of these may have contributed to the decline of this species (2; 3).

DISTRIBUTION   Formerly known from the Hawaiian Islands of Kauai, Oahu, Molokai,
Lanai, Maui and Hawaii.   Now occurs only very locally on Kauai and Hawaii (2; 3).
In Kauai it is found in the central core of the Alaka'i Swamp at an elevation
of about 1,220 m, between the upper Koaie Stream drainage and the upper Waialae
Stream drainage (3; 4; 5; 6; 7).   In Hawaii the species was sighted in the 1950s
and 1960s and most recently in 1974 at about 1,220 m above sea level in the Ola'a
Tract, which is administered as wilderness by the U.S. National Park Service
(W. Banko 1974, pers. comm.).   Systematic surveys in 1977 revealed its existence
north of the Ola'a Tract and into the Hilo Forest Reserve (J.M. Scott 1977, pers.
comm.).

POPULATION   This species was once considered relatively abundant, with a population ratio of about 1:20 compared with the Amakihi Viridonia (Loxops) virens, now
perhaps the second most numerous of the Hawaiian honeycreepers (3).   Recent visits
to the central Alaka'i Swamp on Kauai have frequently yielded sightings of one or
two birds, but almost never more and they are usually seen in the same immediate
area (4; 5; 6).   A single bird of this species was also seen on Hawaii in 1974
(W. Banko 1974, pers. comm.).   In 1977, a remarkable observation of 61 birds,
possibly more than the combined total of the numbers sighted in at least the last
half-century, was made during a series of forest surveys conducted by the U.S. Fish
and Wildlife Service in Hilo District and spanning 35 km of rainforest between 1160
and 1400 m elevation (J.M. Scott 1977, pers. comm.).   The total population for the
two islands is unknown but thought to be exceedingly low, although on Kauai it may
still reach the low hundreds.

HABITAT   Wet native forests between 915 m and 1,375 m in altitude, especially
where Ie'ie (Freycinetia) vines, which the species often selects for feeding (3),
are plentiful.   Birds seen in 1977 were often feeding on Tetraplasandra trees
(J.M. Scott 1977, pers. comm.).

CONSERVATION MEASURES TAKEN   The species is protected by federal and state law
from killing, capture or harassment.   The 4,050 hectare Alaka'i Swamp Wilderness
Preserve, established by the State of Hawaii, includes its entire present range on
Kauai.   The Ola'a Tract on Hawaii, which is of about the same size and provides
the species with one of its last known refuges in that island, is similarly
protected and administered as a Wilderness by the U.S. National Park Service
(2; W. Banko 1974, pers. comm.).

CONSERVATION MEASURES PROPOSED   U.S. endangered species recovery teams were
preparing a plan for the rehabilitation of this species in 1976.

REFERENCES   1.   Warner, R.E. 1968.   The role of introduced diseases in the
                  extinction of the endemic Hawaiian avifauna.   Condor 70:
                  101-120.
             2.   U.S. Dept. of Interior Bureau of Sport Fisheries and Wildlife,
                  1973.   Threatened Wildlife of the United States.   U.S. Bur.
                  Sport Fish. and Wildl. Res. Pub. 114.
             3.   Berger, A.J. 1972.   Hawaiian Birdlife.   Honolulu:University
                  Press of Hawaii.
             4.   Huber, L.N. 1966.   Alaka'i Swamp, Kauai, March 1965.
                  Elepaio 26: 71.
             5.   Gauthey, J.R., Atkinson, I. & Huddleston, C. 1968.
                  A Trip to the Alaka'i Plateau.   Elepaio 29: 19-20.
             6.   Mull, W.P. & Mull, M.E. 1971.   Sighting of the 'O'u on Kauai
                  trip.   Elepaio 32: 51-54.
             7.   Gagne, W. & Hart, A. 1974.   East Alaka'i Swamp.   In Kauai
                  Christmas Count, A. Hart, compiler.   Elepaio 34: 119-122.
             8.   Haley, D. 1975.   The last Oo.   Defenders 50: 476-479.

MONA YELLOW-SHOULDERED BLACKBIRD

Agelaius xanthomus monensis Barnes, 1945

Order PASSERIFORMES   Family ICTERIDAE

STATUS   Vulnerable.   Known from Mona Island, between Puerto Rico and Hispaniola,
West Indies, where its population is very small and threatened by proposals for
developing the island as a deepwater superport and oil refinery or using it as a
Navy bombing range.   The Shiny Cowbird Molothrus bonariensis, which has recently
begun to parasitize the nests of the nominate subspecies on Puerto Rico (4), was
reported from Mona in 1972 (H. Raffaele 1973, pers. comm.).

DISTRIBUTION   Confined to Mona Island where this subspecies has been found both
on the inland plateau and the coastal plain (1).

POPULATION   No early estimates.   Current estimate is 100-200 and there is no
evidence of any changes in abundance (2; 3; H. Raffaele 1973, pers. comm.).

HABITAT   Arid scrublands of the central plateau and coastal strip (1).

CONSERVATION MEASURES TAKEN   The subspecies is protected under Puerto Rico
Commonwealth law and by the U.S. Endangered Species Act of 1973.

CONSERVATION MEASURES PROPOSED   Elimination of Shiny Cowbirds from Mona if it
becomes clear that the blackbird has become a preferred host of that species (1).

REMARKS   The nominate race on Puerto Rico is also rated as Vulnerable.

REFERENCES   1.   Raffaele, H. 1973.   Assessment of Mona Island avifauna.
                    In Isla Mona, Vol. II, Appendix K.   Commonwealth of
                    Puerto Rico: Junta de Calidad Ambiental.
              2.   Post, W. 1974.   Proposal to U.S. Fish and Wildlife
                    Service for research on the population ecology of
                    the Yellow-shouldered Blackbird.
              3.   Post, W. & Wiley, J.W. 1976.   The Yellow-shouldered
                    Blackbird - present and future.   Amer. Birds 30: 13-20.
              4.   Post, W. & Wiley, J.W. 1977.   Reproductive interactions
                    of the Shiny Cowbird and the Yellow-shouldered Blackbird.
                    Condor 79: 176-189.

PUERTO RICO YELLOW-SHOULDERED BLACKBIRD

Agelaius xanthomus xanthomus (Sclater, 1862)

Order PASSERIFORMES   Family ICTERIDAE

STATUS   Vulnerable. This blackbird has declined markedly in abundance in
Puerto Rico, and it is now quite local. Drainage of freshwater wetlands is
thought to have been a primary cause of its decline, while predation by rats and,
more recently, brood parasitism by the Shiny Cowbird Molothrus bonariensis
(established on Puerto Rico only since 1955) are other factors now operating.

DISTRIBUTION   Once widespread in the entire coastal plain of Puerto Rico, but
now largely confined to the south-west coast near La Parguera and Cabo Rojo (1-4).
A small population is resident at Ceiba on the east coast. However, nesting on
the mainland is now very rare and most breeding occurs on small rat-free off-shore
islets. In the recent past competition for nest sites by Pearly-eyed Thrashers
Margarops fuscatus may have restricted the blackbird's breeding range (4).

POPULATION   This blackbird was once quite common in lowland Puerto Rico but has
declined in abundance during the last 60 years and there are now only about 2200
left, mostly in the south-west except for about 100 on the east coast. Brood
parasitism by the Shiny Cowbird has decreased the chances of a substantial
recovery (4; 5) and the annual rate of decline has been calculated at 20 percent
(W. Post 1977, pers. comm.).

HABITAT   Formerly freshwater wetlands, fields, mangroves and open woodland
throughout the Puerto Rican lowlands (2; 3). All but one of the wetland areas
have been drained (C.B. Kepler 1974, pers. comm.). The subspecies nests in
coconut palms and mangroves, now predominantly on offshore islets. Only coconut
palms with rat guards are utilized. The bird is most frequently seen in arid
scrubland around the south-west coast.

CONSERVATION MEASURES TAKEN   The subspecies is protected under Puerto Rico
Commonwealth law and by the U.S. Endangered Species Act of 1973. Research into
its status and biology has been undertaken by the Commonwealth of Puerto Rico Dept.
of Natural Resources.

CONSERVATION MEASURES PROPOSED   Further research to determine the best means
of mitigating the effect of brood parasitism by Shiny Cowbird (W. Post 1976, pers.
comm.).

REMARKS   The other subspecies A. l. monensis of Mona Island is also listed in the
Vulnerable category.

REFERENCES   1.   Post, W. 1974.   Proposal to U.S. Fish and Wildlife Service
                   for research on population ecology of the Yellow-shouldered
                   Blackbird.
              2.   Wetmore, A. 1916.   Birds of Porto Rico.   U.S. Dept. Ag.
                   Bull. 326: 1-140.
              3.   Danforth, S.T. 1925.   Birds of the Cartagena Lagoon,
                   Porto Rico.   J. Dept. Ag. Puerto Rico 10(1): 130 pp.
              4.   Post, W. & Wiley, J.W. 1976.   The Yellow-shouldered
                   Blackbird - present and future.   Amer. Birds 30: 13-20.
              5.   Post, W. & Wiley, J.W. 1977.   Reproductive interactions of
                   the Shiny Cowbird and the Yellow-shouldered Blackbird.
                   Condor 79: 176-184.

OLIVE-HEADED BRUSH-FINCH

Atlapetes flaviceps Chapman, 1912

Order PASSERIFORMES   Family FRINGILLIDAE

STATUS   Indeterminate.   Nothing is known of this distinctive species, collected
in 1911 in Colombia.   Forest destruction in the area where the species was
collected may well have affected it adversely.

DISTRIBUTION   Known only from the Rio Toche at an altitude of 2175 m on the
trail leading to the Quindio Pass and the western slope of the central Andes near
the north-western boundary of Tolima Department, Colombia (1).

POPULATION   Unknown.   The type and one other specimen were taken on successive
days in October 1911 and nothing more has been learned of this species (1).

HABITAT   Subtropical forest.   Much of this forest in northern Tolima Department
has now been cleared (R. Ridgely 1977, pers. comm.).

CONSERVATION MEASURES TAKEN   None known.

CONSERVATION MEASURES PROPOSED   None known.

REFERENCE   1.   Chapman, F.M. 1912.   Diagnoses of apparently new
                   Colombian birds.   Bull. Amer. Mus. Nat. Hist. 31:
                   139-166.

SÃO MIGUEL BULLFINCH

Pyrrhula pyrrhula murina Godman, 1866

Order PASSERIFORMES   Family FRINGILLIDAE

STATUS   Endangered. This distinctive subspecies is restricted to one island in
the Azores where it has been excessively rare for more than a half-century and may
now in fact be extinct.   Shooting to protect budding fruit trees caused its
actual or probable demise.

DISTRIBUTION   Known only from the eastern end of São Miguel (760 sq. km), the
north-easternmost island of the Azorean archipelago (1; 2).

POPULATION   Although from about the middle of the 19th century a bounty was paid
for beaks or heads of this bird on the grounds that it was a pest, it remained
tolerably abundant until at least 1866 (3).   However, by 1903 it was already
considered close to extinction (2), in spite of which a professional collector took
53 in 1907 and 5 were collected as lately as 1927.   Searches for the bird in
1953-1954 and in 1963 yielded only second-hand information suggesting that the
subspecies still existed and had been seen by reliable observers within the past
year or two (1).   This information was dramatically confirmed by the news of
birds captured in 1968 (6) and 1971, while there is an unconfirmed report that two
bullfinches were heard in 1975, singing their distinctive song (J.M. Alvarez
Cabral 1977, pers. comm.).

HABITAT   Forests of eastern São Miguel, and also nearby orchards when fruit
trees are in blossom (1).

CONSERVATION MEASURES TAKEN   Despite strong protests and representations by
professional ornithologists to the Portuguese government in the 1920s (4; 5), the
subspecies remained unprotected and it is only quite recently that hunting of this
bullfinch has been prohibited.

CONSERVATION MEASURES PROPOSED   None known.

REMARKS   The nine other subspecies ranging through most of the Palearctic are not
known to be at risk.

REFERENCES   1.   Bannerman, D.A. & W.M. 1966.   Birds of the Atlantic
                    Islands, Vol. 3.   Edinburgh and London: Oliver and
                    Boyd.
              2.   Hartert, E. & Ogilvie-Grant, W.R. 1905.   On the birds of
                    the Azores.   Novit. Zool. 12: 80-128.
              3.   Godman, F.D. 1866.   Notes on the birds of the Azores.
                    Ibis (new series) 2: 88-109.
              4.   Lowe, P.R. & Bannerman, D.A. 1930.   The extermination
                    of the Azorean Bullfinch.   Ibis (12)6: 374-379.
              5.   Murphy, R.C. & Chapin, J.P. 1930.   Letter to editor
                    of Auk.   Auk 47: 300-301.
              6.   van Vegten, J.A. 1968.   The Azores Bullfinch not extinct.
                    Ardea 56: 194.

RED SISKIN

Spinus cucullatus (Swainson, 1820)

Order PASSERIFORMES   Family FRINGILLIDAE

STATUS   Endangered.   This siskin from northern South America is under intense
pressure from trappers for the cage bird trade.   Its range and populations have
declined markedly in recent years, a trend unlikely to be changed until the last
bird has been trapped.

DISTRIBUTION   The species is very patchily distributed in northern Venezuela
from Monagas state westwards to Falcon, Lara and Trujillo (P. Schwartz 1974, pers.
comm.), on Trinidad in the north-western peninsula and north centre, and on
adjacent Monos and Gasparee islands (2), and in north-east Colombia in the Norte
de Santander division (1).   It is now absent from the more accessible areas of
Venezuela and there is only one recent record from Trinidad and none from Colombia
since 1947.

POPULATION   Unknown, although there has clearly been a major decline.   The
species at one time formed flocks and dispersed to more accessible areas in
northern Venezuela after breeding, but in the past decade trapping pressure has
stepped up and birds of both sexes are now sought in remote mountain areas during
the breeding season.   Formerly only males were trapped (P. Schwartz 1974, pers.
comm.).   Specimens were taken at Villa Felisa, 20 km south of Cúcuta, Colombia,
near the Venezuela border, in 1947 (1).   Two birds were seen in 1960 in the Arima
Valley, north-central Trinidad (2).

HABITAT   Tropical forest, open scrub and pastureland.   As the more inaccessible
forest is opened up, trappers take advantage of the situation and quickly deplete
populations of this species.

CONSERVATION MEASURES TAKEN   The species has legal protection in Venezuela,
but clandestine capture of it for sale continues unabated (W. Phelps 1974, pers.
comm.).   It is listed in Appendix 1 of the 1973 Convention on International Trade
in Endangered Species of Wild Fauna and Flora.

CONSERVATION MEASURES PROPOSED   None known.

REMARKS   The great demand for this siskin (a male fetched $50 in Venezuela in
1974) arises from the fact that it is the source of the highly sought after red
pigment in domestic canaries, with which it readily hybridizes.

REFERENCES   1.   de Schauensee, R.M. 1966.   The Species of Birds of South
                     America and their Distribution.   Narberth, Pa.: Livingston
                     Publishing Co.
              2.   ffrench, R. 1973.   A Guide to the Birds of Trinidad and
                     Tobago.   Wynnewood, Pa.: Livingston Publishing Co.

TUMACO SEEDEATER

Sporophila insulata Chapman, 1921

Order PASSERIFORMES   Family FRINGILLIDAE

STATUS   Indeterminate.   There are no records of this species, known from one
island off the coast of Colombia, since the type series was collected in 1912.
The island is now covered by a large city and the species may be extinct.

DISTRIBUTION   Known only from Tumaco Island, Nariño Department, south-eastern
Colombia.

POPULATION   Unknown.   Four specimens were collected in 1912 (1).

HABITAT   Tumaco Island was "dry, sunny, and sandy with only stunted vegetation,
and, on one side, mangroves" in 1912 (1).   Today the island is almost entirely
covered by the city of Tumaco (J. Hernandez 1974, pers. comm. to M. Rylander).

CONSERVATION MEASURES TAKEN   None known.

CONSERVATION MEASURES PROPOSED   None known.

REFERENCE   1.   Chapman, F.M. 1921.   Descriptions of proposed
               new birds from Colombia, Ecuador, Peru and Brazil.
               Amer. Mus. Novit. 18.

PINK-BILLED PARROTFINCH

Erythrura kleinschmidti (Finsch, 1878)

Order PASSERIFORMES   Family ESTRILDIDAE

STATUS   Rare. Restricted to moist indigenous forest on Viti Levu, Fiji, where
it has been observed in recent years in several localities both in the central
mountains and in the lowlands (1-3). It is nowhere abundant, but why it is so
rare is not yet understood.

DISTRIBUTION   Confined to Viti Levu, Fiji, where it has been seen with some
regularity during the last ten years on the Nandrau Plateau in the centre of the
island (1-3) and also north-west of Suva in the lowlands (2; 4; 5). The species
may be more widely distributed than previously thought; much of Viti Levu's
rainforest has not been properly explored by ornithologists.

POPULATION   Not known with certainty but undoubtedly low. A recent estimate
of at least 400 birds was based on surveys on the Nandrau Plateau (1). There is
no evidence that this parrotfinch has decreased since its discovery and it has
recently been shown to be rather common in certain localities (5).

HABITAT   Rainforest, both in the lowlands and at an altitude of about 915 m on
the Nandrau Plateau. The species has been noted as feeding on ripe fruits of two
species of figs (Ficus). Much of the indigenous forest, on which it and many
other endemic Fijian birds depend, has been cut or poisoned, and exotic trees have
been planted to replace indigenous ones. Nevertheless, substantial areas of the
original forest remain.

CONSERVATION MEASURES TAKEN   The species has legal protection in Fiji. Several
thousand hectares of forest are protected as reserves on Viti Levu (3).

CONSERVATION MEASURES PROPOSED   Establishment of more extensive forest reserves
on Viti Levu to protect this and other forest-dwelling endemic Fijian birds.

REFERENCES   1.   Ziswiler, V. undated.   Die Bedrohung der Landvogelfauna
                   südwestpazifischer Inseln.   Final Report to WWF on
                   Project No. 391.
              2.   Clunie, F. & Perks, I. 1972.   Short notes on Fijian birds:
                   Notes on the Pink-billed Parrot-finch of Fiji.
                   Notornis 19: 335-338.
              3.   Holyoak, D. undated.   Notes on the birds of Viti Levu and
                   Taveuni, Fiji.   Unpublished ms.
              4.   Ziswiler, V., Güttinger, H.R. & Bregulla, H. 1972.
                   Monographie der Gattung Erythrura Swainson, 1837 (Aves,
                   Passeres, Estrildidae).   Bonner Zool. Monog. 2.
              5.   Clunie, F. 1973.   Pink-billed Parrot Finches near
                   Nailagosakelo Creek, southern Viti Levu.   Notornis 20:
                   202-209.

PALAU BLUE-FACED PARROTFINCH

Erythrura trichroa pelewensis Kuroda, 1922

Order PASSERIFORMES   Family ESTRILDIDAE

STATUS   Indeterminate. This subspecies was described from a single specimen
taken on the largest island of the Palau group and only very recently has been seen
again on two of the smaller islands.   The reasons for its scarcity are not
understood.

DISTRIBUTION   Recorded on Babelthuap (397 sq. km) in the Palau group (1).   In
1976 this subspecies was sighted on Arekabesang, just south of Babelthuap, and
also on Ngermeaus, a small island toward the southern end of the group (R. Owen
1976, pers. comm.).

POPULATION   This subspecies must have already been quite rare when first
discovered for, since that time, it has only been seen again on two occasions, the
first a single bird and the second four birds (R. Owen 1976, pers. comm.).
Expeditions to the Palaus in 1931 and 1945 failed to find it (1).

HABITAT   The species is found in open areas in woodlands, along forest edges,
grasslands, gardens and wherever there is grass in seed (2).   The precise
habitat requirements of the Palau subspecies are unknown but are presumed to be
similar to those of other subspecies.

CONSERVATION MEASURES TAKEN   None known.

CONSERVATION MEASURES PROPOSED   The subspecies has been proposed for the U.S.
Trust Territories list of endangered species (R. Owen 1975, pers. comm.).

REMARKS   Of the 10 subspecies presently recognized, no others are known to be at
risk.   The species ranges from the Celebes through New Guinea and Northern
Australia to the Carolines, New Hebrides and Loyalty Islands.

REFERENCES   1.   Baker, R.H. 1951.   The avifauna of Micronesia, its
                   origin, evolution and distribution.   Univ. Kansas Pubs.
                   Mus. Nat. Hist. 3(1):   359 pp.
              2.   Ziswiler, V., Güttinger, H.R. & Bregulla, H. 1972.
                   Monographie der Gattung Erythrura Swainson, 1837
                   (Aves, Passeres, Estrildidae).   Bonner Zool. Monog. 2.

RODRIGUES FODY

Foudia flavicans Newton, 1865

Order PASSERIFORMES   Family PLOCEIDAE

                                    Subfamily PLOCEINAE

STATUS   Endangered. Restricted to the island of Rodrigues, easternmost of the
Mascarene group, Indian Ocean; it is seriously reduced from its former abundance.
Competition from the introduced Madagascar Fody Foudia madagascariensis may be an
important factor in its decline, and extensive destruction of forest habitat in the
1960s has undoubtedly worsened its situation (1).

DISTRIBUTION   Widespread on Rodrigues in the 19th century, by 1930 it had become
confined to the wooded areas on higher ground (2).   By 1965 the fody could be
found only at Solitude, Cascade Pigeon and Sygangue (1; 3-5) although an isolated
pair was seen on Ile Crabe off the south-west coast in 1970, but not subsequently
(4; 5).

POPULATION   Described as abundant last century, the species remained at least
not uncommon until the 1950s and early 1960s. Following upon the subsequent
cutting or clearing of many forest plantations and indigenous woodland areas and
the direct effects of cyclones, its population then rapidly declined.   Surveys in
1974 revealed its presence at 36 sites (three-quarters of them in only 15 ha of
forest plantation at La Solitude, where the species outnumbered the introduced
Madagascar Fody by 3 to 2), giving an estimated population of 20 to 30 pairs, plus
some unpaired males (4).   By 1978, the population had risen to about 100 pairs,
the area occupied at Solitude and Cascade Pigeon having expanded considerably (5).
A very severe cyclone in February 1979 reduced its numbers by about 40 percent (5).

HABITAT   Formerly all kinds of scrub or woody vegetation, but now tall mixed
hardwood forest, where the species apparently competes most effectively with the
Madagascar Fody.   All areas presently occupied are north-facing, which may be due
to the fact that this aspect gives greater protection from destructive cyclones.
The Mauritius Forestry Department has recently been replanting areas cleared in the
1960s with Vitex and Tabebuia (two species utilized by the fodies) as a watershed
protection measure (1), though illegal cutting is still a problem.

CONSERVATION MEASURES TAKEN   Part of the habitat is protected as "mountain
reserve" and areas of potential new habitat are being created by the Forestry
Department's planting program (1).   Cascade Pigeon was declared a nature reserve
in 1975 and in the same year legal measures to protect the fody from killing or
disturbance were initiated.

CONSERVATION MEASURES PROPOSED   It has been suggested that forest management
programs should take more specific account of habitat requirements of this and
other endemic species (6).   Another suggestion recommends the translocation and
establishment of a 'reserve' population of the Rodrigues Fody elsewhere, preferably
on Mauritius where it is argued that the differing habitat requirements of the
equally endangered Mauritius Fody would preclude undesirable competition between
the two species (1).

REMARKS   Several pairs are now held by the Jersey Wildlife Preservation Trust
and by the Government captive breeding aviaries on Mauritius itself, their capture
for that purpose having been approved by the Mauritius Government in 1978 (5).

REFERENCES   1.   Cheke, A.S. (in press).   Observations on the Surviving
                    Endemic Birds of Rodrigues.   Report of the Brit. Ornith.
                    Union's Mascarene Islands Expedition.
              2.   Vinson, J. 1964.   Quelques remarques sur l'Ile
                    Rodrigue et sur sa faune terrestre.   Proc. Roy. Soc. Arts
                    and Sci. Mauritius 2(3):   263-277.
              3.   Gill, F.B. 1967.   Birds of Rodriguez Island (Indian
                    Ocean).   Ibis 109:   383-390.
              4.   Staub, F. 1973.   Birds of Rodrigue Island.   Proc. Roy.
                    Soc. Arts and Sci. Mauritius 4(1):   17-59.
              5.   Cheke, A.S. 1979.   The Rodrigues Fody Foudia flavicans -
                    A brief history of its decline and a report on the 1978
                    expedition.   Dodo 15:   (in press).
              6.   Cheke, A.S. 1978.   Habitat Management for Conservation
                    in Rodrigues (Indian Ocean).   Cyclostyled Conservation
                    Memo. No. 4 (B.O.U. Mascarene Expedition).

MAURITIUS FODY

Foudia rubra (Gmelin, 1789)

Order PASSERIFORMES   Family PLOCEIDAE

                                               Subfamily PLOCEINAE

STATUS   Endangered.   Restricted in range, declining in numbers and now seriously
threatened with extinction.   The main factors responsible are habitat destruction,
competition with introduced birds and nest predation by introduced mammals.

DISTRIBUTION   Confined to the Indian Ocean island of Mauritius where the species
is now only to be found in the limited areas of indigenous forest remaining in the
south-western corner of the island.   These comprise the montane evergreen forests
on the uplands surrounding the Black River Gorges and along the adjacent southern
escarpment of the island, especially between Mount Cocotte and the Savanne
Mountains (1; S. Temple 1976, pers. comm.).   At one time the species was
undoubtedly more widespread (2) but as long ago as 1911 its range was quite
restricted (3).

POPULATION   At one time considered as common, although no estimates of numbers
were made, it had already become rare by 1911 (3) and by 1974 the total population
probably numbered less than 300 birds, or around 100-120 pairs (S. Temple 1976,
pers. comm.).   By 1978 the number appeared to have fallen considerably (A. Cheke
1979, pers. comm.).

HABITAT   Almost exclusively, indigenous montane evergreen forest and scrub,
although the species is occasionally found in exotic second growth vegetation
adjacent to native forests (1).   Forest once covered most of Mauritius but now
less than five percent of the island supports native vegetation (4; 5).   Introduced Madagascar Fodies Foudia madagascariensis may compete seasonally with the
Mauritius Fody for food, and introduced Crab-eating Macaques Macaca irus and Black
Rats Rattus rattus, which abound in the indigenous forests, are serious nest
predators (1).

CONSERVATION MEASURES TAKEN   The species is fully protected by laws forbidding
the killing or capture of native birds and a large portion of its range is within
officially declared reserves.   Ecological studies to define its status and
requirements were undertaken during the period 1972-1975.   An experimental project
for capturing and translocating a few pairs from insecure habitat in Mauritius to
extensive areas of suitable habitat on Réunion was attempted in 1975 (8).

CONSERVATION MEASURES PROPOSED   Continuation of the measures for protection and
management of remnant areas of native vegetation which are essential for the fody's
survival.   A management plan for nature reserves and national parks has been
prepared and was submitted to the Mauritius Government in 1974 (7).

REFERENCES   1.   Temple, S.A., Staub, J.J.F. & Antoine, R. 1974.   Some
                    background information and recommendations on the
                    preservation of the native flora and fauna of Mauritius.
                    Unpublished Report submitted to Mauritius Government.
              2.   Newton, E. 1861.   Ornithological notes from Mauritius,
                    part II.   Ibis (1)3: 270-277.
              3.   Meinertzhagen, R. 1912.   On the birds of Mauritius.
                    Ibis (9)6: 82-108.

4. Vaughan, R.E. & Wiehe, P.O., 1937. Studies of the vegetation of Mauritius, part I: A preliminary survey of the plant communities. J. Ecol. 25: 289-343.
5. Temple, S.A. 1974. Wildlife in Mauritius today. Oryx 12: 584-590.
6. Temple, S.A. 1975. In World Wildlife Yearbook for 1974-75, pp. 210-212. Morges: World Wildlife Fund.
7. Procter, J. & Salm, R. 1975. Conservation in Mauritius, 1974. Unpublished IUCN Report to the Mauritius Government.
8. Cheke, A.S. 1975. Proposition pour introduire a la Réunion des oiseaux rares de l'Ile Maurice. Info-Nature, Ile Réunion 12: 25-29.

SEYCHELLES FODY

Foudia sechellarum Newton, 1867

Order   PASSERIFORMES   Family   PLOCEIDAE

                                       Subfamily   PLOCEINAE

STATUS   Rare.   The species is now confined to three small rat-free islands in
the Seychelles archipelago, but is fairly common on each, the island which has the
highest population of these fodies being a Strict Nature Reserve.

DISTRIBUTION   Known to have included Marianne, La Digue, Frigate, Cousin,
Cousine and, possibly, Praslin: the species was extirpated from Marianne,
presumably when the forest of that island was destroyed last century; by 1867 only
a secondhand report confirmed its presence on La Digue and it was not found there
subsequently (1; 2); and two specimens collected in 1907 are the only evidence of
its occurrence on Praslin.   It is now only to be found on Frigate, Cousin and
Cousine, which have a combined area of 400 ha (2; 3).   Five individuals translocated to D'Arros in the Amirantes in August 1965 were still alive in 1968 (3).

POPULATION   Abundant on Marianne at the time of its discovery in 1867 (1), the
species was last observed there in 1890 although it has been suggested it only
became extinct there shortly before 1940 (2).   In 1867 it was reported as sparse
on La Digue (1) and apparently vanished shortly afterwards.   In all cases where it
has disappeared introduced rats seem to be chiefly to blame.   In 1959, the
populations were estimated at 250-300 on Frigate, 105 on Cousin and 80 on Cousine
(4).   The 1965 estimates produced much the same figure, 250-300, for Frigate, but
substantial increases on Cousin (400-600) and Cousine (100-150) (5).   In 1975 it
was believed that its numbers on Cousin had reached about 1000 (6).

HABITAT   Originally consisted mainly of primary lowland forest, but with the
general replacement of such forest by coconut and cashew plantations and scrub,
the species adapted itself to habitats dominated by this exotic vegetation.   The
introduced Madagascar Fody Foudia madagascariensis is now found on all three
islands where the Seychelles Fody survives, but competition between the two is not
considered to be a factor in the reduction of the range of the endemic species (2).

CONSERVATION MEASURES TAKEN   Legally protected from hunting or capture.   Cousin
Island, where this species is now most plentiful, was made a Strict Nature Reserve
in 1975.

CONSERVATION MEASURES PROPOSED   The continued exclusion of cats and rats from
Cousin and Cousine is considered important, although on Frigate the fody has
survived despite the presence of cats, most of which have now been eliminated
during efforts to save the endangered Magpie Robin Copsychus sechellarum (see
relevant data sheet Code 134) but which were formerly quite common.

REMARKS   It is possible that in its rat-free last strongholds this Fody suffers
some predation from native snakes and lizards, which is however unlikely to be
very serious.

REFERENCES   1.   Newton, E. 1867.   On the land-birds of the Seychelles
                     Archipelago.   Ibis (2)3: 335-360.
                2.   Crook, J.H. 1961.   The fodies (Ploceinae) of the Seychelles
                     Islands.   Ibis 103a: 517-548.

3. Penny, M. 1974. The Birds of Seychelles and the
    Outlying Islands. New York: Taplinger Publishing Co.;
    London: Collins.
4. Crook, J.H. 1960. The present status of certain rare
    land birds of the Seychelles Islands. Seychelles
    Government Bulletin. 5pp.
5. Gaymer, R., Blackman, R.A.A., Dawson, P.G., Penny, M.
    & Penny, C.M. 1969. The endemic birds of Seychelles.
    Ibis 111: 157-176.
6. Diamond, A.W. 1975. Cousin Island Nature Reserve
    Management Plan, 1975-1979. London: ICBP.

CLARKE'S WEAVER

Ploceus golandi (Clarke, 1913)

Order PASSERIFORMES   Family PLOCEIDAE

                                          Subfamily PLOCEINAE

STATUS   Rare. Known only from one Kenyan forest which has suffered continuing reduction in size as the result of uncontrolled exploitation of forest products and clearing for agricultural development.

DISTRIBUTION   Confined to the Arabuko-Sokoke Forest in lowland south-eastern Kenya. In the decade preceding 1966 the extent of this forest was cut by half. In 1976 it was estimated that only 360 sq. km remained. (1-3; 6; 7).

POPULATION   Unknown but the species seems quite common within its restricted range, having been seen in flocks of up to 100 birds; this may be quite a significant proportion of the total population, which has been estimated to be not more than 1000-2000 pairs (4; 5; P. Britton 1979, pers. comm.).

HABITAT   Dry and mainly deciduous lowland forest typical of the East African coastlands. The weaver has been recorded, often wandering through in flocks, in all the different kinds of vegetation comprising the Arabuko-Sokoke Forest. Its nest has so far eluded discovery. The place where five specimens were collected in 1964 has now been cleared of forest by agricultural development.

CONSERVATION MEASURES TAKEN   The species is protected by Kenyan law. Out of the 400 sq. km of the Arabuko-Sokoke Forest Reserve 40 sq. km have been classified as nature reserve, in which disturbance of any kind is prohibited.

CONSERVATION MEASURES PROPOSED   Reservation of an additional 20 sq. km of forest as nature reserve to ensure that adequate representative samples of all main forest habitats are protected. Modification of Kenya Forestry Department policy, with special reference to avoiding the replacement of indigenous forest of major scientific or conservation value by exotic timber species (4).

REMARKS   Morden's Scops Owl Otus ireneae, the Sokoke Pipit Anthus sokokensis and the Amani Sunbird Anthreptes pallidigaster are other bird species entirely or largely restricted to the Arabuko-Sokoke Forest.

REFERENCES   1.   Clancey, P.A. & Williams, J.G. 1959. On the unknown female dress and specific relationships of Ploceus golandi (Clarke). Ibis 101: 247-248.
              2.   Hall, B.P. & Moreau, R.E. 1962. A study of the rare birds of Africa. Bull. Brit. Mus. (Nat. Hist.) Zool. 8(7): 313-378.
              3.   Ripley, S.D. & Bond, G.M. 1971. Systematic notes on a collection of birds from Kenya. Smithsonian Contrib. Zool. 111.
              4.   Brown, L.H. et al. Undated. A report on threatened bird species in East Africa. Mimeo. 12 pages.
              5.   Williams, J.G. 1957. The re-discovery and status of Ploceus golandi. Ibis 99: 123-124.
              6.   Britton, P.L. 1976. Primary forestland destruction now critical. Africana 5(12): i-ii.
              7.   Turner, D.A. 1977. Status and distribution of the East African endemic species. Scopus 1: 2-11.

USAMBARA WEAVER

Ploceus olivaceiceps nicolli Sclater, 1931

Order PASSERIFORMES   Family PLOCEIDAE

                                            Subfamily PLOCEINAE

STATUS   Rare.   Entirely restricted to two East African mountain ranges, in each
of which the accelerated rate of destruction of the forest cover since the mid-
1960s has posed a serious threat to the survival of several other birds in addition
to this subspecies.

DISTRIBUTION   The Usambara Mountains in north-eastern Tanzania and the Uluguru
Mountains 275 km to the south, in east-central Tanzania (1; 2).

POPULATION   A decline is believed to have taken place, although this weaver has
never been known to be numerous.   Thus the original collector only saw it half a
dozen times in his first three years (1929-1931) of residence at Amani in the East
Usambaras; he in fact collected it outside his office, on the edge of the forest
by which Amani at that time was almost entirely enclosed.   It is now considered
exceedingly rare and perhaps declining, the most recent sighting being of three in
the West Usambaras in 1977 (4).   The total Usambara population is unlikely to
exceed 1000 (S. Stuart 1978, pers. comm.).   Evidence of its presence in the
Ulugurus still rests on two specimens taken in 1952 and 1961 (2; 5).   It has been
suggested that competition from the much more common forest-dwelling Dark-backed
Weaver P. bicolor may partly account for its rarity (S. Stuart 1977, pers. comm.
to P. Scott).

HABITAT   Evergreen cloud-forest at elevations between 1600 and 2100 m.   In both
the Usambaras and the Ulugurus such forest has been seriously reduced since the
mid-1960s by clearing for subsistence agriculture and the cultivation of tea and
cardamom (3; 4; S. Stuart 1978, pers. comm.).

CONSERVATION MEASURES TAKEN   None known.

CONSERVATION MEASURES PROPOSED   Up to date survey of the remaining cloud forest
in the two mountain ranges and of the status and distribution of the endemic birds
which depend on this habitat is the essential prerequisite of recommendations for
the creation of reserves or other appropriate conservation measures (S. Stuart
1978, pers. comm.).

REMARKS   The nominate race of this weaver is found in the Brachystegia woodlands
of southern Tanzania, Mozambique and Malawi and is not at risk.   Some authors have
considered that differences in the habitat requirements and head color of the two
forms would justify them being treated as separate species.

REFERENCES   1.   Sclater, W.L. 1931.   Ploceus (Symplectes) nicolli, sp.
                   nov.   Bull. Brit. Ornith. Club. 52: 26-27.
              2.   Ripley, S.D. & Heinrich, G.H. 1966.   Comments on the
                   avifauna of Tanzania, Part I.   Postilla 96
              3.   Brown, L.H. Undated.   A report on threatened bird species
                   in East Africa.   East African Wildlife Society.
              4.   Stuart, S.N. & Hutton, J.M. (eds) 1977.   The avifauna
                   of the East Usambara Mountains, Tanzania.
                   Cambridge University expedition report.
              5.   Britton, P.L. 1978.   The Andersen collection from Tanzania.
                   Scopus 2: 77-85.

PONAPE MOUNTAIN STARLING

Aplonis pelzelni Finsch, 1876

Order PASSERIFORMES   Family STURNIDAE

STATUS   Vulnerable.   Known only from Ponape, Caroline Islands, western Pacific,
where it has apparently decreased and is now rare and local.

DISTRIBUTION   Now restricted to the mountains of Ponape (334 sq. km), near the
eastern end of the Caroline Islands chain; but formerly also extending to the
lowlands (1).

POPULATION   Although no population estimate has been made, the species was
presumably more abundant when it ranged into the lowlands.   By 1930 it was
confined to the mountains and was apparently not uncommon, for a series of 59
specimens was collected.   However, in 1948 it was described as very rare, only
two birds being seen, one of which was collected (1).   Another was collected in
1956 by J.T. Marshall, Jr. and in 1975 at least one bird and possibly two or
three more were seen (R. Owen 1975, pers. comm.).   The high mountains of Ponape
have not been thoroughly surveyed since 1930, so it is possible that it is still
quite common there.

HABITAT   Mountain forests at altitudes of over 200 m, although in the past the
lowland forests were apparently also inhabited by the species (1).   It has been
suggested that the related Kusaie Starling Aplonis corvinus became extinct as the
result of rat invasion of that island (2) and rats of two species (R. rattus and
R. exulans) are known to be present on Ponape.   However, a subspecies of another
related species, the Micronesian Starling Aplonis opacus ponapensis, is numerous
on Ponape despite predation by rats and despite being hunted for food.   Its
nesting sites, holes in trees, are similar to those of A. pelzelni, but the
Micronesian Starling is more aggressive and has been observed to drive away the
Mountain Starling (1), so this may well be a factor contributing to the latter's
rarity.

CONSERVATION MEASURES TAKEN   This species is on the U.S. Department of Interior
list of endangered species and is therefore fully protected by the U.S. Endangered
Species Act of 1973.   It is also protected by the U.S. Trust Territories
Endangered Species Act of 1975.

CONSERVATION MEASURES PROPOSED   No additional proposals have been reported.

REMARKS   A thorough survey of the status of this and other endemic birds of the
U.S. Trust Territories is long overdue.

REFERENCES   1.   Baker, R.H. 1951.   The avifauna of Micronesia, its origin,
                   evolution, and distribution.   Univ. Kansas Pubs. Mus.
                   Nat. Hist. 3(1): 1-359.
              2.   Greenway, J.C. Jr. 1958.   Extinct and Vanishing Birds of
                   the World.   Amer. Comm. Internat. Wildlife Prot. Spec.
                   Pub. 13.

SANTO MOUNTAIN STARLING

Aplonis santovestris Harrisson and Marshall, 1937

Order PASSERIFORMES   Family STURNIDAE

___

STATUS   Rare and local. Thinly distributed in the interior highlands of
Espiritu Santo, New Hebrides.   Not known to be in danger of extinction but only
three pairs have been located in four searches for the species in the last few
years (1).

DISTRIBUTION   Restricted to higher elevations, above 1,160 m, of Mount Wataimasan
and the Tabwemassana Massif on Espiritu Santo, in the New Hebrides archipelago,
South-west Pacific, where it is very sparsely distributed (1; H. Bregulla 1974,
pers. comm.).

POPULATION   Not known precisely but thought to be quite low.   There is no
indication of a decline but an expedition to Espiritu Santo in 1971 failed to find
it and during three more recent visits by ornithologists to the Tabwemassana Massif
only three pairs have been found (H. Bregulla 1974, pers. comm.).

HABITAT   Montane moss-forest at altitudes exceeding 1,160 m (1; 2).

CONSERVATION MEASURES TAKEN   The species is protected by law, as are almost all
endemic birds of the New Hebrides (1).

CONSERVATION MEASURES PROPOSED   A continuing effort to educate the people of the
New Hebrides towards a better appreciation of the value of their unique endemic
avifauna (H. Bregulla 1974, pers. comm.).

REMARKS   The clutch laid by this species is said to be the abnormally small one,
for a starling, of only two eggs.

REFERENCES   1.   Harrisson, T.H. & Marshall, A.J. 1937.   Bull. Brit.
                   Orn. Club 57: 148-150.

ROTHSCHILD'S STARLING

Leucopsar rothschildi Stresemann, 1912

Order PASSERIFORMES   Family STURNIDAE

STATUS   Endangered. With its range now restricted to only quite a small
portion of the island of Bali, Indonesia, this starling continues to be captured
for the cage-bird trade, despite legal protection therefrom and despite the fact
that the impact of this exploitation on the wild population has never been
properly assessed. However, the most serious threat to it probably stems from
human occupation of much of its former range; the partly consequential increase of
competition from another species of starling may also be an adverse factor.

DISTRIBUTION   Now confined to the area from Tjelukan Trima to Bubunan on the
north-west coast of Bali (1; 2) and to the small island of Nusa Penida off the
south coast (3). The starlings are believed to move between these two areas
(F.W. King 1976, pers. comm.), although their discovery on Nusa Penida is only
quite recent, an expedition in 1938 not having found them there (10). The area
occupied by the starling in the north-western corner of Bali in 1976 was estimated
at about 200 sq. km (11).

POPULATION   In 1925 'hundreds' were seen in areas of greatest concentration (2);
in 1976 a total of 127 were counted in 9 localities covering about one-third of
the total range, on the basis of which the total population was estimated at 500
birds and certainly no more than 1000 (11). Excessive capture for the cage-bird
trade was suggested as the reason for the declining population (4) but it has been
shown that clearing of forest lands for human settlements has driven this starling
from all but a small fraction of its former range, its numbers falling accordingly
(11).

HABITAT   Forest and forest edges. As noted above there has been much forest
destruction, an influx of human population to north Bali from Java having in
particular increased the pressure on the starling and its habitat (5; 11). In
1925, the entire western third of Bali except for a few towns was covered by
primary forest (2); in 1976, there were still substantial areas of forest formerly
occupied by the species (L.M. Talbot 1976, pers. comm.), but the modifications to
the forest cover which accompany human settlement had apparently encouraged the
spread of Sturnus melanopterus, a closely related starling of strikingly similar
appearance. In 1926 S. melanopterus did not occur within L. rothschildi's
range, but it is now three times as abundant as L. rothschildi in the latter's
area of maximum abundance, which comprises a mosaic of untouched forest, coconut
plantations and corn fields and is the least heavily settled portion of Bali (11).

CONSERVATION MEASURES TAKEN   The species is protected in Indonesia under the
Nature Protection Ordinance which came into force in 1957 (6). Its capture,
shooting and export were all expressly prohibited in 1971. It is also listed in
Appendix 1 of the 1973 Convention on International Trade in Endangered Species of
Wild Fauna and Flora. Part of its range lies within the 20,000 ha Bali-Barat
Nature Reserve (3).

CONSERVATION MEASURES PROPOSED   The Government has been planning the removal
elsewhere of the 4,500 people living within the boundaries of Bali-Barat Reserve
as at 1976. Prohibition of any further human settlement, of woodcutting and of
animal husbandry (especially around water sources) and the careful control of
ever-increasing tourism have also been recommended (11).

REMARKS   Rothschild's Starling was first bred in captivity in 1931 and captive specimens have become increasingly abundant since the mid-1960s (4). In 1964, out of 50 held in 17 collections, five (10 percent) had been bred in captivity (7). By 1973, 27 percent of those held in collections were captive bred (8), a proportion which had risen to 36 percent, or 190 of the 526 held in 84 collections, in 1974 (9). The successful rearing of second and subsequent generation captive birds has now been recorded in some zoos (G. Greenwell 1978, pers. comm.) and the species is on its way to being self-sustaining in captivity, which, when achieved, should reduce the demand for wild-caught birds.

Four pairs were released on the 40 ha Lokrum Island, Yugoslavia, in 1975. Two pairs were found on the adjacent mainland some days later, suggesting that 10 hectares per pair of the habitat available on the island was insufficient to meet the spacing requirements of the species (11).

REFERENCES   1. Stresemann, E. 1912. Bull. Brit. Ornith. Club 31: 4-6.
              2. Von Plessen, V. 1926. Verbreitung und Lebensweise von Leucopsar rothschildi Stres. Ornith. Monatsb. 34: 71-73.
              3. Hartmann, F.R. 1970. Bali and its Mynah. Animal Kingdom 73(3): 26-29.
              4. Fisher, J., Simon, N. & Vincent, J. 1969. Wildlife in Danger. New York: Viking Press; London: Collins.
              5. Harrison, C.J.O. 1968. Rothschild's Mynah: An appeal for cooperation. Avicult. Mag. 74: 19-20.
              6. Somadikarta, S. 1967. Bird conservation in Indonesia. Bull. ICBP. 10: 167-175.
              7. Jarvis, C. (ed.) 1965. Census of rare animals in captivity. Int. Zoo Yearbook 5: 371-392.
              8. Duplaix-Hall, N. (ed.) 1975. Census of rare animals in captivity, 1973. Int. Zoo Yearbook 14: 396-429.
              9. Duplaix-Hall, N. (ed.) 1975. Census of rare animals in captivity, 1974. Int. Zoo Yearbook 15: 397-405.
             10. Van Bemmel, A.C.V. 1974. Balispreeuwen. Artis (Amsterdam) 20e: 134-137.
             11. Sieber, J. 1978. Freilandsbeobachtungen und Versuch einer Bestandaufnahme des Bali Stars Leucopsar rothschildi. Journ. f. Ornith. 119: 102-106.

SOUTH ISLAND KOKAKO

Callaeas cinerea cinerea (Gmelin, 1788)

Order PASSERIFORMES   Family CALLAEIDAE

STATUS   Critically endangered.   Only a handful of unconfirmed and widely
scattered sightings in the past two decades give hope that it still exists on South
Island, New Zealand.   Predation by introduced mammals, competition for food from
exotic herbivores and destruction of forest habitat are quoted as causes of its
decline, but why they should have affected the South Island subspecies more
seriously than the North Island one is unclear.

DISTRIBUTION   This subspecies was distributed widely throughout South Island and
on Stewart Island, New Zealand, at the time of arrival of European settlers early
in the 19th century.   It declined rapidly and extensively thereafter, and by the
turn of the century was considered a very rare bird.   In the past thirty years it
has been reported from a number of districts of South Island and Stewart Island
(1), but the most persistent reports have come from the Marlborough district in the
north-eastern corner of South Island (G. Williams 1976, pers. comm.).

POPULATION   At the time of its discovery this subspecies was considered common in
optimum parts of its South Island range.   By 1900 it was very rare and, since 1945,
there have been only nine unconfirmed reports (1; 2).   There is some question at
present whether it is still extant.

HABITAT   Mature forests; on Stewart Island also subalpine scrub (1).   These
habitats have been invaded by introduced mustelids, cats and rats, all likely
predators of this bird, its eggs and nestlings.   In addition exotic herbivores
probably compete with it for food, while much of its forest habitat has been
destroyed (2).

CONSERVATION MEASURES TAKEN   The New Zealand Wildlife Service has undertaken
extensive faunal surveys of the forests of New Zealand, in the course of which
special efforts have been made to find this subspecies, but so far without success.
The Kokako species as a whole has full legal protection.

CONSERVATION MEASURES PROPOSED   Follow-up of all unconfirmed sightings in the
hope of finding an isolated population.

REMARKS   The North Island subspecies, C. c. wilsoni, is still widely distributed
on North Island and Great Barrier Island, but rated as vulnerable.

REFERENCES   1.   Falla, R.A., Sibson, R.B. & Turbott, E.G. 1967.   A Field Guide
                    to the Birds of New Zealand and Outlying Islands.   Boston:
                    Houghton Mifflin Co.; London: Collins.
              2.   Ellis, B.A. 1975.   Rare and endangered New Zealand birds:
                    the role of the Royal Forest and Bird Protection Society of
                    New Zealand Inc.   ICBP Bull. 12: 173-186.

NORTH ISLAND KOKAKO

Callaeas cinerea wilsoni (Bonaparte, 1851)

Order PASSERIFORMES   Family CALLAEIDAE

STATUS   Vulnerable. Still widely distributed on North Island, New Zealand, but
nowhere common and slowly decreasing due to continued cutting of remaining
indigenous forests and to predation by introduced mammals. The possible effects
of competition for food between Kokakos and introduced herbivores are also under
investigation.

DISTRIBUTION   In the 1840s, at the time of the first large-scale European
immigration, the Kokako was still widespread over much of North Island and adjacent
Great Barrier Island. Although the range of the subspecies has declined
considerably, it is still found in a number of relict stands of mature forest.
Unfortunately, its discontinuous and restricted distribution, coupled with weak
powers of flight which inhibit its colonization of new areas, place it at
considerable risk (1; 2).

POPULATION   Once quite common, this subspecies rapidly declined in numbers after
the coming of European settlers. The current population estimate is about 1,000
birds, divided into a number of discrete subpopulations. At least some of these,
especially in more extensive areas of suitable habitat, are stable, but others are
still declining (1; 2).

HABITAT   Extensive mature indigenous forest on level or gently sloping terrain
below 600 meters elevation, and most frequently in areas where the thick forest
canopy is broken by natural openings. Introduced predators, including mustelids,
cats and rats, have infiltrated into these habitats. Introduced Australian Brush-
tailed "possums" (the Phalanger Trichosurus vulpecula), introduced deer and feral
goats are likely to compete with the species for food. Only one-tenth of the
original indigenous forest, on which the species depended, remains today (1; 2; 3).

CONSERVATION MEASURES TAKEN   The species has legal protection throughout New
Zealand and the Wildlife Service has undertaken an extensive survey of remaining
forests to determine, with some precision, the location of surviving populations
of this subspecies. As many of these are in State forests, cooperation between the
Wildlife Service and the Forest Service has led to the establishment of several
forest reserves, some permanent, others temporary, for the protection of the Kokako
and its habitat. Competition for food between this species and possums, deer and
goats is being studied.

CONSERVATION MEASURES PROPOSED   Upon completion of the New Zealand Wildlife
Service's distributional surveys a series of Kokako reserves will be established for
the conservation of existing populations and distribution patterns, and of
representative Kokako habitats. Further research is planned to ascertain the
Kokako's exact habitat requirements, so that the reserves can be suitably managed
(G. Williams 1976, pers. comm.).

REMARKS   The nominate subspecies C. c. cinerea is on the brink of extinction in
South Island and there are no recent confirmed reports of its existence.

REFERENCES   1.   Crook, I.G. 1971.   Will Kokako survive in the North Island?
                  Wildlife - A review 3:   35-38.
             2.   Bell, B.D. 1975.   The rare and endangered species of the New
                  Zealand region and the policies that exist for their management.
                  ICBP Bull. 12:   165-172.
             3.   Fisher, J., Simon, N. & Vincent, J. 1969.   Wildlife in Danger.
                  New York: Viking Press: London: Collins.

NORTH ISLAND SADDLEBACK   Creadion carunculatus rufusater (Lesson, 1828)

SOUTH ISLAND SADDLEBACK   Creadion carunculatus carunculatus (Gmelin, 1789)

Order PASSERIFORMES   Family CALLAEIDAE

STATUS   Recovering. The Saddleback, while by no means fully restored in numbers
or range, has improved in status sufficiently since its nadir in 1964, to warrant
a green sheet. Island populations of both subspecies have been established and
have increased, the North Island form so much so that only occasional surveys need
to be carried out to check that population levels are being maintained. The South
Island subspecies will need to be established on two or three more islands before
it is altogether out of danger. Relocation on predator free islands formerly
within its range is the technique which has been used by the New Zealand Wildlife
Service for this highly successful rehabilitation of the Saddleback (1; 2; 3).

DISTRIBUTION   Formerly widespread in North, South and Stewart Islands, New
Zealand. With the arrival of European settlers and introduced predators, both
subspecies rapidly lost ground. Early this century the North Island form only
survived on Hen Island (484 hectares) in the Hen and Chickens group off the eastern
coast of Northland, the South Island form only on Big South Cape Island (911
hectares) and two adjacent islets south-west of Stewart Island (1; 2; 3).   Black
rats Rattus rattus became established on Big South Cape Island in about 1962 and the
ensuing rat population explosion accounted for the extermination of five species of
birds, three of which were found nowhere else.   The North Island subspecies, still
flourishing on Hen Island, has now also been successfully reintroduced on Middle,
Big Chicken, Red Mercury and Cuvier islands, and the South Island subspecies on
Big, Kaimohu, Betsy, Putauhina, Womans and North islands, all off Stewart Island.
However, two attempts to introduce the latter subspecies to Inner Chetwode Island
in Cook Strait have not succeeded (1; 2; 3).

POPULATION   Saddlebacks were abundant throughout New Zealand when European
settlers arrived early in the 19th century, but by the end of the century had
completely disappeared from the main islands (2). The population of the North
Island form on Hen Island, before the program for reintroductions was launched, was
estimated at 500 pairs; it is now double that figure.   The population of the
nominate race in Big South Cape Island off Stewart Island was largely exterminated
by rats in 1964 or 1965, but not before the New Zealand Wildlife Service had
successfully relocated 36 birds to two nearby predator free islands.   After 1965,
only 7 males survived in Big South Cape Island, one or two of them until 1970, but
further introductions, at two-year intervals, of the progeny of the relocated 36
birds to additonal islands have built up a total population of about 200 birds (1).

HABITAT   Coastal scrub forest and understory vegetation (2).

CONSERVATION MEASURES TAKEN   The Saddlebacks have been given full legal protection.
All islands to which they have been introduced are reserves.   The relocation
program has been one of the classic success stories in the short history of management of endangered species.   Removal of introduced predators by the New Zealand
Wildlife Service preceded some of the introductions; natural revegetation of the
islands also followed the suspension of farming or burning. Cropping of successful
populations for a continuing series of reintroductions on additional islands has
now provided a substantial margin of safety for both subspecies.   Earlier attempts,
in 1925 and 1950, to relocate the North Island subspecies failed, in the first case
because the islands selected for release had cats and rats on them, and in the
second because too few birds were released.   Subsequent research into the ecology

of the species and refinements in capture and transport techniques proved essential to the success of relocation (1; 2; 3). Both subspecies have bred in captivity, the North Island one at the Mount Bruce Native Bird Reserve on North Island, and the South Island one in a privately-run aviary; but in neither case was a self-sustaining stock developed and only one of the young birds raised of the South Island form has so far reached maturity (1).

CONSERVATION MEASURES PROPOSED   Reintroduction of the South Island Saddleback to two or three more islands, preferably some distance from the islands around Stewart Island where it now occurs. Monitoring all islands to check that populations are not declining and that no alien mammals have reached the islands concerned (G. Williams 1976, pers. comm.).

REMARKS   The officers of the New Zealand Wildlife Service who so capably carried out the management plan outlined above, deserve the congratulations of all conservationists for their work.

REFERENCES   1. Merton, D.V. 1975. Success in re-establishing a threatened species: the Saddleback, its status and conservation. ICBP Bull. 12: 150-158.
2. Merton, D.V. 1973. Conservation of the Saddleback. New Zealand Wildlife Service. Wildlife - A review 4: 13-23.
3. Merton, D.V. 1975. The Saddleback: its status and conservation. In R.D. Martin, ed., Breeding Endangered Species in Captivity, pp. 61-74. London, New York, San Francisco: Academic Press.

PALAU WHITE-BREASTED WOOD-SWALLOW

Artamus leucorhynchus pelewensis Finsch, 1876

Order PASSERIFORMES   Family ARTAMIDAE

STATUS   Rare.   This conspicuous bird occurs locally in the Palau group, South
West Pacific.   Reasons for its apparent scarcity probably relate to the limited
area of its preferred habitat.

DISTRIBUTION   This subspecies has been collected on the islands of Babelthuap
(397 sq. km) and Angaur (8.4 sq. km) (1) and although sighted on most of the other
islands of the Palau archipelago is restricted almost exclusively to the interior
of Babelthuap (2; R. Owen 1976, pers. comm.).

POPULATION   In 1931, 8 birds were collected, all that were seen by the Whitney
South Sea Expedition during its 2½ months in the Palaus.   In 1945 none were found
on two separate surveys (1), but three were seen on Babelthuap in 1946 (S.D. Ripley
1977, pers. comm.) and two collected in 1950.   A biologist resident in the Palaus
has seen the species only six times in 25 years but more recently it has been found
regularly in small groups of two to ten birds in the more remote of the savannah
woodlands of Babelthuap (2).

HABITAT   Inland savannahs are the favored habitat of this subspecies, but its
strong flight takes it occasionally to every kind of habitat in the Palau islands.
Birds perch in the tops of trees, often on dead branches which makes them
conspicuous, and roost communally at night.

CONSERVATION MEASURES TAKEN   Protected by U.S. Trust Territory Law.

CONSERVATION MEASURES PROPOSED   The subspecies has been placed on the U.S. Trust
Territories endangered species list as a preliminary to the application of
conservation measures.

REMARKS   The ten other subspecies which have been described range widely from
Fiji through New Guinea to Northern Australia and north to the Philippines,
Indonesia and Andaman Islands.   None of them is believed to be at risk.

REFERENCES   1.   Baker, R.W. 1951.   The avifauna of Micronesia, its
                  origin, evolution and distribution.   Univ. Kansas
                  Pubs. Mus. Nat. Hist. 3(1):   1-359.
             2.   Engbring, J. 1979.   Field Guide to the Birds of Palau.
                  Unpublished ms.

LORD HOWE CURRAWONG

Strepera graculina crissalis Sharpe, 1877

Order PASSERIFORMES   Family CRACTICIDAE

STATUS   Endangered.   Very rare and decreasing.   Confined to Lord Howe Island,
South West Pacific.   The cause of its decline is unknown (1).

DISTRIBUTION   This subspecies is sparsely distributed over most of the 13 sq. km
of Lord Howe Island (2; 3).

POPULATION   At one time considered fairly large (2), a steady decline has brought
the population down to between 30 and 50 (1).

HABITAT   Subtropical rainforest on the mountain slopes of Lord Howe Island;
areas in the lowlands are, however, also frequented (2; 3).

CONSERVATION MEASURES TAKEN   The whole island was gazetted as an Ordinary Faunal
District in 1939 (3).   The Australian Museum undertook a detailed survey of the
island's environment for the Australian government in the early 1970s (1).

CONSERVATION MEASURES PROPOSED   National Park status for the greater part of
Lord Howe Island has been recommended: the future development of the island's
tourist potential should take account of a management plan proposed by the
Australian Museum's survey team, which aimed at reconciling such development with
the preservation of the assets derived from the island's remarkable natural
history (4).

REMARKS   Three other subspecies in eastern Australia are widespread and common.

REFERENCES   1.   Recher, H.F. 1974.   Colonization and extinction: the
                   birds of Lord Howe Island.   Australian Natural History
                   18(2): 64-68.
              2.   Hindwood, K.A. 1940.   The birds of Lord Howe Island.
                   Emu 40: 1-86.
              3.   Disney, H.J. de S. & Smithers, C.N. 1972.   The distribution
                   of terrestrial and freshwater birds on Lord Howe Island, in
                   comparison with Norfolk Island.   Austral. Zool. 17: 1-11.
              4.   Recher, H.F. & Clark, G.S. 1974.   Exploitation vs.
                   conservation.   Austral. Nat. Hist. 18(2): 74-77.

MARIANAS CROW

Corvus kubaryi Reichenow, 1885˙

Order PASSERIFORMES   Family CORVIDAE

STATUS   Endangered.   Depleted and apparently declining on both the islands in
the southern Marianas from which it has been recorded.   The reasons for the decline
are unknown.

DISTRIBUTION   This crow is endemic to Guam (541 sq. km) and Rota (85.5 sq. km),
southern Marianas.   In 1945, it was distributed throughout Guam, except in the
immediate vicinity of the military cantonments (1).   It is now only to be found
north of a line between Mangilao and Tumon Bay, particularly at Pati Point and
around Andersen Air Base.

POPULATION   In 1945 this species represented 2.4 per cent of the total number of
birds counted in surveys along the roads of Guam (2) and was also considered fairly
numerous on Rota (1).   The populations on both islands are now estimated to be
less than 100 (N. Drahos 1976, pers. comm.).   One observer who made many visits to
Rota between 1954 and 1974, saw it only three times (R. Owen, pers. comm.) but
twelve were heard calling by a more recent visitor (N. Drahos 1976, pers. comm.).

HABITAT   Forests and coconut plantations (1).   The extent of forestland on Guam
has declined since 1945, but is still considerable.

CONSERVATION MEASURES TAKEN   The crow has been given legal protection and is on
the Guam Endangered Species list, although the list remains to be incorporated in
the Guam Endangered Species Act of 1975.   Nearly 600 ha of the area where it is
still frequently found are within the Pati Point Natural Area and adjacent Anao
Conservation Reserve.

CONSERVATION MEASURES PROPOSED   This species has been recommended for inclusion
in the U.S. Trust Territories list of endangered species (R. Owen 1975, pers. comm.).

REMARKS   Comprehensive surveys of the status of this and other endemic birds of
Guam and the U.S. Trust Territories are long overdue.

REFERENCES   1. Baker, R.H. 1951.   The avifauna of Micronesia, its origin,
                  evolution and distribution.   Univ. Kansas Pubs. Mus. Nat.
                  Hist. 3(1): 1-359.
              2. Baker, R.H. 1947.   Size of bird populations at Guam,
                  Mariana Islands.   Condor 49: 124-125.

HAWAIIAN CROW or 'ALALA

Corvus tropicus Kerr, 1792

Order   PASSERIFORMES   Family   CORVIDAE

STATUS   Endangered.   A relict population still occurs on the island of Hawaii.
The causes of the precipitous decline of this species are obscure, but are thought
to be due largely to grazing of cattle and goats.   Numbers of this species have
been shot by hunters, but this has probably not been responsible for the species'
decline.   Bird diseases, including avian malaria and birdpox, are another likely
cause of decline.   Two just fledged young captured in 1970 suffered from birdpox
(1; 2).

DISTRIBUTION   Apparently always confined to the island of Hawaii between 300
and 2,440 m elevation in Kau and Kona districts, especially on the slopes of
Mt. Hualalai.   The population in Kau is now largely or entirely gone.   Breeding
now restricted to forest between 1,035 and 1,525 m elevation; ranging somewhat
lower and higher when not breeding, but no longer approaching the elevation
extremes of last century (3; 4).

POPULATION   Possibly as many as 70 birds.   Common as recently as the 1930s,
although no more widespread (3).

HABITAT   Wet and dry forests.   The extent of these forests has diminished, but,
more importantly, they have been invaded by feral pigs, cattle and goats, which
has caused some plant species favored by crows to become rare.   The arboreal
black rat Rattus rattus has also been introduced, as have the vectors of certain
avian diseases known to affect native Hawaiian birds.

CONSERVATION MEASURES TAKEN   Protected by federal and state law from killing,
capture or harassment.   A study of the ecology of this species has been undertaken.

CONSERVATION MEASURES PROPOSED   Continue study of population, life history, and
ecological requirements of species (1).

REMARKS   Two just fledged birds were captured in 1970.   One succumbed to disease;
the second responded to treatment, but died in 1974.   Three were captured in 1973
and captive breeding is being attempted.

REFERENCES   1.   U.S. Department of Interior Bureau of Sport Fisheries and
                    Wildlife, 1973.   Threatened Wildlife of the United States.
                    U.S. Bur. Sport Fish. Wildl. Res. Pub. 114.
              2.   Berger, A.J. 1972.   Hawaiian Birdlife.   Honolulu: University
                    Press of Hawaii.
              3.   Banko, P. Ms. dated 1974.   Report on 'Alala (Corvus tropicus).
              4.   Baldwin, P.H. 1969.   The 'Alala (Corvus tropicus) of western
                    Hawaii Island.   Elepaio 30: 41-45.

Date Due